Existential–Phenomenological Perspectives in Psychology

Exploring the Breadth of Human Experience

With a Special Section on Transpersonal Psychology

Edited by

Ronald S. Valle

John F. Kennedy University
Orinda, California

and

Steen Halling

Seattle University
Seattle, Washington

With a Foreword by James F. T. Bugental

KLUWER ACADEMIC/PLENUM PUBLISHERS
New York • London • Dordrecht • Boston

Library of Congress Cataloging in Publication Data

Existential–phenomenological perspectives in psychology: exploring the breadth of human experience: with a special section on transpersonal psychology / edited by Ronald S. Valle and Steen Halling; with a foreword by James F. T. Bugental.
    p.   cm.
   Bibliography: p.
   Includes indexes.
   ISBN 0-306-42979-9. — ISBN 0-306-43044-4 (pbk.)
   1. Phenomenological psychology. 2. Existential psychology. 3. Transpersonal psychology. I. Valle, Ronald S. II. Halling, Steen.
BF204.5.E94 1989   88-39126
150.19′2 — dc19   CIP

© 1989 Plenum Press, New York
A Division of Plenum Publishing Corporation
233 Spring Street, New York, N.Y. 10013

Printed in the United States of America

Existential–Phenomenological Perspectives in Psychology

Exploring the Breadth of Human Experience

With a Special Section on Transpersonal Psychology

To Christin and the Only One
— RV

To my parents, Poul and Margit Halling
— SH

Contributors

Marc Briod, Department of Philosophy, Oakland University, Rochester, Minnesota

Emily Davies, P.O. Box 671264, Chugiah, Alaska

Judy Dearborn Nill, Department of Journalism, Seattle University, Seattle, Washington

Constance T. Fischer, Department of Psychology, Duquesne University, Pittsburgh, Pennsylvania

William F. Fischer, Department of Psychology, Duquesne University, Pittsburgh, Pennsylvania

Robert Frager, Institute for Culture and Creation Spirituality, Holy Names College, Oakland, California and Institute for Transpersonal Psychology, Menlo Park, California

Amedeo Giorgi, Saybrook Institute, 1772 Vallejo Street, San Francisco, California

Steen Halling, Department of Psychology, Seattle University, Seattle, Washington

Bernd Jager, New School for Psychoanalysis, Santa Rosa, California

Mark King, School of Social Work, University of Pittsburgh, Pittsburgh, Pennsylvania

Michael Leifer, Seattle Mental Health Institute, Seattle, Washington

Ralph Metzner, California Institute of Integral Studies, 765 Ashbury Street, San Francisco, California

Donald Moncrieff, 84 Glendale Avenue, Toronto, Ontario, Canada

Donald Moss, Haight Clinic Psychological Services, 109 South Jackson Street, Spring Lake, Michigan

Donald E. Polkinghorne, Graduate Department of Counseling/School Psychology, California State University, Fullerton, California

Dianne Powers, Highline Evaluation and Treatment Center, Seattle, Washington

Robert D. Romanyshyn, Department of Psychology, University of Dallas, Irving, Texas

Jan O. Rowe, Department of Psychology, Seattle University, Seattle, Washington

Susan Schneier, Graduate School for the Study of Human Consciousness, John F. Kennedy University, Orinda, California

Ronald S. Valle, Graduate School for the Study of Human Consciousness, John F. Kennedy University, Orinda, California

Jeanne van Bronkhorst, Pierce County Health Department, Tacoma, Washington

Rolf von Eckartsberg, Department of Psychology, Duquesne University, Pittsburgh, Pennsylvania

Frederick J. Wertz, Department of Social Sciences, Fordham University, College at Lincoln Center, New York, New York

Brian J. Whalen, University of Dallas, Rome, Italy

Bryan Wittine, Graduate Program in Transpersonal Counseling Psychology, John F. Kennedy University, Orinda, California

Foreword

When I began to study psychology a half century ago, it was defined as "the study of behavior and experience." By the time I completed my doctorate, shortly after the end of World War II, the last two words were fading rapidly. In one of my first graduate classes, a course in statistics, the professor announced on the first day, "Whatever exists, exists in some number." We dutifully wrote that into our notes and did not pause to recognize that thereby all that makes life meaningful was being consigned to oblivion.

This bland restructuring—perhaps more accurately, destruction—of the world was typical of its time, 1940. The influence of a narrow scientistic attitude was already spreading throughout the learned disciplines. In the next two decades it would invade and tyrannize the "social sciences," education, and even philosophy. To be sure, quantification is a powerful tool, selectively employed, but too often it has been made into an executioner's axe to deny actuality to all that does not yield to its procrustean demands.

The objectivist view of psychology is very like the precolumbiam view of the world: It regards all that is not familiar as dangerous, mythical, or nonexistent. The whole western hemisphere of human life, the subjective, is thus feared, treated as illusory, or denied. (I use this term, *subjective,* to refer to the whole "internal" or personal realm of experiencing.) Such subjective or experiential processes as values, purpose, ideals, intention, dreams, fantasy, love, courage, and dread are reduced to epiphenomena by the radical objective view. (Strange that those who so vigilantly—and often ruthlessly—advance this myopic view seldom note their own subjective processes!)

In this vein, it is worth remembering the words of Paul Tillich: "Man resists objectification, and if man's resistance is broken, man himself is broken" (1951, p. 98). Clearly, the very essence of being human is the capacity for subjectivity, for inner living, inner experiencing, and inner intending.

In the 1950s, the effort to model psychology on nineteenth century physical science came increasingly to dominate academic and research centers. Yet in consulting rooms there was a less visible but growing counterforce: the movement of psychologists from preoccupation with testing into the practice of psychotherapy. Thus the experience component of our field was being kept alive.

The cultural revolution of the 1960s and early 1970s brought further attention to emotional responses, fantasy, and consciousness (especially its altered states). These are, of course, subjective experiences, and so the way was prepared for the reentry of the exiled dimension of life.

Today we are beginning to emerge from what is, in the long view, a relatively brief interregnum of radical positivism and its consort, psychological behaviorism (Bugental, 1975–1976). The emergence is certainly far from complete, and many academic citadels are still occupied by those who doggedly seek to produce a science in the model of an earlier century's notion of physics. Still the recognition that this is a truncated and distorting perspective is gaining ground steadily.

It is astonishing to see a well-known objectivist researcher forced to attack caricatures of viewpoints that value inner experiencing in an effort to excuse the paucity of results from his or her own orientation—one that rejects all but overt behavior (Skinner, 1987). Still it is instructive to observe how feeble a psychology becomes when it tries to deny human inner life. Behaviorists so readily slide into an objective–subjective dichotomy that smacks of the good–evil preachments of fundamentalist religionists!

More can be learned about this change by comparing the contents of this book with an earlier, related volume. A clear evidence of the renewal of concern with internal processes was the 1978 publication of *Existential–Phenomenological Alternatives for Psychology* (Valle & King). A decade has passed since then, and the title of the present volume is *Existential–Phenomenological Perspectives in Psychology*. The difference between *alternatives for* and *perspectives in* signals a significant evolution in our discipline. No longer is the existential–phenomenological perspective an outsider that may optionally be considered. It has become a recognized view in psychology—a development to which that earlier volume significantly contributed.

Looking back again, we need to note that 30 years ago Rollo May's *Existence* burst on the psychotherapy scene with an impact that caused many to reexamine, and a number to open, their conceptual frameworks (no small achievement that!). For me and for others, May's words spoke to what we were daily experiencing in our consulting rooms but what seemed to be blind spots in the dominant literature of the psychoanalysts and behaviorists. (Rogerian thinking had been helpful but too incomplete and light-sided for the deeper, more tragic and destructive material into which our work took us.)

The 20 years between *Existence* and the first of the two books I compared before saw the rise of many psychotherapeutic schools and systems. Though they shared little else, many of these necessarily gave priority to the subjective realm. While psychoanalysis and behaviorism, essentially efforts to objectify human beings, largely dominated the field, this earlier book marshaled the evidence of the consulting room to support the appropriateness of the more subjective perspective.

Change continues, of course, and so our conception of the subjective realm has grown as well. A significant portion of the 1978 volume was given to six existential therapists. An almost equal portion is now given to the developing field of transpersonal psychology—a topic not even listed earlier in either the table of contents or the index. Clearly, experience, in all its myriad forms, is an important area of psychology again.

What does it mean to be concerned with *experience* as contrasted with *behavior*? It means to attend to the person as a subject rather than an object. It means to recognize that this subject is indeed a source of what is actual and not solely the receptacle of contingency. It means to affirm that the human is a different order of phenomenon than any other. It means that the hope of an objective impersonal science is revealed as vain, partial, and self-defeating.

Many years ago, Franz Kafka pointed out a primary difference between an object and a person—to understand why a stone rolls down a hill, we must look to see what force loosened it from its place at the top, but to see why a person climbs the hill, we must discover what that person seeks at the top. It is the contrast between causation and intention that distinguishes the subjective or experiential realm.

Because humans are physical objects in part, we are subject to gravity as are all objects. However, because we are not only objects, we can also make gravity subject to our intent. Thus—although the law of gravity has not been repealed—we are able to use its force to send our kind to the moon, to send a probe through and beyond our solar system.

The key to this more-than-objective nature of the human lies in our reflexive awareness. The sunflower is aware—but probably not conscious—as it follows its lord across the sky. The deer is aware as it evades the hunter, and it is conscious is some measure. But the human—when most truly human—is not only aware but aware of being aware. This throws wild cards into the deck and provides a powerful counterforce to contingency.

Narrow scientistic psychology has had to deny the reality of reflexive awareness. It simply would ruin most research designs. Similarly, the human "organism" must usually be treated as though it is empty and inert until the experimenter "stimulates" it. The fact that a person is a process, always intending, always evolving, and continually observing and reinterpreting what is going on puts persons quite completely outside of the range of anything like adequate experimental controls. So the experimentalist prefers to pretend none of this is true, and in the laboratory reduces the human to an object.

In the ecology of our world, human beings play a unique and important part: We are—so far as we know—the only creatures to be aware of being aware. This is the miraculous quality of our subjectivity. From this gift (which can often seem a curse) come our capacities to have intentions, to reinterpret experience, to bring into being newness, and to create/discover meaning. The universe is not meaningless, for we are part of the universe and we are the meaning creators.

Subjectivity, inner experiencing, the essence of being human, demand that we take account of experience. Only in that neglected realm can we come to grips with the great issues of our lives. The neglect has resulted in our understanding of ourselves falling far behind our understanding of the physical world. We must mobilize all our potential if we are to prevent that discrepancy from destroying us all. It is to this task that this book contributes as it celebrates the subjective with skill, breadth of vision, and wisdom.

REFERENCES

Bugental, J. F. T. (1975–1976). Toward a subjective psychology: Tribute to Charlotte Buhler. *Interpersonal Development, 6,* 48–61.

Skinner, B. F. (1987). Whatever happened to psychology as the science of behavior? *American Psychologist, 42,* 780–786.

Tillich, P. (1951). *Systematic theology* (Vol. 1). Chicago: University of Chicago Press.

Valle, R. S., & King, M. (Eds.). (1978). *Existential–phenomenological alternatives for psychology.* New York: Oxford University Press.

James F. T. Bugental

Novato, California

Preface

This volume is both a new book and a revised version of *Existential–Phenomenological Alternatives for Psychology* (Valle & King, editors), published in 1978 by Oxford University Press. Twelve of the 20 chapters contained herein are completely new, and the 8 chapters retained from the original have been updated and substantially revised. Plenum Press is now the publisher, a section on transpersonal psychology has been added, and one of the editors, Steen Halling, is new to this project.

Even with these substantial changes, however, the book's basic format remains much the same, as does the impetus behind the book's development. Our aim is to provide a unified and accessible presentation of the existential–phenomenological approach to a wide range of topics in psychology that may be helpful to students as well as our colleagues. It is as true today as it was in 1978 that there are few, if any, psychology texts that provide a comprehensive overview of this approach at an introductory level (i.e., one that does not assume prior knowledge of existential phenomenology). In terms of its content, this book addresses many of the standard topics in psychology (e.g., research, perception, learning, development, personality, social psychology, psychopathology, and psychotherapy) from an existential–phenomenological perspective. In addition, there are chapters addressing issues central to human life (i.e., forgiveness, the passions, aesthetic consciousness, and spiritual awareness) that have received little if any systematic attention in mainstream psychology.

Since 1978, the existential–phenomenological approach has gained much ground and has become an increasingly significant and accepted force in most psychological circles. We have chosen the word *perspectives* (rather than *alternatives*) for this book's title to acknowledge this growth and reflect the nature of this change in our field. Signs of this development include the greater number of presentations on existential–phenomenology and related topics at the annual convention of the American Psychological Association; articles that present and discuss the existential–phenomenological approach in the APA's principal journal, *American Psychologist;* the existence of at least four journals in North America that focus on phenomenology (the *Journal of Phenomenological Psychology, Methods, Phenomenology and Pedagogy,* and the *Review of Existential Psychiatry and Psychology*); and the continued success of professional gatherings such as the International Human Science Research Conference (held annually since 1982). In addition, discussions of existential phenomenology are more common (even if often less than adequate) in textbooks for courses in abnormal, social, developmental, and introductory psychology.

Even with this increased visibility, however, misunderstandings of existential–phenomenological psychology continue to abound. The discussions in textbooks are seldom written by scholars with a solid background in this approach, existential–phenomenology being presented, all too often, as if it studied experience to the exclusion of behavior, and/or as nothing more than another approach to psychotherapy. Yet, this continued misunderstanding should not be too mysterious because the existential–phenomenological approach involves not only a change in what one thinks, but, more to the point, in how one thinks and feels (i.e., how one approaches life as well as specific psychological issues). In reading this book, then, the reader is being implicitly asked to adopt a new attitude, to "look upon the world anew." This invitation to a new perspective echoes the central theme of the phenomenological philosopher Edmund Husserl, who called upon his followers to set aside their theories and preconceptions and come "back to the things themselves," to life as we actually experience it.

The contributors to this volume have been carefully chosen, each chapter having been written specifically for this book. In accordance with the basic phenomenological insight that style and content coconstitute one another (they form an indissoluble unity), we felt that it was most appropriate for each author to write in the style most fitting for him or her given the topic being addressed. Being careful, therefore, not to alter style or content unnecessarily, our editing focused primarily on the coherence and clarity of the material being presented. Implicit in this stylistic diversity, however, is an underlying unity or common thread that reflects the contributors' commitment to an existential–phenomenological approach to psychology. With regard to the five authors discussing transpersonal psychology, their commitment to a transpersonal/spiritual perspective reflects the connecting thread behind their distinctive approaches.

This book is organized into six sections, each consisting of at least three chapters preceded by a brief editors' commentary that introduces the chapters in that section. The first five sections deal with the approach of existential–phenomenology, whereas the last contains five chapters that present transpersonal approaches to psychology. This last section is also preceded by a discussion of the reasons for bringing transpersonal psychology together with the existential–phenomenological approach in this volume.

We strongly recommend that readers who are not familiar with existential–phenomenological psychology begin by reading Chapter 1 as this chapter presents and discusses the key names and concepts necessary for a fundamental understanding of this approach. These names and concepts, as well as others, are identified throughout the book in two detailed indexes. These indexes are thereby designed to assist those using this book as a reference work.

Finally, we wish to point out that each of us is equally responsible for the overall organization and development of this book. Our joint editorship represents a growing friendship, a process whereby the sharing of our similarities and differences along the way has contributed to a positive and transformational experience for us both.

Ronald S. Valle
Steen Halling

Walnut Creek, California
Seattle, Washington

Acknowledgments

I wish to thank two groups of individuals: Those who continue to believe in and promote the power and value of integrating the existential/phenomenological perspective into psychology, and those who, with equal commitment, are dedicated to bringing the transpersonal perspective and spiritual awareness into our field. Both groups represent psychologists who are devoted to the increased understanding of the human condition and to the relief of suffering on this planet. It is because of them that this book is possible.

R.V.

I am grateful for the release time Seattle University has given me through a Faculty Fellowship for the summer of 1986 and a sabbatical leave for the fall of 1987. This support made possible the completion of this project.

I am indebted to the psychology department staff, Erik Lausund, Karen Lawrence, and Jean Morrison-Pace, who graciously and efficiently typed countless versions of sections of this book, and to my colleagues, whose respect for the human spirit continually inspires me. Above all, I want to thank my wife Mical for patiently affirming the value of exploring human experience.

S.H.

Contents

I

Introduction and Foundational Issues

The first three chapters of this text present foundational issues in existential–phenomenological psychology. They are all general in their scope, whereas the chapters that follow deal with more specific topics and applications.

The first chapter by Valle, King, and Halling presents the basic theoretical ideas that constitute the foundation of this book's approach. Because most of the other chapters assume a working knowledge of these basic concepts, we suggest a careful reading of this chapter.

The second chapter by Romanyshyn and Whalen examines the assumptions underlying the approach of contemporary American psychology. They discuss the philosophy and attitude of psychology as a ''science'' as it is traditionally defined and as it is exemplified in current textbooks. In the context of this discussion, they provide important insights into existential–phenomenological thought with their careful consideration of the visible and invisible nature of both behavior and experience as well as the common misunderstandings traditional psychology has regarding these foundational concepts.

The third chapter by Polkinghorne provides a rich and detailed presentation of various methods in existential–phenomenological research. He gives the reader a concrete sense of the value of this research in terms of its findings and interpretations and shows its relationship to its theoretical grounding. Anyone planning to carry out phenomenological research will find this chapter a helpful guide.

1

An Introduction to Existential–Phenomenological Thought in Psychology

Ronald S. Valle, Mark King, and Steen Halling

Almost all present-day psychology textbooks begin their project either explicitly or implicitly discussing the nature of men and women and what there is about them as living, sentient beings that can indeed be studied systematically. Our discussion will also begin in this fashion by comparing the foundation which underlies mainstream psychology with that of the existential–phenomenological approach. As you know, psychology, as it is typically presented, is heavily indebted to the natural sciences both for its understanding of human phenomena and its methods. The ground or foundation for psychology offered in the present volume is existential–phenomenological philosophy, and whereas this particular philosophy has a long history, it is only in recent times that systematic attention has been given to its implications for psychology. Many of you will undoubtedly find some of the ideas introduced to be quite new and, more than likely, somewhat discordant with your presently held views. At the same time, you may also find that existential–phenomenological psychology fits with your intuitive sense of human nature as well as your vision of what psychology should be like if it is to do justice to the realities of human life.

Even though our set purpose is to expose others to this alternative view of human beings and not to convince them of its validity *per se,* we also expect that your thoughts concerning what potentials the individual person (and, in fact, the world he or she lives in) has will undergo change. We hope that our discussion will significantly address your experience of both self and others and that your view of what the human being is will expand to encompass new horizons.

NATURAL SCIENTIFIC PSYCHOLOGY

In the first version of this book (Valle & King, 1978), it was posited that mainstream psychology is primarily behavioristic in emphasis. The situation today is somewhat different. Although there continues to be a strong behavioristic emphasis in some texts, more typically there has been a shift toward a cognitive perspective. According to one introductory text, this means that in psychology: "[W]e study the observable behavior of people and of animals. From that observable behavior we construct logical inferences about the kinds of internal mental processes that underlie the observed behavior" (Darley, Glucksberg, Kamin, & Kinchla, 1984, p. 5). A few textbooks even contain an overview of what they call the "existential–humanistic" perspective (e.g., Darley

Ronald S. Valle • Graduate School for the Study of Human Consciousness, John F. Kennedy University, Orinda, California 94563. *Mark King* • School of Social Work, University of Pittsburgh, Pittsburgh, Pennsylvania 15260. *Steen Halling* • Department of Psychology, Seattle University, Seattle, Washington 98122.

et al., 1984; Smith, Sarason, & Sarason, 1982), and there have been several articles on existential and phenomenological psychology in otherwise traditional journals such as *American Psychologist* (e.g., Faulconer & Williams, 1985; Jennings, 1986). We are gratified that psychology has opened up in this way in the last decade. Nonetheless, the natural scientific model is still the mainstay of contemporary psychology and, although interest in existential–phenomenological psychology has increased, few psychologists have an accurate appreciation of what this approach involves.

What follows is designed to refresh your memory about the nature and origins of the natural scientific approach to psychology. As you read through this section, keep in mind that psychology is a good deal more pluralistic (and therefore more confusing) than it used to be. One introductory text speaks of: "the sprawling fields of psychology, a loosely federated intellectual empire that stretches from the domains of the biological sciences on one border to those of the social sciences on the other" (Gleitman, 1983, p. 504). Nonetheless, some generalizations can still be made with respect to natural scientific psychology.

In asking the question, What is there to know about people anyway?, we very often in our everyday speculations conclude that there are two quite different aspects: (a) the outward, observable side of others; that is, what they do and what they say, commonly referred to as their physical or verbal behavior; and (b) the inward, unobservable side of others; that is, their thoughts, emotions, and sensations, commonly referred to as their private world of experience. Some behavioral psychologists who are interested in studying the aspects of human life that are typically thought of as belonging under the rubric of *experience,* prefer to speak of "covert behavior" rather than "experience." In principle, they argue that *experience* need not be private insofar as the physiological and chemical changes that accompany the experience in question can be observed and measured.

In examining the development of psychology as a separate discipline, it is readily apparent that a majority of its thinkers and practitioners utilize this everyday view of "what there is to know about people anyway" in their work (after all, psychologists are everyday people, too!). Behavior and experience came to be viewed as two separate aspects within psychology (and in many cases, opposing aspects) forming a behavior–experience polarity. That is, behavior and experience were viewed as essentially two different kinds of "stuff"—the first including all there is about a person that others can see or hear (if they have an inclination to either look or listen) and the second including all there is about a person that is inaccessible to others (no matter how hard they try to either

look or listen). Behavior, therefore, came to represent the objective ("object-like") aspect of people, whereas experience came to represent the subjective ("subject-like") aspect. This brand of philosophical dualism (the famous Cartesian split between the observable, accessible body and the unobservable, inaccessible mind) is still foundational to most theory and practice in psychology. That this remains, for the most part, an unexamined and unquestioned foundation makes it all the more powerful.

Let us pause here for a moment and examine the direction that psychology has been following for the past 50 years or so. We live, and have been living, in a world in which we believe that what is unknown or unusual to us will be explained or accounted for by the natural sciences in general (e.g., physics, chemistry, and biology) and by the methods and techniques they employ in particular. This natural scientific approach makes a number of assumptions. The three most crucial to the present discussion are: (a) the phenomenon (i.e., that which is to be studied) must be observable (i.e., we must be able to perceive it with one or more of our senses)—for example, rocket engines, salt, and roses are all observable phenomena; (b) the phenomenon must be measurable (i.e., we must be able to quantify the defined properties of the observed phenomenon)—for example, we can talk about the weight of a rocket engine, the amount of salt in a given chemical solution, or the size of a rose; and (c) the phenomenon must be such that it is possible for more than one observer to agree on its existence and characteristics—for example, all competent observers can agree that the rocket engine exists and weighs 15,000 pounds. (For a more thorough treatment of such natural scientific assumptions see Giorgi, 1971.) Psychology, formed by individuals embedded in this very same natural science world was, therefore, fashioned as a natural scientific psychology.

What are the implications of psychology conceived as a natural science for the behavior–experience polarity previously discussed? The implications should now be quite apparent! Insofar as the individual's experiential world is conceived of as private and experienced only by him or her (i.e., by the one who is undergoing the experience), it is not observable and, therefore, cannot be quantified by observing others. As we have seen, some behaviorists try to get around this problem by speaking of "covert behavior," whereas cognitive psychologists are willing to make inferences about "internal mental processes." In contrast, behavior is readily observable, quantifiable, and its existence and characteristics can be independently agreed upon by two or more observers. You and I cannot only see a person run and hear him or her yell but also measure how fast and how much, respectively.

Psychology, which literally means "science of the

mind,'' became, for many years, nearly synonymous with behaviorism. In more recent times, however, as illustrated by the following excerpts from the opening chapters to several introductory psychology textbooks, there has been a movement toward including both experience and behavior in the definition of psychology:

> Psychology, then, can be broadly defined as a complete science of human experience. (Ornstein, 1985, p. 4)

> Psychology deals with the nature of human experience and behavior, about the how and whys of what we do, think, and feel. (Gleitman, 1983, p. xx)

Yet the natural scientific emphasis remains predominant:

> Psychology may be defined as the scientific study of behavior and its causes. (Smith *et al.*, 1982, p. 6)

> Psychology is the study of the mind and behavior based on a set of rigorous scientific procedures that, when applied, allow professionals to study and predict behavior in order to improve the lives of all of us. (Hothersall, 1985, p. 4)

One of the aims of the natural sciences is to investigate *spatio-temporal* entities and the interrelationships that exist among them (Colaizzi, 1973). Given that it is concerned with basing its work on an observation of behavior, does mainstream psychology also have spatio-temporal entities as its subject matter? Behavior, being both observable and measurable, is certainly spatial in nature (any individual, for example, occupies a given space). This is also true, in principle at least, of the physiological processes which are assumed to underlie behavior. But in what sense is behavior temporal? One must examine the methodology of natural scientific psychology for a clue.

In the actual practice of mainstream psychology, hypotheses are formed and then tested, if at all feasible, in a rigorous experimental fashion. The formulation of hypotheses is the key. An hypothesis is, in general, a statement about the relationship between two entities or variables. In particular, it is a prediction about the cause–effect relationship between the first or *independent variable* (the proposed cause that the experimenter can manipulate) and the second or *dependent variable* (the proposed effect that is observed). Usually a proposed hypothesis will take this cause–effect form directly as in the specific example: ''Lack of sleep will lead to an increase in one's aggressive behavior;'' that is, the cause (lack of sleep) will lead to an effect (an increase in aggressive behavior). Hypotheses may take other forms, also, such as an if–then statement: *If* one doesn't get a proper amount of sleep, *then* one will become more aggressive. A more general case would include two notions with which we are all familiar: stimulus and response. The *stimulus* (that which impinges on the organism's

senses) is usually thought to elicit (cause) the *response* (the motor, perceptual, or cognitive effect). In any case, the important point is that an unstated *linear temporality* is implied in any proposed attempt to determine a cause–effect (or stimulus–response) relationship. One predicts that the effect will follow directly in time the presence of the cause. Similarly, if the proposed cause is absent, the effect will not occur. Another way to put this is that natural scientific psychology, in proposing hypotheses, is essentially asking the question *Why?* (If we return to our example: ''Why does aggressive behavior increase in this situation and not in this other one?'')

Since the 1960s, psychology has moved away from this simple stimulus–response analysis of behavior and has embraced a stimulus–organism–response model instead (Schultz, 1987). The organism refers to the internal processes—whether these are constructed in cognitive or physiological terms—that intervene between the stimulus and the response. In the present example, subjects' thoughts and feelings toward aggression would mediate between lack of sleep and consequent behavior. Those persons with strong inhibitions against aggressive behavior might show patterns of withdrawal or irritation with themselves, rather than aggression, when deprived of sleep. Nonetheless, mainstream psychology does examine spatio-temporal relationships (the connection between condition(s) and subsequent behavior(s)) as do any of the natural sciences. We return to this conclusion later on.

If, in fact, mainstream psychology attempts to unravel the ''if–then'' relationships evidenced in ongoing behavior, one more question must be raised: In what form is behavior manifested to the traditional psychologist? Or, in other words, What are counted as valid psychological phenomena [variables] by the traditional psychologist?

As discussed previously, the criteria that phenomena must fit in order to be considered valid variables are that they be observable and measurable. That is, the psychologist must be able to define exactly what behavior he or she will consider as evidence of a given variable. To use the more common expression, the variable in question must be operationalizable. How to *operationalize* a given variable is a critical issue facing natural scientific psychologists. For example, which of many observable and measurable behaviors will we agree to as evidence for the presence of aggression in our laboratory? Is it the number of times the subjects shake their fists? The number of heated words they use? How red their faces get? How hard they are breathing? The level of their blood pressure? How fast their hearts beat? Or, perhaps, two or more of these together? In one sense, *all* of these may be valid operationalizations of aggression. The point here is that

traditional psychologists must treat their given operationalizations *as identical* to the variable in question for
the duration of their particular experiment. That is, for a
given study, aggression *is* the number of times subjects
shake their fists, or learning *is* the score subjects get on a
written examination, or sorrow *is* the length of time that
subjects shed tears, and so forth. Michael Lewis (1972),
himself a natural scientific psychologist, recognizes the
confusion that often results from equating a phenomenon
with its measurement:

> It is clear from the literature that any exact definition of
> state is not easily forthcoming. Because of the un-
> willingness to deal with introspective description, inves-
> tigators have been forced to define state in terms of orga-
> nism behavior, which they believe accurately reflects
> some underlying condition. That is, there has generally
> been a confusion between measurement and definition.
> This can be seen most often in the literature where at-
> tempts at definition start with state in quotation marks,
> soon giving way to taxonomy, then replaced by measure-
> ment of specific behaviors. From that point on state no
> longer appears in quotation marks. (p. 96)

The type of question infrequently raised by mainstream psychologists and the one never answered by natural scientific methods, however, is, Just what is being
aggressive anyway?, or What is the experience of learning?, Or What is being sorrowful? The reason that natural
scientific psychology cannot even begin to deal with this
kind of question (i.e., *What?* not *Why?*) is because natural
scientific methodology is designed to deal with only one-
half of the behavior–experience polarity—behavior. In
order to address the important questions raised here,
questions relating to human experience as well as to
human behavior, we must turn to another approach in
order to complement natural scientific methodology.

EXISTENTIAL–PHENOMENOLOGICAL PSYCHOLOGY

Having briefly reviewed the traditional approach to
psychology, in addition to having asked why a new approach would be fruitful (and perhaps even necessary),
we now attempt to answer the question, What is this other
approach? From its very name, existential–phenomenological psychology is quite obviously the result of blending two interrelated perspectives, existentialism and
phenomenology. Although existentialism and phenomenology constitute complementary approaches, certain distinctions can be made between them.

The Danish thinker Søren Kierkegaard (1813–1855)
is generally regarded as the founder of existential philosophy, whereas Edmund Husserl (1859–1938), a German
philosopher, is credited as the primary proponent of phe-

nomenology. For Kierkegaard, it was imperative that philosophy address itself to the concrete existence of the
individual person and attempt to elucidate the fundamental themes with which human beings invariably struggle.
Husserl's aim was more academic: phenomenology
meant the rigorous and unbiased study of things *as they
appear* so that one might come to an essential understanding of human consciousness and experience. The
development of specific methods for studying human experience is one of the primary contributions of phenomenology.

Recognizing the inability of positivistic, natural scientific thinkers in the social sciences to deal adequately
with basic human issues (e.g., joy, despair, love, freedom, and choice), twentieth-century existentialists, such
as Jean-Paul Sartre, turned to the methods developed by
phenomenology, for the aim of phenomenology is to allow us to contact phenomena as we actually live them out
and experience them (Husserl, 1970). One of the first
thinkers to bring together existential concerns and phenomenological methodology was the German philosopher Martin Heidegger (1889–1976) who, as a student of
Husserl, also drew inspiration from Kierkegaard. Unlike
Sartre, Heidegger (1962) was not interested in psychological issues *per se,* even though he deeply influenced two
phenomenological psychiatrists, Ludwig Binswanger
and Medard Boss.

Here, then, was an appropriate methodological approach with which to examine the content of existential
philosophy. Phenomenology, therefore, became an almost perfect complement to existentialism (in many ways
phenomenological methods underlie all existential philosophical inquiries, but this issue is well beyond the scope
of the present discussion).

Joined together in this fashion, *existential phenomenology* can be viewed as that philosophical discipline which seeks to understand the events of human existence in a way that is free of the presuppositions of our
cultural heritage, especially philosophical dualism and
technologism, as much as this is possible. Representatives of this joint tradition include Maurice Merleau-Ponty, Karl Jaspers, and Gabriel Marcel.

When applied more specifically to human psychological phenomena, existential phenomenology became
existential–phenomenological psychology, and, as such,
has become that psychological discipline that seeks to
explicate the *essence, structure,* or *form* of both human
experience and human behavior as revealed through essentially *descriptive* techniques including disciplined reflection. The remainder of this chapter attempts to clarify
and expand on this "definition" of existential–phenomenological psychology, these particular ideas and
terms, providing a foundation for the specific issues dis-

cussed in the chapters that follow. (It is important to note that in contemporary writings—including those in this book—"phenomenological psychology" is often used as an abbreviated form of "existential–phenomenological psychology.")

The Foundational Concepts of Existential– Phenomenological Psychology

Examined in terms of the natural scientific viewpoint and its underlying assumptions, existential–phenomenological psychology would be bad natural science. Some questions that the natural scientist might ask are, How can purely descriptive techniques be rigorous in revealing cause–effect relationships?, or How can an objective science hope to reveal such an apparently subjective phenomenon as essence?, or Is not disciplined reflection merely a throwback to purely subjective approaches such as introspectionism? These inquiries would be valid if the differences between existential–phenomenological psychology and natural scientific psychology were merely surface distinctions. But they are not! In fact, existential–phenomenological psychology has a quite different basis, quite different "roots." A closer look reveals that its conception of the human individual, the questions it poses, and its methods are all grounded in carefully articulated, different philosophical assumptions. Although our task here is one of psychology and not philosophy *per se,* an examination of these different assumptions is necessary.

The major (and perhaps most critical) issue is that people are not viewed as just objects in nature. Rather, the existential–phenomenological psychologist speaks of the total, indissoluble unity or interrelationship of the individual and his or her world. The existential man or woman is *more* than simply natural man or natural woman. In the truest sense, the person is viewed as having no existence apart from the world and the world as having no existence apart from persons. Each individual and his or her world are said to *coconstitute* one another. In traditional psychology, people and their environment are seen, in effect, as two separate and distinct things or poles. This traditional conception is rejected by the existential–phenomenological psychologist, in favor of the previously mentioned unity.

This notion of co-constitutionality can be a difficult one to grasp. Let us begin with a simple perceptual example. Figure 1 illustrates the popular "vase and faces" drawing. In this picture, one can either treat the center portion as "figure" and the outer surrounds as "ground" (in which case one sees a vase), or one can treat the center as "ground" and the outer surrounds as "figure" (in

Figure 1. The "vase and faces" drawing.

which case one sees two facial profiles facing one another). In this drawing, then, it is quite clear that the vase and the faces cannot exist without one another. Remove one and the notion of the other has no meaning. So it is with people and their world; if one is discarded, talk of the others is meaningless. This is to say that the human individual is contextualized. It is impossible to conceive of a person without the familiar, surrounding world (house in which that person lives, trees among which that person walks, sky upon which that person gazes, others to whom that person talks, etc.). It is through the world that the very *meaning* of the person's existence emerges both for himself or herself and for others. The converse is equally true. It is each individual's existence that gives his or her world its meaning. Without a person to reveal its sense and meaning, the world would not exist as it does. Each is, therefore, totally dependent on the other for its existence. This is why, in existential–phenomenological thought, existence always implies that being is actually "being-in-the-world" (Heidegger, 1962).

You might ask on what is this total interdependency based? To the existential–phenomenological psychologist, the answer lies in the notion of *dialogue.* People and the world are always in a dialogue with each other.

For this reason, people can be seen as partly active because they are always acting in their world in a purposeful way, and partly passive because the world is always acting on them (i.e., the world presents situations in which the person must act). This relationship is diagrammed in Figure 2. As soon as this notion of a *dialogal relationship* between people and the world is understood, other insights begin to appear. For example, people are seen by the existential–phenomenological psychologist as being "condemned to choice." Within the world (i.e., the world as situations that are presented to each of us which we did not necessarily request), one must always make choices. The only "choice" one cannot make is the choice of not choosing (which is really *choosing* not to).

This leads to another important characteristic of existential–phenomenological psychology; because the world is always acting on people, the model of the person with absolute free will is rejected to the same degree as is the model of the totally objectified, completely determined individual. (Recall that determinism is that philosophical doctrine that posits that one's choice of action is not free but, rather, is preordained or determined by a sequence of causes independent of one's will). Rather than having complete personal freedom on the one hand, or being completely determined by the environment on the other, each person is said to have *situated freedom;* that is, the freedom (and obligation) of making choices within, and oftentimes limited by, a given situation that the world has presented to him or her. In the following chapters, these notions of coconstitutionality and situated freedom will be expanded on and applied in specific psychological contexts.

Another critical issue involves how the *nature of consciousness* itself is regarded. In the everyday experimental work of the psychologist, the nature of consciousness as an issue is rarely raised. If it is brought up, consciousness is usually either equated with what makes up one's experience at a given point in time (i.e., consciousness is thought to be identical with what is presently being thought or felt), or it is thought of as a "container" that "fills up" with contents (new facts, sensations, feelings, etc.). In either case, consciousness is objectified. The notion *loses consciousness,* for example, implies that consciousness is some *thing* that can be lost (or regained at a later time, for that matter). In addition, consciousness is viewed as having a creative function. We speak of "digging things up from memory" or "synthesizing a new idea." Our experiences are often thought as put together or categorized somehow in our mind. In fact, to some (e.g., Brunner, 1957), the very meaning of that which we perceive is a direct product of categorization (i.e., the meaning of a new phenomenon is derived from that category in our mind in which we place it).

Existential–phenomenological psychologists reject this view of consciousness in favor of a perspective more in keeping with their view of the human individual (as described before). For most of them, this different view of consciousness is a derivative of (if not identical to) the thinking of the phenomenologist Edmund Husserl. Husserl's insights and innovations are often difficult to understand, partly because they are so foreign to our natural scientific, causal view of the world. At the same time, these insights are more faithful to basic human experience than natural scientific interpretations.

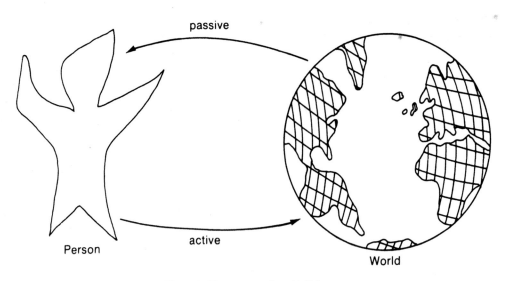

Figure 2. The person and world dialogue.

The major focus of Husserl's (1970) attention was not on the world as interpreted and thus created by scientific fact and theory. Rather, his concern was with the world of everyday experience as expressed in everyday language; that is, with the world as given in *direct and immediate experience* (hence Husserl's slogan, "Back to the things themselves"). One could say that Husserl's domain was the domain of phenomena—pure phenomena independent of and prior to any reflective interpretation, scientific or otherwise. This realm of naive experience, then, is not the external environment of the natural sciences, but, rather, the *Lebenswelt*[1] or *life-world*. This is the world as lived by the person and not the hypothetical external entity separate from or independent of him or her.

The *Lebenswelt*, being given directly and immediately in human experience, is the starting point or ground for the existential–phenomenological psychologist. The life-world is the foundation upon which existential–phenomenological thought is built (no assumptions are made as to what might be behind or cause the life-world); in the truest sense, the *Lebenswelt is the beginning.* It is, therefore, not at all like the world of the natural scientist which is constructed or built up for explanatory purposes (e.g., the way in which simple ideas are first molded into hypotheses and then into complex theories through the direct employment of cause–effect thinking). These constructions are the result of a creating cognitive activity (recall that the natural scientist views consciousness as having a creative function). The life-world is not a construction of consciousness: It is co-constituted or co-created in the dialogue of person and world.

As stated, naive experience is not based on anything else; there is nothing from which it could be constructed. Hypotheses, theories, and the causal thinking on which they are based are, therefore, not the subject matter that

constitute the life-world *per se* as they are not given in direct and immediate experience. They are higher order, less basic, derived notions; that is, they are, like all ideas, derivatives of the life-world.

Left unexamined, without insight into its derived nature, cause–effect thinking can be not only limiting but also misleading. Consider the perspective of Alan Watts (1966):

> We believe that every thing and every event must have a cause, that is, some *other* thing(s) or event(s), and that it will in its turn be the cause of other effects. So how does a cause lead to an effect? To make it much worse, if all that I think or do is a set of effects, there must be causes for all of them going back into an indefinite past. If so, I can't help what I do. I am simply a puppet pulled by strings that go back into times far beyond my vision.
> Again, this is a problem which comes from asking the wrong question. . . . [Consider] someone who has never seen a cat. He is looking through a narrow slit in a fence, and on the other side, a cat walks by. He sees first the head, then the less distinctly shaped furry trunk and then the tail. Extraordinary! The cat turns round and walks back, and again he sees the head, and a little later the tail. This sequence begins to look like something regular and reliable. Yet again, the cat turns round, and he witnesses the same regular sequence: first the head, and later the tail. Thereupon he reasons that the event *head* is the invariable and necessary cause of the event *tail*, which is the head's effect. This absurd and confusing gobbledygook comes from his failure to see that head and tail go together: they are all one cat. (p. 26)

This brings us to another important point. Even when we as traditional experimental psychologists discuss the formulation of hypotheses and theories from our empirical,[2] natural scientific approach, we are usually aware of our thinking or *reflecting* process. We reflect on different ideas and ponder over them, trying to see how they might fit together (e.g., "Are variable A and variable B related?" and, if so, "Does A cause B?" "Does B cause A?" or "Does some unthought of variable C cause both simultaneously?"). These hypotheses are then tested in an experimental fashion, the design of the experiment also being the result of reflective thinking (e.g., Is this particular control group necessary?, Have I operationalized this variable appropriately?). All knowledge derived from the scientific method is, therefore, knowledge born of reflective thought.

It was mentioned before, however, that the life-world is the foundation or ground for this scientific thinking, that it is *prior to* reflective thought. It is because the

[1]*Lebenswelt* is one of many, usually German or French, words that you will encounter in existential–phenomenological writings that express the total interrelatedness or mutual dependence of a phenomenon's distinguishable aspects (e.g., that the person and his or her world coconstitute one another as described before). As there are no comparable words in English that express this implied unity, contrived terms are, therefore, used as the only possible translation. The usual form these English equivalents assume is a relatively literal translation of the meaning of each word, the words then being connected with a hyphen (as in life-world). Other examples include Heidegger's notions of "being-in-the-world" and *Dasein* (literally "there-being"), and Merleau-Ponty's "body-subject." The suggestion of separateness between the person (as "life," "being," or "subject") and the external environment (as "world," "there," or "body") is not entirely dissolved, however, by this method of hyphenation and so these expressions, although quite necessary, continue to appear somewhat artificial or contrived.

[2]*Empirical* as a descriptor of one's approach has been used, not only by the natural scientific-oriented researcher (in this common, often-cited manner) but also by the existential–phenomenological psychologist. See W. Fischer, Chapter 8, for a discussion of these two different ways in which one's investigation may be considered "empirical."

life-world is prior to and the foundation of reflective thought that the existential–phenomenological psychologist describes the life-world as being of a *prereflective* nature (as giving birth to our reflective awareness). In this way, then, the Lebenswelt is both independent of knowledge derived from reflective thought processes, and yet, being *prereflective* (*before*-reflective), it is also the indispensable ground or starting point for all knowledge. Scientific knowledge could not exist without the prereflective life-world. This is the paradoxical nature of the Lebenswelt.

As one example, consider the following passage from Prescott (1974):

> In my senior year in college I took a philosophy course in logic. As I worked through a problem to its final solution, I not only knew that the problem was being worked out correctly or incorrectly based upon my knowledge of certain well-articulated rules, but rather, I knew the problem was correct or incorrect (indeed, I understood, had knowledge of, these rules), because I "knew," I could feel, I could *sense* the harmony or disharmony within the entire problem. To give another example: there will be times in the middle of writing a paper when I am at a loss for words, for articulate meaning and yet I "know," I have a *sense* of what I want to say. What does this experience of sensing involve? At this point in my reflections it would seem it involves feeling meaning, knowing in a bodily way. I experience this knowing, this meaning, almost as a diffusion of a sensation through my chest, my arms, and the back of my head. Sometimes I find that breathing, inhaling deeply, or moving my arms slowly through space heightens or clarifies "knowing" in this mode. It is as if meaning, knowing, has touched me within, throughout my body. I have been affected with and by meaning. I know, I *sense* meaning affectively within my bodily being. Articulate, verbal meaning usually arises for me if I allow myself to stay with this sensing, this felt meaning. As I read over what I eventually do write, attempting to see if it "makes sense" (to use an old, familiar phrase), I actually find I am trying to see if what I have said harmonizes with the sense of meaning, that is, the bodily knowing I feel. (pp. 172–173)

In this particular example, the meaning as "sensed" is essentially of a prereflective nature, whereas the articulated, verbal meaning is this prereflective "sensing" on the level of reflective thought. *Thematic* verbalization or languaging is a reflective process.

Consider this second example. Albert Einstein (1952), whose name conjures up an image of a great scientist and a reflective thinker, once described his own thinking process:

> The words of the language as they are written or spoken do not seem to play any role in my mechanism of thought. The physical entities which seem to serve as elements in thought are certain signs and more or less clear im-

ages . . . these elements are, in my case, of a visual and in some of a *muscular type.* Conventional words or other signs have to be sought for laboriously only in a *secondary stage.* (p. 43 [emphasis added])

Again, Einstein is speaking of an initial prereflective sensing followed, only later, by language.

This is not to suggest that language, because it is critical to reflection, operates solely at the level of reflective awareness or that it primarily serves to "impose" meaning upon the world of perceptual experience. In fact, Merleau-Ponty (1962) reminds us of the intimate connection of language and perception: "As has often been said, for the child the thing is not known until it is named, the name is the essence of the thing and resides in it on the same footing as its colour and its form" (pp. 177–178). The articulation and clarification of meaning changes what is seen: That which was somehow vaguely known, at a preverbal, bodily, level becomes clearly evident.

At the level of the prereflective, speaking is a form of expression that is almost an action, a dimension of our relationship to ourselves, the world, and others that pours forth spontaneously (and, at times, surprisingly). If you notice, for example, that a pedestrian is about to step into the path of an oncoming car, you immediately yell, "Stop!" Had you paused to reflect on the situation, you might have spoken too late.

This example brings us back to our daily lives. As we go about our everyday tasks, we do not normally think of that which surrounds us as being pure phenomena, that is, as being given in our direct, naive experience, as made possible by our very presence. Rather, we think that the world and the objects around us exist independently of us—that what we experience is a direct reflection of what is "out there." We somehow forget that our experience is just that—*our* experience. Husserl (1970) referred to this naive belief in the independent existence of what is given in experience as the *"natural attitude."* In the modern world, the natural attitude includes those beliefs adopted from science, namely that the interrelationships and functioning of objects follow certain discovered or to-be-discovered laws. And it is in pursuit of these laws that we categorize, organize, and interpret our perceptions.

The existential–phenomenological psychologist, however, assumes a different position or vantage point (i.e., one other than this "natural attitude"), a position that Husserl (1962) refers to as the *"transcendental attitude."* How does one assume this transcendental attitude? In order to understand a given phenomenon, one attempts to suspend or put in abeyance one's preconceptions and presuppositions (i.e., one's biases). In phenomenology, this process is called *bracketing.* In order to bracket one's preconceptions and presuppositions, how-

ever, one must first make them explicit—one must "lay out" these assumptions so that they appear in as clear a form as possible to oneself. This is illustrated by the case of a therapist working with an angry young man. The therapist took it for granted, at an early point in the therapy process, that his client's attitude of hostility was a function of the client's childhood experiences of abandonment, as if hostility were an automatic response to such events. Then, later, the therapist realized that he had made the assumption that the hostile attitude and the life events were directly related. At this point, the clinician started to ask whether this original assumption was necessarily true, and a series of other ways of looking at the situation emerged.

These processes of bracketing and explication of assumptions have been found to interact in a dynamic fashion. It seems that as one brackets his or her preconceptions, more of these emerge at the level of reflective awareness (i.e., that which is of the prereflective level becomes accessible at the level of reflective thought). As these newly discovered assumptions are then bracketed, this leads to the emergence and subsequent realization of still other assumptions, and so on. Continuing with our clinical example, the therapist further started to wonder if his client's stories about abandonment might not cover over other aspects of his life (not everyone abandoned him), and if the constant expression of anger might not be a diversion from other feelings.

This process of bracketing and rebracketing is the manner in which one moves from the "natural attitude" toward the "transcendental attitude." This process of adopting the transcendental attitude is called the reduction, as one quite literally reduces the world as it is considered in the natural attitude to a world of pure phenomena or, more poetically, to a purely phenomenal realm. This process of bracketing is one that never ends, and so a complete reduction is an impossibility.

In the reduction, therefore, one does not categorically deny the existence of the natural world—the client did not simply fabricate the events he or she described—but rather one puts in abeyance one's belief that the world is independent of each individual person. (Remember, the existential–phenomenological psychologist views the individual and the world as coconstituting one another and, in this context, we all help to make the story of our lives what it is.) The world, as a result of bracketing the natural attitude, becomes phenomenal in nature—it is not an external conglomeration of entities any longer (i.e., it is no longer the objectified, physical world) but rather a world-for-consciousness (one again, the hyphens illustrate the total interdependency implied—there is no world without a consciousness to perceive it and, similarly, no consciousness without a world to be conscious of).

We have come full circle and have now returned to the notion of consciousness. To the existential–phenomenological psychologist, objects have their basis in and are sustained by the constituting power of consciousness (if one considers for a moment only the consciousness "side" of the world-for-consciousness interdependency). That is, consciousness is not seen as either a creating force of sorts or as an objectified "thing" in itself. Rather it is regarded as a making present. Consciousness is that forum in which phenomena show themselves or are revealed. It is not some mysterious entity or power by which objects are created. As discussed before, the notion and labeling of external objects done in the natural attitude are seen to be of a higher-order, derived, reflective nature; this notion of objects as external is derived from the prereflective phenomena that are present to consciousness when one engages in the reduction.

In addition, the existential–phenomenological psychologist also points out that we are never merely conscious but are always conscious of something. Saying that consciousness is always a "consciousness of" means that it always has an object (an object, that is, that is not consciousness itself). This object may be of a concrete nature such as a chair, a tree, or another person; it could be any one of a number of dream images, or it could be an abstract idea or concept. Consciousness is, therefore, said to be intentional in nature or to be characterized by intentionality. That is, when speaking of consciousness, one is either implicitly or explicitly referring to its intended object as well.

The existential phenomenologist's use of "intentionality" is a specialized one that has a different meaning than the word intention has in everyday speech. Whereas intention normally refers to a purpose or agenda that we have, intentionality addresses the ongoing dimension of our consciousness, that we are always in relation to that which is beyond us. Merleau-Ponty (1962) points out that intentionality extends to our whole bodily being; the way a person walks or carries himself or herself speaks to that person's continual relationship to his or her surroundings.

Zaner (1970) presents the idea of intentionality in an interesting fashion. Examining Figure 3, we can identify two poles: (a) the noetic (i.e., the subjective, the perceiving)—in this case, seeing-of-tree, and (b) the noematic (i.e., the objective, the perceived)—in this case, tree-as-seen. Zaner, in his discussion of this classical distinction, indicates that if we take a reflective stance toward this process we become aware not of two separate poles per se but of a complex affair: the process of consciousness (or, as Zaner refers to it, consciousing) with its specific object. In our example, the specific object would be "the-reflected-on," or, more specifically, "seeing-of-tree-as-seen." Zaner states:

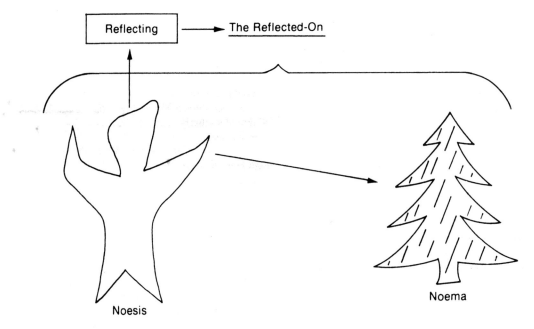

Figure 3. The noetic–noematic complex.

My reflecting, then, is by no means a seeing of the tree, nor simply a grasping of the seeing alone. *It is rather an apprehension of the entire noetic-noematic complex.* Most striking about this complex is just this *correlation.* The most generic feature, we shall say, of any possible consciousing is that it is "intentive" to objects, and these objects are "intended by" the consciousing. (p. 134)

The idea of total interrelatedness, this "correlation" as Zaner calls it, is again apparent. It is by consciousness that objects are made present (are "intended"), yet, equally as true, it is by objects that consciousness is revealed or elucidated. Without a consciousness (as "consciousing") through which they can show themselves, there are no objects. Similarly, without objects revealing themselves, there is no consciousness. They form an indissoluble unity characterized by their mutual intentionality.

As a final point of clarification, consider Zaner's (1970) description regarding another feature of the consciousness–object relationship:

My reflecting reveals that my mental processes are essentially intentive, that they are intentive toward objects of various types, and that different processes can have the same object. Thus, I can see my dog, Irving, remember the house I once lived in, love my family, feel pride in my profession, and so on. I can also see my dog, remember him, love him, feel pride in his uniqueness, defend his peculiar traits before skeptics, and the like. I can also see

the dog, see the grass where he lies sprawled, see the trees behind, and the like. Different consciousings can have the same or different objects, and the same type of consciousing can have the same or different objects. (p. 134)

Intentionality, then, does not just characterize single issues or content. Within existential–phenomenological psychology, and in using phenomenological methods for investigating and describing phenomena, the intentional nature of things seems to be present everywhere you turn.

Implications for Psychological Inquiry

It should be readily apparent from our earlier discussion that existential–phenomenological psychology is not objective or positivistic in nature. From our talk of the life-world or *Lebenswelt* and the intentional nature of consciousness, it should be equally evident that existential–phenomenological psychology is not subjective or introspectionistic in nature either. Existential–phenomenological psychology is, in one way then, a middle ground or, in a more active sense, a thrusting between the purely objective and purely subjective approaches that have taken form in psychology. By treating perception as intentional in nature, the objective and subjective are seen as inseparable, one unable to exist without the other. Any approach that is solely objective or solely subjective is viewed, therefore, as necessarily limited in scope and as doing, in fact, an injustice to the essential nature of the indissoluble subject–object unity. In other words, an approach that is totally objective or totally subjective confuses and distorts the very phenomena it seeks to explain and/or describe.

From this discussion of the life-world and intentionality, it should be clear that phenomenology does not view causality in the same way that traditional psychology does. In fact, the existential–phenomenological psychologist rejects the notion of causality in its linear or additive form (i.e., rejects the belief that change is initiated and directed by external events). Thus the individual is studied without the proposing and experimental testing of cause–effect relationships. These cause–effect relationships have no place in the elucidating of the life-world. In fact, they are meaningless in such a context because the person and his or her world co-constitute one another rather than events in one realm causing events in the other. At best, one could speak of sequences of behavior, but it is impermissible to derive causality from sequence as Alan Watts has so simply illustrated in the "cat and fence" example cited previously.

Even with reference to our own thoughts and feelings, Merleau-Ponty (1962) has pointed out that "the 'cause' of a 'psychic fact' is never another 'psychic fact' . . ." (p. 115). Recalling the "vase and faces" example, one can speak of their mutual dependency, but one would be hard pressed to talk of the vase causing the faces or the faces being the cause of the vase. Or, as another example, the existential–phenomenological psychologist would never speak of something that happened in an individual's past (such as the physical punishment a child may have received from his or her parents) as a cause for later behavior (his or her aggressive nature as an adult). The meaning of both events may be of interest, but this does not justify one's thinking that the first event caused the second.

If the notion of linear causality is rejected as a basis for studying the individual, then hypothesis formation and experimentation (including all that it implies, such as control groups, independent and dependent variables, operationalization, etc.) are also rejected. Hypotheses as proposed functional relationships are not utilized because they imply something hidden is producing (causing) that which is apparent. For the existential–phenomenological psychologist, only that which has its base in naive experience is real and, therefore, only that which is revealed or disclosed as pure phenomena is worthy of attention. Hypothesizing is a cognitive exercise as is the testing of hypotheses though experimentation. The true experiment's whole purpose is to test proposed cause–effect relationships and, so, it also falls by the wayside.

The Nature of Structure

What then is the goal of the existential–phenomenological psychologist? At the very beginning of this section, we stated that the existential–phenomenological psychologist seeks to reveal the structure of experience through descriptive techniques and, as alluded to, does this by asking the question, What? That is, he or she seeks to understand phenomena in their perceived immediacy and is not concerned with explaining, predicting, or controlling them—the question, Why?, is not asked as this question implies an underlying causal view of the world. Description through disciplined reflection, therefore, replaces the experiment as method, whereas structure replaces cause–effect relationships as the content of existential–phenomenological psychology. Let us, then, examine this notion of structure.

Structure (sometimes referred to, whether interchangeably or with subtle philosophical differences, as essence or form) is a basic, foundational concept in the existential–phenomenological approach to psychology. Phenomena, as they are present to us, seem to reveal themselves in different ways, depending on how we look at them or "take them up" in our many, varied perspectives and life situations (as discussed before by Zaner, 1970). Regardless of which of the phenomenon's particular variations is revealed at any given time, this phenomenon is seen as having the same essential meaning when it is perceived over time in many different situations. The perceived phenomenon is analogous to a mineral crystal that appears to have many different sizes and shapes depending on the intensity, angle, and color of the light that strikes its surface. Only after seeing these different reflections and varied appearances on repeated occasions does the constant, unchanging crystalline structure become known to us.

Consider an example from the psychological realm: "being anxious" is an experience we all recognize as it has meaning for us (see W. Fischer's Chapter 8 on this topic). Being anxious, however, never arises in exactly the same way; we may be anxious before taking an examination that we have not studied for, or when anticipating the ending to a horror movie, or before going to the dentist, or, very often, for no apparent reason at all. These are all different manifestations that constitute the meaningful experience that we label as being anxious. This form, recognized despite its many variations, is evident in each one of these different instances. This communality among instances is the "what" referred to earlier; that is, it is the structure of the particular phenomenon.

Merleau-Ponty (1963), who addresses the notion of structure or form throughout many of his writings, defines it as:

. . . total processes which may be indiscernible from each other while their "parts," compared to each other, differ in absolute size; in other words the systems are defined as transposable wholes. We will say that there is form whenever the properties of a system are modified by every change brought about in a single one of its parts and, on the contrary, are conserved when they all change while maintaining the same relationship among themselves. (p. 47)

Another example, that of the notion of *melody* in music, should help to clarify these points. Melody has a common meaning as it is something that almost all of us have experienced; and once a particular melody has been heard, most of us are remarkably good at recognizing it again when it is played by different instruments, in different physical settings, and at different times. Melody is more than just an experience, however, as one can abstract the particular musical notes that comprise it by marking down the order of these notes, their loudness, and their duration on a musical scale. The melody or musical theme from the first movement of Tchaikovsky's Fifth Symphony, presented in Figure 4, is an easily recognized one and can be used to illustrate the notion of structure.

If any one of the "parts" (notes) of this melody is changed (e.g., if any single note is moved up or down any distance on the musical scale while the other notes remain fixed), then a new and different melody is created. If you are musically inclined, you may wish to play the original melody as written and then again with the one-note alteration. This new melody may sound pleasing, or it may not (depending on which note was moved and by how much), but it should be apparent that the structure of the original musical theme is different, that is, a new melody has been created. The "properties of the system" would also be altered if the loudness or duration of any one of the notes was altered. Again, every change in a single part modifies the whole.

On the other hand, if *all* the the notes of this melody were moved up or down on the musical scale the same distance (i.e., if the whole melody was transposed), then

Figure 5. A melody from the first movement of Tchaikovsky's Fifth Symphony transposed one octave.

its structure would remain invariant. For example, the melody in Figure 5 is the same melody pictured in Figure 4 only it has been transposed down one full octave (the distance the set of notes was moved up or down the musical scale is not important for this example as long as all the notes were moved the same distance and in the same direction; a third or a fifth would have done just as well as an octave). Although the melody in Figure 5 is comprised of a whole new set of notes (and not just one as in our previous example), it will be recognized as the same musical theme (i.e., as the same melody) as the one in Figure 4. In this case, all the parts were altered, yet their relationship stayed the same; therefore, the structure remains unchanged. Again, actually playing the notes in Figures 4 and 5 should convince you of this fact. As it is with melody, so it is with human experience, regardless of the particular phenomenon (i.e., experience) being investigated. We might even say that there is a distinctive melody or theme to each of our many experiences.

The structure of a phenomenon is, then, the commonality running though the many diverse appearances of the phenomenon. Giorgi (1970) states: "One of its [structure's] values for us is that it is precisely structure that is the reality that one responds to at the phenomenal level" (p. 179). Recalling that structure is made present to us as *meaning,* one can now rephrase the task of the existential–phenomenological psychologist as one of disclosing the nature of structure in the form of meaning. That is, through description the prereflective life-world is brought to the level of reflective awareness where it manifests itself as psychological meaning. This is done both for the purpose of understanding phenomena and because, as Colaizzi (1973) states, "Without thereby first disclosing the foundations of a phenomenon, no progress whatsoever can be made concerning it, not even a first faltering step can be taken towards it, by science or by any other kind of cognition" (p. 28).

Hermeneutics

The term *hermeneutics* has been appearing in the psychological literature with increasing frequency in the

Figure 4. A melody from the first movement of Tchaikovsky's Fifth Symphony.

def.

last decade or so. Although there are a number of hermeneutical perspectives, they are all concerned with meaning and interpretation. The origin of the word *hermeneutics* suggests as much. In Greek mythology, the god Hermes had the task of bringing messages from the gods to humans. This task was far from a simple one because the gap between the world of the gods and the world of mortals precluded that Hermes simply hand over messages. Instead, Hermes was both messenger and interpreter. In fact, as Palmer (1969) points out, any reading of a message or a text involves at the very least a spontaneous interpretation of its meaning. Similarly, an actor or actress has to interpret a character in his or her own way in order to play this specific character.

At a basic level, then, hermeneutics can be defined as "the study of understanding, especially the task of understanding texts" (Palmer, 1969, p. 9). But understanding a text is not possible if one approaches it in a purely academic or intellectual fashion. Consistent with this, a group of scholars within this tradition (e.g., Gadamer, 1975; Polka, 1986) emphasize the critical role of one's own personal, existential engagement with the text. Thus "a work of literature is not an object we understand by conceptualizing or analyzing it; it is a voice we must hear, and through 'hearing' (rather than seeing) understand" (Palmer, 1969, p. 9). Here it is important to note that the Bible was the text around which the hermeneutical approach developed as a formal perspective. With the Protestant Reformation and its repudiation of Papal authority (including its authority to interpret scripture) arose the need for developing guidelines and principles for proper interpretation of the Bible. And the Bible, by its very nature, is the text that demands a personal response from its readers (Polka, 1986).

How does hermeneutics pertain to psychology? The examples we have given so far may provide an initial clue. But we want to make the connection more explicit by suggesting that the words *behavior, situation, client,* or *data* be substituted for the words *text* or *literature.* Even more broadly, one could say that life is a text that human beings are constantly involved in reading and interpreting. This perspective brings to mind Husserl's (1970) project of elucidating the structures of the life-world. In the words of a psychologist who uses a hermeneutical approach to research, "hermeneutics seeks to elucidate and make explicit our practical understanding of human actions by providing an interpretation of them" (Packer, 1985, p. 1086).

At this point, it is evident that hermeneutics and existential phenomenology have much in common: Both are concerned with being faithful to texts and phenomena, respectively. In addition, they share a common heritage. One of the most significant hermeneutical thinkers in this century, Hans-Georg Gadamer (1975), was a student of Martin Heidegger who himself described his approach to the study of human existence as hermeneutical.

But if these two traditions have so much in common, what justifies the study of hermeneutics as a distinct contributor to psychology? First, and most generally, we would suggest that the questions that have arisen for existential–phenomenological psychologists, in the context of research as well as therapy, are questions that have been addressed, although from a somewhat different vantage point, by the scholars who have been engaged for several centuries in the study of what it means to interpret texts. Many of the contributors to this book have benefited, directly or indirectly, from the insights of the hermeneutical tradition. Second, two specific hermeneutic concepts, the hermeneutical circle and preunderstanding, illustrate the implications of hermeneutics for psychology. A discussion of these concepts follows.

When one initially approaches a text (or a situation or a person), one necessarily sees or reads only part of it, and lacking a sense of the whole, one partly or completely misunderstands the text. Imagine, for example, reading a letter written by someone about whose life you know virtually nothing. Only as you gain an understanding of the whole (i.e., the person's life) do you come to a reliable understanding of the part (i.e., the letter). Yet there is no whole, as such, in that one moves from parts toward a comprehension of the whole, and thus it can be said that one cannot understand the whole without understanding the parts (Hoy, 1978). It is this process of repeatedly moving from the parts to the whole that is referred to as the *hermeneutical circle.*

Accordingly, it may seem that this is not a hermeneutical circle but a vicious one! In practice though, as readers, we move, however gropingly and uncertainly, toward a deeper understanding of a text as we struggle with it. One reconsiders the meaning of a part in light of exposure to additional parts, and one's sense of the whole likewise undergoes change. As a result, it may be more helpful to think in terms of a spiral where one returns to the point of origin again and again, but never at the same level.

The extent to which one deepens one's understanding has to do with one's willingness and ability to reflect on one's *preunderstanding* of the text. The notion of preunderstanding figures significantly in the work of Gadamer (1975). He argues that one brings to any text (or any situation) a set of presuppositions that are a function of one's cultural and personal background and experiences. The text, also, stands within a tradition and a history. Thus, most hermeneutical approaches place considerable emphasis on the inescapable historicity of human understanding (Husserl's work lacks this strong historical

self-reflection

emphasis). For Gadamer, it is not a problem that interpreters or texts are historically rooted (how else could it be?), but this reality becomes a problem if it is not taken into account. It is critical that readers be ready to ask questions about their own preunderstanding, questions such as: "What have I already assumed which may account for my failure to make sense of this section?" or "Are there specific assumptions which this writer takes for granted, and which someone from my tradition would not take for granted?" This process of self-reflection, which is very similar to the process of becoming aware of one's preconceptions discussed above with regard to bracketing, is essential to many human endeavors including international negotiations, developing a relationship with a disturbed client, or coming to know any other human being more fully.

CONCLUSION

The most fundamental claim of existential–phenomenological psychology is that it provides us with an approach that leads to a deeper and fuller understanding of human existence, ourselves, and others. Chapter 2 presents an historical overview of the development of the natural–scientific attitude in psychology. How this development has led to our present conception of existential–phenomenological psychology is then discussed in some detail. The remainder of the text illustrates the theoretical and empirical work of a number of existential–phenomenological psychologists. A number of chapters address topics that are usually addressed in traditional psychology (e.g., research, perception, learning, social psychology, and psychotherapy) so that the reader can readily make a comparison between these approaches. We have also included chapters on topics typically overlooked in psychology (e.g., aesthetic experience, passion, and forgiveness) as well as several chapters on transpersonal psychology, a relatively new approach in psychology that addresses issues such as optimal functioning and spiritual experience.

REFERENCES

Brunner, J. S. (1957). On perceptual readyness. *Psychological Review, 64,* 123–152.

Colaizzi, P. F. (1973). *Reflection and research in psychology: A phenomenological study of learning.* Dubuque: Kendall-Hunt.

Darley, J. M., Glucksberg, S., Kamin, L. J., & Kinchla, R. A. (1984). *Psychology* (2nd ed.). Englewood Cliffs, NJ: Prentice-Hall.

Einstein, A. (1952). Letter to Jacques Hadamard. In E. Ghiselin (Ed.), *The creative process* (pp. 43–44). New York: Mentor.

Faulconer, J. E., & Williams, R. N. (1985). Temporality in human action: An alternative to positivism and historicism. *American Psychologist, 40*(11), 1179–1188.

Gadamer, H. G. (1975). *Truth and method.* New York: Seabury Press.

Giorgi, A. (1970). *Psychology as a human science.* New York: Harper & Row.

Giorgi, A. (1971). Phenomenology and experimental psychology: I. In A. Giorgi, W. F. Fischer, and R. Von Eckartsberg (Eds.), *Duquesne studies in phenomenological psychology: Volume 1* (pp. 6–16). Pittsburgh: Duquesne University Press.

Gleitman, H. (1983). *Basic psychology.* Columbus, OH: Charles E. Merrill.

Heidegger, M. (1962). *Being and time.* New York: Harper & Row.

Hothersall, D. (1985). *Psychology.* Columbus, OH: Charles E. Merrill.

Hoy, D. C. (1978). *The critical circle: Literature, history, and philosophical hermeneutics.* Berkeley: University of California Press.

Husserl, E. (1962). *Ideas: General introduction to pure phenomenology.* New York: Collier.

Husserl, E. (1970). *The crisis of European sciences and transcendental phenomenology.* Evanston: Northwestern University Press.

Jennings, J. L. (1986). Husserl revisited: The forgotten distinction between psychology and phenomenology. *American Psychologist, 41*(11), 1231–1240.

Lewis, M. (1972). State as an infant-environment interaction: An analysis of mother-infant interaction as a function of sex. *Merrill-Palmer Quarterly of Behavior and Development, 18,* 95–121.

Merleau-Ponty, M. (1962). *Phenomenology of perception.* London: Routledge & Kegan Paul.

Merleau-Ponty, M. (1963). *The structure of behavior.* Boston: Beacon Press.

Ornstein, R. (1985). *Psychology: The study of human experience.* New York: Harcourt Brace Jovanovich.

Packer, M. J. (1985). Hermeneutic inquiry in the study of human conduct. *American Psychologist, 40*(10), 1081–1093.

Palmer, R. E. (1969). *Hermeneutics: Interpretation theory in Schleirmacher, Dilthey, Heidegger and Gadamer.* Evanston, IL: Northwestern University Press.

Polka, B. (1986). *The dialectic of biblical critique: Interpretation and existence.* New York: St. Martin's Press.

Prescott, M. P. (1974). Interpretation of Rorschach determinants: Exploration of an alternative view. In E. L. Murray & A. Giorgi (Eds.), *Duquesne papers in phenomenological psychology, Volume 1* (pp. 170–181). Pittsburgh: Duquesne University Department of Psychology.

Schultz, D. (1987). *A history of modern psychology.* New York: Academic Press.

Smith, R. E., Sarason, I. G., & Sarason, B. R. (1982). *Psychology: The frontiers of behavior.* New York: Harper & Row.

Valle, R., & King, M. (1978). An introduction to existential-phenomenological thought in psychology. In R. S. Valle & M. King (Eds.), *Existential–phenomenological alternatives for psychology* (pp. 6–17). New York: Oxford University Press.

Watts, A. W. (1966). *The book, On the taboo against knowing who you are.* New York: Collier.

Zaner, R. M. (1970). *The way of phenomenology.* New York: Pegasus.

2

Psychology and the Attitude of Science

Robert D. Romanyshyn and Brian J. Whalen

INTRODUCTION

Knowledge and the Organization of Knowledge

The organization of knowledge is not neutral with respect to that knowledge. What we know of something is reflected in the way in which we express it. This is seen, for example, in the act of speaking or writing. When we are trying to say something of which we are not sure, we are hesitant and groping. We look for a way to organize what we want to say, and this organization reflects what we will say and what we will not say. On a deeper level, it reflects what we *can* say because of what we know and what we cannot say because of what we do not know. The organization of knowledge, then, is in one sense the knowledge, and knowledge is in one sense its organization.

This relation of knowledge and its organization is clearly present in any textbook. Indeed, a textbook presents not only the facts of a discipline but also the structure of organization within which those facts are a meaning. A text, then, is an *attitude* toward a particular subject, but it is presented as the definitive facts of a discipline. The facts are visible, whereas the attitude that organizes those facts, and even initially selects them, generally remains invisible. Thus a text has a hidden as well as a visible side, not unlike, one might say, the relation of the skeleton to the flesh. The organization of a text therefore is like its backbone.

But the skeleton of a text that is hidden in this way is not completely invisible. On the contrary, the organization of a text, its attitude, is betrayed in that part of a text that we usually ignore or pass over. This is the *table of contents,* for here, perhaps more than with any other part of a text, we can glimpse its anatomy. Indeed, in this chapter we present an "anatomy of psychology," that is, an investigation not primarily of *what* psychology knows but *how* it knows it, a study of its attitude or its way of organizing knowledge.

An attitude not only *organizes* knowledge, it also expresses *presuppositions* and *values* about what is known. For example, as we shall see, the way in which psychology[1] organizes its knowledge is in relation to a specific attitude—the attitude of science. The adoption of this attitude, however, contains presuppositions about the nature of human beings, which in turn lead to a definition of psychology's subject matter in particular ways and with specific implications. Thus psychology is often defined as the science of behavior, and behavior is often defined as a thing or an object of analysis that implies and requires a priority of method in the discipline. Further, the adoption of this attitude with these presuppositions reflects a certain set of values. For example, psychology first commits itself to being a science before it commits itself to being faithful to its subject matter—humanity. This is what Koch (1969) means when he says that: "At the time of its inception psychology was unique in the

---

[1] Throughout this chapter we will use the term *psychology* to refer to traditional psychology, that is, to psychology modeled on the attitude of the *natural* sciences. Rather than constantly repeat the adjective or the qualifying phrase, however, we will at times simply use the noun. The context, however, will make our meaning clear.

Robert D. Romanyshyn • Department of Psychology, University of Dallas, Irving, Texas 75062 *Brian J. Whalen* • University of Dallas, Rome, Italy 00166.

extent to which its institutionalization preceded its content and its methods preceded its problems'' (p. 64).

Hence, the way in which a discipline organizes its knowledge is a key to how that discipline currently understands itself, and the lock for this key is, as we have suggested, the textbooks of a discipline. Thomas Kuhn (1962), in fact, has pointed out that the way in which modern science understands itself is most clearly expressed in its educational texts, for it is here that a discipline seeks to introduce the neophyte not only to the facts of the discipline but to *a way of seeing* those facts. Introductory texts, therefore, are not worthless exercises in scholarship. On the contrary, they are instrumental in establishing and maintaining a tradition, or what Kuhn calls the *procedure of normal science*. Introductory texts establish a tradition for the student who first enters a discipline by admitting the student to its organized way of knowing. For the discipline itself, this tradition is maintained.

But, in these two senses, the reading of an introductory text can be dangerous both for the student and the discipline because it *can* prevent the growth of new knowledge while perpetuating the old. Introductory texts, then, *can* be dangerous to learning, and clearly an anatomy of introductory texts is called for as a way of initiating students into a discipline. This anatomy can balance the emphasis on what a discipline knows with *how* it knows and can balance the facts of a discipline with its attitude.

In proposing such a task, we are particularly mindful of its necessity in psychology for two reasons: First, there are a great number of introductory and survey-type texts in psychology where the attitude of science is uncritically assumed to be *the* anatomical structure of the discipline; second, psychology is directly about us. Indeed, most students, we think, enter a discipline for the first time with some preknowledge about what that discipline is and what it will and can teach them. Moreover, they often have hopes and expectations for the discipline that are dimly related to their life goals and projects of the moment. But whereas this is probably true of all disciplines (e.g., mathematics, physics, and the natural sciences in general), it is probably even more true of psychology. Not all of us are or imagine ourselves to be junior mathematicians or physicists, but everyone more or less fancies himself or herself to be an amateur psychologist.

In line with this fancy, everyone believes he or she knows at least something of what psychology is. This preknowledge, or, if you prefer, this *lived knowledge* of the psychological, is extremely important, because traditional psychology tends to dismiss this lived knowledge and to substitute in its place the fascinating facts of a science. In beginning psychology, then, one can lose his

or her first contact with the psychological, and one can run the risk of losing much of what constitutes the meaning of humanity.

In the next section, a concrete example of the points already presented is given. Our intentions are to show first, that a text is indeed not only the presentation of knowledge but of an attitude as well; second, what this attitude is and third, what presuppositions and values it reflects. For these intentions, we choose perhaps one of the more classic and one of the more popular texts in present use, Morgan, King, Weisz, and Schopler's (1986) *Introduction to Psychology*.

The Anatomy of a Text

In Morgan *et al.* (1986), the authors offer two distinct parts to a definition of psychology, one that suggests that ''psychology is the science of human and animal behavior,'' and the other that suggests that ''psychology has its applied side—that is, it is often used to solve 'real-life' problems'' (pp. 4–5). In the first chapter of the text, these two distinct parts of the definition are divided into separate discussion sections. First, the authors explain the scientific nature of psychology and then proceed to suggest that psychology may be applied to life itself. Given what has been said about knowledge and the organization of knowledge, this division bears a closer look.

Imagine for a moment, a textbook in physics with a division between a ''science-oriented course'' and a ''nature-oriented course.'' Here the division would immediately strike one as strange, and one would be surprised to find this arrangement. This is so, because, in general, we have come to accept as a fact that nature is what science says it is, although even here this fact is itself a philosophical point of view. Nevertheless, such a distinction between the science of nature and nature would seem out of place, primarily because we have come to regard the two as equivalent.

The case with psychology, however, is not the same, and Morgan *et al.*'s division reflects a rather fair and open-minded admission of a distinction between psychology as a science and the tasks, goals, and aims of human life. This distinction, moreover, suggests that psychology, when it is organized as a science, is somehow different from psychology when it is organized around human life. But if this is so, why then is psychology a science, and in what sense is it a science?

These are the main questions to be addressed in this chapter. To begin, however, we should notice the actual organizational plan of the text that Morgan *et al.* (1986) present in their table of contents. Here, as we suggested, we can discover something of the hidden anatomy of the text.

The text is divided into 16 parts:

1. What psychology is like
2. Biology of behavior
3. Sensory processes and perception
4. Principles of learning
5. Memory
6. Thinking and language
7. Motivation
8. Emotion and stress
9. Social perceptions, influences, and relationships
10. Attitudes
11. Development during infancy and childhood
12. Development during adolescence, adulthood, and old age
13. Psychological assessment and testing
14. Personality
15. Abnormal psychology
16. Therapy for psychological distress

In Part 1, the authors begin with a section entitled "The Methods of Psychology" in which they make clear psychology's commitment to the attitude of science. Here they review experimental methods and systematic observation as a way of elucidating how psychology discovers "new knowledge about behavior" (p. 8). The authors stress that as "the science of behavior" (p. 7), psychology depends upon the methodology of science. Thus at the very outset, Morgan et al. indicate that the attitude of science is their organizational scheme.

Within the context of this attitude, they proceed to present a brief history of psychology, thereby indicating that the attitude adopted even organizes the selection and interpretation of psychology's history. Here is a rather clear example of how the attitude that a discipline adopts is the key to its own self-understanding. Of course, history is always read from a particular perspective, and our point, therefore, is not that the history of psychology *as a science* is wrong. On the contrary, our point is only that this is one of many possible readings of psychology's history, and not *the* history, and that the history that is in fact written is in relation to a particular stance or point of view.

As an alternative example, one could initially adopt the attitude that psychology is the disciplined study of typical human actions in typical situations, and from that perspective one would construct its history from the different books of etiquette and manuals of practical action that have been written in every historical age. In this historical lineup Machiavelli's *The Prince* might then replace Descartes's treatise, *The Passions of the Soul*. But again we are not advocating this particular attitude, nor

are we dismissing the one adopted by Morgan *et al.* On the contrary, we wish to indicate only that the organization of knowledge is an attitude toward the subject matter of that knowledge, and more specifically in this instance, that this organization is focused around the attitude of the natural sciences.

Returning to the table of contents, we would suggest that the division between Parts 4, 6, 7, and 8 indicate that the authors organize their knowledge about humans in such a way that they separate learning and thinking from motivation and emotion. One may, of course, point out that this separation merely reflects the inability to speak about everything at once, and that the richness and complexity of human life require some distinctions. Such a point, however, would miss the point of our discussion, or would be beside the point, because our consideration of this table of contents is not for the purpose of arguing against separations *per se* in favor of some ill-founded but impossible conception of unity.

On the contrary, there are distinctions in life, and there are separations to be made, so that we are in fact not questioning this fact of separation but rather the ways in which the separations are made. Faced with a whole pie, for example, a glutton and a gourmet will slice it differently, and each in relation to his or her attitude or point of view, just as psychologists faced with the whole of human life will "slice" it differently. What is important, then, is not that slicing is done, but the way in which it is done. It is the slices and not the slicing that reflect a point of view, an attitude, or a plan of organization. One is entitled, therefore, to question the resulting division and to seek in it a clue to the authors' conceptions about the nature of psychology and the meaning of human beings.

Morgan *et al.* do not include even a brief reference to motivation or emotion in their chapters on learning and thinking. In effect, therefore, these authors are suggesting that, in their consideration of human behavior, thought is and can be separated from affect. This is an old and time-honored position in psychology, but such a view reflects a choice, a philosophical commitment, and not a scientific fact, for one could choose and defend with equal plausibility the point of view that learning occurs only within the context of an affective life situation.

Indeed, this is precisely what Merleau-Ponty (1964) has shown in his essay, "The Child's Relations with Others." Using the data of psychoanalysis, he gives the example of the young child who comes to learn the use of the future and past tenses of her native language within the context of the birth of a brother. His point is that here the learning of language occurs within the total context of an affective life situation. Quite obviously, then, learning is not divorced from affect, just as it is not for those of us who have ever learned to speak a foreign language while visiting a foreign country. In both cases, what is demonstrated, we think, is that a word is a situation and that the learning of language is always within the context of an emotional relation to one's world.

The principles of learning that are presented by Morgan *et al.* do not, however, even allude to this relation, or to the place of learning within the larger context of life. Therefore, although much of the material that they present is relevant to what human learning is, the fact remains that *the organization of their knowledge* in terms of the distinction between learning and motivation *reflects an implicit attitude and not an established scientific fact*. The result, therefore, is the somewhat awkward position of the introduction, which first states that psychology is a science and then immediately thereafter adopts an attitude toward human action that is not a fact of science at all. But given the general hiddenness of a text's attitude and given the typically casual way in which a reader passes over the attitude as revealed in a table of contents, the unsuspecting reader is likely to miss this discrepancy. The reader is apt to come away from his or her first encounter with psychology convinced that cognition and affect are separate and separable realms of the human person and that this distinction of cognition and affect is an established fact of the science of psychology. An assumption rooted in a particular attitude toward humans is mistaken, therefore, as a fact of science. For the unsuspecting reader, the very first assumption—psychology is a science—is also wrongly taken as an established fact, when it is in fact an attitude toward the study of humanity. Thus psychology organizes its knowledge around the attitude of science, but this organization itself and its consequent divisions are not scientific facts but the result of this attitude.

In principle, the same sort of questioning can be applied to the other divisions in the table of contents, and in each case the separations would indicate some of the presuppositions in psychology's attitude toward human beings. Because, however, our purpose in this section is only to provide a specific example, we want to consider just one other aspect of this text's anatomy. And in this case, rather than considering the separations *between* sections, we offer a microanatomy of sorts by considering the separations *within* a particular section. For this purpose, we choose the section entitled "Sensory Processes and Perception" that addresses our "way of knowing about the world around us" (p. 85). This section is subdivided into two main chapters, one named "Sensory Channels," which addresses the five senses, and the other named "From Sensory Processes to Perception," which discusses "perceptual processes that modify sensory input" (p. 85).

In organizing their material in this way, the authors are adopting the attitude that knowing is a two-stage process of sensation and perception, with the latter serving a kind of judging function in the arranging of pure sensory data. Such an attitude, of course, reflects a biological bias that in turn allows psychology to introduce into its study of human knowing concerns that are, strictly speaking, physiological in character. Thus, an experience like seeing a tree can be broken down into the "mechanics" of the visual process *plus* the associative contributions of past experiences provided by the judgments of perception.

Although there are many important issues that are raised by this attitude, the one that is most important here concerns the abstract character of a concept like sensation. Sensations, like a visual sensation of red or a tactile sensation of cold, are *constructions*, much like the atom is in physics. We tend, however, to regard the atom as a *discovered* reality and, in this sense, as a real thing that already exists in nature. But the atom does not exist *in* nature. Rather it exists *in relation to* an attitude toward nature. Atoms are not real but are ways of *realizing* nature. They are not only a something to be seen but are *also* ways of seeing. The observed is what it is in relation to the attitude of the observer. In this sense, the atom can be called a *construction*.

Moreover, we do not mean that, as a construction, the atom is an idea. The relation of the observed to the observer is not the *creation* of the observed. Atoms are neither facts of nature nor ideas of consciousness. Rather, as a construction, atoms are *meanings* that reflect both what can be seen in nature *and* a way of seeing it. Hence the term *construction* as used with respect to atoms and/or sensations indicates that these realities reflect and require a specific attitude toward the world, a specific way of standing in the world, seeing it, and speaking about it (Romanyshyn, 1973, 1975a). The term *construction* indicates that knowledge of what is is inseparable from its style of organization.

Psychology, however, either does not understand sensation as a construction or it forgets this constructed character of sensation. A sensation, then, becomes a real event, and one no longer simply makes believe that seeing, for example, is "like" a physical stimulus transformed into physiological process. Rather, one believes it. In other words, one forgets that this is a way of seeing, as one believes that this is what seeing really is in itself. In short, psychology proceeds *as if* sensations were the real and most basic units of experience. Such a procedure enables psychology to locate the foundations of experience in the nervous system and hence to speak about the biological basis of behavior, as, in fact, Morgan *et al.* do in Part 2 of their text.

The forgotten constructed character of a notion like sensation is not, however, its only difficulty. It is also an abstraction far removed from the living of life. Indeed, if one is talking about *human experience,* and if by that term one means the way in which a human being experiences the world as he or she lives it, then the construction of sensation is inappropriate and in fact unnecessary. In everyday experience, for example, one does not have a visual experience of red and/or a tactile experience of cold; rather one is always experiencing a red apple or a red dress, just as one is always touching a cold ice cube or a cold piece of chicken.

Moreover, it little profits psychology's position to insist that these experiences are the combined results of pure sensory processes and perceptual judgments based on prior experiences, for here the recourse to perception, either as a judgmental or organizing function, is an *ad hoc* hypothesis designed to save the original notion of sensation. In fact, therefore, what the authors' position comes down to is the *assumption* of the notion of sensation as the first and most basic process of knowing, an assumption that is presented, however, as if it were a scientific fact. *But sensation is not a scientific fact, it is the result of a specific attitude toward human beings and world.* Psychologists do not discover sensations; they construct them.

Approached in a slightly different way, the question being raised here concerns the starting point of psychology. Do we, as psychologists, begin with experience as it is given, or do we begin with experience as it is already analyzed prior to and in advance of experience? The former approach begins with descriptions of experience and seeks to discover in experience its meanings and variations. The latter begins with notions assumed to be facts about experience and seeks to discover its mechanism. Merleau-Ponty (1962) has done much to clarify this difference in his major work, *Phenomenology of Perception,* as Erwin Straus (1963) has also done in his major work, *The Primary World of the Senses.* Both of these works constitute existential–phenomenological critiques of sensation.

It is obvious, however, that contemporary psychology chooses the latter as its starting point. In seeking to understand why this is so, we look to psychology's adoption of the attitude of science, for this attitude requires the notion of sensation, just as the notion of sensation endorses the scientific character of its attitude. Sensation allows psychology to investigate the nervous system and the biological foundations of behavior. It is the path or the royal road to the brain and the sense organs. And, a discipline that follows this path is fairly well assured of being given the status of a science. To tinker with the workings of the nervous system in an investigation of memory, for example, certainly seems more scientific than to ponder the variations of memory's meaning.

Again, we are *not* objecting to this *particular* starting point or plan of organization. The attitude of science as a way of organizing knowledge is certainly a *legitimate* attitude for the discipline of psychology to adopt. We are objecting to the *confusion* between what is a fact and what is an attitude. Thus what is presented as a fact of science, in this case that all the psychological processes that are studied in the text are biologically based, is, indeed, an attitude, an attitude that presumes, moreover, that psychology is a science only when it translates its data into biological terms.

But is it, after all, a scientific fact that if one succeeds in knowing the brain physiology of a phenomenon like learning, for example, then one also knows, thereby, what human learning is? Is this a fact of science, or is it a choice from within a particular attitude? And, if the latter is the case, then is it not equally permissible to choose another attitude, another way of organizing one's knowledge, and to suggest, for example, that the meaning of human learning, although not unrelated to its biology, is an altogether different understanding of the biological and hence a different way of seeing and approaching this phenomenon? The issue, then, is not whether the biology of psychological processes is a fact or not a fact. The issue is *the way* in which this fact is a fact, the attitude or stance within which this fact is established. It is only when this question is raised that one can consider if the data of psychology are treated in an *adequate* and appropriate manner.

In principle, of course, this anatomy of a text could continue, and it could be extended to other texts as well. Such a procedure, however, would be unnecessarily time-consuming and beside the point of our intention: to indicate in a specific and concrete way that factual knowledge is indeed the organization of knowledge and that this organization expresses an attitude toward the subject matter of a discipline that contains presuppositions and values about that subject matter.

This section has demonstrated that knowledge and its organization are inseparable and has also indicated that the attitude of organization in psychology is the attitude of science. Moreover, this means that psychology believes that real knowledge equals the methodical pursuit of knowledge as practiced in the natural sciences and that, to understand human beings, means to study them scientifically in this way. Such a position, however, is questionable. Is the attitude of science as practiced in the natural sciences the only way to organize knowledge and the only way, or even the best way, to understand human beings? One could hardly answer *yes* to these questions, considering the vast knowledge disciplines like history and economics have about humans. Yet psychology in its organization uncritically appends itself to the natural sciences. For example, Lester A. Lefton (1985), in his introductory text entitled *Psychology*, says that "psychologists recognize that many factors, both biological and environmental, contribute to behavioral disorders," and he suggests that "many behavioral disorders have a biological, genetic, or even nutritional basis" (p. 30), thus linking psychology with the natural sciences.

But why does psychology relate to the natural sciences rather than history, philosophy, literature, or others? Psychology's claim that it is and/or should be a science is an unexamined prejudice, particularly when one considers that the meaning and understanding of the term *science* and the attitude associated with it are also generally unexamined. In the next section, therefore, we want to interrogate this claim and some features of this attitude in more detail. We want to do this so that the reader can better understand the attitude that psychology uses to organize its knowledge. Someone once said, with respect to science, that nature is not organized the way universities are; it can also be said, with respect to psychology, that human life does not seem to be organized the way psychology textbooks are.

PSYCHOLOGY AND THE ATTITUDE OF SCIENCE

Science and Common-Sense Experience

In his textbook, *Fundamentals of Psychology*, Geldard (1962) states that "psychology is defined as the *science* of human nature" (p. 8) (our italics). This author's understanding of science is made quite explicit when he contrasts this view with the view of common sense. "It was once common sense that the sun . . . must daily pass around the earth . . . [and] that the earth, stretching out . . . in all directions, must therefore be flat," he says. But then he adds, "the youngest schoolboy nowadays *knows* better" (p. 1 [emphasis ours]). Despite the fact that this text was published some 25 years ago, Geldard's view of psychology as a science that is different from common sense still prevails in the field today. For example, this distinction between common sense and the science of psychology appears in Charles Morris's (1982) text, *Psychology: An Introduction*. Morris raises the question, "How does the psychologist's knowledge differ from common sense?" (p. 9) and proceeds to suggest an answer through the following story:

> Psychologists are scientists, and like all scientists they are skeptics. If you met your friends on your way across campus and told them that you were depressed because you had an exam, they would probably believe you. But you may be always depressed. You may feel bad because you were up all night studying or because you skipped breakfast. Before psychologists would accept your simple statement, "I am depressed because I have an exam," they would have to rule out all other possible explanations. This is the essence of the *scientific method*. (pp. 9–10).

The contrast here between common sense and scientific knowledge is quite apparent, but what is not quite so apparent is that this contrast involves some unexamined presuppositions about knowledge and about the real and the nature of the real. This state of affairs is apparent in Geldard's example about the earth and the sun. He seeks to show that the difference between science and common-sense experience involves the position that *seeing* is distinct from knowing, that in fact *seeing is a kind of not knowing,* or an ignorance. We see the sun move, and we see a more or less flat earth, but, according to Geldard, such seeing amounts to not knowing the truth. For what everyone "knows" is that the earth moves and that it is round. Yet, there is a presumption here, for to know these facts is to engage in a kind of not seeing, because to "know" that the earth is round or that it moves requires that we *forget* the evidence of our seeing. Hence Geldard's (1962) and Morris's (1982) contrast between common sense and scientific knowledge not only implies that common sense is a kind of not knowing, it also implies that science as a way of *knowing is a kind of not seeing.* This latter implication, which is an intrinsic feature of this attitude of science, is, however, not admitted.

Geldard's view is also based on the assumption that our everyday perception of reality, according to which we daily see the rising and the setting sun, is a mistaken interpretation rather than true knowledge. Thus, according to this contrast, we live not only in *ignorance* but also in *error*. Moreover, from this perspective, true knowledge, real knowledge, scientific knowledge, demands that one turn away from the given appearance of things and toward some supposedly true reality or reason *behind* them. *Psychology becomes science therefore when it produces the reasons for the errors of our everyday perceptual life,* when it teaches us, for example, that the two lines of the Mueller–Lyer figure (Figure 1) are really equal and only mistakenly appear to be of different sizes because of the context of the arrowheads.

But this corrective explanation is true only if one agrees to ignore the figure as it is given and to see it in that special way as being two lines *plus* reversed arrowheads. In other words, this corrective explanation is true only if one agrees to turn away from the figure as it appears and to substitute in place of this seeing that special knowledge of the lines as *metrically* equal. But to agree to this, to adopt this aspect of the attitude of science, is to adopt the

Figure 1. The Mueller–Lyer illusion

stance according to which true knowledge lies *behind* the everyday errors of appearance. Obviously, however, the everyday experience of things can be treated as an error only if reality as it is experienced has been previously "doctored" in some way, only if it has been previously envisioned in a particular and specific fashion. In the case of our example, the error is charged to the way the lines appear from the perspective of the lines as they are measured. From the special point of view of the ruler, then, the reality of what appears is a deception.

Within this contrast of common sense and scientific knowledge with its false dichotomy between seeing and knowing, psychology does not elucidate human experience, the common sense world of everyday action, but *ignores* it. In fact, to be more faithful to the spirit of Geldard's and Morris's remarks and to be more accurate about the meaning of the attitude of science, we should say that psychology does not merely question the common-sense world, the world as experienced, but it also *corrects* it. Indeed, the ignorance and error in which we live sets psychology its tasks. Because we live in ignorance and error, psychology's tasks are to ignore that ignorance and to correct that error. In completing these tasks, psychology substitutes the mistakes of experience with the facts and laws of scientific knowledge.

The completion of these tasks requires, however, a method, and the method that psychology uses is the experiment. Moreover, situating itself within the tradition of the natural sciences, psychology already understands an experiment in the peculiarly *modern* way as the application of a preplanned experience (Romanyshyn, 1973). An experiment structures experience in advance of what is experienced, and as Morris (1982, p. 12) and Morgan *et al.* (1986, pp. 9–13) note, this procedure involves three conditions: the isolation of phenomena, the systematic variation of variables, and repetition. Of the three conditions, however, the first is by far the most important, because the other two follow from it.

The method of isolating the phenomenon to be studied involves the position that the further one is able to neutralize the given context of a phenomenon, that is, the more one is able to abstract a particular phenomenon from its context of appearance and to substitute an experimentally created context, the more one has understood the

phenomenon. This procedure is as old as the attitude of modern science. Werner Heisenberg (1958), the great nuclear physicist and Nobel Prize winner, has noted that the genius of Galileo was shown by the fact that he was the first to realize "that individual natural processes can be isolated from their context in order to be described and explained mathematically" (p. 8). This procedure proved to be a great boon to the progress of science because it allowed the natural sciences to construct laws of general validity and to find, beneath the changing appearance of things, a regular uniformity. Thus Galileo, as one of the founders of the attitude of modern science, was able through this procedure to disregard the particular circumstances and situations of an object's fall, and to discover, beneath these varying appearances, the idea that all bodies fall equally fast. Certainly this was and is a remarkable achievement!

But what is so remarkable in this way is, at the same time, but from a different perspective, quite foolish, because this procedure presupposes an identity of law behind the most obviously disparate phenomena. Thus Galileo was ridiculed for suggesting that the birds of the air and the fish of the sea obey the same laws of motion. And, even further, one can suspect that he was eventually tried by the Church for suggesting that the swinging of an incense lamp obeys the same mathematical law as the swinging of a pendulum, although of course this specific detail was never in the indictment. The point we wish to make is that, from the point of view of everyday experience, these phenomena are unrelated. Judged from this perspective, Galileo's achievements are foolish. But judged from the perspective of the achievements, they are quite remarkable, and it is this criticism that is foolish. Obviously, then, one cannot take up either perspective *exclusively* because the success of science supports these claims, whereas the evidence of everyday experience continues to refute them. What must be said, therefore, is that, although the experimental procedure of isolating phenomena from their context is successful, it is so only from a specific point of view and at the cost of some particular assumptions.

The price that one pays for achieving the success of this method is much clearer and higher in psychology than it is in the natural sciences. In physics and psychology, for example, the practice of this method requires that the investigator remove the phenomenon he or she is studying from its natural context. Natural events, however, like the falling of an apple from a tree, are apparently more easily removed from their context than are human actions. But we say apparently, because, in strict fact, it may not even be true of natural events. The scientific study of nature has resulted in a univocal conception of nature, nature as science sees it, and it may be that the crisis of the environment is "nature's protest" to being decontextualized in this way.

In any case, the meanings of human action do depend on their context for their meanings. For example, if one adopts the view that human action is like a text to be read, then it is clear that the context of the "words" of this text is all-important to the meaning because the meaning of the word cannot be divorced from the context within which it occurs. True, the meaning is not equal to the context, but it is also not separable from it. We might say, then, that the price of isolating human actions from their given context is related to the issue of meaning.

Psychology does not bypass the issue of meaning but simply understands it in such a way that it can preserve its own methodological procedures. In place of viewing human action as a text to be read, it adopts the view that human action is a natural event like other events of nature. With this view, the problem of meaning is "solved" because it can be handled in the same way as it is in the natural sciences. Thus context can be ignored because the meaning of behavior as a natural event does not depend upon its context.

By adopting this expedient alternative, however, psychology in fact "chooses" to ignore that human behavior is *not* a natural event. Psychologists' assertions that human behavior can be studied as a natural event are themselves already beyond that definition—a falling apple, for example, does not initiate or interrogate the natural law of falling. In adopting this procedure, psychologists must begin their study of human behavior with a *practiced ignorance* of what that behavior is as it reveals itself to them in their own behavior. In a full, but closed, circle, therefore, psychology begins its study of human beings by assuming that experience leaves one ignorant of the world and then proceeds to adopt a practiced ignorance toward this initial ignorance. In other words, because psychology *begins* by assuming that experience leaves us in ignorance of the world, this practiced ignorance is easily justified. "Common sense is not an adequate source of facts about behavior" (p. 2), Edwards (1972) says in echo of Geldard and Morris. And here, as we have seen, lies the start of psychology's task and its meaning as a science.

This discussion of the attitude of science, as contrasted with the attitude of common-sense experience and the correction of the errors of the latter by experiment, has brought us to the issue of meaning. In the next section, we discuss this theme and its implications.[2]

Meaning and Behavior

We have already indicated that traditional psychology, in its adoption of the attitude of science, engages in a practiced ignorance toward the meaning of behavior as it is lived and that it does so primarily through the methodological procedures that comprise this attitude. This preferred ignorance is quite clear in James Deese's (1964) text, *Principles of Psychology*. Rejecting the obvious

---

itself but is rather *a way of experiencing* the world. In an earlier work, Romanyshyn has developed this theme within the context of the metaphorical character of modern science. Much of the discussion of the previous pages could be summarized by saying that, in its inception, psychology has uncritically adopted the metaphor of science and, thus, has continued the development of modern science as a metaphorical description of the world that takes itself literally. Science, including psychology, is a metaphorical speaking of the world that forgets that it speaks metaphorically. For a full treatment of this issue, readers are referred to Romanyshyn's (1982) *Psychological Life: From Science to Metaphor.*

Second, in critiquing this arrangement in psychology through the comparison with common-sense experience, we do not mean to suggest that *existential–phenomenological psychology* is simply a return to common-sense living. Nothing could be further from the truth of what existential–phenomenological psychology is. Indeed, through its own procedures, called *epoches* or bracketings, existential–phenomenological psychology seeks to return to common-sense experience, to the world as it is first lived, *in order to* interrogate the *genesis* of its meaning. In ordinary common-sense experience we tend to live the world forgetfully and uncritically, in a taken-for-granted fashion. This style of straightforward living in things is called the *natural attitude,* and, in this attitude, the objectivity of the world, things, and other people is *assumed*. A type of *naive realism* animates this attitude, according to which the independence and separation of human beings and the world seems guaranteed and unquestionable. Moreover, this naive realism, which Merleau-Ponty (1968) calls the "perceptual faith" (p. 3 ff.), is precisely that upon which the attitude of science builds. It presumes this perceptual faith, and thus it does not elucidate it.

But existential–phenomenological psychology takes up this task of elucidation, and in its interrogation of the natural attitude, of common-sense experience, it seeks to describe the advent of experience's meaning prior to any commitment to the philosophical positions of realism and idealism. In this sense, the world that we as psychological persons experience is not explained either as a fact or an idea. On the contrary, it is described from the point of view of its first appearance in the dialogue between human beings and the world. Experience, in existential–phenomenological psychology, is, then, the conversation between an embodied intention and the world as meant and intended.

Readers who wish to pursue this theme are referred to Merleau-Ponty's (1962) *Phenomenology of Perception,* Giorgi's (1970) *Psychology as a Human Science,* and J. H. van den Berg's (1970) *Things.* An introductory approach to the philosophical issues in existential phenomenology in general can be obtained from Richard Zaner's (1970) *The Way of Phenomenology.*

---

[2]This discussion of scientific experience and common-sense experience has two implications that cannot be fully explored, however, in this text. First, our discussion strongly suggests that science is not an experience of *the* world as it really is in

Cartesian dualism between mind and body as an out-moded one, Deese adopts a position that, however, can be seen only as a denial that human behavior has any intrinsic significance. "Because individual minds are private affairs," he says, "they are not the subject for scientific observation . . . [and] are beyond the techniques of the scientist" (Deese, 1964, p. 2). More recently, Morris (1982) implies a similar view: "Obviously psychologists cannot put your depression under a microscope or dissect your anxiety . . . but they can study you scientifically in other ways" (p. 10). And Morgan *et al.* (1986) echo this view: "*Behavior* includes anything a person or animal does that can be observed in some way. Behavior, unlike mind or feelings, can be observed, recorded, and studied. No one ever saw or heard a mind, but we can see and hear behavior" (p. 6).

Already it is apparent that this dualism, which in fact is inappropriate and outmoded, is rejected by Deese, Morris, and Morgan *et al.* on grounds other than its obsolescence, on grounds that any interior dimension of behavior is not subject to psychology's methods. Thus, along this same line, Deese (1964) continues and adds that "any psychologist, however, can see and hear what you do and say, and from his observations that psychologist can construct a theory of what your mind is like" (p. 2). And Morgan *et al.* (1986) express a similar view:

> From what is done and said, psychologists can and do make inferences about the feelings, attitudes, thoughts, and other mental processes which may be behind behavior. In this way, internal mental events can be studied as they manifest themselves through what people do—their behavior. Thus, it is through behavior that we can actually study and come to understand internal mental processes that would otherwise be hidden from us. (p. 7)

The primacy of methodological convenience is again apparent, indicating that psychology studies behavior because of its easy accessibility.

But what comes easy in this way does not come cheap, for this *method-centered definition of behavior* requires the psychologist to ignore behavior's own interior significance. True, behavior is visible for the observer, and this makes it a fit object of study. But before this observation, behavior is not without significance or meaning. The behaving individual does not need the observing psychologist to construct his or her "mind"; he or she already "has one." And yet this is precisely what Deese's, Morris's, and Morgan *et al.*'s positions entail. Correctly rejecting mind in its *substantive* aspect of Cartesian thought, these authors proceed, however, to dismiss the meaning inherent in behavior. But behavior has or is an interior significance; it has or is a depth and not merely a surface meaning visible to the other. If it is not,

then the significance of these authors' own behavior, like the writing of their books for example, awaits our own construction. In short, their books, which are the outcome of their behavior of writing, would not be meaningful until we observed the books and constructed their meaning. Obviously, however, these authors themselves intended a meaning. What must be occurring, then, is that, in the interest of being a science, this "mindful" aspect of behavior is being ignored—psychology is not being mindful of behavior.

Psychology's commitment to method, therefore, forces it to begin its study of behavior's meaning by disregarding any interior aspect of behavior or, as Skinner (1971) does in *Beyond Freedom and Dignity*, by dismissing this aspect as an illusion and as not contributing to either the conduct or the understanding of behavior. Approached in this way, human behavior is seen as only an outside, visible, external event whose meaning is to be inferred by the observer. In the best tradition of psychology, then, *mind* either as substance *or* interiority, is a hypothetical construct. As Deese (1964) explicitly says again, "It [mind] is a theoretical mind, one that has the features it has because they are *useful* in interpreting the facts of behavior" (p. 2, emphasis ours). Thus behavior has no meaning until the psychologist infers one, and a particular inference is chosen according to the criterion of utility.

Questions, however, arise concerning for whom these inferred meanings are useful and for what reasons. Are they useful for the observer or the actor or both? And are they useful for making psychology into a science and/or for helping us to understand behavior's meaning? In general, the criterion of utility is for the former reasons in each question. In any case, the adoption of this criterion already implies that the psychologist in the act of inference *betrays* the interiority of his or her own behavior, an interiority that in principle he or she has already denied to the behavior of the other and to behavior in general. Deese (1964), Morris (1982), and Morgan *et al.* (1986), like Skinner or like any psychologist who adopts only an exterior point of view in his or her chosen ignorance toward behavior, can explain, therefore, everything in behavior *except* that which makes this behavior of explaining possible, the interiority of behavior, or the intention to explain.

We are not saying here that the intention to explain cannot be understood but only that this intention to explain cannot itself be explained in any *external* or fully *causal* way. Every explanation is itself an intention that itself eludes the explanation. To explain the intention of an explanation is itself intended and would require another explanation that is in its turn also intended, leading to an infinite regress or endless circle. The only way out of this impasse, therefore, is to *see its root in the attempt to maintain a consistently external point of view.*

We cannot do this with respect to ourselves, however, because the adoption and maintenance of this external point of view is itself an expression of our interiority. Psychology, however, does attempt to maintain a consistently external viewpoint, and, in this sense, psychology becomes a *psychology of the other one,* a psychology of alienation. Its practiced ignorance refers therefore to the psychologist's deliberate forgetfulness of what he or she knows about behavior from his or her own behaving.

The criterion of utility, however, is not the only methodical way in which psychology expresses its natural ignorance of behavior. Davidoff (1980), for example, presents another criterion when she says that psychologists "use *scientific procedures,* including systematic observation and experimentation, to gather *publicly observable data*" (pp. 3–4, emphasis ours). In this statement, we are given a criterion for what constitutes the scientific study of behavior, and this criterion perpetuates psychology's ignorance of behavior by determining in advance the prior conditions according to which a problem can be admitted for study. In this methodological maneuver, Davidoff demonstrates that aspect of the attitude of science that *takes in advance* those phenomena or those aspects of a phenomenon to be studied. Fulfilling its goal of being *precise,* the attitude of science *decides in advance* the nature of the phenomenon that it studies.

In this sense, the attitude of science begins by turning away from the way things are in order to begin with how they have already been defined. Science begins with the possible rather than the actual; it begins by first ignoring the real (Romanyshyn, 1973). Although this procedure has met with great success in the natural sciences, its results in psychology are questionable. In beginning with the possible rather than the actual, psychology practices an ignorance toward what behavior actually is as it is lived.

Davidoff (1980) expresses this ignorance by insisting on behavior's visibility for the other. The happy fact that behavior *is* visible for the other does not, of course, change the fact that this position says that behavior *must be* visible in this way. In this sense, therefore, the real criterion is *visibility for the other,* and the *privileged position of behavior* in the definitions of psychology is, then, a consequence of the *privileged position of the observer.* Accordingly, therefore, if by some feat of technology, minds or souls could become visible for the other, then they, too, would be admitted into the study of psychology. Conversely, because behavior is defined as the only visible and experience as only invisible, the latter is generally ruled out of investigation. Thus it is not the subject matter in psychology that is privileged but its methods

and its attitude. Psychology is a science not because of what it studies but because of its methods of study.

Such a view is by no means as natural and unquestionable as it sounds. Indeed, as numerous historians of science have shown (Burtt, 1954; Butterfield, 1950; Whitehead, 1925), this view of science, as defined by its methods rather than its subject matter, has its historical origins in the Renaissance, and, most explicitly, in the work of Descartes. What we so naturally take for granted today is, in fact, a historically chosen attitude toward studying the world.

These methodic criteria concern psychology's attitude toward behavior's meaning, and each (in one way or another) allows (even requires) that psychology begin its study of behavior by practically ignoring its meaning, that is, by ignoring it for all practical purposes. Earlier in the discussion, however, we indicated that psychology *infers* behavior's meaning. Thus psychology, in its practiced ignorance toward behavior, does not ignore or bypass the issue of meaning as such. Rather, it dismisses behavior's actual meaning as it appears and then substitutes in its place the observer's inferred meaning. But this seemingly innocuous concept of inference hides many sins, and, for the purpose of understanding psychology, an understanding of this process is indispensable.

Meaning: Inference and Interpretation

The process of inference is apparent in Davidoff's (1980) discussions of mind, or what may more neutrally be called the experience side of human action. In other words, the assumption of the hypothetical character of mind indicates that the starting point of inferential thinking is the belief that behavior is an empty, external event upon which the observer constructs his or her laws. This process of inference proceeds according to a formula: *from* the observer *to* the observed. Inference is a kind of deduction, and what psychology deduces is the meaning of a behavior that it has at first already ignored. What is ignored in the beginning of its analysis is then reestablished on the basis of a deduction. In one sense, therefore, it can be said that, as a science, psychology is a tissue of inferences.

One can also approach this process of inference by contrasting it with the process of interpretation, for each embodies a different attitude with respect to the meaning of behavior. To infer means to place or to posit something that by definition is not yet there, whereas to interpret means to read something that by definition is there. The former process assumes that behavior first lacks meaning and requires the constructions of the observer for behavior to be meaningful, whereas the latter assumes that behavior is a meaning to be read. The one is closer to an image of behavior as a blank page on which meaning is to be inscribed, whereas the other is closer to the image of behavior as a text. Moreover, whereas inference implies deduction, interpretation implies a kind of induction, in the sense of behavior as a meaning in constant genesis, a meaning that is always being recast in light of time.

The differences between *inference* and *interpretation* can be seen, moreover, in the root meanings of the terms. *Infer* means "to bring into," whereas *interpret* means "agent or negotiator." It can be said that the interpreter is an agent of meaning and/or that the meaning of observed behavior is an act of negotiation. Because, however, negotiation *actively* involves at least two parties, the interpretation of behavior indicates a stance in which meaning occurs *between* the observer and the observed. There is something of a reciprocal, dialectical relation involved in the interpretation of behavior, whereas inference, in its root sense, indicates more of a one-sided, unidirectional relation. In interpretation, meaning passes both ways; in inference, it flows in one direction only. Interpretation requires mutual participation; inference requires a passivity on the part of the observed.

Inference and interpretation, therefore, differ with respect to the way in which behavior means (monologue versus dialogue) and how it arises (unilaterally or dialectically). Although these differences do exist, the fact of the matter is that every inference always involves an interpretation at one level or another, whether or not it is admitted or recognized. Thus, even when the strictest behaviorally oriented psychologist infers the meaning of a behavior, this inference already involves a prior, often implicit, interpretation of that behavior. Indeed, it is only on the basis of this interpretation that the inference is and can be made. Meaning, then, is always "brought into behavior" but always through "negotiation." Psychology's meaningful dilemma about meaning, therefore, is *not* that it engages in this process of inference but that it believes that this process is really a one-sided, unidirectional ascription of meaning to empty behavior by the observer.

As understood and used by psychology, the process of inference prejudges the "meaning" of behavior as only an external and visible event. Indeed, the two issues are co-relative so that the process of inference guides the meaning of behavior in this way, whereas this meaning of behavior requires this process of inference. Behavior, however, is not the only issue that is affected by this process of inference, for this process also influences psychology's understanding of experience. Morgan *et al.* (1986) say, for example, that "psychologists can and do make *inferences* about the feelings, attitudes, thoughts, and other mental processes which may be *behind* the be-

havior" (p. 7, emphasis ours). Thus experience, when it is admitted at all into the study of psychology, is already prejudged as *only* an inside, invisible domain that requires a process of inferring its meaning from the visible outside of behavior. Indeed, all of what we have said so far converges on this theme of experience and behavior. The attitude of science that psychology adopts views meaning in a certain way. Indeed, the process of inference by which it views meaning results in a *spatializing* of behavior and experience. Behavior and experience, however, are not spatial domains, and these spatial metaphors inadequately grasp the meaning of human psychological life.

The next section considers an *alternative* to these spatial metaphors. As an *existential–phenomenological* alternative to a traditional view of behavior and experience, this discussion introduces a *shift in attitude* rather than the introduction of new content.

Attitudes and Perspectives: The Visibility of Experience

The *visibility of experience* is not understandable within a traditional psychological view. Indeed, to understand this claim, it is first necessary to appreciate that traditional definitions of behavior and experience rest on the unwarranted assumption of each term's real spatial existence. Behavior, however, is not real, nor is experience, in the traditional sense of a something that exists independently of an attitude. On the contrary, behavior "and" experience are perspectives on the meaning of human action, and "each" represents not merely a reality that is there to be seen but also a way or a stance of seeing.[3]

Behavior "and" experience, then, are as much statements about an *attitude* toward human action as they are about human action itself. They refer not only to *what* human action is but also to *how* it is *what* it is. What seems most obvious is that traditional psychology's definition of behavior presumes a forgetfulness of attitude, that is, a forgetfulness that human action is always given as a perspective in relation to a particular stance or point of view. In short, behavior "and" experience are not independent realities, real things in themselves; they are perspectives, ways in which human action can be seen, human action as it appears in relation to a particular and specific attitude. What follows is a consideration of each of these perspectives and the attitudes that inform them.

[3]The quotation marks around words like *and* and *each* are essential to our point. They indicate that psychology deals with a reality, a human action, whose two faces are *distinguishable but not separate*.

Adopting the *attitude of the observer,* human action reveals itself as behavior. Moreover, this behavior is visible. On the other hand, this same action that reveals itself to the observer as visible behavior is, from the point of view of the actor, an experience that is, indeed, also visible to him or her. How the actor's experience is visible to himself or herself and even the fact that it *is* visible, are, we agree, usually unnoticed. But the fact remains that the actor's experience is visible in the behavior of the other as behaved by that other. The other then reflects my experience of my own behavior back to me in his or her own behavior as behaved by him or her, and vice versa.

To behave in the presence of the other, then, is to discover the visibility of one's own experience in the "face" of that other. One's experience of being angry, for example, is visible in the other's face of fear. And, the same process is also evident when one is dealing with a thing, for here too the face of the world, its "behavior," reflects one's experience. For example, if while one is standing on a hilltop, admiring the sunset, one says, "The sun is magnificent," then what one has displayed in this brief utterance is something like one's own experience of humility in the face of this grand spectacle. In the magnificent radiance of the sun's "behavior," one finds one's experience of humility, just as one's experience of humility is reflected in, and carried by, the sun's majesty.

Stated as a principle, we would suggest that, from an existential–phenomenological perspective, it is accurate to say that *my experience is your behavior as behaved by you, whereas my behavior is your experience as behaved by me.* We do not, of course, mean to imply a one-to-one correspondance here between my experience and your behavior or to imply an identity. My experience is your behavior *but as behaved by you.* The reflection, then, of my experience *in* your behavior but also *as* your behavior is more properly understood as a *refraction.* Your behavior not only "registers" my experience, it *transforms* it. In any case, what is behavior from one point of view is experience from another, and vice versa.

This visibility of behavior "and" *experience* is, however, only half the story, for experience "and" *behavior* are also invisible. Taking the *actor's attitude,* my experience is visible for me in your behavior as behaved by you, *whereas my own behavior is invisible.* From the observer's point of view, it is just the opposite: *my experience is invisible,* whereas my behavior is visible. And the same is true for the observer's position. His or her behavior, of observing, for example, is invisible for him or her but (can be) visible for me, whereas his or her experience (of observing my visible behavior) is visible for him or her (*in* my behavior *as* behaved by me) but invisible for me. Thus it appears that experience "and" behavior are both visible and invisible, and each in specific ways or in

relation to specific attitudes. *To the attitude of the observer belongs the visibility of the other's behavior and the invisibility of the other's experience, whereas to the attitude of the actor belongs the visibility of his or her own experience and the invisibility of his or her own behavior.* Depending on one's stance, as observer or actor, behavior and experience will appear in different ways.

Although the preceding seems to imply that the terms *actor* and *observer* are spatial positions, these terms are not, in fact, spatial positions at all but attitudes toward human action. In other words, they are not really places to stand but ways of standing (attitude) and ways of seeing human action. Consequently, in addition to the observer's attitude toward the other, *there is the possibility of an observer's attitude toward oneself,* just as there is *the possibility of an actor's attitude toward the other* in addition to that attitude toward oneself. One can, for example, take the observer's attitude toward oneself by *imagining* one's behavior as it is seen by the other, a kind of methodological version of seeing oneself as others see one. And one can take the actor's attitude toward the other by *imagining* his or her experience, a kind of methodological version of placing oneself in the other's shoes. Any subject, therefore, can adopt the attitudes of the actor and observer interchangeably and with respect to himself or herself as well as the other.

But given this freedom, it nevertheless remains true that the *observer's attitude,* whether toward oneself or the other, is *privileged* with respect to the *behavioral* meaning of human action, just as the *actor's attitude* is *privileged* with respect to the meaning of human action as *experience.* Moreover, within each attitude, there is the further privilege associated with the *focus* of the point of view that is adopted. Thus, the observer's attitude *on the other* is the privileged perspective for behavior, whereas the actor's perspective *on himself or herself* is the privileged one for experience. And, these are the privileged attitudes because in each one the *visibility* of human action, either as behavior "or" experience, is most clear. My behavior is, therefore, most visible for you as the observer, whereas my experience is most visible for me as the actor.

Experience is visible, and behavior is invisible. But it is also true that experience is invisible and behavior is visible. Traditional psychology would have no difficulty with the latter but would, however, have difficulty accepting the former. In this discussion, we have tried to suggest that this difficulty arises because we easily forget that behavior's "or" experience's visibility or invisibility are not absolute but relative determinations. Behavior is visible *and* invisible depending on the attitude (observer of the other, actor toward himself or herself) of the investigator. Its *relative* visibility and invisibility means, therefore, its way of appearing *in relation to* a point of view.

Understood in this way, the terms *outside* and *inside* can no longer be seen as synonomous with *visibility* and *invisibility*. Outside/inside, or external/internal, are not *fixed,* spatial domains. On the contrary, rethought as visible/invisible, the outside/inside spatial *dichotomy* becomes a *dialectic* in which either term receives its meaning only in relation to an attitude or point of view. Thus, as we have said, what is "inside" from one point of view (behavior for the actor and experience for the observer) is "outside" from another point of view (behavior for the observer and experience for the actor) and *vice-versa.* Outside/inside are not, therefore, real places, and behavior is not something "over there" whereas experience is something "over here." On the contrary, behavior is "here" and "there" simultaneously, as is experience. A dualism of behavior *and* experience is replaced, therefore, by a duality *within* human action. Psychology, then, is not the study of either of *two* realities, behavior or experience, nor is it the study of one reality that masks or hides another, experience behind behavior. Rather, it is the study of one reality, human action, seen in two different ways.

In this regard, we can draw an analogy between this understanding of behavior "and" experience as perspectives on the meaning of human action and Niels Bohr's principle of complementarity in physics. Just as light is neither *really* a wave nor a particle in and of itself but rather what it is in relation to an attitude or style of questioning, so too is human action neither *really* behavior nor experience, but what it is in relation to an attitude or point of view. That which is studied is not totally separable from the *manner* in which it is studied, and the researcher participates in defining the researched. We are *not* saying the attitude *creates* the reality observed or researched, only that the observed or the researched is not simply *discovered.* This psychological version of the principle of complementarity indicates a conception of the relation between observer and observed that is not adequately described by notions of discovery or creation.[4]

But even if traditional psychology would accept the views that behavior "and" experience are not real entities, but perspectives on the meaning of human action, and that experience is visible in relation to the attitude of the actor toward himself or herself, this psychology could still insist that the perspective of behavior in relation to the observer remains privileged because it seems to be the only way in which *observability by the other,* the criterion previously cited by Davidoff (1980), appears. In other words, psychology could still *negate* the significance of experience's visibility by arguing that this visibility is not given to the other. On the surface, this seems a serious objection, and if we are to preserve the significance of this alternative view, therefore, we must meet this objection in some way. In other words, we must show that experience's visibility is *also* for the other.

We have, however, already suggested that experience is visible *also* for the other. This is the case when the other takes up the attitude of the actor, when the other imagines himself or herself in the actor's shoes. Obviously experience's visibility in this case is *indirect.* But remember the criterion to be met here is observability by the other. Whether visibility is direct or indirect, therefore, is not at issue. Of course, in order to appreciate this last fact, traditional psychology must give up its strong, implicit, but erroneous tendency to imagine that the observer is a location. Our previous remarks about observation as a way of standing, rather than a place to stand, are important, therefore, to counteract this tendency to presume that the observer is a point over there from which behavior is directly visible.

Experience is not only indirectly visible for the other but also visible for the other in a *direct* way and herein lies the real significance of the existential–phenomenological alternative. Experience is visible in behavior, and, up to this point, we have limited ourselves to this kind of formulation. *Stated more generally,* however, this statement really means that experience is visible as a world. Or, to say it most accurately, *experience is visible in the world as a world.*[5] Consider the experience of anxiety, for example. Whatever else anxiety may be for a traditionally based psychology, it is also true that anxiety is a change in the face of the world, an alteration in which the world changes while remaining the same (see W. Fischer, Chapter 5, for a more detailed discussion of "being anxious"). The dentist's office that one visits with a friend, for example, is the same but also different when one returns there again with an aching tooth. One's anxiety in

---

[4]Because the development of this point would take us too far afield from our main theme, we can only say that a good description of this point can be found in Norwood Hanson's (1972) excellent book, *Patterns of Discovery.* Despite the title, Hanson's account of Kepler and the *abduction* of the elliptical orbit of Mars describes a style of thinking that is between creation and discovery.

[5]To live in *the* world as *a* world is to live the world *metaphorically.* A phenomenology of experience would reveal that human experience metaphors the world and that the structure of experience is that of metaphor. Merleau-Ponty's (1962) *Phenomenology of Perception* strongly implies this direction, and, in a publication subsequent to the original version of this article, Romanyshyn (1982) has developed the metaphorical character of psychological life. An earlier version of this theme also appears in Romanyshyn (1975b).

this case is *in* the world, and in the world as a *perceived difference,* as a difference that one lives.[6]

In this sense, existential–phenomenological psychology speaks of experience as a structure *in* and of the world, where structure is understood neither as a preexistent something to be *discovered* in the world nor simply a *created* idea. On the contrary, a structure is a *perceived difference,* a difference that one lives before one knows it and makes it real as a thing or idea. It is a difference between a subject and the world, a difference that is realized between them.

Being anxious, therefore, or for that matter any psychological experience, is a world, and whoever has lived that experience has also lived that world. It is in this sense that another can and does have *indirect* access to experience, because having lived that world, one has already participated in that situation. Experience is visible, then, for the other because your experience and my experience meet *in* the world as a world.

But being anxious, and emotional experiences in general, tend to remain ''worldly'' in very transient ways. In other words, we do not tend as a culture to stabilize these experiences in any permanent fashion. There are, however, other psychological experiences that are permanently enshrined *in* the world, and it is through these that experience becomes visible for others in a very *direct* way. The ways in which a culture builds its buildings, for example, are an indication of the ways in which it embodies certain *typical* experiences.

Consider the location and design of a hospital. Approached from the psychological point of view of experience, a hospital's design and location reveal the ways in which a society experiences illness and health as well as the relationships and boundaries between them. Michel Foucault (1965), for example, has demonstrated this point with regard to psychological illness in discussing the variations in the building of mental hospitals in Europe between the sixteenth and nineteenth centuries. Churches provide still another example, for they reveal the experience of the sacred and the holy for a culture at a particular time. Schools, libraries, and even zoos, which express how a city experiences the irrational and the primitive, are examples as well.[7]

Regardless of the particular example, one point remains the same: There is as much, and perhaps even more, (genuine) psychology in a building than in a brain. We might even say that a genuine human psychology *should* concern itself more with culture and humanity's symbol-making achievements than with biology and reductive explanations of behavior and experience. Be that as it may, what is more important than the examples is their significance, for they allow existential–phenomenological psychology as the study of experience to meet this criterion of observability by the other in a very direct way. A building is not merely a thing; it is a perceived difference. Moreover, as the embodiment or fleshing out of a particular structure of experience, it is quite observable by others. The psychologist, then, who is a reader of buildings is no different from, and is faced with no more or less a difficult task, than the psychologist who is a reader of behavior. In each case the psychological is an observable to be interpreted.[8]

Experience is visible, and there is an important sense in which it is even directly visible for the other. This section has considered this theme, and, as an alternative approach to traditional psychology, it has also suggested that behavior ''and'' experience are not *real* events but perspectives on the meaning of human action. As a summary of this section, consider the following three points:

First, psychology is not the study of either behavior *or* experience nor the study of behavior *and* experience in some additive way. Rather, it is the study of human action as behavior ''and'' experience, where the term *and* is understood as the dialectic behav*ed*-experience, experienc*ed*-behavior. In this sense, it is proper to say that human action is behavior because it is experience ''and'' experience because it is behavior. Furthermore, it is also proper to say that, as a dialectic, experience is the *lateral depth* of behavior, behavior the lateral depth of experience.[9] Or experience is the context or setting of behavior,

---

[6]Being anxious, or psychological experience in general, is *in* the world but not like coffee in a cup. Hence the use of italics with the preposition *in* in order to indicate that experience is not in the world as a thing. The preceding remarks about structure and metaphor are relevant here as well.

[7]Concerning zoos, we might also suggest that there may be a relation between the way in which a city embodies its experience of the primitive and the level of violence within that city. In other words, we are suggesting that a visitor to a new city, for example, may find a clue about that city's violence in the structure and placing of its zoo.

[8]This direct access to experience *modifies* our previous remark that the actor's perspective on himself or herself is the privileged one for experience. When one is dealing with psychological experiences that are *not* enshrined or embodied in a permanent way, this earlier remark remains valid. However, when one is dealing with these kinds of experiences, then the attitude of the observer on the ''other'' rather than the actor on himself or herself is the privileged one. In this sense, these more or less permanent structures of experience provide psychology with general norms in much the same way that a traditional psychology of behavior establishes general norms. Thus, an existential–phenomenological psychology of experience has a double relation to a traditional psychology of behavior. On the one hand, it *complements* it when it concerns itself with the actor's experience. On the other hand, it is a *counterpart* to a traditional psychology of behavior insofar as each concerns itself with *typical* meanings, the one on the side of behavior and the other on the side of experience.

[9]Lateral depth is another issue implied by this existential–phe-

just as behavior is the context or setting of experience. Between them, therefore, there is not a relation of cause and effect, nor even a relation of the manifest to the latent. Rather, their relation is perhaps most clearly understood as one of figure to ground, like those reversible figure–ground examples in gestalt psychology. Thus in the study of human action, the attitudes of observer and actor, respectively, become ways of enhancing the figures of behavior ''or'' experience, even although it is possible, with a shift in the focus of one's attitude, to recover the ground of each figure. In this sense, the issue of the maximum visibility of behavior ''or'' experience that we discussed turns out, in fact, to mean the perception of the *figures* of human action.

Second, this discussion of the visibility of experience further indicates that psychology is a discipline of the world, that psychology is, in fact, a study of the environment. But environmental psychology has a particular meaning here, for it refers exclusively to the human psychological environment, that is, to the world as experienced or to *the* world as *a* world. The environment we are talking of here refers, then, to the environments of psychological action, and on either the transient or permanent level. Thus, in order to understand memory, for example, it becomes necessary to describe the structures of the remembering world. And, on the permanent level, as indicated previously, one task of psychology is a recovery of the psychological as it is fleshed out in the buildings, tools, and accoutrements of contemporary life. In this sense, we would suggest that the architect or city

planner is an implicit psychologist of a culture and of an age.

Third, the previous discussion has also strongly suggested that, insofar as the psychological is a world, the discipline of psychology changes as the world does. In this sense, we would say that the discipline of psychology must be rewritten in every age. Moreover, we would even suggest that there is a closer relationship between psychology and history than there is between psychology and the natural sciences. History, in fact, may be viewed as a past implicit psychology, and psychology as an implicit present history. If nothing else, they are reciprocal disciplines.

Having discussed this alternative, it is now time to return to the main theme of this chapter. In traditional psychology, behavior is a real something in itself, a visible, external event, and psychology, as the study of behavior, is a discipline that infers behavior's meaning. In other words, as a pure external something, meaning is brought into behavior from the outside. Traditional psychology has had three major ways of practicing this style of inference. The next section considers these three styles.

Styles of Inference

Inference is the bringing of meaning into behavior, the exporting of meaning *from* the observing psychologist *to* the behavior observed. In traditional psychology, meaning has been brought to behavior in three general ways. Stated in other terms, the process of inference in psychology has had three major styles. The first can be called *evolutionism,* the second *physiologism,* and the third *naturalism.* A discussion of each of these styles will further advance our understanding of the meaning of the attitude of science in psychology.

Evolutionism

Evolutionism is clearly expressed in the text of Smith, Sarason, and Sarason (1982). Indicating what psychology is and should be, the authors say that ''evolutionary theory has had a profound influence on the study of psychology. . . . If human beings are viewed as an elaborate form of animal life, then it should be possible to learn certain things about them by studying lower forms . . . research with animals is an important tool for obtaining knowledge about human behavior'' (p. 34). For these authors, it is very clear that their commitment to natural science expresses itself in an evolutionary perspective that christens the process of inference with a particular character.

nomenological alternative. Insofar as one understands that experience is visible ''in'' the world as a world, then one is also implying a revision of the notion of depth from the vertical to the lateral. Experience, in other words, is not *behind* or *beneath* (as unconscious, for example) one's behavior. On the contrary, the dialectic behav*ed* experience, experienc*ed* behavior is *between us in the world.* As we previously said, what I call my behavior, you call your experience, and so forth. Indeed, in the world in which we live, it is really impossible to say where one's experience ends and his or her behavior begins, just as in conversation it is impossible to say with absolute finality and certitude who is listening and who is speaking. The fact of the matter is we do both, just as we are simultaneously behaving experience and experiencing behavior. In addition, this *depth* of the lateral should not be confused with the *distance* of the horizontal. The image of lateral depth, therefore, is not a line but a spiral. As such, the lateral depth of human action is temporal, and the dialectic of behavior ''and'' experience in the present is the crossing in the present of the past and the future, of one's history and expectations with that of the other. Readers who wish a fuller discussion of this notion of lateral depth are referred to Romanyshyn (1983), where the psychoanalytic notion of the *unconscious* is approached in an existential–phenomenological way. In addition, Merleau-Ponty's last work, *The Visible and Invisible* (1968), is filled with provocative suggestions along this line.

By adopting this point of view, psychology is able to understand the appearance of human behavior by attributing to it a knowledge that has been gained from the study of other organisms. Meaning becomes a condition or cause of behavior, value a stimulus to behavior, and purpose a goal-directed activity. In more specific and concrete terms, the evolutionary perspective leads to an understanding of a phenomenon like human learning in terms of conditioning. The principles of learning that are established in the study of rats and pigeons in the Skinner box are thus assumed to be transferable to human learning in all situations. Skinner (1957), himself, for example, has advocated in *Verbal Behavior* that even the learning and using of language is a product of reinforcement, and the widespread popularity, use, and apparent success of the teaching machines and programmed instructions based on these principles seem to substantiate his view.

Natural science has extended its range over nature by establishing a *continuity* of laws across the diverse appearance of natural events so that, for example, the falling of an apple from a tree is governed by the same laws as the orbiting of the earth around the sun. In much the same way, psychology seeks and apparently achieves the same extension by establishing a *continuity* of laws over the range of animal and human behavior. But what appears as a successful achievement is, in fact, only a partial vision or insight into the understanding of human action, an insight, moreover, that is gained at the price of reducing the complexity of human action to this preestablished conviction.

Human learning, then, is and can be conditioned, but the very establishment of this fact, and the program of conditioning, indicate that learning is more than a product of its consequences. For if this were not the case, then the programs of conditioning designed by humans to teach others would themselves be conditioned, or accidental, robbing them of any intrinsic validity. Moreover, the designing itself would not even be possible; it would merely occur according to the conditions that would stand *outside* any human understanding. Thus, just as the biological *theory* of evolution indicates our *double* relation to this condition, psychology's evolutionary perspective reveals the same meaning. Human action, like the human body, is the object, the result, the effect of external influences that act upon it, but it is also the understanding of this possibility. And, in expressing this understanding, we simultaneously express our "transcendence" of these conditions, with *transcendence* understood not as our total freedom but only as the negation of our total bondage. For again, if we were totally determined by the world, would we ever be able to establish this condition as a fact for our understanding? Psychology's evolutionary

perspective announces a truth, therefore, but in announcing it in the way in which it does, that is, as indicating *only* the *continuity* between human beings and other organisms, it undercuts the possibility of its own statement.

Magda Arnold (1964) has stressed this same point when she says that "psychologists have insisted again and again that human beings differ from animals only quantitatively and not qualitatively. . . . As a result, they have increasingly avoided terms which would imply a qualitative difference; so reasoning has become problem-solving, desires become drive or needs, willing turns into striving." She adds that "one is almost forced to conclude that experiential evidence is not respectable in psychology or that there is a prior assumption that man and animal have like natures" (p. 33). In fact, as we have seen previously, both conclusions are operative, for the prior assumption of evolution rules out experiential evidence, and the ruling out of experiential evidence is grounded in this prior assumption.

One should note what the dismissal of this experiential evidence involves. What, for example, occurs in transforming the phenomenon of human desire into drives or the experience of wishing into a psychology of needs? To be more specific, what, after all, is gained by translating the phenomenon of sexual desire into the instinct theory of psychoanalysis? Must we not say that, in each instance, we are, in fact, presented with a *metaphor* and that, in each case, the metaphor is forgotten such that the instinct of Eros becomes the *explanation* for the experience of sexual desire? And further, must we not say, therefore, that the experiential evidence of which Arnold speaks indicates that there are two levels of meaning that are operative in these instances, levels moreover that cannot be reduced one to the other? The physiology of sexual desire, then, is neither the equivalent of nor the explanation for the experience. Indeed, the experiential evidence teaches us that the continuity that does exist between humans and animals is in fact "balanced" by a *discontinuity* that also exists between us.

As a style of inference, evolutionism, which traces only the continuities between human beings and other behaving organisms, is one-sided because there is neither a total identity nor a total separation between human behavior and the behavior of other organisms. In the following two sections, this notion of a discontinuous continuity between human action and the action of lower organisms will be alluded to in other contexts. At this point, therefore, let us simply repeat for the sake of emphasis that human action is not only *identical* with the action of other organisms—humans and frogs both blink—but also *different* from it—a human's blink can become a wink. The style of inference called *evolutionism* must somehow retain the paradox of identity/difference if the *human* sense of human action is to be preserved.

Physiologism

This second way of inferring behavior's meaning is already implicit in the previous style because evolutionary continuity is, in fact, primarily established by psychology at the level of the functioning of the nervous system. It is, in other words, at the level of physiology that psychology can find justification for its evolutionary view. A clear example of this identity is found in a remark made by B. F. Skinner (1975). Defending the science of behavior, he says that "it is, I assume, part of biology." "The organism that *behaves*," he continues, "is the organism that breathes, digests, conceives, gestates, and so on." "As such," he concludes, "the *behaving* organism will eventually be described and explained by the anatomist and physiologist" (Skinner, 1975, p. 42 [emphasis ours]). For Skinner, then, behaving is like breathing, with respect to the lawful *continuities* that exist between species. But, whereas breathing may be able to be reduced to a matter of the lungs—although even here the breathing human is not the equivalent of another breathing organism, as anyone who in the depths of anxiety has ever struggled for the breath of life realizes—behavior is always a matter of meaning.

Physiologism, however, does more in psychology than merely *justify* the evolutionary style of thinking, for it provides its own specific context within which psychology can and does infer behavior's meaning. Consider Haber and Runyon's (1983) interesting discussion of *nightmare* in their text, *Fundamentals of Psychology.* This example demonstrates the physiological understanding of a psychological phenomenon, and, in line with this example, we invite the reader merely to recall his or her own experience of nightmare as he or she reads the traditional explanation of it. To orient the discussion let us pose as the central question, What is a nightmare?—a legitimate question that psychology should be expected to address.

Haber and Runyon's (1983) discussion of nightmare occurs within the context of their discussion of the four stages of sleep and its physiological foundations. According to the sleep-monitoring equipment described, a nightmare is a disturbance in sleep that occurs in an individual who is partially awake. The readings of the monitoring equipment reveal an increase in eye and brain activity and a soaring heart rate, whereas other readings indicate that the elapsed time of the nightmare is usually less than one minute.

In answer to the question, What is a nightmare?, the authors offer these physiological facts. With this answer, however, one is still left in the dark with regard to both the meaning of having a nightmare *as well as* the significance of these facts. At first glance, it appears that these facts are unrelated to the experience of nightmare, and that they do little, if anything, to extend our understanding of it. But such a conclusion would be both premature and erroneous, for whereas it is true that *the physiology of nightmare does not* equal the psychological experience of it, it is also true that these *two levels of meaning*, physiology and psychological experience, *are related.*

Psychology, of course, traditionally understands this relation of physiology and psychological experiences by substituting the former for the latter. For psychology, therefore, this physiology of nightmare *is* the psychology of it. Such a relation is, however, untenable, for the simple reason that these physiological facts themselves are significant only because the authors *implicitly* situate these facts within the ordinary context of human life. However crude the authors' lived understanding of a nightmare may be, it is, nevertheless, this context that draws together the meaning of these physiological facts. In and of themselves, these graph readings are insignificant, for even on the most obvious level, the experimenter must *first* have demonstrated that his or her subjects were having a nightmare in order to understand the facts in this way (i. e., as the physiology of nightmare).

Of course, *after* establishing the physiology's significance, the facts themselves can be "interpreted" without recourse to the subject's experience. In this sense, the physiologizing of psychological phenomena establishes a certain *generality,* or a certain general level of meaning, that is *continuous* across many subjects in many situations. This is to be expected because the psychological subject is a body. But this does not change the initial fact that the physiology's significance is situated within the context of lived meaning. And, this fact can never allow one to substitute the physiology of experience for its psychology, because, even at the most general level of meaning, the physiology of an experience is not identical to the psychology of that experience.

Haber and Runyon (1983) themselves reveal their implicit reliance on this lived context of meaning when they speak of nightmares as "sufficiently arousing or *frightening*" (p. 249, emphasis ours). Nothing in the physiological facts speak, in and of themselves, of fear. Fear belongs not to physiology but to meaning. Hence, it is only in their implicit *recontextualizing* of this physiology into the living context of a nightmare that this phenomenon is, and can be, understood as frightening. The physiological facts, therefore, *borrow* their significance from the lived world of experience. Thus the relation between physiology and experience must in fact be reversed.[10]

This reversed relation between physiology and experience, which indicates that the former is always situated within the context of the latter, can be seen in a more specific way if one considers some of the individual facts uncovered in this physiological explanation of nightmare. The soaring heart rate and increased eye and brain activities make sense because the experience of nightmare is, among other things, the experience of panic. Anyone who has ever had the unfortunate experience of panic realizes that, in this experience, one is hyperalert, aroused, and quite active. Indeed, in its primary sense, the experience of panic is closely tied to the act of fleeing. For the dreamer, therefore, the experience of nightmare is this panicky condition in which his or her body quite naturally participates. The physiological facts, therefore, are in accordance with the subject's experience, and his or her bodily behavior at this level of physiology fits this panicky world. Again, the physiology does not "establish" the meaning of this experience; it reveals it.

Approached in this way, the original question, "What is a nightmare?", has two answers. On the one hand, a nightmare is a physiological event, and on the other hand, it is a human meaning. Moreover, the two answers are related, for an understanding of the former answer rests on an understanding of the latter. In this sense, the physiological facts that psychology establishes are not "always" wrong or even irrelevant. They are, however, insufficient, for they provide only an implicit understanding of the phenomenon as it is lived. *The physiology of nightmare is not identical to the psychology of nightmare.*

In spite of these answers, what remains at issue is the question of which answer provides the proper psychological perspective. Notwithstanding traditional psychology's choice of the physiological answer, a genuine psychology of human beings must ultimately situate itself with the human meaning. Again, this does not mean that the former answer is to be ignored, for we have seen that, within the proper context, it provides additional information regarding the experience. The latter answer must be adopted, therefore, because the psychological perspective is essential to the physiological perspective itself. Physiology is not prior to experience. Indeed, an understanding of lived experience is indispensable to understanding physiology. Thus psychology cannot infer the

meaning of behavior or experience from physiology. Rather, it must interpret physiology on the basis of lived behavior *and* experience. The issue of physiology and experience turns out, therefore, to be completely *reversed* from the way traditional psychology sees it. In place of speaking about the physiological foundations of behavior (as Haber and Runyon do), this discussion suggests that psychology should speak about the "psychological foundations of physiology."

Before concluding this section, an additional point of clarification should be made. Although it is true that the physiological perspective is, in and of itself, not wrong, its use can at times lead to erroneous conclusions. In fact, the way in which it has generally been used in psychology has led to a confusion between physiological facts and psychological meanings and to an appropriation of the latter by the former. An example of this confusion is in Haber and Runyon's (1983) statement that the time of the nightmare is usually less than 1 minute. This is what the graph shows of the brain's activity during a nightmare. But this time is the time of the clock, the objective time of one who does not participate in the phenomenon. If this is taken, however, as the real time of the nightmare, and the authors suggest that it is, then the physiological fact has supplanted the experienced meaning, for the real time of a nightmare is its endless duration.

Commenting on the nature of psychology, E. G. Boring (in Deese, 1964) has said: "To understand man, the doer, we must understand his nervous system, which activates his muscles and glands" (p. 38). This statement best summarizes the real confusion that the physiological perspective introduces into psychology, for its application often results in the originary character of psychological phenomena being studied in nonoriginary ways. The only way in which physiology can serve psychology, therefore, is if the traditional relation between physiology and human action is reversed. We need a psychology of physiology to complement our physiology of psychology.

Naturalism

Naturalism is the third way in which psychology *imports* meaning into behavior, and, as a style of inference, it is closely related to the other two styles just discussed. Morgan *et al.* (1986) express this perspective when they say that "psychological researchers simply make the most exacting and systematic study they can of *naturally* occurring behavior" (p. 14, emphasis ours). These authors go on to compare this approach with the perspective of the natural sciences, in saying that "psychology shares this approach with a number of other sciences," including geology and environmental science,

---

[10]The work of Merleau-Ponty is extremely important in this regard. In *The Structure of Behavior* (1963), for example, he makes a similar point, with more extensive discussion, about this *recontextualizing* of physiology through examining the work of Pavlov and his descendents. Readers are referred particularly to Chapters 1 and 2 of that volume.

which try to describe "behavior as it occurs *naturally*" (p. 14, emphasis ours). This view of human action as a natural event already presupposes that it is *continuous* in its meaning with the events of nature, a view that has close ties with the evolutionary perspective.

Naturalism, however, also brings its own unique contributions to psychology's attitude toward behavior. More specifically, this perspective raises the question of whether human behavior is not only a natural event but also an historical action. Stated more generally, this perspective raises the issue of the relation between behavior's context and its meaning. Ultimately, the perspective of naturalism asks whether psychology is more properly allied with the discipline of history than with science, because the former discipline also takes as its subject matter the actions of men and women in time. The following discussion considers these themes in reverse order, from the most general to the more specific.

The British historian, R. G. Collingwood (1956), provides us with a convenient example with which to consider the first issue. That Caesar crossed the Rubicon, he says, is historical fact and, as such, it can be viewed as an event of history. But Collingwood rightly points out that the significance of this event for the historian does not lie in the actual event itself as such; the significance does not lie in the fact, but rather, the fact is a significance. Collingwood's point is that in order to penetrate to this significance, the historian must distinguish between the outside and the inside of events.[11] Events are not actions, nor are actions mere events; each, on the contrary, belongs to a different domain or order of reality. In confusing the two, "the science of human nature, from Locke to the present day, has failed to solve the problem of understanding what understanding is" (Collingwood, 1956, p. 208). In our own terms, the science of psychology, in modeling itself on the natural sciences, has understood understanding in terms of inference rather than interpretation, and in doing this, it has conceived of human action *as if* it were merely an external event.

But what does it mean to distinguish the inside of an event? For Collingwood as historian, and for psychology, it means acknowledging that the facts of history, like the facts of human action, are more than facts. Caesar's crossing of the Rubicon, like John's winking at that beautiful girl, are facts because they are also not facts. The outside of the event is the fact of history, or the fact of behavior, the crossing and the winking; but the inside, as

Collingwood calls it, is not a fact, but an intention, or a motive, if one prefers. In Collingwood's example, the event can only be understood within the context of the intention to defy Republican law; in John's case, the event can only be understood within the context of his intention to attract that beautiful girl. Caesar's crossing, like John's winking, is not a spasm of the neuromuscular apparatus, and, in general, human movements, human actions, are not subject to the same laws that describe the "movements" or "actions" of inanimate bodies. To call human behavior a natural event, therefore, covers over the recognition, given in experience, that *the events of* human action are also *advents of meaning*. John's wink is not a blink, and the event of blinking as a winking is the coming-to-be of a meaning.

Collingwood's considerations are important, therefore, because they strongly suggest that history and psychology are faced with similar problems, and thus, also, that perhaps psychology is more closely allied to history in its attitude toward its subject matter and its methods than it is to science. Both disciplines are faced with the task of interpreting human actions and with the necessity of carrying out this interpretation within the context of the action's occurrence. Each discipline is faced with the same necessity to consider that "an action is the unity of the outside and inside of an event" (Collingwood, 1956, p. 213). Whatever the differences between history and psychology, and there are many, it seems that psychology can learn much from this related field. At the very least, it would be profitable to consider, as an alternative approach to psychology as a natural science, the approach of psychology as historical or hermeneutical discipline.[12]

One of the shared problems of psychology and history concerns the relationship between human action's meaning and its context. In traditional psychology, the perspective of naturalism presupposes that the event of behavior, like that of nature, has a meaning that is independent of its given context. For example, it matters little to the scientific study of natural events whether the establishment of the law of the acceleration of a falling body makes use of an apple in a tree or a ball on an inclined plane in a laboratory. In each case, the law can be established because, beneath the two apparently different phenomena, physics discovers a link. It discovers the link because it is able to ignore the context of the falling; in the natural sciences, *what falls* is always secondary to the *falling*.

Psychology has imitated this practice and has

---

[11]One could question whether or not Collingwood understands the inside of an event in a nonspatial way. But, whatever Collingwood's view, the reader should be clear that we understand and use these terms in light of the previous discussion. In any case, however, our use of Collingwood here is not to further discuss that point but to discuss this issue of naturalism.

[12]The term *hermeneutics* can most generally be taken to mean the science of interpretation. See von Eckartsberg's Chapter 6 and Valle, King, and Halling's Chapter 1 for more detailed discussions of hermeneutics.

adopted this principle. Its use is most visible in psychology's commitment to the experimental method, for one of the principal features of the experimental method is the isolation of phenomena, their removal from the given context of their occurrence. The phenomenon of human learning provides a good example. Haber and Fried (1975) tell us that "it is possible to talk about learning in terms of *the kinds of things learned*" (p. 139, emphasis ours), and, as examples, they suggest learning a route to a destination or hitting a baseball. But then they add: "It is equally possible to talk about learning in terms of general principles, *in the hope that these principles will apply to all kinds of learning*" (p. 139). They conclude by saying that "we will take the latter course . . . , focusing on the two general models of learning, those of classical and operant conditioning" (p. 140).

The prejudice of naturalism is apparent in these statements because the authors clearly indicate their preference for learning over what is learned, as well as their preference that *all kinds of learning* will be subject to the same general principles of conditioning. But one can rightly ask what these general principles and models of learning actually describe because, it is equally apparent from the point of view of experience that learning to drive a car is not equivalent to learning the style, moods, and feelings of one's beloved. For whatever common principles may be operative in each of these situations, it is of equal importance to note the contexts of these examples of learning that modify those principles. It is not that the principles are wrong but that they assume too much, precisely in presuming that learning is a natural event subject to invariant natural conditions. In the end, psychology winds up learning much about the conditions of *performance* but less about the meaning of learning as a human experience.

Another example of this naturalistic perspective is provided by Giorgi's (1967a) critique of the learning of nonsense syllables. This is a particularly good example because nonsense syllables have long been a favorite medium for psychology to establish its general laws of learning via the neutral and democratic conditions of the experiment. In traditional psychology, the learning of nonsense syllables involves a process of association or series of associations *between* the syllables themselves. By going directly to the subjects, however, Giorgi discovered that the syllables are learned not according to any naturalistic laws of association, but percisely because they make sense to, or for, each subject. Indeed, then, the syllables are not nonsense—this is only true from the experimenter's perspective that assumes this in line with his or her intention to demonstrate the laws of learning. Rather, the subject constructs a *context* of meaning

around each syllable. Learning, then, is a highly active, participative attempt to structure a situation, and not at all the passive outcome of some external laws. In a later article Giorgi (1967b) says: ". . . behavior is to experience what figure is to ground or a word is to its context . . . Just as . . . a word [can] be taken out of context, so too can any behavioral act be considered as an entity in itself" (p. 172). But ". . . while a specific word can mean many things in isolation, usually it can have only one meaning in context" (p. 173). He concludes: "To know what a given behavioral act means, one must consider it in the light of the *experiential* context of the participating subject" (p. 173) [our italics]. In short, learning is not only an event, but also a meaning in which the essential and significant role of context cannot be ignored.

As a final example of the importance of context to the understanding of human action, consider the following statements of action:

1. John *kissed* his father good-bye.
2. John *kissed* his girlfriend.
3. John *kissed* his boyfriend.
4. John *kissed* his boss Fred hello and good-bye.

What is amusing about these statements are the suggestions that each one reveals about John. Within the perspective of naturalism a kiss is a kiss, the contact of two pairs of mucous membranes. Within the perspective of human life, a kiss is a meaning that depends upon, among other things, to whom you give it.

Context, therefore, seems indispensable to a proper understanding of human action, and for psychology to adopt this perspective and, thereby, to reject the perspective of naturalism is to acknowledge that human behavior is an *historical action*. In other words, *history is the context of human life, and the historical is the context of the psychological.*

Consider Collingwood's (1956) notion of the "inside" of an event. Speaking psychologically, and in light of the remarks made in the previous section on the visibility of experience, the inside of an event can be called *experience*. Approached in this way, Collingwood's concern as historian for the inside of Caesar's crossing the Rubicon is a concern for Caesar's experience, which is the ground of this "observed" behavior of crossing. Obviously, however, this experience is not something that is private to Caesar alone, for if experience was private in this way, then neither a true history, nor psychology, of that "event" could be established. This experience is, therefore, understandable in light of its wider horizon of meaning, in the historical institutions that were challenged by that act. All of that is Caesar's experience, which gives background to the behavior of crossing, and his experience is visible in this background. Stated most generally, human experience always has an historical horizon around it, and one can, therefore, interpret the experience if one knows its context.

This, of course, does not mean that this historical context determines that experience or that, if one knows that context, then one has "captured" the pure meaning of that experience. For, in addition to this historical horizon of experience, there is also the actor's intentional horizon, the reason why he or she takes up these historical norms in this way. And here one must rely on Caesar himself, on his own spoken or written "explanations" of his action. Although these reasons are themselves also historical, the point is that one can never *reduce* an action to its history even though that action is not understandable outside the context of that history. History as the context of human action is, therefore, "only" the acknowledgment that time weaves together the fabric of human life; it is not a surrender to the external point of view discussed previously.

Summary

The three styles of inference—evolutionism, physiologism, and naturalism—all contribute to defining the attitude of science that psychology adopts as its point of view toward its subject matter. Throughout this chapter, we have attempted to present this attitude as psychology itself uses it, raising questions along the way concerning the meaning of its use.

CONCLUSION

Morgan *et al.* (1986, p. 4) say that psychology is a science, and they also clearly map out their definition of psychology as a science. Psychology, they tell us, is rational and empirical, objective and quantitative, experimental and systematic:

1. Although *rational* simply means reasoned, *organized* knowledge, a criterion that is certainly desirable and necessary, "rational" has taken on a very special and very narrow meaning in psychology. Psychology is rational insofar as it organizes its knowledge as science, that is, according to the attitude of science. In fact, the criterion of rationality is redundant because psychology is a science because it is rational, and it is rational *only* because it is a science. There are, however, other ways to

be rational, other ways to organize knowledge; the discipline of history is only one example. Thus psychology's exclusive identification of rationality with the attitude of science is itself an historical choice to organize its knowledge in a particular way.

2. The criterion of *empirical* also presents special problems because it, too, has taken on special meanings in psychology. On the one hand, the term *empirical* has become identified with experiment, as opposed to its wider context of experience, and on the other hand, it has become identified with observation by the other. The first identity raises the problem of context because an experiment essentially means the isolation of phenomena. And the second identity prejudges what behavior and experience are. Psychology comes to identify the psychological with behavior that is understood in the narrowest way as a visible and exterior event in and of itself. Any understanding of behavior *and* experience as perspectives on human action is ignored.

3. The criterion of *objectivity* rests on the prejudice of the objective world. In adopting this criterion, psychology does not question the genesis or becoming of objectivity but simply takes it for granted. This position merely extends and builds on the unquestioned objectivity of everyday experience, leaving the origin of that experience unclarified. In this regard, psychology first proceeds to *ignore* common-sense experience and then to *correct* it through its styles of inference.

4. The *quantitative* aspect of psychology is a concrete way of carrying out its other criterion of being empirical. Numbers provide the neutral context of meaning that allows psychology to abstract a phenomenon from its given context of meaning. Although this is not the only way that psychology achieves this abstraction, it is still true that measurement generally substitutes for meaning in psychology.

5. The criterion of being *experimental* is already discussed in the criterion of being empirical. One can add that the experimental procedures of psychology have been all-important in justifying its physiological style of inference, whereas the physiological investigations of psychology have found support in this criterion of being experimental. The experimental equipment in Haber and Runyon's (1983) study of nightmare, for example, already determines in advance that nightmare is a physiological event.

6. The criterion of being *systematic* is an internal one because psychology believes itself to be systematic when it is being rational, empirical, objective, quantitative, and experimental in the ways we described. In the last resort, psychology is systematic in the way it *organizes* its knowledge, so that this criterion brings us full circle again

to our original starting point: *The organization of knowledge is not neutral with respect to that knowledge.*

Psychology claims to be a science, and this is the way in which it organizes its knowledge. In this chapter, we have offered a *systematic* and *critical* dialogue with this claim from the point of view of existential–phenomenological psychology. Examining the spatial metaphors that underlie psychology's understanding of the terms *behavior* and *experience,* an understanding that means that psychology becomes a discipline of inference, we have also suggested how existential–phenomenological psychology is an *alternative* to traditional psychology. Having come this far, are we justified in concluding that psychology is not a science, or as Sigmund Koch (1969) has said: "Psychology cannot be a coherent science"?

We think not. Indeed, we trust that the reader realizes that what has been at issue throughout this chapter is a *view* of science that psychology adopts. Understood in this light, we would say that at least two options are open for psychology. Either psychology can understand itself as a science with a different and broader interpretation of this attitude, or it can understand itself as another kind of discipline, that is, as a discipline that organizes its knowledge in another way. Whichever option it chooses, however, we think that, in the last analysis, the real issue is not the claim itself but rather the relevance of the plan of organization to its subject matter. And, in this regard, we believe that existential phenomenology makes two essential contributions. First, it insists that the demands of the subject matter shape the plan of organization of a discipline rather than the other way around. Second, it begins its investigation of the psychological with human action *as lived* rather than with an attitude of practiced ignorance toward it. In this regard, a systematic–critical investigation of the view of science that psychology adopts forces psychology to another *alternative*—existential–phenomenological psychology. Psychology's own self-critical momentum takes it toward an existential–phenomenological approach, and this, we hope, is demonstrated in this chapter.

REFERENCES

Arnold, M. (1964). Basic assumptions in psychology. In A. Walters (Ed.), *Readings in psychology* (pp. 31–37). Westminister: Newman.

Burtt, E. A. (1954). *The metaphysical foundations of modern science.* New York: Doubleday.

Butterfield, H. (1950). *The origins of modern science: 1300–1800.* London: Bell.

Collingwood, R. G. (1956). *The idea of history.* New York: Oxford University Press.

Davidoff, L. L. (1980). *Introduction to psychology.* New York: McGraw-Hill.

Deese, J. A. (1964). *Principles of psychology.* Boston: Allyn & Bacon.

Edwards, D. C. (1972). *General psychology.* New York: Macmillan.

Foucault, M. (1965). *Madness and civilization.* New York: Pantheon.

Geldard, F. (1962). *Fundamentals of psychology.* New York: Wiley.

Giorgi, A. (1967a). A phenomenological approach to the problem of meaning and serial learning. *Review of Existential Psychology and Psychiatry, 7,* 106–118.

Giorgi, A. (1967b). The experience of the subject as a source of data in a psychological experiment. *Review of Existential Psychology and Psychiatry, 7,* 169–176.

Giorgi, A. (1970). *Psychology as a human science.* New York: Harper & Row.

Haber, R. N., & Fried, A. H. (1975). *An introduction to psychology.* New York: Holt, Rinehart & Winston.

Haber, R. N., & Runyon, R. P. (1983). *Fundamentals of psychology.* Reading: Addison & Wesley.

Hanson, N. R. (1972). *Patterns of discovery.* London: Cambridge University Press.

Heisenberg, W. (1958). *The physicist's conception of nature.* London: Hutchinson.

Koch, S. (1969). Psychology cannot be a coherent science. *Psychology Today, 3,* 4, 14, 64–68.

Kuhn, T. S. (1962). *The structure of scientific revolutions.* Chicago: University of Chicago Press.

Lefton, L. A. (1985). *Psychology.* Boston: Allyn & Bacon.

Merleau-Ponty, M. (1962). *Phenomenology of perception.* New York: Humanities Press.

Merleau-Ponty, M. (1963). *The structure of behavior.* Boston: Beacon.

Merleau-Ponty, M. (1964). *The primacy of perception.* Evanston: Northwestern University Press.

Merleau-Ponty, M. (1968). *The visible and the invisible.* Evanston: Northwestern University Press.

Morgan, C. T., King, R. A., Weisz, J. R., & Schopler, J. (1986). *Introduction to psychology.* New York: McGraw-Hill.

Morris, C. G. (1982). *Psychology: An introduction.* Englewood Cliffs, N. J.: Prentice-Hall.

Romanyshyn, R. (1973). Copernicus and the beginnings of modern science. *Journal of Phenomenological Psychology, 3*(2), 187–189.

Romanyshyn, R. (1975a). The attitude of science and the crisis of psychology. In A. Giorgi, C. T. Fischer, & E. L. Murray (Eds.), *Duquesne studies in phenomenological psychology* (Vol. II, pp. 6–18). Pittsburgh: Duquesne University Press.

Romanyshyn, R. (1975b). Metaphors and human behavior. *Journal of Phenomenological Psychology, 5*(1), 441–460.

Romanyshyn, R. (1982). *Psychological life: From science to metaphor.* Austin: University of Texas Press.

Romanyshyn, R. (1983). The unconscious as a lateral depth: Perception and the two moments of reflection. In H. Silverman, J. Sallis, & T. Seebohn (Eds.), *Continental philosophy in America: Prize essays* (pp. 227–244). Pittsburgh: Duquesne University Press.

Skinner, B. F. (1957). *Verbal behavior.* Salt Lake City: Appleton-Century-Croft.

Skinner, B. F. (1971). *Beyond freedom and dignity.* New York: Knopf.

Skinner, B. F. (1975, January). The steep and thorny way to a science of behavior. *American Psychologist*, 42–49.

Smith, R. E., Sarason, I. G., & Sarason, B. R. (1982). *Psychology: The frontiers of behavior.* New York: Harper & Row.

Straus, E. (1963). *The primary world of the senses.* New York: Free Press.

van den Berg, J. H. (1970). *Things.* Pittsburgh: Duquesne University Press.

Whitehead, A. F. (1925). *Science and the modern world.* New York: Macmillan.

Zaner, R. M. (1970). *The way of phenomenology.* New York: Pegasus.

3

Phenomenological Research Methods

Donald E. Polkinghorne

PSYCHOLOGY AND PHENOMENOLOGICAL RESEARCH

Research methods are plans used in the pursuit of knowledge. They are outlines of investigative journeys, laying out previously developed paths, which, if followed by researchers, are supposed to lead to valid knowledge. These paths are drawn on maps based on assumptions about the nature of reality and the processes of human understanding. The map developed for Western science during the past three centuries is based on the notion that reality consists of natural objects and that knowledge is a description of these objects as they exist in themselves. The purpose of the paths laid out on this map is to eliminate the distorting influence of personal perspective and the subjective properties of researchers.

Phenomenological research methods are drawn on a different map. It is a map developed in the first half of this century by Edmund Husserl and subsequent members of the phenomenological movement (Spiegelberg, 1976). The phenomenological map is not antithetical to the mainstream natural science map, but it marks different features of the terrain. It locates geological features of human awareness and reminds us that the research journey needs to attend to the configurations of experience before moving on to assumptions about independent natural objects. Because the descriptions of natural objects are derived from experience, experience itself must be clear-

ly understood before a firm foundation can be established for the sciences studying the natural world.

The approach of Western science includes the commonsense assumption that experiencing is unproblematic and consists of sense data reflecting the objects of the world along with subjective bias and feeling. These subjective elements can be sifted out through methodological techniques that recognize only those experiences consisting of directly perceived objects on which there is intersubjective agreement. In this model of experience, the knower is a passive recipient of reflective sensations from natural objects. Phenomenological philosophy, however, calls this assumption into question. It holds that experience involves the operation of active processes that encompass and constitute the various contents that become present to awareness. These contents include not only the objects of perception but also those of memory, imagination, and feeling.

Phenomenological Philosophy

The phenomenological map refocuses inquiry, concentrating not on descriptions of worldly objects but on descriptions of experience. This requires a change in the attitude or attunement of the researcher from a natural perspective to a phenomenological perspective. In the phenomenological perspective, questions about the existence and character of the objects that are experienced are put in abeyance while the researchers attend, instead, to what is present or given in awareness. This suspension or reduction (also called the first or phenomenological *epoche* [bracketing]) of the commonsense thesis that an independent reality "explains" experience locates the

Donald E. Polkinghorne • Graduate Department of Counseling/School Psychology, California State University, Fullerton, California 92634.

research in the phenomenological realm [Husserl, 1913/1931, pp. 107–111]. It removes the distraction, the need to look outside of awareness for sources that "cause" experience.

In the return to the investigation of experience itself, phenomenological philosophy has produced an understanding of experience that undercuts some of the commonsense assumptions that inform Western science. The form and continuity of experience are products of an intrinsic relationship between human beings and the world. The error of the traditional approach is the result of separating mind and body into two independent spheres. This separation has produced two contradictory pictures. On the one hand, the world is understood to be made up of the random buzzing of electrical particles, and it is mind that imposes the notions of form and substance on this confusion. On the other hand, the world itself is understood as ordered and structured, the mind making no special contribution to experience and merely passively mirroring the natural order (Rorty, 1979). The phenomenological correction holds that experience consists of the reception of worldly objects by the processes of consciousness to constitute what presents itself in awareness.

In awareness, objects appear *as* something. That is, things appear as "chairs," "tables," and so forth; they do not appear as mere sense data. The notion of independent sense data is derived from a secondary abstracting process that constructs out of an originally given whole perception a deficient mode of seeing. Experience, as it is directly given, occurs at the meeting of person and world. For example, as I experience two objects, one appears nearer to me than the other. The seeing of the one thing as nearer than the other requires both that the object exists in the world and that a person exists who is the locus of the experience. Understanding experience merely as a mental projection onto the world (the idealistic fallacy) or as a reflection of the world (the realistic fallacy) misses the necessity of the person–world relationship in the constituting of experience. Experience is a reality that results from the openness of human awareness to the world, and it cannot be reduced to either the sphere of the mental or the sphere of the physical.

The realm of experience consists of both particular occurrences and the meanings of which they are instances. The commonsense approach assumes that the real is only particulars—that is, that individual things make up the hard-core facts of reality. For example, things like this particular pencil I am holding are ultimately what make up reality. But this particular is also an instance of "pencilness," a category of meaning. Phenomenology recognizes the experiential reality of meanings as well as concrete particulars. A meaning remains constant in spite of factual variations in the experience of

its particular manifestations. For example, particular experiences of the meaning *triangle* may show up as drawings on a blackboard, three pieces of metal connected together, or a marking on my dog. What remains constant is the structure of "triangleness" that presents me with the particular experiences of triangles. Erazim Kohák (1978), in commenting on Husserl's differentiation of particulars and principles, writes:

> Our direct awareness includes not only particular, factual instances but also the necessary principles they embody. In ordinary experience as I live it, I am aware of every object both as a particular and "in principle," as the instance of a type. (p. 14)

The investigations of phenomenological philosophy have concentrated on describing these structuring activities of experience. Husserl (1913/1931) uses the terms *eidos, Wesen,* or *essence* to refer to these structures of experience. Although we do not experience a particular without perceiving it as an instance of a structure—that is, as a kind of something—we can examine these typical ways of being in isolation, apart from any instantiation. "It is possible to know something 'in principle' without having any particular instance in mind" (Kohák, 1978, p. 15). The investigation of conscious (or "lived") structures involves distinguishing those aspects of an experience that are invariant and essential, making the experience show up as the kind it is—that is, as the typical way in which a phenomenon presents itself in experience. For example, for a figure to be seen as a triangle, the essential elements are three intersecting straight lines. Other elements, such as a particular color or size, or the particular size of the angles, or whether it is the outline of an actual object or a drawing in chalk, are unessential. These unessential elements are not necessary for experiencing something *as* a triangle. Instead, they serve to differentiate particular experiences of triangles from one another.

Husserl (1913/1931) held that knowledge of the structures of consciousness was not a matter of induction or generalization from a sample but was the result of a "direct grasp" of "eidetic seeing." I need only one instance (even an imaginary one) to grasp or "see" (not in the sense of visual sighting but of apprehending) the principle and inner necessities of a structure. In practice, the process leading to grasping the essential pattern of a structure usually requires a careful working through and imaginative testing of various descriptions of an essence, until the essential elements and their relationship are differentiated from the unessential and particular.

Phenomenological philosophy has concentrated its investigations on descriptions of those essential structures that are inherent in consciousness and are necessary for human experience to have the general appearance it has.

In this sense, it is concerned with the universal elements and relationships that constitute experience in general. Phenomenological philosophy holds that consciousness is intentional in the sense that an essential characteristic of experience is that it is always an experience of something. Consciousness is an activity guided by human intention rather than determined by mechanical causation. It acts to constitute its contents (*noemata*) in various modes (*noeses*)—including imagination, recollection, and hallucination—as well as in perceptual awareness. Husserl (1913/1931) has investigated the principles of consciousness that constitute our experience of physical objects as unified wholes, given that what appears at any moment to awareness is a one-sided perspective of an object. Husserl (1928/1964) has also identified the elements of temporal protention and retention, which are necessary to constitute experiences of temporal wholes such as melodies and sentences.

With Martin Heidegger's (1927/1962) investigation, *Being and Time,* phenomenological philosophy began to merge with the philosophy of existence. Existentialism, whose roots go back to Kierkegaard and beyond (Friedman, 1964), can be defined by its central theme, *existence,* a term used in a new, more limited sense by Kierkegaard, for the way in which a single individual experiences his or her being-in-the-world. Existential phenomenology maintains that existence can be approached phenomenologically and studied as one phenomenon among others in its essential structures.

Phenomenology and Psychology

Thus far, I have discussed phenomenology and existentialism as philosophies, not psychologies. It is important to differentiate phenomenological *philosophy* from phenomenological *psychology.* As a philosophy, phenomenology has been concerned with providing descriptions of the general characteristics of experience, with a particular focus by existentialists on the experience of being human. Giorgi (1985b) expressed the need "to translate the fundamental and valuable insights of [philosophical] phenomenology into a concrete program of psychological scientific research" (p. 45). Underlying the particular sciences, such as psychology, are philosophical positions regarding the nature of reality and ways that reality can be known. Phenomenological psychology is a perspective that acknowledges the reality of the realm of meaningful experience as the fundamental locus of knowledge. It differs from mainstream psychology by holding that human behavior is an expression of meaningful experience rather than a mechanically learned response to stimuli.

Phenomenological psychology is not a subfield of philosophy; it is a psychology that draws on the philosophical insights of phenomenology. As a psychology, it assumes its place within the psychological and scientific traditions that have preceded it. It selects for study the phenomena relevant to psychology and investigates these phenomena in a methodical, systematic, and rigorous way. The translation of the philosophical methods developed by phenomenology into functioning research practices for psychology is unfinished. Suggestions for this translation are offered in later sections of this chapter.

Although the structures investigated by *philosophical* phenomenology are universal and required for the appearance of consciousness itself, phenomenological *psychology* investigates structures that are typical or general for groups of people. The method of *philosophical* phenomenology retains the traditional philosophical use of self-reflection or "armchair philosophizing" that psychology broke away from when it became a science, but phenomenological *psychology* places the emphasis on descriptions from research subjects (see Giorgi, 1985b, pp. 46–53), instead of the researchers' self-reports.

The tradition of psychology has held the examination of conscious experience as one of its critical tasks. In its early decades, psychology dealt with practically nothing but consciousness, and in the past two decades it has returned to the investigation of consciousness under the aegis of cognitive science; it was only during its middle decades that psychology was redefined by behaviorism to exclude conscious experience.

Psychological Research on Consciousness

During the era of behaviorism, from the 1920s to the 1960s, mainstream psychology, for the most part, abandoned the attempt to study consciousness and limited itself to data available to direct public perception. In the last two decades, however, psychology has returned to consciousness as a major object of study, with electronic computers and information theory replacing Wundt's chemistry model. Cognitive psychologists—for example, Kosslyn (1980)—have developed computer programs that purport to simulate human responses. These are based on the assumption that because both the computer and human beings respond similarly to the same inputs, the mind must function like a computer program. Although computer analogies of consciousness were thought to hold great promise, the limits of this approach are becoming apparent (Gardner, 1985), as we shall see later.

Other psychologists (for example, Hirai, Izawa, & Koga, 1959) have attempted to study consciousness by examining brain-wave measurements, assuming that changes in brain-wave activity correlate with different types of mental activities. And split-brain researchers have studied patients who have had their corpus callosa surgically severed, attempting to correlate types of conscious activity with the right- and left-brain hemispheres. Despite the wide attention given to this research program and the initial excitement surrounding it, split-brain studies (see Bakan, 1978) have proved to be of limited value in comprehending the structures and contents of consciousness. Mainstream research investigating consciousness has retained a commitment to the philosophical principles of positivism. After initial successes, these programs have developed problems (Gardner, 1985) as they have moved to study the more complex activities of consciousness, such as musical and other artistic abilities.

The difficulties that mainstream psychological research has encountered in these studies can be attributed to inadequacies in the understanding of consciousness in its foundational philosophy—positivism. Phenomenological psychologists hold that the general description of consciousness developed by phenomenological philosophers provides a firmer base from which to develop research designs to study consciousness and its flow of experiences. Psychological research based on phenomenological philosophy uses a different approach to the study of consciousness than is used in mainstream psychological research; epistemological principles attuned to the special characteristics of human experience are applied. The aim of phenomenologically informed research is to produce clear and accurate descriptions of a particular aspect of human experience. Recognizing that consciousness is different in essence from the objects of nature, it rejects the positivists' ideal of a single and unified scientific method that will be able to yield all knowledge. Phenomenological research holds that the unique characteristics of consciousness require a distinct kind of science, utilizing data-gathering procedures and processes designed specifically for developing general descriptions of experiential processes.

Phenomenological psychological research uses a different set of epistemological principles than the set used in positivist psychology, and its use of the general terms of knowledge generation—for example, *method, research*—is sometimes misinterpreted because the meanings assigned to these terms in phenomenological research are not the same as are assumed by mainstream psychologists. For example, the term *method*, as used in positive science, refers to a specific sequence of technical procedures, an algorithm, designed to protect the investigator from error and insure the production of reliable knowledge. Such an algorithm has been of limited usefulness when applied to the study of consciousness. Methods based on phenomenological principles, by contrast, function as general guidelines or outlines, and

researchers are expected to develop plans of study especially suited to understanding the particular experiential phenomenon that is the object of their study.

Research is another problem word. To many, the term *research* connotes laboratory experiments, quantified data derived from sophisticated instruments or questionnaires, and statistically described relationships among operationally defined variables. Psychological researchers using phenomenological principles, however, often conduct open-ended interviews. Working from long interview transcriptions, they search out meaning units and use "thought experiments." (A thought experiment involves varying a thought or perception in one's imagination and observing the outcome. For example, I can vary my image of a chair so as to "see" it without legs to find out if such an imagined image would still be experienced as a chair.) Their products are general descriptions of the features and structures common to interview examples. Although some have suggested that such terms as *inquiry, study,* or *investigation* might be clearer for phenomenologically grounded research, I believe that the term *research* should not be confined to studies using the natural-science model. All psychology researchers, both phenomenologists and positivists, are expected to share a commitment to scientific values and the search for truth. They engage in systematic and rigorous searches seeking a depth of understanding that extends beyond a cursory view and commend their findings to the scientific community for review and critique.

Descriptive and Qualitative Research

Phenomenological research is descriptive (Ihde & Silverman, 1985) and qualitative (Bogdan & Taylor, 1975; Schwartz & Jacobs, 1979), but it has, in addition, a special realm of inquiry—the structures that produce meaning in consciousness. Simple identification of phenomenological research with descriptive or qualitative research overlooks the important differences between phenomenology and the other sciences that use descriptions and natural language data.

Although phenomenological research is sometimes identified with other "descriptive" and "qualitative" approaches, it differs from them because its focus is on the subject's experienced meaning instead of on descriptions of their overt actions or behavior. Phenomenology maintains the critical distinction between what presents itself as part of a person's awareness and what might exist as a reality "outside" of our experience.

The term *descriptive research* usually refers to all those inquiries whose goal is to give a neutral, close, and thorough account of the topic they are investigating (Ihde & Silverman, 1985). Instead of approaching topics with predetermined hypotheses, they look to discover the essential attributes of phenomena and then express the results in verbal portraits. In addition to phenomenological research, the case study (Yin, 1984) and field research (Crane & Angrosino, 1974) are included within the category of descriptive research. Descriptive research can also refer to studies whose findings are given as taxonomic descriptions. Thus the natural sciences—botany and ornithology, for example—whose practices include establishing classification schemes for the objects of their realm can be called *descriptive*.

In general use, "qualitative research" refers to a particular perspective on the nature of the human realm (Ashworth, Giorgi, & de Konig, 1986, p. vii), and is not simply a category of research designs. From the qualitative perspective, the richness and profundity of human reality is seen as closely related to the structures and meanings of natural language. Thus in the broad context of research strategies, *qualitative* is identified with a commitment to the logic of natural language as the preferred form for understanding human affairs. Qualitative research uses natural language descriptions (for example, unstructured interviews) for its data and usually presents the results in natural language. Descriptive and qualitative research are overlapping categories with most descriptive studies done from a qualitative perspective. Besides phenomenological research, with its focus on the realm of experience, other kinds of studies can be carried out from a qualitative perspective. These explorations of the human realm approach their topics from the commonsense or natual attitude viewing their phenomena as existing in the world. Examples of nonphenomenological or "quasi-phenomenological" qualitative research are *Children of Crisis: Vol. 1* (Coles, 1967), *Intimate Strangers* (Rubin, 1983), *Habits of the Heart* (Bellah, Madsen, Sullivan, Swidler, & Tipton, 1985), and *Vital Involvement in Old Age* (Erikson, Erikson, & Kivnick, 1986). (The special use of nominal or qualitative variables in developing statistical data, Reynolds, 1977, is usually not included as part of the qualitative research perspective.)

Doing Psychological Research from a Phenomenological Perspective

The locus of phenomenological research is human experience, and it approaches the topics of interest to psychology through their presence in conscious awareness. Instead of studying the body as an organic object, it studies the experiences people have of their bodies. In this sense, the subject matter of phenomenological research is limited. The exclusive focus on experience, however, provides access to all that can be directly known because all knowledge is ultimately grounded in human experi-

ence (Husserl, 1936/1970). There is no viewpoint outside of consciousness from which to view things as they exist independently of our experience of them. (The theory of intentionality, however, has been extended by Merleau-Ponty, 1945/1962, to include subconscious bodily behaviors and by Ricoeur, 1960/1967, to the unconscious structures of volition and action. Studies in these areas require interpretative or hermeneutic methods as a supplement to the phenomenological inquiry of directly conscious experience.)

Phenomenologically based inquiries can be divided into two basic types: (a) those that ask how objects are present to the various modes of conscious experience, such as perception or memory, and (b) those that ask how meaning presents itself in experience. Although there are examples of the first type—for instance, Richer's (1978) study of how perceptual objects are given to experience and Casey's (1976) study of the presence of objects in imagination—most phenomenological researchers have been interested in investigating the presence of meaning in experience. In experience, events appear as meaningful—both the appearance of worldly objects and happenings and our own thoughts and feelings. Although experience is meaningfully ordered, the structure and order of meaning are difficult to describe. The purpose of phenomenological research is to produce clear, precise, and systematic descriptions of the meaning that constitutes the activity of consciousness.

The psychological study of the processes of consciousness is problematic in three ways:

1. Consciousness differs in fundamental ways from natural objects. It cannot be picked up and held or examined under a microscope. The contents of consciousness are in continuous flux; they cannot be easily grasped. Consciousness is an activity, not an object, and it presents itself as a fleeting trace or indication, a mere wisp. Romanyshyn (1982) has proposed that consciousness is analogous to a mirror reflection.

2. Consciousness is always filled with contents and is an integrated ensemble of modes of presentation, such as perceptions, remembrances, and imaginations. It is present to us as a complex of interacting strata—levels of abstraction, awareness, and control. The presence of these contents is the result of the constitutive work of consciousness with its openness to itself, others, and the cultural and physical existents in the world. We have direct access to the finished work of our conscious processes, yet in our everyday existence we are not aware of the operations that make up the integrated flux of experience.

3. Access to consciousness is also problematic, and the data a researcher collects are several times removed

from the actual flow of experience. For one thing, the act of reflecting—by researchers on their own or by subjects on their experience—effects a change in awareness. The initial nonreflective, direct engagement with the flow of experience (the object of study) is replaced by the self's relocation to a point of observation that is removed from the experience. For another thing, the report of what was witnessed requires that the observation of experience be described in a language. Thus the verbal or written report is not a duplication of what was seen; it is a culturally conventional system of signs that indicates or points toward the prereflective reality. In addition, we have direct awareness of only one consciousness, our own. Care must be taken by researchers as they interpret reports from others describing their experiences.

These problem areas confront any attempt to comprehend the operations and productions of consciousness. The task of psychology—generally held to be the understanding of human existence—requires knowledge of the structures that are implicit in the experienced or lived realm out of which our actions and expressions arise.

A general format for the phenomenological investigation of consciousness by psychologists follows a three-step procedure. The investigator must:

1. Gather a number of naive descriptions from people who are having or have had the experience under investigation.
2. Engage in a process of analyzing these descriptions so that the researcher comes to a grasp of the constituents or common elements that make the experience what it is.
3. Produce a research report that gives an accurate, clear, and articulate description of an experience. The reader of the report should come away with the feeling that "I understand better what it is like for someone to experience that."

The following sections will discuss these steps in detail. I will use, as an example, Fischer and Wertz's (1979) study of being criminally victimized. This study demonstrates how the results of a phenomenological research inquiry can be used to effect changes in public policy and, thereby, in the quality of our lives.

DATA GATHERING

In psychological research based on a phenomenological perspective, the usual purpose of data gathering is to collect naive descriptions of the experience under investigation. The descriptions provide specific instances

from which the researcher can tease out the structure of consciousness that constitutes the experience.

Phenomenologists need reports of the experience as it actually appears in a person's consciousness. These reports are different from commonsense descriptions that are aimed at depicting things or happenings as they exist independently of a person's experience of them; thus, the production of phenomenological protocols requires that subjects' awareness be redirected toward their own experiencing. The way the researcher frames questions can help subjects to report their experiences rather than to give worldly depictions. By asking, What did you experience? or, What was it like for you? instead of, What happened?, the investigator is more likely to elicit experiential data.

Phenomenological researchers can draw on three sources to generate descriptions of experiences: (a) the researchers' personal self-reflections on the incidents of the topic that they have experienced; (b) other participants in the study, who describe the experience under investigation either orally, in response to interview questions, or in written statements; and (c) depictions of the experience from outside the context of the research project itself—for example, by novelists, poets, painters, choreographers, and by previous psychological and phenomenological investigators.

Data from Self-Reflection

Although phenomenological philosophers often make exclusive use of self-reflection in their studies, in phenomenological psychological research, self-reflection, when used, is typically only a preparatory step to gathering data from research subjects. Colaizzi (1973) has called self-reflection the individual phenomenological reflection (IPR). The researcher will often jot down these reflections for reference during data analysis. They are important for locating the presuppositions and biases the researcher holds as well as clarifying the parameters and dimensions of the experience before beginning subject interviews. The Fischer and Wertz (1979) project began with an initial self-reflective process by its research team.

> [We] agreed, as a sensitizing exercise, to jot down notes about our personal experiences of having been the victim of crime. Then we met to discuss, among other issues, what we thought we were likely to find. The recorded anticipations alerted interviewers to possible themes that might require clarification if alluded to by subjects. They also allowed us to become aware of our presuppositions regarding the phenomenon so that we could attempt not to impose them upon our subjects. Later we found that some of our notions had been fulfilled (albeit always in special ways), some modified, and some disconfirmed. (p. 138)

Phenomenological research emphasizes approaching the topic afresh without preconceived notions about what one will find in the investigation. The data from self-reflection can be used by researchers to help them become aware of and bracket out the presuppositions and assumptions they bring to the investigation. This awareness, in itself, provides some protection against the imposition of the researchers' expectations on the study.

Data Gathered from Participants

A primary difference between phenomenological philosophy and phenomenological psychology is the use of other persons as the primary source of original naive descriptions of an experience. Although psychological research might include a researcher's personal descriptions, its focus is on data generated from subjects.

This major modification in the philosophical method for psychological research is supported on philosophical and pragmatic grounds. Strasser (1969) has proposed that phenomenological research needs to include the experiences of others if solipsism is to be overcome. Emphasizing that the meaning and contents of experience are not *within* but *between* persons, he has proposed a dialogic phenomenology that would search for what *we*, rather than *I*, experience. The full exploration of the attributes of a meaning structure, he said, requires an understanding of how it operates among us and creates a meaningfully shared experiential world. Spiegelberg (1964) has also argued for a phenomenology through vicarious experience in which descriptions of experience by others are accepted. He cites the important phenomenological investigations of psychopathological experiences by researchers who have no previous personal knowledge of these experiences as a demonstration of the value of using vicarious descriptions. Giorgi (1985b) has described the practical reasons for using descriptions from others in phenomenological psychology:

> The reason that descriptions of experienced situations by others are so critical, on a pragmatic level, is that the climate of self-understanding in psychological science is still such that a description of an experience and the analysis of it by the same person (the researcher) is simply not acceptable because of the fear of "subjective bias." (pp. 49–50)

He proposes that the original data for psychological studies should consist of "naive descriptions, prompted by open-ended questions, of experiences by subjects unfamiliar with the researcher's theories or biases" (p. 69).

Researchers have gathered descriptions from subjects in various forms, the two most common ones being written statements and (the preferred method) interviews. The face-to-face interaction of the interview allows the researcher to help the subject move toward nontheoretical descriptions that accurately reflect the experience. Stevick (1971) explains her preference for interviews: "Written questionnaires employed in the pilot studies yielded responses of a distant and highly reflective nature. The experimenter's [written] questions also pre-structured the phenomenon for the subjects. Recorded interviews were found to correct these problems" (p. 135).

I will be using the term *subject* to refer to he or she who provides written statements or participates in interviews for the research project even though there has been some move against this term and for its replacement by *co-researcher, research partner, research collaborator,* or *co-author.* The reason for the move had been to emphasize that phenomenological research interacts in a personal manner with those asked to provide examples from their experience. People are not to be treated as experimental objects for the use of the researcher; the role and responsibility of the participants is to share their experiences with the researcher. They are not, however, primarily involved, nor held responsible for, the analysis and conclusions of the study. It is the researcher who plans, implements, and writes up the study. Participants open their subjective experience to the researcher, but they are not "subjects" of the researcher. Participants are human subjects—that is, they are actors (the subjects of sentences); they are not objects (passive recipients of stimuli).

Selection of Subjects

Subjects are chosen who are able to function as *informants* by providing rich descriptions of the experience being investigated. The first requirement of selection is that a subject has had the experience that is the topic of the research. Many topics, such as "being angry" and "feeling understood," are part of the general experiences of most people. Some topics, however, are limited to specific groups—for example, the experiences of being criminally assaulted or being the sibling of a schizophrenic. The second requirement is that a subject has the capacity to provide full and sensitive descriptions of the experience under examination. Adrian van Kaam (1969) has proposed that this capacity requires subjects to have six important skills: (a) the ability to express themselves linguistically with relative ease, (b) the ability to sense and to express inner feelings and emotions without shame and inhibition, (c) the ability to sense and to express the organic experiences that accompany these feelings, (d) the experience of the situation under investigation at a relatively recent date, (e) a spontaneous interest in their experience, and (f) the ability to report or write what was going on within themselves (p. 328). This last skill requires an atmosphere in which subjects can find the necessary relaxation to enable them to put sufficient time and orderly thought into the reporting or the writing. Colaizzi (1978) states: "Experience with the investigated topic and articulateness suffice as criteria for selecting subjects" (p. 58).

The logic of the selection of subjects in phenomenological research differs from the logic of statistical sampling theory. The statistical demands of making inferences from a sample to a population require that subjects be chosen randomly from the population for which the study is designed. The purpose of phenomenological research is to describe the structure of an experience, not to describe the characteristics of a group who have had the experience. Rather than seeking to describe the mean and standard deviation of a group as it relates to the experience, the phenomenological concern is with the nature of the experience itself.

The purpose of selecting subjects in phenomenological research is to generate a full range of variation in the set of descriptions to be used in analyzing a phenomena, not to meet statistical requirements for making statements about distribution with a group of subjects. Phenomenological researchers use subjects to generate a fund of possible elements and relationships that can be used in determining the essential structure of the phenomena. (Besides gathering the empirical descriptions from subjects, phenomenological researchers generate additional descriptions through imaginative thought experiments.) The point of subject selection is to obtain richly varied descriptions, not to achieve statistical generalization. The error that phenomenological researchers can make in selection is to choose subjects that produce a narrow range of descriptions. The researcher needs to choose an array of individuals who provide a variety of specific experiences of the topic being explored.

The issue of generalizability for phenomenological findings is not one of population characteristics but the specificity of the essential description. For example, if a researcher is investigating the experience of "being anxious" and uses descriptions from students anxious about grades, the question of generalizability is whether the essential structure developed in this particular situation would hold for "being anxious" in other situations, such as public speaking. Researchers who want to claim that their findings apply to other situations than that represented by their subjects, must overcome the readers' doubts that the application or extension of the findings to other situations is appropriate. The argument would need to be made that the essential constituents of the phenomenon they have identified from the imagined and empirical variations of the experience would not be altered in another situation. Strategies for this argument can be based on the use of a stratified sample of people selected as representative or prototypical of those to whom the findings are said to hold. For example, a researcher studying the experience of "being healthy" could choose to interview athletes, physicians, hospital patients, and the disabled in order to gather sufficient variation in the descriptions of the experience.

The *number of subjects* selected for phenomenologically based studies varies considerably. At one end of the continuum is van Kaam's (1969) use of 325 written descriptions from high-school students in his study on the experience of "really feeling understood." In the mid-range are Stevick's (1971) use of 30 interviews in her study of the experience of "being angry" and Mruk's (1983) use of 25 descriptions of "being pleased and displeased with self" in his study of self-esteem. At the other end is de Konig's (1979) use of three subjects to generate the data for his study of the experience of "being suspicious."

For a specific example of the selection of subjects for a phenomenological psychology study, we can return to the Fischer and Wertz (1979) study of people who had been criminally assaulted. At the request of the researchers, representatives of a police department in the Pittsburgh area telephoned a stratified sample of persons who had reported crimes during the previous 3 years. Eighty percent of the people called agreed to participate in either personal or telephone interviews. People whose victimization was rape, attempted murder, or corporate crime were excluded. Six members of the research team conducted 50 interviews that were taped and transcribed.

The Interview

In the interview, subjects were asked to describe in detail examples of their experience with the topic being investigated. In Fischer and Wertz's study, the victims were asked to describe what was going on prior to the crime, what it was like for them to be victimized, and what had actually happened. The researchers reported that "questions were restricted to requests for clarification or elaboration of what the victim had already said" (p. 138).

Characteristically, interviews are open-ended and unstructured, requiring enough time to explore the topic in depth—usually from a half-hour to an hour, although sometimes lasting for several hours. In some studies, subjects are interviewed more than once. The length of the interview depends on both the amount of self-reflection the participant feels comfortable with and the topic of study. Some studies require extensive interviewing with only a few people; others need a greater variety of descriptions, and so a large number of people are interviewed. Interviews are taped and transcribed.

The theory behind phenomenological interviewing differs from the theory behind survey-questionnaire interviewing. Survey interviewing is considered a stimulus–response interaction; the interviewer's question is the stimulus, and the subject's answer is the response. According to survey-interview theory, it is assumed to be possible and desirable for the questioner to present a constant stimulus to all subjects. Thus the questions must be worded exactly the same in each interview, the questions must be presented in the same order, and the interviewer must not respond in a manner that would bias responses.

The phenomenological interview, in contrast, is conceived of as a discourse or conversation (Mishler, 1986). It involves an interpersonal engagement in which subjects are encouraged to share with a researcher the details of their experience. The researcher's behavior, although individualized, is also disciplined in its focus on the research question. Most interviews used in phenomenological studies have been conducted face-to-face; at times, however, logistics require the use of telephone interviews. The Fischer and Wertz (1979) study used both personal and telephone interviews.

Kvale (1983) has outlined aspects of the phenomenological interview. The focus of the interview is on the life-world or experience of the interviewee and is theme-oriented, not person-oriented. The interview seeks to describe and understand the meaning of the central themes of the experience being investigated. The interview is qualitative in aiming at obtaining nuanced descriptions that are precise and stringent in meaning and interpretation. The interview seeks descriptions of the experience itself without the subject's interpretation or theoretical explanations. To keep the focus on non-theoretical descriptions of the experience, the interviewer takes care to remain open to the presence of new and unexpected constituents in the description and does not shape the questions as tests of ready-made categories or schemes of interpretation. Rather than seeking general opinions, the interview focuses on specific situations and action sequences that are instances of the theme under investigation so that the essence or structure of the theme will emerge and show itself. When the statements of an interviewee are ambiguous, it is the task of the interviewer to seek clarification. The interview is a temporal process, and descriptions may become richer and clearer in the latter portions of the interview.

Colaizzi (1978, p. 58) suggests a procedure by means of which interviewers can generate questions to be used in the phenomenological interview. The first step is to engage in self-reflection on the topic to be investigated; this allows the interviewer to uncover *prima facie* dimensions for exploration. The second step is to conduct some initial interviews in the manner of a pilot study; these interviews might add dimensions that have been overlooked in the self-reflection. The integration of these two steps can generate a list of research questions designed to tap the subjects' experiences in their fullness.

Other approaches to gathering descriptions from subjects include Spiegelberg's (1975) procedure of "cooperative or group phenomenology" and the "think aloud" technique that Christopher Aanstoos (1986) used in studying the thought processes involved in a game of chess. Spiegelberg's group data-gathering procedure brought subjects together in groups ranging in size from 6 to 16 people and lasting from 2 days to 2 weeks. (These groups are similar to the focus groups used in contemporary marketing research.) The researcher led the group, moving the process from individual written descriptions by each member to a final general structural description reflecting the group as a whole.

The "think aloud" technique involves asking the subjects to "think out loud as completely as possible all of the thoughts you are having throughout the game . . . exactly as they occur to you" (Aanstoos, 1986, p. 83). While engaging in an activity, each subject "thinks aloud," describing any thought that comes to mind, and the subjects' descriptions are tape-recorded and later transcribed. (In the Aanstoos study, the subjects' opponents listened to music through headphones so they would not hear the subjects' reports and strategies. In addition, the chess moves were written down so that the subjects' thoughts could be linked to their moves.)

Researchers may also set up particular events for subjects, such as watching a motion picture or observing children at play, and then ask them to report the experiences that they had in engaging in the event. The more usual procedure is to ask subjects to recall their experiences of incidents from the past.

As mentioned previously, one of the epistemological tactics of philosophical phenomenology is the phenomenological reduction. In this reduction, attention is reduced from the natural concern about the independent existence of what appears in experience to concern with a description of the appearance itself. The data of phenomenological research are descriptions of experience as it presents itself, not descriptions of objects and actions as they are assumed to exist outside of experience. In gathering protocols from subjects, researchers take the subjects' reports as descriptions of their experience, not as statements about an independent reality. Thus, even when researchers doubt the existence of the objects being described, their interest remains focused on the subject's experience. An extreme case would be a subject's report of a hallucination where the researcher knows that the experience being reported is an illusion. The point of gathering phenomenological data is to obtain example descriptions of the experience under investigation, not to ascertain if these descriptions correspond to an independent reality.

The principle of the phenomenological reduction maintains that the protocols needed for phenomenological research are descriptions of what is present in a person's consciousness when he or she attends to the particular experience under investigation. These descriptions are different from commonsense descriptions that are aimed at depicting things or happenings as they exist independently of a person's experience of them; thus the production of phenomenological protocols requires that subjects' awareness be redirected toward their own experiencing. The way the researcher frames questions can help subjects to report their experiences rather than to give worldly depictions. By asking, What did you experience? or, What was it like for you?, instead of, What happened?, the investigator is more likely to elicit experiential data.

Data from Previously Developed Descriptions

Characterizations of the experience under investigation can be drawn from a variety of sources within one's tradition, ranging from philosophical texts and research articles (using either phenomenological or natural science methods), to creative literature (such as poetry, plays, and novels), and nonliterary art forms. Philosophical studies have often combined the use of data gathered from self-reflection and from philosophical writings. Casey's (1976) study on imagination, for example, used self-reflection and philosophical texts, including Sartre's (1940/1966) *Psychology of Imagination* and various works of Romantic authors.

Creative writers and cultural myths can provide psychological researchers with very sensitive, rich descriptions. Steen Halling (1979), for example, used two of Eugene O'Neill's plays as the source of data for his study of the experience of forgiveness, and Bernd Jager (1979) used the Greek myth of Dionysus for his study of passion. Literary descriptions, however, often contain sophisticated metaphors and images requiring considerable interpretion if the researcher is to gain access to the depth of understanding they offer. This interpretive or hermeneutic work requires an understanding of how genre, historical context, author's intent, and reception by the reader contribute to eliciting the meaning of a literary work. The editors of *Duquesne Studies in Phenomenological Psychology, Vol. 3* (Giorgi, Knowles, & Smith, 1979) point out differences between the use of data

gathered directly from subjects and the use of literary sources:

> Up to now, empirical-phenomenological psychology proceeded by collecting protocols descriptive of the subjects' experience (e.g., learning, envy, anxiety, etc.), and then systematically and rigorously interrogating these descriptions step by step to arrive at the structure of the experience. Hermeneutical psychology suggests another data source and a different method of analysis. . . . Does a hermeneutical work of this type depend solely upon the singular talents of the individual author, or can the hermeneutical procedure be in some way specified and standardized so that it can be communicated to others for reduplication? (pp. 179–180)

The editorial comment suggests caution in using literary protocols as the data base for phenomenologically grounded psychological research. I have a more positive attitude to this type of data, especially when used in combination with protocols gathered from subjects. Literary data often offer deeply penetrating descriptions, and they allow the researcher access to protocols from a variety of geographical and historical settings.

The Results of Data Collection

The data-gathering process produces a collection of experiential descriptions of the topic under investigation. The very process of gathering the data allows the researcher to learn about the experience and to obtain some notions about its structure. In phenomenological research, therefore, investigators commonly consider it essential to participate directly in data gathering. The gathered descriptions—whether personal reflections by the researcher, reflections from subjects, or previous descriptions—are converted to written form. The stage of data collection often results in hundreds of pages of written material, which is then analyzed in the data-analysis stage to tease out the essential descriptions of the experience under investigation.

DATA ANALYSIS

The aim of phenomenological inquiry is to reveal and unravel the structures, logic, and interrelationships that obtain in the phenomenon under inspection. Data analysis is the core stage of research efforts in phenomenological psychology. Its purpose is to derive from the collection of protocols, with their naive descriptions to specific examples of the experience under consideration, a description of the essential features of that experience. The researcher must glean from the examples an accurate essential description of their contents and the particular structural relationship that coheres the elements into a unified experience.

Essential Structures as Findings

The finding of phenomenological research is a description of the essential structure of the experience being investigated. The essential structure is made up of the elements or constituents that are necessary for an experience to present itself as what it is. The finding is called a "general structural description" or "synthetic description." For example, van Kaam's (1969) study of the experience of "really feeling understood" produced as its finding:

> The experience of "really feeling understood" is a perceptual-emotional Gestalt: A subject, perceiving that a person co-experiences what things mean to the subject and accepts him, feels, initially, relief from experiential loneliness, and, gradually, safe experiential communion with that person and with that which the subject perceives this person to represent. (pp. 336–337)

The finding of Stevick's (1971) study of "being angry" produced this general structural description:

> Anger is the pre-reflective experience of being made unable by another who prevents us, and it is the counteraction of this sense of inability by an affective transformation of the other and of the relationship with the other. The body is experienced as bursting forth, and expresses itself, publicly or privately as each person's pre-reflective restrictions allow, in expansive, explosive, nontypical behavior. (p. 144)

The phenomenological position is that the sphere of experience appears at the intersection of person and world. This sphere has common features that structure the person–world interaction so that contents, not buzzing confusion, appear, and these contents appear *as* meaning something. Experience is not indistinct and unstructured chaos; it appears as differentiated and structured. Phenomenological research is the search for those processes of consciousness that give the objects that appear in awareness meaning, clarity, and discrimination.

Phenomenological *philosophers* are primarily concerned with providing descriptions of the universal structuring processes of consciousness. They are interested in the structures that produce a common appearance and similar characteristics to each person's experience. Their investigations are directed to the level of universal structures—for instance, those that constitute a differentiation among the appearances of natural objects, persons, and self. Although the specific experiences of human beings are culturally and historically variable, experience appears to have a primary and basic common structure.

Psychological research does not usually focus on these universal structures; instead, it examines the level of structures that constitute psychological meanings in particular contexts or situations. If a psychology researcher were to collect descriptions of "the experience of being in a classroom," the focus of interest in the analysis of the experience of this situation would be placed on its psychological structures. The same descriptions could possibly be used to analyze the sociological or anthropological structures of the experience.

A Search for Lived-Structures or Essences

Various terms have been used to designate the process through which the researcher moves from a collection of naive descriptions to a structural description. Husserl (1913/1931) calls the process the eidetic *epoché*. (This *epoché* differs from the phenomenological *epoché* where the question about the independent existence of the contents of consciousness is suspended). The eidetic (essence) *epoché* (abstention) is a "bracketing" of interest in the particular and specific instances of an experience in order to grasp its structural principles. It is also referred to as the "reduction" or "reducing" of specific descriptions to their fundamental structures. The use of the term *reduction* in this context is unfortunate because positivistic science refers to *reduction* as a type of explanation that accounts for characteristics of an object by providing descriptions of its most primitive parts. The purpose of Husserl's reduction is to disclose a nonreductive structure that unites the invariant elements of an experience into a whole.

Van Kaam (1969) refers to the process used to grasp the essential structure of an experience as "explication." He states: "By explication, implicit awareness of a complex phenomenon becomes explicit, formulated knowledge of its components" (p. 316). The term *thematization,* borrowed from qualitative research, has also been used to describe this process; in phenomenological research, it denotes that the search for essential structures involves identifying the constituents or themes that appear in the descriptions.

The Steps in the Analysis

The movement from a collection of protocols to an accurate, clear, and informative structural description can be a complex and difficult process. Because a whole protocol or a collection of protocols cannot be analyzed simultaneously, they have to be broken down into manageable units, and a process of sequential steps must be delineated that can assist the researcher in developing general structural descriptions.

The type of steps used in the phenomenological analysis of a set of subject descriptions can be understood by reviewing the development of the methods of protocol analysis. This section will summarize three studies that portray the development of psychological research methods based on phenomenology. The studies to be reviewed are van Kaam's (1969) study of "really feeling understood," Colaizzi's (1978) study of "being impressed by reading something to the point of modifying one's existence," and Giorgi's (1975a, b) study of "what constitutes learning for ordinary people going about their everyday activities."

Van Kaam's study was originally completed in 1958 as a doctoral dissertation at Western Reserve University, and its publication as part of his *Existential Foundations of Psychology* (1969) was influential in the revival of qualitative research in psychology. The study retains aspects of research based on content analysis with its use of a large number of subjects, intersubjective concurrence of judges, and attention to the percentage of protocols in which a constituent occurs. Van Kaam, who was a faculty member at Duquesne University, did not continue with the development of phenomenological research methods. Instead, this work was undertaken by another group of scholars at Duquesne. Under the leadership of Giorgi, and working independently of van Kaam, this group sought to develop methods more directly grounded on phenomenological philosophy. The procedures outlined in Colaizzi's (1978) study are representative of the work of the Duquesne group during the 1960s. The procedures in Giorgi's (1975a, b) study are the further outgrowth of his work with the Duquesne group and of his own reexamination of the phenomenological literature undertaken during his 1969 stay in Europe. The direction of the evolution of procedures for phenomenologically grounded psychological research has been toward a stance more completely grounded in phenomenological insights and away from positivistic assumptions. The process of development remains open-ended and unfinished.

Van Kaam (1969, pp. 325–328) used six steps or operations in his study of "really feeling understood":

1. *The classification of the data into categories.* A "sufficiently large random sample of cases" is taken from the pool of protocols, and a list is developed that contains "every basically different statement made by the subjects." Van Kaam suggests that the use of several judges drawing selections from the same data can help "insure the validity of this procedure." The final listing must be agreed on by the judges. The list consists of the concrete, vague, intricate, and overlapping expressions as they occur in the protocols. Examples given by van Kaam are "I feel a hundred pounds less heavy" and "[I have] a load off my chest." In addition to creating a list of

the various statements, van Kaam also calculates the percentage of the protocols in which each item on the list has appeared.

2. *The reduction and linguistic transformation of the selections into more precisely descriptive terms* (p. 326). The shift from the subjects' original language given in the raw data to descriptions in the words of the researchers is a crucial procedure in the analysis of qualitative data. The transformation is not accomplished by technical procedures as it is in quantitative analysis, such as the transformation of a group of raw scores into standard deviation and mean scores. Linguistic transformation is carried out by means of the ordinary human capacity to understand the meaning of statements. One can move from a statement to its referent—the experience to which it points—and redescribe that experience from a different perspective. In this case, the experience is redescribed from a perspective concerned with precise description, and it shows how the experience relates to the topic under investigation—the feeling of being understood.

In van Kaam's example, the original protocol statements identified in Step 1, "I feel a hundred pounds less heavy" and "A load off my chest," are transformed by identifying them as instances of "a feeling of relief." The move in this step is to reduce the lists given in the language of the original transcriptions to a list in the language of the researchers describing elements that might be parts of the experience of feeling understood. To increase the intersubjective validity of these transformations, van Kaam has sought the agreement of judges that the "reduced elements" are accurate reflections of the original selections. (Van Kaam uses *elements* and *constitutents* interchangeably; in Giorgi's nomenclature presented later they have distinct meanings.) The percentage of protocols containing these reduced elements have then been calculated—for example, "perceiving signs of understanding from a person" occurred in 87% of the protocols.

3. *The elimination of those reduced statements developed in Step 2 that are probably not inherent in the experience of feeling understood.* Elements that merely express aspects of the experience that relate to a specific situation and elements that are a blending of several parts are removed from the reduced list.

4. *The first hypothetical identification.* After the first three operations—classification, reduction, and element elimination—are completed, the resulting list is taken as the first hypothetical identification and description of the experience.

5. *Application.* The hypothetical description of Step 4 is applied to randomly selected protocols. The description is tested to determine if it contains more than

the necessary and sufficient constituents of the topic under investigation. It may also be that some of the protocols contain elements inherent to the experience that have been left out of the hypothetical description. In such instances, the hypothetical description is revised to reduce or expand its elements. Step 5 may have to be carried out several times with the hypothetical description undergoing changes until it characterizes the inherent elements in the structure in a new random sample of protocols.

6. *Valid identification.* When the previous steps have been carried out successfully, the hypothetical description can be considered to be a valid identification and description of the experience. Van Kaam reminds the researcher that "it is evidently valid only for the population represented by the samples" (p. 327). The validity lasts until new cases of the experience can be shown not to correspond to the necessary and sufficient constituents contained in the formula.

Colaizzi (1978, pp. 58–62) describes his use of similar steps in his study of the experience of "being impressed by reading something to the point of modifying one's existence." After reading all the protocols to "acquire a feeling for them," he extracts the phrases or sentences that directly pertain to the experience. The next step he describes is similar to van Kaam's reduction in which the phrases as they appear in the protocol are transformed into the words of the researcher. In Colaizzi's version, the meaning of each protocol statement is extracted, and the result is a list of "meaning" or "significant" statements reflecting the essential point of each original statement. Regarding this step, Colaizzi writes:

> This is a precarious leap because, while moving beyond the protocol statements, the meanings he [the researcher] arrives at and formulates should never sever all connection with the original protocols; his formulations must discover and illuminate those meanings hidden in the various contexts and horizons . . . in the original protocols. (p. 59)

Colaizzi's next step is to cluster the individual themes to produce a further reduction into general themes (theme clusters) that are common to all the subjects' protocols. The clustering process is similar to van Kaam's Step 5 in that it makes use of a zigzag procedure. The researcher moves back and forth between the meaning statements and the successive revised hypothetical "exhaustive" lists until the themes are accurately reflected in the clusters. The final result of the zigzag process is the finding of the research, the essential structural definition. The following is a portion of Colaizzi's final description of the experience of "changes through reading":

> The already known becomes seen in a new light, allowing hidden meanings of the familiar to emerge. . . . Re-

gardless of the book's content, it ultimately refers back to the reader himself. . . . The ordinary is all radically restructured, and for a long time afterward the reader is occasionally reminded of the extraordinariness of the commonplace in some area, about which he is convinced that the author has established some truth, and to which he is converted, at least temporarily. (p. 65)

A final step, missing in van Kaam's formulation, is added in Colaizzi's method of analysis. The researcher returns to each subject and asks, "How do my descriptive results compare with your experiences?" and "Have any aspects of your experience been omitted?" Any relevant new data that emerge from these follow-up interviews are worked into a revised, final description. Colaizzi, unlike van Kaam, did not use independent judges in the analysis of his data and thus did not include the aim of intersubjective concurrence in the reductive steps. He also did not calculate the percentages of the occurrence of statements across the protocols.

Giorgi's (1975a,b) account of his study of "what constitutes learning for ordinary people going about their everyday activities" offers another set of steps to be taken to produce a description of a general structure of experience. Giorgi, instead of seeking universal essences, emphasizes the psychological perspective of his research and his interest in structures that are context-related or relevant for typical situations or typical personalities. This move introduces a dependency on contingencies that universal essences do not have and makes the structural descriptions more subject to change; nevertheless, his research remains within the phenomenological framework because it produces descriptions that transcend the specific experiences on which they are based.

In the description of his study of learning, Giorgi describes the six steps he used in working with a single protocol (for example, the transcribed text of one complete interview). The protocol he uses to illustrate the steps was generated in an interview with a woman who selected as her example of learning the insights she gained about interior design from her friend:

1. The researcher reads completely through the protocol to get the sense of the whole.

2. The researcher reads through the protocol again and divides the transcript into units (blocks) that seem to express a self-contained meaning from a psychological perspective. This is accomplished by recording each time a transition in meaning is perceived—for instance, a change in subject matter or a change in activities being described. This is not an automatic or technical process; it requires the researcher's judgment. Although the researcher reads from the perspective of his or her discipline's interests (in this case, psychology), care must be taken to treat the text as a naive and nontheoretical presen-

tation of the subject's experience and to seek those divisions that are part, in fact, of the subject's own experience. The divisions are to be those that naturally cohere in the text rather than those imposed by the expectations of a researcher's theoretical position. Each block is referred to as a "meaning unit." The meaning units are constituents of the experience, not elements, in that they retain their identity as contextual parts of the subject's specific experience. In the example, the meaning refers to learning about interior design by this person at this time, not to learning in general. (An element implies a contextless discrimination and results from a reduction of a constituent.)

Giorgi (1975b) found that the woman's protocol (the one he used as an illustrative example) divided into 15 meaning units. The opening meaning unit was the following portion of the protocol:

> [In response to the question, "Could you describe in as much detail as possible a situation in which learning occurred for you?"] The first thing that comes to mind is what I learned about interior decorating from Myrtis. She was telling me about the way you see things. Her view of looking at different rooms has been altered. She told me that when you come into a room you don't usually notice how many vertical and horizontal lines there are, at least consciously, you don't notice. And yet, if you were to take someone who knows what's going on in the field of interior decorating, they would intuitively feel there were the right number of vertical and horizontal lines. [The next sentence of the protocol was marked as the beginning of a second meaning unit.] (pp. 88–89)

3. In Giorgi's third step, after having delineated the natural meaning units, the researcher tries to state, as simply as possible in his or her own language, the meaning that dominates the natural unit. This is a concise description of the meaning unit and is the first transformation of the data from the subject's words to the researcher's words. The researcher tries to express in an explicit way the implicit psychological aspects of the meaning unit and then writes out a sentence in his or her own words that expresses this discovery. These transformations, stated in the third person, retain the situated character of the subject's initial description and are the psychological equivalents of the meaning units of Step 2 that were originally expressed in the subject's own words.

Where van Kaam and Colaizzi move directly from the delineation of the protocols' natural meaning units to a search for the essential elements of the general experience under investigation, Giorgi's transformations (Steps 3 and 4) and first synthesis (Step 5) retain the situated context in which the experience has occured to an individual subject. Only after developing a situated structural description of the experience for each subject does Giorgi move to a general transsituational description of it (Step 6).

In the third step of the example, Giorgi identified the constituent in the opening meaning unit as "role of vertical and horizontal lines in interior decorating." At this point, the analysis has produced a division of the protocol into 15 units, each accompanied by the statement of its situational theme in the words of the researcher.

4. The next step is to interrogate each meaning unit and its theme in terms of the specific topic of the study. The researcher works with the meaning units (Step 2) and their first transformations (Step 3). The question of the study (in this case, "What is learning?") is put to each unit and its accompanying first transformation. This is a second transformation in which the researcher draws out from each unit of the protocol those aspects that are related to the topic under investigation and redescribes these aspects in the language from the perspective of psychological science (in this case, in the psychological terms related to learning).

Even though the subject's original description has been given in response to the research question, it often contains sections unrelated to the question. If there is nothing explicit about the topic in a meaning unit, the researcher can pass it over. Giorgi's (1975b) description of the central meaning about learning found in the first meaning unit is:

> The awareness of vertical and horizontal lines and their importance for interior decorating as described by a friend was the content and one of the goals of the learning experience. (pp. 91–92)

5. Once the meaning units have been transformed into psychological language, the researcher works to synthesize and tie them together into a descriptive statement of essential, nonredundant psychological meanings. The transformed meaning units are related to each other and to the sense of the whole protocol. This structural description continues to include the concreteness and the specifics of the situation in which the subject's learning took place. The description answers the question, "What is the psychological structure of learning as it presented itself to this subject in this particular situation?" The description of the situated structure of learning developed for the whole protocol being considered here is:

> S[ubject] becomes aware through a friend that rooms have vertical and horizontal lines and that these lines are important for interior decorating. Having acquired this knowledge, S[ubject] looks for and perceives the lines in her own living room and then rearranges the furniture in the room in accordance with her perception of the lines. Afterwards the room really looks different to her and this fact is confirmed by her husband, who however, does not know why the room looks different. S[ubject] describes her own learning as knowledge application, and a certain way of looking, and implicitly acknowledges that there may be levels of learning. Explicit awareness of specific

criteria for determining the proper room rearrangement were not present; only the general intention to rearrange the room. The readiness to learn about the relationship between lines and interior decorating made possible the recall of relevant past experiences about European cathedrals and their lines. (pp. 94–95)

6. Only after completing the situated descriptions does the researcher develop a description at the general level from the protocol. The construction of the general structural description leaves out the particulars of the specific situation reported in the protocol. Instead, it centers on those aspects of the experience included in the protocol that are transsituational or descriptive of learning in general. Although the description does not claim to be of a universal structure of consciousness, it does claim a general validity beyond the specific situation of the subject. The general description of the situated structure derived from the example protocol is:

> Learning is the ability to be present to, or exhibit the "NEW" according to the specific context and level of functioning of the individual. This awareness of the "NEW" takes place in an interpersonal context and it makes possible the sustained appreciation of a situation in a fuller way, or the emergence of behavior that reaches a different level of refinement in a sustained way or both. (pp. 94–95)

Giorgi's example finishes with the analysis of this single protocol. For this reason he retains the delimiting term *situated* in the title of the general description. He does, however, advocate the use of multiple subjects in phenomenological psychological research. In addressing the point of multiple subjects, Giorgi (1985a) writes:

> One would rarely conduct research of this type with only one subject. It is important to realize this because it is most difficult to write an essential general structure with only one instance. The more subjects there are, the greater the variations, and hence the better the ability to see what is essential. (p. 19)

The researcher moves through six steps with each subject's protocol, developing a separate general description of the situated structure for every one. If the researcher begins, however, with multiple protocols, Giorgi allows that producing a general description for the situated structure for each protocol may not be necessary.

7. Thus an additional step is required to produce a single general structural description. For this final description, the term *situated* can be dropped if all of the subjects "can be subsumed under one typology" (p. 20). In this step, the researcher directly synthesizes the transformed meaning units from the various protocols into a final general description.

Giorgi's steps, like Colaizzi's, do not include van Kaam's percentages or the comparative validity of multi-

ple judges. All three researchers, however, employ a similar series of steps: (a) The original protocols are divided into units, (b) the units are transformed by the researcher into meanings that are expressed in psychological and phenomenological concepts, and (c) these transformations are tied together to make a general description of the experience.

The Transformation and Synthesis of the Data

Transformations

One of the most difficult aspects of the data-analysis process to explain is the transformation of a meaning unit, which is given in a subject's everyday langauge, into a statement using psychological terms to describe the phenomenon being investigated. The transformations are necessary because the original descriptions given by subjects are usually naive regarding psychological structures and often include multiple and blended references.

The transformation is not accomplished through abstraction or formalization. It does not remain at the level of the linguistic expressions, as does traditional content analysis with its use of word counts (Krippendorff, 1980), but focuses on the experiences to which the language refers. The transformation "goes through" the everyday linguistic expressions to the reality they describe, and then it redescribes this reflective reality in the language appropriate to a phenomenologically based psychology. One difficulty for this redescription is the current vocabulary of psychology. This vocabulary is tied to nonphenomenological perspectives—for instance, behaviorism and psychoanalysis. Thus phenomenological psychologists generally use the language of commonsense enlightened by a phenomenological perspective for their redescriptions.

"Going through" concrete expressions to the experience itself is accomplished by two thought processes: reflection and imaginative variation. The process of reflection involves a careful and sensitive reading of an expression to answer the questions, What is truly being described in the meaning unit? and What is absolutely essential to understand the psychological dynamic operating here? The researcher then tests the answers he or she first proposes by imaginative variation.

Imaginative variation is a type of mental experimentation in which the researcher intentionally alters, through imagination, various aspects of the experience, either subtracting from or adding to the proposed transformation. The point of free variation is to imaginatively stretch the proposed transformation to the edges until it no longer describes the experience underlying the subject's naive description. The use of these processes is to enable the researcher to produce meaning transformations on which there is consistent intersubjective agreement. Van Kaam's study did not use imaginative variation and thus is closer to a logical deduction from the given protocols than a phenomenological analysis of a structure of experience.

A test of the correctness of a meaning transformation is that one can work backward from the transformed expression to the original naive expression. An adequate transformation should not be simply an idiosyncratic process in which the results are unique to the particular researcher producing the redescription. They must be publicly verifiable so that other researchers will agree that the transformed expression does describe a psychological process that is, in fact, contained in the original expression. (Giorgi, 1985b, reports that when the transformation is carried out on the same protocol by different individuals and the results are compared, the degree of "intersubjective agreement is surprisingly high" [p. 73].)

Synthesis

Transformations are redescriptions of meaning units. Synthesis involves tying together and integrating the list of transformed meaning units into a consistent and systematic general description of the psychological structure of the experience under investigation. Synthesis is the process of phenomenological eidetic reduction. It involves an intuitive "grasping" of the essential psychological elements that incorporate the redescribed psychological meanings, and it is thus different from an inductive or simple generalization procedure. Van Kaam's study derived its final synthetic description by collating the predominant features of the experience. The phenomenological process of synthesis is different from a process that adds or lists together elements; it requires an eidetic seeing of the whole. In the grasp of the whole, the elements are understood.

The procedure of synthesis calls for the researcher to read through the redescribed meanings and then to formulate what might be a general description of the structure underlying the variations in the meanings. The researcher again conducts "thought experiments" in which proposed formulations are imaginatively varied to the point at which an imagined structural description no longer fits the meanings. The proposed formulation is then compared to the transformed meanings again to see if it is supported. This procedure of zigzaging between the transformed meanings and a proposed general description goes through several rounds, the formulation becoming more refined each time until the meanings clearly support the final general description.

As in the case with the transformations, the synthesis can be tested by other researchers. By examining the redescribed meanings along with the final general description, other researchers should be able to agree that the product of the synthesis is accurate and clearly presents a possible description of the essential structured elements of the experience being investigated.

EXPRESSIONS OF THE FINDINGS

The finding of a phenomenological study is the general structural description. In phenomenological research, the researcher has the freedom to express the finding in multiple ways. Giorgi (1985a) makes the point that "to a large extent how the findings are presented [depends] very much upon the audience with whom one is communicating" (p. 20). The same essential findings are expressed in each case, but they are geared to the background and vocabulary of the audience.

Fischer and Wertz's (1979) study, referred to previously, investigated the experience of "being criminally victimized." Because their project called for dissemination of their results at public forums, they produced five expressions of their findings, all responding to the different communicative needs of their various audiences. For example, the first expression of their findings was a typical description of the general structure, which they called "general condensation." It was four paragraphs in length, and "evolved from half a dozen drafts, each giving up more detail, and varying the way of presenting each constituent [feature] so as to evoke its relation to the whole" (p. 150). They concluded that, because of its succinctness and compactness, the general condensation necessarily lost the richness and concreteness contained in the raw data. Although the general condensation was too dense and technical for use at public presentations and nonprofessional discussions, it provided the basis for the more useful reporting formats.

As a second expression, they distributed individual case synopses. (The example they used in their report was two and a half pages in length.) Each case synopsis, produced by using the person's own words or a very close approximation of them, described what was "personally critical to a particular victim's experience" (p. 140) and was intended to provide the audience "with concrete examples that reverberate with their own lives" (p. 143).

The Research Report

The phenomenological research report must include a description and documentation of the procedures employed by the researcher to collect the data (including a description of the subjects used in the study) and the steps applied to move from the raw interview data to a general description of the experience under investigation. Examples should be provided of original protocols and transformations, and arguments should be given to support the synthetic conclusions. Readers can then follow the researcher's analytic process and thus understand how the transformed meanings and structural description have been arrived at. Although the documentation does not *prove* that the conclusions of the study are correct, they can allow the reader to check to see if the general description is indeed supported by and derived from the data.

The research report should also include a review of the previous research and theory pertaining to the topic. This is done to set the scholarly context in which the study will be carried out and to justify why an additional study, using phenomenological methods, is needed on the topic. The implication of the phenomenological findings for psychological theory and application should conclude the report.

Issues of Validity

The phenomenological researcher needs to be concerned throughout the investigative process with whether the findings are "valid"—that is, whether or not the findings can be trusted and used as the basis for actions and policy decisions. The concept of validity ordinarily refers to the notion that an idea is well-grounded and well-supported and thus that one can have confidence in it. Some confusion exists in the literature about how to apply the notion of validity to phenomenological research. In mainstream social science research, measuring instruments (including questionnaires) generate types of data that can be analyzed by using statistical procedures. There the concept of validity has been specifically delimited to refer to confidence in the measuring instruments. Are they measuring accurately what they claim to measure?

Phenomenological research, however, approaches validity from a more general perspective—as a conclusion that inspires confidence because the argument in support of it has been persuasive. Not all arguments persuade with the same power, though. A "sound" argument persuades because it is able to resist attack. A "convincing" argument is stronger than a "sound" one; not only can it withstand attack, but it can also silence the opposition. A "conclusive" argument is still stronger; it puts an end to all doubt or debate. For example, the syllogism is a "conclusive" argument: Conclusions derived from syllogistic arguments (given the acceptance of the premises) cannot be doubted. The degree of validity of the findings of a phenomenological research project, then, depends on the power of its presentation to convince the reader that its findings are accurate.

Researchers must persuade readers (including the community of scholars) that the two types of inferences that they have made in reaching their findings are powerfully supported: (a) the transformation of the raw data into phenomenological, informed psychological expressions and (b) the synthesis of the transformed meaning units into a general structural description. The reader must be able to follow the thought processes that have led to the conclusions and to accept them as valid. In those cases where the phenomenon is one that the readers have experienced, the findings must also correspond to the readers' own experiences of the phenomenon.

The validity of phenomenological research concerns the question, "Does the general structural description provide an accurate portrait of the common features and structural connections that are manifest in the examples collected?" The doubts to be addressed include:

1. Did the interviewer influence the contents of the subjects' descriptions in such a way that the descriptions do not truly reflect the subjects' actual experience? (See Mishler, 1986, for a survey of the research on interview outcomes.)
2. Is the transcription accurate, and does it convey the meaning of the oral presentation in the interview?
3. In the analysis of the transcriptions, were there conclusions other than those offered by the researcher that could have been derived? Has the researcher identified these alternatives and demonstrated why they are less probable than the one decided on?
4. Is it possible to go from the general structural description to the transcriptions and to account for the specific contents and connections in the original examples of the experience?
5. Is the structural description situation-specific, or does it hold in general for the experience in other situations?

The phenomenological researcher works in the linguistic realm and cannot draw on a reader's commitment to the conclusive power of statistically expressed arguments. Thus reports of phenomenological research need to include reasoned and convincing responses to the questions that responsible readers are expected to ask of the research and to make explicit the philosophical ground and specific world view on which the research is based.

The Usefulness of Phenomenological Research

Natural scientific research aims to produce the kind of knowledge that allows one to predict and control the topic under investigation. Phenomenological research is quite different; it seeks understanding for its own sake and addresses the question *what?* not *why?* Productive phenomenological research supplies a deeper and clearer understanding of what it is like for someone to experience something. The research results amplify our understanding of these experiences and lead to several consequences: (a) we can appreciate and be more sensitive to those involved in these experiences, a particularly significant consequence for those in the helping professions; (b) some of the understandings derived from logical-mathematical theories and research can be enlarged on, deepened, and, in some cases, corrected; and (c) social action and public policy can be amended so as to be more responsive to the way in which we experience various situations.

One of the reasons I chose to use Fischer and Wertz's (1979) study of the experience of being criminally victimized is that it provides an example of how the results of phenomenological research can affect policy changes. Fischer and Wertz's results were useful in several ways:

1. Their descriptions helped other victims of crime to understand and to come to terms with their own experiences.

2. Their results helped counselors who work with crime victims to be more sensitive and responsive to their clients. For example, victims typically respond first by taking action—they call insurance companies, change locks, arrange for replacements of licenses and credit cards, and so forth—and only later—days, weeks, sometimes months—are they ready to reflect on what has happened to them and what it has meant to them and to society. Without this reflection, victims do not fully recover a sense of being in charge of their lives. This finding implies that counselors should make themselves available later in the process of adjustment and not limit their presence to the initial police response.

3. Their results provided authorities with information on the type of response victims previously thought they would receive. For example, victims expected the police to investigate reported crimes immediately and were disappointed and angry when this did not happen. Thus the findings make it clear that victims should be told just how long they can expect to wait before the police will begin their investigation of a crime.

4. The purpose of the illustrated narratives was to provide public officials with "an immediate sense of the full sweep of the personal meaning of being criminally victimized" (p. 145). This understanding has increased the officials' motivation to instigate changes in public policy and has provided them with insight into what policies need to be changed. For example, "it is apparent that if the victim is to integrate, i.e., overcome, the experience, he requires something different than such current efforts as financial compensation and child care services while testifying in court" (p. 150). Assistance needs to include community members with whom the victim can talk about the experience, and the community agencies need to understand victims' feelings of vulnerability and guard against victimizing them further through inconsideration or ineptitude.

It is important to include in the phenomenological research report an implication section where the significance of the findings for practice and policy is spelled out. Wertz (1984) has written about the need for an implication section: "A further moment [extention] of research is required to relate the findings to various sectors of the lifeworld within which the research is situated" (p. 45). He mentions that, in addition to consequences for public policy, phenomenological researchers often relate their findings to other psychological theories and practices. Giorgi's (1975b) and Colaizzi's (1973) studies on the "experience of learning" imply that changes are needed in the convention pedagogical strategies used in schools. Aanstoos's (1983) research on thinking carries critical implications "for information processing theories" and Wertz's (1982) study of perception for visual theories.

In addition to the findings of phenomenological research, participation in the process itself can be useful for subjects. Wertz (1984) has described the beneficial effects that sometimes accrue to the interview participants in the research. In his study with Fischer (1979) on victimization, the process of engaging in the interview was itself helpful for the subjects in restoring their broken sense of community.

The phenomenological research methods reviewed in this chapter are designed to yield clear and accurate descriptions of the structures of consciousness that constitute what appears in human experience. The research methods of other sciences are constructed to produce information about objects and human activities as they exist in themselves, outside of their appearance in human experience. Phenomenological methods are devised to investigate another realm of reality, the realm that comes into being at the intersection of consciousness and the world—human experience. Phenomenological methods have characteristics whose purpose it is to provide researchers clear access to this realm. These methods are also designed, however, to produce knowledge that meets the commitment to truth shared by all the sciences. The development of psychological research methods based in phenomenology is in a beginning phase. With more experience and effort, these methods will gain in sophistication and clarity.

RECOMMENDED READING

In recent years, an extensive body of literature has developed that contains psychological studies that are based on the phenomenological perspective and that include discussions of phenomenological methodology. I suggest that those who want to learn more about the phenomenological perspective on psychological research go directly to this literature. The two primary sources are the *Journal of Phenomenological Psychology* and the four volumes of the *Duquesne Studies in Phenomenological Psychology* (Giorgi, Fischer, & von Eckartsberg, 1971; Giorgi, Fischer, & Murray, 1975; Giorgi, Knowles, & Smith, 1979; Giorgi, Barton, & Maes, 1983). Papers from the biennial meetings of the International Association for Qualitative Research are published regularly as *Qualitative Research in Psychology* (Giorgi, 1986). Additional edited books include Spiegelberg's papers in *Doing Phenomenology* (1975); *Exploring the Lived World: Readings in Phenomenological Psychology,* edited by Aanstoos (1984); *Phenomenology and Psychological Research,* edited by Giorgi (1985a); and von Eckartsberg's survey of phenomenological methods, *Life-World Experience: Existential-Phenomenological Research Approaches in Psychology* (1986) A new journal, *Methods,* is another source for articles that addresses the methodological issues of phenomenological research.

REFERENCES

Aanstoos, C. M. (1983). A phenomenological study of thinking. In A. Giorgi, A. Barton, & C. Maes (Eds.), *Duquesne studies in phenomenological psychology: Vol. 4* (pp. 244–256). Pittsburgh: Duquesne University Press.

Aanstoos, C. M. (Ed.). (1984). *Exploring the lived world: Readings in phenomenological psychology.* (West Georgia College Studies in the Social Sciences, Vol. 23). Carrollton: West Georgia College.

Aanstoos, C. M. (1986). Phenomenology and the psychology of thinking. In P. D. Ashworth, A. Giorgi, & A. J. J. de Konig (Eds.), *Qualitative research in psychology* (pp. 79–116). Pittsburgh: Duquesne University Press.

Ashworth, P. D., Giorgi, A., & de Konig, A. J. J. (Eds.). (1986). *Qualitative research in psychology.* Pittsburgh: Duquesne University Press.

Bakan, P. (1978). Two streams of consciousness: A typological approach. In K. S. Pope & J. L. Singer (Eds.), *The stream of consciousness* (pp. 159–184). New York: Plenum Press.

Bellah, R. N., Madsen, R., Sullivan, W. M., Swidler, A., &

Tipton, S. M. (1985). *Habits of the heart: Individualism and commitment in American life.* New York: Harper & Row.

Bogdan, R., & Taylor, S. J. (1975). *Introduction to qualitative reserach methods.* New York: Wiley.

Casey, E. S. (1976). *Imagining: A phenomenological study.* Bloomington: Indiana University Press.

Colaizzi, P. F. (1973). *Reflection and research in psychology.* Dubuque, IA: Kendall Hunt.

Colaizzi, P. F. (1978). Psychological research as the phenomenologist views it. In R. S. Valle & M. King (Eds.), *Existential-phenomenological alternatives for psychology* (pp. 48–71). New York: Oxford University Press.

Coles, R. (1967). *Children of crisis* (Vol 1). Boston: Little, Brown.

Crane, J. G., & Angrosino, M. V. (1974). *Field projects in anthropology.* Morristown, NJ: General Learning.

Erikson, E. H., Erikson, J. M., & Kivnick, H. Q. (1986). *Vital involvement in old age.* New York: W. W. Norton.

Fischer, C. T., & Wertz, F. J. (1979). Empirical phenomenological analyses of being criminally victimized. In A. Giorgi, R. Knowles, & D. L. Smith (Eds.), *Duquesne studies in phenomenological psychology: Vol. 3* (pp. 135–158). Pittsburgh: Duquesne University Press.

Friedman, M. (Ed.). (1964). *The worlds of existentialism.* Chicago: University of Chicago Press.

Gardner, H. (1985). *The mind's new science: A history of the cognitive revolution.* New York: Basic Books.

Giorgi, A. (1975a). Convergence and divergence of qualitative and quantitative methods in psychology. In A. Giorgi, C. T. Fischer, & E. L. Murray (Eds.), *Duquesne studies in phenomenological psychology: Vol. 2* (pp. 72–79). Pittsburgh: Duquesne University Press.

Giorgi, A. (1975b). An application of phenomenological method in psychology. In A. Giorgi, C. T. Fischer, & E. L. Murray (Eds.), *Duquesne studies in phenomenological psychology: Vol. 2* (pp. 82–103). Pittsburgh: Duquesne University Press.

Giorgi, A. (Ed.). (1985a). *Phenomenology and psychological research.* Pittsburgh: Duquesne University Press.

Giorgi, A. (1985b). The phenomenological psychology of learning and the verbal learning tradition. In A. Giorgi (Ed.), *Phenomenology and psychological research* (pp. 23–85). Pittsburgh: Duquesne University Press.

Giorgi, A., Fischer, W. F., & von Eckartsberg, R. (Eds.). (1971). *Duquesne studies in phenomenological psychology: Vol. 1.* Pittsburgh: Duquesne University Press.

Giorgi, A., Fischer, C. T., & Murray, E. L. (Eds.). (1975). *Duquesne studies in phenomenological psychology: Vol. 2.* Pittsburgh: Duquesne University Press.

Giorgi, A., Knowles, R., & Smith, D. L. (Eds.). (1979). *Duquesne studies in phenomenological psychology: Vol. 3.* Pittsburgh: Duquesne University Press.

Giorgi, A., Barton, A., & Maes, C. (Eds.). (1983). *Duquesne studies in phenomenological psychology: Vol. 4.* Pittsburgh: Duquesne University Press.

Halling, S. (1979). Eugene O'Neill's understanding of forgiveness. In A. Giorgi, R. Knowles, & D. L. Smith (Eds.), *Duquesne studies in phenomenological psychology: Vol. 3* (pp. 193–208). Pittsburgh: Duquesne University Press.

Heidegger, M. (1962). *Being and time* (J. Macquarrie & E. Robinson, Trans.). New York: Harper & Row. (Original work published in 1927)

Hirai, T., Izawa, S., and Koga, E. (1959). EEG and Zen Buddhism: EEG changes in the course of meditation. *EEG Clinical Neurological Supplement, 62,* 76–105.

Husserl, E. (1931). *Ideas toward a pure phenomenology and*

phenomenological philosophy (W. R. B. Gibson, Trans.). New York: Humanities. (Original work published in 1913)

Husserl, E. (1964). *The phenomenology of internal time-consciousness* (J. S. Churchill, Trans.). Bloomington: Indiana University Press. (Original work published in 1928)

Husserl, E. (1970). *The crisis of European sciences and transcendental phenomenology* (D. Carr, Trans.). Evanston, IL: Northwestern University Press. (From original work published in 1936)

Ihde, D., & Silverman, H. J. (1985). *Descriptions.* Albany: State University of New York.

Jager, B. (1979). Dionysos and the world of passion. In A. Giorgi, R. Knowles, & D. L. Smith (Eds.), *Duquesne studies in phenomenological psychology: Vol. 3* (pp. 209–226). Pittsburgh: Duquesne University Press.

Kohák, E. (1978). *Idea and experience.* Chicago: University of Chicago Press.

Konig, A. J. J. de (1979). The qualitative method of research in the phenomenology of suspicion. In A. Giorgi, R. Knowles, & D. L. Smith (Eds.), *Duquesne studies in phenomenological psychology: Vol. 3* (pp. 122–134). Pittsburgh: Duquesne University Press.

Kosslyn, S. M. (1980). *Image and mind.* Cambridge: Harvard University Press.

Krippendorff, K. (1980). *Content analysis: An introduction to its methodology.* Beverly Hills, CA: Sage.

Kvale, S. (1983). The qualitative research interview. *Journal of Phenomenological Psychology, 14,* 171–196.

Merleau-Ponty, M. (1962). *Phenomenology of perception* (C. Smith, Trans.). New York: Humanities Press. (Original work published 1945)

Mishler, E. G. (1986). *Research interviewing: Context and narrative.* Cambridge: Harvard University Press.

Mruk, C. J. (1983). Toward a phenomenology of self-esteem. In A. Giorgi, A. Barton, & C. Maes (Eds.), *Duquesne studies in phenomenological psychology: Vol. 4* (pp. 137–149). Pittsburgh: Duquesne University Press.

Reynolds, H. T. (1977). *Analysis of nominal data.* Beverly Hills, CA: Sage.

Richer, P. (1978). A phenomenological analysis of the perception of geometric illusions. *Journal of Phenomenological Psychology, 8,* 123–135.

Ricoeur, P. (1967). *The symbolism of evil* (E. Buchanan, Trans.). New York: Harper & Row. (Original work published 1960)

Romanyshyn, R. D. (1982). *Psychological life: From science to metaphor.* Austin: University of Texas Press.

Rorty, R. (1979). *Philosophy and the mirror of nature.* Princeton: Princeton University Press.

Rubin, L. B. (1983). *Intimate strangers: Men and woman together.* New York: Harper & Row.

Sartre, J. (1966). *Psychology of imagination* (B. Frechtman, Trans.). New York: Washington Square. (Original work published 1940)

Schwartz, H., & Jacobs, J. (1979). *Qualitative sociology.* New York: Free Press.

Spiegelberg, H. (1976). *The phenomenological movement: A historical introduction* (2nd ed., Vols. 1 and 2). The Hague: Martinus Hijhoff.

Stevick, E. L. (1971). An empirical investigation of the experience of anger. In A. Giorgi, W. F. Fischer, & R. von Eckartsberg (Eds.), *Duquesne studies in phenomenological psychology: Vol. 1* (pp. 132–148). Pittsburgh: Duquesne University Press.

Strasser, S. (1969). *The idea of dialogal phenomenology.* Pittsburgh: Duquesne University Press.

van Kaam, A. (1969). *Existential foundation of psychology.* New York: Image Books. (Original work published 1966)

von Eckartsberg, R. (1986). *Life-world experience: Existential-phenomenological research approaches in psychology.* Washington, DC: University Press of America.

Wertz, F. J. (1982). Findings and value of a descriptive approach to everyday perceptual process. *Journal of Phenomenological Psychology, 13,* 169–195.

Wertz, F. J. (1984). Procedures in phenomenological research and the question of validity. In C. M. Aanstoos (Ed.), *Exploring the lived world: Explorations in phenomenological psychology* (pp. 29–48) (West Georgia College Studies in the Social Sciences, Vol. 23). Carrollton: West Georgia College.

Yin, R. (1984). *Case study research.* Beverly Hills, CA: Sage.

II

Classical Topics in Psychology

The following three chapters represent existential–phenomenological examinations of selected topics in some classical areas of psychology. Moss's Chapter 4 challenges the often held view that existential phenomenology, given its foundational philosophy that repudiates causal analysis and reductionism, has nothing to offer the physiological psychologist. Moss initially reviews several traditional treatments of body image and then, using the notion of the lived body, offers insights that only an approach that acknowledges the central importance of human experience can provide.

In Chapter 5, Wertz examines the connection between a phenomenology of perception and ideas about perception suggested by the psychologist Abraham Maslow. Although a phenomenological study of perception shows specific limitations of Maslow's notions of deficiency and growth cognition, both phenomenological psychology and Maslow bring us to an awareness of the fragmentation and impoverishment of perception induced by contemporary technological culture and point to the possibility of a recovery from this state of affairs.

Giorgi's Chapter 6 on learning and memory similarly proceeds from a careful study of these phenomena as they are experienced by the human subject. This approach enables him to clarify, for example, the inner connection between performance and insight. His conclusion shows in what sense phenomenological psychology and mainstream, laboratory psychology are both scientific.

4

Brain, Body, and World
Body Image and the Psychology of the Body

Donald Moss

This chapter discusses the psychology of body image as an example of the phenomenological attempt to overcome dualistic notions of body and mind. The chapter: (a) outlines the history and concepts of the psychology of body image, (b) surveys the evolution of neurological and neuropsychological theories and research on body image, and (c) introduces the phenomenological concepts of the lived body, lived space, and the personal world. We begin with an introduction to the phenomenological approach in psychology.

CONCEPTUAL APPROACHES TO BODY AND MIND: BEHAVIORISM, NEUROPSYCHOLOGY, AND PHENOMENOLOGY

Chapter 1 presents the tendency prevalent in natural–scientific psychology to make a strict division between body and mind, behavior and experience, and the objective and subjective aspects of the human being. Behaviorism is the approach to psychology that chooses to study the body, behavior, and what is objective and observable to the senses; it also, for many years, chose to exclude from study the mind, experience, and what is subjective and inaccessible to others (Watson, 1979). Physiological psychology and neuropsychology, in turn,

represent an attempt to explain the functional bases of behavior and experience through neurophysiological and neurochemical mechanisms and systems.

Phenomenological psychology, in contrast, offers a holistic viewpoint, looking at the human being as a unity of body and mind, behavior and situation. Because of the early roots of phenomenological philosophy in the idealistic tradition (Husserl, 1965), many psychologists incorrectly believe that phenomenology studies only subjective experience, and what is mental ("inside the person's head") and inaccessible to observation. These psychologists often claim that phenomenology is a form of "introspection," that is, an examination of thoughts and feelings that ignores the body and behavior.

In actuality, however, phenomenology within psychology has attempted to study the whole individual, including behavior, body, and a personal world of experience. In phenomenology, the person is considered an embodied "being-in-the-world" (Merleau-Ponty, 1962). This means that human action and human experience are not split up to be studied separately. Merleau-Ponty (1963), a prominent French phenomenologist, described what is "mental" as the meaningful structure of our actions in the world. Viewed in this way, the mental and the body are not separate and cannot be understood except as a unity.

The physiological understanding of the body is also addressed by phenomenology. In fact, the phenomenological understanding of the human being begins by drawing on advanced concepts from neurophysiology. Even in its "up-to-date" form, however, neurophysiology pro-

Donald Moss • Haight Clinic Psychological Services, 109 South Jackson Street, Spring Lake, Michigan 49456.

vides only a limited perspective on the body. Phenomenology, therefore, introduces the idea of the "lived body" (Madison, 1981, p. 22) to give a broader, more adequate perspective on the body of the human being. This idea is not an attempt to replace physiological psychology with a phenomenological approach. Rather, it is an attempt to complete the picture of the human being and his or her body that physiological psychology begins.

Further, careful phenomenological investigations can provide a corrective to neuropsychological explanations that do not do justice to the actual structure of a psychological phenomenon such as body image (Moss, 1981, pp. 160–162). Or, one might define a phenomenologist as Hebb (1951) did, as "one of those who, at the extreme, do not like existing theories (and perhaps never will) but are interested in attacking them and finding evidence that is hard to handle" (p. 47). Hebb's remark was intended ironically, yet it is true that the method of phenomenological description is a useful tool for uncovering the inadequacies of psychological constructs and models and thus compels researchers to advances in theory building (Straus, 1982).

When researchers begin independently, proceeding from the phenomenological and the latest neuropsychological viewpoints, and attempt to construct a comprehensive structural understanding of "body–mind," they occasionally come into an uncanny convergence. Karl Pribram (1986, pp. 508–510), a prominent figure in contemporary neuropsychology, has observed the parallel conceptual frameworks developed by Merleau-Ponty in his work *The Structure of Behavior* (1963) and by Miller, Galanter, and Pribram in their work *Plans and the Structure of Behavior* (1960). Just as phenomenology was forced to take account of human embodiment and world, behaviorism found itself compelled to the study of "cognitive behavior," "covert behavior," and the structure of mental life (Pribram, 1981, pp. 142–146). As scientists, one begins within a specialized, partisan vocabulary, captive to a chosen point of view, but one is compelled by the investigatory dialogue with the concrete phenomena of psychological life to transcend these starting places and derive a more adequate conceptual framework.

The phenomenological ideas of an embodied-being-in-the-world and of the lived body will be presented more fully later in this chapter with the viewpoint of Merleau-Ponty as our primary frame of reference. First, however, let us review some older understandings of the body from the history of psychology.

BODY IMAGE

Since the turn of the century, a group of syncretistic and awkward terms have appeared in the literature of both neurology and psychology. Body image, body schema, body ego, body concept, and somatognosis are a few of many such terms (Fliess, 1961; Head, 1926; Schilder, 1933) that represent efforts to reunite the apparently dual realms of body and mind into their living unity. Scientific psychology knew no alternative path to a more holistic concept and tried to stretch the old concepts of medicine and philosophy to fit the new phenomena. Thus "body image" describes a phenomenon showing properties of both body and mind.

Body image is generally understood as "the picture that the person has of the physical appearance of his body" (Traub & Orbach, 1964, p. 57). Body image refers to the individual's *explicit* picture of the body. *Body schema,* an alternate term, refers to the *implicit* knowledge the person has of the position of his or her body. The body schema is the knowledge of the body's current position and possible future positions, which the individual utilizes during movement, without even thinking. Because body schema includes the implicit knowledge about both actual and possible positions of the body, it is also a *disposition to action* in certain directions.

We will come to see that this body image as picture and this body schema as disposition to action are very closely related. You can observe this interrelation for yourself. Most human beings have a more differentiated and precise control over the highly useful fingers of the hands than of the toes of the feet; the mental picture an individual has of his or her hand with its fingers is also usually more detailed. Thus the hand is more completely organized both in the body schema that organizes activity and in the body image, one's picture of one's own body. The neural representation of the body in the motor cortex of the brain, the so-called Penfield–Boldrey "homunculus" depicted in textbooks of neurology and physiological psychology, is a functional organization established in the course of early development and reflects the actual life history of each individual (Restak, 1984, p. 77; see Figure 1).

Consequently, athletes, ballet dancers, and other agile individuals have a more highly developed body image than do the less agile, especially for those parts of the body involved in self-produced movement (McKinney & Rabinovitch, 1964). Here again, the close relationship between the body image and the body schema is evident.

Past Misconceptions

Let us first dispose of a misconception about body image that originates in the commonsense viewpoint of everyday life. Common sense frequently assumes that the human being perceives his or her own body in the same way a disinterested onlooker notices anything in the surrounding world—a tree, a rock, an automobile. This dis-

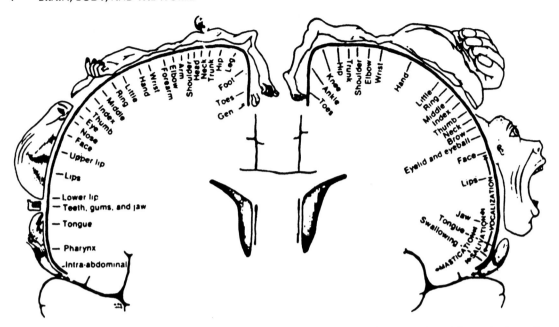

Figure 1. The motor homunculus showing the neural representation of the body in the brain's motor cortex. It is organized according to the functional importance and sensitivity of body parts; the hands and fingers are represented over a wider area of the cortex than are the hips or legs. (From *The Brain* by R. Restak. Copyright 1966 by Bantam. Reprinted by permission.)

interested perception of the casual bystander is taken as the basic process by which each individual knows his or her body.

The objective, supposedly neutral observation of the laboratory scientist is a further refinement of this disinterested perception. Having striven so long as scientists to cultivate this "objectivity," we confuse this highly sophisticated and specialized knowing for the primary basis of all knowledge and perception. Completely disinterested perception ("objectivity") is a late achievement of the trained, mature adult, yet we often treat it as the basis for all perception. We assume that all deviations from this objective perception come about by a secondary addition of subjective, personal, or emotional qualities to an originally objective picture.

Objectivity

Even the so-called objective knowledge of science is riddled with interpretation and subjectivity. Goethe, the German poet, pointed out that with each attentive glance into the world we already theorize (Goethe, cited by Straus, 1926, p. 26). Feyerabend (1978), a contemporary philosopher of science, observed that:

On closer analysis we find that science knows no "bare facts" at all, but that the facts that enter our knowledge are already viewed in a certain way and are, therefore, essentially ideational. (p. 19)

Erwin Straus, the phenomenological psychiatrist, and Jacob von Uexküll, a phenomenologically oriented biologist, both showed that all knowledge is dependent on a prior posing of questions; the question in turn shapes the answers—the results of the so-called "objective" observation (Straus, 1982, pp. 12–13; von Uexküll, 1928, pp. 3–4). Straus studied the phenomenon of a disinterested "knowing," of detached contemplation, and found it to be an elaborate and complex human achievement, by no means automatic or universal, far more demanding than the usual pathic involvement of the human being—as a creature in need—in a world of goals and destinations (Straus, 1952, 1965).

The philosophy of science has pursued this line of thinking and investigated how research carries out a construction or shaping of facts. Kuhn introduced the idea of a scientific "paradigm" that shapes what the individual researcher discovers; Lakatos replaced the concept of paradigm with that of the "research program"; and Laudan radicalized this concept further to look at "research traditions" that involve a family of theories all sharing a common history, ontology, and methodology (Gholson & Barker, 1985).

Further, the critique of the naive belief in objectivity has spawned a rich tradition of research on the social psychology and sociology of the research situation, including studies on the so-called "Rosenthal effect" (Rosenthal & Rosnow, 1969), the role of values in shaping research findings (Howard, 1985), and the controversial view of "social constructionalism" that scientific knowledge is no more than a process of consensus formation (Berger & Luckmann, 1966; Gergen, 1982, 1985). Most theoretical psychologists would now agree with Scarr (1985, p. 499) that "like other scientists, psychologists construct knowledge. To sensory data we attribute meaning in theoretically-guided inventions of facts."

Yet the psychologist approaching body image typically takes "seeing" for granted as a simple transmission of information from the object to the observer's brain.

The history of psychology even provided an elegant physiological rationale for the commonsense view of objectivism (Tibbets, 1969). Psychological theory assumed that "sensations" are the primary data of consciousness and that there is a one-to-one correspondence between one incoming sensory stimulation in the world and one sensation in my head. This assumption, called the "constancy hypothesis," proposes that "what is" or "actuality" is transmitted automatically to our sensory apparatus and then, in the process of interpretation involved in perception, subjective distortions take place, and subjective meanings are added on to the objective sensations.

According to this misconception, human beings start out with an objective, disinterested visual picutre of the body and then subjective meanings are stuck on later to produce the final body image. The findings of 70 years of neurological, physiological, and psychological research have long ago undermined this view (Hochberg, 1969). Nevertheless, this view has powerful roots in the commonsense attitude of everyday life—and in the natural scientific world view. It has therefore continued to haunt scientific research long after every trace of evidence for such a theory had vanished. For example, Traub and Orbach (1964) concluded: "Since the individual has access to accurate mirrors, his body image ought to depend in large part upon data derived from such reflections" (p. 54).

We encounter here two assumptions: first, that the individual *should* form his or her body image from objective, disinterested information; and second, that a person looking into a mirror is obtaining that objective, disinterested information about his or her body. Neither of these assumptions corresponds to the way an individual typically perceives his or her own body. Think for just a moment about the last time you looked in a mirror and consider what highly selective details you saw—a mis-

placed hair, a slight paunch, sleepy eyes, or a pimple. An extreme example would be a young woman with anorexia nervosa, who stares in the mirror at her emaciated body, selectively focuses on a fold of fat on her thigh, and bemoans how grossly obese she is. As we see in the next section, there is a marked selectivity in the human being's perception of his or her body; the individual does not merely register "what is there."

Merleau-Ponty's Answer to Past Misconceptions

The phenomenological view of body image put forth by Merleau-Ponty (1962, 1963) stands in sharp contrast to the misconceptions just discussed. Merleau-Ponty abandons both the idea of an original objective picture of the body and the idea of a pure process of sensation subject to secondary distortion (i.e., the "constancy hypothesis").

According to Merleau-Ponty, one's body image is not a matter of acquired objective or accurate knowledge concerning the body; in fact it is fundamentally not a matter of *reflective knowledge* at all. Prior to reflecting about the body, the individual forms a familiarity with his or her body. This takes place at the prereflective (before reflection) level; this is the "taken-for-granted" level at which humans act and experience prior to thinking about their action or experience. Prior to *reflecting* on his or her body and prior to *knowing* about the body, the child *lives* the body, develops its capacity for action, and builds up a familiarity with the body as a vehicle for action. In so doing, the child does not explicitly focus his or her consciousness on the body but acts through the body in an action-oriented focus upon some object. The body comprises one's earliest capacity for relating to the world of objects.

This lived familiarity has a priority both in one's individual developmental history and in everyday life. The infant builds up a lived familiarity with the *hands as instruments of grasping and pointing*, before acquiring the knowledge that this is a hand or that the hand has a muscle called the "palmar brevis" and a bone called the "trapezium." In everyday life, the human being draws on this lived familiarity with the hand's various *potentials for action*, without referring to knowledge about the hand. In fact, too much thinking about the function of the "palmar brevis" or the "trapezium" during our action may interrupt the attempt to grasp or point.

Merleau-Ponty (1962) called the individual's body, as it is lived and experienced, a *lived body* (or "own body," *corps propre*). He distinguished this lived body from the body as objectively known by science or by disinterested observation. The hand, as an instrument of grasping and pointing, is part of the lived body; the hand, as dissected, is part of the objective body. Similarly, German researchers use the word *Leib* for the lived, personally meaningful body and *Körper* for the objective factual body studied in the laboratory (Plügge, 1967, 1970).

For Merleau-Ponty, the body image is considered in light of the lived body. The body image is built up around the immediate, prereflective familiarity with one's own body and with the network of actions possible for one's body. An objective, visual picture of the body, if it is acquired at all, is a later achievement, based on the already existing prereflective familiarity. In other words, the objective picture of the body comes later, after explicit reflection on one's body and its position in the world. Such a reflection presupposes that one has already formed a basic acquaintance with one's own body. The hand studied with such rigorous objectivity in the mirror is already a hand that has an intimate meaning for the individual in everyday life. It is already familiar as the means by which one feeds oneself, waves to a departing friend, and turns the doorknob to a closed room. It is this *hand as meaningful in everyday life* that figures in the individual's image of his or her own body.

Lacan (1968, 1977) and Ver Eecke (1984, 1985) described a specific "mirror stage," between the ages of 6 and 18 months, when the child first recognizes its own mirror reflection as such and utilizes this visual image as an ideal framework gathering much of the prereflective familiarity with its own body into the unity of one ideal identity. Thus Lacan conceived the human being as *identifying* with and as actively *appropriating* his or her body in the course of development. He asserted that the recognition of the mirror image as oneself plays a formative and indispensable role in the development of human identity, comparable to the case of the female pigeon that cannot develop further unless it catches sight of a member of its own species. Research on self-recognition in primates has pointed in parallel directions (Gallup, 1977; Gallup, McClure, Hill, & Bundy, 1971).

Gallup's primate studies address a central question: Is the viewing of the reflection of the organism's own body *instrumental* in establishing a more integrated identity? Or, as Gallup's work suggests, is the ability of the primate (and perhaps the human) to recognize its body in the mirror merely a sign that a solidified identity has already developed? (Gallup believes that this process of identity formation most likely proceeds through contact with other members of the species.)

In related studies, Merleau-Ponty (1964a,b) showed that the child's reflective appropriation of the body during the "mirror stage"—recognizing, labeling and owning it as *mine* and *myself*—takes place within the context of intimate relationships with others. Thus the child acquires the physical image of his or her own body in the context of "seeing him- or herself in others' eyes." Moss (1982, 1984) investigated the ongoing reappropriation of the body as *mine* in adult life, in the face of stigma and social trauma. These studies point to the matrix of intimate interpersonal relations and identifications, especially within the child's family, that support the formation of a solid body image and identity. This interpersonal dimension of body image cannot be addressed in detail here, but the reader is referred to Paul Schilder's (1950) perspective: "We may take parts of the bodies of others and incorporate them in our own body-image. . . . We may take in parts of the bodies of others by identifying with them" (p. 72). A review of recent empirical research on body image by Van der Velde (1985) further examines the role of interpersonal relationships in the formation of body image.

This phenomenological theory of body image (Merleau-Ponty, 1962, 1963; Plügge, 1967, 1970; Straus, 1966, 1967) is based on a careful study of research in physiology and psychology. It presupposes the recognition of the close link between body image—the individual's picture of his or her own body—and body schema—the body's disposition to action. Yet, this view also goes beyond the understanding of body image prevailing in physiology and psychology. In their investigations, Merleau-Ponty, Plügge, Straus, and other phenomenologists often drew out implications of experiments that the researchers, handicapped by obsolete assumptions, had overlooked.

However, before examining examples of the kinds of research on which Merleau-Ponty based his theory, we can demonstrate quite simply that the body image does not originate as an objective, disinterested visual picture. Begin by drawing a picture of your own body. When you examine this picture closely, you will see that some parts of the body are more prominent than others—pictured in more detail, perhaps emphasized by shading or heavy lines, or perhaps even disproportionately large.

You will also probably notice that you have spent more time on one part of the picture than another—most likely your face and your hands, but perhaps some other part had absorbed your attention as well. A clinical psychologist interprets such emphases symbolically. For example, an emphasis on the teeth is taken to indicate aggression and hostility. Erasure around the genitals is interpreted as ambivalence or conflict about one's sexuality. Such interpretations must be made cautiously and must be understood in the context of the person's own experiences. Let us leave these symbolic interpretations and consider the theoretical significance of this self-drawing.

A camera is an objective, disinterested recorder of what is there, though it is used by a photographer who selects what will be included, what will be excluded, and what will occupy the foreground. The camera itself does not emphasize one feature over another; it does not sketch a face in more detail than feet. For the camera, all parts of the body are equal. One's own perception of the body does, however, select out, emphasize, highlight, and omit. To draw a so-called "objective" self-portrait, following the laws of visual perspective and proportion, is actually a difficult achievement realized only by a few after much discipline. Notably, those parts of the body that play a central part in one's dealings with the surrounding world—for example, hands, eyes, and mouth—are often larger in one's body image. The parts of one's body that are important in qualifying one as attractive in social relationships, such as a woman's figure, hair, and facial features, also often have a special prominence in the body image. A bodily stigma that disqualifies one as unattractive also has prominence; it may be left out entirely or given a central place beyond its visibility for others, depending on the individual's way of coping with the stigma. Scars, acne, obesity, and congenitally deformed limbs are examples of such stigmata.

The picture one has of one's own body, then, is not based on a passive visual perception of "what is there." Rather, the picture is built up around those parts of the body that have a special relation to the world of things and of other people. This priority of the activity and functioning of the body in shaping the body image is also evident in children's drawings, which select out the parts of the body important in the child's experience—for example, a head, eyes, or arms. The configuration of a child's drawings often makes sense only in terms of the child's experience of the activity. Many early scribbles are gestural representations of motion and not just poor attempts at "pictures" (Gardner, 1980; Winner, 1986, pp. 25–27). Later, children frequently draw arms and hands coming out of the face (Linn, 1955). This appears to reflect the young child's experiential sequence—"I reach to put into the mouth"; the reach of the arm is an extension of the mouth. Only later in the child's development does the picture come to resemble an objective visual reproduction. Even then, seemingly "objective" perception is affected by developmental and "subjective" factors. For example, Mueller, Heesacker, and Ross (1984) showed that research subjects with a more developed image of their own body also performed better on a face recognition task. The commonsense viewpoint, which believes that the objectively accurate picture comes first, is thus topsy-turvy.

Let us return to the phenomenological understanding of the body. The human being makes a radical distinction between "*my own body*" and all other objects. Consequently, the present chapter will rely extensively on first person pronouns (*I, me, mine*) in referring to the individual's experience of "my own body," and to the experience of being physically rooted in "my" situation and "my" world, in the belief that this uniquely personal perspective is central to illuminating the psychology of the body and body image.

My own body does not present itself as an object completely accessible to my perception. It is, at the same time, the only thing that is always with me, and the only thing I never encounter in the world before me.

Unlike all other objects, my body is also something I *live* and only secondarily *know*. I act through it, exist through it, perceive the world and others through it, without explicitly reflecting on the body. Thus my body, as I live it, inhabits the prereflective realm of the human *lifeworld* and not the objective world that exists for scientific knowledge. We make a strict distinction here, between the objective body as the object of external observation and of laboratory scrutiny and my own body as I experience it, animate it, and live it. It is one's *own body* that phenomenological psychology calls the *lived body*. It is a body integrated into human life and expressive of character; it is the "living envelope of our actions" (Merleau-Ponty, 1963, p. 188).

The phenomenological perspective turns the commonsense viewpoint upside down. The commonsense viewpoint assumes that one starts out with an objective picture and then distorts it by adding subjective elements. The phenomenological view holds that the prereflective familiarity with the lived body and with a network of possible actions in one's world comes first, and the objective picture is later built up on this prereflective foundation. What, then, can this new viewpoint mean for the psychological understanding of the body?

A summary look at the fields of contemporary neurology and neuropsychology, fields within which the concept of body image has matured, may clarify what is meant. In these fields, we will discover concepts of body, human action, perception, and world much more sophisticated and adequate than those prevailing in the mainstream of academic psychology. We will discover also that these more sophisticated concepts require the new view of body image introduced here.

EVOLUTION OF NEUROLOGICAL AND BODY IMAGE CONCEPTS

The origins of the body image concept lie in the field of neurology. Neurologists developed the concept of "body schema" to account for the operational organization of the orientation and movements of the various body parts and organs in space and the parallel concept of the "body image" to account for the experiential, conscious sense of one's body as a unity. The understanding of what is implied by body image has evolved along with the rest of the field of neurology. The development of neurological concepts went through several phases: strict localization theories, integration and "Gestalt" theories, and theories of fluid and dynamic structures.

Strict Localization Theories

In the beginning of this century, crude, albeit elaborate, anatomical localization theories were commonplace. Global faculties of mind, not subject to further analysis, were understood to be mysteriously located in discrete areas of the brain. In the extreme, this meant that one spoke not only of general areas such as speech and vision but even of specific locales for discrete abilities such as "ideas of number," the "understanding of words and phrases," and even the "personal and social ego."

Figure 2 shows a localization chart from the German psychiatrist Kleist (1934; reproduced in Luria, 1973, p. 24) that illustrates the extreme form of such localization theories, prevalent as late as the 1930s and 1940s. These theories assumed that "for every mental act there was a neural element, either identical with it or in exact correspondence" (Head, 1926, p. 65).

These early neurologists utilized analysis into elements as their instrument, and they "fell into the subtle error of assuming that the elements reached by analysis could be treated as independent entities which had entered into combination" (Head, 1926, p. 66). That is, the individual human was analyzed as a series of separate faculties or abilities, and a *parallel* localization in the brain was charted as the basis for each. This attempt to analyze the person into elemental parts may be called "mental atomism" because an effort is made to discover the mental atoms out of which the person is built. Each mental atom is treated as if it were independent of the others. Thus the ability to read and the perception of space would be separate mental atoms—to be studied separately. The

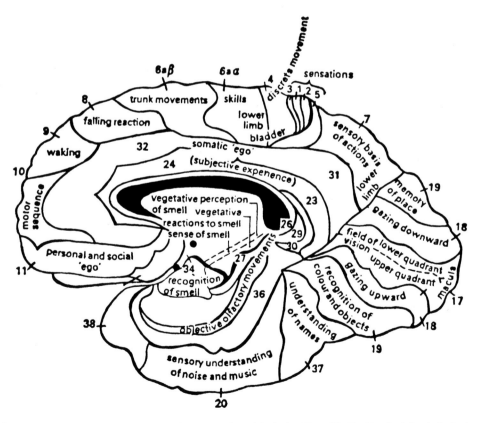

Figure 2. Kleist's localization chart: Medial representation of the brain. (From *The Working Brain* by A. R. Luria. Copyright 1973 by Penguin Press.)

tendency in psychology to study one function in isolation reflects this "atomistic" bias. Luria (1966) points out that, although clinical study of brain injuries and the resultant symptoms were utilized in drawing such map of the brain, the *parallelistic* concept involved is hardly distinguishable from the medieval teaching of the three ventricles of the brain as the sites of the three faculties of mind.

In accordance with this localization theory in neurology and with the mental atomism that is the corresponding psychological theory, body image was first understood as no more than the collection of a number of visual, tactile, and kinesthetic sensations of the body.[1] Body image development was thought, therefore, to be an increase in associations among these already existent and discrete sensations (Merleau-Ponty, 1962, p. 99).

Integration and "Gestalt" Theories

Neither this localization theory in neurology nor the corresponding notion of body image as a collection of discrete sensations provided an adequate basis for understanding the abnormal phenomena—often the consequences of brain injury—that have been scrutinized by modern neurology. A new notion of body image and body schema developed that described them as a *Gestalt*,[2] or structure, that serves to coordinate and organize both the functioning of various organs and body parts and our awareness of these organs and their functions.

Henry Head (1926), an eminent British neurologist, pointed out that when a human being moves about, the *afferent* nerve processes[3] cannot even evoke a perception of the movement until the incoming nerve processes are integrated into the structural body schema:

> By means of perpetual alterations in position, we are always building up a new postural model of ourselves which constantly changes. Every new posture of movement is recorded on this plastic schema, and the activity of the cortex brings each fresh group of sensations

evoked by altered posture into relation with it. (Head, 1926, p. 605)

Thus each movement is registered anew on an ever-adapting schema of our place in space, just as "on a taxi-meter the distance we have travelled is presented to us as already translated into schillings and pence" (Head, 1926, p. 488).

When this process of integration into a "body schema" does not occur, the individual's awareness of his or her movement is missing, and the coordination of the movement also breaks down. More recent research has supported this view and brought into prominence the role of the explicit image the individual has of his or her body. For example, after the amputation of a limb, the tactile sensitivity of the remaining portion of the limb varies according to *how the individual pictures the stump* (Haber, 1955). As the individual alters the way he or she pictures the limb, the distribution of sensitivity in the limb is reorganized. This discovery revised the previous understanding of body image. There is not first an objective body sensation passively received by the brain, and only then an effort to associate various sensations. Rather, the initial reception of "messages" from the body already takes place through the central organization of the person's body image.

A different understanding of the brain's involvement in psychological functioning also emerges from the emphasis on the total structure of an activity. Neurologists noticed that after an injury to the brain, the individual almost never lost one function entirely. Rather, many structurally related functions were usually partially impaired. In many cases, the activity—be it writing, reading, or conversation—could still be performed, but the *structure* of the activity was altered. The patient might still read but would go about reading differently. For example, the patient might find that he or she could only understand the text when reading aloud. There is not a single "ability to read" that is affected; it is rather one component of reading, which involves the interpretation of what is visually perceived, that is impaired. Some new method for reading is substituted that involves auditory and not visual comprehension.

Other activities drawing on the same component (visual comprehension) will be similarly affected in their total structures. To discuss such findings, neurologists drew on the work of Hughlings Jackson, a nineteenth-century neurologist far ahead of his time (Luria, 1973, p. 25). They came to speak not merely of the presence or absence of a function due to the intactness or impairment of a specific brain locale but rather of the structural disintegration of a function, or of the reorganization of a func-

---

[1]*Kinesthetic.* Having to do with the perception or awareness of muscular state or muscular movement.

[2]*Gestalt* is the German term for configuration, structure, or organization. The Gestalt school for psychology, having a theoretical viewpoint similar in many respects to that of phenomenology, emphasizes the total organization of mental processes, and not just the component parts.

[3]*Afferent* nerve processes carry nerve impulses from the sense receptors inward to the brain; they are also called *sensory* nerve processes. *Efferent* nerve processes carry excitations from the central nervous system outward to the peripheral *effectors* (muscles or glands); they are frequently called *motor* nerve processes.

tion, or of the descent of a function to a more primitive structural level (Luria, 1966).

Body Image: A Fluid and Dynamic Structure

A further refinement of the concept of body image came with the recognition that the individual does not have one single static image of his or her body. Rather, the body image is continuously in process of revision, being shaped according to the current situation of the individual (Head, 1926; Schilder, 1950). We introduce a factor central to the phenomenological understanding of body image when we emphasize that this continuous process of body image formation occurs through the individual's activity directed toward a personal world: "There is no doubt that this process of structuralization is only possible in close contact with experiences concerning the world" (Schilder, 1950, p. 113). Van der Velde (1985) has taken this concept farther to show that each individual develops innumerable body images, as products of various roles of the body within interpersonal relationships, and that these body images serve as "fundamental dynamisms" in the ongoing formation of self-concept.

The Neuropsychology of A. R. Luria

Up to this point, we have reviewed the evolution of neurological notions of neural organization and body image in a schematic and general way. However, A. R. Luria, a figure in contemporary Russian neurology, has evolved a sophisticated notion of neural and behavioral integration. Presentation of his position will lay a foundation for the remainder of this chapter.

A specific understanding of body image and body schema may be derived from Luria's position. Luria (1973) introduced several concepts to revise neurological theory. First, Luria clarified the notion of localization. He rejected the simplistic notion that each psychological function is located in a single, specific brain tissue—the *strict* localization theory, and he put forth instead a theory of *dynamic* localization. The various zones of the brain are specialized in their operations, and specific zones are crucial for certain psychological functions such as speech or visual perception. However, these zones do not function in isolation from one another. No single zone is capable on its own of supporting a human activity. For any single human activity, many zones of the brain join together as component parts of "*a complex functional system.*" This functional system has a *complex total structure* in its operation, and each zone of the brain

involved contributes to supporting some aspect of this total structure.

This complex functional system is characterized by a relative *mobility of component parts.* For example, all of the same zones of the brain are not involved each time a single human activity such as walking, writing, or talking is performed. Walking does not involve the same overt movements of the body on a sidewalk as it does on mountainous terrain; nor are the zones of the brain involved strictly identical. Study of the victims of brain injury and laboratory experiments with animals have demonstrated the capacity of the brain to reorganize its functioning (Luria, 1973). Should one zone contributing to an activity be injured, another zone may take its place, consequently altering the total structure of the activity. Thus there is no fixed chain of neural responses in the brain or motor responses in the body that is waiting to be triggered off whenever the same action is elicited. Rather, there is a complex and dynamic process by which various "working zones of the brain" are integrated into a functional system to facilitate the action demanded by the current situation. This ongoing process of integration presupposes the *continuous orientation of the body to the situation of the individual.* This is the work of body image and body schema.

According to Luria's viewpoint, higher mental processes are recognized to be *formed in a long process of historical development.* Neither the neurological nor the psychological structure of these processes is constant from the beginning of our development. The anatomical brain is a flexible organ, subject to continuous revision in its functional organization. It operates not according to reaction patterns fixed from birth but according to patterns of integration that are established in the course of individual and historical development.

The higher mental processes are also recognized to be *social in origin.* External aids, or historically originated devices, such as language, the digital counting system, or the multiplication table "are recognized as essential elements in the establishment of functional connections between individual parts of the brain" (Luria, 1973, p. 31). In other words, such external aids serve to unite various zones located in completely different and often distant areas of the brain into a single functional system in order to perform some action. As Luria (1973) put it, "historically formed measures for the organization of the brain tie new knots in the activity of man's brain" (p. 31). This principle discredits attempts to reduce all cultural, social, and intellectual achievements to brain and physiological activity. It recognizes that social forms, historically arrived at operations, and linguistic structures are appropriated by the individual. Once appropriated, they serve to bring independent areas of the brain, not contiguous to one another, into single functional systems. There is thus a strict dependence of neurological functioning on historically and socially formed structures.

Luria's colleague, Lev Vygotsky (1978), called these external forms "psychological tools." He investigated how the child and even the adult, in the course of development, take over such "tools" from the social milieu, internalize them, and utilize them as the foundations for the higher mental processes. The neuropsychology of Luria and Vygotsky is thus a cultural psychology: "Every function in the child's cultural development appears twice: First, on the social level, and later, on the individual level; first, *between* people, and then *inside* the child" (Vygotsky, 1978, p. 57).

Vygotsky and another Russian psychologist, Leontiev, developed a concept of "activity" as "object-oriented" that parallels in many respects the phenomenological understanding of "intentionality" (Kozulin, 1986; Leontiev, 1978). The direction, motive, and organization of any activity are determined by the specific nature and meaning of its object. This understanding of activity also served as the basis for a structural theory of consciousness (Vygotsky, 1979).

We cannot go into great detail on the kinds of historically and socially formed structures that serve to organize human activity and the activity of the brain. Consider one example: Every language selects a narrow range of actual sounds from the range of vocal sounds available and organizes them along recurrent patterns into meaningful configurations. Without a lengthy introduction into the complex, historically originated structure of a given language, we cannot even *hear* the sounds that are utilized. An American cannot hear the intonations that are crucial in determining the meaning of a Chinese verbal expression. The structure of speech activity depends not only on the zones of the brain that are involved but also on the phonemic and syntactic systems of a given language.

A study of neurology, according to Luria, then, does not tell the full story of our mental life. The structure of human mental activity is supported on the one side by the working zones of the brain within and on the other by external forms, which are appropriated from the society in the surrounding world. Should either side be undermined, by brain damage on the one side or by ignorance of external form on the other, the activity would collapse. A qualitative change on the one side necessitates a change on the other side as well (for example, the neuropsychological disposition adequate to learning one's own language as a child is inadequate to scholarly study of ancient Hebrew).

In accordance with his new understanding, Luria was able to speak of a theory of *dynamic localization.* Localization is neither static nor constant. Rather, it "moves about essentially during development of the child and at subsequent stages of training" (Luria, 1973, p. 31). Behaviorally, writing is a structurally different activity when the adult casually signs a signature than it is when the child laboriously copies over letters one at a time. What begins as a choppy and poorly integrated chain of isolated motor impulses becomes what Luria calls a single *kinetic melody.* (Chapter 1 introduced the phenomenological concept of the *structure* of a particular phenomenon by a comparison to a musical melody. Here we discover the same idea of melody applied to human movement.) "In the course of such development, it is not only the functional structure of the process which changes, but also, naturally, its cerebral organization" (Luria, 1973, p. 32). In the higher mental processes, an "*interfunctional organization*" also occurs, as tasks once elementary in structure are performed with the close participation of higher forms of activity. Whereas damage to areas of the visual cortex in the child leads to underdevelopment of higher zones involved in visual thinking, "a lesion of these same zones in the adult can cause only partial defects of visual analysis and synthesis, and leaves the more complex forms of thinking, formed at an earlier stage, unaffected" (Luria, 1973, p. 33).

In order to illustrate his concepts, Luria discussed the neurological disorder of *apraxia* (an inability to make purposeful movements due to brain injury). The ability to make purposeful movements relies on several "working zones of the brain" acting in unison. Depending on the zone that is injured, the structure of movement is affected differently. An injury to one area (called the postcentral cortex) results in an inability to place the hand in the proper position for movement. When another area (the basal ganglia or the premotor cortex) is injured, there is a lack of smooth consecutive organization of the various hand motions into one "kinetic melody." Damage to different areas affects the structure of the activity in other ways. Thus each concertedly working zone in the brain makes "its own contribution to the performance of the movement and supplies its own factor to the structure. Complex manipulation of objects can thus be disturbed by lesions of various cortical areas (or subcortical structures); however, in each case it is disturbed differently" (Luria, 1973, p. 38).

Luria gives further examples to show how an understanding of the neuropsychological organization of behaviors—demonstrated by the effect of dysfunction of various cortical areas on different behaviors—contributes to understanding the "internal composition" of psychological processes. "Apparently identical psychological processes can be distinguished, and different forms of mental activity can be reconciled'' (Luria, 1973, p. 41).

For example, when a hemorrhage occurs in the left temporal area, the disparate structure of musical hearing and speech hearing is revealed by the selective deterioration of speech hearing, whereas musical hearing and composition are unimpaired. In another example, a lesion to the left parieto-occipital region of the cortex results in the simultaneous impairment of such apparently disparate activities as spatial orientation, arithmetical calculation, and the understanding of complex logico-grammatical structures. This simultaneous impairment reveals a commonality of structure. Thus an insight into the cerebral organization of an activity may also lead us to a more differentiated understanding of the qualitative structure of a behavior.

Luria's Structuralism and Phenomenological Psychology

In this presentation of Luria's position on neuropsychology, we may note that one central principle is common to both his position and the phenomenological position—the emphasis on the "internal composition" or *structure* of psychological processes. Luria's structural perspective in neurology requires as its complement a structural approach to psychology. As Merleau-Ponty (1963) has shown, the psychological level of human experience and behavior reveals a richness of organization that parallels but surpasses the more primitive organization evident at the levels of reflex formation or neurologic function: The challenge of phenomenological psychology is to explore that higher level organization of psychological life.

Several other conclusions also follow from Luria's work. Human mental activity is social and historical in origin and has a structural organization distinguishing it from animal behavior (Luria, 1966, p. 21). This also represents a phenomenological position. Further, Luria's research shows that we are dealing not with immaterial "faculties of mind" linked to discrete brain tissues but rather with complex and dynamic functional systems both at the behavioral and neural levels (Luria, 1966). The role of social and linguistic forms in organizing neural activity means that physiology is only fully comprehensible in the context of psychological, sociological, biographical, and linguistic perspectives. Bodily processes are structured along lines shaped socially and biographically.

For these reasons, we deny that anatomy determines or causes behavior in a linear fashion. Ultimately, Luria's view returns us to the examination of: (a) concrete behaviors, (b) the matrix of everyday life events, and (c) individual and social history. Although neuropsychology may indicate the crucial importance of these factors for understanding human mental activity, the exploration of these factors is outside the scope of neuropsychology. A phenomenological psychology is necessary to complete the picture.

Phenomenological psychology emphasizes the *total structure of our activity and experience*. It also discloses the structural interdependence between: (a) the individual's lived body and its surrounding place, (b) the individual's actions and experiences, and (c) those actions and the organization of the personal world. These themes, which we will explore later in this chapter, complement the principles of neurological functioning introduced in the present section. Phenomenology, however, focuses its study on concrete, meaningful experiences in everyday life and not on the functioning of the nervous system. The points of view of neuropsychology and phenomenology diverge greatly; the structural understandings that result are both compatible and complementary.

Neural Functioning and the Body Schema

Each of the conclusions we have reached concerning neural function applies as well to the body schema. This schema is one further instance of a dynamic functional system. Luria (1973) has also made the following specific remarks on the neuropsychology of the body schema, referring particularly to Hughlings Jackson.

In 1874, Hughlings Jackson "postulated that the right hemisphere, although unconnected with speech functions or with logical forms of organization of consciousness dependent on speech, participates directly in perceptual processes and is responsible for more direct visual forms of relationship with the outside world" (Luria, 1973, p. 165). The right hemisphere is also concerned with analysis of information received from one's own body, and is "more closely connected with direct sensation than with verbally logical codes" (Luria, 1973, p. 165). Lesions of the right hemisphere lead seven times more frequently than lesions of the left to disturbances of the body schema. It is this kind of lesion to the posterior or midzones of the right hemisphere that is involved in "left-sided hemianopia" or inattention to the left side of the body.

In many cases, these disturbances are accompanied by a true disturbance of the body image in which the proportion of various parts of the body to one another in perception is distorted. These disturbances extend also to the individual's orientation in space. Familiar spatial relationships become strange. Even the individual's recognition of objects and of people may be disturbed. These "gnostic disturbances" associated with injury to the right hemisphere are "characterized by a much less marked modal specificity and they are much more frequently global and polysensory in character'' (Luria, 1973, p. 167) (see Sperry, 1966, Gazzaniga, 1970, and Blakeslee, 1983, for discussion of more recent findings corroborating the significance of the right hemisphere of the brain).

Luria (1973) makes the reservation that the most important function of the right hemisphere is the ''general perception by the patient of his own body and his own personality'' (p. 167). A corollary to Luria's statement is the observation that, indeed, psychologically as well as neurologically, the individual's perception of his or her body and personality are intrinsically bound up with orientation in space, the direct experience of one's own body, and the potential movement of the body in space. The perception of body and self is the perception of a web of relations to the world and a web of possible actions. Each of these processes of orientation, perception, and behavior is marked by the global and polysensory character Luria has described. They also involve in each case the operation of dynamic functional systems.

Once again we find here a neurological confirmation for the phenomenological principle of the structural interdependence of behavior, perception, and orientation in space, yet traditional psychology often attempts to separate these phenomena from one another and study them in isolation.

THE PHENOMENOLOGY OF THE BODY

In the last section, we reviewed the development of neurological theory from the strict localization theories through the more complex viewpoint of Luria. According to Luria, the total structure of behavior must be comprehended, and this total structure depends on a complex integration of many working zones of the brain. This integration takes place with the help of social, historical, and linguistic forms as ''the basis for the construction of new and more complex behavioral processes, which would be impossible without it'' (Luria, 1966, p. 56).

Having broadened our understanding of the role of the brain and physiology in human activity, we may now return to the phenomenological theory of the lived body and present it more fully. In doing so, we are not looking for a way to refute such theories as that of Luria. Rather, we are undertaking the more direct exploration of the meaningful structures of human action and experience that the most advanced neurological theories call for. Generally, in neuropsychology, ''structure'' connotes the organization observable in neural and mental processes; in phenomenology, ''structure'' connotes the prereflective organization of the individual's activity, as he or she lives it. Phenomenology emphasizes that the orga-

nization of our mental life is meaningful and explicable in the context of the individual's situation. The two connotations of structure overlap and share a basic emphasis on the organization and interrelation of the parts within any total activity.

Karl Pribram (1960), the American neuropsychologist, has also spoken of the necessity of taking into account the ''experiential components'' and the ''situational determinants'' that contribute to the final structure of behavior. Further, Pribram (1971) has defended the inclusion of the individual's ''awareness'' in psychological research, the use of ''mental language,'' and the need for a wider base of data than the ''neurohumoral.'' He also warned of the ''danger that a range of problems is ignored if the focus of inquiry is purely behavioristic'' (1971, p. 104). We are proceeding, then, from the contemporary recognition by neuropsychologists that we need a structural understanding of the human being at the psychological level of behaving and experiencing in order to complement the structural concepts of modern neuropsychology. The phenomenology of the lived body and its unique surrounding space provides a complementary understanding.

The Body and Human "Lived Space"

Paul Schilder (1933) has pointed out that the space around the body image is different from the space of physics. The space of physics has to do with the objective *position* of an object in a mathematically charted space. My own body's spatiality has to do with specific human *situations,* and with attitudes and actions I may take up toward these situations. Just as phenomenology speaks of a *lived body* (or ''corporeality''), so, too, it speaks of *lived space* (or ''spatiality''), which is this space of human action lying all about us. The space of physics is a reflectively *known* space—the space known by natural science and mathematics. Human space is *prereflective,* which means that we move about in it, orient ourselves in it, experience it, and live it before even thinking about it. We falsify human action and experience when we treat them theoretically as if they occurred in and are determined by the objective physical setting. If we wish to comprehend an individual's actions, we must comprehend this space about the person—as he or she experiences it.

The dimensions of human ''lived space'' are not the three Cartesian dimensions that are absolutely equivalent with each other—the dimensions x, y, and z graphed in a high-school geometry class. Rather, they are functional and meaningful dimensions of human action; each dimension has its specific character with respect to our biological and psychological being. ''Up and down'' and ''forward and backward'' constitute dimensions in human lived space that are not the same as the vertical and horizontal dimensions in objective space. To be ''high'' or ''low,'' to ''come up in the world,'' to be ''upright,'' to ''fall behind,'' or to be ''ahead of oneself'' all have their specific significance in human lived space.

Erwin Straus (1982) emphasized that both the biological space of animals and human lived space are not homogeneous as is the known space of physics: ''Animal and human locomotion are significant only in relation to non-homogeneous space, in which the goods of life are unevenly distributed'' (p. 150). In terms of our everyday experience, this nonhomogeneity means that for the hungry individual, the 20 feet to the refrigerator are meaningful in a way that the 20 feet in the opposite direction are not. For the thirsty man in the desert, the 20 square feet on which a freshwater spring stands are of more value in that moment than the 20 square miles around it. In these examples, we see the nonhomogeneous nature of the lived space around the individual. We also see that *lived space is organized around human activities and the places or objects that are their targets.*

Lived space is the space toward which we are oriented in a tangible, bodily way. Just as the lived body is a body disposed to possible actions, the lived space about that body is an organized network of routes, pathways, and obstacles to those actions. It is not the space of geometry, full of points charted against a three-dimensional system: It is, rather, a human space full of hospitable oases and dangers to be circumnavigated; of familiar settings and alien territory; and of points of departure and destination. In each moment, before we think about what we are about to do, we discover that we are oriented toward some destination with our body.

For example, when we are saying goodbye to someone after a visit, we often discover ourselves reaching for the doorknob as though to leave, before we have finished saying our goodbyes. With our bodies, we are oriented toward immediate departure, before we have reflectively recognized our impatience to leave. We also become apprehensive in our bodies in the face of a threat, breathing rapidly and shallowly, before we reflectively consider what constitutes the threat. We move through lived space in the way a football player navigates the field, moving spontaneously toward openings and sidestepping opponents, before he ever has a chance to rationally calculate what he is about to do.

You will notice that the words we use here to discuss the organization of lived space—words such as *destination, opening, threat, danger,* and *oasis*—refer to some actual or possible human action. Without reference to human action, such words are meaningless. What is a destination with a journey? It is only through human ac-

tion that the organization of lived space is constituted. When we understand the lived body as essentially the *potential for certain actions,* we understand the *intimate relation between the lived body and the lived space around it.*

Motility and Perception

Another manner of understanding the spatiality of the body is to turn to the relation between motility[4] and perception. *Perception* is a term largely dropped out of the modern behavioristic stimulus–response (S-R) schema. According to the behavioristic view, the external stimulus conditions or causes the behavioral response. One speaks of sense receptors, but these are viewed as *passive* receptors merely registering the independently existing stimulus. The individual is seen as having *no active control* over this process.

In opposition to this, the unequivocal primacy of perception is a recurrent theme in Merleau-Ponty's phenomenology. This primacy is the necessary consequence of the discovery by neuropsychology of the *circular relationship between perception and motility.* ''Every perception is connected with an attitude and every perception has its motility'' (Schilder, 1950, p. 34). The stimulus–response schema is based on an outmoded view of nerve operations. We now know that the sensory receptors and afferent (incoming) nerve processes are under efferent (outgoing) control from the central nervous system. In other words, our senses are not entirely passive; the individual exercises an active control in selecting what the senses receive. This shift in our view of nerve processes is important because along with it there is a new view of the active role of the animal and human organism in shaping its own effective environment:

> The shift is from the notion that an organism is a relatively passive protoplasmic mass whose responses are controlled by the arrangement of environmental stimuli to a conception of an organism that has considerable control over what will constitute stimulation. (Pribram, 1960, p. 4)

Once again we are discovering an intimate unity between two processes that are usually separated by traditional psychology. Perception and action are usually studied in isolation from one another. Yet both neurologically and at the level of human action in lived space, we discover that they are intertwined.

The German neurologist, Viktor von Weizsäcker (1973), introduced the concept of the *Gestaltkreis* (*Gestalt* circle) to describe this circular involvement of per-

---

[4]*Motility* is a psychological and physiological term for any movement or activity on the part of an organism.

ception and action and to illuminate the intimate rapport between the human subject and the environment. To be underway in some action is to organize our perception toward some object, and inversely, to perceive a situation in the world is to be invited into active involvement in that situation. With every step forward, our view of the situation is adjusted; with every adjustment in our view, we are invited to step forward anew.

Merleau-Ponty (1963, pp. 209–211) has called this continuous interplay between subject and world a *dialectic*. In this dialectic between person and world, it is difficult to distinguish strictly between perception and action:

> The plunge into action is, from the subject's point of view, an original way of relating himself to the object, and is on the same footing as perception. (Merleau-Ponty, 1962, p. 110)

The body schema is a fluid and dynamic process by which the whole organism is oriented and directed toward the world. Neurologically, afferent and efferent impulses are integrated within a "dynamic functional system" (Luria, 1973). Psychologically, the body schema entails both an ongoing process of perception and a continuous disposition to action.

Body Schema and World

Our discussion of lived space and of the circular relation of motility and perception leads us into a third area. Heinz Werner (Wapner & Werner, 1965) has pointed out the "interdependence of the structure of the body self and the structure of one's environment" and the interdependence of the "characteristics of the person as a bodily entity and the characteristics of the world around him" (p. 6). Once again, we are departing from the behavioristic view of an independently existing stimulus causing the behavior of an organism in isolation. Rather, we highlight here the circular relation between the individual and the world. This concept of circularity once again reiterates a central theme of phenomenological psychology. The human being is never separate from the world. They are in a constant dialogue with each other. The human being is partly active—shaping the world—and partly passive—being shaped by the world. The human being and the world "co-constitute" each other.

For the physicist there is one world, objectively given and identical no matter who studies it. For phenomenological psychology, there is a *world for each embodied organism*—a world formed by the organism's bodily attitude and activity toward its world. The body, in this sense, is a system of possible movements that radiates from the organism to its environment. To use a previous example, the hungry body organizes about itself a world

in which the routes or pathways to obtaining nourishment have a particular prominence. In fact, as research on eating behavior has shown, an individual for whom the pathway to the kitchen has a special prominence *is hungry*—even if the stomach is physiologically satiated (1971). The body in action is the means by which the individual takes hold upon space as a field of action and shapes for him- or herself a personal world. It is this intimate behavioral bond between body and world that phenomenology calls *embodied-being-in-the-world*.

The personal world for each individual is an extended, more global version of the lived space he or she experiences in each moment. The personal world is the *organized totality of the situations and regions of one's life*. When we encounter one human being, we are coming into contact with a being whose actions and experiences all occur within a personal world. These actions and experiences have meaning for the person only in relation to this world. We said earlier that we must comprehend the lived space around the individual, if we wish to comprehend his or her actions. So, too, we must come to understand the *meaningful organizations of the individual's personal world,* if we are to understand who the individual is, for him- or herself and for others. To explore this personal world is to confront continually the role of the *lived body* in organizing the personal world.

The "Mineness" of the Body

In the past three sections, we have elaborated on the phenomenological theory of the body. Let us turn now to the advantages of this phenomenological viewpoint by examining certain privileged human phenomena that traditional psychology overlooks because it finds them difficult to comprehend. The individual's experience that this body is "*my own*" body is one such phenomenon. From a behavioristic or a strict physiological perspective, this "mineness" of the body is a subjective quality to be excluded from scientific scrutiny. Let us look more closely at this phenomenon.

Erwin Straus (Straus, 1967; Straus & Griffith, 1967), in criticizing typical understandings of body image, emphasized that the human lived body is never experienced anonymously as *the* body, but rather as *mine,* as *my own* body with a kind of intimacy exceeding by far the mineness of property that one might dispose of. He regarded this experience that the body is mine as of fundamental importance; for Straus (1966), this possessive experience marks the transition from biology to true psychology (p. 150). Further, Straus (1966) believed that "the experience of the body as mine is the origin of possessive experience. All other connotations of possessive relations are derived from it" (p. 151).

Yet the "mineness" of the body is an achievement and not a given, something established in the course of child development, easily undermined by later events (Schilder, 1950). Straus, too, showed that in pain or physical illness, one's own body is alienated from oneself. The patient experiences disease as a foreign power or entity within, attacking and overpowering him or her (Straus, 1969, pp. 45–47).[5]

In many forms of psychopathology, this owning of the body and its parts as "my own" is greatly disrupted. In standard psychiatric terminology, this pathological phenomenon is called *depersonalization*. Aspects of the body are disowned—as are the regions of the world and of experience to which they are functionally related. The mineness of the body presumes a cultural and biographical history of construction and integration of the body and a conventional and plastic establishment of boundaries between what is *mine* and what is *other*. Depersonalization of the body, common, for example, in obese persons, merely carries the original process of differentiation and warding off of "external reality" to an untenable extreme, untenable because the not-me body refuses to stay behind as the individual attempts to disown it and leave it behind.

In research with medical patients who are so obese as to be incapacitated and immobilized, one frequently encounters this phenomenon of depersonalization (Moss, 1982, 1984). Earlier it was said that the human lived body is unlike all other objects in the world. Yet the obese individual who depersonalizes his or her body views it precisely as a brute object and uses impersonal, third-person language for the body: "it," "this body," "that thing," or "this stuff I am trucking around." This is a sign of a severe disorder in self-world relations because, as we have said, when part of the body is depersonalized and disowned, the same happens to functionally related regions of the world.

When obese patients draw pictures of themselves, they often focus on the facial features and hair while only sketchily drawing a torso. Arms and legs, hands and feet, the organs by which we take a stand and act on the world, are often missing entirely or are incomplete. This emphasis on the head and lack of emphasis on the body is called a "head/body split." Examples of drawings by obese patients are included in Figures 3 to 6. Figures 3, 4, and 5

Figure 3. Self-drawing by obese adult woman.

show an emphasis on facial features with arms and legs incomplete. Figure 6, also by an obese patient, reveals a severe underdevelopment in the entire body image. Figure 7, by a nonobese adult, and 8, by a nonobese 9-year-old child, are provided for contrast.

In these drawings, notice the variations in emphasis on diverse parts of the body. The lines in the figures vary in darkness, thickness, and sketchiness. Even the *size* of the figures and their position within the page varies. Each of these factors is given a significance by the clinical psychologist in his or her interpretations. For example, one often finds that an individual who hesitantly and reluctantly lingers around the edge of a social setting, such as a party, will also draw himself or herself reluctantly as a tiny presence up in the left-hand corner of the page.

The "head/body split" in a self-drawing often corresponds to a head/body split in everyday life. For example, one woman reports that "from here up" (the neck up) she is valuable, competent, and a real human being, whereas "from here down" (the rest of her body) she feels disgusting, useless, and even less than human. *To this division in her body corresponds a split in her world!* There are "head areas"—professional activity where her

---

[5]*Body image and illness.* How a person images his or her body has practical consequences for health and well-being documented by medical and psychological research. (See the following sources for a sampling of this research: Fisher & Cleveland, 1968; Simonton & Mathews-Simonton, 1975; Simonton, Mathews-Simonton, & Creighton, 1980; Freeman, Beach, Davis, & Solyom, 1984; Weathers & Billingsley, 1982; and Sands, 1982.)

Figure 4. Self-drawing by obese adult woman.

directly examined. Consider these examples: We must ask, for example, how it is that the bodily alterations undergone in illness or surgery occasionally lead an individual to remark, "I'm a different person than I was before." Almost everyone has had the experience occasionally of awakening to find oneself sluggish, feverish, in pain, otherwise "not normal," and may have found oneself remarking, "I'm not myself today." We might dismiss this as merely a manner of speaking, by which the individual excuses any consequent inadequacies or unpleasantries in mood or behavior.

To dismiss such a remark too lightly, however, is to dismiss that whole realm of experience we label variously as *ego, self, subject,* or *person.* There are days when the "not-myself" experience is so intense that an individual really does not recognize "myself." What is the significance of personal tempo, favored familiar patterns, and mood such that human beings differentiate "myself" and "not myself"? Obese persons, sick persons, and surgery patients are just a few examples of people for whom these differences are intensely experienced as really *making a difference.*

Here again, in raising such a question, the indissolu-

"mind" is important to her and social activity where her "personality" is important. In these areas, she feels she is as competent as anyone else. She tells herself that her body is not relevant in such activities. Then, there are "body areas"—more physically involving activities such as heavy household work, everyday events such as climbing the stairs, and physically demanding sports. These areas, when she has not had to give them up entirely (sports), are areas of struggle, effort, and trial for her (household work, stairs). There are also regions of shame for her—areas where she is self-conscious about the visibility of her obese body for others, such as swimming and dancing.

When a part of the world has already become a region of futility, incapacity, or shame, that region is relinquished and the related parts of the body are often disowned as "not me" or as "that thing I am helplessly encased in." With this loss of a region of the world comes mourning, grieving, and tears. Here, we discover once again that intimate behavioral bonding of body and world.

In returning to this theme of the behavioral bond with the world, this phenomenon of *mineness* can be more

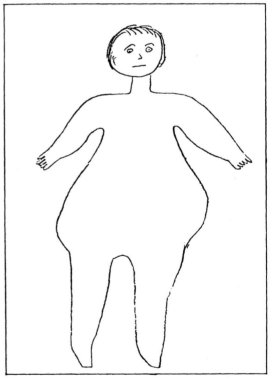

Figure 5. Self-drawing by obese adult woman.

Figure 6. Self-drawing by obese adult woman.

unexpected obstacle, or when the odors of percolating coffee and frying bacon do not lure one forth in the usual way but rather cause one to recoil and feel queasy in the stomach. This behavioral bonding of body and world provides the assurance—when nothing is "wrong"—of *being-myself-in-my-world.*

This bond between the way the human being lives his or her body and personal world can perhaps best be seen when some change is made in the objective body. When this change happens, there is a *lag* in the reorganization of these behavioral bonds with the world. A man with his leg newly amputated not only still feels that he has a leg, but he also still lives in a *world whose organization is based on his having his leg.* This is the "phantom limb" phenomenon that has been an object of argumentation in neurology for decades (Plügge, 1967, 1970). In discussing a double amputee with "phantom" legs, Schilder (1951) reports seeing him sit on a high chest. This amputee "did not realize that he did not have his two legs and jumped down and hurt himself badly" (1951, p. 54). His world was perceived in relation to the legs he no longer had; the distance from the chest was "jumpable" with the legs. The leap has nothing to do

ble unity of perception and motility—so falsified when questions of perception are only investigated using subjects seated immobilized in a chair—must be recognized. Traub and Orbach (1964) manufactured a mirror that distorted the reflection of the subject's body in various fashions. Subjects were seated in front of this mirror and asked to guess when the mirror accurately reflected the subject's own body. Traub and Orbach rightly concluded that this mirror was a useful instrument for the quantitative measurement of body image—just as the self-drawing technique does. Yet we must not forget that research while seated in a chair gives only a reflective, static picture of the dynamic, fluid process of body image formation while engaged in activity.

The sense of self or the alteration in the body must not be viewed in isolation; rather, these experiences must be reintegrated into the world that the body inhabits. To behave and feel differently is to be denied access to the familiar world and to be thrust into a strange world. To move around sluggishly with influenza is to inhabit something like a "world with the flu." One may recognize illness for the first time only when the stairs present themselves not as the usual path to breakfast but rather as an

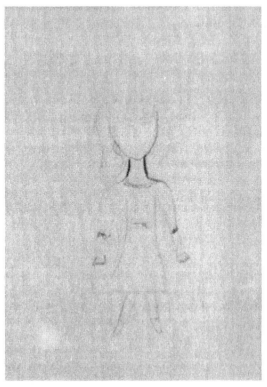

Figure 7. Self-drawing by nonobese adult woman.

Figure 8. Self-drawing by nonobese 9-year-old girl.

with the measurable distance of physical space. This man did not go through the calculations of a scientist before leaping. His action has to do, rather, with the lines of possible movements radiating out from the body to the world.

Consider this last example of a body image lag, based on obesity. When weight loss happens rapidly, as in medically managed starvation, there is often a *lag* in reorganizing the body schema and the world. Newly thin individuals often speak of having a "fat mind in a thin body"; they also occasionally speak of still living in a "fat man's world." Glucksman and Hirsch (1969) stated that one patient "reported that he continued to feel self-conscious about occupying most of the seat on a bus, even though he could easily share it with another passenger" (p. 369). Such patients often move about in an awkward way as though they still weighed 400 pounds. Their world is still perceived in terms of narrow places to be traversed, tight fits, and steep stairways even though their physical girth no longer requires such concern. A patient I interviewed after a period of weight loss reported finding herself several times sliding the carseat all the way back in order to get into the car. She then laboriously lifted her legs up into the car with her arms—one leg at a time. She

did this even after her reduced bulk no longer demanded the extra space and after her knees had become capable of lifting the weight of her legs without aid.

Let us review. It is not the objective, measurable body that constitutes the human world but rather the body as I live it, *my own* body engaged in action oriented to *my* world. This behavioral bonding of body and world takes place at a *prereflective* level. We have sought an understanding of this behavioral bonding of body and world through a series of abnormal examples because, in normal experiencing, the relation of my body to my world is taken for granted. It is lived and not known. The experience that this body is my own stands out most vividly against those cases where the body is experienced as *other,* as *not-me,* and as *disowned,* where my familiar, personal world is called into question. Phenomenological psychology provides a useful perspective for understanding such human psychological phenomena as depersonalization, body image, and identity that are so essential in our everyday existence because phenomenology does not isolate the subjective from the objective nor the feeling of "mineness" from the ongoing behavior in the world. Only by investigating both this crucial experience of "mineness" *and* the individual's activity in his or her world can these phenomena be understood. Natural–scientific psychology, when it separates out this or that aspect to study in isolation, transforms and truncates the phenomena before the research begins.

For phenomenological psychology, the question, *Who am I?,* is inseparable from the question, *What kind of world do I live in?* To be at home with myself is to be at home with my personal world. To be ill at ease with myself is to be ill at ease with this or that region of my personal world. This continuous, essential unity of the individual, the body, and the personal world is the basis for the concept of the human being as an *embodied-being-in-the-world.*

CONCLUSION

This chapter utilizes the topic of body image to introduce current concepts in a phenomenologically informed psychology of the body. Readers who wish to pursue study of body image in greater detail may consult several available texts. The most far-reaching technical exploration of body image to date remains that of Schilder (1950). The development of the concept of body image has been reviewed by Gerstmann (1958) and Kolb (1959). Fisher and Cleveland (1968) present a comprehensive review of the empirical research on body image. An anthology of articles on body image edited by Wapner and Werner (1965) is also helpful. Van der Velde (1985) summarizes and synthesizes more recent research. Finally, Merleau-Ponty (1962) and Plügge (1967, 1970) present rich, philosophically oriented investigations of body image from the phenomenological standpoint.

The phenomenological understanding of the body goes beyond the original concept of body image and beyond the concepts of modern neuropsychology to undertake a concrete exploration of the activity of the lived body and the structure of the human world. It is an attempt to transcend outdated, dualistic concepts of an objective physical body and a subjective mind existing in separation. The various concepts such as body image, body ego, and body concept emerged from a time of crisis in psychology in the early decades of our century, when the available concepts were inadequate to describe a phenomenon that had properties of both body and mind. Phenomenological psychology has pursued an understanding of the body, space, action, perception, and world that addresses this original dilemma.

What results is a dialectical viewpoint. The phenomenological idea of a behavioral bonding of body and world is useful throughout in understanding that *the* body image and *the* body schema do not exist as such. They are schematic ways we have of speaking about a fluid and dynamic dialogue doing on between body and world. The world about me presents me with an invitation—I respond. That invitation itself is only explicable in light of an original question my body has put to the world. We may turn back and forth and become dizzy in our turning, but we will not discover an absolute priority in either body or world. I am free to act in the face of my world; my freedom is shaped in turn by this world. There is neither absolute freedom nor an absolute and passive determinism. There is only the reality and life of a "situated freedom" (Merleau-Ponty, 1962). I am free in and through my situation. My body is, at the same time, the means by which I am free and the outside limit of my freedom. It is the only means by which I have a world and act on my world; it is as well the carrier of my mortality.

REFERENCES

Berger, P., & Luckmann, T. (1966). *The social construction of reality.* Garden City, NY: Doubleday.

Blakeslee, T. R. (1983). *The right brain.* New York: Berkley Books.

Feyerabend, P. (1978). *Against method.* London: Verso.

Fisher, S., & Cleveland, S. E. (1968). *Body image and personality.* New York: Dover.

Fliess, R. (1961). *Ego and body-ego: Contributions to their psychoanalytic psychology.* New York: Schulte Publishing.

Freeman, R. J., Beach, B., Davis, R., & Solyom, L. (1984). The prediction of relapse in bulimia nervosa. *Journal of Psychiatric Research, 19*(2–3), 349–353.

Gallup, G. G. (1977). Self-recognition in primates: A comparative approach to the bidirectional properties of consciousness. *American Psychologist, 32,* 329–338.

Gallup, G. G., McClure, M. K., Hill, S. D., & Bundy, R. A. (1971). Capacity for self-recognition in differentially reared chimpanzees. *Psychological Record, 21,* 69–74.

Gardner, H. (1980). *Artful scribbles: The significance of children's drawings.* New York: Basic Books.

Gazzaniga, M. (1970). *The bisected brain.* New York: Appleton-Century-Crofts.

Gergen, K. J. (1982). *Toward transformation in social knowledge.* New York: Springer Verlag.

Gergen, K. J. (1985). The social constructionist movement in modern psychology. *American Psychologist, 40*(3), 266–275.

Gerstmann, J. (1958). Psychological and phenomenological aspects of disorders of body image. *Journal of Nervous and Mental Diseases, 26,* 499–512.

Gholson, B., & Barker, P. (1985). Kuhn, Lakatos, and Laudan: Applications in the history of physics and psychology. *American Psychologist, 40*(7), 755–769.

Glucksman, M. L., & Hirsch, J. (1969). The response of obese patients to weight reduction. III. The perception of body size. *Psychosomatic Medicine, 31,* 1–7.

Haber, W. B. (1955). Effects of loss of limb on sensory functions. *Journal of Psychology, 40,* 115–123.

Head, H. (1926). *Aphasia and kindred disorder of speech* (Vol. I). Cambridge: Cambridge University Press.

Hebb, D. O. (1951, September). The role of neurological ideas in psychology. *Journal of Personality, 20,* 39–55.

Hochberg, J. E. (1969). Effects of the Gestalt revolution: The Cornell symposium on perception. In P. Tibbets (Ed.), *Perception: Selected readings in science and phenomenology* (pp. 118–136). New York: Quadrangle.

Howard, G. S. (1985). The role of values in the science of psychology. *American Psychologist, 40*(3), 255–265.

Husserl, E. (1965). Phenomenology as rigorous science. In E. Husserl, *Phenomenology and the crisis of philosophy* (pp. 71–147). New York: Harper & Row.

Kleist, K. (1934). *Gehirnpathologie.* Leipzig: Barth.

Kolb, L. C. (1959). Disturbances of body image. In S. Arieti (Ed.), *American handbook of psychiatry: Vol. I* (pp. 749–769). New York: Basic Books.

Kozulin, A. (1986). The concept of activity in Soviet psychology. *American Psychologist, 41*(3), 264–274.

Lacan, J. (1968). The mirror phase as formative of the I. *New Left Review, 51,* 71–77.

Lacan, J. (1977). *Ecrits.* (A. Sheridan, Trans.). New York: W. W. Norton.

Leontiev, A. A. (1978). *Activity, consciousness, and the personality.* Englewood Cliffs, NJ: Prentice-Hall.

Linn, L. (1955). Some developmental aspects of the body image. *International Journal of Psychoanalysis, 36,* 36–42.

Luria, A. R. (1966). *Human brain and psychological processes.* New York: Harper & Row.

Luria, A. R. (1973). *The working brain.* London: Penguin Press.

Madison. G. B. (1981). *The phenomenology of Merleau-Ponty.* Athens: Ohio University Press.

McKinney, J. P., & Rabinovitch, M. S. (1964). *Development of body image.* Unpublished manuscript cited by Traub and Orbach (1964).

Merleau-Ponty, M. (1962). *Phenomenology of perception.* London: Routledge & Kegan Paul.

Merleau-Ponty, M. (1963). *The structure of behavior.* Boston: Beacon Press.

Merleau-Ponty, M. (1964a). The child's relations with others. In J. M. Edie (Ed.), *Primacy of perception* (pp. 96–155). Evanston: Northwestern University Press.

Merleau-Ponty, M. (1964b). Maurice Merleau-Ponty a la Sorbonne. *Bulletin de Psychologie. 236*(XVIII), 3–6.

Miller, G. A., Galanter, E., & Pribram, K. (1960). *Plans and the structure of behavior.* New York: Henry Holt.

Moss, D. (1981). Phenomenology and neuropsychology: Two approaches to consciousness. In R. Valle & R. Von Eckartsberg (Eds.), *The metaphors of consciousness* (pp. 153–166). New York: Plenum Press.

Moss, D. (1982). Distortions in human embodiment: A study of surgically treated obesity. In R. Bruzina and B. Wilshire (Eds.), *Phenomenology: Dialogues and bridges. Selected studies in phenomenology and existential philosophy: Vol. 8* (pp. 253–267). Albany: State University of New York Press.

Moss, D. (1984). *Appropriation of the obese body as exemplified by female intestinal bypass patients: A phenomenological investigation.* (Doctoral dissertation, Duquesne University). (University Microfilms No. 8502511).

Mueller, J. H., Heesacker, M., & Ross, M. J. (1984). Body-image consciousness and self-reference effects in face recognition. *British Journal of Social Psychology, 23*(3), 277–279.

Plügge, H. (1967). *Der Mensch und sein Leib* [Man and his body]. Tubingen: Max Niemayer Verlag.

Plügge, H. (1970). *Vom Spielraum des Leibes* [The action space of the human body]. Salzburg: Otto Muller Verlag.

Pribram, K. H. (1960). A review of theory in physiological psychology. *Annual Review of Psychology, 11,* 1–40.

Pribram, K. H. (1971). *Languages of the brain: Experimental paradoxes and principles in neuropsychology.* Englewood Cliffs, NJ: Prentice-Hall.

Pribram, K. H. (1981). Behaviorism, phenomenology, and holism in psychology. In R. Valle & R. Von Eckartsberg (Eds.), *The metaphors of consciousness* (pp. 141–151). New York: Plenum Press.

Pribram, K. H. (1986). The cognitive relationship and mind/brain issues. *American Psychologist, 41*(5), 507–520.

Restak, R. (1984). *The brain.* New York: Bantam.

Rosenthal, R., & Rosnow, R. L. (Eds.). (1969). *Artifact in behavioral research.* New York: Academic Press.

Sands, D. V. (1982, July). The role of health locus of control, cancer health beliefs, and body-image in breast self-examination. *Dissertation Abstracts International, 43*(1-A) 84, ISSN 04194209.

Scarr, S. (1985). Constructing psychology: Making facts and fables for our times. *American Psychologist, 40*(5), 499–512.

Schachter, S. (1971). Some extraordinary facts about obese humans and rats. *American Psychologist, 26,* 129–144.

Schilder, P. (1933). *Das Körperbild und die Sozialpsychologie. Imago, 19,* 367–376.

Schilder, P. (1950). *The image and appearance of the human body.* New York: International Universities Press.

Schilder, P. (1951). *Brain and personality.* New York: International Universities Press.

Simonton, O. C., & Mathews-Simonton, S. (1975). Belief systems and management of the emotional aspects of malignancy. *Journal of Transpersonal Psychology, 7* (1), 29–47.

Simonton, O. C., Mathews-Simonton, S., & Creighton, J. L. (1980). *Getting well again.* New York: Bantam.

Sperry, R. W. (1966). Brain bisection and mechanisms of consciousness. In J. C. Eccles (Ed.), *Brain and conscious experience.* New York: Springer Verlag.

Straus, E. (1926). *Das Problem der Individualität* [The problem of individuality]. In T. Brugsch & F. H. Lewy (Eds.), *Die Biologie der Person. Ein Handbuch der allgemeinen und speziellen Konstitutionslehre: Vol. I* (pp. 25–134). Berlin-Vienna: Urban und Schwarzenberg.

Straus, E. (1952). The upright posture. *Psychiatric Quarterly, 26,* 529–561.

Straus, E. (1965). Born to see, bound to behold. *Tijdschrift voor philosophie, 27e*(4), 659–688.

Straus, E. (1966). *Phenomenological psychology: Selected papers.* New York: Basic Books.

Straus, E. (1967). *Phantoms and phantasmata.* Paper presented at the Fourth Lexington Conference on Phenomenology, Pure and Applied, Lexington, Kentucky.

Straus, E. (1969). Psychiatry and philosophy. In M. Natanson (Ed.), *Psychiatry and philosophy* (pp. 1–83). New York: Springer Verlag.

Straus, E. (1982). *Man, time, and world.* Pittsburgh: Duquesne University Press.

Straus, E., & Griffith, R. M. (Eds.). (1967). *Phenomenology of will and action: The second Lexington conference.* Pittsburgh: Duquesne University Press.

Tibbets, P. (Ed.). (1969). *Perception: Selected readings in science and phenomenology.* New York: Quadrangle.

Traub, A. C., & Orbach, J. (1964). Psychophysical studies of body image. *Archives of General Psychiatry, 11,* 53–60.

Van der Velde, C. D. (1985). Body images of one's self and of others: Developmental and clinical significance. *American Journal of Psychiatry, 142*(5), 527–537.

Ver Eecke, W. (1984). *Saying no: Its meaning in child development, psychoanalysis, linguistics, and Hegel.* Pittsburgh: Duquesne University Press.

Ver Eecke, W. (1985). Lacan, Sartre, Spitz on the problem of the body and intersubjectivity. *Journal of Phenomenological Psychology, 16*(2), 73–76.

von Uexküll, J. (1928). *Theoretische Biologie* [Theoretical biology]. Berlin: Springer Verlag.

von Weizsäcker, V. (1973). *Der Gestaltkreis* [The Gestalt-circle]. Stuttgart: Suhrkamp Taschenbuch Wissenschaft.

Vygotsky, L. (1978). *Mind in society. The development of higher psychological processes.* Cambridge, MA: Harvard University Press.

Vygotsky, L. (1979). Consciousness as a problem of psychology of behavior. *Soviet Psychology, 17,* 5–35.

Wapner, S., & Werner, H. (Eds.). (1965). *The body percept.* New York: Random House.

Watson, J. B. (1979). *Psychology from the standpoint of a behaviorist.* New York: St. Martin's.

Weathers, C., & Billingsley, D. (1982). Body-image and sex-role stereotypes as features of addiction in women. *International Journal of the Addictions, 17*(2), 343–347.

Winner, E. (1986). Where pelicans kiss seals. *Psychology Today, 20*(8), 25–35.

5

Approaches to Perception in Phenomenological Psychology:
The Alienation and Recovery of Perception in Modern Culture

Frederick J. Wertz

Nothing is more difficult than to know precisely what we see.
Merleau-Ponty (1962)

Perception is so continually present, close to us, and diverse in its forms that it is one of the most challenging themes for psychological reflection. We are so captivated by what we perceive that the *hows* and *whys* remain in the background. In the wilderness of everyday life, perception can easily embarrass the investigator who ceases to take it for granted, for attempts at conceptualization seem alien, in one way too crude and in another too sophisticated in their complexity. Perception, therefore, tends to elude the grasp of knowledge and to remain a great mystery.

The study of perception in psychology has a long and complicated history. Much has been learned about the anatomical and physiological characteristics of the sense organs, the kinds and amounts of physical stimulation to which human beings respond, the principles governing the organization of meaningful forms, and, to some extent, the role of the brain in these processes (Boring, 1958; Dember & Warm, 1979). Phenomenological philosophers and psychologists have criticized

much of this work for failing to carefully *describe* perception in natural situations. By beginning with the physical aspects of typically artificial stimuli in the laboratory and postulating abstract intellectual explanations, psychology has missed the concrete richness and essence of perception and has had little to tell of its role in the life of the perceiver and in human cultural history. These criticisms and the attempts by phenomenologists to provide a more faithful and revelatory study of perception may be found in the works of Merleau-Ponty (1962, 1964), Straus (1963), Gurwitsch (1964), McConville (1978) and Wertz (1982, 1983, 1987).

This chapter will examine the connection between a phenomenology of perception and the ideas about perception suggested by Abraham Maslow who, himself unsatisfied with the psychoanalytic and experimental traditions of psychology, attempted to launch what he called the "third force" in psychology with the explicit goal of a more complete grasp of the human being. Phenomenological psychology may be considered one of the various orientations within the broad, third force or humanistic movement. My aims are: (a) to offer conceptualizations of perception that vividly reflect its every day life, (b) to demonstrate the similarities and differences of two approaches to perception within third force psychol-

Frederick J. Wertz • Department of Social Sciences, Fordham University, College at Lincoln Center, New York, New York 10023.

ogy—those of Maslow and phenomenological psychology, and (c) show how the humanistic movement in psychology arises in response to the cultural-historical crisis of human alienation and attempts to aid humankind in its quest for a fuller contact with the world.

MASLOW'S TYPOLOGY OF PERCEPTION

Motivation and Cognition

Maslow's consideration of perception occurs within his general concern about different kinds of motivations. He asserts, as do traditional motivational theorists, that people attempt to fulfill *basic needs*—deficiencies of food, safety, sex, affection, and self-esteem. However, when these "prepotent" needs are consistently gratified, people engage in a process of *growth* that is qualitatively different from any attempt to fulfill a lack or to reduce the tension of needs. "The psychological life of the person, in many of its aspects, is differently lived out when he is need-gratification bent and when he is growth-dominated or 'meta-motivated' or self-actualizing" (Maslow, 1968, p. 27). In the area of behavior, for instance, Maslow (1954) calls *coping* any attempt to eliminate a deficiency, such as twisting a cap off a bottle in order to get a drink of water. In contrast, behavior is said to be "expressive," as in dance, when the person moves not to fulfill any deficit but simply delights in the movement itself:

> Activity can be enjoyed either intrinsically, for its own sake, or else, have worth and value because it is instrumental in bringing about a desired gratification. In the latter case, it loses its value and is no longer pleasurable when it is no longer successful or efficient. More frequently, it is simply not enjoyed at all, but only the goal is enjoyed. (Maslow, 1968, p. 31)

These considerations also apply to cognition, leading Maslow to distinguish *deficiency cognition* from *being cognition*. Presumably, memory may serve as an instrumental function, as when one recalls how to open a Chinese-puzzle box containing money. Or, one may remember simply for the joy of the recollecting, as when pondering last summer at the lake. "Deficiency-cognition can be defined as cognition which is organized from the point of view of our basic or deficiency needs and their frustration or gratification," whereas being cognition takes up its object "in its own right and its own being without regard to its need-gratifying or need-frustrating qualities, without primary reference to its value for the observer or its effects on him" (Maslow, 1968, p. 203). There is gratification in both kinds of cognitions, but they involve different *kinds* of pleasure—relief in deficiency cognition and ecstacy in being cognition. Although much

of our contact with the world is dictated by our needs, Maslow finds a different psychological structure in our moments of growth.

Deficiency Perception and Being Perception

Maslow (1968) says that perception may turn out to be the most important of all areas in which deficiency and growth orientations are found. The first is instrumental, attuned to objects that fulfill the perceiver's needs, whereas the second, more rare, embraces the total being of the object. "Being-perception is a momentary thing ordinarily. It is a peak, a high spot, an occasional achievement. It looks as if human beings perceive most of the time in a deficiency way. That is, they compare, they judge, they approve, they relate, they use" (Maslow, 1968, p. 92). One is more likely to see the ominous character of dark, approaching rain clouds and run for cover than to gaze in fascination at their richly patterned and marvelously changing texture. Yet "it is in principle possible to admire the beauty of a flood or the tiger the moment before he kills" (Maslow, 1968, p. 93). Perception may either guide a person in fulfilling physiological, safety, belonging, and self-esteem needs, or it may operate in a "meta-motivated" apprehension of the *suchness* of objects, in which case it is no longer useful but nonetheless witnesses what exists.

Maslow contends that psychology has stressed the instrumentality of perception to the exclusion of its potentiality for bringing people closer to being. He suggests that our understanding of perception and the perceived world would be much changed by a careful study of both need-interested and "desireless" perception. First, the object of being perception is seen as a whole with an internal richness that is fully attended to. The object is seen as complete—detached from relations, utility, expediency, and purpose; it is a universe unto itself. The perceiver is fascinated and completely absorbed, as a mother may be when she views her baby with wonder and minute care. The connoisseur of fine painting looks again and again, each time seeing something new. The details and many-sidedness of the object, in which nothing is unimportant, are embraced. As opposed to the usual consequences of repeated experience (boredom, familiarity, loss of interest), being perception affords an ever-enriching intensification of one's contact with the object. In contrast, deficiency perception tends to note only what relates to one's needs and goals, often glibly rubricizing the object. The same baby is seen in a more limited way when the mother notices that its diapers need to be changed and sets about solving the problem.

Whereas deficiency perception actively abstracts or selects aspects of the object that are familiar, threaten, or promise fulfillment, being perception is more passive and concrete, patiently surrendering and submitting itself to the uniqueness of the perceived without evaluation or classification. The perceiver respects the object and perception is "gentle, delicate, unintending, and undemanding, able to fit itself passively to the nature of things as water gently soaks into crevices. It must not be the need-motivated kind of perception which shapes things in a blustering, overriding, exploiting, purposeful fashion, in the manner of a butcher chopping a carcass" (Maslow, 1968, p. 44).

Because being perception emphasizes the object's being rather than the perceiver's needs, the object is given as independent of the ego, as an end in itself, rather than in terms of its utility, something to be feared and reacted to. Cancer may look beautiful and intricate through a microscope, a mosquito wondrous, whereas, in instrumental perception, these would be seen as dangerous or irritating things to be destroyed. Being perception's selfless, noninterfering, let-it-be style paradoxically allows a merging of the perceiver and the perceived. It evokes lofty, Godlike awe, amazement, and humility in the face of the universe that is usually seen as something we fear, control, and use for our selfish human needs.

Healthiness and Veridicality in Perception

Maslow relates perception to his concern for health and truth in his "psychology of being." Indeed the first characteristic of health is "a superior perception of reality" (Maslow, 1968, p. 26). Healthy people transform their activity into end experience so that even instrumental acts are intrinsically enjoyed and the person gains a sense of true being (Maslow, 1954). "To the extent that perception is desireless and fearless . . . it is more veridical . . . [N]eurosis, psychosis, stunted growth are cognitive diseases as well, contaminating perception" (Maslow, 1968, p. 203). Maslow stresses that an emphasis on deficiency perception in living not only precludes experiencing the finer aspects of reality but involves gross distortions and blindness:

> Especially when the structure of the person or the object seen is difficult, subtle, and not obvious, this difference in style of perception is most important . . . to perceive the intrinsic nature of the world is to be more receptive than active, determined as much as possible by the perceived. . . . Do we see the real, concrete world or our own system of rubrics, motives, expectations, abstractions, which we have projected? Or to put it bluntly, do we see or are we blind? (Maslow, 1968, p. 90)

Despite this harsh commentary on deficiency perception, Maslow recognizes the necessity of instrumental activity and points to a corresponding danger in being perception,

namely that it is potentially useless and impractical, which may be equally perilous. "The surgeon who gets lost in peak wonder at the beauty of the tumor may kill the patient. If we admire the flood, we don't build the dam" (Maslow, 1968, p. 118).

A PHENOMENOLOGICAL APPROACH TO PERCEPTUAL TYPOLOGY

Husserl

The phenomenological approach to perception was begun by the philosopher Edmund Husserl (1900, 1913, 1948), who throughout his career never ceased to be fascinated by perception. This section will focus on the concept of *intentionality* and some insights into perception that have provided an historical and theoretical foundation for later work on perception. First, however, a brief word about Husserl's approach is in order.

Husserl believed that psychology must begin with a description of the essences of its phenomena as they appear in everyday life. In order to do so faithfully, the psychologist must abstain from or "bracket" not only theoretical preconceptions of the subject matter (particularly those that might be taken over from natural sciences) but judgments of what really exists or does not exist. These *epochés* would enable the psychologist to view the experienced world purely as such and to learn about the process or *how* of experience (Husserl, 1954). Through a method called free imaginative variation, the investigator can intuit or see the *eidos,* or *essence,* of the experiential process under consideration.

Perhaps no phenomenological notion is more obvious and yet elusive than that of intentionality, which Husserl found through the previously cited method to be the essence of conscious life. When one imagines the possible variations of mental life, one is struck by something fundamental that, however miraculous and inexplicable, cannot be ignored without great cost: *consciousness is conscious of something other than the consciousness itself.* Although this may seem to be a mere twisting play of words, the insight gained is that our mental aliveness—whether in imagining, thinking, remembering, anticipating, feeling, wishing, behaving, perceiving, or indeed any imaginable experience— "transcends," goes beyond itself, aims at and contacts something other than itself. Although a rock or any nonconscious thing merely rests within itself and remains enclosed within its own impassible boundaries, consciousness in its very essence reaches out and inhabits *a world.* I do not merely see, move, and remember; I see a chair, I push it toward the table and remember to get some things from the store. According to this description, the objects that concern us are not represented in our minds (nor in our brains) but are yonder, in the world, and consciousness genuinely contacts and encounters them.

Perceiving is, for Husserl, a very special kind of experiencing. In a sense, it is our most original relationship with the world because, through perception, we apprehend things existing and immediately present "in the flesh." And yet, just as surely as we perceive our situation in its undeniable reality, we do so only partially, in a limited way, from specific perspectives rather than in totality. I see the world from where I stand, with some things appearing clear and close, others obscure in the distance, and some out of sight altogether. I see the chair now from this side, then from that side, then from the top, then I sit on it and feel its sturdy supportiveness beneath me, and then, after gazing at the dying fire across the cold room, I look back at the chair and notice how nicely burnable its wood is. The angle and orientation from which I perceive renders some aspects of the thing visible and others hidden. At any given moment, perception may surpass its limits and explicate more of the object's meaning, but it is always limited, perspectival. It is thus of the very essence of perceptual objects to appear in profiles, partial aspects that, taken all together, constitute the total object. This implies that every perceptual object, and indeed the perceptual world at large, is inexhaustible, always containing "more to perceive." Perception's partialness, however, is by no means a defect; it is our very power and means of successfully contacting reality.

Merleau-Ponty

Maurice Merleau-Ponty (1962, 1964, 1968) built upon the work of Husserl and, in doing so, made original contributions to the phenomenology of perception, including the central focus of this section, the notion of the *body subject*. How is it, Merleau-Ponty wondered, that this marvelous apprehension of reality takes place? It is, he observed, by virtue of a *bodily* subjectivity. Usually when we think of the human body, we mean a physical thing. No matter how well we understand the complexities of neurophysiology, however, the body conceived this way remains closed within itself, as are all merely physical things. This body object is not the *intentional* entity that the psychology of perception must recognize as the way perceiving "takes place." And yet for Merleau-Ponty, neither could the concept of mind, equally interior, help us understand the transcending, reality-contacting nature of perception.

When Merleau-Ponty (1962) calls our attention to the body *as the subject* of perception, he has in view not a

material object in space nor a mental idea of space but an intelligent participation through which space originally emerges. Even the most elementary perceptual qualities of objects, Merleau-Ponty stresses, require the body's dynamic participation. There is no "weight" without lifting, no "smoothness" without a caress, no "circle" without a curving glance, no "depth" without reach, and no "distance" without gait. Unobtrusively in the background of every perceptual field is a body gearing into, both undergoing and actively engaging in, the situation. Lighting does not merely strike a passive retina; the gaze ranges through space and sweeps over contoured surfaces much like a blind man's cane. The body can confront, strike, capture, follow, and mimic the world of things because it is one of their kin. Things move and I move, too. In following their movement and moving against them, I understand their way by a primal participation in that way.

Yet unlike mere things, the body freely traverses the situation in which it is bound as a *praxic power*. Its various "parts" each have their own potentials for acting and sensing, together orchestrated in the unity of enveloping, practical intentions. In order to strike a bull's eye with an arrow, I glance around for the bow, grasp it with my hands, and, after threading the arrow with the string, direct my gaze along its axis to the target, anticipating its flight, that is literally an extension of my body through the situation.

No mere thing, the body is a point of view on things. The different sensory modalities of the perceiving body give access to different features of the world. The cohesive unity of the body's different parts is immediately reflected in the variegated cohesion of the perceptual world, which is at once tangible, visible, sonorous, fragrant, and palatable. These qualities become differentiated and articulated by means of globally organized "work." *Work* is an intentional or relational term that implies both an existing situation and our *potentialities* for making something more out of that situation. As I brush my hair, I can feel the same bristly texture of a brush with both my left and right hands as well as my scalp. I can also see the texture and even hear the bristly sound as the brush glides over my hands. The "different" senses, communing in this unitary intention (to brush my hair), are aimed and bound together as they coherently approach *the thing*. The body subject tacitly subtends the entire figure/ground organization of our lived space, forming a practical system with the world it reveals and transforms.

The body skillfully comports itself through time and space, giving birth to a multilayered order. As a body subject, I am at once an anonymous, momentary, and immediate presence. And yet I am also an habitual, personal, and cultural–historical dilation of being-in-the-world. Spontaneously engaged in tasks from the start, I-as-body originate meaningful work in my confrontation with the world. Through my individual history and in the company of and guided by the others with whom I live, I explore this great world that progressively opens further. One worldly matter I may explore is myself. Far from finding a disembodied spiritual essence, I double back on my reality, locating myself by touch, sight, smell. In what Merleau-Ponty (1968) calls the fundamental *chiasm,* I find myself to be paradoxically both a thing amid things and yet always on the hither-side, the zero point and gnostic precondition of their revelation.

As I disclose the positions, substantiality, weight, size, and movement of things, they hold me, support me, and set the coordinates for my self-recognition. I may gaze at myself in the mirror on the wall and touch my own hands. Perceiver and perceived at once form an inextricable proximity and an irremediable distance as they turn about each other in mutual revelation, meeting but never coinciding completely. Again, perception is always imperfect and incomplete, never merging with its surroundings, and yet forming a relatively stable disclosure from within the real.

Different Ways of Perceiving

In my own study (Wertz, 1982, 1983), I tracked human perception through a diverse array of situations in everyday life and attempted to understand how each person's perceptions unfolded. Perception does not operate at random, nor does it run through all its possible variations in a logical way. Typically, a person's way of perceiving and the objects perceived occur in strict conformity with their relevance to the person's goal. For instance, one of the subjects set out in a department store to buy a new sofabed. After focusing on the store directory, she made her way through the aisles until she saw the furniture section in the distance. After approaching the sofabeds, she focused on one after another through sight and touch, noticing the color and texture of the fabrics, the softness of the cushions, the inner construction, the ease of manipulation, and the price of each. Almost nothing else in the store caught her attention. I call this type of perception *pragmatic* because it plays the role of a means to the task's end. The other general type of perception, which I call *appreciative,* encounters the situation with an affirmative intent, dwelling closely with what is perceived rather than utilizing it for a distant goal.

Pragmatic Perception

Here the perceptual activity and the appearance of the perceived are not the person's ultimate aim; they are merely a necessary means to achieve a goal that lies beyond them. One of the subjects in a supermarket does not *thematize* (i.e., focus upon as distinct objects) each of the people at all; they remain in the background of her perceptual situation because they are irrelevant to getting groceries. She reads her list, scans the shelves for needed foods, yet once an item is found and placed in her basket, she perceives it only vaguely in the background. As another subject walks to his hotel room to go to sleep, he notices very little of his surroundings thematically. He does not focus on the desk clerk at all, for instance, as he passes through the lobby; but when his key fails to open his door, he looks for the clerk for help. Even when he perceives the clerk in accord with a newly acquired relevance, the subject does not focus on his eye color, dress, style, age, or mood because these features are task-irrelevant. He notices "a quizzical look on the clerk's face" and his "calling to a porter" because they pertain to the solution of his problem.

Pragmatic perception operates precisely according to the type of work to be done, within which it is integrated, and it is curtailed as soon as the work no longer requires an apprehension of the surroundings. I see a doorknob in order to turn it, so that I may open the door, and I cease to perceive it thematically as soon as the door opens. Indeed, the opening itself is focused upon only so long as it serves my exit, and it slips into the perceptual background as soon as this is accomplished.

Appreciative Perception

In this case, the aim of the person's overall engagement in the situation is simply to perceive something; one lives to perceive rather than vice versa. Other psychological processes (e.g., behavior, anticipation) either take a back seat or operate in the service of perception, thus reversing the order of priorities found in pragmatic perception. As one subject listens to a symphony, hearing is his aim, and if he adjusts his posture in the chair or scratches his head, he does so with the intent of achieving a comfort and concentration that allows a more complete devotion to the music.

One might argue that one listens to a symphony or gazes at a painting solely for relaxation. When this is the case, perception is indeed pragmatic, but it is also possible that listening is the ultimate end, in which case any concomitant relaxation merely serves to heighten the perceptual contact with the object. Van den Berg (1972) notes that after being ill and bedridden for some time, we begin to notice "the little things" in our surroundings—the light patterns cast by the rising sun, marks on the ceiling, the wallpaper, chirping birds, the sounds of housework. This is so inasmuch as perception no longer serves the routine pragmatic activities in which these "little things" are irrelevant.

An extreme case of appreciative perception occurs in the "psychedelic" experience, wherein the person finds ordinary objects compelling. When asked to pass someone an ashtray, a person may become fascinated with it instead of handing it over. Perception takes up an open devotion to its object—one is "all eyes and ears"—and things are a wonder. One abandons work and falls in love with the world. People on vacation, tourists, can often be identified because they are the ones "always looking around at everything."

But illness and trips are not the only occasions for appreciative perception. The perception of the loved one by the lover is a multisensory unfolding of the former's infinite array of qualities. Had our subject been a woman in love with the desk clerk, she might not have only seen his quizzical look or heard him call the porter; she might have noticed the twinkle in the clerk's eyes, the noble style obscured by his ill-suited uniform, or a sadness in his voice.

Subtypes of Pragmatic and Appreciative Perceptions

Subtypes of pragmatic perception develop various forms or organized structures in the service of different kinds of tasks. The perceiver may be engaged in moving, manipulating, appropriating, or making, each of which requires specific ways of perceiving and specific thematic spheres. In transportation, for instance, the perceiver is primarily oriented toward the direction of intended movement. Rather than focusing upon one object in the visual field, the perceiver looks around openly, keeping pathways in view and spotting the most traversable way to the destination with attention to obstacles and openings. There is a special attunement to other moving objects, particularly those in or approaching the path. Fleeting glances span the surface of the field of movement.

Perception varies according to the particular manner of transportation—walking, roller skating, driving a car. The narrow space between a bus and the curb that the driver of the car does not notice is immediately thematized as "wide enough" for the bicycle rider, who in turn fails to focus on the manhole cover that the roller skater spots and jumps over. The work of a surgeon requires a much more narrow thematic field and an intently

active scrutiny of the details in this strictly circumscribed space. I have elsewhere (Wertz, 1982) analyzed such typical regularities of perception in the human work world as walking, driving a car, information gathering, and problem solving. McConville (1978) discusses perception in moving furniture, playing football and golf, and estimating distance.

In appreciative perception, the kinds of objects and their perceived characteristics may also vary widely, but here the determining principle is the perceiver's intrinsic interest. A person may be interested in the natural, human, or cultural surroundings, with an intense devotion or an idle curiosity. One of our subjects spent an afternoon in a forest, wholly taken in by nature, whereas another listened intently to a symphony. In line at the supermarket, another subject watched people who are "always more interesting than magazines like the *Enquirer*." Different personal cares are lived through different perceptions. At a musical comedy, one audience member may almost exclusively focus upon a friend in the show, scrutinizing her every move and blush of emotion, whereas another may thematize the chorus line, then the music, then the set construction in a more varied and yet more fickle and superficial manner.

Because no practical task dictates relevance, a given perceptual process may vary rather fluidly according to the perceiver's changing rays of affirmation. On a trip to the Grand Canyon, one might be absorbed for some time in the rocky cliffs, the hues of purple and orange shadowing through the deep, magnificent, and immense canyon, only then to turn and watch the children playfully feeding the mules and petting their foreheads. Thus, according to the personal interests of the perceiver, the thematic field may be diversely open or restricted.

Interconnections and Syntheses of Types

In a given situation, the different types of perceptions can operate in close proximity and even unitary fusion. Because a person may engage in more than one task—unrelated tasks, a family of tasks, or a hierarchy of tasks—perception manifests multiple modes of operation and achievements. An automobile driver, once direction and safety are established, can idly appreciate the pedestrians or storefronts. He or she may even be able to see the speed and angle of the car cutting in front of him or her in order to establish optimal distance as well as noting the car's special characteristics—"a nicely restored old Ford"; pragmatic and appreciative perception are then indistinguishable.

Some activities require an alteration or syncretic fusion of pragmatic and appreciative perception, such as painting and sculpting, wherein both behavioral (e.g., handle ability) and aesthetic (e.g., beauty) aspects of the object are crucial. Leisure-time activities, such as the one listed next, often contain the dual presence of pragmatic and appreciative perception.

One of the subjects engaged in a lake-fishing situation in a leisurely, aesthetic way while his father drove the boat. "The sun is beginning to climb the clear blue sky. I feel the fresh chill of the air, still cold from the lake, whose flat smooth, glassy surface still holds traces of mist from the morning fog." He sticks his hand into the cold water up to his wrist and feels "its solid pushing force swirl between my fingers." Then, for a moment, the subject enters a pragmatic mode of perception as he looks for "a good spot to fish." Now he sees the lake not as an end in itself but as a means to catching fish. He finds a shady spot "that doesn't look too deep," and, after pointing it out to his father, he returns to appreciate the surroundings—"the trees whispering in the breeze and the lake, though calm, lapping in an eternal lullaby." After the boat stops, however, he takes up the task of fishing and, rather than dwelling with the situation as an end, he begins to see it in a practical manner as a means for fishing. He looks at the boat's anchor and finds it "heavy and troublesome" as he throws it overboard. Then he looks for and finds his rod and the canister of worms, perceiving the latter in a both pragmatic and appreciative way at once. He focuses on the "soft, black mud" and pulls out a "wet, slimely worm squirming like crazy." This perception is pragmatic inasmuch as the thematization of the worm-to-be-grasped is a means to catching fish, but the worm is also valued for its aesthetic, animate qualities as intrinsically interesting. In much of his fishing perception, it is impossible to distinguish utility from appreciation.

It may be that the differentiation of these types of perceptions is a late development in cultural history. Primitive peoples have been noted for the syncretic fusion of use, aesthetic, and spiritual characteristics in their perceptual worlds (Werner, 1948); for instance, a spear's power to strike and kill requires feathers manifesting strict aesthetic and religious characteristics.

Project as the Ground of Perception

Examining the basis of these typical regularities of perception offers further insight. Perception is part of a larger structure of human life that includes behavior, anticipation, remembering, imagination, thought, and other nonperceptual moments. Each of these aspects of mental life is orchestrated with the others in an overarching *project* (cf. Sartre, 1943). A person aims, through each situation, at a still outstanding state of affairs; this striving constitutes the person's project. The subject in the department store, for instance, was seeking to own a new sofa bed.

A person lives through the project with a specific kind of *presence:* One may be hurried, agenda-oriented, and discerning, as is the case of the previously mentioned subject. In this large-order unity, such tasks as walking to the car, driving to the department store, looking at sofa beds, imagining each in the living room, calculating finances, and deciding on the right one are organized. Within this project, perception participates as a pragmatic means in the tasks of walking, driving, and assessing the relevant aspects of the sofas, thus contributing its part in the person's overall projective presence in the world.

This context of perception must be interrogated in the assessment of its type. The clearest examples of appreciative perception occur when the goal of the person's project is the perceptual experience of the immediate situation. Pragmatic perception occurs when the project's goal is not achievable by perceiving alone but requires contact with the perceptual situation in order for the person to proceed to the project's end. The subject who wants to go to a concert must first find a newspaper, pick a concert to go to, walk to the hall, buy a ticket, and find his or her seat. He or she perceives pragmatically until the concert begins, for only then does perception coincide with the project's end.

Although, in the symphony example, perception is the key mode of actualizing the project's end, often a project is ambiguous or involves multiple determinations. For the subject in the woods, perceiving nature is her primary end and also a means to recollecting her past, entering reverie, and engaging in spiritual reflection. Thus the stream is at one moment a glistening wonder for appreciative perception but is at other times a reminder of her childhood and a symbol of eternally flowing life. Multiple aspects of a project may be expressed in the interconnections and fusions of different types of perceptions, as occurs in the case of our fisherman, who sets out not only to catch fish but to embrace his natural surroundings, and in the case of the hunter who aims not only to kill but to harmonize with the spiritual powers of the hunt.

The family of projects constituting the person is reflected through perception. Although perception always manifests the person's life-historical process, it also discloses the situation as independent of the person's projective presence. The particular qualities of sofa beds, the concert, and the forest are not created by the project, which may even be frustrated. In each perception, we find both the life-historical movement of the person, with all its multidetermination and ambiguity, and the autonomous reality of the world. Perception is, therefore, a meaningful meeting and intertwinement of the person and universe, wherein the latter's brute contingency appears according to the former's projective presence.

MASLOW AND THE PHENOMENOLOGICAL PSYCHOLOGY OF PERCEPTION

Convergences

Both Maslow and the phenomenological description agree not only that perception is related to motivation but that the latter abides in the very organization of the former. Although experimental psychology views motivation as a variable independent of perception, exerting a causal influence on it from outside (e.g., Ashley, Harper, & Runyon, 1951; Erdelyi, 1974; Eriksen, 1960; McClelland & Atkinson, 1948), both third force approaches recognize that *perception itself is teleologically structured.* Both consider valuing to be an essential constituent at the heart of perceptual perspectivity.

This recognition leads to the discovery of two distinct types of perceptions, one that involves intrinsic or affirmative valuation and another that involves instrumental or practical valuation of its object. Both views also testify to perceptual processes that are at once both affirmative and instrumental. Maslow and the phenomenological investigation both relate these types of perceptions to the larger structure of mental life. Finally, both point to the greater empirical frequency of instrumental perception over perception for its own sake as well as the emphasis upon the former by psychology from Bruner and Goodman (1947) to Skinner (1974).

Divergences: A Critical Analysis

Although, on first inspection, the convergences of the two typologies are striking, a deeper comparison shows great differences. The source of these are the schools' divergent approaches. Giorgi (1970) has used the term *approach* to designate how psychology is conceived or understood and what assumptions are made concerning the nature of the human being. A school's approach to psychology includes its goals and philosophical presuppositions as they interrelate with its methodology and subject matter. Although Maslow addresses perception from the perspective of a theory of motivation, phenomenological psychology attempts to set aside all abstractive preconceptualizations and describes perception concretely. In a sense, these approaches are the inverse of each other because the latter investigation began

with individual perceptions and progressively opened its scope to the whole of mental life, whereas Maslow began with a theory of motivation (i.e., the basic needs for survival and the human capacity for growth) and deduced its implications for perception. A phenomenology contributes to a more precise description of types and attempts to distinguish them *eidetically* (i.e., according to their essential qualitative structures), whereas Maslow brings a systematization to the various constituents of motivational life.

First, we must ask if what Maslow calls *deficiency* and *being perception* are the same as pragmatic and appreciative perceptions. It appears that the phenomenological terms have a broader reference, are more comprehensive than Maslow's. Clearly, all examples of deficiency perception provided by Maslow are examples of pragmatic perception in my sense. However, we find examples of pragmatic perception that do not include deficiency motivation. For instance, our subject going to hear a symphony clearly perceives the situation in a pragmatic way as he spots the newsstand, buys a magazine, selects a concert, finds his way there, gets his ticket, and locates his seat, yet he is not fulfilling any deficit of food, safety, belonging, love, or self-esteem. This concert goer lacks something, the music, but it is not needed in Maslow's sense. If need can be spoken of, it is what Maslow calls a growth or meta need, the need to *be* at a concert, and yet perception is clearly instrumental.

On the other hand, whereas Maslow's cases of being perception are all examples of appreciative perception in my sense, it is doubtful that Maslow would consider my instances of casual or idle appreciation to be cases of being perception. As my subject waits for a porter and glances superficially over the lobby, noting a group of schoolchildren passing through, perception has no instrumental value and therefore could not be considered deficiency perception. On the other hand, its rubricizing— lack of intense devotion to the unique—and absence of growth motivation exempt it from Maslow's category of being perception. There are many such instances of perception that correspond to neither of Maslow's types and remain anomalous without the broader typology provided by the phenomenological analysis.

Next, we must ask if Maslow's characterizations of perception are adequate even in the instances in which his typology clearly applies. Maslow calls being perception a total, veridical experience of the object in contrast to deficiency perception, which is blind and distorting in its "projection, creation, and manufacture" of its object. These characterizations do not withstand careful conceptual scrutiny. No perception, including what Maslow calls being perception, ever apprehends the *total* being of the object. Perception is always limited in its grasp; the object always extends beyond those profiles that are apprehended. This is precisely why being perception never tires of its object; the waterfall provides mysterious, inexhaustible richness for perceptual wonder. This does not imply, however, that perception is merely blind, contaminated, or distorted, for all perception, including deficiency perception, also provides an objective perspective on the real. Even the most strictly deficiency-oriented perception, say spotting a water fountain to get a drink, does not project, create, or manufacture but apprehends reality. Because perception is always both partial and true, seeing is a perpetual overcoming of blindness that is never total but genuinely progressive. From this point of view, Maslow's assertions about being perception are too naively realistic and those about deficiency perception are too intellectualistic to be true of any perception, let alone to differentiate two types of perceptions with eidetic rigor.

If these types of perception cannot be distinguished as the veridical from the projective, what about the adequacy of Maslow's other characterizations? In many cases, Maslow's attempt to contrast the types discloses something that is often empirically true, or true in a certain sense, but that remains inessential or equivocal in the final evaluation. For instance, Maslow stresses that an exclusive focus on or absorption in the object occurs only in being perception. It is *often* the case that this is *more* true of being perception than deficiency perception, but it is hard to imagine anyone more absorbed in the immediate perceptual field than a surgeon, whose perception is instrumental. Being perception is also supposed to apprehend the many sidedness of its object, and this too is often true, but the buyer of a sofa bed or dinner meat may consider these objects far more thoroughly than a perceiver meditating on a tree from a single vantage point. Further, being perception is not necessarily passive, and deficiency perception is not necessarily selective, for one may actively focus on the aspects of symphony music or a painting and be passively assaulted by a chilling wind. Being perception is often more attuned to uniqueness, whereas deficiency perception often rubricizes, but this is not always so. Our subject in the woods looks from water to the shore, trees, and sky, viewing each in their typical, even universal characteristics, whereas the surgeon takes the spatial idiosyncrasies of the cancer into detailed account.

All perception, not just being perception, reveals an object that is transcendent to the act of perception. The food I eat, though viewed from hunger, is still seen as independent of me and my perception, that is, as existing regardless of whether I perceive it or not. It is also not only being perception that lacks differentiation of subject and object; deficiency perception of "thirst-quenching water" shows its own sort of fusion. The "quenching" character of the water, like the "comfortableness" of a chair and the "slipperiness" of the icy sidewalk, imply the perciever's intentions—drinking, sitting, walking—in their very perceptual qualities.

Some of Maslow's characterizations reflect empirical frequencies, and others require more precise clarification. Both types of perceptions show their own kinds of explicitation, selectivity, activity/passivity, typification, ego transcendence, and fusion with the world. The essential difference between the types lies instead, as Maslow does stress, in their teleological structure. This, however, can only be understood by considering the *context* of perception, the overall *intent* of the perceiver, the *values* inherent in perception, and its place in the perceiver's *project*. While walking down the street, I am struck by some good-smelling pizza. Which type of perception is this? It could be either or both, depending on whether I utilize the smell in my search for dinner or simply affirm the wonderful smell for its own sake.

These considerations lead us to the question of whether the terms *being* and *deficiency* are appropriate to the difference between the types. In view of the breadth of the phenomena we wish to comprehend, abandoning realistic and idealistic biases, and sharpening our eidetic intuition, concrete description discloses being and deficiency in all perception. Heidegger (1927) shows that equipment, the sphere of utility, manifests its own *kind of being,* which he calls "readiness-to-hand" (*Zuhandenheit*). Indeed, things *are* manipulable, edible, and safely traversable. We can also extend Sartre's (1943) analysis of doing, making, and having to include all pragmatic pursuits and conclude that all are most basically projects of being, wherein perception is a *revelation of being.* In other words, even seeing a thirst-quenching water fountain is a perception of being. The essential difference between the types of perceptions lies, then, in their different *relations to being,* whether being is merely utilized or affirmed.

On the other hand, deficiency is manifest beyond the "basic needs" specified by Maslow, and it can be found in all perception, even cases he designates as being perception. Our subject's going to a concert felt a lack, a desire to hear a symphony. Deficiency goes beyond our "basic needs" and may even be experienced in the realm of growth, the pure appreciation of being. Therefore, it appears that the dialectic of deficiency/striving and fulfillment/end experience is also quite general and applies in its own way to both types of perceptions.

Maslow, who himself characterizes the process of

growth as ''endless,'' would probably agree with the phenomenological anthropologies that assert that nonbeing is immanent not only in perception but in all our activity. Sartre (1943) says that nothingness lies coiled at the heart of human being like a worm. This ontological lack (as opposed to the physiological and psychological kinds stressed by Maslow), which Sartre later develops as a practical condition of humanity called ''scarcity'' (1960), is never ultimately fulfilled. Heidegger (1927) says that a human being is *at issue, at stake, in question* in its very existence. To this extent, even peak experiences, our ''Godlike'' moments when we come closest to a sense of ultimate completion, are but steps along the way, moments in our becoming. In the only final end, death, far from gaining being, we lose it. Hence our existence is both precious and precarious, to be used and appreciated in its imperfect and yet revelatory mortality.

Perhaps what is most distinctive about Maslow's insights, the very passion that in part led to some of the difficulties noted before, is his sense of the problematic, pathological, and even dangerous character of instrumental motivation and his strong belief in the value of affirmation in human life. We must be careful not to overlook the profound significance of this driving force in Maslow's analysis as we strive for conceptual clarity.

Why study perception after all? Maslow stresses that the style of perception is a crucial part of and reflects a person's total way of existing; further, he believes that we perceive and exist too much in the instrumental mode and do not caringly affirm the world enough. In relating to other people, we too often view the other person simply as a pragmatic tool for selfish needs without perceiving, let alone respecting the other as a whole. Equally true in relation to ourselves and our natural surroundings is *how we perceive matters.* Maslow is imploring humanity to perceive the world more faithfully, fully. These concerns, which lie close to the heart of Maslow's consideration of perception, provide us with a clue to the ground that lies at the root of both approaches to perception.

PERCEPTION, PSYCHOLOGY, AND MODERN LIFE

Since Kuhn (1962), it has become almost commonplace to say that scientific paradigms rest upon and express cultural themes. By identifying these, this section will explore the deepest convergence of Maslow and phenomenology. After a brief characterization of the relationship between traditional psychology and modern life, an account will be taken of the contemporary movement that attempts a critique of psychology and a broadening of

basic values. Finally, the cultural crisis of perception that forms the foundation of the previously mentioned contributions in psychology will be elaborated.

Traditional Psychology and the Alienation of Perception

Merleau-Ponty (1962), in the *Phenomenology of Perception,* stresses our difficulty in knowing precisely what we see. Doubtless, in days gone by, we did not even need to know scientifically what we saw. We simply saw, and that was enough. Inasmuch as the appreciative and instrumental aspects of perception have become dissociated from each other in human life, with the latter predominating, we move so quickly beyond perception, to nonperceptual modes of existing such as behavior and thought that our perception is largely forgotten.

That appreciative perception has been overlooked by psychology attests to contemporary values. The psychophysical paradigm expresses the reduction of perception to functional efficiency. Behaviorism's emphasis on the operant goes even further in placing priority on functional effectiveness by reducing humanity to behavior and thereby excluding perception as such from psychology. Perhaps the reign of behaviorism is now coming to an end (Mayer, 1981) because behavior itself, in the prescientific reality of production processes, is becoming obsolete, replaced by machines. Psychology has changed inasmuch as the ''cognitive revolution,'' as an outgrowth of computer technology, has now surpassed behaviorism, but times have not changed to the extent that this ''revolution'' expresses only a more sophisticated emphasis on functionality, that of calculative thought. Once again a legitimate topic in psychology, perception is now being viewed as an information-processing, cognitive function.

To the extent that perception is an intrinsic and not just an instrumental aspect of human existence, to the extent that it has a reality of its own apart from the sheer mechanics of behavior and the logic of calculative thought, much of psychology has followed our culture and lost touch with perception. Traditional psychology, from behavioristic to cybernetic, cannot but deepen our loss of contact with our surroundings because its theory and research on perception have presupposed the dichotomy of perceptual life, exalted the pragmatic, and ignored the appreciative. Perhaps even more dangerous is that psychology itself has assumed an instrumental, technological stance in its treatment of human beings, in accordance with its stated goals of ''prediction and control'' (in contrast to ''understanding''). Even in considerations of ethics in the treatment of research subjects, the cost-benefit model entails a fundamentally utilitarian approach to humanity.

Instrumental Existence and the Recovery of Affirmation

For van den Berg (1961), the deepest meaning of modern psychology (and he is not referring to a mere appendage of management technology) is that of an emergency bridge back to the lived world, from which we have become alienated. Third force psychology attempts to address this eclipse of the human being and point the way to a fuller existence. Like any knowledge, it can be but small compensation for a fragmentation and loss of life that has left us impoverished.

Maslow is right in saying the quality of life as a whole varies according to whether it entails an instrumental or affirmative posture. Modern industrial culture's almost exclusive concern with functional efficiency and its forgetfulness of all else has been identified by many thinkers (e.g., Colaizzi, 1978; Heidegger, 1927; Marcel, 1948). As this general atmosphere is recognized as a constriction of human presence in particular localities, a movement toward the recovery of affirmative values arises. Although many examples could be cited, a few representative examples will give the flavor of this trend.

Heidegger (1966) distinguishes between calculative and meditative thinking along the same lines as our typology of perception and has testified to an overemphasis on the former in both everyday life and science. *Calculative* thinking in organizing, research, and planning always reckons with given conditions that serve specific purposes in order to achieve prescribed results. It moves from one prospect to the next, without ever collecting itself, as it computes ever more promising and economic possibilities. Heidegger (1966) puts it this way:

> The world now appears as an object open to the attacks of calculative thought, attacks that nothing is believed able any longer to resist. The world becomes a gigantic gasoline station, an energy source for modern technology and industry. This relation of man to the world as such is in principle a technical one, developed in the seventeenth century first and only in Europe. It long remained unknown in other continents, and it was altogether alien to former ages and histories. (p. 50)
> Modern science has followed and in turn deepened this narrowing. We still seem afraid of the exciting fact that today's sciences belong in the realm of modern technology and nowhere else. (p. 14)

Heidegger (1966) considers the situation nothing less than perilous to the extent that, for a humanity that is captivated and beguiled by the technological revolution, calculative thinking may someday "come to be accepted and practiced as the only way of thinking" (p. 56). This uprootedness and loss of the sense of being's mystery can only be prevented by an unrelentingly courageous practice of *meditative* thinking, which contemplates the meaning reigning through what is:

> Anyone can follow the path of meditative thinking in his own manner and within his own limits. Why? Because man is a *thinking, meditating* being. Thus meditative thinking need not be "high flown." It is enough that we dwell on what lies close and meditate on what is closest; upon that which concerns us, on this spot of home ground; now, in the present hour of history. (Heidegger, 1966, p. 47)

Throughout modern culture, there have been many such critiques of the totalization of instrumental modes of existence and the loss of appreciative forms, as well as attempts at renewing the fuller existence. Two domains especially dominated by instrumentality are nature and the body. Ecologists, to the extent that they are concerned not merely with preserving more resources for consumption, but rather with the intrinsic value of the natural environment for its own sake, also manifest a countercultural trend, placing affirmation on at least an equal footing with efficient management. Perhaps more impressive by virtue of its transcendence of the very dichotomy of affirmation and instrumentality is Leboyer's (1975) work in medicine, a field that has been almost completely dominated by the efficiency attitude. He introduces an obstetric knowledge that recognizes the infant. His work implies not only an overthrow of the view of the infant as a physiological being but medical practices that promote the developmental unfolding of the traditionally traumatized personhood of the newborn (Wertz, 1981).

Psychology can follow suit in every subject matter it encounters. Good examples may be found in Fischer's (1985) work in human assessment, von Eckartsberg's (1971) ecopsychology, Colaizzi's (1973) learning theory, and Rogers's (1965) approach to psychotherapy. Third force psychology is distinctive in its concern for the total being of the person that is implicit in all psychological phenomena but that is perpetually in question and perhaps more than ever in jeopardy.

Perception in the Life-World

Conversations in the film, *My Dinner with Andre* (Shawn & Gregory, 1981), express this crisis in contemporary life, and the eclipse of perception in particular, as well as the struggle to resolve it through an enhanced, more open perceptual relationship with the world.

My Dinner with Andre carries us through the interchange between two friends, who had not met in some time, as they converse over dinner. Wally is a struggling playwright/actor whose recent days have been wholly taken up with such practical necessities as finding work, paying the bills, and getting the next meal on the table. He dreads this meeting, which he expects to be a kind of mercy mission, for he has enough problems of his own without confronting those of the troubled, off-beat Andre, whom a mutual friend had reported to be in very bad shape. Andre, at the height of supreme success as a director, had dropped out of the theater, left his family, and traveled to odd parts of the world in search of something beyond the material and social security that Wally is struggling so single-mindedly to achieve. What follows is a fascinating series of encounters between two people with strikingly different perspectives as they discuss their lives and try to understand each other, our culture, and the ultimate meaning and value of existence.

Andre, deeply disturbed with everyday life in New York City, dwells repeatedly on the way people perceive. For instance, he describes a visit to the Public Theater during which many people told Andre how wonderful he looked, until one woman noticed how horrible he looked and asked him what was wrong. She, partly because she had recently been through a personal tragedy in her own life, saw him with perfect clarity, whereas others saw only his tan, his shirt. Such restrictions of perception are examples of the impoverished and unreal relationships Andre has found in much of modern life:

ANDRE: It's like what happened just before my mother died. We had gone to the hospital to see my mother, and I'd been in to see her, and I saw this woman who looked as bad as any survivor of Auschwitz or Dachau, and I was out in the hall sort of comforting my father, and this doctor, who was a specialist in the problem she had with her arm, went into her room and came out beaming and said to us, ''Boy, don't we have a lot of reason to feel great? Isn't it wonderful how she's coming along?'' Well all he saw was the arm. . . .[We became] confused and frightened, because the moment before, we saw somebody who looked already dead, and now here comes this specialist who tells us that everything is great. I mean, they were literally driving my father crazy. . . . [T]he doctor didn't see my mother. The people at the Public Theater didn't see me. We're all walking around in some sort of fog. (Shawn & Gregory, 1981, pp. 61–62)

Such is the fog of what is no longer a universe but a pluriverse, made of specialized, fragmentary realities (e.g., the medical) with no common relevance. People's projects are discontinuous, possess diverse pragmatic aims, and lack an appreciative dwelling with the fuller meaning of situations. Behavioral functionality is often accorded a privileged status, whether one is attempting to appear respectable at a social gathering or curing an arm, and the world is perceived only in its relevance for those limited ends.

Shawn and Gregory (1981) discuss role playing and

careerism, which despite (or is it because of?) their efficacy, preclude genuine communion.

ANDRE: And I mean, it may be, Wally, that one of the reasons that we *don't* know what's going on is that when we're there at one of those parties we're all too busy *performing*. We're concentrating on playing our own roles and giving a good performance so we *can't* perceive what's going on around us. That was one of the reasons Grotowski gave up the theater, you know. He just felt that people in their own lives were now performing so well that performance in the theater was sort of superfluous and in a way obscene.

WALLY: We just put no value at all on perceiving reality. On the contrary, the incredible emphasis we place now on our careers automatically makes perceiving reality a very low priority because if your life is organized around trying to be successful in a career, then it just doesn't matter what you perceive or experience. You're just thinking, well, have I done the thing I planned? Have I performed the necessary action for my career? And you really can shut your mind off for years ahead in a way. You can sort of turn on automatic pilot. Just the way your mother's doctor had on this automatic pilot when he went in and looked at the arm and totally failed to perceive anything else. Our minds are focused on plans and goals, which in themselves are not reality.

It is not that modern existence is without the benefits of comfort. Our technology has been highly gratifying and in this way a supreme success, but on the other hand, the beneficiaries are paying a high, however subtle and concealed, price for the comforts upon which many people now depend. We are no longer at home beyond the realm of our instrumental control.

WALLY: Debbie and I were given an electric blanket. And I can tell you it's such a marvelous advance over our previous way of life, and it's great. But *it's* quite different from *not* having an electric blanket, and sometimes I wonder, well, what is it doing to me? I mean I sort of feel—I'm not sleeping in the same way.

ANDRE: Wally, that's the kind of comfort that sets you apart from reality in a very direct way. I mean, if you *don't* have an electric blanket, your apartment is cold, and you need to put on another blanket or to go to the closet and pile up coats on top of the blankets you have, well, then you know it's cold . . . and that sets up a link of things. You have compassion for the person—is the person next to you cold? Are there other people in the world who are cold? What a cold night! . . . I can snuggle up to you even more because it's cold. . . .

But turn on that electric blanket and its like taking a tranquilizer . . . I mean, what does it do to us, Wally, to live in an environment where something as massive as the seasons and the cold and the winter don't in any way affect us? That means that instead of living under the sun and the moon and the sky and the stars, we're living in a fantasy world of our own making. . . . We're having a lovely time with our electric blankets and meanwhile we're starving, because we're so cut off from reality that we're not getting any real sustenance. Because we don't see the world. We don't see ourselves. We don't see how our actions effect other people. (pp. 77–78)

Van den Berg (1962) describes how we have largely removed such uncomfortable realities as sickness and death from our world and unwittingly, by eliminating precariousness, also lose the sense of *preciousness*. Can we appreciate the being of our modern environment with its concrete sidewalks, sterile architecture, livestock slaughterhouses, and the ever-more functional artifacts? "If we allowed ourselves to see what we're doing everyday, we might just find it too nauseating" (Shawn & Gregory, 1981, p. 81).

What many people now appreciate is isolated in theaters, museums, and zoos or perhaps away from home altogether in an affair or a vacation. No one would ever confuse modern utensils or furniture with works of art or see in them any intrinsic value. We appreciate rare situations and simply function in most. The dichotomy of types of perceptions is culturally inscribed in our world. The modern artist who mounts a picture frame on the wall and sticks a cafeteria fork in the center is challenging the habitual fragmentation of perceptual life that our typology reflects, as are craftsmen who make tools that are interesting to look at and feel in their own right. Still we need vacations.

WALLY: Why do we require a trip to Mount Everest in order to be able to perceive one moment of reality? Isn't New York real? I mean, I think if you could become fully aware of what existed in the cigar store next to this restaurant, it would blow your brains out. Isn't there just as much reality to be perceived in the cigar store as there is on Mount Everest?
ANDRE: I agree with you, Wally, but the problem is that people can't see the cigar store now. (p. 90)

Though the prospects may sound silly, it is as if we need a perceptual reeducation in order to restore full potential.

ANDRE: [The Scottish mathematician Roc] had a whole

series of exercises, very simple ones, that he invented just to keep seeing, feeling, remembering. . . . [I]f you go to a Buddhist meditation center, they make you taste each bite of your food so that it takes you about two hours—it's horrible—to eat your lunch. If you're just eating out of habit, you don't taste the food. (p. 75)
. . . We're going to have to learn how to go through a looking glass into another kind of perception, in which you have a sense of being united to all things, and suddenly you understand everything. (p. 95)
WALLY: . . . to somehow strip away every scrap of purposefulness from selected moments, and the point of it [is to] then be able to experience somehow *pure* being. In other words, . . . discover what it would be like to live for certain moments without having any particular thing that you were supposed to be doing. (p. 104)

Berger (1972), who traces the modern crisis of perception to its roots in capitalism, believes that a more careful and full seeing of the world, far from being an idle aestheticism or an individual exercise, is already a radical, grassroots, political action.

Perhaps it is still possible to perceive being appreciatively as Heidegger suggests that we think meditatively. It is possible, because the human is a *perceiving being,* to begin with what is closest and dwell perceptually on this home ground. Clinical writers from Rogers (1965) to Kohut (1977) trace the ills of contemporary humanity to the absence of affirmative, interpersonal perception, which they then place at the center of their liberating, growth-facilitating practice. In a broadening restoration of our contact with other people, we might ourselves rescue what is precious from nonbeing. Only in this way can we transcend the isolation and aloneness implicit in our mortality.

ANDRE: I've acted the role of the friend. I've acted the role of the writer, director or whatever. I've lived in the same room with this person, but I haven't really seen them.
WALLY: [T]he other person's face could turn into a great wolf's face for seconds, and it wouldn't even be noticed.
ANDRE: I have this picture of [my wife] Chiquita that I always carry with me, and it was taken when she was about twenty-six or something, and it's summer, and she's stretched out on a terrace in a sort of old-fashioned long skirt that's kind of pulled up and she's slim and sensual and beautiful, and I've always thought about just how sexy she looks. And this last year I realized that the face in that picture was the saddest face in the world. That girl at the time was lost, so sad, and

so alone. And I've been carrying this picture for years and not every really seeing what it is. (p. 107)

ANDRE: At least attempt it—even if you can't make it, attempt it—even if you're going blind, do some exercises for your eyes or, you know, something. But of course there's a problem, because the closer you come, I think, to another human being, the more really completely mysterious that person becomes, and the more unreachable. You know you have to reach out to that person, you have to go back and forth with them, you have to relate, and yet you're relating to a ghost. Or something. I don't know. Because *we're* ghosts. *We're* phantoms. Who are we? . . . [T]hat's to face the fact that you're completely alone and to accept that you're alone is to accept death. . . . Have a real relationship with a person that goes on for years—well, that's completely unpredictable. Then, you've cut off all your ties to the land and you're sailing into the unknown, into uncharted seas. And I mean, people hang on to these images of father, mother, husband, wife because they seem to provide firm ground. But there's no wife there. What does that mean, a wife? A husband. A son. A baby holds your hand, and suddenly there's a huge man lifting you off the ground, and then he's gone. Where's that son? You know? (pp. 111–113)

The third-force psychology of perception arises from this exigency within human life as an attempt to recover, in the sphere of general knowledge, this most basic way in which we encounter *the real*, to remind us of its inexhaustible richness and its transcendence of all our practical pursuits and intellectual categories. The aim is to call us to our full potential for witnessing the precious and yet so precarious world, and to humble us before its endlessly emerging, changing, and vanishing being.

SUMMARY AND CONCLUSION

This exploration of the views on perception provided by Maslow and the phenomenological psychologists has led us to recognize that there are many ways in which people may perceive the world. In perceiving, we utilize and/or affirm our immediate situation. Each perception, with its concrete style, meaning, and teleology, is embedded in an individual's larger biographical context, which is in turn embedded in the great cultural history of humankind. Psychology, likewise, arises out of this latter broad nexus. The search for the roots of the humanistic psychology of perception has led us to the contemporary critique of, and emancipation from, the instrumental existence so dominant in our culture. This alternative to traditional,

natural scientific psychology grows out of a revolt against the excessive emphasis upon functional efficiency in our highly specialized, technologically oriented era, which tends to cast aside the affirmative and holistic recognition of existence.

This human psychology testifies to the ravages and forgotten values of our vulnerable humanity. In approaching perception, this psychology reminds us of the centrality and meaning of perceiving and stresses the importance of a broadly affirmative perception in our relations with the human and natural environments. The unity of the third force lies in its seeking to regain contact with, and thereby help revive, humanity by testifying not only to our utilitarian pursuits but to the full array of potentialities in our quest for being.

REFERENCES

Ashley, W. R., Harper, R. S., & Runyon, D. C. (1951). Perceived size of coins in normal and hypnotically induced economic states. *American Journal of Psychology, 64*, 564–572.

Berger, J. (1972). *Ways of seeing*. New York: Penguin.

Boring, E. G., (1958). *A history of experimental psychology*. New York: Appleton..

Bruner, J. S. & Goodman, C. C. (1947). Value and need as organizing factors in perception. *Journal of Abnormal and Social Psychology, 42*, 33–44.

Colaizzi, P. F. (1973). *Reflection and research in psychology*. Dubuque, IA: Kendall/Hunt

Colaizzi, P. F. (1978). *Technology and dwelling*. Pittsburgh: Paul F. Colaizzi.

Dember, W. N., & Warm, J. S. (1979). *Psychology of perception*. New York: Holt, Rinehart & Winston.

Erdelyi, M. H. (1974). A new look at the new look: Perceptual defense and vigilance. *Psychological Review, 81*, 1–25.

Eriksen, C. W. (1960). Discrimination and learning without awareness: a methodological survey and evaluation. *Psychological Review, 67*, 279–300.

Fischer, C. T. (1985). *Individualized assessment*. New York: Brooks Cole.

Giorgi, A. (1970). *Psychology as a human science*. New York: Harper & Row.

Gurwitsch, A. (1964). *Field of consciousness*. Pittsburgh: Duquesne University Press.

Heidegger, M. (1927). *Being and time*. New York: Harper & Row.

Heidegger, M. (1966). *Discourse on thinking*. New York: Harper & Row.

Heidegger, M. (1967). *What is called thinking?* New York: Harper & Row.

Husserl, E. (1900). *Logical investigations*. London: Routledge & Kegan Paul.

Husserl, E. (1913). *Ideas: general introduction to pure phenomenology*. New York: Collier.

Husserl, E. (1948). *Experience and judgement*. Evanston, IL: Northwestern University Press.

Husserl, E. (1954). *The crisis of European sciences and transcendental phenomenology*. Evanston, IL: Northwestern University Press.

Kohut, H. (1977). *The restoration of the self.* New York: International Universities Press.

Kuhn, T. S. (1962). *Structure of scientific revolutions.* Chicago: Phoenix Books.

Leboyer, F. (1975). *Birth without violence.* New York: Knopf.

Marcel, G. (1948). *Philosophy of existence.* London: Harvill.

Maslow, A. H. (1954). *Motivation and personality.* New York: Harper & Row.

Maslow, A. H. (1968). *Towards a psychology of being.* New York: Van Nostrand Reinhold.

Mayer, R. E. (1981). *The promise of cognitive psychology.* San Francisco: W. H. Freeman.

McClelland, D. C. & Atkinson, J. W. (1948). Projective expression of needs I: Effects of different intensities of hunger drive on perception. *Journal of Psychology, 25,* 205–222.

McConville, M. (1978). The phenomenological approach to perception. In R. S. Valle & M. King (Eds.), *Existential-phenomenological alternatives to psychology* (pp. 94–118). New York: Oxford University Press.

Merleau-Ponty, M. (1962). *Phenomenology of perception.* New York: Humanities Press.

Merleau-Ponty, M. (1964). *The primacy of perception.* Evanston, IL: Northwestern University Press.

Merleau Ponty, M. (1968). *The visible and the invisible.* Evanston, IL: Northwestern University Press.

Rogers, C. (1965). *Client centered therapy.* Boston: Houghton-Mifflin.

Sartre, J-P. (1943). *Being and nothingness.* New York: Philosophical Library.

Sartre, J-P. (1960). *Critique of dialectic reason.* London: NLB.

Shawn, W., & Gregory, A. (1981). *My Dinner with Andre.* New York: Grove.

Skinner, B. F. (1974). *About behaviorism.* New York: Vintage.

Straus, E. (1963). *The primary world of the senses.* Glencoe: Free Press.

van den Berg, J. H. (1961). *The changing nature of man.* New York: Delta.

van den Berg, J. H. (1962). *Psychology of the sickbed.* Pittsburgh: Duquesne University Press.

Von Eckartsberg, R. (1971). Towards an ecological social psychology of the individual and the idea of life-style. In A. Giorgi, W. F. Fischer, & R. Von Eckartsburg (Eds.), *Duquesne studies in phenomenological psychology, Volume I* (pp. 373–394). Pittsburgh: Duquesne University Press.

Werner, H. (1948). *Comparative psychology of mental development.* Chicago: Follet.

Wertz, F. J. (1981). The birth of the infant. *Journal of Phenomenological Psychology, 12*(1), 205–220.

Wertz, F. J. (1982). Findings and value of a descriptive approach to everyday perceptual process. *Journal of Phenomenological Psychology, 13*(2), 169–195.

Wertz, F. J. (1983). Revolution in psychology: Case study of the new look school of perceptual psychology. In A Giorgi, A. Barton, & C. Maes (Eds.), *Duquesne studies in phenomenological psychology, Volume IV* (pp. 222–243). Pittsburgh: Duquesne University Press.

Wertz, F. J. (1987). Cognitive psychology and the understanding of perception *Journal of Phenomenological Psychology, 18*(2), 103–142.

6

Learning and Memory from the Perspective of Phenomenological Psychology

Amedeo Giorgi

INTRODUCTION

The primary purpose of this chapter is to demonstrate an alternative approach to the psychology of learning and memory. Although I shall stress the differences from mainstream psychology, there are occasions to show certain common touch points as well because the approach being articulated does claim to be within the purview of science.

The necessity for an alternative approach has arisen because a number of psychologists are becoming increasingly aware that not all of the legitimate questions that psychologists are interested in pursuing can be subsumed under the perspective of a natural scientific psychology. For example, the emphasis on quantification and the sensory–perceptual aspects of concrete phenomena has left, until recently, the qualitative aspects and the experienced meanings almost untouched. Yet, theoretically, the latter belong as much to the phenomena of learning and the memory as do the former.

I also want to be clear in stating that the manner of asking questions and pursuing them in this chapter does not exhaust alternative strategies, nor does the scope of the presentation given here reach the limits of the perspective adopted. There are more variations than can be considered. Rather, what is said here should be considered as the tip of an iceberg, as exemplifications of dimensions of learning and memory that could be explored in more depth. In brief, what follows are suggestions of how phenomena of psychology can be approached phenomenologically and some hint of the value that such an approach can have.

Finally, another limit of the presentation is that learning is approached from a theoretical and research perspective. No attempt is made to incorporate clinical or applied literature on learning and memory because it would take far too much space.

LEARNING

Context

Science proceeds by systematically questioning the phenomena in which it is interested. However, it is rare that a particular set or family of questions can ever exhaust a phenomenon. Because of the tendency to establish traditions in science, it often happens that one set of questions dominates the research within a given subfield. This has happened in the psychology of learning, although certain substreams are discernible. The common tradition is the natural scientific approach, and the subfields that were established early are the verbal learning approach, begun by Ebbinghaus (1885/1964), the conditioning ap-

Amedeo Giorgi • Saybrook Institute, 1772 Vallejo Street, San Francisco, California 94123.

proach that had its roots in the work of the Russian physiologists Sechenov (1863/1965) and Pavlov (1897/1910) and was initiated in the United States by Thorndike (1898) and Small (1899), and the motor skills and performance approach, begun by Bryan and Harter (1897). The one thing common to these three traditions is that they have all been laboratory-based. Although research in naturalistic settings had been attempted with animals and with humans in other disciplines, it seems not to have been an option within the research tradition in academic psychology. This omission is based upon a methodological bias, a bias that the research presented later counteracts.

Before beginning the actual presentation of the research, let me be explicit about a problematic point. In order to be understood properly, three critical issues need to be addressed: the presentation of the data, the comparison of descriptive research with traditional learning and memory, and finally, the scientific interpretation of the descriptive method. I shall touch upon all three points by first presenting the research itself and then demonstrating its scientific legitimacy through dialogue with some aspects of mainstream research.

Learning Descriptions

The first problem in beginning descriptive research in learning was the determination of the learning situation. After considering several alternatives, I decided to let the subjects define it for me. This meant that they had to describe the learning situation retrospectively as they believed it occurred to them. In principle, this is not a problem because, phenomenologically speaking, a psychological situation is not defined by objective time and space but by how a situation and its dimensions are experienced by the subject. Objective characteristics, however, can indirectly be helpful to the extent to which they help a researcher discern the sense of experiential givens.

Thus, the exclusive data in the research project consisted of retrospective reports by subjects concerning situations that *they* defined as experiences of learning. Five descriptions will be presented, one in its entirety so that some concrete sense of the data can be obtained but only synopses of the other four. The following description depicts a rather ordinary social situation but an atypical one with regard to learning:

> During August, I spend 10 days in San Francisco, staying with a couple I had not met before. They were friends of the person I was traveling with. Both of these people are professionals, busy in their respective occupations. They were also caring for the 2½-year-old son of the man. During our stay, Michael and Marika gave us the use of one of their cars and urged us to enjoy ourselves in the city. They shopped, cooked, cleaned, and also

worked. My friend and I took care of our own possessions, trying to interfere as little as possible with the rhythm of the home. I offered throughout the first 3 days of our stay to help with the maintenance chores, and each offer was politely refused. The five of us were also sharing lots of playtime together.

> I began to feel uncomfortable with not contributing more to the process of meeting the needs of all of us in the house. I talked with my traveling companion about my discomfort, and he reassured me, saying that Michael and Marika would ask if/when they wanted help. I still felt that Michael and Marika really did want assistance and that they were not asking for it. I was experiencing some awkwardness with just going ahead and doing things in the kitchen, etc., as I was afraid of messing up plans for meals or being to forward in any way. I was also afraid to check out my suspicions with Michael and Marika directly because they appeared to be at ease with what was happening. I continued to offer assistance, and the refusals continued also.

> The evening of the fifth day of our stay, my friend and I came back from a day in the city. Michael and Marika were painting their kitchen. As I walked in the house and saw them, I felt the fear and awkwardness around actually assisting in some way come over me again. I went into the living room, frustrated that the good feelings of the day were dissipating; my friend came in and sat down with me, asking me what was wrong. I explained that I wanted to help but that I felt sure my offer would be refused. My friend asked me if I really did want to help. I started thinking, "Yes, I do, and I would enjoy helping." I had been feeling like a guest and offering to help as if I didn't really have much to offer. I reviewed mentally my approaches to Michael and Marika in the last few days and realized that I had been expecting refusals from the beginning. I thought that in my own home, I'm more likely to refuse help from a guest or not ask for it even when I wanted it. Still, inside, I felt very positive about working with them to create an easier time with more sharing for us all, and I decided that I had been inhibiting myself out of fear instead of stating what I wanted. I went into the kitchen and said I wanted to help cook dinner. Michael heard me, and I felt that this was because I had made a positive statement. I learned that in this situation I had been inhibiting myself by judging what their response would be in advance.

The other four descriptions can be summarized as follows:

> A subject described learning to drive a car. The situation consisted of being taught in an empty parking lot by an older friend. The subject described learning the displays on the dashboard, then trying to move the car, and finally being able to go out in real traffic. He described initial phenomenal distortions (car seemed too big) but with learning, things began to seem normal.

> Another subject described learning to make yogurt. She and a friend received instructions from a third party, and the subject merely memorized the steps. When she went to make it, it did not turn out right, and so she invented a correction based upon an assumption about what went wrong, and then it turned out correctly. Later she was with the friend who also received instructions and,

watching her make it, saw a step she hadn't done. She asked her friend about it and realized that she had not followed those instructions, that her correctly made yogurt turned out well for the wrong reason. She was able to figure out why her yogurt turned out correctly and realized that only then did she know how to make it.

Another subject gave his son his treasured chess set, and he attached great significance to the passing of the chess set as part of family tradition. The father assumed that the son would carry on the tradition, and initially it appeared from his behavior that he would. However, later behavior did not support the initial impression, and the father learned from another son that the reason the first son wanted the chess pieces was because of the lead weights in them. The father then realized that there can be two perspectives on the same situation and that the son had the right to receive the gift according to his perspective.

This subject had set himself up in a restaurant for his retirement years, and he assumed that all was going well. One night when business was good he discovered that there was not as much money in the register as he had assumed, and then he discovered that his waitresses were cheating him. This made him realize that unless he changed some things, his retirement project would collapse. He realized that he would have to learn to be a tough boss.

These data were obtained from nonacademic subjects of both sexes from ages 20 through 50. No attempt was made to control for such specific variables at this stage because the primary interest was in the general psychological meaning of learning as experienced by the learners regardless of personal differences.

Outcomes

The original descriptions of the data presented here were analyzed according to a phenomenological psychological method. A full explication of the method cannot be given here (see Giorgi, 1985, for an extended discussion), so a summary is provided.

The method proceeds as follows: First, the entire description is read to get the sense of the whole protocol. Second, once the sense of the whole has been grasped, the researcher goes back to the beginning and reads through the description once more with the specific aim of discriminating "meaning units" from within a psychological perspective and with a focus on the phenomenon being researched, in this case, learning. Functionally speaking, a "meaning unit" is determined whenever the researcher experiences a significant shift in meaning in the description being analyzed and he or she notes all such shifts. Third, once the meaning units have been delineated, the researcher rereads the meaning units again and with the help of free imaginative variation (Husserl, 1913/1962), expresses the psychological insight contained within them, if any, more directly. Because the psychological

insights being expressed in the description are usually implicit, imagining alternative ways of expressing them helps to determine the most precise expression. Finally, the researcher, again with the help of free imaginative variation, describes the structure of which each transformed meaning unit is a part, which can be done on the basis of an individual, typical, or general perspective, providing what is called a structure of the experience of learning. In this study, it was done on a typical basis, that is, the types of learning each description represented were determined, and then the individual descriptions were grouped accordingly.

Two basic typical structures were the outcome of this study; one may be called the "experience of adequate performance" and the other, "the experience of learning by detecting inadequate assumptions." There was one description that belonged to the former category (learning to drive) and four for the latter category in general. Of the latter four, two belong to one subtype that includes evidence of behavioral change (descriptions two and three) and two to a subtype that lacked that quality (descriptions four and five) because evidence of behavioral change was not present.

The descriptions of the typical structures found in this study are presented next. Because the adequate performance type is based on only one description and therefore is less complicated, it is presented first:

> Learning is the gradual achievement of mastery over the control of a task, with the help of an expert other, which was experientially organized around three successive phases that eventually became integrated: the discrimination of relevant parts, the selective functioning of the parts in safe conditions, and finally, the performance of the task in normal conditions. At the beginning of each phase, Subject was simultaneously thrilled and fearful, and learning was expressed in terms of movement from distorted perspectives on the situation to balanced perspectives as S moved from fear of, to confidence with, the task.

For the "detection of inadequate assumptions," where evidence for behavioral change is lacking, the structure reads:

> Learning consists in the clarification of a situation lived ambiguously and erroneously in such a way that prior inadequate assumptions due to lack of knowledge, conflicting possibilities, or uncritical positing are discovered with the help of a significant other. The learning consists of the perception of the problem and the direction in the adequate solution with the resolve to act adequately in the future.

Where evidence for behavioral change is included, the structure of the "detection of inadequate assumptions" reads as follows:

> Learning consists in the clarification of a situation lived ambiguously and erroneously in such a way that prior

inadequate assumptions due to lack of knowledge, conflicting possibilities, or uncritical positings are discovered with the help of a significant other, and then removed so that adequate behavior and understandings can ensue.

The difference between the two structures is reflected in the last sentences. Where evidence for behavioral change is lacking, the learning focuses on the experienced insight that wrong assumptions were posited. In the other case, the behavioral changes can be referred to. These and similar data strongly suggest that almost any human situation can be experienced as a learning situation. What is necessary for learning to be experienced is that a situation be organized around a new personal discovery that includes the implication that the consequences of the discovery will go beyond the specific situation in which it was experienced. By speaking of a new "personal" discovery, what is meant is that the discovery one makes does not have to be absolutely new but only new with respect to the subject's experiential history. To speak of a discovery means that an experiential or behavioral possibility now exists for the subject that did not exist before. To call it a possibility also implies that the new experience or behavior can be applied in future situations. Finally, as an experiential datum, learning presents itself as a mode of organization, and in order to be identified, that mode of organization has to have certain constant descriptive features that the structural description is meant to capture.

These points can be clarified by reference to the data. To begin with the last point, like most human phenomena, the mode of organization of learning falls into certain types. Thus, we saw that the five descriptions yielded two types of learning. The "adequate-performance" type reveals a structure containing a ministructure of nearly identical form but ever-widening content. One could describe the ministructure as discriminate, practice, perform. Thus, first the relevant parts of the car are discriminated and, with practice, mastered; then the behavioral actions for moving the vehicle are identified and with practice, mastered; and finally, the aspects of driving within traffic are identified and mastered. But with each widening of content, the previous discriminations that were thematically experienced become automatically lived and integrated, and what were separate aspects become unified by the subject. Moreover, the "reality" character of the last integration brings a certain finality to the experience (Subject said it was most frightening). There are no second chances here, and one must perform adequately.

The four "inadequate assumptions" descriptions show themselves to be of a common structure with context-laden variations but of a different type from the "adequate performance" structure. In these four cases, each time, the inadequate performance revealed itself first, and the subjects had to make sense of what was going on. (Sense making was no problem for the "adequate-performance" type; only performance was.) For the subtypes in which there was evidence for behavioral change, once insight was achieved, the false assumption was corrected, and adequate performance followed. With the other two subtypes, the possibility for correct performance offered itself, but there was no indication in the description that the possibility was taken up. From a phenomenological point of view, however, the fact that the possibility of correct performance presented itself to the subject's awareness is not a small matter. Without that awareness, it is certain that the subject would continue to behave less than adequately; with it, the subjects could meet the situation in an objectively adequate way and thus improve their lives.

We are discussing the importance of the awareness of possibility, and the main point is that the awareness of the possibility of more adequate behavior belongs to the experiential structure of learning. Thus the woman who visited San Francisco with her friend realized that she was uncomfortable, and it was only when she thought of the possibility that perhaps she was doing something wrong that her actual behavior in the world transformed. Before the actualization of the possibility, its sheer presence acts as a kind of guide; after correct actualization, it settles into the background and sediments itself as the appreciation of the total context of the situation. After all, the example of the subject who made the yogurt shows that correct performance in and of itself is not sufficient to constitute learning either. Robust learning is performance plus understanding, but the genesis of learning can include understanding alone or performance alone, and, as psychologists, it is important for us to understand the totality of the process, including incipient phases.

Finally, what is "new" for the subject can be quite varied, but it must be meaningfully appropriated and of sufficient significance so that there is a transformation in the structure of the experience. Thus the father who gave the chess set to his son was troubled about his own future when he discovered that his son was not using the gift as a chess set and then was able to be more at peace with himself when he realized that he did not automatically have the right to impose his interest in chess on his son. This "new" insight enabled him to live with himself and his son more comfortably. The driver had to learn how to use his body in new ways in order to drive a car successfully. These possibilities of the body always existed, but what was new was the actual accomplishment of these possibilities.

What makes all of these descriptions examples of the

experience of learning, however, is that they show the ability to overcome an opacity that blocks immediate achievement in experience or behavior that, relative to the situation, requires a significant amount of time. In other words, the prolonged temporal acquisition, discovery, or implementation process seems to be the organizational feature that distinguishes the phenomenon of learning. This same feature came out in another study (Giorgi, 1986), and it seems to be what distinguishes learning from correct insight and behavioral competence, both of which emerge immediately and adequately. This feature does not exhaust the experiential characteristics of learning, of course, but it does seem to be an essential feature of the phenomenon of learning as experientially understood.

MEMORY

Context

Memory, like learning, is subject to several approaches. Sometimes psychologists seek the mechanisms of memory (John, 1967) through physiological or chemical research, although ontogenetic or developmental approaches have also been utilized (Nagy, 1979). These are basically approaches that seek what underlies memory, but they do not directly probe it. Cognitive psychological approaches (e.g., Cohen, 1977; Ellis, 1972/1978) look at memory itself, but they describe it in terms of a cognitive model of mind and use terms that meet the demands of the model first (e.g., encoding, storage, retrieval, etc.), and, even though these terms are partly adequate in terms of fitting the lived phenomena of memory analogously, the adequacy is not a concrete one but a formal and abstract one. And, there is the verbal-memorizing tradition begun by Ebbinghaus (1885/1964) that depends upon the actual exercise of memory on restricted tasks. This tradition uses a quantitative approach almost exclusively and tries to understand memory in terms of the conditions of the laboratory situation. There are some isolated qualitative, even empirical, studies of memory (e.g., Bartlett, 1932), but they do not form a tradition in the sense that the other streams referred to do. Thus the need to look at memory directly still exists.

Interestingly enough, the oldest of the traditions just mentioned is the one begun by Ebbinghaus. Although he was explicitly interested in memory, he also began the learning tradition (mentioned before) because he wanted to use new materials for memorizing purposes and wanted all of his experimental inquiry to be contained within a single situation. Thus the acquisition of the material became learning, and its recall became a test of memory.

Putting the matter so directly helps us to see that, in a way, both "phenomena" are abstract; they belong to concrete situations that are larger than themselves.

When Ebbinghaus invented nonsense syllables in order to create material that would be ahistorical (so that subjects could learn material with as little bias as possible in order to see how memory could function "purely"), the situation was precisely one in which he wanted to see how memory would function for its own sake, just as the learning of nonsense syllables is learning for its own sake. But that is not how these phenomena usually manifest themselves in the everyday world. One remembers or learns in order to accomplish something, and the potential accomplishment is often very relevant to whether or not learning or remembering takes place as well as how it takes place. Thus, by turning to concrete descriptions of memory as the basis for research, one can capture the phenomenon in its natural context, and this will reveal dimensions of the phenomenon that the "purer" situations cannot capture.

Another interesting facet of experience is revealed by comparing learning with memory, and that is the presentational–representational difference. Whatever complications are associated with the study of learning, the description provided by the subject primarily refers to the perceptual situation in which the subjects finds him- or herself. By definition, memory has to refer to something that is not in the subject's immediate perceptual environment. This leads to a more complicated analysis, as follows.

PSYCHOLOGICAL PHENOMENOLOGICAL ANALYSIS OF MEMORY

Findings

Phenomenological analyses begin by turning to concrete experiences because they do not want to be impositional with respect to experience and because they want to be faithful to the way experiences are lived. Consequently, as with the learning research, this research begins by asking subjects to describe specific experiences of memory. The precise question was, Please describe for me a situation in which you remembered something. Please be as concrete and detailed as you can. Three typical but brief responses to the question will be used as examples:

Subject 1

I was asked to recall a time when I had to remember something, giving a full account of that process. I went to a meeting out of town. As I was walking down the hall, the woman in front of me turned around and immediately called me by name and asked about my family. The woman's face was familiar, but I couldn't remember what her name was or where I had known her. We parted, and I was left trying to figure out the puzzle having not admitted my lapse of memory. As I couldn't recall her name by merely trying to bring it up, I began to think about the places I had lived and tried to place her there. I was sure it wasn't in Antioch where I now live, perhaps it was in Concord where I had lived 9 years ago. Then all of a sudden I saw her standing at her front door and I moved into her living room, kitchen, and back outside where I turned and looked across the street and could see the home of other friends. It was Bakersfield! At that moment I knew her name was Joan and her husband Don. I could then see him, too, though not plainly; his facial features were hazy as if looking at him without my glasses. It was as if placing her in context gave me her name.

As I was thinking about the places I might have known her, I tried different names most of which began with *J*, and various environments flashed by, none of which seemed just right. Sometimes my mind would be dark or blank while I had the feeling of my mind casting about for something. As I was trying different names the faces of the people I named would appear. The whole process took about 10 minutes.

Subject 2

Today as I walked across the lawn from Stevenson Hall to the bookstore I decided to walk on the grass because it looked like a carpet. As I walked hurriedly at first, I looked down upon the grass and took joy in the greenness of it. I slowed down and began to remember a time over 15 years ago when a boyfriend and I used to sit on the lawn at SRJC and have lunch together. The very same sort of yellow dandelions were on that lawn, and he used to pick them and make minibouquets for me. I felt myself fill with the warmth of the emotion I felt then— and as I got to the bookstore I was smiling in a most peaceful way and felt very loving towards others.

Now, I did not consciously call the memory to me— maybe the smell of the grass, the color, the yellow flowers—who knows for sure. It was a moment of remembrance with a nice payoff.

Subject 3

I was getting ready for the senior ball, and I asked for my mother's help. (I really wanted her to look at me, admire me, praise me—but mainly to be *happy* for me). I wanted her validation.

She refused to do so. I felt empty inside—and no matter what I looked like in the mirror—it was translated into ''not good enough.''

Suddenly I remembered, vividly, standing before my mother at age 4½ begging and crying to continue in kindergarten. She was refusing, loudly screaming and threatening me—complaining that I got my dresses too dirty with watercolors to be able to continue school. I cried hysterically and then stopped short as my mind found one loophole: the one that told me that I would

have to go to school in first grade and that she'd have to let me. I would somehow feel present at school, if not always pleased within myself *in* school.

I flashed back to the dress I was in and decided to go to the dance despite my mother's attempt to prevent me from attending with her approval inside of me. I would be present and functioning, if not exactly comfortable with myself for going.

In order to highlight the psychological aspects of the concrete descriptions of the subjects written from an everyday life perspective, the Situated Structure of the Memorial Experience for each subject is presented. The situated structure, in principle, tries to be faithful to the concrete experience of the subject, whereas, at the same time, making clear the organizational features of the experience. These structures are:

Subject 1

The subject accepts the research task and repeats the instructions. *Memorial Situation I* then appears as subject recalls a situation in which she is walking down a hall and she is addressed by name by a woman who is familiar to her, but whom subject cannot place. Subject then tries to come up with the identity of the woman and approaches the task in the manner of a puzzle. She goes through places she has lived and eliminates her current location.

Suddenly subject visualizes a scene in which *Memorial Situation II* arises and subject sees herself at a house where the woman who addressed her is standing and, as subject walks through the house, she recognizes the neighborhood as Bakersfield. Then the woman's name comes to her mind [Joan]; then her husband's name, and she is even able to visualize him vaguely. Subject suggests that the visualized context seemed to provide the name. But it also is true that a name could provide an image [as with her husband].

Subject then describes some strategic procedures: She thought of places she lived in order to locate the woman; somehow she thought of trying different names beginning with *J*; she states that various scenes flashed by; she also described moments in which her mind was dark, even though she was aware that it was casting about; finally, she was trying to correlate names with faces.

It is not clear why this memory appeared to subject, but it obviously served to meet the demands of the research situation.

Subject 2

Subject accepts the research task and describes *Memorial Situation I* in which she sees herself walking across the lawn on her campus toward the bookstore, motivated to do so because it looked like a carpet. She walked hurriedly at first, but then took joy in the greenness of the grass and slowed down, and then *Memorial Situation II* appeared, and subject visualized a scene from more than 15 years earlier when she and her boyfriend used to sit on such a lawn and have lunch and make minibouquets for her.

Subject then goes back to *Memorial Situation I* and describes herself as smiling, peaceful, and full of warmth for others. Subject is not sure why *Memorial Situation II* arose, but she suggests possibly the smell of the grass or the colors, etc. She is sure that she did not consciously choose to recall it, but it was a pleasant memory that left her full of warmth toward others.

Subject 3

Subject accepts the research task and remembers *Memorial Situation I* in which she was getting ready for the senior ball and asked for her mother's help. She really wanted her mother's validation but her mother refused. Subject remembers feeling empty inside, and no matter how she looked in the mirror, she recalled that she felt not good enough.

Subject then becomes present to *Memorial Situation II* in which she visualizes herself as 4½ years old standing before her mother crying hysterically because she wanted to continue kindergarten and her mother was refusing allegedly because subject got her dress too dirty. Subject recalls that she cried and then stopped as she thought of a loophole: Her mother would have to let her go to school in first grade. Until then she would somehow make herself feel present at school, even if not always pleased with herself at school in such a mode.

Subject then flashes back to *Memorial Situation I*, and she uses a similar strategy to solve her problem there as she used when she was 4½. She will go to the ball despite her mother's refusal to "validate" her, but she will try to carry her mother's approval inside of her. She remembers interpreting this as meaning that she should somehow be present at the senior ball and functioning, even if this meant that she would not be exactly comfortable with herself.

It is also interesting to note that all three descriptions contain two memorial descriptions, with intricate relationships between them as well as with the time of the remembering itself. Because the structure of the temporality of the memorial experiences for each subject is similar, only the temporal structure for the first subject are presented, in Figure 1, as a model for all three subjects.

Discussion of Findings on the Experience of Memory

Before discussing my own findings, I want to acknowledge that Casey (1987) has recently published an interesting phenomenological analysis of remembering, but it would take us too far afield to compare our psychological analysis with his philosophical analysis. Instead, I refer briefly to the difference in the two types of analyses in order to indicate why they are not identical.

Philosophical phenomenology tries to come up with the most fundamental structures of experience, whereas psychological phenomenology presupposes those struc-

tures rather than thematizing them. In other words, the phenomenological psychologist attempts to thematize, among other things, the typical features of an individual's phenomenal world. It is not so much the objective reality as understood by a disinterested consciousness that is the concern, as it is the very specific way in which things and events are experienced and their implications. Of course, the philosophical "objective" perspective is often helpful for discriminating psychological aspects because it provides a comparative framework. At the limit it, too, can be the object of psychological scrutiny if a subject experiences a situation or an event precisely in an objective way. However, these problems are best left for purely theoretical discussions, and I shall now turn to the findings presented previously.

The intentionality of consciousness is key for phenomenological analyses. Intentionality means that conscious acts are always directed to objects that transcend the acts in which the objects appear. It also means that the "act–object," or "noetic–noematic," structure is intrinsic to consciousness, and this must be respected in analyzing memorial descriptions as well. The major implication of this fact is that a person who describes a situation in which he or she remembered something previously is also referring to a situation in which an act with an intentional structure is evoked. Thus, in the first example, the subject is at her home writing about a remembered situation in which she went to a meeting in another town and was called by name by a woman whom she recognized but could not remember by name nor the context within which she knew her. In remembering the hall, the subject is remembering a perceptual situation that is given to an act of perceiving that is being re-presented memorially. Noetic aspects appear when the subject says, "I had the feeling of my mind casting about for something," and noematic aspects emerge when she says, "And various environments flashed by, none of which seemed just right."

There is, therefore, a certain iterativeness or repetitiousness with consciousness that is most pronounced with representational phenomena. The subject from her home directs her consciousness toward a time in the past when she remembered something (which is an intentional act), and the object of the act of memory is a past-lived event that has its own intentional acts and objects. Amazingly, this subject regained access (as we all can do with various degrees of success) to the original perceptual act and recovered aspects of it that were obviously lived but not thematized initially. To use a grammatical analogy, this type of remembering is like a sentence with independent, or even dependent, clauses that have their own subject and verb and have a relative autonomy even while being dependent upon the main sentence. Another way to

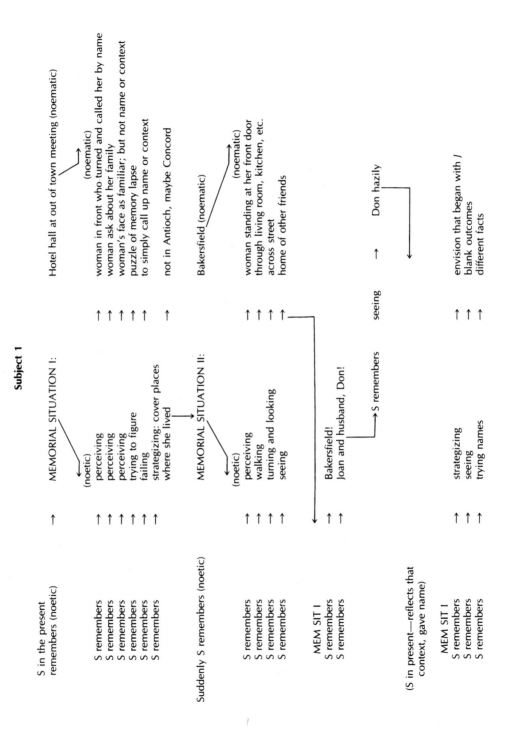

Figure 1. Threefold temporal structure of memorial experiences (Present, Memorial Situation I, Memorial Situation II) demonstrated through subject one.

highlight this intriguing fact is to say that all of the conscious processes that happen in waking life can occur again within memory. Thus we can think, perceive, desire, feel, and so forth but with a memorial index. To attach the memorial index means that we reawaken our own earlier "thinkings," perceivings, desirings, and the like. This is what differentiates memory from other iterative modes of consciousness such as imagination or dreaming consciousness.

It is also interesting to observe that, whereas the researcher asked for *a* memory description, two were always contained within the descriptions provided by the subjects. In part, this is due to the nature of the research, which is retrospective, and part to the nature of consciousness, which, as I mentioned, is iterative.

Of course, what is especially of interest psychologically is the relationship between the memorial situations that appeared to each subject. In terms of formal structure, all three descriptions are alike insofar as they reveal the noetic–noematic relationship. Thus we must look at the context in order to see if we can detect a reason for the emergence of the two memorial situations.

In the first description, the subject basically employs a rational strategy. She is greeted by a woman who is familiar to her, but she can recall neither the context nor the name. She relates the woman to places she has lived and systematically retraces her dwellings, while, at the same time, being guided by the letter *J*. As she was working through this process, suddenly a scene emerges in detail in which she recognizes the woman, her husband, and the place, and everything comes together for the subject. The detailed scene emerged suddenly and prior to the subject's full recognition of it, but it clearly is related to the whole direction of the search she was undertaking. It was the sought-after intentional object that did not come forward at first, but its psychological meaning is clear: It is the detailed answer to the subject's search regarding the identity of the woman and the context within which the subject knew her.

In the second description, the second memory is more of a welcome surprise to the subject. She is walking hurriedly across the grass and then slows down and begins to enjoy the greenness of the grass and from that joy there wells up the joys she used to share with her boyfriend when they picnicked together on just such a lawn. She also realized that the warmth and joy of the memory had an effect on her current mood because she felt much more warmth towards others after the memory than when she was merely heading for the bookstore in a pragmatic way. The series of intentional relations in this description seems to run as follows: the awareness of the greenness of the grass and its accompanying joy (noetic, Memory Time 1) leads to the memory of picnics with her boyfriend

on lawns (noematic, Memory Time 2), which in turn intensifies the joy that the subject feels (noetic, Memory Time 1), which in turn, is spread to the perceptual world at large (noematic, Memory Time 1). Thus, it seems as though the different memorial presentations are sustained by the continuity of joyous noeses.

Description 3 is similar to description 2, except that the feelings involved are on the ambiguous or negative side and the memories more poignant. The subject chooses, as a memory description, a time when she was getting ready for her senior ball and she wanted her mother to tell her that she looked well in her dress and to affirm her in this important moment of her life, but her mother refused to do so. The subject then said she felt empty inside and that she could not appear "good enough" to herself, and it was at that moment that the second memory suddenly and vividly appeared. The subject was 4½ years of age and she was crying because her mother would not let her do what she wanted, and the reason was that she got her dress too dirty. In this case, the memory that ties the two memorial presentations together is practically identical. Each time the subject is seeking approval for an activity (going to the ball; going to kindergarten; each time the mother refuses), and each time the subject's relation to her dress is important (to look pretty enough in it; to wear it without getting it dirty).

What is also amazing is that the subject solves each situation by the same strategy. As a child, she stopped crying when she realized that her mother would have to let her go to first grade, and until then, she would "somehow feel present at school" until she could go, even though she would not always feel pleased about it. It is at that moment that she flashes back to *Memorial Situation I* and says that she decided to go the ball anyway and tried to attend with the feeling of her mother's "approval inside of me," but again, not fully comfortable with this decision. Thus, the two memories seem to be supported by a common intentional structure: When the subject wants to fulfill conflicting desires, she decides to fulfill one and makes up the lack of the other through pretense (in one case her presence at school; in the other her mother's approval), even though she is simultaneously aware that the pretense is not the real thing. (In passing, one can note the problem with this attitude: The subject is *deciding* to fulfill her desires rather than experiencing them *as fulfilled*.). In any event, that Memories 1 and 2 should be present in that particular subject's description is not surprising. This description also helps us to understand why the awakening of memories can be helpful to people with problems in the present.

The preceding discussion, of course, raises the question of why the first memory was chosen to begin with. What is the relationship between the subject's present and

Memorial Situation I that the subject chooses to describe? Unfortunately, I do not have the data to answer this question, but now that I am sensitive to the issue, I shall be more inclusive in the data-gathering phase of the research.

Overall, however, the data seem to suggest that the relationship between the two memorial presentations in the subjects' descriptions are related by meaning, though in varied ways. For the first subject, the presence of a detailed partial meaning both fulfills and enlightens the guiding framework. For the second subject, the feeling of joy finds another instance that then outruns itself. And for the third subject, as has just been demonstrated, an invariant meaning structure seemed to subtend the two instances. Obviously, these relations will have to be explored further in order to be described more precisely.

Another interesting psychological aspect of the memory descriptions is the way in which the concrete descriptions exceed the original motivations even though sustaining them. The first subject, for example, goes on to describe how she went on to her neighbor's living room, kitchen, and outside the backdoor where she turned and looked across the street. She saw the home of the other friends, and then she went on to describe her neighbor's husband. All of the "bonus" description she gives not only shows how memories exceed the intentions that precipitate them but also their potential relevance. The details indicate how new, perhaps relevant, aspects of our experience can come before us. The subject, after all, was only trying to remember the name of the woman she met in the hall, and she ends up describing, however vaguely, her neighbor's husband. Perhaps seeing him evoked his name and that, in turn, his wife's, the original object of the search. It shows that the memorial presences that are awakened belong more to the earlier perceived intentional acts rather than to the contemporaneous memorial intentional act. This might help us understand why one can come up with new insights with memories of one's own lived experiences: In remembering, one reawakens intentional acts that are still related to their original noemata.

A closer analysis reveals another dimension of the intentional perceptual "act–object" structure that is evoked through the memorial intentional act. The first subject admitted that even while her mind was "blank," she had the "feeling" that she was simultaneously "casting about for something." This, and other statements, indicate that experience is functioning at different levels as well. (She also said that while she was thinking about different places, she tried different names, most of which began with *J;* as the different "places" flashed by, she was also aware that they were not quite right, and so on. The degree of complexity being expressed here is too great to be accounted for sequentially.)

In addition to the levels, there are also a series of "feelings" that can be interpreted as the noetic source of the presences. In other words, the presences that come up with their "fringes" of being close, being off, seeming right, and the like have, as their correlate, "noetic acts" that are rooted in feelings, which brings us to the role of the body in memory. After all, the first subject "walked through" the house of her neighbor and "perceived" the street where other friends lived and "looked" at the husband as though she were not wearing her glasses, and so on. The second subject "saw" the minibouquets that her boyfriend made; the third subject was present to her own crying for not being able to continue kindergarten. Because these are previously lived perceptual acts that are being reawakened, it is not surprising that there should be a bodily role. Often, the feelings that the awakened perceptual acts evoke reverberate back to the present and subjects re-experience in the present the feelings that are being evoked in the memory. It is as though the body is the silent carrier of these meanings through feelings, and I am struck by how often this appears in memorial descriptions.

Consider these examples from other subjects:

(Subject 4). As I recall this incident, I feel pain . . . I find that I really don't want to remember it, and yet it remains a vivid memory of a day in my life. . . . Neither of us spoke, but as I sat there, I remember as clearly today as then, and that I felt very close to him [her son].

(Subject 5). It was sunset, and the warm breeze that had been drifting through my window all afternoon was becoming chilly. It sent a shiver through me. . . . A similar cold breeze was coming in the house through the back screendoor. The cold air sent a shiver through me, and as I got up to close the back door, I saw my fiance coming up the back walk.

(Subject 6). This event took place 31 years ago. A minimal amount of background seems necessary, and I feel a little anxious about getting to hard parts of the story; I start tightening up around my center. . . . Bodily, when remembering about this, my head wants to sink down into my shoulders—I feel like closing up, disappearing. . . . [Subject was required to leave a pet squirrel behind because of state laws and she abandoned it in a forest. Part of the description of the event at that time reads:] I can feel the cage wire hurting my fingers, and the difficulty of walking up that hill. I feel tight, like I am trying to keep from falling.

All three of these partial descriptions show that memory of feelings provoke feelings in the present and that they are capable of bringing up memorial presences as noematic objects of such feelings.

My present commentary has just begun to tap the richness that these protocols contain with respect to memory. It is, indeed, a problem with descriptive research that it cannot be reduced and communicated more efficiently.

Unlike traditional research with tables and figures that reduce findings, the communication of descriptive research requires elaboration of the given. It focuses on the richness of the data and its implicatory relations. In this context, therefore, this chapter does not represent an exhaustive analysis of the findings. It is written merely with the intent to indicate some of the possibilities of the phenomenological approach to memory.

Some Contributions of the Phenomenological Approach

There are complementary and unique aspects to the phenomenological approach to learning and memory. By beginning concretely and allowing the fullness of the experience to count as such, the critical dimensions for any experience to be a human experience can be accounted for as these dimentions are lived. I am speaking here about the sociality, historicity, and the meaning-giving characteristics of human subjectivity. For example, in all five learning descriptions, the presence of a significant other was important for learning to take place. To take two examples, the teacher of the student learning to drive told him that he was ready to move to the next level when he wished to remain at the some level longer, thus instilling in the learner the confidence he needed. With the San Francisco couple, it was only when her friend asked the subject if she really wanted to help, that she was able to be decisive about her approach to her hosts. I have found this facilitative role of another person to be a key factor in the experience of learning when it occurs positively.

The contents of the three memory descriptions also intrinsically involved others. For the first subject, it was a casual acquaintance who triggered off the memory process and with the other two subjects, the memorial presentations involved significant others. Although the limited data of this research did not reveal the impact of sociality on the noetic processes of memory, it is very likely that there are such influences, thus revealing the pervasiveness of the sociality of memory.

Historicity is present because the subject, in his or her description of a learning situation, always reveals enough of his or her previous experience to make the interpretation of the current situation at least minimally meaningful. Thus we know that the driving learner never drove on his own before and that the San Francisco lady as a hostess tended not to expect guests to help with household chores. Without some knowledge of these historical factors, a sense of learning could not be obtained.

Last, the attribution of meanings in experience is so intrinsic that any ignoring of it would violate the experience being examined. Thus the driving learner believed that cars were huge, and the San Francisco subject thought that the couple did not really want help. These attributes were lived by the subjects, and, without taking these personal meanings into account, we would have been unable to understand these experiences precisely as learning experiences.

The meanings lived by the subjects are also important for the understanding of memory. Thus the first subject recognized the house and the neighborhood as "Bakersfield" and that led to the woman's name. Probably only the second subject could see dandelions as potential minibouquets because of her relationship to her former boyfriend. With the third subject, her ability to make "things the way she wants" despite circumstances gives a psychological meaning to her memory that one would not perceive if one did not know her history.

The combination of these three factors—sociality, historicity, and meaning attribution—help make the analysis of experience possible and relevant as a complement to performance studies by mainstream psychology.

In contrast to this approach, the traditional model sees sociality, historicity, and meaning attribution as factors to be controlled by the experimenter. They are seen as relatively independent and abstract variables that can be maniuplated, whereas the phenomenological approach recognizes the fact that these factors can only count insofar as they are *interpreted or understood by the subject*. Thus, in the San Francisco couple learning description, we can assume that our subject has had many experiences as a guest and host, but only the knowledge that she has lived that relation with the attitude that she does not expect a guest to be helpful can help us understand part of the reason that the situation she described could become a learning situation. Overall, then, there is a convergence of values between the descriptive approach and mainstream psychology because they both respect sociality, historicity, and meaning attribution, but these dimensions are treated differently in the two perspectives. The major difference is that the descriptive phenomenological approach includes these variables only as they are interpreted by the subject, whereas the mainstream approach relates them to subjects as objectively controlled variables.

There is another way in which convergence and divergence can be shown. The mainstream psychology of learning has concentrated on performance in relation to criterion, especially in terms of time, trials, and/or errors. These factors are also present in the descriptive data, but their objective determination does not stand out as the crucial factor. From the descriptive perspective, how long it took or how many times the subject had to look at the dashboard to make proper discriminations is less important than the fact that he or she can get an articulated comprehensible grasp. In other words, amount of time and number of attempts are important only insofar as they allow the possibility of such a comprehensible grasp. The pivotal point here is not the number of trials or errors but the quality of the experience that leads to clarity or competence.

With respect to errors, their phenomenol presence is everywhere. The driving subject said that his car seemed like a huge boat and that the street seemed very narrow. These experiences, and others like them (e.g., the San Francisco subject's initial perception that her hosts would not accept help), are the experiential correlates of behavioral errors. Once learning is achieved, the perceptions and expectations involved are in line with the objective givens just as when, on the performance side, no flaws are present. From this perspective, the number of errors is less interesting than their specific nature.

A unique contribution of the descriptive approach is the concept of "subjective learning." The two subjects whose descriptions lacked evidence of correct performance after insight bring up the issue of "degrees of learning." Sometimes the experience of learning is robust and objective; at other times it is relative to the subject's personal history only and is very meager on an objective scale. For example, if the driving subject's learning ended after he had discriminated the dashboard instruments, he could hardly call himself a driver, yet it would be an achievement vis-à-vis his personal history and thus cannot be wholly discounted experientially speaking. There is evidence that the development of the learning process has structurally consistent transition points that define phases, although the phases are correlated with types of learning. These delineated phases of the experiential learning process can help determine intervention points when needed. Once again, there can be convergence with mainstream psychology because performance data also reveal such breaks, but the experiential perspective gives a clearer meaning to the phases *for the subjects.*

Perhaps the difference between the two approaches can be seen even more vividly in the case of memory. We said that the natural-science research tradition emphasized quantification and an external perspective, whereas the phenomenological tradition emphasizes experience and meaning. This is clearly seen with respect to the mainstream memory studies we outlined previously. To seek a physiological or chemical model is to try to understand memory externally and nonpsychologically. An attempt to measure memory would be a quantification of it and would presuppose the lived experience. The cognitive approach is descriptive, but it is more faithful to the model, which is formal and abstract, and thus the descriptions remain external to the lived experience. The closest is the Bartlett (1932) type of study, where it will be re-

called, Bartlett had subjects learn stories, anecdotes, discussions, and other types of "realistic" materials, that is, materials that were identical to those encountered in everyday life. However, even though Bartlett's materials were meaningful in themselves, they are still somewhat distant because the meaning does not intrinsically spring from the subject's relation to the materials, but rather, the subject has to relate him- or herself to a story, which he or she has not chosen and may or may not find personally meaningful. It would be different if the subjects had to generate their own stories, but that is never done. Thus, within the research tradition, only the phenomenological approach captures the intrinsic relation of the subject to his or her memory.

Perhaps one example will suffice to demonstrate this point. If we take the subject who remembered preparing for the senior ball and then flashed to crying to stay in kindergarten, what question would a researcher want to put to her? Should one ask about her memory span? Should one examine her brain? Should a researcher measure the speed of the two memories, or how long each one lasted? How could any of these questions penetrate the meaningful relationship between the two memories? This is what is meant when it is said that the very questions put to psychological phenomena by mainstream psychology remain external to them.

Nevertheless, one must respect both the convergences and divergences between these two scientific traditions. They cannot easily be brought together, nor can they be wholly distanced from each other because they both point to the same fundamental human phenomena. Thus a few words on their relationships seems in order.

PSYCHOLOGY AND SCIENCE

Mainstream psychology depends upon that form of research known as "experimentation," and it does so for three basic reasons: (a) to utilize the precise form of control that experiments afford; (b) to discover relationships and facts; and (c) to verify findings. The aims of descriptive research overlap with the aims of mainstream psychology without being identical to them. The primary difference is simply that those who espouse descriptive psychology are not necessarily convinced that research in its experimental form as it historically evolved is the best form of research for psychological phenomena. Those who adopt a phenomenological approach are convinced that there are logical grounds for approaching psychological phenomena descriptively. Even if it is not experimental in the strict sense, a descriptive approach with qualitative analysis is a legitimate form of research that can meet the three criteria of control, discovery of relationships, and verification (although in different ways). Before considering this point, however, let us look at how the context a researcher posits is so very important for understanding the relevance of his or her research.

At the beginning of this chapter, it was stated that what was common to the learning traditions, as with the memory studies, was the natural scientific approach. That the values of this perspective dominated research in learning can be seen from Hilgard's (1951) summary:

> To study learning in the lab, it is necessary to discover or invent situations in which graduated improvement may occur, so that scores can be obtained. Such situations exist in familiar tasks like typing and piano. In these it is possible to score success according to the time required or errors made, or repetitions needed. Rote memorizing lends itself readily to this kind of study. All that is needed is the introduction of measures of progress such as the number of promptings needed after different amounts of study. It was natural that the earliest quantitative studies of learning made use of these familiar experiences. (p. 517)

Thus, it was necessary that situations be chosen that would allow the researcher to "score progress" or count errors or measure time. The activities that would meet such criteria could serve as the subject matter, and, in a certain sense, the activity in and of itself was less important than the situation. Nonsense syllables, learning of telegraphy, problem boxes, and mazes entered, therefore, psychological history.

The main point, however, is: Change the criteria and the situation changes. Phenomenological psychologists are interested in the organization of experience and the meanings it holds for the experiencer and in how those meanings vary for different phenomena and different individuals. The structure of the descriptive research situation is as fitting for its purposes as traditional research situations are for theirs.

But still the question remains: Can descriptive research be as scientific as the traditional approach? The answer is an affirmative one and can be demonstrated by returning to the three points just mentioned. Recall that, in descriptive research, one seeks meanings. In the same way, the meeting of the criteria is through meanings. Thus the descriptions provided by the subjects are guided by the meaning of the instructions and questions put to them. This is a form of control. Subjects are asked, for example, to describe learning experiences and not just any experience, or, within learning, they are asked to describe a specific type of learning, and so forth. Second, by means of descriptions, systematic discoveries are made about the experience of learning. It was found before that wrongly posited assumptions constitute a category of learning as experienced and that the relationship to a significant other was an important factor in learning.

These are gross findings, of course, in need of differentiation and refinement (which are possible within the methodology being proposed), but they are genuine systematic discoveries.

Finally, let us turn to the question of reliability and validity. The latter is possible because most of the descriptions obtained are descriptions of learning as judged by a postresearch analytic criterion. Occasionally, one does find a description that purports to be learning, but, in fact, is not, according to the postresearch criterion, just as in running nonsense syllable experiments one occasionally finds subjects that fail to meet the criterion. Overall, however, a sense of validity is present because the description can be subsumed under the concept of learning. Reliability is equally present because, whether one is working within a subject or across subjects, the same question elicits comparable descriptions. In other words, variations of the phenomenon are obtained, but it is the same phenomenon being described. In addition, reliability is also present across researchers. Many different researchers following the same method and using the same data can come up with comparable findings.

Overall, a major difference between descriptive and traditional research is that, in descriptive research, one tries to satisfy the criteria of psychological meaning; it is not a matter of measurement. The criteria are more akin to logical coherence even though they are not necessarily logical in the formal sense. Thus, if the descriptive approach, both logically and practically, can yield findings that meet its own criteria, why should it not be included within the totality of methods of psychological science? It seems that prejudgment plays an important role in keeping psychology from being open to more diverse possibilities of research.

One purpose of this chapter is to show that descriptive research can be practiced rigorously and systematically and that it is based upon logic and sound theory. Even if a future integration with traditional psychological approaches is possible, what matters now is how descriptive research meets its own qualitative criteria and not those of traditional metric psychology.

REFERENCES

Bartlett, F. C. (1932). *Remembering: A study in experimental and social psychology.* Cambridge: Cambridge University Press.
Bryan, W. L., & Harter, N. (1899). Studies on the telegraphic language: The acquisition of a hierarchy of values. *Psychological Review, 6,* 345–375.
Casey, E. S. (1987). *Remembering: A phenomenological study.* Bloomington: Indiana University Press.
Cohen, G. (1977). *Psychology of cognition.* New York: Academic.

Ebbinghaus, H. (1964). *Memory* (H. A. Ruger & C. E. Bussenius, Trans.). New York: Dover. (Originally published 1885.)

Ellis, H. C. (1978). *Fundamentals of human learning, memory, and cognition.* Dubuque, IA: William C. Brown. (Originally published 1972.)

Giorgi, A. (Ed.). (1985). *Phenomenology and psychological Research.* Pittsburgh: Duquesne University Press.

Giorgi, A. (1986). A phenomenological analysis of descriptions of concepts of learning obtained from a phenomenog'aphic perspective. *Publikationer* from *Institution for Pedagogik, Gotegorgs Universitet, Fenomenografiska Notiser* 4.

Hilgard, E. R. (1951). Methods and procedures in the study of learning. In S. S. Stevens, (Ed.), *Handbook of experimental psycholgoy* (pp. 517–567). New York: Wiley.

Husserl, E. (1913). *Ideas.* Gibson, TX: WRB. (German original, 1913)

John, E. R. (1967). *Mechanisms of memory.* New York: Academic.

Nagy, Z. M. (1979). Development of learning and memory processes in infant mice. In N. E. Spear & B. A. Campbell (Eds.), *Ontogeny of learning and memory* (pp. 109–133), Hillsdale, NJ: Lawrence Erlbaum.

Pavlov, I. P. (1910). *The work of the digestive glands* (W. H. Thompson, Trans.). London: Charles Griffin. (Originally published 1897.)

Sechenov, I. M. (1965). *Reflexes of the brain* (S. Belsky, Trans.). Cambridge: M.I.T. Press. (Originally published 1863.)

Small, W. S. (1899). Notes on the psychic development of the young white rat. *American Journal of Psychology, 11,* 80–100.

Thorndike, E. L. (1898). Animal intelligence: An experimental study of the associative processes in animals. *Psychological Monographs, 2*(8).

III

Development, Emotion, and Social Psychology

The next three chapters examine specific issues within closely related areas of psychology: development, emotionality, and social psychology.

Beginning with the reminder that we were all children at one time, Briod's Chapter 7 raises the issue of gaining access both to the child we once were as well as to the ongoing experiences of children around us. This is a critical question because, in Briod's view, the developmental literature contains too many preconceptions about the lives of children. As a corrective, he offers an illuminating study of the child's relationship to past, present, and future based on the accounts of children of various ages.

William Fischer's Chapter 8 considers the phenomenon of ''being anxious'' as an example of human emotionality. This chapter provides an excellent example of the kind of insights generated by the use of protocol analysis, insights that are of potential benefit to both the anxious person as well as the professional psychologist. Toward the end of his chapter, Fischer clarifies how all forms of being emotional provide opportunities for self-understanding.

Von Eckartsberg's Chapter 9 on person perception is unique in that it is the only chapter in this volume to utilize ''story telling'' as its medium of presentation. This form is especially apt in that the chapter itself is a perfect example of the dialogal-existential approach that it advocates. The chapter also provides a comprehensive overview of recent innovations in the theory and practice of social psychology.

7

A Phenomenological Approach to Child Development

Marc Briod

And the children in the apple-tree
Not known, because not looked for . . .
—T. S. Eliot

THE POSSIBILITY OF A PHENOMENOLOGY OF CHILD DEVELOPMENT

That it is even possible to take a phenomenological approach to child development rests upon a radical empirical fact: To be human means that one is or was once a child. The experience of being or having been a child is known to every person as an essential condition of his or her existence. This knowledge is accessible either directly to children who are currently living through their own developing childhoods or indirectly to adults who recollect childhood experiences out of the fabric of their already developed life-worlds. It is the radicality of this "world fact" (Wild, 1959) concerning childhood that makes possible a phenomenological approach to child development. For one cannot make sense of the world of a developing child without existential grounding in the experience of living or having lived as a child. And one cannot hope to communicate with others about the meaning of the developing child's world unless those others, too, are or have been children.

But the idea of child development usually connotes the development of someone else's world, not one's own.

How, then, does phenomenology bridge the gap between one's remembered youth and the immediate presence of other children? If each child inhabits a child world that adults live in the mode of having-been, then we share that world with children insofar as both experience its manifestness. Adults experience the manifestness of childhood indirectly, through having been a developing child; children experience it directly, through the now-being of a developing child. Both these ways of experiencing childhood are modalities of being-in-the-world; one is as an adult, the other, as a child.

There is no question here of needing to discover that we adults inhabit the same planet, breathe the same air, or have the same overlapping life spans with children. Rather, phenomenology returns us to the experienced roots of our existences, so that we may find there a deeper commonality, a sense of similitude among our "subjective" awarenesses of life. Along with awakening us to such existential commonalities as the possibility of our own death, the radical freedom and responsibility for our own existence, or the primacy of the lived body, phenomenology offers a way of drawing us toward our common rootedness in the world of the child. This gravitational pull can, in turn, provide the basis for a profound sense of being-in-the-world-with-others, and in particular, with those special others who are currently developing as children.

Mark Briod • Department of Philosophy, Oakland University, Rochester, Minnesota 48063.

But if the possibility for a phenomenology of child development rests upon our capacity to regain access to our own childhoods, then we must ask whether and in what respect we can ever rediscover the child we once were. Is the autobiographical remembering of one's childhood a reliving of it? Clearly not, because as Lippitz (1986) points out, "to do that, I would have to be in a position to put out of action the person I have become" (p. 59). We can reopen ourselves to our remembered childhoods but only to "the child of the *remembering* adult," not the original child, which "remains lost to us forever" (p. 56). So if we try somehow to "bracket" or "suspend" our adult awareness in order to reconnect with the child within, we will find that such bracketing can only occur from the thicket of our daily living *as* remembering adults.

If phenomenology can help us draw closer to the experiences of childhood, how might the development of those experiences be understood? A phenomenological approach is merely a series of still portraits unless it uncovers the child's world as changing in and through time. Throughout this chapter, but especially in the concluding sections, the development of the child is taken to be an organic aspect of his or her life-world as a temporal existence, the continual unfolding of a life that is always already open to its own future, as well as to present and past.

CULTURE AND PHENOMENOLOGY

Not only is childhood rediscovered from one's position as a remembering or observing adult, but it is revealed in and through the particular circumstances of one's culture. The task of the phenomenologist is to identify those existential "essences" that define the developing world of the child and that inhere within the texture of the child's unique culture. Yet it is not a matter of ignoring or abstracting from the conditions of a given human setting. A phenomenology of childhood seeks to understand the experience of development as the child lives it through. This goal is not accomplished by distilling out a set of universal characteristics but by uncovering the essential or invariant features of a child's developing world through different narrative examples.

So the primary aim of a phenomenological account is not to draw attention to the specific cultural influences that affect the way each child develops but to gain a deeper understanding of what it invariably means to live and develop *as* a child in various human settings and circumstances. The intent is to uncover the meaning of the experience of being a child, the sense or flavor of a child's world as it is lived out of a particular time and place. In this way, a felt awareness of children's development may be evoked in the reader rather than an antiseptic awareness of "universal stages" of development. The latter is hypothetical and objectified, not about the life-world of children who inhabit different cultures, but about isolated characteristics of cognition, affect, socialization, and morality, distilled from both the life-world and its attendant cultures.

The life-world is the ground of all that is empirical, and certain sources of data remain especially close to that world as it develops. Sources that may offer glimpses into the child's development include biography, autobiography, written accounts by clinical psychologists, therapists, psychoanalysts, teachers, parents, as well as accounts by children themselves, and the occasional powerful narratives of childhood summoned forth by novelists and poets. Perhaps the richest sources of data come from the reports of analysts whose work with neurotic patients often yields significant childhood memories. A difficulty with psychoanalytic reports, however, is their deep entanglement with the theories of neurosis, ego formation, defense mechanisms, oedipal fantasies, self-esteem, and the like. What is needed are inumerable cross-cultural scenes, episodes, moments—narratives lovingly drawn from involved conversations with children and from awakened childhood memories. The goal is to glean something of the texture of the child's development as it is lived through various cultural conditions, not as it appears problematically to the clinician or theoretically to the scientist.

CHILDREN AND CHILDHOOD

The idea of child development commonly connotes two things: (1) human beings do, in fact, experience a delineated period of life known as childhood, and (2) childhood changes over time, progressing through increasingly complex stages of behavior and experience, in a predictable sequence of transformations, and according to certain presumed laws of human development.

The first idea, that human life is developmentally divided into two main phases, cannot be uncritically accepted. Historian Philippe Aries (1962) argues that before late Medieval times there was little awareness of childhood as a distinct period of life. The biological dependency of infants upon their mothers usually ended by age 5. Thereafter, the little ones were expected to make their own way in life, without special coddling or attention from older members of the family or community. They were still children: relatively young, immature, inexperienced, uneducated. But *as* children, they were given no special attention, affection, or care by older members of the family or community. After infancy, their dress became indistinguishable from that of adults, their exact ages were rarely known, and their segregation from adult settings and activities was unimaginable. Children were given no designated times or places to play, to invent games, or to receive special training. In short, children had no socially visible childhoods.

The reason for this inattention to children, which Aries calls "a feeling of indifference towards a too fragile childhood" (p. 39), may stem in part from the very high child mortality rates during Medieval times. Societies with lower child mortality rates and better living conditions cultivated livelier interests in their children. But here is the larger point: Although phenomenologists seek to disclose the life-world as having a past, their primary aim is not the historical reconstruction of cultural circumstances that surround people's lives. Aries only indirectly reveals to us a significant feature of the lived world of the developing Medieval child. That world is merely implied by his reports of adult disinterest toward their children. His discovery that Medieval children were taken for granted and not coddled does not show that their worlds were qualitatively the same as that of adults. Rather he shows us in a powerful way how much of the child's experience may be culturally defined and is therefore subject to change across time and place.

The aim of the phenomenologist is to understand the invariant existential aspects of the developing world of the child. These aspects are the human conditions of the child's life-world, conditions that children bring to their cultural circumstances. They may be revealed in the memories of adults, in narrative reports from children, or in adult narratives about children. But invariant themes are not found independent of the concrete cultural settings in which children find themselves. For instance, a phenomenologist may observe that each child's manner of learning from adults varies according to different traditions (whether it be learning to shoe a horse, read a map, or do arithmetic). Yet he or she may also notice the essential fact that each child betrays a decidedly child's way of learning from adults, a way that is always already woven into the conditions of the child's experience.

So, although childhood as a distinct phase of life may be a modern cultural invention or discovery (in Europe, at any rate), we are not thereby entitled to assume that young people have not always inhabited a world that develops in certain essentially childlike ways, permeating the cultural environment, and best elucidated through phenomenology.

STAGE THEORIES OF DEVELOPMENT

The idea of child development also commonly connotes a changing and dynamic life, one that progresses from simpler and relatively "immature" levels of behavior and experience toward more and more complex stages of growth. Most of the major developmental psychologists have formulated their theories about personality, selfhood, intelligence, morality, and so forth on the basis of such stages or levels.

But stage theories of child development tend to rigidify our ways of looking at children. As one researcher puts it, "we do not often see or hear real children any more; rather we see *stages* of advancing development, stages of readiness, stages of moral judgment" (Polakow-Suransky, 1984, p. 1). A phenomenological approach, on the other hand, resists the positing of theoretical constructs about levels of development and thus keeps us open to seeing children (as well as our remembered selves) in fresh and vibrant ways.

Many practitioners who are both reflective and open to children's lived experiences are rightly skeptical of developmental theories. In an autobiographical account of how he became a teacher, Herbert Kohl (1984) says:

> I've learned [that] . . . a child is not an abstraction that can be fitted neatly into some scheme or theory, for growth never quite fits the laws of development psychologists invent. You have to discover who a child is by tapping and probing gently . . . before a plan for construction or reconstruction can be developed. And you have to love to see a beautiful structure emerge. (p. 4)

Some child researchers, too, have begun to conclude that developmental stage theories are not firmly enough grounded in children's experiences. For example, Piaget's theory (1950) that a child's intelligence undergoes predictable transformations of reasoning was based upon his conversational encounters with children. His method of posing open-ended questions to children brought him close to a phenomenological approach. But his structuralist theory of cognitive development has met with major criticism by empiricists like Gareth Mathews (1980) and Margaret Donaldson (1978), who have noticed children's propensities (like adults) for displaying intelligent thought or action primarily in the context of their own meaningful life experiences or in the train of questions or ideas that the children themselves have opened to reflection.

Both these researchers have noticed, for instance, that deductive reasoning (part of Piaget's highest stage of intelligence) turns up in the situational and speculative language of very young children, occurring many years in advance of what a Piagetian would predict. Similarly,

Lawrence Kohlberg's (1969) cognitive theory of moral development is considered insufficiently empirical by critics who point out that his structuralist assumptions predefine his stages of moral reasoning, thus precluding the relevance of many significant experiences recounted by his developing subjects (Prescott & Valle, 1978).

Stage theories in psychology also tend to assume continuous growth over time. Erik Erikson's (1980) eight-stage theory of psychosexual development is a case in point. The child who moves, say, from the third stage of psychosocial development (involving a chronic "crisis" of initiative vs. guilt) to the fourth stage (involving a new "crisis" of industry vs. inferiority) is said to be shifting psychosexually from a search for a sense of purpose by means of sex-role identification at home, to a sense of competence by means of self-esteem in school. This is one of the eight knots in the continuous thread of development from infancy to old age, according to Erikson. It is deemed crucial that each knot be untied in timely fashion by the developing child, although any given stage may become a Gordian challenge if a child's environment fails to provide the emotional and social support needed for successful disentanglement.

Erikson assumes a continuity of change from level to level that is characteristic of most stage theorists. Phenomenologists, on the other hand, bring no such assumption to their research on children. As J. H. van den Berg (1961) has pointed out, the idea that human life grows in a structured, continuous, and gradual way is a modern bias that is rarely questioned. Before continuous development became part of our modern orthodoxy: ". . . discontinuity, which means a nongradual transition, a leap, an unconnectedness, and which implies accidental or free occurrence, was accepted in every respect as possible and real" (p. 54). Phenomenologists remain open to the possibility of major discontinuities in "normal" human development in spite of what current theories seem to preclude.

STAGE THEORY AND THE OBJECTIVE FRAME

A few objective researchers on development have begun to voice their own concerns about the theory of stage sequences. Jerome Kagan (1984) observes that developmentalists have always had faith in some form of connectedness between earlier and later patterns of human behavior. This faith, says Kagan, must always be put to the test:

Despite the attractiveness and seeming utility of regarding development as being composed of slowly growing, connected stages, we should remain open to the velocity of the transitions and the degree of connectedness among them.

I do not claim that there are no structurally preserved elements in development—there must be some; I suggest only that it is unlikely that every actor in the first scene of the play has a role in the second act. (p. 91)

But Kagan's skepticism here is firmly within the tradition of rational scientism, which never questions its aim of gaining a knowledge that can help to explain child behavior. The aim of the phenomenologist, to gain an understanding that stays as close as possible to meanings that inhere in the textures of ordinary life-world experiences, is brushed aside in favor of the grander aim of acquiring objective knowledge that explains and predicts.

This form of hard-nosed social science often results in the sort of scepticism that is so evident in Kagan's writings. The goal of science, he tells us, "is to generate statements in the objective frame" (p. 24); but private experience often "represents an odd fragment of what is present" (p. 21) because "each person's frame is unique and limited in scope and illuminates only a small part of the event to be understood in the objective frame." (p. 24). This leaves it to the objective scientist to piece together the "real" connections and meanings that make experience truly intelligible in the objective frame.

The contrast between this sort of scientism and a phenomenological approach is clear-cut. For example, a few phenomenologists have tentatively begun to mark out the way that children experience lived time (Briod, 1986; Lippitz, 1983; Merleau-Ponty, 1964). They describe the textured world of a child's lived time as an intentional presence to things, events, and people, disclosing past and future horizons within a unitary, holistic field of time consciousness. But Kagan, by virtue of his unwavering goal of seeking objective stages, tries to step outside the child's life-world in order to see it as it "really" is. He thereby slices the temporal wholeness of that world into disconnected time periods that must somehow be objectively reconnected if research on development is to achieve scientific respectability. The result is a net that has been so widely cast upon the ocean of human behavior and experience that it yields little meaningful or useful knowledge of how children *live* their development. Thus Kagan himself refers to the science of development as a "temporary period of relatively weak theory and an insufficient number of trustworthy facts" (p. 25). But to a phenomenologist, objective facts about children are always untrustworthy, because they are at least one step removed from the life-world of the child. The subsequent weakness of theory is the chronic result of this untrustworthiness of facts. The alternative is not to rely instead on merely subjective facts but rather to return to lived experience as the only reliable evidence about what it is like to develop as a child. The life-world is, of necessity, the primordial source of all experience and knowledge, out of which emerges the very distinction between subjective and objective frames of reference.

THE OPENING OF A CHILD'S WORLD

Van den Berg (1961) speaks of the possibility for accidental or free occurrence in development, and Kohl (1984) refers to seeing a beautiful structure emerge. Neither writer mentions objective laws or stages. Rather, development is regarded as the child's open, creative venture of living toward the future.

Kohl acknowledges the limitation of his "building" metaphor when he adds, "People are not buildings, and that's what makes observing their growth so interesting. Buildings do not build themselves, but people do" (p. 45). Here he is perhaps overcorrecting for the tendency among theoretical psychologists to employ biological metaphors of maturing, flowering, ripening, becoming, and so on. This tendency is based on the presumption that the life sciences offer an epistemologically sound model for knowing about our world and that any psychology of child development founded on biological images will share in that soundness. Kohl's overcorrection suggests that children somehow build or create themselves, with assistance from facilitating adults who can help "develop" them. For Kohl, the prevailing metaphor for development shifts from the biological to the technocultural. Development becomes an act of making, constructing, building, as if the developed child were a product or artifact created by the social environment or by his or her own efforts. Not surprisingly, psychologists who try to emulate the life sciences lean toward biological metaphors of growth and maturation, whereas practitioners (especially educators) who regard development as a manifestation of culture or technology lean the other way, toward metaphors of making and fashioning.

Some terms, like *growing, developing,* and *forming,* carry a felicitous double meaning, drawn from either biological or cultural ways of looking at the child. Still other terms, like *changing, transforming,* and *restructuring,* lose the flavor of both perspectives because they suggest no temporal direction for the child's world (which is toward the future, if not always explicitly toward adulthood).

Metaphors for development are a necessary and appropriate part of the language of the child researcher. When we become conscious of them, we are reminded of the poetic ground of our thinking about children. The choice of a metaphorical way into the child's lived world is a choice that must be reflected upon and explicitly determined in accordance with one's existential sense of what it is to *be* in that world.

My own searchings for a root metaphor often return me to the image of "opening" because it suggests a movement of lived time that seems inherent in child development. The opening of a child's horizons of lived time connotes changes in and through the child's awareness of the world, just as an artist or poet becomes more and more open to experience through eye and mind. Neither biology nor culture predominate here, though both are implicated, and either perspective *may* be called upon by the phenomenologist in order to further elaborate a child's development, provided the sense of the child's world opening to itself has already been carefully described.

Opening, of course, suggests the expanding, widening, enlarging, or emerging of children's lives, as well as Martin Heidegger's (1962) fecund notions of dis-closing, dis-covering, making manifest, letting be, and so on. So child development is perhaps most adequately conveyed by a language of disclosure. But it would be accorded its special metaphorical flavor of growing, flowering, emerging, making, and so forth in light of the narrator's sense of the texture of each developing life. Moreover, it would be described as a life of creative openness, not self-made, but creative in the exact degree to which it is open to the newness and freshness of experience, and to its own life as a continual return to the sedimented layers of existing intentionalities, meanings, and projects.

Every metaphor for development has its opposite term: decaying, declining, regressing, destroying, shrinking, collapsing, closing, covering over, and so forth. A phenomenological approach to child development does not rule out the employment of any and all metaphors, including their opposites. But at the most fundamental level of narrative and hermeneutical work, the child's experience is best regarded as opening, revealing, or disclosing a world, in keeping with the phenomenological approach to *any* lived experience, first mapped out by Husserl (1962) and later given existential underpinnings by Heidegger (1962), Merleau-Ponty (1962), and others.

So we arrive at a view of child development that is closely aligned with the humanities and arts as ways of perceiving the textures of human life. To put it another way, a phenomenological approach to child development presumes less distance between the sciences and the arts than has been traditionally the case. Given the often unforeseeable patterns of growth in children, science (the art of discovery) is hardly a more disclosing approach to development than are the discoveries of art, especially the narrative and poetic forms (Koestler, 1978, pp. 131–161). For the dis-coveries of art are unabashedly grounded in the lived world of the artist, and make no pretense about generalizing (by means of inductive reasoning) to unwarranted theories or laws about human experience. So the aim of understanding child development may well be achieved more honestly and empathically through literary forms such as biography than through scientific thinking that is far too quick to leap from the rich and bewildering varieties of concrete experience to abstract generalities about types or laws of normal development, cognitive development, personality development, moral development, and so forth.

PHENOMENOLOGY THROUGH CHILD BIOGRAPHY

As a biographer, one first attends to the development of a child's world through the remembrance of childhood. One seeks to uncover glimpses of children growing— glimpses that are given through the recollection that life is founded in having been a child. One seeks to open up the larger story of growth toward a future of no-longer-being-a-child. To do this, one searches for themes of meaning and intentionality in the lives of children. Although each life is unique in much the same way that every work of art is particular, nonetheless, there is an underlying trajectory that is shared by every developing child, namely, the drift of an existence that eventually becomes less and less childlike. It is this common course that the phenomenologist qua biographer seeks to capture through descriptions and interpretations of diverse stories about children growing.

The key to researching child development through biographical explorations is that researchers must become aware of the interplay between the glimmerings of their own childhoods and the stories of children around them, such that each emergent world sheds light on the others:

> Biographies must not be allowed to degenerate into the supplies of material which aim to satisfy preconceived theoretical notions. One can *learn from the concrete and particular*. . . . The universal activity within it can be traced (and at the same time, without removing it from its context entirely) and made amenable to the intersubjective test. In this way every concrete pedagogical practice, and also every biography, attains an exemplary character because it may potentially instruct me. From the biographies of others, I learn by trying to make them comprehensible to me. At the same time, they disclose my own history to me, which otherwise may have remained in the dark without the help of the others. (Lippitz, 1986, p. 61)

A phenomenology of child development through biography requires movement back and forth between remembering one's childhood years of becoming and lived experiences among children who are presently develop-

ing. Phenomenological biographies need not involve extended and detailed life stories in the grand tradition of biographical writings. What is sought is the exemplary moment when the child experiences a sense of openness to a new way of being-in-the-world, a transition to an enlarged, or at least unfamiliar, condition of living.

Some life-span psychologists seem drawn to a biographical orientation as well as to "moments" or "episodes" rather than "stages" as markers of development. John Kotre (1984), calling himself a narrative psychologist, uses this approach:

> Elegant and compelling though stage theory is, it has fit poorly any life I have studied. To describe moments and episodes in lives has certain advantages over describing stages. Moments imply nothing about the proper age for the appearance of a motive, nor about its duration or ascendancy, nor about its foundation in the successful completion of previous tasks. Moments make room for accidents in what Klaus Riegel calls the outer-physical dimension of life and for chance encounters that dramatically alter a life's direction—in other words, for surprise. A vocabulary of moments and episodes keeps one from the developmental determinism that has been the occupational hazard of life-span psychologists from Freud on down and from behaviorists' unwarranted expectations of prediction and control (pp. 262–263).

In order to show that a moment in the developing life of a child is not accidental, but an essential invariant theme, the phenomenologist must observe and describe the situation out of which the moment arises, consider episodes in other children's lives that bear at least a family resemblance to the exemplary moment, and try to recall any similar pivotal moments from his or her own childhood. This is one form of the "intersubjectivity test" referred to earlier by Lippitz. The intersubjectivity test implies that knowledge about the development of children is not acquired by means of inductive generalizations from objective samplings of children. Rather, intersubjective comparisons tend to expose similar meanings that inhere in many children's lived worlds. Primordial meanings are discovered through paradigmatic stories about growing children, stories that are interpreted and compared to other narrative stories until a similitude is disclosed among developing children in various times and places. (Giorgi, 1983)

The sort of knowledge that results from a phenomenological approach to child development is clearly different from the knowledge achieved through standard social science procedures. It is an empathic, imaginative sense of what it is like to live as a developing child—a deepened sentiment about, and understanding of, the child's unfolding life. It is decidedly not a purely objective form of knowledge because phenomenological insight stays as close as possible to the originative, rich, concrete textures of individual existences.

AN EXEMPLARY APPROACH: THE OPENING OF LIVED TIME

The central thesis of this chapter is to suggest that child development can best be understood through richly worded descriptions and interpretations of individual children's developing life-worlds. There are no scientific shortcuts to knowledge about the growth of children. Objective research can, of course, discover many patterns and generalities about the "normal" growth of a child's body, a child's social activity, or even a child's cognitive experience (within any given culture). But the child-in-the-world cannot thereby be pieced together from these various strands of objective evidence. In the end, there can be no substitute for multifarious, attentive, and reflective accounts.

Let us undertake a description of lived time as our way "into" the developing world of the child. Lived time has been a major preoccupation among all the major phenomenologists since Husserl, simply because articulation of the everyday experiences of time is central to any full-bodied account of what it means to exist as a human being. Yet very little work has been done with children, perhaps because the child's life-world has been seen as a pale or immature version of adult awareness.

If we expect to understand the living time of the child, we must attend to moments or episodes that reveal the way past, present, and future become manifest to children in the course of their ordinary living. And we must show how their lived time grows open as a *world* of temporal experience.

The following narratives were drawn from the lives of three children: my daughter, Nina (6), and her friend, Jamie (3), both of whose episodes were written down by me in a journal form; and Arthur (9), whose childhood remembrances from Hungary, 1910 to 1914, are a part of Arthur Koestler's autobiography (1974).

These accounts were selected because they represent a 3-year-age difference between each child, thus inviting developmental comparisons. In addition, there are obvious cultural differences between Arthur's Hungary at the turn of the century and the Midwestern settings of Nina and Jamie some three generations later. So the essential invariants in their worlds emerge from the narratives in spite of the cultural gap between them.

Jamie (3)

Last spring our family took a weekend camping trip. We enjoyed it so much that we went on a second vacation 3 weeks later. As we were backing down the driveway, 3-year-old Jamie came running toward the car:
"Can Nina play?"
"No, Jamie, we're going on a vacation."
"Why are you going on a vacation?" There was a note of disappointment in her voice.
"Because we want to see new places, and swim, and walk in the forest, and things like that."
"Oh." She wore a sad expression on her face, and there followed an awkward moment of silence. Then suddenly she brightened: "Do you remember when you went away on a vacation before, and then you came back?"
And she happily waved goodbye to us as we drove on down the street.

During that long moment of silence after Jamie learned that Nina could not come out to play, her sadness turned to acceptance as soon as she formulated a question that released and expressed the memory of the previous weekend. She saw that Nina's departure would soon be past, but she also saw that it would become the past of a future that would again come around. And she believed in this link between past and future, because she had seen it work just 2 weeks earlier when Nina had left home on Friday and returned on Sunday. So already at 3 years of age, Jamie was able to look around the corners of her immediate world to see the horizon of her past in one direction and her future in the other. Looking across the axis of her present moment of lived time, with the past on one side, and the future on the other, she was calmed by the assurance that the desired future would arrive soon enough.

Nina (6)

For the first time in her life, Nina showed a keen interest in a news item on television. She saw a flash bulletin that the body of a previously kidnapped child had just been discovered in an isolated wooded area. The older children in the neighborhood had been buzzing about this kidnapping for several weeks. Nina had been listening to all their talk, and now she became the message bearer: "Guess what, Sarah? [a friend] They found the boy who was kidnapped, and he's dead." But Sarah was skeptical. "No really, Sarah, it's true. It just happened, and his house is here in Birmingham, or anyway, it's close to here. I saw it on TV." Nina was in awe of the power of her own announcement. She sensed that she was the local carrier of a fearful and threatening news item. She looked again into Sarah's face. This time she saw a hint of shock and anxiety and immediately broke off from her insistent message.

Like her younger friend, Jamie, Nina found herself in the dramatic presence of a simultaneous field of past and future occurrences. She envisioned the frightening possibility of the kidnapper's entering her neighborhood from a previously far-away place. But then she gained control over that feared possibility by seizing the opportunity to become a feared one herself, a harbinger of danger in her own right. When she saw that she was believed and that her message was upsetting her friend,

Sarah, she immediately stopped pressing her claim. Here we can see the intensification of Nina's sense of lived time, reflected in her attempt to speak about their shared presence in a world suddenly turned dangerous. (''Right now, here in Birmingham, a kidnapper.'')

> A few weeks later, Nina was playing at Jamie's house when word came by phone that Jamie's grandmother had just died after a long illness. Jamie had never known her grandmother except briefly as a bedridden, sickly old woman. So this call drew little reaction from her, and both girls returned to their playing. But in the evening, Nina announced to her family at dinner that she had been in Jamie's house when the call came through. An excited, nervous grin crossed her face, as though she felt that she'd been witness to a privileged piece of humbling news. She was aware of having been there at a time of great significance, the very moment when Jamie's own grandmother was pronounced dead. Nina knew perfectly well that people die every day, and that a few of her own relatives had, in fact, died during the past several years. But this was different. It was Jamie's grandmother, and it was the first time that someone who had been alive one minute, was dead the next. It made a deep impression, but not as a personal loss, since she hadn't known the old lady. There was no hint of sadness. But there was a telltale awkward grin (or was it a grimace?) at having lived through a fateful event in the life of her friend, even if (as Nina noticed) Jamie was too young to sense its larger meaning in a way that Nina herself was beginning to feel.

We observe Nina gazing upon both sides of her temporal field. On one side, a living grandmother; on the other, a dead one. The moment of the phone call and its immediate aftermath became for her a lingering moment of great presence, a present event truly worth pondering and speaking about. Had it been her own grandmother's death, it might have hit too close to home, pushing her into a cloying condition of fear, confusion, and loss. Instead, it was a death that seemed to strike next door, not too far and not too close, but just enough distance away to embolden her to speak openly. Her trembling voice betrayed a feeling of awe and gave indication of her struggle to absorb its powerful significance. Thus, as with her heralding of the kidnapper murder, Nina seized the chance to bring under closer scrutiny and control her own emerging images and feelings about the possibility of death. We see her moving toward a fuller awareness of the finite, creaturely condition of the lives of people around her, and possibly, of her own life as well.

Arthur (9)

If we now look at a child's emerging experience of lived time through the lens of an adult's memory, we may begin to notice a certain affinity to the three preceding episodes. Arthur Koestler (1974) recalls a tonsillectomy he endured when he was just 5 years old:

> I was made to sit in a kind of dentist's chair; then, without warning or explanation, my arms and legs were tied with leather straps to the frame of the chair. This was done with quick, deft movements by the doctor and his assistant, whose breathing was audible in the silence. Half senseless with fear, I craned my neck to look into my parents' faces, and when I saw that they, too, were frightened, the bottom fell out of the world. The doctor hustled them both out of the room, fastened a metal tray beneath my chin, pried my chattering teeth apart, and forced a rubber gag between my jaws.
>
> There followed several indelible minutes of steel instruments being thrust into the back of my mouth, of choking and vomiting blood into the tray beneath my chin; then two more attacks with the steel instruments, and more choking and blood and vomit. That is how tonsillectomies were performed, without anaesthesia, A.D. 1910, in Budapest. . . .
>
> Those moments of utter loneliness, abandoned by my parents, in the clutches of a hostile and malign power, filled me with a kind of cosmic terror. It was as if I had fallen through a manhole, into a dark underground world of archaic brutality. Thenceforth I never lost my awareness of the existence of that second universe into which one might be transported, without warning, from one moment to the other. The world had become ambiguous, invested with a double meaning; events moved on two different planes at the same time—a visible and an invisible one—like a ship which carries its passengers on its sunny decks, while its keel ploughs through the dark phantom world beneath. (pp. 173–174)

Arthur was faced with a second appendectomy after the first attempt had failed. Indelible memories of the barbarous tonsillectomy and failed appendectomy overwhelmed him, and he found himself in ''profound fear of the ether mask, or a repetition of the choking agony before going under'' (p. 177). He was alone with his fears, cut off from his parents, who had ''trapped and betrayed'' him into the two previous operations. But then, as we saw with Jamie and Nina, Arthur began to think back and forth across the axis of his personal time. Memories of two painful operations, accompanied by images of parental abandonment, loomed from his past. They assumed greater significance in light of yet another surgical disaster whose uncomfortable imminence bore down on him from the future. His awareness swung from past to future, future to past, across the poignant line of his lingering presence to a world that seemed suspended, poised in a limbo of time before his impending operation. As with the younger children, Arthur's awareness of time was intensified by the sense that he was in danger, threatened by a circumstance over which he could exert no direct control.

Suddenly, as he continued to think laterally across his drifting field of time, he stumbled upon a story that offered the gift of special meaning: He found in it the key for controlling his fear during "the choking agony" when the ether mask would again be thrust on his face:

> Then, one day, while reading the *Tales of Munchausen*, I had an inspiration. The chapter I was reading was the delightful story of the boastful Baron falling into a bog and sinking deeper and deeper. When he has sunk down to his chin, and his remaining minutes seem to be counted, he saves himself by the simple expedient of grabbing his own hair and pulling himself out.
>
> I was so delighted with the Baron's escape that I laughed aloud—and in that same instant found the solution to the problem which had been haunting me. I was going to pull myself out of the bog of my fears by holding the ether mask myself over my face until I passed out. In this way I would feel that I was in control of the situation, and that the terrible moment of helplessness would not recur. (pp. 177–178)

Arthur arrived at his "solution" through a lateral drift and letting-be of his own thinking-in-time. By the day of the appendectomy, his parents had been primed to ask the anaesthetist to permit his request to hold the ether mask, which was granted. Koestler recalls that he felt no fear when he finally put the mask on his face "under the encouraging grin of the anaesthetist" (p. 178).

Here again we see the link between a child's existence and thinking in time and his or her emerging or "developing" control over threats to his or her existence. Arthur did not deliberately search for a solution, nor did he define his problem. His thinking ran beneath the flow of rational consciousness. It was as much a way of being as a style of reflection. It was a radical openness to his lived world, his own lived time *as* problematical. This openness of thought was what enabled him to immediately "see" the connection of the Baron-in-the-bog story to his own life. He sensed its synchronistic meaning, its singular gift of timely presence after the long period of agonizing exile from his parents, squeezed as he had been between a painful past and a fearful future.

Looking back on this episode from his vantage point as an adult, Koestler opens himself to still other meanings. In addition to his "second universe" account, he proposes other retrospective interpretations, one in the language of psychoanalysis, the other in a mythic vein. First, Koestler the analyst:

> Since that episode I have learned to outwit my obsessions and anxieties—or at least to come to a kind of *modus vivendi* with them. To arrive at an amicable arrangement with one's neuroses sounds like a contradiction in terms—yet I believe it can be achieved, provided one accepts one's complexes and treats them with respectful courtesy, as it were, instead of fighting them and denying their existence. (p. 178)

The second adult voice, Koestler the mythicist, speaks of the "archaic horror" of his early and brutal tonsillectomy:

> This was my first meeting with "Ahor"—the irrational, Archaic Horror—which subsequently played such an important part in the world around me that I designed this handy abbreviation for it. (p. 174)

After describing the two appendectomies, during which "the old enemy, Ahor, had appeared in a new guise" (p. 177), Koestler elaborates upon this mythological interpretation:

> It is my profound belief that man has the power to pull himself by his own hair out of the mire. The Baron in the Bog, abbreviated "Babo," conqueror of "Ahor," has become for me both a symbol and a profession of faith. (p. 178)

Koestler's diverse interpretations serve to remind us that there need not be any singular account of what "really" happens to a child. Each interpretation is a version, rendering, or construal, of what is primordially experienced. But a truly hermeneutical account uses language that attempts to stay as close as possible to the sense of the original experiences, which are disclosed aspects of a holistic, seamless web of lived existence. Koestler borrows from the psychoanalytic wing of theoretical psychology for one interpretation, then abruptly jumps from the language of psychological science to the language of myth for the second interpretation. Neither account is wrong, misguided, nor inappropriate. How could they be, when both are Koestler-on-Koestler? But the psychoanalytic version conveys a notion of psychodynamic determinism, whereas the mythic story offers an image of self-determination and voluntary action. Both accounts are "hermeneutical" to the extent that they "preserve a liaison with the originary stream of experience" (Schrag, 1980, p. 66).

A DEVELOPMENTAL COURSE

When we look at these three children, what developmental changes can we discern from the youngest to the oldest? There are obvious existential affinities: Each is a world of lived time poised before an arresting circumstance that calls into question a future that is partly foreshadowed by the past. And in each case, the circumstance is rendered less imposing through the thinking and languaging of the child. Even with the 3-year-old, we see how reflecting upon the past (through posing a question) mitigates her momentary sense that the immediate future may be disappointing.

Developmental continuities are also discernible.

The sheer extent and elaboration of thinking through language is a major sign of growth. It reflects the developing way that these children maintain or reduce their sense of personal vulnerability. Jamie reassures herself that Nina will shortly return from a weekend trip by recalling out loud that Nina had, after all, returned from a previous one. Nina, who had been hearing (and probably worrying) for several days about the missing kidnapped child, seizes her chance to become the threatening voice of imminent doom toward her friend, Sarah, when she boldly repeats the television bulletin. She also brings to her family ill tidings about another death, as if to gauge by her parents' reaction the extent to which their and her presence in the world is exposed to danger. Arthur is profoundly shaken by the realization that he must undergo another suffocating invasion of his body. He roams his "house of thought" until he finds a story that offers the empowerment that he implicitly seeks: Help comes when he is finally ready to verbalize a request to his parents that they support his wish to anesthetize himself.

So a major line of development from Jamie through Nina to Arthur is the increasing sense of responsibility for, and control over, their own lived existences. This progression is linked to the emerging capacity to live in and through a symbolic world, the world of words heard, spoken, and read. It is mainly by means of words given and received that children gain a voice and a protection for their sense of being-in-the-world (Becker, 1971). The lived body, as "the base of operations and the center of concernful projects" (Schrag, 1980, p. 58), gradually armors itself and takes flight in language.

The emerging verbal self is the outward expression of the child's expanding temporal horizons. Jamie uses only a few words to state her discovery of the trusted link between a recent event and her immediate future. Nina draws upon a broader range of language resources to announce two recent deaths as present menaces to her family and neighbors. And Arthur finds himself mired in a painful past that has implications for his endangered future. He drifts in and out of narrative language for many weeks before he uncovers the knifelike words that sever his anxious thinking from the problematical surgery that seems ever hovering near his future horizon. Those few printed words, laden with a meaningful message that he is well primed to decipher, immediately restore a lightness to his sense of being-in-the-world.

CONCLUSION: STATE OF THE ART

A phenomenological approach to child development differs profoundly in intent and style from the theoretical approaches that have become widespread in psychology.

A phenomenological account seeks to evoke in the reader an understanding of childhood that is infused with a felt awareness, a sense of similitude, an imaginative bonding with the growing child through the incisive uses of language. The style of this approach has more in common with certain narratives and reflections found in the writings of the humanities than it does with the objective methods of the social sciences. But, as a radical empirical procedure, it may also remain within the purview of the social sciences. It is, therefore, a hybrid orientation that straddles the fence between the often imaginative insights about childhood found in biography, poetry, novels, and meditations, on the one side, and the attempts at a science of strictly clinical observation and interpretation, on the other.

Until very recently, there was considerable hesitancy among phenomenologists to describe and interpret the life-worlds of children, presumably because the experiences of childhood seemed too far removed from their own. The major phenomenologists, from Husserl to Ricoeur, have taken as their point of departure an adult way of being-in-the-world. Yet the lived experiences of children (concerning time, death, work, freedom, sexuality, etc.) appear to be unique and cannot be deduced simply by subtraction from the more "developed" experiences of adults.

Because most phenomenologists have been reluctant to investigate children's life-worlds, very little in the current literature reflects a truly phenomenological orientation to childhood. Some analysts, like Alice Miller (1981), occasionally report their patients' language about remembered childhood. But these reports are frequently paraphrasings that become absorbed into a neo-Freudian frame of reference, such as the defensive repression of painful childhood memories, which often seems to be the tacit topic for consideration. The works of child analysts such as Erik Erikson (1980) are usually written in a similar style, rarely permitting the reader an opportunity to linger over the nuances in the child's language because the author moves quickly to elaborate upon a developmental theory that purports to place the drift of the child's words in a larger objective frame. Moreover, language about childhood that emanates from the analyst's couch or therapist's office is often deeply troubled language, not the best gauge of what it is like to live and speak from relatively ordinary life circumstances.

The chronicles of teachers may offer a better source of accounts of children's life experiences. They are effective narratives to the extent that they are not primarily about "problem children" and include faithful renderings of children's discourse. The writings of Paley (1981) and Dennison (1969) are examples of this genre. The weakness of such chronicles is that they often (but not always) seem unable to move beyond pure description or else they lapse into current jargon about schooling, learning psychology, and development. My own teaching at a university has afforded me the opportunity to invite teachers and parents to keep journals about children's experiences of time as they become mentioned in the routine course of home and school conversation. Together we then work at the difficult task of interpretation, which yields to few rules, and does not come easily in an intellectual atmosphere that is rife with preexisting theories about the already known nature and development of the child.

As we have seen, another promising source of insight into children's life-worlds is biography and autobiography. Biography is one of the most commonplace forms of literature, though rarely do we read a biography that is about a commonplace individual. It is only in retrospect that we can see continuities or discontinuities between an exceptional adulthood and a singular child— a child who may give every appearance of having developed in an ordinary everyday way. For this reason, it is an unending source of fascination to read about the childhoods of socially recognized people, which helps to explain the popularity of anthologies of childhood biography (McCullough, 1987; Milgram & Hawkins, 1974).

The voices of children may be heard most directly in the stories they tell. Such stories reflect the developmental progression of life concerns among children of differing ages. Several anthologies (Pitcher & Prelinger, 1963; Sutton-Smith, 1980) are a plentiful resource of children's imaginative storytelling, though the reader is left to speculate on the way that the stories express something meaningful about the child's life-world.

Works in English that might qualify as full-fledged phenomenologies of childhood are few in number. Sometimes they are attempts at freeing original descriptions of lived experience from excessively theoretical presuppositions, thus letting those descriptions stand out more fully as expressions of being-in-the-world (Knowles, 1986). Sometimes they are the basis for a larger ethical and political treatise on the treatment of young children in our society (Coles, 1986; Polakow-Suransky, 1982). And sometimes they are attempts at interpreting the experiences of children as they themselves converse about them (Mathews, 1980, 1984; Merleau-Ponty, 1964, 1973). But the most fully elaborated phenomenological accounts of the child's developing life-world have yet to be composed.

REFERENCES

Aries, P. (1962). *Centuries of childhood*. New York: Random House.

Becker, E. (1971). *The birth and death of meaning*. New York: The Free Press.

Briod, M. (1986). The child's sense of time and the clock. *Phenomenology & Pedagogy 4*(1), 9–19.

Coles, R. (1986). *The moral life of children*. Boston: Atlantic Monthly Press.

Dennison, G. (1969). *The lives of children*. New York: Random House.

Donaldson, M. (1978). *Children's minds*. New York: W. W. Norton.

Eliot, T. S. (1943). *Four quartets*. New York: Harcourt, Brace, and World.

Erikson, E. H. (1980). *Identity and the life cycle*. New York: W. W. Norton.

Giorgi, A. (1983). Concerning the possibility of phenomenological psychological research. *Journal of Phenomenological Psychology 14*, 129–169.

Heidegger, M. (1962). *Being and time*. London: SCM Press.

Husserl, E. (1962). *Die krisis der eupaischen wissenschaften und die transzendentale phanomenologie* (2nd ed.). The Hague: M. Nijhoff.

Kagan, J. (1984). *The nature of the child*. New York: Basic.

Knowles, R. (1986). *Human development and human possibility: Erikson in the light of Heidegger*. Lanham, MD: University Press of America.

Koestler, A. (1974). Selections from arrow in the blue. In J. I. Milgram and R. P. Hawkins (Eds.), *Childhood revisited* (pp. 170–181). New York: Macmillan.

Koestler, A. (1978). *Janus*. New York: Random House.

Kohl, H. (1984). *Growing minds*. New York: Harper & Row.

Kohlberg, L. (1969). Stage and sequence: The cognitive-developmental approach to socialization. In D. Goslin (Ed.), *Handbook of socialization theory and research* (pp. 347–480). Chicago: Rand McNally.

Kotre, J. (1984). *Outliving the self*. Baltimore: Johns Hopkins University Press.

Lippitz, W. (1983). The child's understanding of time. *Phenomenology & Pedagogy 2*(3), 172–180.

Lippitz, W. (1986). Understanding children, communicating with children: Approaches to the child within us, before us, and with us. *Phenomenology & Pedagogy 4*(3), 56–65.

Mathews, G. B. (1980). *Philosophy and the young child*. Cambridge, MA: Harvard University Press.

Mathews, G. B. (1984). *Dialogues with children*. Cambridge, MA: Harvard University Press.

McCullough, D. W. (1987). *American childhoods: An anthology*. Boston: Little, Brown.

Merleau-Ponty, M. (1962). *Phenomenology of perception* (C. Smith, Trans.). New York: Humanities.

Merleau-Ponty, M. (1964). The child's relations with others (W. Cobb, Trans.). *The primacy of perception* (pp. 96–155). Evanston: Northwestern University Press.

Merleau-Ponty, M. (1973). *Consciousness and the acquisition of language*. Evanston: Northwestern University Press.

Milgram, J. I., and Hawkins, R. P. (Eds.) (1974). *Childhood revisited*. New York: Macmillan.

Miller, A. (1981). *The drama of the gifted child*. New York: Basic Books.

Paley, V. B. (1981). *Wally's stories: Conversations in the kindergarten*. Cambridge, MA: Harvard University Press.

Piaget, J. (1950). *The psychology of intelligence*. London: Routledge & Kegan Paul.

Pitcher, E. G., and Prelinger, E. (1963). *Children tell stories*. New York: International Universities Press.

Polakow-Suransky, V. (1982). *The erosion of childhood.* Chicago: University of Chicago Press.

Polakow-Suransky, V. (1984). *The social landscape of play: The child as researcher.* Paper presented to The American Education Research Association in New Orleans, April 23, 1984.

Prescott, M. P., & Valle, R. S. (1978). An existential-phenomenological look at cognitive-development theory and research. In R. S. Valle and M. King (Eds.), *Existential-phe-* *nomenological alternatives for psychology* (pp. 153–165). New York: Oxford University Press.

Schrag, C. O. (1980). *Radical reflection and the origin of the human sciences.* W. Lafayette, IN: Purdue University Press.

Sutton-Smith, B. (1980). *Folkstories of children.* Philadelphia: University of Pennsylvania Press.

van den Berg, J. H. (1961). *The changing nature of man.* New York: W. W. Norton.

Wild, J. (1959). *Human freedom and the social order.* Durham: Duke University Press.

8

An Empirical–Phenomenological Investigation of Being Anxious

An Example of the Phenomenological Approach to Emotion

William F. Fischer

INTRODUCTION

Whether one reflects upon the language of the current media or simply takes stock of one's chats with friends and neighbors, one soon realizes that, for the most part, contemporary living is described in the language of emotion. Television dramas and magazines, even the lyrics of popular music, offer characterizations as well as analyses of various fears, frustrations, guilts, shames, jealousies, and contentments of everyday life. Moreover, popular books and periodicals abound in prescriptions for living happily, for keeping one's mate satisfied if not in love, for avoiding guilt or embarrassment, for staying unaffected or in control of one's emotions, for steering clear of depression, and for coping with despair. In everyday life, the varieties of emotional living are unequivocally acknowledged as significant, even if occasionally problematic.

Although a few psychologists have been loathe to study the phenomena of emotional living as *sui generis,* that is, as constituting in their own right legitimate domains of investigation and theorizing, most have come to recognize the practical as well as the theoretical value of attempting a systematic understanding of these ways of being human. In an academic symposium that represented a number of perspectives, one presenter asserted:

> I want to start with the proposition that our reasons for interest in feelings and emotions are not merely theoretical or scientific, strong though these may be. The sources of interest, I believe, exist also in the fact that the most important problems of modern society are, in many respects, emotional problems. Both directly and indirectly is this so. Directly because of the fact that, in our modern world, there are such powerful and widespread feelings of aloneness, rejection, insecurity, discouragement, alienation and resentment, rather than positive emotions which people might prefer to have. Indirectly in that, if it be protested that the crucial problems of modern society are problems of international conflict, economic waste and exploitation, racial discrimination, population explosions, and the like, the answer that might well be made is this: What underlies these other problems in considerable degree, are emotional factors such as fear of other nations with different ideological orientations, difficulties in making emotional readjustments regarding what constitutes a satisfying, heart-warming size of family, and emotional commitments to special privileges on the part of far too many groups within society. (Leeper, 1970, p. 151)

Still, despite the fact that psychological theories of emotion have been propounded since the pioneering work

William F. Fischer • Department of Psychology, Duquesne University, Pittsburgh, Pennsylvania 15282.

of James (1884) and despite the fact that philosophers have been offering analyses of the meanings of emotionality, particularly in its relation to reason, ever since the time of Plato, agreement upon the basic dimensions of these phenomena does not exist. In the preface to her comprehensive, two-volume study, *Emotion and Personality* (1960), Magda Arnold writes:

> There is no adequate theory of emotion today, that is, no theory can integrate the psychological, neurological and physiological aspects of affective phenomena and place emotion in its proper perspective as a factor in personality organization. (p. v)

Thirteen years later, in the introduction to his text, *The Psychology of Emotion* (1973), Strongman summed up the situation as follows:

> Emotion is feeling, it is a bodily state involving various physical structures, it is gross or fine-grained behavior, and it occurs in particular situations. When we use the term we may mean any or all of these possibilities, each of which may show a wide range of variation. This points to the major difficulty which besets the academic study of the subject. Different theorists have taken differing starting points. Any theory of emotion or any empirical research on emotion deals only with some part of the broad meaning that the term has acquired. Some theorists stress psychological factors, some behavioral, some subjective. Some deal only with extremes, some say emotion colors all behavior. *There is no consensus of opinion: at present emotion defies definition* (pp. 1–2 [italics in original]).

I would suggest that Strongman's characterization of the situation is as suitable today as it was in the early 1970s. As the title of this chapter suggests, it is my intention to focus upon the phenomenon of being anxious. Although I considered the possibility of contrasting and comparing a number of recent phenomenological–psychological studies of specific modes of being emotional, for example, Ramm's analysis of being jealous (1979), or Stevick's of being angry (1983), I abandoned this project for several reasons, the most important of which was that it did not afford the reader an opportunity to follow the thinking of a phenomenological psychologist as he or she researches a specific instance of being emotional. Hence, I have settled upon three interrelated goals, and these motivate the content as well as the limitations of this chapter. They are: (a) to offer a general description of my empirical–phenomenological approach to the study of human emotionality, (b) to briefly contrast and compare that approach with its more typical counterparts in natural scientific psychology, and (c) to concretely exemplify my approach by schematically describing how I solicit, analyze, and reflectively grasp a specific description of an individual's situated experience of being anxious.

ON THE MEANINGS OF MY EMPIRICAL–PHENOMENOLOGICAL APPROACH TO HUMAN EMOTIONALITY

Readers may be somewhat surprised that I describe my phenomenological approach as empirical. In many circles, phenomenological modes of researching the subject matter of psychology are dismissed as antiempirical, or as imprecise, arm-chair alternatives to a genuinely empirical scientific approach. A clarifying digression, even if it be brief, seems to be in order.

Among traditional psychologists, being empirical means that researchers utilize as data *only that which has been perceived by them through their senses*. As Bergmann and Spence (1944) have clearly articulated:

> Scientific empiricism holds to the position that all sciences, including psychology, deal with the same events, namely, the experiences or perceptions of the scientist himself. (p. 3)

The experiences or perceptions of the subjects, on the other hand, are held to be questionable at best. In most researches, they are not even solicited. When they are, they are not treated as comparable to, that is, as potentially informative as, the experiences of the researcher. In fact, when subjects' experiences are utilized as data, they are supposed to be transformed according to the image of human being that is consistent with natural scientific philosophy. Again, Bergmann and Spence (1944) are quite specific on this matter:

> The empiricist scientist should realize that his behavior, symbolic or otherwise, does not lie on the same methodological level as the responses of his subjects, and consequently that he should not in reporting the latter use any mentalistic terms which have not been introduced from a physicalistic meaning basis. (p. 4)

In other words, subjects' experiences, insofar as they are not reduced to the language of physics and in contrast to those of the researcher, are preconceived to be mixtures of fact and fancy; they are assumed, *a priori*, to be pervaded with distortions due to operative drives, previously acquired habits, and biasing attitudes. Hence, traditional natural scientific psychology is empirical to the extent that it is open to phenomena as experienced by researchers, who, it is assumed, are struggling to incarnate neutral, objectivating attitudes.

As an empirical–phenomenological psychologist, I espouse a somewhat different understanding of being empirical. For me, all experiences of a phenomenon of interest are potentially informative, regardless of who lives and describes them. There is no *a priori* reason to disparage or dismiss the descriptions that are offered by subjects. Although it must be acknowledged that some perspectives provide a better access to the phenomenon of interest than others, *this is true for researchers as well as subjects, that is, regardless of who lives them.* Hence, the first task of the empirical–phenomenological researcher is to determine, typically through pilot studies as well as reflection, which perspective(s), which mode(s) of access, might be most informative, that is, promise to yield the richest descriptions of the phenomenon of interest. For example, if one is researching the psychological meanings of being courageous, then one will discover that empathically present observers have a direct access to the phenomenon; they can immediately experience another being courageous; subjects who are actually living a situation courageously do not experience themselves as so engaged. Still, they, too, can have access to the phenomenon; when they do not live frightening and/or dangerous situations courageously, they can experience themselves as lacking courage and can describe the meanings of being courageous as that which they find themselves to be lacking. Hence, the researcher interested in the phenomenon of being courageous can be most empirical when he or she determines how each of the varying modes of presence to, or perspectives upon, the phenomenon of interest is capable of being informative. Of course, this implies that researchers must not dismiss in advance any particular perspective.

Continuing with this schematic characterization, I would say that the adoption of my approach constitutes an effort to reawaken, to thematize, and to reflectively understand the phenomena of being emotional. Pursuant to that effort, it is necessary to reanimate the question, *What is being emotional, that is, how does one actually experience and live out a particular situation when one is being emotional?* Not only must this question be asked anew, it must be elevated to its rightful position of priority. Moreover, only when it is clearly and carefully answered can a psychologist turn to such related queries as "Why does this particular way of being emotional occur now, at this time, in this situation?" The implicit, taken-for-granted answers to the first question that have been proposed by most psychologists, especially those committed to the anthropologies of natural scientific thought, are limited at best, and generally inadequate. As an example of this, I would cite the manner in which Dustin (1969) has attempted to characterize the *whatness* of anxiety:

> To help us understand anxiety, we will first describe a related emotion—fear. Fear is an emotion produced by danger. As the danger increases so does the fear. Taking a driving test, interviewing for a job, or walking down an unlighted street at night may produce some fear, but it will be easily controlled. As the danger increases, however, symptoms such as pounding of the heart, a sinking feeling in the stomach, shaking and trembling, and cold sweat become more difficult to control. In extreme fear, or panic, thought deteriorates into a nightmare of distorted mental images, and the person may run wildly about, crying, shouting and laughing in rapid succession. Though you probably have experienced panic, you may not recall just how excruciatingly unpleasant it was because it is usually forgotten soon after the crisis is over. Fear is natural in dangerous situations and so it is not puzzling to us. But if these same emotional reactions occur where there is not enough danger to warrant them, these same emotions are called anxiety, and they are very puzzling indeed. (pp. 1–2)

In general, Dustin's style of thinking about anxiety is rather typical. It is shared by many psychoanalysts as well as most experimental psychologists. In this regard, I would suggest the following:

1. Anxiety or being anxious is not approached directly; it is not allowed to speak for itself. Instead, prior to any inquiry or experimentation, it is grasped and characterized as a peculiar form of fear. Still more precisely, it is preconceived as fearfulness that seems to be unwarranted by the situation in which it occurs. I would like to ask: unwarranted for whom? Certainly not for the person who is living it out. According to Dustin, it is experienced and judged as unwarranted by the observing psychologist. But doesn't that imply that it is only the observing psychologist, the "expert" other, who has the authority to determine the real meanings of the situation as well as the appropriateness of the behaviors that occur in relation to it? Only he or she has the right to assert how things really are. If we grant this, how are we to understand the anxiousness of the individual in the situation? If we decide, solely on the basis of our own experience, that his or her fearfulness is unwarranted and therefore label it as *anxiousness,* how will we ever make sense of its occurrence in the first place? Have you ever tried to convince an anxious person that his or her anxiousness is uncalled for?

2. The situation in which the fearfulness/anxiousness occurs is, on *a priori* grounds, grasped as independently antecedent to and causally productive of the emotional way of being that emerges. It is as if Dustin understands this danger as inhering in the situation, independent of any individual's experience thereof. Hence, when someone is exposed to such a situation, one that has already been predefined as dangerous in itself, it is said to produce or otherwise cause the emotion in the person, presumably in some repository such as a psyche or central nervous system. Further, bodily phenomena, such as a pounding of the heart, or a sinking feeling in the stomach, are grasped as symptoms of the emotion. In other words, the bodily phenomena are also

predefined as to their meanings; they are products of the emotion; they are its alleged effects. The reader should notice that in all of these characterized relationships, Dustin has arbitrarily divided the phenomena of being fearful/being anxious into three discrete realms: the situational, the inner emotional proper, whether this is located in a psyche or a nervous system, and the bodily. Moreover, the relations between these realms are arbitrarily described in a language of productive causality.

3. Phenomena of each of the three realms are thematized only in terms of their quantitative profiles. Hence, situations are simply more or less dangerous; no reference is made to the possibility of qualitative differences. That is to say, there is no suggestion that the danger that threatens in fearfulness might be qualitatively different than the danger that threatens in being anxious. Further, emotional responses to the danger situation are differentiated solely on the basis of quantitative thinking. Hence, panic is charactered as extreme fear; it is not really different, it is just more of the same.

4. Finally, Dustin suggests that, whereas fear is natural, anxiety is not. Presumably, it is always puzzling, always unwarranted. Is this really so? Does such a thesis truly correspond to our experience? In fact, is not this characterization of anxiety an arbitrary, even if logical, by-product of a definition that is more concerned with being consistent with the principles of natural scientific anthropology than with being faithful to the phenomena of human living as they actually show themselves?

As an empirical–phenomenological psychologist, I would suggest that the task of approaching and scientifically characterizing the phenomena of being emotional does not demand that the researcher preconceive of them in terms of *elementally discrete realms* such as the situational, the inner emotional, and the bodily. Nor does it require that the relationships between these realms be defined in advance as causally productive. Moreover, it is both arbitrary and reductive to thematize only those profiles of phenomena that can be described quantitatively and mechanistically. Obviously, they are not the only ones that deserve to be elevated to the status of the real.

It seems to me that the diverse forms of being emotional can and should be explored in their multiple, even inexhaustible aspects or profiles, that each should be interrogated as to how its particular aspects refer to, allow for, and typically blend into each other. Further, as I have already stated, researchers should be concerned with how the various forms of being emotional show themselves to subjects as well as to psychologists. Empirical–phenomenological research seeks to interrogate and understand the bases, or grounds, of the various aspects or profiles of phenomena. It agrees that actor–subjects and

observer–subjects experience being anxious differently, but it asks why should the perspectives of the observer–subjects, especially if they are the psychologist–observer–subjects, be accorded scientific status exclusively? It is not the case that the two perspectives are in competition; they are not incompatible; we do not have to choose between them. Rather, researchers must realize that these two perspectives complement each other; through each, one is present to the phenomenon under study, albeit by means of diverse profiles.

If we are to comprehend faithfully human emotionality as it is actually lived and experienced, we must return to description. We cannot resort to arbitrary preconceptions or definitions. We must insist that our conceptualizations be responsive to the ways in which human beings live their everyday lives. The worlds that they cocreate and live out with others cannot be subordinated to the *a prioris* of natural science.

As I have suggested before, Dustin arbitrarily divided the phenomenon of being anxious into three discrete realms: the situational, the "inner" realm of the emotion proper, and the bodily. If readers recall the excerpts from both Arnold (1960) and Strongman (1973), they will realize that these theorists, as well, subscribe to this Cartesian dissection of the phenomenon. In fact, it is a standard strategy among most, if not all, natural scientific approaches to this topic. Stated somewhat more elaborately, one could assert that theorists and researchers of this general orientation have typically assumed that emotions are entities or states whose locus is literally inside the person, whether this is conceptualized as intrapsychic or intradermal. Further, they have assumed that these entities or states are produced by external, antecedent situations (stimuli) that are said to interact with internal drives or motives, thereby producing bodily changes either by way of an "inner emotion" or concurrent with it.

When one adopts an existential–phenomenological understanding of human beings, one realizes that the various forms of being emotional are actually diverse ways of being-in-the-world. Hence, although it may be true that being emotional involves self, world, other, bodily, and behavioral constituents, it is not true that these must be treated as discrete and hence, as causally related. Rather, the existential–phenomenological psychologist recognizes that each form of being emotional, as it is actually lived and experienced, is a coherent whole, or structure, the meaning of which is given in the interrelations of its self, world, other, bodily, and behavioral constituents. Thus, for example, the worldly meanings of a particular instance of being emotional are neither external nor prior to that instance; still less do they cause it. Rather, it is the world in its personal significance that is expressed and lived out by the individual in his or her bodily as well as behavioral style of being emotional. Hence, from an existential–phenomenological perspective, being emotional is a particular way of being in a situation, one that shows itself through a specific intertwining or configuration of situational, self, bodily, and behavioral themes.

AN EMPIRICAL–PHENOMENOLOGICAL INVESTIGATION OF BEING ANXIOUS

Almost 70 years ago Freud (1917/1963) wrote:

> The problem of anxiety is a nodal point at which the most various and important questions converge, a riddle whose solution would be bound to throw a flood of light upon our whole mental existence. (p. 393)

Today, many, if not most, clincial psychologists would agree with Freud's estimation of the significance of anxiety. However, as I have documented elsewhere (Fischer, 1970a), there continues to be little, if any, consensus as regards its constituents or their conceptualization. Truly, it is a paradoxical situation. How can so many people agree upon the importance of this phenomenon when they are utterly unable to concur in characterizing its meanings?

In the remainder of this chapter, I describe, as well as exemplify, my empirical–phenomenological approach to the meanings of being anxious. Readers who would like to familiarize themselves with alternative approaches, methods, and/or conceptualizations of this phenomenon should consult the writings of Dustin (1969), Fischer (1970a, 1974, 1982), May (1977), and Spielberger (1966).

Unlike Dustin or any of the other natural-science psychologists who have attempted to study being anxious (consistent with their philosophical perspective, they would refer to it in "thing" language, i.e., as anxiety), I do not begin my research with an arbitrary definition. In fact, it is the very *whatness* or meaning of being anxious, as people actually live and experience it, that I seek to comprehend. Hence, after reflecting upon and rendering explicit my own preconceptions as to the meaning of being anxious, thereby thematizing my starting place as well as sensitizing myself to the potentially determinative influences of what I already believe, I turn to others, such as relatively naive undergraduate students. To be more specific, I tell them that I am interested in how people experience and live out particular instances of being anxious, and I ask them if they would help me in this project. That is to say, I ask them if they would each describe, in writing, a concrete instance of being anxious as they recall having experienced and lived it. Needless to say, I

also tell them that some descriptions may be shared with colleagues or published but that, in such a case, I would first change or delete all identifying names and references to places.

The reader may realize that the utilization of these procedures thematizes another interesting difference between empirical–phenomenological research and that which is typically actualized by more traditional psychologists. In the former, subjects and researchers are collaborators in an enterprise whose meanings and purposes have been revealed and openly discussed. There is no effort to deceive subjects as is too frequently required in the case of natural scientific research designs. One could say that in the latter, researchers tend to be all-knowing, but personally unknown, whereas human subjects tend to be kept in ignorance, yet may be personally exposed.

As an empirical–phenomenological psychologist, I do not believe that the data that I collect will be contaminated by the active, knowing participation of my subjects. Neither do I assume that these subjects' experiences of phenomena, in this instance, being anxious, are merely subjective, that is, unreliable and riddled with irrelevant if not distorting influences. Clearly, each subject's personal knowledge of, attitudes toward, and feelings about being anxious contribute to his or her experience of its meanings and, hence, must be recognized as in some sense determinative of said meanings. But this is true of everyone's experience of being anxious, including mine. All experiences of phenomena are perspectival, and one must take into consideration that which is constitutive of each perspective. It is naive to believe that one can eliminate or minimize, whatever that would mean, the perspectival character of human modes of presence to phenomena. The so-called neutral or objective stance of the researcher is itself a perspective, one that decisively influences which aspects or profiles of a given phenomenon he or she will experience.

From the preceding, it follows that I do not assume, as do natural scientific psychologists, that the "real" meanings of a phenomenon are independent of all human (or animal) presence. Hence, I do not believe that the pursuit of objectivity requires the researcher to try to separate the presence of the subject from the phenomenon, a state of affairs that is not only impossible but meaningless. Instead, I seek to illuminate the meanings of phenomena, in this instance, being anxious, as they are actually lived and experienced. Thus, when I ask the students to submit descriptions of situations in which they, themselves, had been anxious, I give them the following instructions:

> Please describe in as much detail as possible a situation in which you were anxious. To the extent that you can, please include in your description a characterization of

how you came to realize that you were anxious, that is, how it showed itself to you, as well as what you experienced and did while you were anxious.

The following excerpt, although rather lengthy, is still fairly typical of the descriptions that were submitted and is especially suited for illustrating the phenomenon of being anxious. The lettered brackets that appear at different points in the description refer to its "scenes," that is, its global units as they were determined in the following analysis:

Before describing my experience of anxiety, I would like to make a few remarks concerning the writing of this paper and to provide some background material that is necessary to an understanding of this particular experience. The experience that I chose to describe constitutes an extremely painful episode in my life, an episode that until this assignment I had for the most part avoided reflecting upon. Therefore, I used this paper as a lever to force open a pain-filled happening to reflection, to learning and I hope to growth.

Now some background material. At the time of this particular experience, I was deeply involved in a search for religious meaning and a sense of the holy in my life. I had always been a religious person, but the period of this occurrence was one of particular fervor. A few months prior to this experience, I had become deeply involved in the Catholic Pentacostal movement. In this structure I experienced God in a new and highly personal way. Jesus Christ had become a hard reality. He was no longer an act of faith—a God way up there. He cared about me and for me; He wanted to and did help me. He was a person whom I could talk to and expect an answer from. Moreover, I had made a commitment to this God–Man and to myself to live by His word and to propagate His teachings. Christ and His Spirit were pervasive influences in my everyday life.

Also at that time, I was struggling violently to realize myself as a sexual being. I had feelings and desires that I could not always reconcile with my religious training. Since I had taken leave of the seminary, my concept of sin had become vague. I did not know exactly how to handle my natural impulses. I could not completely buy the standard Catholic teachings on morality and sex that had been inculcated into my being and yet, when I would engage in some illicit activity such as petting, I felt guilty and uneasy until I would go to confession. I had no criteria—I was in the process of developing one. This developmental process was in a strange, hands-off stage. I could neck passionately as long as my hands did not roam. To add to the confusion, I had started to view most sexual activity as a breach of trust with my newfound God. Further, I was completely captivated by a girl who I had known throughout high school but had only become involved with during the summer between my freshman and sophomore years at college. During the preceding year, our relationship had vacillated. At the time of the experience, we were desperately searching for a sense of balance for we were almost polar-opposite personalities. She had no religious qualms and was hoping to establish and cultivate good sexual relations with me. My hesitancy to act constituted an unspoken problem between us

and was frustrating in not allowing logical climax in an often passionate relationship. I was fully aware of her desire for intercourse.[A]

Keeping this background material in mind, I would now like to consider the situation and my anxious experience of it. It was a humid rainy August night. The whole world was sweating and still. P. and I were watching television at my house. My family was not home; they had gone to spend a week's visit with my uncle. We were quite alone. I had my shirt off and was lying on a couch with my head in her lap. The air was thick. A candle flickered in the far corner of the room, the only light besides the television's unblinking eye. The rain beat monotonously on the roof; the television set droned on and on. I became a little drowsy. All motion was suspended. Suddenly, P. began to tickle me. I retaliated, and we rolled off the couch and onto the floor. The mock battle continued for several minutes until we were left laughing and breathless. A short silence ensued. I then became aware of our proximity. I was lying partially on her and partially on the floor. I raised my head and looked into her eyes. Her face was flushed, her hair mussed seductively, framing her features. The top button of her shirt had become undone, and her full breasts rose and fell rhythmically; we began to kiss passionately.

The whole situation became undone. I felt like I was on fire; I had a burning desire to touch and be touched. I began to think about sin. I remember saying to myself things like, "be careful" and "I'll stop when I have to." But soon I drew what I can only describe as a reflective blank. I was devoid of reflection. I had no organized thoughts of sin or even of what I was doing at the time. It was a sort of tranquil nothingness in which I was focally aware of only my hardening penis and the fullness and warmth of her responsive body. I unbuttoned her shirt and fondled her breasts. She opened my pants and slowly slid her hand into my crotch. I kicked my pants off, and we necked violently for an indeterminate length of time. I started to slide my hand down the front of her jeans and the next thing that I knew was I was sitting naked facing a half-naked P. who was telling me that it was the end of her period, that she would be safe, and that she would be back as soon as she took her tampon out. "Mister, you've got something that I want," and she walked out.

I was kneeling naked in the center of my living room; the television was a disinterested eye, it was a noise in the distance that was growing more and more annoying. The candle cast uncanny patterns over the ceiling and distorted my shadows on the wall. I angrily slapped the television off. But these things, and indeed the whole room quickly faded. I stared into the darkness.

The full realization of what was happening came in a fragmentary manner. I had not even considered intercourse this evening. It was just not a real possibility for me before this moment because she was not on the pill, because I had no condom, and because I did not know that it was her period. I had led myself on saying, "I'll stop when I have to." And yet, here I was waiting for the girl that I loved to return and allow me the final embrace. I was stunned. I felt funny, tight, but especially in my chest and stomach; in fact, my stomach felt queasy, and I was trembling all over.[B]

[Having presented the situation, I now turn to my experience of myself being anxious in it. The only way that I could properly describe my anxiousness is to recreate it in the first person. Hence, the next section is presented as a stream of consciousness.

"Dammit! What am I going to do? You know exactly what you're going to do. Come on, get serious. I can't do that. How long is it taking her? Damn! Damn! What'll I say when she gets back? She's really up. She's going to be disappointed; so am I. Why did I let it go this far? Where is she? What if somebody comes to the door? Who's going to come now? Maybe the phone will ring. Damn, it's up to me, yes or no? Nobody is coming or calling. I've got to do it or talk her out of it. Why did I have to go this far? What will I tell Father F. when I see him? I'll have to go to confession sooner or later. But if I do it now it will be easier the next time. We'll go on and on; she'll end up on the pill, and I'll be trapped. What will I tell Z. and C. [friends in the movement]? Some Christian I am; big time Pentacostal who made a real commitment to the Lord. I was going to preach the word and show the world how good it can be. How will I be able to go to the prayer meetings if I don't stop this once and for all. Hell, there'll be no point in going to confession if I can't say that I'll never do it again. Somehow, this isn't going to be a one-night stand. If I only didn't love her so much. Where is she? Come on P., no one-night stand. The Holy Spirit's really filled me. I really live in rotten good faith. How can I be such a hypocrite? By their fruits you shall know them! If you love me, keep my commandments. It's a choice, the world or Him. I can't make her, not tonight, not ever. Hell, I'd give anything for her. Stop it! Stop it! I'm not going to make her; I've done enough, cut myself off from Christ already. Haven't I hurt Him enough for one night? 'If you love me keep my commandments.' Yes Lord, I know, I've got to make a stand here. Help me, Jesus, help me, please. I know You can, I know I'm wrong. Help me stop here; give me the strength. Oh Lord, if you mark inequities, who can stand? Forgive me, forgive me, Jesus. I'm sorry. Why didn't I stay away from her? I knew it, Goddammit, I knew it. I won't, I won't do it, help me, please. She's going to be pissed; can't blame her. Why can't she understand? She'll never understand; she'll never know what I know. She hasn't gone to the prayer meetings and felt the presence of the Spirit; she doesn't know the people who were cured; she doesn't know the Spirit or Jesus. She doesn't care either. Why can't she understand? Damn! What am I going to do? Where is she? God, I feel sick. I'm shaking. Where is she? I'd give anything to make it with her. Maybe I should get dressed before she comes back. I really love you P. That makes it all right doesn't it? Why not? It's natural! Maybe she won't be so bitchy if we do it. What am I saying, I can't. Get dressed! Don't do this to Jesus. What'll she think of me? What if she laughs? What if she leaves me? I can't take this."[C]

P: I guess the first thing I'll do is take all my clothes off.
F: You're back.
P: You don't sound very enthused. I expected more; I thought you wanted me.
F: God knows I do P, but . . .

P: Don't worry silly, I can't get pregnant [drops her pants and lies down on the couch]. Come here.

I walked over to the couch and stood over her, staring down at her body. I was torn and trembling. My body was tense and my penis throbbed. I wanted to, I can't; I'm a man, it's natural. It aches; her hand. It feels so good. I love her, I love her, I love her. Hypocrite, what about Christ? I thought, "I can't.''[D]

The next thing that I remember is opening my eyes and seeing her kneeling over me caressing my face. P. said, "It's all right, love. It's all right.'' How much time elapsed I don't know. I woke up in a kind of dream. My body was limp, and I was completely wrung out. I was trembling slightly and just wanted to sleep.[E]

Having presented the situation and my anxious experience of it, I will speak of how I came to realize that I was anxious. When my bodily state became the focal point of my awareness, I first realized that I was anxious; I felt funny, tight, my stomach was quesy and I was trembling. But these intrusions only brought my anxiousness into focus for fleeting seconds. The second awareness of my anxiousness came only after P had gone home and I had begun to attempt to make sense out of what happened. I thought about the whole incident and realized that I had blown it and that I had really fallen apart. These thoughts were accompanied by the wish that I had kept my cool throughout the whole incident. In other words, at this time I was removed from the situation and made sense of it by realizing that I had been very anxious.[F]

Before proceeding with a characterization of my analysis of this description, I would like to remind the reader of the intentions that guide my phenomenological researches of being anxious. As I have suggested before, I want to answer the question: What is the psychological meaning of being anxious? Hence, I ask subjects to describe specific situations in which they came to realize that they were anxious, to include in their descriptions some characterization of how that realization occurred, and to portray concretely what they experienced and did while they were anxious.

At this point, some reader might remark, "But what can you do with these descriptions? They were written by different people; they describe diverse situations in which widely divergent issues were at stake; some of them are much more articulate than others, etc." My response would go something like the following: "Everything that you have said is true, but each description characterizes being anxious as it was actually experienced and lived by a particular person in a particular situation. That is to say, each description or protocol describes a specific, situated instance of that general human possibility that we refer to when we speak of being anxious. Hence, my task, as a researcher, is to analyze these specific instances in such a way that I am able to comprehend that which constitutes them as concrete and yet diverse examples of this general human possibility.''

Essentially, my method, which is described in detail elsewhere (Fischer, 1974, 1982), consists of a series of four successive yet interrelated reflections. In the first, each subject's description, which may have been elaborated in the context of a follow-up interview, is regarded as a story that characterizes his or her involvement with the phenomenon of interest, in this case, being anxious. I read and reread the description or story asking, ''What's happening here? How did the subject's involvement with being anxious arise and unfold? What are the global units of that unfolding?'' When I have realized a sense of those units—I refer to them as scenes of the story—I mark them off with brackets on a typewritten copy of the subject's description. This is what I have done with the description presented previously.

When I have delineated the scenes of the description, I again reflect upon them and attempt to state their respective meanings, but now from my own perspective, that is, from the perspective of a researcher who is trying to comprehend the subject's lived through experience of being anxious. Although this was accomplished for all of the scenes, concerns for space do not permit me to present each of the meanings that were determined. Hence, I will offer as examples of this part of the analysis the meanings of scenes A, C, D:

Scene A

Founding the subject's possibility of becoming anxious in this situation were his recently enacted, deeply felt commitment to the Catholic Pentecostal movement, his current, ''violent struggle'' to realize himself as a sexual being, and his intensely lived relationship with a girlfriend who was seeking unconflictedly to develop a satisfying sexual relationship with the subject and in relation to whom the latter had been hesitant to respond, concerned that he would violate his religious commitment.

Scene C

While waiting for his girlfriend to return from her preparations for their anticipated lovemaking, becoming anxious meant that the subject was gradually paralyzed by his anticipations of disappointing her and suffering her rejection, of losing the respect of his confessor and friends in the movement, and of realizing himself as a hypocrite who had shamefully betrayed his own commitments. Hence, he could not decide whether to go ahead as he desired or whether to try to explain to his girlfriend how their love making would violate his religious commitments.

Scene D

When his girlfriend returned and invited him to join her in an embrace, being anxious meant that he now experienced the total bodily character of his paralysis. Faced

with a situation that he could not face, that was impossible, he fled, that is, he fainted.

In the third reflection, I utilize the meanings of the scenes in an effort to synthesize an answer to the question: What was the psychological meaning of being anxious as it was experienced and lived by this subject in this situation? This answer is referred to as a *situated structural description*. In the instance of the description presented above, it was as follows:

For this subject, the possibility of becoming anxious arose when, together with an other, he passionately, albeit ambivalently, cocreated a situation that invited him to realize that which he desired, yet also signified him as a betrayer of friends and commitments, as well as a shameful hypocrite. Being anxious meant that he was paralyzed in the face of these irreconcilable possibilities, that he experienced the bodily character of his paralysis, that he could neither act out his desire nor affirmatively stand with his friends and commitments. Being anxious was surpassed, at least temporarily, by his unacknowledged flight from the situation—he fainted.

In the fourth and final reflection of my method, I ask, What is the psychological meaning of being anxious as a possibility that human beings may live and experience? My answer, which is called a *general structural description* of being anxious, has been realized by contrasting and comparing over 25 situated structural descriptions with each other, always looking for that which seems to be essential to all of them, even if present less articulately in some. It may be stated as follows:

An anxious situation arises when the self-understanding in which one is genuinely invested is rendered problematically uncertain and hence, possibly untrue. Two variations of this situation may be delineated: In the first, an essential constituent of that self-understanding, one that expresses one's identification with a state of affairs that one is endeavoring to realize, for example, becoming a PhD candidate in one's graduate program, is now experienced as possibly unattainable, and thus the entire self-understanding that one is living is called into question; in the second, a meaning that one is living as either never-to-be-true-of-one or as no-longer-to-be-true-of-one, for example, being someone who ''gives in'' to the desire to masturbate, has emerged as possibly (still) true, thereby undermining the self-understanding that is, at least in part, founded upon its absolute exclusion.

Initially, becoming and being anxious in either of these situations means that one experiences a sudden loss of momentum, a sense of being blocked, an inability to move forward undividedly. Confronted with multiple, problematic, and often contradictory meanings of the situation, one is captured, at least temporarily, by its ambiguity, its lack of a univocal meaning. Expressing this sense of being blocked and captured is a burgeoning uncertainty as to what to do, for that matter, as to one's ability to do anything effectively.

Breaking through this more or less articulate confusion, one experiences the alien, dysfunctional character of one's body as it resonates to the uncertainties of the situation. It is important to note that how one relates to these bodily resonances, for example, the dryness of one's mouth, the feeling of weakness in one's knees, and/or the sense of "butterflies" in one's stomach will prefigure whether one will explicitly acknowledge and feel one's anxiousness. Moreover, even if that anxiousness is explicitly acknowledged and felt, one may not take it up with an interest in genuinely discovering its significations, that is, take it up as revealing something important about the present situation and one's projects thereof.

Most typically, one will make an effort to turn away from what one's body is announcing. That is, one may engage in a flurry of action, usually aggressive, directed at some aspect of the problematic situation, for example, at an other or at some aspect of oneself in the form of disparagements. Or, one may acknowledge the fact of one's anxiousness but refuse to recognize, let alone explore, the situation as its reciprocally implied source. Hence, to state the matter somewhat differently, one may not allow one's anxious body explicitly to signify the problematic significances of the situation.

Beyond this general characterization, two diverse styles of being anxious may be delineated. In the first, one feels paralyzed, in imminent danger of being overwhelmed by the unthinkable, the inescapably problematic character of one's self-understanding; one is unable to even consider its implications. Hence, one continues, often adamantly, to turn away from the possibility of reflecting upon it. The situation is lived as if there was nothing to be learned from it; nothing has really changed, only the familiar is acknowledged.

In the second style of living out being anxious, one gradually acknowledges, speaks to, and affirms the problematic possibility/meaning as really true. It might be noted that this typically occurs in the presence of some empathic friend or other. Now, in uncertainty and trepidation, one explores and appropriates the ambiguity that has been revealed. Resolving to be oneself, even if "I'm full of contradictions, at least for now," one recommits oneself to one's projects of one's world-with-others, trusting that the future will bring with it a sense of coherence. One's understanding of who one is, of what one's relations with the world are all about, has undergone at least a modest transformation, and, in one's desire to get comfortable with that, one will frequently seek out others with whom to explore it.

CONCLUSIONS

At this juncture, it seems appropriate briefly to recapitulate the principal meanings of my empirical–phenomenological approach to the study of being emotional. Following this, I will exemplify how being anxious, as I have described it, concretely instantiates some of the general themes of being emotional. At the same time, I will present certain of the findings of Frankel's (1985) investigation of anger and Ramm's (1979) study of jealousy, relating these as well as to the previously mentioned general themes.

In the opening section of this chapter, I acknowledged that when I adopt an empirical–phenomenological approach to the study of being emotional, I grasp any given example thereof, for example, being anxious, as a particular way of being-in-a-situation. In researching these examples, I seek to comprehend the concrete interrelated meanings of subject and situation as they are actually lived and experienced. Hence, I solicit subjects' descriptions of particular situations in which they actually experienced themselves as living through this phenomenon. Moreover, in keeping with the phenomenological imperative to let that which one is studying show itself in its own terms, I do not tell subjects what to focus upon other than the situation, as they experienced and lived it, including their perceptions, thoughts, feelings, actions, and the like. Nor do I suggest to them how to describe the interrelations of what they experienced and lived. For example, I do not ask them what caused or made them feel anxious.

I might also mention that I have asked still other subjects to describe their experiences of persons other than themselves whom they grasped as being anxious. [*from observer*] This has allowed me to obtain access to the experience of the other-being-anxious (Fischer, 1974). Clearly, both perspectives, that is, the experience of oneself as anxious and the experience of the other-being-anxious afford researchers access to the phenomenon of being anxious as people live and experience it. Thus there is neither the felt need nor the desire to follow Dustin (1969) and others by defining being anxious in advance as a special type of fear, or as a particular concatenation of physiological processes, or as the product of some intrapsychic conflict.

How does being anxious, as I have described it, concretely instantiate some of the general themes of being emotional? For example, how does an anxious situation constitute a particular exemplification of what we mean when we speak of an emotional situation? If we begin with the meaning of the latter, we can say that an emotional situation is a state of affairs that is experienced and lived as signifying the current standing of at least one of one's projects of the world-with-others, that is, its realizability, its uncertainty, or its unrealizability. Now, if readers look once again at the general structure of being anxious that I have presented, they will find that it describes an anxious situation as an ambiguous and contradictory state of affairs that subjects live as signifying the problematic uncertainty of at least one of the projects upon which their respective self-understandings are founded. That is to say, in calling into question, at least temporarily, the realizability of a project that founds some constituent of an individual's self-understanding, an anxious situation renders that self-understanding problematically uncertain.

Of course, not all projects are lived as foundational for a person's self-understanding. For example, Frankel (1985), in her empirical–phenomenological study of being angry, determined that her subjects were struggling to realize projects of having and/or doing, rather than projects of being. Moreover, their situations were lived as angry ones insofar as they were experienced as signifying that the subjects had been "unfairly caught, violated, and rendered ineffective in their projects" by certain others who, although able and expected to treat them with greater consideration, did not.

For the most part, being emotional is lived as a way of expressing how one is, rather than as a mode of being informed about one's projects and relations of the world-with-others. That is to say, except where one stays with and reflects upon the feelings that will sometimes punctuate one's instances of being emotional, one tends to live out, rather than learn about, the diverse aspects of one's situation in their significances for one's projects. In the instance of being anxious, one invariably turns away from the possibility of discovering, let alone exploring, what one's transformed body is announcing. Typically, it is only where there is a close friend or some compassionately empathic other that one is able to endure the discomfort of being anxious and reflect upon its significance.

In the instance of being angry, Frankel tells us that subjects are absorbed with the felt necessity, the demand, to get through to the other, to attribute blame and to insist upon redress. They have neither the time nor the inclination to stop and genuinely reflect upon what is happening to them; why the other is apparently indifferent to their desires, and so forth. Ramm tells us that, typically, jealous subjects do not question or reflect upon the self-significations of their projects to be the center of their significant others' worlds. Rather, they struggle to convince themselves that either the other's distraction by a third was only momentary and hence of little consequence, or that their significant others only appeared to be interested in them but were never actually so. In either case, they continue with their projects.

The empirical–phenomenological approach to the psychology of emotion is in its infancy. We want to explore and analyze people's experiences of particular modes of being emotional; we also want to clarify the psychology of feeling, a way of being-in-a-situation that is related to being emotional but cannot be reduced to it. Readers who are interested in examining other examples of the empirical–phenomenological approach to being emotional might read Ramm (1979), Fischer (1970a,b, 1974, 1982), Schur (1978), Deegan (1981), Stevick (1971, 1983), and Frankel (1985).

REFERENCES

Arnold, M. (1960). *Emotion and personality.* New York: Columbia University Press.
Bergmann, G., & Spence, K. W. (1944). The logic of psychophysical measurement. *Psychological Review, 51,* 1–24.
Davitz, J. (1969). *The language of emotion.* New York: Academic Press.
Deegan, P. (1981). *The use of diazepam to transform being-anxious: An empirical-phenomenological study.* Unpublished doctoral dissertation, Duquesne University, Pittsburgh.
Dustin, D. (1969). *How psychologists do research: The example of anxiety.* Englewood Cliffs, NJ: Prentice-Hall.
Fischer, W. F. (1970a). *Theories of anxiety.* New York: Harper & Row.
Fischer, W. F. (1970b). The faces of anxiety. *Journal of Phenomenological Psychology, 1,* 31–49.
Fischer, W. F. (1974). On the phenomenological mode of researching being-anxious. *Journal of Phenomenological Psychology, 4,* 405–423.
Fischer, W. F. (1982). An empirical-phenomenological approach to the psychology of anxiety. In A. deKoning & F. Jenner (Eds.), *Phenomenology and psychiatry* (pp. 63–84.) London: Academic Press.
Frankel, C. (1985). *The phenomenology of being-angry: A multiperspectival study.* Unpublished doctoral dissertation, Duquesne University, Pittsburgh.
Freud, S. (1963). Introductory lectures on psychoanalysis. In *Standard edition of the complete psychological works of Sigmund Freud (Volume XVI)* (pp. 243–496). London: Hogart Press. (originally published 1917)
Giorgi, A. (1970). *Psychology as a human science.* New York: Harper & Row.
James, W. (1884). What is an emotion? *Mind, 9,* 188–205.
Leeper, R. (1970). The motivational and perceptual properties of emotions as indicating their fundamental character and role. In M. Arnold (Ed.), *Feelings and emotions: The Loyola symposium* (pp. 151–168). New York: Academic.
May, R. (1977). *The meaning of anxiety.* New York: W. W. Norton.
Ramm, D. (1979). *A phenomenological investigation of jealousy.* Unpublished doctoral dissertation, Duquesne University, Pittsburgh.
Schur, M. (1978). *An empirical-phenomenological study of situations of being-disappointed.* Unpublished doctoral dissertation, Duquesne University, Pittsburgh.
Spielberger, C. (Ed.). (1966). *Anxiety and behavior.* New York: Academic.
Stevick, E. (1971). An empirical investigation of the experience of anger. In A. Giorgi, W. F. Fischer, & R. von Eckartsberg (Eds.), *Duquesne studies in phenomenological psychology. Volume 1* (pp. 132–148). Pittsburgh: Duquesne University Press.
Stevick, E. (1983). *Being-angry within the context of an intimate relationship: An existential-phenomenological investigation.* Unpublished doctoral dissertation, Duquesne University, Pittsburgh.
Strongman, K. (1973). *The psychology of emotion.* New York: Wiley.

9

The Social Psychology of Person Perception and the Experience of Valued Relationships

Rolf von Eckartsberg

I want to tell the story of a semitraumatic experience that I had teaching a class on social psychology on the undergraduate level at Duquesne University. It was one of those events, neither planned nor anticipated, that befalls us. Yet, in coping with the contingencies that arose, I learned a lot about the students, myself, and the scholarly discipline.

I have used a standard text as a starting point to illustrate the way in which "traditional social psychology" speaks and conceptualizes the domain of social psychology. This can be illustrated by the table of contents of a traditional textbook—which is pretty much the same in all the textbooks—a survey of which shows a social psychology that does research and presents results. In my teaching, the name I give to this way of doing social psychology is *experiment and laboratory-based social psychology*. I point out that it is characterized by an attempt to analyze the events of everyday social living into their constituent processes (such as attitude formation or person perception) and then produce these processes under controlled laboratory conditions, so that systematic variations can be introduced and changes in the process observed in response to particular induced influences. I note that this is done with preselected groups of subjects, sharing some characteristic measured by testing, so that

comparisons between groups and comparisons between experimental treatments and controls can be made using appropriate statistical procedures. I attempt to bring forth the fact that this type of social psychology tries to grasp cause–effect sequences and ultimately aims to make prediction and control of human behavior possible.

Pointing out that this is the model that has worked so well for the natural sciences, namely, bringing natural processes into the lab and studying them under controlled conditions, I note that this method is taken over as an approach to human social processes. And within this model, human social processes are identified as human behavior, that is, responses that are intersubjectively observable and measurable. Finally, we discuss the fact that within this paradigm, the laboratory situation is assumed to be sufficiently similar to the real-life situation, and thus, generalizations from lab to life can be confidently made, noting that much ingenuousness and even copyright-idea procedures have been produced in this fashion.

This is usually the first step in my introductory "spiel" to the whole realm, that is, the multiple worlds called social psychology that I want to portray for my students. I want to locate the tradition fairly and honor its contribution. Generations and lifetimes of effort go into this careful work and buildup of scholarly disciplines. Channels of communication such as journals, books, and conferences are set up to bring out the new information and to keep it in circulation. The field is packaged in

Rolf von Eckartsberg • Department of Psychology, Duquesne University, Pittsburgh, Pennsylvania 15282.

many textbooks and special studies that are then presented to new students in the appropriate slot of their psychological curriculum. Thus, the discipline becomes perpetuated. It can also become frozen, when it does not continue to grow in the direction of questioning its own identity as a discipline and use the fidelity of personal experience as its guideline for this questioning. This is a controversial issue that I then introduce as the next step.

There are other approaches that criticize the traditional experimental approach by pointing to the essential flaws, omissions, and downright falsifications that ensue from studying social living under the "inspectoscope" of the experimental approach. The first such criticism came from field theory as developed by Lewin (1951). A further development of this approach has been pursued by Roger Barker, called *ecological psychology* (1968), and it is to this work that I turn next. I name this: *ecological and field-oriented social psychology*.

I have found Barker (1968) particularly helpful because he puts his finger right on the sore spot: "What is the nature of the data that you deal with?" he asks the traditionalists. He goes on to point out that the data of the tradition have a special character. He calls them *operator data* because they are produced by a special *operation* on the part of the social psychological experimenter and are the *outcome* of this special operation. The experimenter creates the experimental situation, and in so doing, decides what the subjects are to do, what performances they are to give, and what they are to respond to. Typically, he or she also prescribes a very limited way in which the subjects can respond and react. These are called *response categories,* and they make comparative counting possible. But they are not self-initiated and spontaneous events in everyday life.

Barker thus calls social psychology back to the field of real life. Through the use of his work, I introduce a new paradigm for social psychology, an approach in which scientists are called upon to do their observations, descriptions, countings, and comparisons of whatever we study *within* the domain of everyday living. I point out that Barker feels this return is necessary for *whatever* social processes and social behavior we are singling out for special scrutiny. We are to be recorders or transcribers of ongoing spontaneous social life events. I emphasize that such descriptions and countings are also data but data of a different sort than the operator data of the experimental approach. Barker calls them *transducer data.* I also note that Barker is aware that language itself is a kind of operation by means of which the experienced reality of one person is made linguistically available to another—a seemingly irreducible problem—but point out that Barker and his cohorts were able to convince both themselves and other critics that they were pretty reliable and, hence,

"objective" in recording aspects of the "behavior stream" (which they called *behavior episodes*). The unit of analysis of behavior thus becomes spontaneously generated observable episodes. Out we go, legions of observers, into the field, and we record everything we possibly can. I emphasize that for Barker we want to study the whole field in *all* its interdependent subsystems, in its multiple situatedness, in its total householding of behavioral energies, in its *total behavioral ecology.* A formidable task quite successfully executed.

In a beginning way and with a promising armamentarium of research strategies, we know "how many" and "how much" of what kinds of behaviors occur "when and where" and for "how long" in what settings, and we compare behavioral output of different settings and whole towns with one another. I note that this kind of naturalistic counting and tabulating is long overdue, both in areas of human social living and in the private flow of personal experience, pointing out that it is nothing less than an embarrassment that we do not know much about human base rates in areas other than the sexual. We do not know the basic behavioral distribution of love and hate, of joy and sorrow, of hope and despair. Nor do we know the incidence of fighting, of caressing, of badmouthing, of praising, of working, or of celebrating. We have some information from surveys, it is true, but it is not systematic and complete, and rarely is is focused on the total householding of one particular person, the personal–behavioral ecology.

Csikszentmihalyi (1975, 1976, 1977, 1978) has published an ingenious body of research based on the sampling of human behavior and experience in real-life settings. He uses an electronic beeper that alerts volunteering subjects at randomly chosen intervals to record the situation in which they find themselves, their activities, and their perceptions, and to make ratings on their feelings and emotions. This research program is beginning to provide us with some vital information regarding the base rates of human activities in selected populations. Csikszentmihalyi includes the experiential dimensions and ratings in his research approach and thus goes beyond the purely behavioristic ecological paradigm of Barker. A decade earlier, Leary (1970) had pioneered a behavior/experience time-sampling method using a kitchen timer to record activity and experience in terms of time, place, behavior, posture, numbers of others present, behavior of others, and a classification of behavior according to a social game framework, finding important ratios that can be related to personality functioning.

I present these ideas to the students to show the open endedness of the field. I am pretty enthusiastic when I get into the integrative vision of an *ecological way of thinking*. At that point, I shift the focus toward the within and the interdependence of the processes of relating, through experience. To me, that is the most exciting horizon upon which to begin to sketch the drama of the flow of life events. So I am always tempted to jump ahead into the consciousness-oriented cinematics of life before I prepare the ground that allows us to lift ourselves off of the gravitational field of behaviorism (to which Barker, even in his ecological emphasis, still adheres). The next step, therefore, is to indicate that merely focusing on observable behavior and thus condemning oneself to an outsider–observer position still leaves the essential reality that is experienced by the actor in the event, untouched.

I point out that, for Barker, we have to stay in the realm of conventional and socially shared meaning and work with what such behavior *typically* signifies. The particular goals the actor pursues, the nuances of feeling that accompany his or her bodily movements, perhaps even the mythical self-aggrandizing imaginings that secretly or even silently accompany the action, all of these most interesting and significant human features must be excluded from Barker's way of collecting data. They are excluded because the only way to understand them would be to include the actor/subject into the research procedure and let him or her tell you what happened. My teacher, Gordon Allport, could never understand why psychologists neglect and even distrust the self-report. He would ask, "Why don't we just ask the person what is going on?" The question still needs to be asked today because very few people have heard it. Why not, indeed?

At this point in the presentation of social psychology, I am always tempted to go into the reasons for distrust. I note that deception plays a great part in social psychological experimenting, with subjects always kept in the dark about what is really going on. They are usually given a phony story, so that they believe that something else is supposedly going on rather than what the experimenter really has in mind. He or she wants to catch the behavior unaware, innocent of intention. I know that it is difficult for students to understand this cat-and-mouse game played by experimental social psychology but try to point out that it has to do with the ideal of scientific objectivity. I emphasize that within this framework we want to discover the immutable laws that govern the production of behavior, that we want them pure, uncontaminated by existential contingencies or chosen, aimed-for goals. There should not be anything personal or subjective in our understanding; the hypotheses must be formulated in terms of if and then and cause and effect, so that they can become subject to control, prediction, and production outside of the awareness (and hence consent and refusal) of the actor. I show that such ultimate motives must lead to what amounts to orthodox Freudian projection: distrust of the subjective. I usually do not go further

than this with the class at this early stage, except perhaps to indicate that there is also a moral issue involved here. You can manipulate and control in out-of-awareness ways, and for some areas of human life, particularly those related to necessary physiological needs, this is indeed the rule—a fact from which Skinnerian behaviorism derives its strength.

I do emphasize, however, that for significant areas of human life, it is always a matter of being as conscious as possible of the meaning and implication of an event in which we are existentially involved. This is an ideal, not always fulfilled, but it does imply that the appropriate way to study human events as they are experienced by the actor himself or herself is to investigate the meaning that the act has for the actor. This mode of approach will include description of the activity as it could have been observed from the point of view of the actor. To tread into these territories of actor descriptions is exciting, inviting, and valid in many ways, though we must always be aware of deliberate or unaware self-deception that is always possible. But that is a matter of the nature of the researcher-researched relationship. I show that if it is optimized as a co-researcher effort consenting to mutual disclosure of experienced and acted-through events, it can be quite fruitful. We may be able to sort out the self-deceptions with the help from our friends who preside over the psychiatric couch.

Now, when I go into this elaboration of the reasons for the distrust of self-reported experience, I have to make clear that we have already entered yet another step, and, with it, have begun to articulate yet another way of doing social psychology, which I usually name *ecological and experiential social psychology*. This work is associated with the literature of existential-phenomenology and dialogal existentialism. The names associated with existential-phenomenology are Husserl (1962), Sartre (1956), Merleau-Ponty (1962), Heidegger (1962), and Schutz (1962), whereas the dialogal existentialists group themselves around the names of Buber (1958), Marcel (1964), and Rosenstock-Huessy (1963, 1969, 1970). I try to make clear that this is, of course, a gross oversimplification because there are so many subtle internal differences among these people that one hesitates in trying to classify them into two schools, but I note that there is some justification for this categorization.

The initial rough difference is that the approach of the existential–phenomenological social psychologists begins with careful descriptions and reflective analysis of human consciousness as given to the individual. The dialogal existentialists are, on the other hand, more impressed with the reality of speech between people and study the use of language generally as well as how it expresses human experiences and activities. I point out that, for the dialogal existentialists, human events are phenomena of meaning articulated in language, that they are stories to be told and listened to, and that these stories are considered the starting point for all further thinking and theory building. I also discuss how consciousness, too, is related to speech, which, because it contains within itself the power of articulation of all of historical humankind, is, in a sense, vastly superior to the consciousness of the individual, although individuals can naturally make a new creative contribution to the whole of humankind's speech. I often use the example of Freud, pointing out that if you are Freud, then you have permanently affected the speech of humankind as well as its consciousness. Indeed, Freudian speech has led us into a partial Freudian world.

I always like this example to bring home to the students that speech and consciousness do matter, that they have real consequences, that they have substance, and that we cannot ignore them. As a matter of fact, I usually exaggerate a little and tell the students that their awareness and their speech are their most precious possessions and powers; they constitute the qualities that make mere behavior into responsible human actions! Hence, I attempt to bring home the fact that we cannot, under any circumstances, ignore the reality of human experience, consciousness, and meaning in the formulation of our social psychology; that it remains incomplete and badly distorted.

I then pick up the ecological emphasis again, for which we honor Barker, Lewin, and Csikszentmihalyi, and connect it with the important phenomenological concept of the life-world, sometimes called "everyday world." I set forth the idea that the place to study social living is where it naturally occurs and in the manner in which it is given to the experience of the participants. So much for the introduction to the kinds of social psychologies we will be dealing with here in this class.

Although students are not entirely describable as *tabula rasa* regarding their knowledge of a discipline such as social psychology, they often act as though they had not the slightest idea of its issues. They show a moving faith—it moves me to see their innocence not to say gullibility—in their teachers and in what their teachers select for them to study. They do not usually question or challenge that "this is the way it is." As a teacher, I am often awed by the power I have in selecting the discussion partners and thinking contemporaries for my students. As a teacher, I decide what will inform the thinking of these young people; I have a hand in shaping the future of social psychology or whatever discipline I happen to teach. In my choice of authors, of textbooks, of a syllabus, of a table of contents, of a set of concepts, I exert a determin-

ing influence on the thinking and approach of the next generation of co-workers. This is sometimes a problem for me when I try to call students into a new paradigm and way of thinking and going about doing social psychology. I have to lead them away from the tradition, whereas, at the same time, I want to honor the tradition for providing the occasion and target for critique. This presentation–critique dialectic is, after all, the essence of scholarship.

Under the scruples of these deliberations, I go overboard in doing justice to tradition the way it is, although in my own conviction, it is really *the way it has been.* My doing so confused the students. At least, that is what must have happened in that class, come to think of it now, in retrospect. But I am getting ahead of myself.

I have to pick up the thread of this narrative, of the story of this class that threw me into a kind of trauma and finally led me to a felicitous resolution. What I have been describing is my own frame of expectations of where students are in the class discussion, into which I am about to involve them. The starting point is very important, and it had always worked fairly well, at least in my perception and judgment. But where students "were" by the mid 1970s had changed, and this class made me realize it. In the particular context of the Psychology Department at Duquesne, where I teach, and where psychology has the reputation and avowed explicit emphasis of a dialogal–existential–phenomenological approach to psychology, even the undergraduate students had already come to expect to hear matters in an "existential–phenomenological" way, whatever that may be. A certain innocent mystique seemed to have arisen and spread as a subtle expectational set. In order to explain what happened in that class, I told myself that I had underestimated this grass-roots movement toward that philosophical set: existential–phenomenological psychology. The students primarily wanted to hear what I, as an existential–phenomenological psychologist, would have to say about social psychology. They were not content—as a matter of fact they were getting impatient—listening for 3 weeks straight to what Hastorf, Schneider, and Polefka (1970)—quickly and ideologically typified as "traditionalist"—had to offer. Underestimating this expectational set was a real "mistake"—in the benevolent sense of miss-take, a minor folly—in my teaching strategy. But I was unaware of all of this, then.

Unaware, miss-taken, or miss-taking the attitude of the students, I proceeded to expound the text very carefully, point by point, chapter by chapter. I was really interested in how Albert Hastorf *et al.* in 1970 were formulating the matter. For 3 weeks, twice a week for an hour and a half, I threw myself with great enthusiasm, textbook in hand, into chiseling out the basic structured argument of this book, yet I was gradually beginning to wonder why most of the students did not seem to share my enthusiasm.

First we got into the treatment of Hastorf *et al.*'s (1970) concept of experience. In order to clarify the often-conflicting usage of the concepts of *perception* and *experience,* Hastorf *et al.* proposes a stratified scheme of three layers:

- Level 1: Raw feelings
- Level 2: Verbally described experience
- Level 3: Scientific experience

Raw feelings are vague and unnamed and constitute a primordial way of relating. They become articulated through labeling activities when we attach verbal labels to events, objects, and qualities of objects, and this is the way we experience everyday life (Level 2). Moving to the third class of experience, scientific experience, we increase abstraction and apply some sort of systematic and theoretical organization. Here, we create abstract categories that are difficult to refer specifically to the external world and that constitute our "ways of thinking about experiences." This, presumably, is the very theory that Hastorf *et al.* propose in the book; that is, a perceiving of others in terms of units called "*intent–act–effect segments of behavior.*" In the language of phenomenology, these would be *phenomena* (i.e., meaning units); in the language of ecological–experiential social psychology, these would be *human events.* According to Hastorf *et al.,* the scientific experience constitutes the highest level, the one to which one aspires, because it gives us a causal–structural understanding of the process of person perception.

As I progressed in the course, after having outlined three major approaches to social psychology, I tried to make cross-references, as I have done here, speaking of one in terms of the others. Therefore, I present structural understanding, as the aim of any systematic effort, whether *natural scientific* (i.e., causal in orientation) or *human scientific* (i.e., intentional in focus). This is another way of making the differentiation between the experimental and the experiential. I try to show that in the experimental, we want to establish cause–effect sequences, whereas, in the experiential approach, we want to delineate and understand the meaning that shapes the action under consideration for the actor.

Hastorf *et al.* (1970), in characterizing the process of perception in general as "being an experience that has structure," as one "taking place in a world of experience that has stability," and as "revealing our world of experience as meaningful," actually make "phenomenologically compatible" statements. Implicitly, Hastorf

et al. consider person perception as a phenomenon of co-constitution, that is, the observer participates actively in the construction of meaning. It is not mere information processing in terms of preestablished codes and categories but a creative constitution born of the situated moment. As Hastorf *et al.* (1970) summarize it:

> We perceive other people as causal agents, we infer intentions, we infer emotional states, and we go further to infer enduring dispositions or personality traits. (p. 17)

Implied in this statement is a complex personality theory using the vocabulary of intentions, emotion, dispositions, and traits. The critical term that points to the person-perceiving process for Hastorf *et al.* is *to infer.* We "infer"; this is the crux of the matter. Is it a complex process of rational judgment like a computer might be programmed to calculate—as in some of the sophisticated cognitive algebra-oriented attribution theories—or is it a reading of possible meanings, as in hermeneutic explication or doing a "hermeneutical study?" Or is it simply some more mysterious process of intuitive apprehension. a sensing and mutual recognition of "elective affinity," the beckoning of a "*possible we,*" or however else we might want to characterize the mystery of encounter?

But back to the story. We, as a class, now proceeded through the assembly hall of evidence that had been accumulating through experimental laboratory work. Following the process-topics of the chapter headings, we looked at accuracy in person perception, impression formation, and, finally, attribution theory. As we continued, the students became progressively disenchanted with the reading and were sometimes openly critical, if not hostile. This initially surprised me, as I myself was engaged on an interesting clue hunt for the inadequacies of proceeding within such an approach. For the students, on the other hand, the meaning of this activity must have been, and was actually reported by some to be, nothing more than "more things to remember that aren't worth remembering," a real ideological response. At first, I did not understand what the student's response meant and pedagogically tried to regain their interest by going into the material in a more detailed manner but that only increased the problem. On the part of the students, there was a real reluctance to let themselves get involved in the details of reported findings or the intricacies of experimental design. Upon probing, I got the "so-what" reaction. "So what? We don't really learn anything more or better about the way we experience people in our lives when we go through these findings, they are so limited and abstract that they don't mean anything to us, anymore."

They had me over a barrel. I had to agree with them

ideologically; in terms of human life, in terms of the actual ongoing human events in which we are involved, these findings make little or no sense. You do not manipulate the warm–cold variable on an adjective checklist when you introduce your friend to your parents. That is just too crude a way of talking about what really matters in an encounter.

But professionally, as a social psychologist, I had to present and represent fairly the tradition and the material that is marketed under this name. Thus I tried to point out to them the social psychological issue at the very heart of the process of the classroom events themselves. This was my characterization:

> You students have accepted the general theory of meaning making that Hastorf *et al.* present in the first part of their book because you believe this already. It describes the presentation of intentional phenomenological evidence, presumably human-event life stories. But this is not forthcoming in Hastorf *et al.* Instead, their book does what every social psychology textbook does with person perception; it tries to make a chapter-heading sequence under which one can collect all the research done on the topic, research areas that have no intrinsic relationship to each other. So then the topics are always something like this: the perception of emotions, attitudes, traits, the good judge, and the accuracy of perception. Everything that is explored is always investigated in an anonymous group-average fashion. Within this context, the full meaning and context of the "event of encounter" that we perceive in our own life, as a meaningful adventure, never gets examined. Yet this is the way that social psychologists, up to now, and however inadequate it may be, have been able to collect the accumulated wisdom of decades of research. And it is based on this particular research paradigm called *experimental social psychology.*

But the students were not impressed. They objected to the manner in which everything was broken down into sketches, photographs, paper-and-pencil judgments, and the like so that any resemblance to everyday life, the way they knew it from their spontaneous ongoing life with people, was lost. So, I was glad to move to the end of Hastorf *et al.*'s (1970) book, Chapter 4: Attribution theory, which promised just that: "to consider the other as we usually come to know him in real life as an active participant with us in social interactions" (p. 61).

Thus, with some hope, but only to become disappointed again, we went into the "phenomenology of social behavior" (one chapter heading) and the intricacies of "attribution theory." Heider (1958) has laid the groundwork for this theory based on commonsense psychology. We delved into the "perception of causality" in either the person or the environment. However, the promised return to the everyday world of interhuman experience really was not forthcoming. Instead, the development of attribution theory, presented in Hastorf *et al.*'s book through Jones and Davis (1965) and Kelley (1967),

seemed to run in the direction of formulating the laws of "cognitive algebra." These authors assumed that complex information-processing procedures based upon multivariate statistical models characterized interhuman relations and judgments. Everybody is made into (assumed to be) a rigorous mathematically oriented scientist performing complex cognitive operations—perhaps unconsciously—in evaluating others, employing difficult mathematical weighting and correlation procedures to arrive at assertions of motives. The real-life experiential context of ongoing social relations and loyalties, of struggles, of fights, of resolutions, of inspired fellowship, have no place in this cognitive scheme. The process becomes one of internal cognitive decision operations, computer simulatable, the picture of the person as one of a prodigious objective information gatherer and evaluator, sitting in judgment, but not really involved in the ongoing passions of life, its risks, fears, hopes, and epiphanies.

The students could not stomach this dry-as-dust empiricism and scientific metaphorizing. It makes cognitive fiction of that intuitively felt nature of humans' existential relationships with each other. It ought to be prefaced with a disclaimer: "Any relationship to real life is purely by accident." And yet, the basic insight of attribution theory, that we perceive human action in terms of human intentions and sometimes in terms of causal inferences regarding the environment or the demand character of the situation, holds true. It is a characterization based upon human meaning and the striving to perceive human meanings, and it is true that we attribute motives and causes to our own and other's actions. As persons, do we act as "intuitive scientists" as Brown (1986) in his *Social Psychology,* claims? In this volume, Brown systematizes the attribution literature and develops the "causal calculus" for predicting the kinds of attributions people make.

Three important psychological dimensions and characteristics of available information are used by Brown (1986) to construct his complex "pocket calculus for predicting causal attribution": consensus, distinctiveness, and consistency. In an impressive fashion, he presents the experimental evidence that has accumulated about the issue to validate his calculus and to discuss attributional styles such as "depressive realism" and systematic biases in attribution. Also, he further articulates a "fundamental attribution error" that lies in the observer's tendency to overestimate dispositional causes and to underestimate situational causes.

Even if this impressive systematization of the complexity of attribution as a calculus had been available in 1975, I doubt that the students in my class would have been satisfied with this way of looking and theorizing. They wanted to get into the concrete description of experience from the actor's point of view.

As a class, we then moved into the descriptive sociology of Erving Goffman (1959), using *The Presentation of Self in Everyday Life*. There was an initial flurry of excitement, particularly due to the vivid descriptive vignettes that liven up Goffman's texts. But after some closer reading, the students experienced the fatigue that accompanies conceptual overelaboration. The prevalent attitude of the students seemed to be that "we don't have to take it apart quite that much." Also, the text did not generate spontaneous and vivid discussion; there was little openness to splice oneself into it. And again, I had to agree with the students. Goffman manifests that strange brand of "emotional attachment to complexity" that characterizes so many of our contemporary intellectuals. It is almost a compulsive and quite thoughtless categorizing and piling-up tendency, a sort of conceptual grabbiness, trying to pull things into line by force, often *tour de force*.

In addition, Goffman's attitude of continual struggle for self-presentation, for role playing, for the theatrics of life, had lost its fascination. By now, over half the semester had passed. We were bravely biting into and chewing through the reading materials, but we lacked excitement and personal involvement. I, as well as the students, felt that we were mired in an alien territory in which there was no opportunity for sharing our humanity. We were moving in the rarified atmosphere of the merely conceptual realities of role playing, interpersonal game playing, and attribution algebra. Any semblance to characters real and alive had evaporated. And we still had Bem (1970)—*Beliefs, Attitudes, and Human Affairs*—to go through.

After 2 weeks with Goffman, we came to a kind of crisis, and even "palace revolution." One day in class, a student raised his hand and said, "So what? We've been reading all this stuff; but it doesn't make much sense for our lives. We want to look at our lives and get into a psychology that speaks to our lives."

Beyond the actual crisis in the class, this brought me to a crisis in teaching as well because it demanded a real change in midstream, at a point when we were not completely through with our material. I was hit by the typical anxiety of a teacher responsible for material to be presented but unable to get it across and had to grope for an improvised strategy to deal with this trauma. What I had planned to do later, that is, speak about ecological and experientially oriented social psychology, had to be done right now. In a way, I was prepared. At the time, I was working with a graduate student, on a PhD dissertation on the phenomenon of "friending," a study of the way in which students describe, dialogue, and reflect together on their experience of what he called *friending*.

It so happened—and sometimes these synchronicities are uncanny—that this student had just sent me some materials from his PhD thesis: the results sections. So, in order to concretize the existential–phenomenological approach (which this student had been using), I reported his study and findings to the class. They listened respectfully to the procedure, which was the reflective analysis of written protocols, but when I arrived at the summary of the findings, and the list of the so-called "essential constituents of the phenomenon of interpersonal friending" (Saravia, 1977)—which is the thesis title—that very title made most of the students almost visibly disappear from the classroom through a recoiling movement of their consciousness. The verbal protest was not far behind. "We can't relate to that either; the concepts don't mean anything to us; it's too abstract."

Why still this verbal protestation? To help bring this out, let me reproduce this student's findings with regard to the phenomenon of "being with friends" as I presented them to the class:

The overall sense of the experience of being with friends is quite similar to that previously articulated as mutual presence—particularly the sense of shared presence to a new space and the absence of a sense of self. Specific new features which emerged at this point in the exploration of being with friends included the following:

First, being with friends involved a sense of "synchronous presence"—a sense of fitting, effortless presence to one another and the world which involved being appropriate (without effort), being reciprocally responsive ("moving at the same pace"), being thorough and complete in perception-action, and being willing to be/act together. This sense was characterized as being in the same space at the same pace without either effort or suppression but with congruence in mood and time.

Second, being with friends involved a sense of receptiveness to the givenness of the other which was characterized as being, feeling, enjoying, and responding in the same world, an approaching of a moment in a shared way in which we realize or find ourselves "in common."

Third, being with friends involved an experiential quality of "being oriented toward the future together." This was a sense of a present experiential moment being a "flowing onward of shared time"—a sense of anticipation of future growing-together in unanticipated ways, or as the perception of a future in the present which seems to pull us together.

The experiences of being together in a growing way were largely identified in their experiential dimensions to those previously articulated in the consideration of mutual presence. Specific new features which emerged at this point in the exploration of being together in a growing way included the three mentioned above as well as the following:

The most outstanding experiential feature was the intentional or deliberate character of this presence. There was a sense of working to be together, or struggling, or seeking, or building toward a presence together. This intentional quality was experienced as being directed not toward the others but toward the world to be shared. In other words, there was a sense of deliberately entering into and becoming a participant in a specific laughing, fantasy, etc. world of meaning. Somewhat more subtly, these experiences also revealed an experienced invitation to enter that particular world, to dismiss other involvements or concerns, and to sustain the space being created. (Saravia, 1977, pp. 122–123)

After the students' criticisms, it dawned on me that, indeed, such summarizing statements do not mean very much unless you can relate them step-by-step to the experience from which they originated. They are the meanings without which the process would not be what it is; they are necessary constituents of the process phenomenon. We cannot but formulate them as conceptual abstractions, as Hector Saravia (1977) did. When you yourself are involved in the search for and naming of the constituents as they appear to you from your reading of the concrete experiential descriptions, that experience remains as a meaning-giving matrix for the named constituents. In other words, if you do the reflective-constitutive work, you know exactly what the constituents, even in their abstract conceptual formulation, refer to. As Hector articulated these things about friending, and as I understood them from my own readings of the protocols, I was aware of the matrix from which they came and to which they referred, that is, the protocols themselves. Yet, the students in my class were not familiar with that grounding material. They had not gone through the work of reflectively renaming the material in terms of essential constituents; they had no experiential access to it, and therefore, it seemed necessarily formal and abstract to them.

When I finally realized this state of affairs, there was only one solution: doing it; doing existential phenomenology together. We had to go through this experience together. This was something I had never attempted with a whole class. My mode of reflection had always been personal; I did the reflecting alone and then published it, thus inaugurating the scholarly critique dialectic. Now I was forced into a new mode, and I was anxious. I did not know whether we could do this—I had never done it. But the work of Hector Saravia had encouraged me to try, and the students positively demanded that we proceed in this way, into uncharted territory.

Thus I started to put into implementation this new and foreign approach. First we became co-equals in deciding what we would be doing. We discussed what process we would study and came to an agreement: We would all study *an event and experience in which we felt we were moving closer to another person.* I cannot exactly trace the process of how this decision came about; it emerged from a group discussion. It seemed a natural move from Hector Saravia's friending. But it also happens that this was the thesis topic of another graduate student with whom I had been working for the year preceding this class, so I am a little suspicious that I might

have had more than co-equal status in the formulation of the focus and pushed to stay in the realm of the familiar. But what is a teacher if he or she had no prefamiliarity with the topic, is he or she still a teacher? That was part of the trauma of this class for me, that I was pushed out of familiar territory and routines into the unknown. We used a simple enough procedure: We had agreed upon the topic, the phenomenon we were to study. It was an experience in a relationship when I felt we—the other person and I—moved closer together.

We also agreed to do this by writing a description of the event as best we could. We would read these descriptions in class and discuss them and tape-record the sessions. Because there were only 18 people in the class, this seemed feasible.

I was surprised, relieved, and deeply moved by what followed. We were all moved by each other's descriptions, deeply moved, and we experienced a real sense of fellowship and communion rarely experienced in college classrooms. I want to express my thanks to the members of this class.

Before we began reading our reports, I had made it a rule that we would engage in "respectful listening to each other." By this, I meant that we were not to interrupt, criticize, or judge each other tactlessly. I emphasized beforehand, and again and again throughout the sessions, that each experience was valid and true and that the categories of good and bad or right and wrong were to be held in brackets. Somehow I feared that this public sharing of intimate experiences and meanings could lead to embarrassment and hurt or tactless judgments. This turned out to be an unjustified presumption on my part. As the stories were read, they and their authors commanded spontaneous respect, deep respect by everybody. We really began to perceive each other as unique persons.

I had each report read twice, and, after the second reading, we gingerly engaged in some conversation, for clarification of points in the story and for sharing of ideas and feelings that the story evoked. It was a very peculiar feeling for me, the teacher, just to sit with the others and listen to the unfolding of a truly dramatic movement between two persons, a genuine touching and intertwining together in consciousness on all levels of subtle nuance that we all knew to be true and felt privileged to be told. These were believable stories, they were true stories, and often simple truth spoke forth and had the power to move us. See for yourself:

THE STORY OF TERRY (19-YEAR-OLD FEMALE)

We have known each other many years. In fact, she had been my teacher in junior high school. We had more than student–teacher relationship and, even when I was in junior high, as I became older, we shared more and more and discussed things that I needed to sort out. She always had the gift to not give me direct answers to my questions and problems. Rather, she could give me information to work with to formulate my own answers. I became very close to her husband and three children also, and, although I saw them infrequently, I had kept in touch by letters and phone. When I sent her a Christmas card a year ago, she called me and told me that she had moved out of the house and was living in an apartment with another woman. I had met this woman before, and Anne [the teacher] said enough for me to get a vague feeling of what was going on without bluntly stating it. She invited me over to the apartment and several weeks later I did go. On the way over, I had pretty good idea of what to expect, but I kept telling myself that it was just because it was easier for her to live in an apartment while going to school. After spending the day with her and V., there was no longer denying the fact that she had left F. (her husband) for a different life-style.

On the way back to the bus, I found myself with a half smile on my face, thinking, well now you know, kid, what are you going to do about it? I didn't honestly see anything wrong with homosexuality, but, from the little bit I heard, I felt obligated to find something wrong with it. So I found my point of attack in: What about the kids? It certainly wasn't original, but it sufficed to get me worked up enough to condemn the whole thing. The easiest thing to do is just forget it, and since I was involved in other things, I managed to somewhat. But I could not deny my feelings for her. Nor did I want to. I knew I had a very dear friend, and I loved and respected her. It wasn't until the following summer when during an argument, I blurted, "You only love me when I live your way," did I realize that that was exactly what I was doing with Anne. I sat down and really thought about it, and then I wrote her a letter. Although I didn't say flatly what I was trying to say, she understood and within a week I received a reply from her. Her letter sounded jubilant; she was so happy with the new house she and V. had bought, being enough for the kids to really enjoy, and other developments in her life. But more importantly, because she knew I had worked through the situation and my love for her hadn't changed. In the meantime, I read everything about homosexuality that I could get my hands on, even law books. And I was amazed that my original response was so stereotyped and narrow-minded. When I finally saw her again, I told her all the research I had done and how I felt. Somehow during the discussion we fell into a serious gaze and our hands fell into each other's. I leaned forward to her, and we embraced, and I began to cry silently. When we looked at each other, we were both crying, but at the same time smiling gloriously. There was a special beauty in our silence and a special meaning, which language cannot begin to touch.

But now, what to do with this? What was I, as a teacher, what were they, as students, supposed to contribute now? What they had presented was, in a way, already perfect. There was no way to "improve" upon such descriptions. Maybe, at best, we could try to amplify and deepen their meaning in some ways. So the conversation

and dialogue toward touching the essential in the stories cautiously began: not a worked-out method to apply, not a "doing-something-specific" with the text, although there are such methods that have been developed (Colaizzi, 1973; Fischer, 1974; Giorgi, 1970, 1975; von Eckartsberg, 1972, 1975a,b, 1985, 1986). They involve a rather careful and elaborate procedure that takes months and years to complete, and it is difficult to do in the context of classroom group work. So we had to improvise some other way of doing existential–phenomenology together in an exploratory way.

We listened carefully and respectfully; we began to hear reverberations; we let questions, insights, and types of experienced movements slowly emerge and gel; we let observations crystallize into tentative verbal formulations. In the course of discussion, the following statements were made in the group discussion in response to listening to all the stories. These are, for the students as well as for me, the teacher, original insights into the phenomenon under study:

> It impressed me how slowly a process like this works. Sometimes it takes six months to linger or to be worked through. And then something happens which only symbolizes what has been kind of slumbering.

> There is a moral decision in there, somehow, an act of courage. You have to come to a clear stand, finally, it must become addressed, faced up to at one point.

> How we are all sometimes trapped within our own thinking, prisoners of our own stereotyped conceptions, which kept us from making contact.

> Thought becomes different when you have to think it through because it concerns your own real life, when it is existential, not playful thinking.

> It has to enter your life or it really doesn't count at all. . . . And then you can't even resolve it for yourself. It has to come up . . . as a confrontation. You know, you say something, in anger, and that's where your true feeling is. And then you take it from there. It has to come between . . . it has to be expressed. Otherwise it's of that lingering . . . quality.

> What I thought was . . . it must have been at first . . . it must have really hurt you. But I think you came through . . . came to your senses . . . that isn't the right way to say it. . . . The rebuff . . . when you're rebuffed you hurt. And you smart and that takes months and months to overcome. That's what's impressive to me about it.

> You have to get into a situation of constraint, against your better judgment or against what you would normally do. Normally you'd beg out before . . . you get into all kinds of strategies to avoid it. . . . There is something here, in each movement, for things, there is a real stoppage that all of a sudden breaks. Transforms everything. The world literally matters. . . . Almost like a red–green light change.

> So in the life course other things come to the forefront which then free the movement. They open the blockage.

The whole thing, the context . . . and it's a matter of timing. Right after, there is like a period of mourning, a period of anger or a period of resentment or something like a period of dissonance; that just has to linger.

It's almost like a bigger force comes into play. Something that grabs both . . . it happened in almost all the ones you mentioned last time. It was something beyond one . . . it's beyond willfulness.

These were some of the shared insights that came up spontaneously in the discussion as we were trying to do existential phenomenology together.

As a teacher, I at first felt pretty helpless being asked to respond to a story that had been read. I had no worked-out answers, no plan, no theory, no hypothesis. I just had to improvise and that really meant that I had to honestly respond to what had happened. In retrospect, it turned out that I kind of led the discussion. After all, the students found it even more difficult to find an opening to a way of relating intellectually to what was being read. Sometimes we were close to being mute, dumbfounded, and just overwhelmed by reality. To give what was presented a Freudian interpretative reading in the presence of the person whose life story it was was felt by me to be inappropriate. The students were glad that I became influential in moving the discussion respectfully toward a universal level, toward the emphasis of what was essential here. It all remained on the level of honest wrestling, and nobody was ahead of anybody else.

In the end, we tried to summarize what we had discovered. Going back to the initial description of Terry, we had to recollect and organize most of what had been said in the spontaneous discussion. When we traced the psychological and actional movement of the people involved and determined on what discernible level of consciousness these movements occurred in relation to the time flow, the situations, and the scenes, this suggested a kind of breakdown into phases: the summary became "metaphorized" as a kind of flow chart. We kept listening to it and musing about it. We glimpsed the dramatic nature of the narrated event, of the story. Who, with whom? There were protagonists and their social groupings. Did what? How? And on what level? The movement, the style, the emphasis, the degree of awareness of the movement had to be explored. To whom or to what? The direction of events, of intentions, of addresses, of targets had to be identified. Where? When? The scenes, the existential sequence, the place and the timing of activities, and then always the why? The motive, the reasons, the cause that could be perceived. Here we heard stories within stories, the story behind the story, the interpretation, our reading of the meaning of the event, the way we make sense of it. Slowly this insight dawned on me, and I have been thinking about it a lot since this class happened.

A real-life-event is a dramatic event; it has the structure of a dramatic narrative, and it is most naturally and best communicated as a story (Brand, 1968; Crites, 1971; Dunne, 1973; Keen & Fox, 1973). Life is a story to be told, and as the story of a real person, it has the power to move us. That is how we experience and judge its truths. This is the foundation of meaning regarding a human event—we understand it as a story. In the existential–phenomenological approach, when we ask people to describe a phenomenon, what we are really asking them is to tell us its story, the story of the occurrence of the event that illustrates the phenomenon about which the researcher asks. In laboratory studies, we also operate on the basis of a story. As a subject, you get to respond; you are given a few lines in experimenters' events. Their experiments are their stories, and you, the subject, have to make up your own story about the meaning of the acts you are asked to perform. Usually, the "being-a-good-subject-for-science" story is sufficient to quell your curiosity.

Thinking further about the essential structure of stories and story lines, I have discovered that each story has a universal but implicit and taken-for-granted structure in its way of relating its minimally necessary constituents to each other. These constituents are revealed as spontaneous responses to implicit questions. The following eight questions are minimally necessary to yield the constituents that compose the drama of unfolding of human action:

The questions	The subject matter they yield
Who? With whom?	The actors and their groups.
Does what?	The experience and actions—experiactions.
How?	Their quality, style, and means.
On what psychological level?	The level of consciousness.
To whom?	The addressees of the action.
When?	The place and time.
Where?	The situation, setting, scene of the action.
Why?	The motivation that guides the action.

In the spontaneous telling of the story, whether we ask these questions explicitly or answer them implicitly, we can be said to be weaving a meaning structure—a dramatic narrative, a story. The story does not make complete sense until and unless it provides an answer to these minimally necessary questions.

We look at the event from the vantage points provided by these basic questions; they can be seen to conceptually enclose the event; they circumscribe it.

We have seen how, in order to understand and to communicate a human event, you have to bring and tell it in the form of a story. When scrutinized as a dynamic unfolding of meaning (i.e., as a narrative story) it turns out that it is the interdependent (i.e., ecological) interplay of eight simultaneous questions that constitutes the birth of meaning of human psychological life. We can use the model of the regular octahedron—a double pyramid—as a perfect ideal figure and imagine it analogously to a laser-generating tube, now extended to eight dimensions, sides, or facets, like an eight-sided double-pyramid-shaped diamond. The eight essential questions in their dynamic and interdependent, simultaneous, poised, and hovering presence allow the meaning of the event to unfold storylike, movielike, fully perceivable within the field of force generated by the questions. This yields the thought figure of a three-dimensional eight-sided double pyramid that surrounds the event on all sides. This ideal structure symbolizes the essential structure of any human event. I call it *the crystal of psychological reality*.

During the summer following this fateful class, I did some research in this direction. This opened up a whole new body of literature for me, in the domain of literary criticism; I finally realized that I had come across something very akin to gems of ancient wisdom, namely Aristotle's six elements of tragedy: plot, character, thought, melody, diction, and spectacle.

Moreover, my thinking was also very similar to the scholasic hexameter, which lists the following questions that must be answered in the treatment of the topic:

[In Latin] Quis, Quio, Ubi,
    Quibus Auxiliis, Cur, Quomodo, Quando
[In English] Who, what, where
    by what means, why, how, when

Kenneth Burke (1945) in his book, *A Grammar of Motives,* has developed a similar approach to the understanding of human action and motives using the concept of the "dramatic pentad":

> Any complete statement about motives will offer some kind of answers to these five questions: what was done (act), when or where it was done (scene), who did it (agent), how he did it (agency), and why (purpose). (1945, p. xv)

Charles Muses (1974) speaks of the "syntax of events" and "the faces of meaning," and he presents a sevenfold classification of questions:

1. Which (kind of)? What?
2. Does what?
3. Where (place or space)?
4. When (time moment and/or time interval or delay)?
5. On and/or to (which kind of)? What?
6. Why (motive and/or reason)?
7. How (manner and/or means)?

I felt good having unwittingly added to this list "on what psychological level?", for that makes it relevant to modern psychological conceptions that speak in terms of levels of consciousness.

After a personal discovery in the realm of thought, one often finds oneself "in good company," joined in the formulation of an idea with other scholars. It lends credibility to the new idea.

Thus, as a social psychologist, beginning within a traditional measurement-oriented approach, I was forced by the logic of events into the company of scholars concerned with storytelling. We understand something when we know its story. Human life is a story to be told. I also realized that our colleagues, the clinical psychologists and psychiatrists, have never lost track of this fundamental human reality and thus, perhaps unwittingly but forced by the logic of "case studies," have kept our psychological profession sane.

Stories do not analyze; they synthesize. They conjure up in the listener the dramatic event, a lived adventure, a real-life people with their deeds, responses, musings, dreams, fears, and exultation. In opening yourself respectfully to what is told, in accepting the gift of the other who makes the effort to tell you the tale with its implicit moral, you allow the story to move you, to make you recognize your spiritual kinship to the events told and the actors named. You find yourself linked in destiny, in inspired fellowship or in motivated animosity.

Listening to the vibrant tension of the continuous, interdependent, open-ended, and forever further-revealing basic questions, the crystal modulates and intensifies the voice of communion, of our spiritual kinship with others, of our personal "existential ensemble," our chosen and avowed social body, the "*we* of our identity" (Who? With Whom?).

Our powerful analytic and experimental procedures have only succeeded in fractionating psychological reality to such a degree that we are at a loss as to how to "put Humpty Dumpty together again." Perhaps we might start again with simple storytelling. In the realm of human meaning, we stay in the realm of human understanding—*Verstehen*—and that has to do with stories, with the dramatic narrative of human events. This is the level at which lay persons and psychological experts can meet and find a common language. All expert jargon somehow has to relate to this primordial level of commonsense psychology, psychology lived as story. For a moment, I glimpsed the vision of a redefinition of psychology: *Psychology is the study of the personal stories of human events.*

Since this classroom experience, I have continued to study the stories or protocols that the students wrote on their experiences of moving closer together. Upon closer reading, the story of Terry reveals itself to be a story of reconciliation, a moving closer together, again, after a conflict. I chose this story to illustrate my hermeneutic–phenomenological research approach that discloses the dynamic *existential process structure* of the phenomenon; how it is a dynamic, unfolding, experienced, and situated event for the participant.

In this approach, there are several steps involved in the process of interpretation. Close attention is paid to the psychological moves and interactions of the protagonists in the story. The real-time referents and the intervals between actions are scrutinized carefully, and the unfolding psychological meaning is articulated by the researcher. The following procedural steps are used:

After I obtained the story, I began the explication and interpretation by identifying and naming chapters and their constitutive subphases and subevents and by summarizing their contents. The explication/guiding question in this step of the interpretation is: What are the chapters and subphases, or episodes, that constitute the plot of reconciliation, and how can they be named?

The second step is to formulate the psychological meaning contained in each phase of the story as an experienced existential process. The explication/guiding question of this step of the hermeneutic reflection is: What is happening in the experience of the protagonist? What concrete existential process is experienced by the actor in the story in the exact sequence of its occurrence?

These questions about what happens in terms of the protagonist's experience emphasize his or her *psychological moves* sequentially over time as an existential process. My hermeneutic work consists in articulating my view of this unfolding process, preserving its chronological character as an unfolding plot.

The chaptering, subphasing, and episoding summarized in the section beginning on page 149 reveal my own process of comprehension and interpretation. I see the story as a long drawn-out personal struggle by the subject, Terry, to save an important relationship, a long-standing mutually satisfying love–mentor relationship. Their relationship had fallen into some neglect over the years but continued underground because it seemed an important milestone in Terry's early development, a lasting bond of what I call *inspired fellowship.* This is a subform of a love relationship in which two people, one older and more experienced, mutually encourage and elevate each other in thinking, feeling, being creative, and valuing. They "bring each other out," help each other grow spiritually as persons, and even challenge each other.

A crisis in the relationship occurs for Terry through the disclosure that Anne is a lesbian. The disclosure leads Terry to struggle with herself and her socialized moral-attitude stereotypes toward such a life-style. She is forced into a moral choice—for or against Anne. She cannot come to a decision in a purely rational and deliberate manner, once and for all. She becomes entangled in the conflict, and it takes a long time and some fortuitous circumstantial happenings in Terry's life for her to find a resolution that leads to reconciliation.

After a sequence of particular psychological moves (being anxious, doubting, delaying, avoiding, feeling conflict, and letting time pass), Terry is confronted with the issue in another social context, the relationship with her mother. In a moment of deep emotional agitation, she comes to the insight about herself that it has been her own warding-off style of denial that had made her repress her love for Anne as a person and mentor. Accepting responsibility for her own self-deception and denial of her deepest feelings and values, she makes an essentially moral decision to respond, live authentically, and risk herself by facing up to the conflict. She takes courageous action to confront her own unknown leanings by establishing personal contact with Anne, to see for herself first by letter, and then face-to-face, on which occasion the "blessing of reconciliation" is experienced by both. This includes a kind of confession of sins, a making speakable between them what had not been shared. The airing of Terry's loss of faith in Anne, her suspicion, erection of psychological barriers, moral condemnation, and anguish helps to reestablish and strengthen their relationship. In retrospect, Terry comes to see Anne's handling of the crisis as another instance of her concern, as a mentor, for Terry, thereby allowing Terry to come to her own decision.

We do not have to move very far into a metalevel of theoretical understanding and discourse to account for the motives operating here. One could attempt a Freudian rendering in terms of latent homosexuality, a Jungian translation in terms of the "wise old person archetype," or a social-learning interpretation in terms of the reinforcement and deconditioning of parental stereotypes. We are here taking an existential position, that is, the perspective of responsible personal agency that holds that people create relationships with each other through acts of moral judgment and commitment in the context of chosen value orientations.

TERRY'S STORY: A HERMENEUTIC APPROACH

Original Story

We have known each other many years—in fact she had been my teacher in junior high school. We had more than a teacher–student relationship even when I was in junior high. As I became older, we shared more and more and discussed things I needed to sort out. She always had the gift to not give me direct answers to my questions and problems but rather could give me information to work with to formulate my own answers. I became close to her husband and three children also, and although I saw them infrequently, I kept in touch by letters and phone.

Chaptering and Subphases

I. From Teacher to Mentor

How, over several years, the relationship between Terry and Anne, her junior high-school teacher, came about and what it meant.

1. Their Initial Relationships. How Terry and Anne came to know each other and established a more than teacher–student relationship: discussing things Terry needed to sort out.

2. Anne's Gift. Anne's gift for Terry: to help her find her own solutions. A mentorship develops.

3. Terry and Anne's Family. Terry became friends with Anne's husband and three children also and stayed in contact over time.

Existential Process Structure

Terry, a young girl, meets a female teacher, Anne, in junior high school with whom she establishes a personal relationship. The teacher becomes her mentor, making her feel welcome and encouraging and guiding her to always find her own solutions. Terry becomes friends with Anne's husband and three children. Terry keeps in touch with Anne over the years by occasional visits and communications and considers herself in a stable and rewarding relationship with her.

Original Story

When I sent her a Christmas card a year ago, she called and told me that she had moved out of the house and was living with another woman. I had met this woman before, and Anne said enough for me to get a vague feeling for what was going on without bluntly stating it. She invited me over to the apartment. And several weeks later I did go. On the way over I had a pretty good idea of what to expect, but I kept telling myself that it was just because it was easier for her to live in an apartment while going to school. After spending the day with her and Jane, there was no longer denying the fact that she had left Bill for a different life-style.

Chaptering and Subphases

II. Complications in the Relationship: Precipitating Events

How, a year ago, Terry realized Anne's change to a homosexual life-style. Serious complications arise in the relationship.

1. The News. A year ago, news of change in Anne's life, her moving in with another woman, comes by way of an exchange of Christmas greetings. Terry writes; Anne calls.

2. The Telephone Call. Terry knew the other woman and was suspicious about what was going on. Terry gets invited to visit.

3. The Visit. On the way over, what Terry expects to find and how she makes up her mind about it.

4. The Realization. After the day's visit, Terry concludes Anne is a lesbian!

Existential Process Structure

A crisis in the relationship occurs for Terry a year prior to the report while Terry is a junior in college. The crisis arises through a hint in a Christmas card sent by Anne, indicating that she was now living with another woman whom Terry also knew. Terry suspects a lesbian bond. Terry's relationship to Anne becomes problematic for Terry and leads to a serious struggle with herself. She experiences the emergence in herself of a social moral attitude and a stereotyped view of a lesbian life-style. But Terry is curious and wants to see for herself, to test out this relationship; she accepts an invitation to visit Anne in her new home several weeks later. She realizes during and after the visit that Anne is indeed living a lesbian life-style, and she finds herself bewildered and confused.

Original Story

On the way back to the bus, I found myself with half a smile on my face, thinking: "Well, now you know, kid, what are you going to do about it?" I didn't honestly see anything wrong with homosexuality, but from the little bit I heard I felt obligated to find something wrong with it. So I found my point of attack in: "What about the kids?" It certainly wasn't original, but it sufficed to get me worked up enough to condemn the whole thing. The easiest thing to do is just to forget it and, since I was involved in other things, I managed to somewhat. But I could not deny my feelings for her. I knew I had a very dear friend, and I loved and respected her.

Chaptering and Subphases

III. Crisis, Avoidance, Conflict

After the visit, Terry lives in conflict and avoidance of Anne and the issue for several months.

> *1. Terry's First Thoughts.* Now, you know, what are you going to do about it?

> *2. Feels Obliged to Take a Stand.* Terry feels socially obligated to reject and condemn homosexuality and justifies it by a stereotyped response.

> *3. Condemnation of Anne.* Terry works herself up to condemn the whole thing.

> *4. Terry's Avoidance.* She keeps herself busy and forgets, almost; she avoids.

> *5. Terry's Love for Anne Surfaces Again.*

> *6. Terry's Hesitation.* Terry reasserts her love for Anne to herself, but she hesitates.

Existential Process Structure

Terry is now forced into a moral dilemma and feels that she has to make a choice: for or against Anne. She cannot come to a decision in a purely rational and deliberate manner, once and for all. She becomes entangled in the conflict and resolves her ambivalence and confusion by condemning Anne, rationalizing her stance in a self-righteous but stereotyped manner. It takes months for Terry to find a way out of her pattern of projecting blame and denial. She "forgets" by keeping busy with other things and avoids the issue. Yet, from time to time, her continuing positive feelings for Anne and her appreciation for her as a mentor surface, and Terry cannot deny them to herself. They are in "gestation" and work "underpsychically." Yet she continues to avoid coming to terms with the relationship with Anne.

Original Story

It wasn't until the following summer, when during an argument [with mother], I blurted, "You only love me when I live your way," did I realize that that was exactly what I was doing with Anne. I sat down and really thought about it, and then I wrote her a letter. Although I didn't say flatly what I was trying to say, she understood, and within a week I received a reply from her. Her letter sounded jubilant. She was so happy with the new house she and Jane had bought, being enough for the kids to really enjoy, and other developments in her life. But, more importantly, because she knew I had worked through the situation and my love for her hadn't changed.

Chaptering and Subphases

IV. The Turning Point in Their Relationship

Terry has the insight and resolves to confront and live through her conflict and ambivalent feelings.

> *1. Terry's Insight.* Last summer Terry realized her one-sided intolerant reaction regarding Anne in an encounter with her mother.

> *2. Contact Again.* Terry writes an explanatory letter to Anne.

> *3. A Positive Reply.* Within a week Anne writes back jubilantly.

> *4. Good News.* Anne "understood," helped her to find her own solution again. Terry's love for her hadn't changed.

Existential Process Structure

After 6 months of avoidance, of denial, of being anxious, and of experiencing conflict and just letting time pass and keeping busy in other directions, Terry finds herself confronted with the issue of conflicting life-styles in another relevant social context, in a confrontation with her own mother, whom she accuses in a spontaneous outburst of anger and frustration, "You only love me when I live your way!" In a moment of deep emotional agitation, Terry makes the connection to her own attitude toward Anne and comes to an insight about her own style of denial that had made her suppress her love for Anne as her friend and mentor. This insight reconfigures her understanding, and she acknowledges to herself that she had avoided the issue by projecting the blame. Accepting responsibility for her actions from that moment of recognition of her own self-deception and self-justification and for denying her deepest feelings and genuine love and respect for Anne, she makes a moral decision to respond, to face up to her true feelings, to live authentically, and to risk herself and her meaning-making habits. She takes courageous action to confront her own unknown leanings and uncertain reactions by initiating personal contact again with Anne and to explain herself to her. She writes a letter and receives an encouraging, understanding, and implicitly forgiving reply from Anne within a week.

Original Story

In the meantime, I read everything about homosexuality that I could get my hands on, even law books, and I was amazed that my original response was so stereotyped and narrow-minded. When I finally saw her again, I told her all the research I had done and how I felt. Somehow, during the discussion, we fell into a serious gaze and our hands fell into each other's. I leaned forward to her, and we embraced, and I began to cry silently . When we looked at each other, we were both crying. but at the same time smiling gloriously. It was a special beauty in our silence and a special meaning, which language cannot begin to touch.

Chaptering and Subphases

V. The Blessing of Reconciliation

Terry overcomes her stereotyped ideas and fears, makes contact again with Anne, and a deep reconciliation and reunion ensue.

1. Homework. Terry reads up on homosexuality and gains insight into her own past narrow-mindedness.

2. Their Reunion. As they meet again, they have a deep personal exchange. Terry confesses her doubts. They have an emotional reconciliation in which they find themselves genuinely close and moved, and they firmly reestablish their mutual love and respect for each other, their ''inspired fellowship.''

Existential Process Structure

Before seeing Anne again, Terry studies up on homosexuality and now fully realizes how narrow-minded, stereotyped, and defensive she has been. When they finally meet again face to face, they both experience the blessing of reconciliation after the following happened: a kind of confession of sins on Terry's part, a making speakable between them what had not been shared, and the granting of mutual forgiveness in a tender moment of mutual recognition beyond words in which both are moved to tears and embrace. Terry's loss of faith in Anne, her suspicions, erection of barriers, rejection, moral condemnation, and unjust projection of blame are aired between them and help to reestablish and strengthen their relationship together. And Terry realizes that Anne has been acting as her mentor all along, allowing her to come to her own insights and decisions, to make her own mistakes, and being accepting of her, concerned and always encouraging, and welcoming her being without pushing her or forcing the issue. Their relationship emerges purified and strengthened through this ordeal, and both are glad over the reconciliation.

We can add another step to our hermeneutical work and try to characterize the achronological, that is, nonsequential, configurational meaning of the phenomenon as the *essential meaning structure*. In this structural configuration attitude, the *metastory of reconciliation* turns out to be the following:

> An ongoing interpersonal relationship of intimacy and mutual importance is ruptured due to a falling out between the partners and made problematic. Ongoing face-to-face contact is disbanded, and a self-righteous construal of the reasons for the break is formulated, which projects the blame for the break on the other partner. There is much denial.

The attribution of blame for the failure or rupture of a relationship is usually external. The other is blamed. I exonerate myself from blame through imaginatively storying the events in this light.

A precipitating event or crisis typically occurs in one of the partners that disrupts the stalemate and reminds that partner of the continuing claim of the relationship, of the living in tension, and in mutual rejection. Bringing the relationship to renewed awareness forces also a reconsideration of one's attitudes, values, and involvements. If one of the partners has a change of heart and/or insight into the situation and can dislodge his or her frozen and stereotyped perceptions and evaluations, owning up to and assuming some of the responsibility for the rupture, then movement toward renewed contact and conciliatory actions becomes possible, that is, imaginable and actualizable.

As long as I blame the other and do not accept part of the responsibility for the rupture in the relationship, no movement toward reconciliation is possible. However, when I move into an attitude of coconstitution, that is, when I assume part of the responsibility for the creation, maintenance, and reconciliation of our relationship and when I can recognize and acknowledge that our lives continue to be linked in valued relationship with an attractive we-feeling quality, then I start working toward reconciliation.

Once initiated, the peace-making overtures must be acknowledged and reciprocated by the other so that a crucial face-to-face exchange can occur. Such an exchange involves confession of sins and stupidity, expression of regret and sorrow, and the asking for forgiveness in so many words and gestures, in a situation and moment of great vulnerability, openness, and risk.

The rupture and the relationship itself, our ''we'' (us together), has to be made speakable directly, face-to-face, here and now. An encounter as a genuine confrontation with its full, explosive mixture of fears, anxieties, guilt feelings, hurt, and anger has to be risked and undergone without any guarantee. I enter this encounter with apprehension and total vulnerability.

The other, when approached, has the right and choice to refuse. The accepting response of the other seals the reconciliation in a dramatic moment of mutual recognition and ongoing shared intimacy, and cocreativity can resume its course in a strengthened relationship.

This characterization of the essential meaning structure of the experience of reconciliation is a provisional statement subject to confirmation, challenge, and modification by further work on other stories. It is subject to revision through further data and research even though there is a presumed shared consensus of meaning tied up in the very concept *reconciliation*. We know the verbal and experiential meaning of this word in a general way but not as a detailed psychological configuration in all its nuances. It is only by using an existential–hermeneutic approach that we can articulate both the unfolding of the *existential process* over time and the *essential meaning structure* of the phenomenon as an idea.

THE TRANSPERSONAL NATURE OF SOCIAL REALITY AND VALUED RELATIONSHIPS

Existentially speaking, we live in valued interpersonal relationships that have an appeal and claim upon us. This holds true both in the *intimate sphere of private life,* that is, in relationships of love, friendship, mentorship, and inspired fellowship—what we might refer to as life in the "existential ensemble"—as it holds true in the *public sphere* in which we hold offices in institutions and play roles in socially prescribed situations. We live in valued relationships that matter to us and that are socially structured and supported. The "we" of family, of lovers, of friendship, of professional-client relationship, of membership in a social body has a demand character that goes beyond our personal wishes. We-relationships carry mutual obligations that transcend our own willfulness and command our commitment and obedience to its rules and values. Valued relationships as social institutions such as professions, religions, the arts, sciences, political parties, sports, and other interest groups have a *transpersonal nature*. They constitute a "higher" reality of calling, commitment, and shared spirit that takes a hold of all its members. The "we" or "us" of relationship and experienced belongingness transcends the control of the individual members.

Spiritual transmission of values has a transgenerational dimension. Generations of individuals are called into succession to carry on a tradition or a specific cultural form of shared activity—a standing-action pattern. Social reality is thus transpersonal and language, as a meta-institution, can be said to be the prototypical example. As individual speakers, we carry on and contribute to the heritage expressed in the institution of language. Particular "language games," such as the sciences, recruit members and thus perpetuate themselves from generation to generation. The spirit of doing science, for example, survives the death of any and every member of the scientific community and can thus be said to be a transpersonal reality. All the arts, political institutions, and the religions show a similar transpersonal dimension. They have power and authority that command our obedience and cooperation, and they achieve a certain limited immortality in human affairs.

Rosenstock-Huessy (1916/1963, 1970) has emphasized and articulated this social meaning of the transpersonal or spiritual dimension:

> We call spiritual only that which concerns and is appropriate to more than one soul. A reality is spiritual (like socialism, the state, the church) when several souls in succession have to occupy a designated position in it. Everything spiritual, therefore, has to be understood as soul-succession. The spirit takes hold of more than one person.
>
> And when the spirit takes hold of only one person, as a genius, for instance, then this happens only so that through this person others are also being affected and moved. The spirit is a power of humankind. The soul is a power in human nature. (1916/1963, p. 798, my translation)

Participation in valued relationships is the giving of oneself over to the *we* of the relationship in a soul-filled time period. Such a commitment and caring for our *we* involves the experience and acknowledgment of a transpersonal power that works in and on the relationship. It has a hold on us and demands our consent and our creative and effortful participation.

The social calendar, which marks our holidays, and its accompanying rituals, ceremonies, and celebrations, provides the social drumbeat that envelops the members of the celebration community and reinforces their experience of belongingness and commitment (von Eckartsberg, 1988). The shared holidays of the community as a social body commemorate what is important about our heritage and tradition—our shared destiny—and they provide structured occasions through which we become aware of the transpersonal nature of our belonging to one another and of being pledged to the values we hold in common. The study of calendars and holidays and its rituals gives us an important access to and insight into the spiritual and value-committed life of a community, to its transpersonal dimensions (Rosenstock-Huessy, 1969). In and through the high times of "concelebrating," we, the communal participants, reaffirm our belongingness and commitment to our shared and transpersonal social identity.

The experience of person perception happens, existentially, in the context of valued relationship over a lifetime. Person perception is not primarily a technical skill to be scientifically analyzed but a power of commitment to be appreciated and cultivated. We have to understand the dynamic process structures of our interpersonal living and also recognize its transpersonal dimensions: love, duty, commitment, devotion, inspiration, spirit.

Looking at the social psychology course described in this chapter in retrospect, I can now see why I had such a hard time in the beginning. When you are talking to students who are experientially oriented—and who are not in the age of mass media life dramatization—and hence, already implicitly committed ideologically to an existential position, you are facing students who expect to learn by participation, by relating what they hear and read to their own experience, by relating it to their own story. That is their point of departure and their point of return. As teachers we have to take cognizance of this fact.

Most social psychology textbooks and professional research journals do not present their material as life story. At best, there is the story of doing the experiment, but this report is often a sordid story of manipulation, deception, and anonymity that retains little, if any, resemblance to a fully human story. It commands no personal respect. Rather, it generates disbelief and a slight feeling of resentment. Variables do not represent what people are, and the correlation of dimensions cannot fill the void of the lack of human drama. After all, we live our lives with real people, and, although we have to make judgments about each other, we judge in the context of sharing a life, with moral consequences, participating in the ongoing existential drama. Most social psychological research in person perception is inconsequential. It is game playing, observer gossip, flip judgment on insufficient evidence, interplay of conceptual phantoms. No wonder it does not answer the needs of many of our students who want to understand and be initiated into the full power of responsible interpersonal reality: real-life partnership.

REFERENCES

Allport, G. (1961). *Pattern and growth in personality.* New York: Holt, Rinehart & Winston.

Barker, R. (1968). *Ecological psychology.* Stanford: Stanford University Press.

Bem, D. (1970). *Beliefs, attitudes, and human affairs.* Belmont, CA: Brooks-Cole.

Brand, G. (1968). *Gesellschaft und personliche Geschichte.* Stuttgart: Kohlhammer.

Brown, R. (1986). *Social psychology: The second edition.* New York: Free Press.

Buber, M. (1958). *I and thou.* New York: Scribners.

Burke, K. (1945). *A grammar of motives.* Englewood Cliffs, NJ: Prentice-Hall.

Colaizzi, P. F. (1973). *Reflection and research in psychology.* Dubuque: Kendall-Hunt.

Crites, S. (1971). The narrative quality of experience. *American Academy of Religion, 39*(3), pp. 291–311.

Csikszentmihalyi, M. (1975). *Beyond boredom and anxiety.* San Francisco: Jossey-Bass.

Csikszentmihalyi, M. (1978). Attention and the holistic approach to behavior. In K. Pope & J. Singer (Eds.), *The stream of consciousness* (pp. 335–358). New York: Plenum Press.

Csikszentmihalyi, M., & Getzels, J. (1976). *The creative vision.* New York: Wiley.

Csikszentmihalyi, M., Larson, R., & Prescott, S. (1977). The ecology of adolescents and experiences. *Journal of Youth and Adolescence, 6*(3), 281–294.

Dunne, J. (1973). *Time and myth.* Garden City: Doubleday.

Fischer, W. F. (1974). On the phenomenological mode of researching "being anxious." *Journal of Phenomenological Psychology, 4,* 405–423.

Giorgi, A. (1970). *Psychology as a human science.* New York: Harper & Row.

Giorgi, A. (1975). An application of phenomenological method in psychology. In A. Giorgi, C. T. Fischer, & E. L. Murray (Eds.), *Duquesne studies in phenomenological psychology* (Vol. II) (pp. 82–103). Pittsburgh: Duquesne University Press.

Goffman, E. (1959). *The presentation of self in everyday life.* Garden City: Doubleday Anchor Books.

Hastorf, A., Schneider, D., & Polefka, J. (1970). *Person perception.* Reading, MA: Addison-Wesley.

Heidegger, M. (1962). *Being and time.* New York: Harper & Row.

Heider, F. (1958). *The psychology of interpersonal relations.* New York: Wiley.

Husserl, E. (1962). *Ideas.* New York: Collier.

Jones, E. E., & Davis, K. E. (1965). From acts to dispositions. In F. Berkowitz (Ed.), *Advances in experimental social psychology* (Vol. 2) (pp. 220–266). New York: Academic.

Keen, S., & Fox, A. (1973). *Telling your story.* Garden City: Doubleday.

Kelley, H. (1967). Attribution theory in social psychology. *Nebraska Symposium on Motivation, 15,* 192–238.

Leary, T. (1970). The diagnosis of behavior and the diagnosis of experience. In A. R. Mahrer (Ed.), *New approaches to personality classification* (pp. 211–230). New York: Columbia University Press.

Lewin, K. (1951). *Field theory in social science.* New York: Harper Torchbooks.

Marcel, G. (1964). *Creative fidelity.* New York: Farrar Straus.

Merleau-Ponty, M. (1962). *Phenomenology of perception.* London: Routledge & Kegan Paul.

Muses, C. (1974). The syntax of events. *Astrologia, 1*(1), 19–30.

Rosenstock-Huessy, E. (1963). Angewandte Seelenkunde [Applied science of the soul] *Die Sprache Des Menschen-Geschlechts.* Heidelberg: Lambert Schneider. (Originally published in 1916.)

Rosenstock-Huessy, E. (1969). *Out of revolution.* Norwich: Argo.

Rosenstock-Huessy, E. (1970). *Speech and reality.* Norwich: Argo.

Saravia, H. (1977). *An existential–phenomenological investigation of the experience of "friending presence."* Unpublished doctoral dissertation, Duquesne University.

Sartre, J.-P. (1956). *Being and nothingness.* New York: Philosophical Library.

Schutz, A. (1962). *Collected papers* (Vol. I). The Hague: Nijhoff.

von Eckartsberg, R. (1972). Experiential psychology: A descriptive protocol and a reflection. *Journal of Phenomenological Psychology, 2,* 161–173.

von Eckartsberg, R. (1975a). The eco-psychology of motivation theory and research. In A. Giorgi, C. T. Fischer, & E. L. Murray (Eds.), *Duquesne studies in phenomenological psychology* (Vol. II) (pp. 155–181). Pittsburgh: Duquesne University Press.

von Eckartsberg, R. (1975b, September). *The psychoecology of culture building.* Paper presented to Division 32 Symposium, American Psychological Association Convention, Chicago, Illinois.

von Eckartsberg, R. (1985). The dialogal–existential we-feeling and nonviolence. *Dharma, 2*(April-June), 147–156.

von Eckartsberg, R. (1986). *Life-world experience. Existential–phenomenological research approaches in psychology.* Washington, DC: Center for Advanced Research in Phenomenology and University Press of America.

von Eckartsberg, R. (1988). R. Schutz's promise for social psychology. In L. Embree (Ed.), *Wordly phenomenology: The continuing influence of Alfred Schutz.* Washington, DC: Center for Advanced Research in Phenomenology and University Press of America.

IV

The Clinical Area

The clinical area within existential–phenomenological psychology has a more widely known and extensive history than any of the other subfields covered in this book. All three chapters in this section address some aspect of this history, point to relationships between mainstream psychology and phenomenology, and richly illustrate their distinctive contributions to clinical psychology with case examples.

Constance Fischer's Chapter 10 presents a detailed discussion of the history of, and current practice in, personality and clinical assessment. She shows how an approach to assessment that is guided by existential–phenomenological principles is able to address the specific features of a client's lived world and thus to open up possibilities for change for both client and clinician. The chapter ends with a complete case report that gives the reader a full and concrete sense of this approach.

In Chapter 11, "Demystifying Psychopathology," Halling and Dearborn Nill posit that, whereas disturbed behavior may appear senseless or irrational, a closer examination will show it to be meaningful. They articulate a fivefold framework for interpreting disturbed behavior that is rooted in existential–phenomenological thought but that also draws from other major psychotherapeutic traditions, such as psychoanalysis and behaviorism.

Moss' Chapter 12 on psychotherapy is similarly integrative in its approach. He presents key insights from a broad range of therapeutic traditions that share a concern for an understanding of human experience. Included in his discussion are an historical introduction to phenomenological and existential influences in psychotherapy and a presentation of the fundamental principles in experientially oriented psychotherapy.

10

Personality and Assessment

Constance T. Fischer

This chapter is written in four major sections. The first provides some historical background to mainstream psychology's approach to the areas traditionally designated as "personality and assessment." The second section focuses on limitations and other difficulties of contemporary notions and practices. The themes running through the first two sections have to do with established psychologists' inclinations to look upon human affairs in terms of natural laws operating independently of human consciousness. From the perspective of other psychologists, who regard humans as being not only *objects* of nature but also as being active *subjects,* the predominant view is not so much wrong as it is incomplete. The incompleteness, however, can have deleterious consequences when it takes the form of either: (a) an explicit reduction of all human events to mechanics and/or electrochemistry, or (b) an implicit technologized comprehension—which occurs in the absence of formal recognition of specifically human characteristics.

The third section of this chapter presents existentially and phenomenologically based departures from the object–science traditions in assessment of personality. The final section overviews my own conceptions and practices of psychological assessment. Excerpts from actual assessments and a sample report illustrate ways in which the psychologist can be scientific and still take into account both the client's and his or her own subjecthood.

Constance T. Fischer • Department of Psychology, Duquesne University, Pittsburgh, Pennsylvania 15282.

THE PAST: PSYCHOLOGY AS NATURAL SCIENCE

No doubt people always have wondered about their differences from one another and devised their own ways of making related judgments. But as formal areas of study, "personality" and "assessment" had their beginnings in the Europe of around the 1860s to the early 1900s. By and during that time, the natural sciences were making many dramatic discoveries. For example, Charles Darwin had sailed on *The Beagle* to the Galapagos in 1831 and had published his biological classifications and theory of evolution in 1859. His lesser known cousin, Sir Francis Galton, a gentleman scholar, undertook a 2-year African voyage, making significant contributions to geography enroute. He was the first publisher of weather maps and the first to describe the anticyclone as a weather system. In 1884 he established the first anthropometric laboratory, where he collected measurements on height, arm span, visual acuity, color discrimination, memory, and numerous other variables—all from intrigued visitors to the laboratory. Galton's interests led to his development of correlation and regression statistical techniques, to construction of mental tests that were to serve as a selection criterion for breeding a superhuman race, to the first psychological questionnaire, to free association as a research technique, to the first stop watch (for timing the associations), and to still more. Evolutionist, geographer, anthropologist, eugenicist, statistician—all self-made; these were times of exciting possibility.

In short, theological and philosophical concerns had given way to a belief that if there were a God, It had set the world in motion according to a logic of objects—an order

157

that could be discovered and manipulated. In biological classification and in mathematical relationships, one could find all the harmony, wonder, and splendor one might wish. Moreover, these explorations occurred in the face of continuing but better mechanized intra-European wars, along with the Industrial Revolution's social unease and productivity. This juxtaposition of chaos with mechanized order presented the challenge of the times.

Physicians, physicists, and anatomists worked to discover how natural laws governed human affairs and, in this effort, established psychology as a formal discipline. Significantly, during this period textbooks appeared with the titles *psychophysiology, physiology as a natural science,* and *psychology as a natural science.* These titles reflect the factual intertwining of psychology with the physical sciences of the day as well as psychology's efforts to claim itself as a legitimate scientific endeavor. Ernst Weber (1795–1878), a physiologist, devoted his work to uncovering the natural laws connecting mind and matter, an area of study designated as *psychophysics.* He assumed that regularities in nonmatter (behavior, perception, emotion, memory, thought) were dependent upon material variables. A typical experiment involved blindfolding a research subject, placing a lead weight on one palm, while varying the heaviness of the weights placed one at a time on the other palm, and asking the subject to judge when a weight exceeded the heaviness of the comparative weight. Weber and his contemporaries experimented with a variety of psychophysical methods forerunning our current ones, such as presenting the stimuli in descending as well as ascending order, in paired comparisons, and for the subject to rank order. Similarly, Weber and other researchers experimented with the relation between mental judgments and other kinds of physical stimuli such as light intensity and the volume of sound. Eventually, Weber formulated his findings into a mathematical law expressing a constant relation between stimulus intensity and perception. Gustav Fechner (1801–1887), a physicist and philosopher, refined Weber's law into one that stated that the magnitude of sensation is proportional to the logarithm of stimulus intensity.

The previously mentioned examples are only a few instances of the work being done in this period. (See Boring, 1957, for the classic text on the history of experimental psychology. See DuBois, 1970, for a history of psychological testing that includes its overlap with the history of experimental psychology.) The present examples are intended to highlight the fact that, during these beginnings, the researchers were not interested in studying individuals as such; they needed individuals only as representatives of the species in order to generate data from which universal laws could be derived. None of the

individuals was an exact exemplar of the law, but data across many people yielded measures of central tendency (such as arithmetical averages) that did provide regularities that could be said to characterize the functions of the mind in general. This search for universal laws provided a major foundation for the later psychological testing movement, that of the area known as "individual differences." Significantly, however, this area, too, is not about qualitative differences. It is the field that studies how prenamed, test-defined characteristics are mathematically distributed among specified populations (gender and age groupings, for example). At a much more sophisticated level, this is similar to the way a teacher presents the distributions of midterm grades as being "curved" so that the most frequent scores are C's, with B's and D's being equally less frequent scores. The specific way a student formulated answers and even the particular character of the answers are lost; the student's performance is expressed by a number that indicates his or her mathematical location among classmates.

Back to the beginnings. It is Wilhelm Wundt (1832–1920), another physiologist, who has been formally acclaimed as the father of experimental psychology. He was the first (in 1879) to open an official laboratory, to direct dissertations in psychology, and to establish a journal for systematic publication of methods and data. Numerous Americans studied with him and with one of his students, an Englishman, E. B. Titchener (1867–1927), who later taught at Cornell University. Although other American psychologists focused on studying and norming human capacities and on developing animal, child, and abnormal psychology, the German tradition pursued studies of the "mind"—universal elements that made up perception, the determinants of reaction time, and so on.

The continuing assumption on both continents was that even consciousness is most appropriately researched via the methods of the physical sciences. Specifically, this meant that researchers regarded themselves as detached observers of events that were determined by laws independent of their efforts to uncover them. Setting up an experiment and the recording and analysis of results were thought to involve only logical reflection—thinking deductively in terms of Aristotelian discrete categories of inclusive and exclusive classes. Put differently, this approach was that of an external perspective—external to the person observing the events apparently happening in observable sequences "out there." In their effort to identify the laws underlying human affairs, psychologists tried to "control-out" "extraneous variables" so they could observe the interaction of the isolatable elements, conditions, or the initiation of an event.

Today one can see the same assumption and goal in the methods of psychological assessment. Assessors have been trained to be scientific—to be standardized in their approach to the assessee, to leave values and personal interests aside. They carefully repeat the test manual's instructions to the client, and, in general, they try to be objective observers. They score tests according to the manuals and plot profiles along preset dimensions (e.g., manifest anxiety, need for succorance, performance IQ, ratio of movement to color responses). The second section of this chapter points out the limitations and restrictions of these otherwise reasonable procedures. But first, some related history should be mentioned.

Contemporary "personality and assessment" has its roots in nineteenth-century medicine as well as in the previously mentioned experimental laboratories. For example, Jean-Martin Charcot (1825–1893) and Pierre Janet (1859–1947) were early-day neurologists, physicians known as alienists—specialists in strange manifestations of natural forces on the mind. Although in an inconsistent manner, Charcot conceptualized hysteria in particular in terms of dynamic, functional, cortical lesions following physical trauma; symptoms were signs of this process as well as of resulting dissociations of ideas from earlier events. Janet spoke in terms of degenerative processes in which a field of consciousness concentrates on one system of ideas while retracting from others. He thus later claimed his own ideas to have predated Freud's concept of the unconscious. Other contemporaries such as Emil Kraepelin (1855–1926) and Eugen Bleuler (1858–1939) assumed that psychological problems were the product of physical disease, but they were less interested in exploring dynamics than in describing clinical signs and developing classification systems. All of these major historical figures were interested primarily in exploring the natural order underlying mental disease in general and only secondarily in the individual patient.

Sigmund Freud (1856–1939), a neurologist, also was interested in uncovering the dysfunctions and forces governing mental (and hence also behavioral) events. But his ultimate method of research (the patient's free association) was simultaneously a method of treatment; unlike his earlier colleagues, Freud also pioneered individual psychotherapy and examination of psychological data in their own right.

Nevertheless, it was his natural-science notions of childhood sexuality and instinctual aggression that received the most immediate attention. Fortunately for psychoanalysis, it met with lessened resistance when its initial opponents realized that even the "irrational unconscious" was said to follow natural laws and that bizarre behavior actually fell into known categories. Although Freud himself was a creative theorist, forever revising his formulations, many of his lesser followers theorized about patients as though they were merely complex machines. It is certainly true that, although often pointing beyond mechanics, Freud's system was explicitly posited in the language of the times (both of the Industrial Revolution and of the new science)—forces, counterforces, energy, mechanisms, productions, power, repression.

One more major person among the many historical figures in "personality and assessment" should be highlighted. Alfred Binet (1857–1911), a French scholar of law, medicine, and biology, was dissatisfied with the "brass instrument" research dominating scientific psychology. Binet's conceptual interests were not in mental structures (Wundt's elements) nor in psychophysical laws but in reasoning processes. He described intelligence as the ability to set and maintain a goal while still being self-critical. Yet, for Binet, too, intelligence was an underlying process, something that accounted for diverse achievements. Nevertheless, practical affairs were of major concern to him; it was as a representative of a group equivalent to a mental retardation association that he petitioned the French Ministry of Education for a grant to develop tests to identify retardates in the school system, in order to provide them with special assistance. The resulting scale (which dealt with mental age, not IQ) was later revised in the United States as the Stanford-Binet.

Binet's influence on American psychology is seen primarily in the vast use of testing as a predictive enterprise. We identify and classify candidates for special education largely in terms of IQ; we admit students to graduate schools on the basis of Miller's Analogy Test scores and assorted other aptitude patterns. American psychology ignored Binet's warnings that scores on psychological tests should not be taken more seriously than school achievement, that the child's ways of reasoning should be observed, and that the statistical techniques employed should not be more sophisticated than our knowledge of the phenomenon being measured.

This particular selective attention has marked American psychology in general. There were, in fact, minority voices such as that of Franz Brentano (1838–1917), a German philosopher, claiming that psychology did not necessarily have to conceive of itself as a natural science; it could instead address human consciousness and action as phenomena to be described and understood rather than to be reduced into lower orders, measured, and manipulated. Moreover, today, careful reading of the works of both historical and contemporary authors reveals that, even where humans are explicitly presented as *objects* like any other objects of nature, implicitly the authors operate on the basis of humans as also being *subjects*— shaping as well as being shaped by the environment. (See Fischer, 1977, for an account of the historical coexistence of psychology as a subject science and an object science.) The most obvious example is that laboratory scientists

have not accounted for how it is possible for them to plan, direct, and evaluate research if they, too, (as humans) are merely the products of the interacting laws of nature. The same point holds for personality theorists and assessors.

THE PRESENT: RECOGNIZING THE RESTRICTIONS OF THE NATURAL-SCIENCE PARADIGM

So far we have seen that the early-day psychologists tried to fashion this new discipline into a natural science—a science of mechanical and reactive objects. The laboratory methods of the physical sciences were borrowed outright or were adapted for measuring the relations among physical stimuli and human responses (for example, the relation between intensity of a flash of light and the amount of time required to perceive it, or the number of reinforcements required for a rat to learn to press a bar, or the amount of intelligence [IQ] required to become an engineer). By the 1920s, American psychologists also were strongly influenced by J. B. Watson's (1878–1958) behaviorism—psychology conceived as only the study of relations between observable behavior and physical environment.

Recent History

This natural-science approach worked well in that we clearly established that there is an orderliness, a comprehensibility of human affairs, one that can be researched and then applied to constructive interventions into those affairs. Indeed, the federal government requested that the American Psychological Association (still under 15 years of age at the time) try to apply its new expertise in testing to devise mass screening procedures for World War I draftees. The resulting Otis group intelligence test was a major contribution to the war effort; it saved lives and training time, lowered accident rates, and increased efficiency of personnel through its screening and placement decisions. After the war, these accumulated data were used for statistical examination of correlations among abilities, differences of IQ among persons of varying national origin, and so on. Group tests were then developed for use in public schools, for industrial purposes, and for the peacetime military.

After the war, three times as many persons as before the war called themselves psychologists and devoted themselves to constructing, administering, and interpreting tests. (See Chapter 2 of Sundberg, Tyler, & Taplin, 1973, Wallen, 1958, and Watson, 1953, for histories of American clinical psychology; note the importance of testing and of the World Wars to its development.) There was great excitement during these times about psychology's success in applying its laboratory methods to practical matters. Psychologists identified themselves as scientists, proud of their methodological objectivity (i.e., that their personal values and opinions were excluded from the publicly verifiable test scores) and of their subsequent success at predicting levels of effectiveness from the test scores. (See Giorgi, 1970, for a discussion of how this approach and method preshaped the kinds of data and issues that psychologists in general would generate.)

This scientific expertise at test construction, research, and use has grounded both clinical psychology's claim to be a science and its unique contribution to the mental health team. As physicians and psychologists began to read Freud's work (he lectured at Clark University in 1909), it was the psychologists who were expected to test whether the posited personality components and dynamics did indeed exist. It was psychologists who were expected to become experts in researching and using the Rorschach test (the inkblots) and other "projective techniques." Moreover, as psychologists worked side by side with physicians in both world wars, especially World War II, pooling their limited knowledge of how to differentiate the malingerers, shell shocked, hysterics, and the brain damaged, psychologists discovered, that from force of circumstances, they were becoming experts in psychopathology, psychodiagnostics, and psychotherapy.

However, interviews, psychotherapy, and projective techniques (relatively unstructured tasks intended to reveal personality, e.g., free associations, drawings, telling stories) have not been particularly amenable to statistical examination. Indeed, consistency among scores of the projectives has been difficult to obtain, and few scores correlate consistently with other criteria (such as IQ, diagnosis, behavior). Nevertheless, in their daily experience, practicing clinicians clearly found projective techniques to be useful and developed them further. They based their rationale largely on the psychoanalytic theory that was being worked out by practicing psychiatrists.

University-based psychologists, on the other hand, identified themselves primarily as scientists and devoted their efforts in large part to laboratory studies of animal behavior—eventually leading to behaviorism as our leading orientation as well as to diverse learning theories, which together form one of today's major personality theories and therapies. The academicians also specialized in designing research strategy and statistical analysis of results. Their development of achievement and aptitude tests was extended into attitude inventories and into tests for a myriad of personality traits. Today, most issues in the areas of personality and ability are explored and argued in terms of test scores.

The preceding evolution is reflected in the organization of contemporary introduction-to-psychology textbooks. Separate units address personality theory and assessment. The personality unit explains that there are three major kinds of theory:

1. *Motivational theories.* These theories are based on drives or needs, or on purposes. Among the former are the theories of psychiatrists such as Freud, Adler, Jung, and Sullivan and of the psychoanalyst Erikson. Behavior is variously explained in terms of sexual and aggressive forces, avoidance of inferiority feelings, needs for interpersonal security and intimacy, and so on. The theorists of purpose are the existentialists and humanistic psychologists, who in recent times are provided increasing coverage. Here action is understood in terms of values, search for meaning, and fulfillment of human potential. In the necessarily brief coverage of introductory textbooks, these and the theories discussed next are presented simplistically and as though they were in competition to prove which has *the* truth.

2. *Trait theories.* These are variations on the theme that "personality is the dynamic organization of traits within the self that determine the individual's unique way of playing his or her social role." Strict trait theory has been thoroughly criticized by psychology in general as not taking environment into account—a person just does not behave the same way in all circumstances. (See Mischel, 1968, for an early and compelling research-oriented critique.) In addition, trait theory has been criticized for circular reasoning. For example, Johnny's poor academic performance also shows up as poor performance on an intelligence test, and then that score is used to explain the other ones. Despite general acknowledgment of these problems, psychologists and the public alike frequently think, at least implicitly, in terms of trait theory. For instance, we still ask whether a person has enough "intelligence," "motivation," and so on, to do such and such. Personality (trait) scores still serve as major diagnostic and experimental criteria.

3. *Learning theories.* These theories conceive of personality as "a construct inferred from the characteristic pattern of behavior exhibited by an individual; a unified system of responding" (Kendler, 1974, p. 736). Some of these theories deal only with patterns of observable reinforcements and behavior. Others include much more, for example, "personality is the organization within an individual of systems of motives and habits that determine characteristic behavior and thinking" (Morgan & King, 1975, p. 464). A major subtheory, cognitive

psychology, examines the self-defeating thoughts that people have learned to tell themselves and teaches them alternative beliefs or thoughts that allow for constructive behavior (e.g., Beck, Rush, Shaw, & Emery, 1979; Meichenbaum & Jaremko, 1983).

The typical introductory psychology textbook's unit or chapter on assessment is in turn broken into its own separate sections. Projective techniques are mentioned last and briefly as tools that have been helpful to many clinicians but that lack empirical validity. Objective assessment is given the greatest coverage. This type of assessment relies on standardized administration and scoring, followed by comparison of the person's scores with those of particular groups (e.g., successful business executives, male freshmen, hospitalized paranoid schizophrenics). The collection of these norms (the pattern of a group's scores) and their use is called the area of *individual differences* mentioned earlier in this chapter. Coverage of objective assessment also includes the importance of reliability (consistency of subject response and of scoring) and of validity (how well the test scores correlate with other tests and behaviors that presumably were similar to what the test was to measure).

After discussion of personality, interest, achievement, and aptitude tests, a part of the objective assessment section is devoted to measurement of intelligence. This part has grown progressively smaller over the years as criticisms from both outside and within psychology have grown. For example, the tests reflect the values of the white professionals who constructed them, and they are thus biased against cultural minorities. Moreover, the in-house arguments about which factors make up intelligence have lost vogue as we realize that our sophistication in constructing tests exceeds our comprehension of what we are testing. Nevertheless, intelligence tests remain among the best-constructed and most widely used assessment devices. (See Anastasi, 1982, for a leading undergraduate textbook on psychological testing; Tuddenham, 1963, for an historical review of the intelligence testing movement; Rabin, 1968, for a standard textbook on projective techniques; and Butcher, 1972, for issues in objective personality assessment, and Butcher & Finn, 1983, for clinical use of objective tests.)

Present Issues

The natural-science paradigm has indeed established psychology as a science, one that has demonstrated an orderliness to human affairs. But that demonstration has been a technological one. In large part, psychological data and theories have been artifacts of our technological methods. For example, psychologists are beginning to realize that much of our literature on intelligence is instead about IQ, which in turn says as much about our research designs and statistical analyses as it does about intelligent behavior.

Another limitation of our technological approach is that, in the search for ultimate laws via statistical precision, we psychologists have ignored the nonpartitive, holistic character of being human. Just as personality theory, objective assessment, and projective techniques have been developed separately rather than through a unified effort, so, too, psychologists have measured intelligence and evaluated affect, defense mechanisms, and overt behavior as though they were separate. The difficulty is that once conceived or evaluated as separate, these distinctions cannot be added back up into a unified person. Moreover, despite recent discussion in textbooks about how only patterns of relationships, and not linear causality, can be discovered by science, our partitive analyses encourage slippage into causal explanations. Two examples are: (a) ''the patient's low IQ precludes success in education therapy''; and (b) ''Samuel's acts of vandalism are a function of his hostility toward authorities, exacerbated by his heightened anxiety over his parents' divorce.''

One more way of describing this dilemma is that, in our efforts to be objective, we have regarded ''secondhand'' events, such as test scores, counts of check marks recorded on observation sheets, and neurophysiological graphs as primary evidence of natural laws. We have lost sight of the fact that test performance is a sample of behavior and that scores and categories are abstractions from sampled behavior. Intelligence tests, for example, are a careful tapping of achievement on school-related tasks. Insofar as present achievement predicts later achievement, the intelligence test is a measure of ''potential.'' But our search for universal laws led us into regarding that ''potential'' as more primordial than, and as mediating as, actual performance. Today, we are aware of the slippage in this sort of reasoning, and some of our textbooks warn against it, but we do not know how to address life events in their own right—as primary data. A practical consequence of the search for universal laws having become a search for underlying variables is that we have lost the individual's particular unified way of being an instance from which such laws (patterns, relationships) were derived. Although scores can be helpful in classifying people into general categories and in making related decisions about them, they do not assist in understanding the individual in his or her particular situation or in making concrete suggestions into that person's actual life.

The preceding account of the strain against our nat-

ural science orientation is representative of widespread concerns within mainstream psychology. But with the exception of existential–phenomenologically grounded efforts to provide human-science foundations for psychology, corrections have come from within the natural-science tradition. Efforts have been restricted to: (a) increasing sophistication about the limits of assessment devices (e.g., instead of looking for alternatives to intelligence testing, we say that the only problem is in its potential for misuse); (b) conducting research into more refined variables and examining their complex interrelations (e.g., studying different kinds of intelligences, such as divergent and convergent, in relation to motivation, background, reinforcements); and (c) applying technology such as the previously mentioned with a humane attitude.

More concretely, the following are specific representative issues with which clinical psychologists are struggling. Each issue exemplifies both awareness that our natural-science orientation is not fully adequate for dealing with people, especially as individuals, *and* hesitance to make radical revisions that would explicitly take into account the more than object character of humans:

1. The ''clinical-versus-statistical-prediction'' research literature has demonstrated that statistical formulas, based on statistical analysis of earlier cases, are more efficient (more accurate and faster) than individual clinicians who classify on the basis of their own examination of the same actuarial, interview, and test data. Examples are prediction of suicide or of diagnostic category. Moreover, scorer reliability and consistency of diagnostic interpretation of projective techniques, such as the Rorschach, have been notoriously low. As a consequence, graduate schools have been dropping their projective-techniques courses altogether, and many graduate programs require only one testing practicum. Practicing clinicians (in contrast to academic psychologists) grumble about this circumstance but rarely point out that perhaps clinicians' proper arena is that of addressing the unique aspects of a client's life and of stepping into that particular life to help the client to redirect him- or herself. This is not to say that clinicians do not also have to make decisions as to whether a client is schizophrenic, brain-damaged, suicidal, and so on but that, as clinicians, their interest is not so much in which preset categories the person best fits but rather in what light such artificially clear-cut organizational devices throw on the person's particular ways of being and on related dangers and options.

2. A similar issue is the controversy surrounding our formal training model for clinical psychologists, the ''scientist–professional'' model (see Kendall & Norton-

Ford, 1982). The idea has been that, in graduate school, the student is trained to be a scientist—an expert in (natural) scientific research design and data analysis. Then, during practicum courses and an internship, the student learns to apply this knowledge and attitude in clinical practices. The problem has been that, instead of serving as a cohesive model, in fact the hyphenated construction ("scientist-professional") represents a divisive tension between the academically oriented ("scientific") and the practicing ("professional") psychologists. Clinicians claim that their university training deals with general trends (e.g., "level of aspiration varies with parents' socioeconomic class"), usually expressed in mathematical terms (e.g., $r = 0.39; p < 0.05$), and that such training does not prepare them for working with clients directly. Academicians, in turn, decry the looseness with which many clinicians formulate their understandings of clients, often without empirically tested referents (e.g., "the spider web response indicates Oedipal conflicts"; "the client's inner need for love must be given expression").

Since the late 1960s, clinicians have established professional schools of psychology, which often grant PsyD rather than PhD degrees in recognition that their emphasis is not so much academic as professional training. Students spend more time in field settings, working with experienced clinicians, and researching applied rather than laboratory problems. Initially, many psychologists feared that the professional schools would prove to be watered-down versions of the old university programs or that they would deal with individual clients without adequate grounding in general trends such as those provided by research studies. By the mid-1980s, however, many of these programs had become fully accredited by the American Psychological Association. In any event, the professional-school movement is part of the strain against psychology's natural-science orientation, but it has not sought a different way to be scientific.

3. A final example of psychology's tension with its traditional orientation is that of its perplexity in the face of mandated "right-of-access" principles such as those in the "Buckley Amendment." State and federal legislation and court decisions increasingly are giving citizens right of access to school records, credit-bureau files, medical charts, and psychoeducational records. The response of professionals, including psychologists, has been to keep dual files (with private notes unavailable to the citizen), to develop code terms with special meanings only to professionals, or to refuse to record anything controversial. The arguments have been varied: clients would not understand our sophisticated records, either because of their problems or because of their lack of expertise; whether or not they understood, clients could be damaged by reading the truth about themselves; explaining records to clients

would be too time-consuming for already overextended staff. The bind that practitioners find themselves in is that they do not know how to translate their scientific conceptions into everyday language. Too often we know more about our technology than about the everyday events they are supposed to elucidate.

THE FUTURE: A HUMAN-SCIENCE APPROACH TO PERSONALITY AND ASSESSMENT

Theory of Personality

Theories of personality attempt to account for the psychological similarities and differences among people. As mentioned before, the prevailing theories are those that conceptualize these similarities and differences in terms of psychodynamics (drives, needs, and coping mechanisms), traits, and learning theories. Each of these perspectives does, of course, highlight particular aspects of how people function. But all of them assume an external viewpoint, looking for explanations in conditions, events, or constructs that are seen as more basic or essential (if not linearly causal) than the person's own experience "and" behavior.[1] Moreover, tests of these theories therefore are in terms of already posited variables (e.g., ego strength, reinforcement history, distorted cognitions, IQ).

In contrast to this natural-science approach, existential phenomenology grounds what I prefer to call a *human-science* approach that attempts to preserve the unity of a person's life while still being an empirical, rigorous discipline. Surely, it is often productive to differentiate biological, behavioral, and experiential aspects of this unity and even to differentiate these still further into, say, cognition, affect, and motivation. What is more, there are no natural or human-science ways to present or examine an organic whole all at once and still be focally attuned to its particular fullness and complexities. But the human-science psychologist remains aware that, when we differentiate, it is for the sake of trying to hold things in manageable form so we can think systematically about them. We should not confuse our own analyzing and organizing devices with an inherent state of affairs. Nor should we slip into thinking that observed events are "merely" manifestations of a more basic underlying reality. It is this sort of slippage that leads to simplistic causal conceptions.

---

[1] "Experience 'and' behavior" is borrowed from R. Romanyshyn; the single quotation marks indicate that the two terms are not meant to be separate but instead are perspectival aspects of a unitary moment.

Accordingly, our human-science theory of personality is a structural one; it accounts for perceived events by describing their *whatness*—the differentiations that can be made within the whole. Thus W. Fischer (1970) has described "being anxious" as being the circumstance in which one feels that he or she absolutely must do something but also feels uncertain about being able to do it. Anxiety exists when all these aspects are present. It is not necessary to locate explanation in external variables such as stimuli, reinforcement history, or past trauma. Once we know the whatness, the "why?" question disappears.

For example, when you know that Mary Anne feels she just has to make an *A* on her chemistry midterm if she is to make it into the premed honorary but she feels she has no way of being sure she will be able to remember the formulas and, for that matter, she does not know what the instructor will emphasize, then you do not ask, "but why is she anxious?" True, you would understand Mary Anne's anxiousness more thoroughly if you knew how her "must" evolved (is she proving herself to a professionally oriented family, for example?). But her past in itself does not determine her present; what counts is how she lives that past now. Similarly, you would understand Mary Anne more thoroughly if you knew her biorhythmic patterns, constitutionally predisposed bodily stress systems, and so on. But again, these biological facts cannot account, by themselves, or even in addition to other facts, for Mary Anne's way of approaching that chemistry midterm. Human-science psychologists do hope to pursue the biological order's participation in the person's lived world. It is this interest and its empirical methods that set human-science psychology somewhat apart from the historical forms of phenomenology and existentialism, even though these philosophies provide its theoretical foundations.

The structural approach, however, does not simply map out static or interactive patterns. It is radically structural in that it takes into account humans' radical (Latin, "at root," "at core") difference from other objects. Specifically, because the experiencing person is never completely determined by "givens" but behaves in large part in terms of personal meanings and their implications for his or her goals, the differentiations within a structure cannot be regarded as constants. It is this particular radicalism that distinguishes human-science psychologists from those scientists who are otherwise similar to us in their denial of any simple, linear, "billiard-ball" notions of causality.

Back to personality theory in particular. As human-science psychologists, we study the individual person living his or her world. "Person-in-world" is the unit of study. Mary Anne's world on the day of the exam is one of time's passing too quickly, of taken-for-granted roommates, and unnoticed winter crocuses. There is no perceivable "real" world independent of our assorted perceptions of it. So the human-science personality theorist is interested in finding ways to conceptualize the particular ways people in general move through their worlds, transforming and being transformed by them. We are interested in transformative processes, restructurations. We explore ways to study and convey the complex realities co-constituted by observers, subjects, and their cultural, historical milieux.

As human-science theorists and researchers, we are interested in developing comprehensions of general phenomena, not just the lived worlds of individuals. For example, we research brain-damaged existence, being ashamed, being embarrassed, being depressed, being in privacy, dieting toward enduring weight loss, the process (in psychodrama) of the possible becoming viable. All such research starts with observations of, or reports from, individuals and then gradually abstracts commonalties. However, these generalities arise from the data rather than being preset categories of classification. Narrative presentation of the findings preserves the structural whole, including the ways that different subjects exemplified the phenomenon.

Human-science psychologists who are interested in personality theory as a discipline are now building a content—systematic interrelated studies. Like mainstream psychology, we know more about clinical deviations than about typical development. (For the former, see de-Konig & Jenner, 1982; W. Fischer, 1985; Fischer & Fischer, 1983; Keen, 1970; May, Angel, & Ellenberger, 1958; for the latter, see Fischer & Alapack, 1987; Knowles, 1986.) Even so, to an unusual degree, existentially phenomenologically grounded research and practices are consistently consonant with theory. In a way, this entire chapter as well as all the others addresses "what does it mean to be human?" "How shall we try to understand how the individual person participates in general patterns? Where are opportunities for change?" The following sections illustrate the unique way that our approach to "personality" sustains the particularity of the individual client even while making use of what we know about generalized situations, kinds of people, test norms, and so on.

Nature of Data

Within human science, both research and applied work begin with different data than that which mainstream psychology has accumulated. Like behaviorists, we do begin with publicly observable events (either behavioral or spoken). However, in contrast, we regard these events as implying the person's lived history, present world, and goals (see Fischer, 1973a). We do use test scores, traditional research, and other theories' constructs to help us expand and refine our understandings of those observed events. But we regard these resources as tools, ones derived from earlier life events. An example: We do not try to explain a student's poor classroom achievement in terms of a low IQ. Rather, we see performance on the intelligence test as a further instance of limited achievement (see Fischer 1969, 1973b, 1974, for human-science approaches to intelligence).

Study of subtest scores, however, might lead the counselor or psychologist into productive hunches about how that student goes about learning and performing, and hence about how teachers might step into that process more effectively. Thus the assessor might note that a student earned higher scores when he could look at an example of what he was supposed to achieve (Block Design, Digit Symbol) than when he had to "work in his head." The assessor might then wonder whether the student has become anxious when left on his own without visible support, whether he has become otherwise distracted when not attending to concrete stimuli, or whether he is organically unable to deal with abstract material. That is, the assessor does not read the scores as literal or determinative statements about the person nor discount the scores as misguided, but, instead, the assessor asks the scores how they might throw light on the student's classroom achievement—how they bespeak the same phenomenon differently. The assessor must then return to the student-in-the-classroom to see if the reflections through theory and tests have refined the assessor's vision in ways that allow stepping into the student's experiaction[2] to help him approach tasks more productively.

The assessor recognizes that the client's experience of his or her situation must be taken into account. The assessor's own experience also is inevitably involved—as historical/cultural context, professional training, personal background, and so on. Instead of trying to standardize his or her conduct so it will be like all other examiners' and thereby can be discounted as a constant variable, the human-science assessor tries to be aware of and to specify his or her approach and access to the client. This biographical presence can be communicated by statements such as: "All together I found him consistently easy to be with and to like—something in the manner of a teacher shaking her head but enjoying a charmingly problematic student" (from a report by Fischer, in Tallent, 1976).

Disciplined, examinable descriptions, then, are achieved not by trying to exclude the assessor's subjec-

tivity (individuality, perspective, involvement) but by explicitly taking it into account. Because biographical presence cannot be "controlled out," the more rigorous standard is to specify it instead. This holds even for computer-administered, scored, and interpreted tests, where the constructors' and programmers' values, goals, and backgrounds are only implicitly present. Specification of biographical presence to an empirical event allows other observers either to adopt a similar approach and arrive at a similar understanding or to specify the differing approaches through which they see somewhat differing profiles. Thus, the basic purpose of objectivity has been achieved: We have assured that an observation has consensual validity, that it is not merely one person's peculiar interpretation. The consistency or reliability provided by this human-science objectivity is one of integrated variations of perspective on an empirical referent (the publicly observable event). We bypass the artificial clarity of the fictive natural science single presence (the objective observer) in favor of dealing with the complexity and ambiguity inherent in our meaning—constituting biographically situated nature.

Human affairs are orderly, but their complexity exceeds Aristotelian clear-cut categories and deductive logic. Human-science assessment, therefore, is not as efficient as traditional ones in its presentation of data. But it is more comprehensive and, in the long run, allows for more effective intervention into a particular person's life. Along these lines, for both applied research and practice, we say that our goals are not the older ones of "predict and control" but of "anticipate and influence."

Whether the psychologist is studying a general phenomenon or a particular client's situation, the subject works collaboratively, insofar as he or she can, with the psychologist. The psychologist guides the investigation but encourages the subject to report additional instances (from other situations) of the events that occur during the assessment. For example, during an assessment, the psychologist might point out that the client has settled for just guessing the number of dots she was supposed to copy from the Bender–Gestalt cards. Having just lived through that experiaction, the client recalls structurally similar instances such as estimating her office budget instead of itemizing it. Upon further exploration, it turns out that, sometimes, this sort of approximation has been effective; at other times, its consequences have been problematic. The latter turns out to have occurred when the client was vaguely afraid that if she slowed down and dealt with details, she would lose her bearings and find out that she did not know enough to finish the project. Discoveries such as these are the "refined primary data," which are available to both assessor and client.

As they continue to explore the client's situated ex-

---

[2]From von Eckartsberg, 1971; the term expresses experience "and" action in their originary unity.

periactions with their various consequences, they also identify landmarks by which the client can come to recognize that he or she is moving into, indeed co-creating, a familiar problematic situation. Having also identified the ways or styles in which this particular client has traversed and shaped his or her world, they can find pivot points at which the client could swing over to an alternate route to his or her goal without losing a step. In other words, they find personally viable, already available, ways for the client to get where he or she was going.

Sometimes it may turn out that the goals themselves should be reevaluated. Always, the client's lived world— its invitations, danger signs, moodedness, and physiognomies—is altered while trying out different routes. In the preceding example, the client might try to slow down on the Bender-Gestalt, deliberately counting the dots, planning the spacing of the designs. As she does this, she finds she still prefers a quick overview, getting started quickly at first, but that she can then slow down to calculate more systematically. For her, the landmarks indicating that she should look for a pivot point back into slowing down and calculating (after acquiring that quick overview) are short breath, rapidity of heartbeat, a sense of wanting to get out of the situation, and so on. Thus sticking to primary data has allowed psychologist and client to work directly into constructive interventions. The client experiences herself not as an object to whom things have happened but as an active subject who has been contributing to her difficulties and who can also work at sizing up and remedying those difficulties.

Granted, thoroughgoing and enduring changes require a thorough interventional assessment, systematic suggestions for living out alternative routes, and time for all this to evolve into integrated habitual patterns—into a restructuration. The interventional assessment, similar to initial or short-term therapy, is a starting place. Sometimes, of course, the assessor is not asked to intervene but to recommend where a client should be placed, such as in a special education class, a locked ward, or a parole program. But, even in these cases, the psychologist bases the decision on refined primary data, includes the client directly in exploring that data, and usually reports concrete constructive suggestions to the staff who will be assisting the client.

The preceding notions can be summarized into six interrelated guiding characteristics of human-science assessment practices. Our approach is:

1. *Structural.* We look for explanation in terms of the whatness of an event.

2. *Contextual.* This structure includes the assessor's comprehension of the person's world-as-lived as well as what the assessor can identify from a public per-

spective as physical (biological, environmental) contexts of the focal events. The contexts in which variations of the event have occurred and of when the event has not occurred at all are also explored.

3. *Descriptive.* The primary data are contextualized life events, with the client's and the observer's perspectives specified. Test scores, constructs, research literature, all are derived data through which the assessor modifies and refines his or her perception of life events. Description via primary data rather than by interpretation into personality traits, defense mechanisms, and such is "representational description"—the client's experiaction is sampled (represented) by re-presenting particular instances relevant to the referral. Both the publicly visible incident and the assessor's particular presence to it are described, thereby evoking the lived worlds of assessor, client, and reader.

4. *Collaborative.* People co-constitute all their situations, and, hence, we encourage the client to be an informed, active participant throughout the assessment, including being a commentator on any written documents. As a co-investigator and co-assessor, the client is acknowledged as partially responsible for his or her past and future and as able to participate in clarifying and redeveloping them.

5. *Interventional.* Assessment, even of the traditional sort, inevitably affects the client—who finds personal meanings in the situation. The human-science assessor acknowledges this, and systematically attempts to intervene constructively into the client's ways of moving through situations. The purpose is both to evaluate current possibilities and to develop further ones. In this way, we are less likely to think of current limitations as being final. By way of contrast, recall that traditional assessment is based on the beliefs that the client has a particular set of abilities and personal characteristics and that these can and should be recorded without influencing them. Also bear in mind that, historically, one purpose of assessment was to classify the individual into already established group norms; psychologists have acted as though individualized understanding and intervention should be reserved totally for a very separate enterprise, that of therapy.

6. *Authentic.* The human-science assessor is keenly aware that circumstances do severely restrict the psychologist's and client's access to each other and to options. Not all clients can collaborate in a reflective, verbal way. Emergencies and heavy case loads often preclude thoroughgoing assessments. But this final guiding principle reminds us that all the previously mentioned ones are just that—guiding principles, to be followed as authentically as possible. *Authenticity,* in the Heideggerian sense, is a striving toward the possible while acknowledging the

necessary (the givens, limits, requirements), pulling back from momentary exaggerations of either (see Heidegger, 1927/1962).

HUMAN-SCIENCE ASSESSMENT PRACTICES

As it happens, there are very few existential–phenomenologically oriented psychologists who are interested in assessment. Theory, therapy, and, more recently, research have been heavily preferred areas. This is probably in large part an overreaction to the problems of traditional assessment, which placed both psychologist and client into objectlike relationships. The psychologist was supposed to assure objectivity by equating assessment with standardized administration of tests. Even "rapport" was an effort to maneuver the client into a condition under which levels of motivation, anxiety, and comfort would be optimally balanced for the production of best intellectual performance and of unguarded psychological (personality) performance. Except in counseling situations, the "test results" rarely were shared with the client. Virtually no psychologists of the traditional assessment orientation give a report to the client. It is no wonder. Such reports have been written in the objectifying language of test scores, psychopathology, defense mechanisms, ability limits, traits, and so on. The individual, as such, is lost as he or she is presented in terms of group norms. The resulting tone is one of limitation and inevitability. So, it could indeed be destructive for clients to read such a report, and admittedly, they probably would not understand much of it.

Many, if not most, psychologists during the past decade have found the preceding circumstance to be dissatisfying—boring in process and providing no assurance that the client will be helped by the report. Indeed, following initial disposition of the client, reports seem to wind up undisturbed in file cabinets. Both trait psychology and strict psychoanalytic interpretation are in disfavor as being (for different reasons) unscientific and nonhelpful. General social consciousness has dissuaded many human-services professionals from contributing further to "the myth of mental illness" (Szasz, 1960) by conducting assessments for diagnostic purposes. Finally, psychologists have discovered a greater reward from helping rather than testing clients, and greater prestige, independence, and income in psychotherapy than in testing. So it is not surprising that testing increasingly is relegated to MA-level technicians when done at all and that it is existential–phenomenological psychologists in particular who have turned their backs on formal psychological assessment (see Craddick, 1975, and Dana & Leech, 1974, as among the rare exceptions).

The purpose of the preceding preface is threefold. First, if the following assessment practices seem rather obvious or commonsensical, remember the objectifying, natural-science tradition to which they are an alternative. Second, although many experienced clinicians often on their own do some of the same things, they typically tack them on the objective assessment rather than developing these practices as part of a thoroughgoing human-science assessment. That is, although dissatisfied with the narrowness and restrictiveness of traditional testing, psychologists have not looked for a radical alternative. Although this section boldly carries the heading, "Human-Science Assessment Practices," these are in reality practices that I worked out for myself in dialogue with existential-phenomenology. Nevertheless, although this is my particular way of conceptualizing the practices, none of them is "brand new" (see Chapter 1 of Fischer, 1985, for an overview of the contributions of like-minded psychologists). Third, the following practices are representative of ways to carry out the guiding principles, but they are not the only way of conducting and describing human-science assessment. Similarly, the examples are intended to provide concrete instances rather than a comprehensive range of my own practices (see Fischer, 1985, for an entire textbook, *Individualizing Psychological Assessment,* and Fischer, 1978, for brief examples and discussion of human-science assessment).

Human-science assessment is appropriate for all clients, but as with traditional assessment, one must be more flexible and innovative with limited clients (e.g., retarded children, mute schizophrenics) and with externally referred clients (e.g., prisoners, "problem children") (see reports by Fischer, 1985, 1987, and in Tallent, 1976, for examples of psychodiagnostic studies).

The Assessment Process

Referrals are typically stated in natural-science terms like "establish IQ," "differentiate between schizoid personality and group delinquent reaction," or "provide a personality picture." I first contact the referring person to find out what events have led to the referral. This "situating the referral" is easier said than done, however, because most often what the referring person has focused on is end results rather than the process leading to them. This problem is conceptualized in abstract, mechanistic terms. In regard to the referrals, when I asked a teacher what the "establish-IQ" referral was all about, I was told that "this student didn't score at grade expectancy on social studies achievement tests, and I thought it might be because he isn't as intelligent as we thought he was."

A counselor clarified the second referral: "Well, this fellow has an arrest record, and I don't know whether it's because he's identifying with street leaders or whether he's schizoid." A psychiatrist explained the third referral: "The patient was admitted as a depressive neurotic with suicidal preoccupations, but has not responded to antidepressants [medication], so I wondered if this could be simply a passive-dependent personality on one hand, or, on the other, if the admissions staff failed to pick up on an underlying agitation."

My best bet for getting back to "primary data" is to ask the referring person what decisions he or she is confronted with. The teacher told me that he did not know whether to encourage his student to try harder or to congratulate him for doing as well as he has. The community mental health counselor said he did not know whether to recommend group therapy or a behavior modification program. The psychiatrist was trying to decide whether to prescribe tranquilizing drugs and whether to encourage his staff to be supportive or demanding with the patient. At this point, it usually is somewhat easier for the referring person to recall events that would support the various sides of the decision. With the teacher, I asked for examples of when the student had met or exceeded grade-level expectations. We discovered that he had held his own on group projects, on homework assignments with which he could check with his mother, and in classroom discussions. It turned out that he had done less well when left totally on his own, whether writing an independent book report or taking a standardized test. The teacher and I agreed that the referral, thus contextualized, should be revised to "explore with Daniel the meanings of working by himself and to suggest ways in which he could be encouraged to extend his active participation in groups to his independent work." Note that IQ as such was no longer an issue. Even had Daniel been working below grade expectancy across the board, the assessor would try to contextualize his performance in order to expand whatever already was working for him into other contexts. This is the realm of life events, to which scores are relevant. But scores are derived from those life events; scores are not produced by separate, underlying, variables.

The language of the sample referrals did help me to think about the clients in light of what the mental health literature has accumulated on general patterns of behavior. But I saw these patterns and categories as generalizations or abstractions, not as deductions about some sort of underlying reality. Life events are the primary data for the human-science psychologist; assessment results are suggested interventions into those life events.

A common misconception about existential–phenomenological (here, human-science) assessment is that the psychologist treats the client as entirely unique. To the contrary, the assessor's contribution is, in large part, his or her personal and academic expertise about general patterns of experiaction. This knowledge informs and shapes inquiries into how the particular individual participates in these general patterns. Of course the assessor does not try to force-fit clients into preexisting categories, and, indeed, his or her understandings of patterns change somewhat after getting to know each client. The assessor is well aware that our present knowledge is not comprehensive. Existing conceptions offer assistance but not answers. It is within this attitude that the psychologist collaborates with the referring person and with the client.

Often, after preliminary contextualizing with the assessor, the referring person decides to defer or cancel testing pending his or her own contextualizing with the client and the latter's helpers. These efforts may include trying out interventions with the client. The psychologist is not a test technician but a consultant, one who integrates knowledge of psychology's accumulated literature with his or her understanding of a particular subject's situated experiaction. The psychologist assists the referring person and the client to help themselves. In the preliminary consultant role, the psychologist may bring the client and referring person together so that all three collaborate at one time. Daniel, for example, helped to identify those times that he felt more comfortable even when working by himself. With that information, he and his teacher agreed that they would work systematically at expanding from his doing workbook assignments (with answers in the back to check against) to his doing rip-out assignments that he could check with the teacher in the morning before class.

A self-referred client and the psychologist work together from the beginning. Either way, when the psychologist settles in to working directly with referred or self-referred clients, he or she quickly rediscovers that these persons, just like the previously mentioned teacher, mental health worker, and psychiatrist, talk in objectifying, totalizing terms. Examples: "I'm an intelligent person, but my inferiority complex blocks me from getting ahead"; "There's nothing wrong with me, it's all these establishment types who are uptight"; "When this impulse breaks out, I can't do anything about it; I wonder if it's hereditary." So here, too, the psychologist inquires into critical situations with which the client is faced and asks for concrete examples of the "inferiority complex," run-ins with the "uptight establishment types," and the "impulse."

The major difficulty in such efforts to describe and to contextualize is that the clients, like all persons who are in defensive or problem-oriented modes, recall in terms of objectifications, that is, categorized persons or events are seen as causing outcomes. Especially in problematic situations, unless we make particular efforts to be open to other possibilities, we all (clients and psychologists alike) perceive and think in terms of objects and forces. Thus, Daniel's teacher says, "I keep thinking that he has more potential, but when he doesn't score well on the achievement tests, I think maybe he's just not intelligent enough after all." At first, this teacher was unable to say just what he had experienced as Daniel's "potential." Eventually, as I encouraged focusing on actual events, the teacher shook off earlier conceptions and discovered more alive recollections of Daniel leaning forward in his seat during lectures, asking questions in an excited manner, and requesting extra resources for a class project. Later, as he watched Daniel in class, he saw with a vision that was attuned to process and context. More on this later.

Sometimes the client, as well as the referring person, finds that discussion has differentiated the problems and options adequately to work further on them him- or herself. More often, however, discussion only circumscribes the issues, bringing client and assessor into agreement about them but only in a rather global, abstract way. It is at this point that I turn to test materials. I do not "administer tests," but I do "use test materials."

In the case of Link, who was referred by the mental health worker, I asked him to copy freehand the nine Bender–Gestalt geometric designs. We had been trying to understand how Link had gotten into trouble even when he has intended to stay clean. We both witnessed the first design's starting on the upper left corner of the paper and the second design's completion in the middle of the page. Already, I realized that, although Link was intending to do a good job, he was going to run out of room. Sure enough, at the seventh design, Link looked up at me, puzzled that there was no space left for it. I looked at him noncommittally, and Link smashed the pencil point on the sheet, angrily shouting that I had tricked him. "Yes," I said, "the same way Mr. Wilkins 'tricked you' into missing your appointment Tuesday." We stared in silence for awhile at the torn Bender sheet and its implicit history of our encounter. Then I asked Link what other times he had gotten himself into being "tricked." It appeared that sometimes he had, in fact, been used as a scapegoat by his sisters, father, and street group. But there were also times more like the Bender incident. For example, his shop teacher had promised to take him to a potential employer if Link would come to class on time, dress neatly, and clean up his area satisfactorily for the entire month. Link had kept his part of the bargain for 2 weeks while the shop teacher congratulated him regularly, but when these reminders petered out, Link began lapsing into prior habits. At the end of the month, Link was told that he had lost his chance. He accused the

teacher of having tricked him and threw a plane through a closed shop window.

With this and other related instances in mind, we returned to the Bender. I asked Link to retrace the figures as he had originally done them but to look ahead for a way to solve his dilemma as he approached the seventh design. As he began, he said, "like what?!"—"Well, where else could the designs go?," I replied. In what I took as a defiant tone, Link announced that he could take another sheet of my paper. As I smiled and nodded and gestured for still more options, Link itemized more, gradually beginning to laugh as he elaborated his options into absurdities (from "using the back of this page" to "cutting down a forest to make my own paper").

Later, in our session, I suggested that Link start from scratch with the Bender designs; I again gave the standard instructions. This time, though, as Link recognized the feeling of "just going along," he stopped to check his progress against the stimulus cards and his remaining space. When there nevertheless was not enough room for the last design, Link snorted, thumped the eraser end of his pencil on the desk, but, recognizing this situation as pivotal, he grinned sheepishly and announced/asked, "Hey, so it's okay for me to put this one on the back, right?"

We proceeded in a similar manner through sections of the Wechsler Adult Intelligence Scale, the Rorschach (inkblots), and some Thematic Apperception Test cards (ambiguously drawn scenes for which the subject makes up stories). As we went, variations of the Bender experience occurred, and we came to call them "going along versus thinking for yourself." Each new occasion led to a reunderstanding of prior instances as well as to a different chance to try out "thinking on his own." Other themes emerged, too, of course, and all modified each other. For example, to my initial surprise, Link did not become angry when I left him on his own, with no feedback, to tell me what sorts of things he could see in the inkblots. When we talked about my puzzlement, Link reported that "well, I knew right from the beginning that I was supposed to do this by myself—it didn't have much to do with you." This turned out to be similar to Link's taking care of his little brother, with whom he had not become angry and with whom he had worked hard without quitting.

Thus the answer to the earlier referral question was that, although Link's difficulties had been the outcome of characterological patterns of experiaction and were not merely typical of all adolescents, he was not grossly out of touch with other persons' perspectives. Link's troublemaking was explained in terms of those circumstances in which he had and had not (the "when/when not") thought for himself, become angry, and so on.

The assessment report also included summaries of our interventions and related suggestions for how the mental health specialist might work with Link.

Comportment through Tests as Access to Process

Let me point out some of the purposes of using test materials in the previously mentioned human-science manner. Clients and I together are able to observe their "tracks" as they move through the tests; I am not looking *at* them; they do not experience themselves as being *obj*ectified (see Fischer, 1971, for a discussion of how this particular looking together into a shared referent precludes invasion of privacy). Along these lines, my preferred seating arrangement is not 180° across a desk but something around 100° and enough distance (6 or so feet) so that we each can see all of the other. I do not make use of a pencil and pad until we are well into a collaborative relationship. Likewise, I do not begin with a question-answer period. Instead I first briefly present what I know of the referral issue and ask clients to fill me in on their version of how the referral came about. As I say little and gesture for the client to continue, he or she shifts from a standard packaged version and begins to recognize gaps, seeming inconsistencies, and ambiguities. The client begins to qualify earlier totalizations and to discover experiactional, multiperspectival contexts. When we reach the limits of this reflective exploration, I turn to the tests.

The test materials allow us to continue breaking through old conceptions. In particular, they help both of us to move out of conventional social modes and speech. As clients comport themselves through some particular test, they find themselves in a context similar to others; the test situation can then serve as a lived metaphor for structurally similar past events. Link's smashing his pencil into the evolving Bender "is" his throwing the plane through the shop window. Through the test activity, we find touch points with phenomena that were previously unavailable for reflection. Sometimes, these phenomena are simply habitual patterns that the person has taken for granted. For example (from a different client): "Well, I guess I do typically ask a lot of questions to be sure what's expected of me; I guess what we're seeing is that sometimes that gets me into trouble . . . at least when supervisors think I'm not independent enough."

But persons' pasts are always present in the ways they co-create their environments, and this co-creation contains all the levels and complexity of what traditionally is known as "the unconscious." To make this point in academic settings, I sometimes contrast my approach with psychoanalytic "depth" psychology by saying that "the unconscious is horizontal"—visible in the ways people traverse their terrain with its personal phys-

iognomies, invitations, and danger signs. Moreover, this travel imagery ("lived world," "pathways," "goals," "territory," etc.) encourages us to observe how people participate in bringing about what "happens to" them.

For example, a paranoid man suspects that people may belittle him or worse, and his self-protection is an aggressive one. He maintains a social distance, stares penetratingly, out-argues authorities, and publicly accuses people of outrageous motives. In this way, he shapes his world into one in which people avoid him, talk behind his back, and do, indeed, experience outrageous feelings in relation to him. Sometimes I refer to this experiactional differentiation/shaping of one's traversed and future territory as a "style" of moving through particular situations. Exploration of this highly contextualized and active process is at the heart of human-science assessment. Seeing style is the different vision that I mentioned earlier.

Understanding that a person's style is part of the process that creates end products (test scores, broken windows, etc.) allows the psychologist to help clients to identify the landmarks that call for change in direction. Intervention can be especially constructive when clients are guided in their movement toward alternatives that they experience as already being personally viable. It is joint involvement in the testing activity that renders style as process visible and accessible to both assessor and client. Note that constructive intervention is also possible, even when the client lives out new variations without cognitive insight.

Use of test materials also provides a common ground, a shared reference point, from which clients can scan into their pasts for other instances like those occurring during the assessment session. In this way, client and psychologist gain access to the life events behind the referral. So long as test comportment is viewed as a specialized instance of similar events (rather than as evidence of underlying conditions), the use of tests helps to keep client and psychologist in the realm of primary data, bypassing both slippage into technocracy and reasons for keeping psychological reports secret from clients.

Further Illustrations of the Assessment Process

The earlier psychiatric referral (depressive neurotic versus passive dependent personality versus underlying agitation) can serve to illustrate some additional aspects of human-science assessment. During the initial contextualizing, I listen for what the client understands as the reasons for the assessment, but I also check on this directly from time to time during the assessment, as the client becomes progressively more open and reflective during our work together.

For example, Mrs. Smyth at first told me that "the

doctor wants to know if he should change my medicine.'' Fairly soon after that, she clarified that he wanted to establish whether or not she were suicidal. Much later, in response to my direct inquiry, Mrs. Smyth acknowledged that she thought my job was to find out if she were ''crazy.'' She herself had wondered if this could be true because, in fact, she was now in a mental hospital. Moreover, she had often been bewildered and frightened at her own sudden anger when people she usually counted on expected too much of her. She had indeed wondered whether this meant that she were crazy and if this craziness could cause her to kill herself. Earlier in our session she had been intent on disproving this possibility to both of us. In short, as a human-science assessor, I do not look for constancies of personality that are evoked by diverse stimuli, but instead I explore and take into account the changing possibilities that vary with the client's perceptions of his or her circumstances.

I prefer performance-oriented tests to multiple-choice tests for gaining access to how certain experiaction evolves into particular finished events. But, in the early stages of an assessment, collaborative profile analysis (from multiple-choice tests) can at least lead to exploration of the *when's* and *when-not's* of problematic events.

Mrs. Smyth's Minnesota Multiphasic Personality Inventory (MMPI) answers were scored and plotted prior to our meeting, and I had tabbed my reference books for pages with descriptions of persons with profiles like hers. I read relevant sections aloud to Mrs. Smyth and asked her in what ways the characterizations were and were not true of her. Even though she was not a particularly introspective or reflective person, she participated effectively. For example, she resolved the seeming contradiction between MMPI descriptions of her as ''dependent'' and as ''knowing [her] own mind'' in the following ways:

> I know what I want, it's just that I shouldn't be expected to do everything by myself. Besides, I do lots by myself—I tend the house and do all the cooking. And when the kids were little, it was my husband [who] was lost. . . . I was in charge of everything about them.

I also use test profiles and background information to formulate preliminary alternative understandings. For example, in this case, the nursing staff felt that Mrs. Smyth was still depressed because of her moody isolation on the unit and her occasional crying spells. They felt that she was too immobilized to be considered suicidal at the time. But I noted on the MMPI that she scored relatively high on scales that usually reflect energized resentment, which led me to suspect that she might indeed make a suicidal effort, not only out of desperation but also in retaliation against those who were failing her. With explicit awareness of such possibilities, the assessor can be alert to related occurrences with performance–test materials.

In this case, further secondary data on which I reflected in order to better understand primary data (actual life events) were research reports on suicide patterns. For example, I noted that, in Mrs. Smyth's case, there was indeed a ''precipitating event,'' one that precluded continuation of her prior ''identification'' and her customary way of relating to her family. Specifically, her two children were now approaching adolescence. They no longer let her ''mother'' them and, instead, maintained a charged distance from which they made demands and derogatory judgments. In addition, Mr. Smyth recently had accepted trucking jobs that took him out of the house for weeks at a time. Because Mrs. Smyth could not see a viable alternative way of being, I felt that she might become one of those persons who ''impulsively'' kills herself. This was consonant with her report that she had gained rather than lost weight. That is, she did not fit the pattern of those depressed clients who eat little, lose weight, and either plan a suicide or allow themselves to be ''accidentally'' killed. Rather, she fit a pattern of distressed persons.

Another resource with which I compared my direct observations of Mrs. Smyth was phenomenological research. As I experienced her as being anxious, I became attuned to how she felt she must continue to be the mother she had been but was desperately uncertain of her ability to do so (see W. Fischer's chapter in this book on being anxious). My own research on crying helped me to recognize that Mrs. Smyth's tears were those of protest as well as of resigned sorrow. These sorts of reflection helped me to see the possibility of an angry and despairing suicide attempt. They also encouraged me to answer the referral by describing Mrs. Smyth as a basically ''dependent'' but giving person, diagnostically more distressed than depressed.

I suggested that the unit staff should meet her where she was, offering compassion and support, but, in addition, pulling her into helping out with tasks and projects around the ward. Group therapy might focus on ways she could maintain her old routines despite her children's turbulence. Older members might hold out the probability that, once the children have grown out of adolescence, they not only might once again allow their mother to care for them but might also encourage her to depend on them for support. Finally, my report emphasized the importance of working with the entire Smyth family to further assess and collaboratively alter Mrs. Smyth's dilemma; her difficulty was as ''environmental'' as it was ''psychodynamic.''

A collaborative approach does not preclude disagreements between client and assessor; each of us is final authority on his or her own opinion. Mrs. Smyth and I agreed to disagree about my impression that she was resentful of her husband's leaving her on her own with the growing children. My report included this disagreement and specified our respective grounds, thereby telling readers not only my understanding but the client's; the latter's helpers would have to approach her through both understandings.

Often the client cannot directly assist the assessor in finding other instances of assessment experiaction. In these cases, I may consult with the client's involved others (family, employer, institutional staff), sharing an observation from the assessment and asking them for similar examples and exceptions. When I mentioned to the nursing aides that Mrs. Smyth had cried in a choking way, protesting that "life isn't fair," and that I had sensed a certain resentment at that moment, a male aide recalled that Mrs. Smyth had glared at him and then yanked a broom from his hand when he had sternly insisted that, sick or not, she was responsible for cleaning her own cubicle.

Access to these nonspecialized, everyday events is facilitated by conducting the assessment in the client's environment. In Mrs. Smyth's case, I got as far as being with her in several of the hospital's settings (her cubicle, the day room, canteen). Link I saw only in my office. I did work with Daniel in his school setting. A more ideal arrangement is one reported later, in which the entire assessment was conducted with a boy and his parents in their home.

Report Writing

Most textbooks on report writing admonish assessors to avoid jargon, to include only information directly relevant to the referral, to write with the background and interests of particular readers in mind, to describe what is specific to the particular client (avoiding universally true statements like "this patient is sometimes anxious"), and to provide specific, concrete suggestions rather than generalities like "therapy could be helpful." However, these standards have been difficult to meet while also trying to model one's assessment on the natural-science laboratory report. Not accidentally, these standards are easier to meet through a human-science approach (see Tallent, 1988, for criticism of traditional reports and for sample reports from a variety of theoretical approaches).

The following characteristics of human-science assessment reports are rarely found in traditional (natural science) reports, although experienced clinicians in private practice at times follow some of these procedures. The report focuses on life events, with test performances presented as specialized instances. The report presents selected examples of both types of data. What was physically visible as well as its meanings to the assessor (in-

cluding his or her sense of meanings to the client) are described. Early in the report, I provide physical descriptions of the client, in part so the reader can picture the client throughout the report. But I try to describe the client in motion rather than statistically, so the reader will be attuned to the ways the person moves through and shapes/is shaped by his or her territory.

This particular form of representational description serves two interrelated purposes: (a) The reader's own "biographical presence" is called into play through the vividness of the description and through my presence as a (necessarily) biographically rooted and involved observer; and (b) objectivity is served, in its broader and more basic sense. The reader senses that we are all referring to the same publicly observable events as we respect the variability within generality of our "participant observations." The reader can see who I was while with the client and can imagine how the latter might be somewhat different with other people. In part to encourage the reader to imagine me as a particular individual (with whom the client appears in the report as he or she does), I use first-person form ("I" rather than "the examiner" and rather than referring only to the client without mentioning the interpersonal context). I also refer to reported events in the past tense in order to evoke a sense of situatedness rather than of pervasiveness ("John worked slowly with the blocks" versus "John works slowly").

The goal of the report is not classification but individualized suggestions that are already partially tried out and carefully geared to the client's available ways of moving through situations. By the time the formal report is written, the client often has already adapted the suggestions made during the assessment and, in that process, further refined his or her understandings of the assessment issues. The written report thus is a progress report—the current state of understandings and suggestions, always refinable through additional perspectives, and always, in a sense, out of date in that events have continued to evolve after the formal assessment.

The client may read the report and offer commentary, sometimes written directly on the report. This opportunity may further the assessment process while also informing other readers of the client's status as a responsible, informed participant. In addition, the recorded commentary highlights any disagreements between the client's understandings and my own.

The length of the report varies with the complexity of the issues and the purpose of the report. If it is a matter of classification (e.g., placement in special education, determination of legal competency), the report can answer the question in one or two pages. But a human-science report usually will continue on to give the reader a sense of the client's style, pivot points, and lived world.

This holds where the client is a primary reader for whom the report is a reminder of understandings and suggestions that were developed during the assessment session or where the readers are persons who will be working directly with the client.

My reports include diagnostic, psychodynamic, or other theory-related phrases when they would be helpful to particular readers. However, I make it clear that these phrases *refer to* specific events but *do not explain* them. Theoretical constructs about "personality" and "ability" are not allowed to seem more real than the actual events described in the report.

A Sample Assessment Report

The following report illustrates many of the previously mentioned assessment and report-writing practices. Names and other identifying information have been changed. It is written in the form of a letter (on my private practice stationery) to the parents. After they had read it, we talked on the phone, discussed some points further, and agreed that I should forward a copy to the boy's new school with a note saying that the parents had reviewed the report and asked for this action. In the meantime, I had enclosed a copy of the report's suggestions to the boy, in a separately addressed envelope, as his own record.

I have chosen this report because there are no esoteric issues. However, even complex cases are of this same form:

Psychological Assessment[3]
ROBBIE MARCH
August 9, 19—

Mr. Henry and Mrs. Joan March
421 Richardson Street
Pittsburgh, Pennsylvania

Dear Mr. and Mrs. March,

The following is a review of the observations, understandings, and suggestions we arrived at together last Thursday as we explored Robbie's school performance. Especially because it includes a couple of afterthoughts, please telephone me not only with any corrections of

[3]Some notes about this particular report: (a) My reports to mental health specialists usually are briefer and more schematic than this; here, the extra detail is helpful to the parents and teacher; (b) in reports to nonprofessionals, I rarely include IQ scores as I do here; in this case the parents and school personnel had already been given an IQ that was drastically discrepant, and I wanted to counter its earlier impact; (c) I do not typically remark to clients, as in my concluding note to Robbie, that I liked them; in this case it was true and seemed important to affirm to Robbie; (d) Telephone follow-up at 2 months and 4 months found Robbie taking initiative, making friends, and achieving well in school except for mathematics. Robbie created his own pseudonym for this chapter.

facts or any additions but also for clarification or possible disagreement. I will then include these in a cover letter with this report to Sister Marion at Ebel School. I have also enclosed an additional note just for Robbie, excerpted from this report.

The Referral and Assessment Situation

By the time Robbie completed fourth grade this past spring with grades of D and F, his parents had decided that patience with the school system and with Robbie was not succeeding. They enrolled Robbie in a local parochial school (Ebel) for the coming fall with hopes that he would benefit both from its concern with the individual child and from its tradition of consistent discipline. They were pleased by their visit to the school, especially by what they heard of its use of small-group instruction. I imagine that they also may hope that a Catholic setting might minimize prejudices against a black student.

Mrs. March works in a personnel office, where Robbie has met the staff socially. These persons had assured the Marches that, from their contacts with him, Robbie seemed like a bright, untroubled, energetic boy, whose school difficulties probably were situational. Nevertheless, during the summer the Marches contacted me, as an independent clinical psychologist, to conduct a formal assessment of Robbie's poor academic achievement.

Mrs. March's overview of the background, which she gave me over the phone, was essentially the same picture I came to through examination of Robbie's report cards and school papers and through my visit in the March's home. Robbie's kindergarten records describe a regular youngster getting along fine. His first-grade report card describes a likable boy who meets academic expectations but who is overly "talkative" for the classroom setting. The second-grade report indicates that the talkativeness and activity level probably are frustrating to the teacher and are interfering with school achievement. Robbie's third-grade class had a series of substitute teachers, who assigned him grades of B and C. During that year, the school reported that Robbie's Otis IQ was 90 (from which teachers would not expect higher achievement than C's and B's). During the past year (fourth grade), Robbie's teacher had described him as "quarrelsome," "a nuisance" to other students, a daydreamer, and as overly talkative. She has regarded him as not being serious about school, as not being "motivated." On the other hand, she seems to have provided little if any positive response to Robbie's efforts. Her comments on his papers are of this sort: "this is not as bad as before." All of her comments (including those on report cards) to the Marches were negative.

My meeting with Robbie took place on 8-7-19— in his home from 10:30 to about 3:15. Mrs. March intercepted me at a nearby crossing that had just been blocked off for resurfacing and guided me to their house. We entered through the recreation room, where my first view of Robbie was at his full set of drums, enthusiastically and loudly producing what seemed to me as high-quality music. Turning off the amplifier, he looked me over and grinned broadly during a comfortable introduction. That image of an alert, energetic but relaxed, smiling youngster has remained with me as representative of Robbie. He led the way upstairs to the kitchen where Mr. March met us. (Both parents had taken the day off from work to be available during the assessment.) My first impression of the Marches held up through our 5 hours together: straightforward, perceptive, unpretentious parents, with high aspirations for their son, eager to help him but also able to confront his limits and difficulties. Physically, all three are slim and evenly featured; all three were dressed neatly in slacks and shirts. I imagine that they are generally seen as being attractive persons.

My representative images of Mrs. March are of her leaning forward over the kitchen table (where most of our work took place), waiting for Robbie to have his own say, but with eyebrow raised and mouth almost forming what she knew that he knew (despite his roundabout way of getting there). My image includes Mrs. March's catching herself in this posture, reflecting, and sitting back. My second representative image of Mrs. March is of her at the sink preparing our lunch: flowing but efficient movement, quietly and quickly carrying out her earlier plan for a light, attractive, refreshing lunch that all four of us would be likely to enjoy. As Mrs. March had mentioned on the phone, her husband was the quieter of them. He sat back into his kitchen chair, eyes following attentively and alertly, but his features otherwise composed for observation rather than interruption. When he did speak or otherwise take initiative, it was done gently but firmly, flowing smoothly and helpfully into the proceedings. The parents deferred equally to one another during discussions, giving me the impression of a long-married couple that has come to terms with differences.

With other families, I have asked to be left alone with the child after initial group interaction, later bringing the parents back into a discussion of what I observed. In this case, finding no disruptive tension among the participants and finding that all four of us were able to observe Robbie's test performance and to try out its implications for alternative approaches as we went, I wound up working with the entire family for most of our time. (Actually, the "entire" family would have included Robbie's married sister, 15 years older than he.) Our discussions centered on Robbie's comportment through the Bender-Gestalt, the Wechsler Intelligence Scale for Children, a drawing, Thematic Apperception Test stories, and responses to selected Rorschach cards. Robbie also showed me his room and several of his drawings and projects.

Robbie as Seen through the Test Materials

Before beginning the Bender, I asked Robbie (who sat across from me at first, and later catty-corner, with a parent at each of the other table sides) to tell me what folks had said about my coming. He sat tall but loosely, with glances at his parents being the only indication of wariness. He hesitated for a moment as though not sure of how to start and then grinned with what struck me as a self-conscious and somewhat playful, "I forgot." As we gave hints, pretty much staying on his ground, Robbie seemed to be both relieved and to take pleasure in our knowing that he knew more than he appeared to. Eventually he announced that I was a "psychologist to help me understand school." Again, he hesitated to elaborate, looked for affirmation from us that his guess would be correct, and then launched into an account of school, from time to time confidently sending his moth-

er out to bring in documents. I found myself appreciating his open enjoyment of our attention and his confidence that his parents would not let him down. But it also seemed that he genuinely looked to them rather than to himself for direction.

As Robbie talked about school, he seemed to wish that he did have better grades, but otherwise didn't know quite what to think about them. He was indignant about being blamed for trouble he didn't start and about students taking his pencil or other belongings. Otherwise, he seemed to regard his school career simply as the way things are.

When I asked Robbie to copy some geometric designs freehand (the Bender-Gestalt), he started right away and then had to erase part of the first design. Similarly, he scattered the designs on his paper, without regard for the total number that would have to go on the page. Midway, I interrupted to identify this continuing pattern. Robbie agreed that *starting without planning* is what leads to messy papers that are so dissatisfying to his teachers. We explored the possibility that he could *stop and think before beginning.* For example, he could have counted the dots beforehand instead of midway as he had done. I suggested that he also could have used an additional sheet of paper, and Robbie mentioned that he could have made each figure smaller. Then he enthusiastically volunteered to start over. This time he numbered the figures, arranged them sequentially, corrected an error from the original sheet, and pronounced that the second sheet was much better (as it indeed was, although both were adequate for a 10-year-old).

Nevertheless, the same pattern of getting started first and only then reflecting, showed up through all of our activities. On the WISC, Robbie tossed out associations first, sometimes stopping there, sometimes (as when I just waited without writing down his answer) working his way to the most appropriate answer. For example: (question): "What do we celebrate on the Fourth of July?"—"Fireworks. Parades. It's independence of America." During our discussions, Robbie readily accepted hints and employed them with practice items, but his older pattern came to the fore as we began a new subtest.

A second theme is that of *looking to adults.* Instead of relying on himself for direction, Robbie habitually looked to one of us for guidance once he had jumped in. Examples: "Do I color in the dots?"; "Did I do that one [acceptably]?"; "Should I start over?" This turning to us was matter of fact and not self-conscious or helpless. But even as he took advantage of our responses, Robbie did not look for principles or for an overview as such but instead worked his way cumulatively to success. During the Bender and WISC, the three Marches and I pursued the notion of Robbie placing himself "in charge," "being the quarterback," "being the captain" (as of a hockey team, or in the Navy). We were trying to help him to try out taking responsibility for making overall plans and for deciding when *his* criteria had been met; but in part Robbie confused these features with "choosing whatever I want." He did proudly bring out a complicated plastic model ship he had built by following the printed instructions and checking only once with a cousin for help. (He also proudly explained that his Dad had been in the Navy.) Both parents recognized these themes as familiar ones. For example, his mother had been encouraging Robbie to set out all the ingredients and to read the entire recipe on his own before he begins to cook.

The third theme is perhaps a variation of the first two. As Robbie made up stories to the TAT pictures, we adults noted independently (and later discussed) that his characters *did not have long-range goals or plans; they rarely took initiative and instead reacted to events or waited for resolutions to happen.* Examples: a man climbs down a rope to escape a fire, a boy goes inside a house only to get out of the heat, a boy doesn't like a gift violin. But on the blank card (where Robbie had to make up a picture as well as a story), he launched enthusiastically into a Flash Gordon adventure. He laughingly agreed to my suggestion that the character be called Robbie Gordon and consistently used that name throughout. Later, when I asked what his three wishes (for anything at all) would be, he named a two-way radio, a Kenmore truck, and finally, after hesitating, said he would like to be a hero. The latter would be like "saving a spaceship from blowing up," or "stopping two trains from hitting each other." I added "hitting a home run that wins a tournament," and Robbie agreed, happily instructing me to "write that down too." At this point, I tried to open a middle ground between Robbie's mundane TAT stories and his fantastic heroes. I asked if he could think of less dramatic ways of "being important." Here Robbie came up with "stopping the innocent from going to jail," "stopping the ocean from flooding a city," and "being an executive (which turned out to mean being a research scientist concerned with ecology, inventing a phonograph record that doesn't wear out, or developing new ways of transporting things from country to country). It seems to me that, at present, Robbie does not conceive himself as able to work his way through the everyday to his own important contributions.

Robbie's TAT stories also contained several *references to false blame that eventually is cleared up by authorities*—parents, police, and "Robbie Gordon." Examples: lying about the main character, others assuming the boy was a killer, "calling him a name." Mr. and Mrs. March and I later agreed that Robbie's being in effect an only child and one with no age-mates on his street, probably has contributed to his sensitivity to blame, both false and accurate. That is, he hasn't had a chance to "build immunity" through give-and-take with siblings and neighbors. This fourth theme is related to the next one: During our time together Robbie made few references to peers. Out of concern for his social isolation, the Marches had enrolled Robbie in Cub Scouts (but the troop has since folded), and this summer he went on an overnight camp, and he played on a Little League baseball team . . . right into an all-star tournament. Robbie proudly showed me a photo of his team, as he had showed me his fourth-grade class picture, his portable tape recorder, encyclopedia set, and camp awards. But he did not speak of special friends. His other prized possessions were related to his parents: crafts projects he has brought home to his mother, a newspaper clipping of the three Marches waiting for Pirate autographs, and his autograph book filled with a range of sports figures contacted through his father or through the family's waiting together at sporting events. When I asked directly if he had any buddies (most 10-year-olds are into fast, if shift-

ing, friendships), he mentioned two youngsters "up the hill" with whom he does sometimes play. I do know that Robbie is sensitive to criticism from peers, but otherwise I can only report this character of his social relations. After all, he also did not mention his Grandmother, with whom he spends his free time while waiting for his parents to come home from work.

Concluding Remarks

From the above sorts of observation, it seems to me that Robbie's "lack of motivation," poor grades, and low achievement scores can be understood in terms of: (a) his confidence in his parents' respect for him and in a world in which authorities see to it that things eventually will be taken care; (b) fourth-grade (and in September, fifth-grade) work requires initiative, planning, and relatively independent follow-through, which are contrary to Robbie's current style. (In retrospect, I wonder whether this style has developed in the face of the Marches doing too much for Robbie while he feels that he has to maneuver them into paying attention directly to him. . . ??); (c) standardized tests do not allow Robbie to check with adults or to correct himself after he leaps in, also, although Robbie works quickly, on my tests he seemed oblivious to being timed; and (d) at that critical fourth-grade stage, Robbie's adults apparently failed to evoke the school-related hero in him or to show him how to get from "jumping in" to being a "captain" with his school assignments.

On the WISC, where the individual administration allowed Robbie to work his way through initial approximations to the correct answer, his IQ (conservatively scored) was 122, placing him within the upper 10% of his age peers. Performance levels on the various subtests were remarkably consistent—an indication of the reliability of the IQ score. Moreover, Robbie worked steadily at these tests for more than 4 hours with only a few detours (to tell me about or show me his various other successes). Robbie clearly is not deficient in "intellectual ability" or in "motivation."

Although I probed for possible psychological fixations, conflicts, and the like, I found none. No doubt, as the Marches and Robbie's teachers begin to work more systematically to help him toward "captaining" his way to achieved importance, then whatever interpersonal family struggles exist for Robbie would come into focus. I suspect these would be related somehow to Robbie's being the sole nonadult in a working family. I also anticipate that the Marches will be more perceptive and constructive than many parents in recognizing and working with these developments.

Suggestions

The following suggestions are grounded in the above themes. The individualized groupings of suggestions for the parents, teachers, and Robbie are overlapping.

Mr. and Mrs. March

1. Your own ideas seem sound to me (such as encouraging Robbie to set out all his cooking ingredients in advance). Also recall our idea about helping Robbie to set up a prominently placed homework chart that would show goals, homework progress (scores on practice tests,

checks for finishing assignments, etc.), and grades as well as other school accomplishments. Remember that the purpose is to help Robbie build up (over time and many activities) his own sense of how he can project achievement and then work his way toward it. It is important that he see his own progress and that he see continuity among school, home, and his adult future. Perhaps his progress with his drums could be included on the chart. Robbie should participate in drafting the chart, with you guiding him to include small enough units to demonstrate progress. If redrafting seems necessary, Robbie can help to plan that too.

2. Perhaps if Robbie felt that you openly affirmed and enjoyed his more childlike interests (horseplay, "being bad, cool," drums, "Robbie Gordon" fantasies), then he might seek his own council in those instances where he now seeks adult attention in the form of help with what he already knows.

3. Continuing to provide the warm support Robbie now receives while at the same time encouraging him to be a captain can be tricky. During projects (homework, cooking, building models), perhaps you could tell Robbie outright that one of you will stay in the same room with him to be readily available but that he should present his questions in the form of "Here's what I think; does that sound right?" Other forms of request that are based on prior reflection should also be honored. Of course, sometimes a 10-year-old needs to know that Mom and Dad will help out just because he's himself; standoffs should be avoided in favor of some give and take.

4. As you continue to look for occasions for Robbie to be with age peers (such as the YMCA programs), you might keep one eye on opportunities for Robbie to bring his acquaintances home. This might promote a sense of closer friendship.

Ebel Teachers

1. Robbie seems eager to get started at Ebel, but he also has mentioned being afraid that he'll be "different"—that he won't know the prayers, that he is black, that he may be called names, that he might goof up through not knowing the rules. Because it is especially important that Robbie get off to a good start, perhaps if reprimanding is necessary, it could be in the form of: "Robbie, here *we all do* thus-and-so" (group model information rather than blame placing). The Marches would be appreciative of any early calls you think might help them to explain or reinforce school principles.

2. Judging from his standardized achievement scores, Robbie may start out in the lower part of his class. This makes it all the more critical that, whenever possible, he receive positive feedback on what he has done correctly. Similarly, acknowledgment of how far he's come in any area goes a long way with Robbie. I anticipate that with such assistance Robbie will be in very good standing by the end of the school year.

3. I don't know how it might be done in a fifth-grade class, but it is important that Robbie be assisted to envision final products, to think ahead, to look for principles before plunging in. One general strategy might be to encourage Robbie to ask his questions in the form of "Is *this* right?" rather than open-endedly eliciting your assurance that he does know.

4. Similarly, an occasional twosome assignment (teaming with another child for such projects as preparing a class presentation or cleaning blackboards) might help Robbie to enjoy planning and accomplishing. As the semester gets underway, perhaps you could identify areas of strength in which Robbie could assist another child. Here, too, he could enjoy taking on responsibility, planning, and seeing his accomplishments, while also developing friendships.

Robbie

When I scored those tests you took, I found out that you know enough and are smart enough to be making B's and A's in the fifth grade. Of course, at first you'll have to work very hard to catch up with your new class. Your Mom and Dad will help you every night with homework and with practicing for tests. Maybe you can even make a big "progress chart" together to keep track of what you practice and how well you're doing. Where would be the best place to keep it? —on your bedroom door, in the kitchen, or where? Anyway, if you practice hard in school and at home, I think you'll learn a lot—enough to be a research scientist. And you'll earn good grades, too.

I think that your Mom and Dad and your teachers will be trying to help you to plan ahead, to stop and think before you get started, like you did on the second sheet of paper with those designs you copied. That means you have to know how you want something to come out before you start, like Robbie Gordon planned his attack on the enemy ship, or like a hockey captain plans his team's strategy. That's the best way to be "cool"—to know who you are and who you want to be, and what you want to do. To help you to be cool that way (to think for yourself), your parents and teachers sometimes will ask you to figure out what *you* think before you ask for help.

I think you're going to have a good year, Robbie. And I think your new teachers and classmates will like you, especially if you work hard and help other people. I know that I liked you very much.

Sincerely,

Constance T. Fischer, PhD

CONCLUDING REMARKS

Looking back to the themes reviewed earlier in this chapter, it is now more concretely apparent that the area of personality and assessment *can* be scientific (empirical, rigorous, accountable) without reducing experi-action to traits, mechanisms, or electrochemistry, and that we *can* escape slippage into technologized practice. We *do* have access to an orderliness within human affairs without imposing classical natural-science conceptions and methods. We *can* engage the client as a responsible collaborator in pursuit not only of this orderliness but of initiating change within it.

The human-science approach to assessment and intervention flowed consistently from its approach to "personality." The various emphases characterizing the major kinds of traditional personality theories were included without elevating any one to primordial status. Specifically, purposiveness was taken into account without rendering it into a drive. Consistency across situations was studied without conceiving it in terms of traits activated by stimuli. We bypassed the circularity of arguing from derived data to a presumed underlying source. We dealt with learning processes without mechanizing them or treating them separately from experience.

The principles and practices of human-science assessment took into account the intersubjective character of objectivity without *objec*tifying the subject matter. Clinical impressions and ''projective techniques'' were included as part of the assessment process but without imputing internal dynamics. Human-science assessment certainly was not boring or demeaning for either client or psychologist.

The training model tension is resolved where the psychologist is (human-) scientific even while attending to the client's existential situation. The ''clinical versus statistical prediction'' controversy is resolved as an artifact of imposing natural-science categories on human goals and processes. Mandated open files are no longer problematic when data are actual life events (about which the client already knows), when understandings are specified as perspectival, and when results are collaborative, concrete suggestions.

Above all, human-science assessment provides a way to work with primary life events without losing their particularity, even as the psychologist makes use of research and theory. That is, as illustrated in the Robbie March report, the person can be described as a particular individual and not just as a location within tables of statistics, as cognition-behavior patterns, or as a series of stimulus–response connections. Personal environment can be included in highly specific suggestions. Representational description allows all of the person's helpers to work within a shared sense of his or her particular ways of living general patterns.

In short, this chapter has reviewed ways that psychologists can more thoroughly, consistently, and justifiably follow their inclinations to actively acknowledge and utilize their clients' and their own subjecthood.

REFERENCES

Anastasi, A. (1982). *Psychological testing* (5th ed.). New York: Macmillan.

Beck, A. T., Rush, A. J., Shaw, B., & Emery, G. (1979). *Cognitive therapy of depression.* New York: Guilford Press.

Boring, E. G. (1957). *History of experimental psychology.* New York: Appleton-Century-Crofts.

Butcher, J. N. (1972). *Objective personality assessment: Changing perspectives.* New York: Academic Press.

Butcher, J. N., & Finn, S. (1983). Objective personality assessment in clinical settings. In M. Hersen, A. E. Kazdin, & A. S.

Bellack (Eds.), *The clinical psychology handbook* (pp. 329–344). New York: Pergamon.

Craddick, R. A. (1975). Sharing oneself in the assessment procedure. *Professional Psychology, 6,* 279–282.

Dana, R. H., & Leech, S. (1974). Existential assessment. *Journal of Personality Assessment, 38,* 428–435.

deKonig, A., & Jenner, F. (Eds.). (1982). *Phenomenology and psychiatry.* London: Academic.

DuBois, P. H. (1970). *A history of psychological testing.* Boston: Allyn & Bacon.

Fischer, C. T. (1969). Intelligence as effectiveness of approaches. *Journal of Consulting and Clinical Psychology, 33,* 668–674.

Fischer, C. T. (1971). Toward the structure of privacy. In A. Giorgi, W. F. Fischer, & R. von Eckartsberg (Eds.), *Duquesne studies in phenomenological psychology* (Vol. 1) (pp. 149–163). Pittsburgh: Duquesne University Press.

Fischer, C. T. (1973a). Behaviorism and behavioralism. *Psychotherapy: Theory, Research, and Practice, 10,* 2–4.

Fischer, C. T. (1973b). Intelligence contra IQ: A human-science critique and alternative to the natural science approach to man. *Human Development, 16,* 8–20.

Fisher, C. T. (1974). Exit IQ: Enter the child. In G. Williams & S. Gordon (Eds.), *Clinical child psychology: Current practices and future perspectives* (pp. 333–350). New York: Behavioral Publications.

Fischer, C. T. (1977). Historical relations of psychology as an object-science and a subject-science: Toward psychology as a human-science. *Journal of the History of the Behavioral Sciences, 13,* 369–378.

Fischer, C. T. (1978). Collaborative psychological assessment. In C. T. Fischer & S. L. Brodsky (Eds.), *Client participation in human services: The Prometheus principle* (pp. 41–61). New Brunswick, NJ: Transaction.

Fischer, C. T. (1985). *Individualizing psychological assessment.* Monterey, CA: Brooks-Cole.

Fischer, C. T. (1987). A phenomenological approach to Mr. A. In M. T. Nietzel & D. A. Bernstein (Eds.), *Introduction to clinical psychology* (2nd ed.) (pp. 59–62). Englewood Cliffs, NJ: Prentice-Hall.

Fischer, C. T., & Alapack, R. J. (1987). Phenomenological approach to adolescent psychology. In V. B. Van Hasselt & M. Hersen (Eds.), *The handbook of adolescent psychology* (pp. 91–107). New York: Pergamon.

Fischer, C. T., & Fischer, W. F. (1983). Phenomenological-existential psychotherapy. In M. Hersen, A. E. Kazden, & A. S. Bellack (Eds.), *The clinical psychology handbook* (pp. 489–305). New York: Pergamon.

Fischer, W. F. (1970). *Theories of anxiety.* New York: Harper & Row.

Fischer, W. F. (1985). Self-deception: An empirical-phenomenological inquiry into its essential meanings. In A. Giorgi (Ed.), *Phenomenology and psychological research* (pp. 118–154). Pittsburgh: Duquesne University Press.

Giorgi, A. (1970). *Psychology as a human science: A phenomenological approach.* New York: Harper & Row.

Heidegger, M. (1962). *Being and time.* New York: Harper & Row. (Originally published, 1927.)

Keen, E. (1970). *Three faces of being: Toward an existential clinical psychology.* New York: Appleton-Century-Crofts.

Kendall, P. C., & Norton-Ford, J. D. (1982). *Clinical psychology: Scientific and professional dimensions.* New York: Wiley.

Kendler, H. H. (1974). *Basic psychology.* Menlo Park: Benjamin.

Knowles, R. T. (1986). *Human development and human possibility: Erikson in the light of Heidegger*. Lanham, MD: University Press of America.

May, R., Angel, E., & Ellenberger, H. F. (Eds.). (1958). *Existence: A new dimension in psychiatry and psychology*. New York: Basic.

Meichenbaum, D., & Jaremko, M. (Eds.). (1983). *Stress management prevention: A cognitive-behavioral perspective*. New York: Plenum Press.

Mischel, W. (1968). *Personality and assessment*. New York: Wiley.

Morgan, C. T., & King, P. A. (1975). *Introduction to psychology*. New York: McGraw-Hill.

Rabin, A. I. (Ed.). (1968). *Projective techniques in personality assessment*. New York: Springer.

Sundberg, N. D., Tyler, L. E., & Taplin, J. R. (1973). *Clinical psychology: Expanding horizions*. New York: Appleton-Century-Crofts.

Szasz, T. S. (1960). The myth of mental illness. *American Psychologist, 15,* 113–118.

Tallent, N. (1976). *Psychological report-writing*. Englewood Cliffs, NJ: Prentice-Hall.

Tallent, N. (1988). *Psychological report-writing* (3rd ed.). Englewood Cliffs, NJ: Prentice-Hall.

Tuddenham, R. (1963). The nature and measurement of intelligence. In L. Postman (Ed.), *Psychology in the making: Histories of selected research problems* (pp. 469–521). New York: Knopf.

von Eckartsberg, R. (1971). On experiential methodology. In A. Giorgi, W. F. Fischer, & R. von Eckartsberg (Eds.), *Duquesne studies in phenomenological psychology* (Vol. 1; pp. 66–87). Pittsburgh: Duquesne University Press.

Wallen, R. W. (1958). *Clinical psychology: The study of persons*. New York: McGraw-Hill.

Watson, R. I. (1953). A brief history of clinical psychology. *Psychological Bulletin, 50,* 321–346.

11

Demystifying Psychopathology
Understanding Disturbed Persons

Steen Halling and Judy Dearborn Nill

It is significant to note that psychiatry pays particular attention to those people with whom other persons have trouble empathizing.
(Savodnik, 1974, p. 96)

INTRODUCTION

Three basic questions are frequently asked in the context of psychiatry and psychology: What kinds of behavior are judged to be abnormal, whether by professionals or lay persons? What are the various patterns or forms of disturbed behavior? How can one make sense of the apparently senseless or irrational behavior of disturbed persons? For existential–phenomenological psychology, which seeks to understand human existence on its own terms and to disclose the significance of behavior for the actor as well as the observer, the last question is the most fundamental and constitutes the major focus of this chapter.

The first question, what distinguishes abnormal from normal behavior, is clearly of practical as well as theoretical importance. In everyday life, it is often raised with a sense of urgency. For example, parents who notice their adolescent son becoming increasingly isolated after he breaks up with his girlfriend are apt to wonder whether this is an ominous development calling for professional intervention. However, as anyone who has examined the literature of psychopathology knows, there is no consensus on criteria that might enable us to differentiate disturbed from normal behavior in an authoritative manner. Textbook concepts of disturbance, such as subjective distress, psychological inability, or violation of social norms (e.g., Price & Lynn, 1986) are obviously incomplete. For instance, although it is true that many people who are psychiatrically disturbed experience "subjective distress," it is also true that the capacity to experience emotional pain or grief is generally regarded as a sign of psychological maturity (see W. Fischer, 1986, for a phenomenological perspective on the nature of abnormality).

Theoretical uncertainty notwithstanding, lay persons and professionals in contact with people who wash their hands hundreds of times a day to "fight off germs" or who hear voices telling them they are damned have no difficulty agreeing that psychological disturbance is real. Of course, cultural relativists (e.g., Ruth Benedict, 1934) argue that behavior such as compulsive hand washing and hearing voices might be regarded as desirable in some cultures. But even they would admit that such abstract considerations have little immediate usefulness for dealing with disturbed people. Moreover, there is a critical flaw in cultural relativism. To say that a particular behavior that most people regard as abnormal—self-mutilation, for example—is acceptable in another society is to assume that behavior is an "in-itself," having a meaning and identity independent of its context. Ritualistic "self-mutilation," following a socially sanctioned and religiously prescribed pattern in the Amazonian jungle, for

Steen Halling • Department of Psychology, Seattle University, Seattle, Washington 98122   Judy Dearborn Nill • Department of Journalism, Seattle University, Seattle, Washington 98122.

179

example, is very different from an act of self-injury in our society. The difference is in the person's own perception of the act as well as in others' response to it.

The second question, concerning the various forms of disturbed behavior, is typically raised once a person's demeanor has been identified as "abnormal." Yet few practices in mental health are as controversial as diagnosis. Members of the general public who have favorable attitudes toward diagnosis expect that once a problem has been classified, the type of treatment to be followed is clearly indicated. This assumption is naive. Nevertheless, clients and members of their families may feel a definite sense of relief once a baffling and distressing problem is named. Therapists may also feel much less anxious when they believe they have recognized a certain pattern already familiar to themselves and their colleagues.

Further, mental health professionals who are advocates of diagnosis point to the current authority, the third edition of the American Psychiatric Association's (1987) *Diagnostic and Statistical Manual of Mental Disorders* (DSM-III-R), as a viable guide. (We will discuss the DSM-III-R at several points in the next section of this chapter.) These advocates say the DSM-III constitutes a striking improvement over previous diagnostic manuals and provides clinicians with a sharply defined set of categories and criteria for identifying various types of mental disorders. But critics of diagnosis argue that all diagnosis is an arbitrary pigeonholing of persons which dehumanizes by disregarding the uniqueness of each individual. They point to studies, such as Rosenhan (1973), that challenge the adequacy of assessments and suggest that, once a diagnosis has been assigned, it tends to stick even if it is incorrect.

However much the word *diagnosis* has taken on either miraculous or pejorative connotations, its etymology is profound: discriminating or discerning knowledge (*dia* = through or between, *gnosis* = knowledge). In this light, the naming or classifying of a person's pattern of disturbance might be one aspect of a more penetrating search for understanding. As such, diagnosis can lead to the third and most significant question: How does one make sense of seemingly senseless or irrational behavior?

To present a framework for understanding disturbed behavior and experience is the primary goal of this chapter. Our approach is broader than any specific theoretical perspective, although it draws upon psychoanalysis, behaviorism, systems theory, and especially existential–phenomenological thought. Our thesis is that even profoundly disturbed behavior is intelligible, potentially at least, if one approaches it in a certain *attitude* and takes into account five basic principles. With respect to this attitude, one must remember that the understand-

ing of another is an interpersonal event; it is not something one can achieve theoretically or abstractly. The British psychiatrist R. D. Laing (1965) has written caustically about colleagues who have great academic knowledge of schizophrenia but who have never come to understand one schizophrenic patient. To arrive at a deeper insight into another person, especially someone who is psychologically disturbed, requires an empathic, disciplined, imaginative, and receptive stance. It also requires that one learn to tolerate one's own puzzlement and confusion in the face of behavior that defies ordinary assumptions about how people live their lives.

The five principles of understanding are not separate from this open, empathic attitude but are the part of the approach that can be laid out more explicitly and systematically. In a sense, the principles are like a map in relation to the countryside it depicts: no substitute for traveling but a trustworthy guide to one's destination. We intend to show through an extended case study that the actual process one goes through in coming to understand more of another person implies the themes we articulate here in a formal way.

Many of the examples in this chapter come from clinical practice. This is not to imply that only psychotherapists can move toward an understanding of disturbed persons. In some instances, the most astute observer of an individual's conduct might be a neighbor, friend, or family member rather than the specialists who have been called upon to provide expert help. But it is most often psychotherapists who have extended close contact with people suffering psychiatric problems and who also write about these experiences.

THE FIVE PRINCIPLES

The five interrelated principles or themes are as follows: (1) *Context:* Behavior and experience are a function of the meaning of situations or contexts perceived by the person. Symptoms do not appear out of the blue; understanding the disturbed person means coming to understand what various events mean to him or her. (2) *Purpose:* Even behaviors and experiences that appear to be dysfunctional, habitual, unwanted, or meaningless can be shown to have a purposive (albeit often unconscious), functional aspect. (3) *Interpersonal drama:* Clients' rigid and easily threatened conceptions of themselves, the world, and others lead them to attempt to direct their relationships according to preconceived "plots." (4) *Critical incidents and phases:* Often, current behavior, goals, and expectations become understandable in light of significant incidents or phases from the person's past. This is not to suggest that past events "cause" present behavior. Nevertheless, clients' approaches to specific challenges and demands grow out of past experiences that taught them (however unhelpfully) about themselves and the world. (5) *Embodiment:* So-called defense mechanisms are never merely mental operations. The repression of fear, for example, may involve constriction in a person's breathing. One's actual understanding of another entails reliance on observations of the other's physical manner and appearance.

Context

The notion of context is the most comprehensive of the principles. Each of the other four refers to a particular dimension of context and the specific ways context is made known. That a person's behavior and experience is in response to the perceived meaning of events and situations is most readily seen with respect to one's own life. Imagine yourself making an abrupt turn onto a side road immediately upon realizing your fuel tank is empty and there is a gas station on that road. Although this behavior is perfectly sensible from your point of view, it is likely to be a source of consternation for your passenger who did not notice the sign for the gas station or the needle on the fuel gauge.

Insofar as the context of one person's behavior is not evident to another, the second is apt to be puzzled. Insofar as a person's behavior is at odds with the context as perceived by another, it is likely to be judged strange or abnormal. Anyone who wants to understand "psychopathology" has to relearn that all behavior is in response to a context, even when it is far from evident what the context might be. The alternatives to searching for the meaning of behavior (that is, its relationship to a context) are to dismiss it as bizarre, explain it with reference to a person's diagnosis—"he's hallucinating because he is schizophrenic"—or relate it to some hypothetical neurological or biochemical process in the individual's brain. The following scenario described by Steen Halling illustrates how easily one can conclude a client's disturbance is unrelated to his or her social and psychological circumstances:

> As a member of the psychology staff in a state hospital, I worked closely with Dorothy, a patient who was diagnosed manic-depressive. As far as the staff could tell, her manic episodes started arbitrarily. Yet Dorothy's behavior did improve when we worked out a treatment plan with her and her husband stipulating that she could visit him for the weekend if she had behaved appropriately during the week. Our major concern was that, while Dorothy was emotionally dependent on her husband, he seemed ambivalent about the prospect of her recovering and being discharged from the hospital.
>
> One day a letter arrived for her and, since I was

going to her ward, I delivered it. Dorothy was as calm and coherent as she had been all week. She took the letter, noted it was from her husband, and went to her room to read it. A few minutes later she came out, her face flushed, rambling incoherently. As she rushed down the hallway, she threw the letter at me. Soon everyone in the building knew that Dorothy was having another one of her "attacks" and that it had come out of nowhere. However, as I looked at the letter, the whole episode became less mysterious. It was clear to me, as it must have been to Dorothy, that her husband was saying indirectly he did not want to see as much of her as her continuing improvement would ensure.

The staff's failure to understand Dorothy's actions and change of mood resulted from their implicit assumption that their own awareness of her circumstances was adequate. Because Dorothy's dramatic change could not be accounted for by anything they noticed, they concluded the change did not make sense.

The philosopher Max Scheler's classic study of interpersonal relations (*The Nature of Sympathy,* 1970) suggests that understanding requires the observer to move beyond his or her preconceived assumptions about self and other. Sadler (1969) summarizes Scheler as follows: "Only as one participates in another's personal act, and only as this participation serves to replace our knowledge of his external characteristics may we have a direct knowing of another" (p. 58).

This insight is corroborated by van Kaam's (1969, Chapter 10) classic study of the experience of "really feeling understood." His subjects reported that the others' co-experience of what something meant to them was critical to their being understood. With Dorothy, the diagnosis of manic-depressive is a prime instance of an "external characteristic." Halling's ability to understand Dorothy's behavior was a function of his prior knowledge of the relationship between Dorothy and her husband and the fact that he was there, almost alongside Dorothy, at the moment of the shift.

To gain insight into Dorothy is to gain insight into her world—what matters to her, how she experiences her surroundings, her body, time, and other people (van den Berg, 1972). This notion of "being-in-the-world," which was developed by the German thinker Martin Heidegger (1962), is critical in phenomenological psychology. Being-in-the-world stresses that human existence is fundamentally relational. To be a person is to be open to, in relation to, concerned about, a world. Admittedly, in everyday language, one speaks of *entering into* a relationship, wherein *relationship* refers to an intimate connection. But at a more general level of meaning, even a person who is deeply isolated has a relationship with others, although it is a relationship of keeping them at great distance.

The emphasis on interpreting human behavior in context rather than in terms of events "inside the person" was championed most admirably by the American psychiatrist Harry Stack Sullivan (1954). For Sullivan, psychiatry is the study of interpersonal relations and not the study of personality *per se*. In his view, the term *personality* makes sense only if it is redefined as "the relatively enduring pattern of recurrent interpersonal situations which characterize a human life" (Sullivan, 1953, pp. 110–111).

The DSM-III and the DSM-III-R do give more attention to the interrelationship between behavior and situations than did their predecessor, DSM-II (American Psychiatric Association, 1968). Clinicians using the new manual are encouraged to include as part of their diagnosis an assessment of the degree of stressfulness of events ("psychosocial stressors") that appear to have contributed to clients' disorders. These events are rated, however, on the basis of how the "average" person would have been affected by them and not in terms of the significance they had for the client.

According to its chief editor (Spitzer, Williams, & Skodol, 1980), the DSM-III is genuinely descriptive and atheoretical, in contrast to the DSM-II, which provides interpretations, frequently psychoanalytically based, of disturbed behavior. But the DSM-III and the DSM-III-R does not consistently adhere to its stated intent of being descriptive, atheoretical, and situational in its approach to psychiatric disorders. Often the DSM-III falls back on the tradition of "descriptive psychiatry" championed by the German psychiatrist Emil Kraepelin. Kraepelin has given us excellent portraits of patient behaviors, especially those he regarded as manifestations of an underlying disease process. However, his guiding assumption was that "mental illness" is organically based. As a result, he had little reason to try to understand patients psychologically and paid little attention to how his patients experienced their own behavior or how their "symptoms" related to their circumstances (Alexander & Selesnick, 1966, pp. 163–166; Kraepelin, 1902).

In a similar vein, the DSM-III (p. 182) tells us that the delusions of the schizophrenic are patently absurd and have no possible basis in fact. Thus we are asked to regard these beliefs as having no relationship to anything that has happened in the client's life. Yet this assumption is contradicted by clinical evidence. Mendel (1976) has pointed out how the delusions of schizophrenics arise from their attempts to make sense of their circumstances and to salvage self-esteem. Laing and Esterson (1970) have demonstrated how such delusions are understandable when viewed in the context of the clients' families. They give the example of a woman who insists her parents are not married, when in fact they are. A closer examination of

the parents' relationship reveals that they are very much "divorced" in terms of their emotional and physical interaction (Laing & Esterson, 1970, pp. 75–106).

Behavioral psychologists would also agree that it is critical to study behavior in relation to the environment. B. F. Skinner (1973, 1974) has insisted that all behavior is a function of the environment in which it occurs and that the way to change behavior is to change the environment. The behavioral analysis that identifies what aspects of the environment need to be changed calls for systematic study of the "subtle and complex relations among three things: the setting or occasion upon which behavior occurs, the behavior itself, and its reinforcing consequences"(Skinner, 1973, pp. 257–258).

The significance of this approach for clinical understanding and intervention becomes evident if one looks at Skinner's definition of a particular consequence, namely reinforcement. A reinforcer is a consequence that increases the strength or frequency of the behavior that precedes it. For example, a therapist who asks a number of personal questions of a client who is suspicious, thereby increasing his or her suspiciousness, is reinforcing the client's suspicious stance. This is not, we would hope, the effect the therapist wants to have, but preoccupation with being helpful may obscure the specific way in which his or her behavior is part of the context within which the client is responding.

The lesson behaviorists hold out for therapeutic psychology can easily be forgotten as therapists become enmeshed in the subtleties of clinical theory as well as their clients' "subjective" experience. Nonetheless, we also recognize that behavioral psychology, with its predilection for reducing human existence to complex stimulus–response configurations, bypasses what is essential in human beings, that is, their very *personhood* (Keen, 1978, p. 240). Fortunately, in practice it is impossible to treat people as if they were mere stimulus–response configurations. Transcripts of clinical interviews done by behavioral psychologists, such as Joseph Wolpe (1982), make it apparent (as many behaviorists themselves would admit) that these clinicians draw their understanding of life from many sources other than behavioral psychology and relate to clients in ways that belie their mechanistic conception of human beings.

The importance of relating behavior to the person's context within a perspective that is holistic rather than reductionistic has been powerfully demonstrated by the psychologist Constance Fischer (see Fischer, 1985, as well as her presentation in Chapter 10 in this volume). She has developed a unique phenomenological approach to the assessment of clients, a key dimension of which is a contextual analysis. This analysis aims to identify the situations in which both the client's problematic and desirable behaviors occur. The psychologist's own interaction with the client as well as the client's and others' reports provide the necessary information. In contrast to the behavioral approach, Fischer seeks to understand and describe as far as possible the fundamental meaning of these various situations for the client.

In the case of Dorothy, contextual analysis would identify patterns of behavior she and the hospital staff regarded as obstacles to returning to the community (e.g., manic "episodes" and explosive ways of expressing anger) as well as those ways of behaving that seemed constructive (e.g., expressing dissatisfaction directly and nonviolently). The context of both kinds of behavior, along with their significance for Dorothy, would then be explored.

Purpose

The significance of context is intimately connected with our second principle, that even seemingly senseless, bizarre, and self-destructive behaviors have a function or purpose in the life of the disturbed person. Failure to address the underlying reasons for clients' attachment to their symptoms, an attachment that is sometimes more puzzling to the clients themselves than to their therapists, can jeopardize the healing process. Paradoxically, a respectful and patient exploration of the psychological function of problematic behaviors and experiences often leads to clients feeling less entrapped or controlled by them. Similarly, the recognition that symptoms are integral to a client's framework for ameliorating distress and coping with the demands of life helps both client and therapist to react with less frustration should apparently resolved symptoms return.

Sigmund Freud pioneered the exploration of the meaningfulness of all human behavior, including psychological symptoms. Throughout his life, he sought to demonstrate that all aspects of experience can be shown to be expressive of unconscious motivation. In the *Psychopathology of Everyday Life*, for instance, Freud (1960) illuminates the connection between various behavioral peculiarities (such as "slips of the tongue") and hidden psychological conflicts. We would argue, however, that one does not have to postulate the existence of forces, such as instincts or drives, to account for seemingly irrational behavior. The Swiss existential psychiatrist Medard Boss (1963, pp. 105–108) has shown that the psychoanalytic preoccupation with causes bypasses what constitutes the speculations of a sophisticated but distant observer. (See Moss's Chapter 12 in this volume for a more detailed discussion of Boss's approach.) Careful description eliminates the need for such speculations, as was shown in the case of Dorothy. Further, although Freud's

own interpretations are often couched in the language of causes, derived from the natural scientific conceptions of his time, these interpretations are as much inspired by the perspectives of the humanities with their concern for human motives and intentions (Bettelheim, 1983).

The DSM-III-R makes occasional reference to the experience of the person being diagnosed and does so with greater fullness than the DSM-II: Obsessions are "not experienced as voluntarily produced, but rather as thoughts that invade consciousness and are experienced as senseless or repugnant" (p. 245); persons diagnosed as suffering from paranoid personality "often have an inordinate fear of losing their independence or the power to shape events in accordance to their own wishes" (p. 338). Insights such as these help us to make sense of otherwise baffling behavior patterns. For example, given the paranoid person's concern with losing independence, his or her rigidity in thought and action and constant suspicion of others' hidden agendas become intelligible as survival techniques.

Particularly memorable accounts of the sense in "nonsensical" behavior have been provided by the psychologists Atwood and Stolorow (1981, 1984) in the tradition of "psychoanalytic phenomenology." These thinkers are deeply influenced by psychoanalysis but want to redefine psychoanalytic ideas and concepts in light of actual therapeutic process. They recognize there are unexamined philosophical presuppositions in Freud's theorizing (e.g., that biological motives are primary in human behavior) that get in the way of the effort to make intelligible the complexities of human experiencing.

In one study (Atwood & Stolorow, 1981), they examine the situation of a very disturbed young woman who had been secretly whipping herself for a period of years. Through exploration of her abusive family background and what she revealed about her inner life in intensive psychotherapy, client and therapist came to understand the significance these whippings had for her. First, the rituals followed acts, such as assertiveness, to which her parents typically responded with anger or physical punishment. By whipping herself, she minimized the feeling of helplessness that accompanies anticipation of attack from outside. Second, over time the self-inflicted pain became her means of ameliorating a deep and frightening sense of losing connection with the physically real world, including her own body. As Laing (1965) has pointed out in his discussion of similar phenomena, a ready-made explanation of self-punishing behavior as masochistic overlooks how pain may be valued by the sufferer for its assurance that one really exists and one really feels. Our goal is not, of course, that this interpretation become the new "orthodoxy." Rather, we are suggesting that the confirmation of any set of interpretations develops out of the clinician's growing awareness of the many facets of a particular client's existence.

In *A Miracle to Believe In*, Barry Neil Kaufman (1980) describes a striking shift in his understanding of Robertito, a young autistic boy. One of the most puzzling aspects of the boy's behavior was the stereotypic, circular (choreiform) movements of his left arm and leg. In accordance with prevailing expert opinion (Blackstock, 1978; Knobloch & Pasamanick, 1975), those who worked with Robertito tended to view the movements as meaningless by-products of a neurological disorder. Kaufman, however, felt there was something strangely familiar about them. One evening he realized there was a similarity between the boy's apparently senseless motions and the kind of rhythmic movements he himself made whenever one of his limbs fell asleep. To test the possibility that Robertito was responding to numbness on the left side of his body, Kaufman gently pricked the boy with a pin on the left and right sides. Robertito responded to the prick on the right side but showed virtually no reaction to the left side. Kaufman tried massaging Robertito's left side and found the boy cooperating, whereas he ordinarily exerted great effort to avoid physical contact.

Kaufman's attentiveness paid off; he allowed himself to observe and be affected by what he saw in a personal, imaginative way. This led to a hunch about the boy's behavior that was confirmed through further interaction. The incident shows that a psychological interpretation is just as relevant to problems with a neurological or organic component (the lack of feeling in Robertito's left side) as to those without such components. Kaufman's growing insight into Robertito's behavior also emphasizes the interpersonal context within which understanding emerges. This brings us to our third principle, that behavior is part of an interpersonal drama.

Interpersonal Drama

Human existence is interpersonal to its very core. Rollo May (1958) writes of Heidegger's notion of *Mitwelt*, one's life with other human beings, as one aspect of "being-in-the-world." We have already referred to Harry Stack Sullivan's thesis that psychiatry is the study of interpersonal relations. A number of existential–phenomenological thinkers, including Max Scheler (1970), Emmanuel Levinas (1969), and Martin Buber (1965), have an equally strong interest in defining the study of the person as the study of the interpersonal. Buber (1965) not only asserts that human life is fundamentally constituted by relationships but that it is through one's engagement in relationships that one's growth as a person takes place (Halling, 1987).

That there is an interpersonal disturbance in the lives of people who are labeled psychologically abnormal is, for the most part, readily evident. In the case of Dorothy, there was a disturbance in her relationship with her husband. The yound woman discussed by Atwood and Stolorow (1981) was reared by pathological parents. Little imagination is required to recognize how upsetting the actions of both these clients were for those around them. Atwood and Stolorow (1981) describe how difficult it was for the therapist to watch his client engage in a pattern of self-abuse. It is not just that one is distressed in a momentary way by what disturbed persons do. As one becomes involved with someone who is disturbed, one is often pulled into a compellingly dramatic relationship. The word *melodramatic* might be more apt because the relationship tends to be simultaneously intense and one-dimensional in the sense described later.

The domain of the melodramatic is discussed by Freud under the rubrics of *transference* and *countertransference*. Transference generally refers to negative or positive attitudes of a client toward the therapist that are disproportionate to the reality of the therapist's actual behavior and presence. A therapist might note, for example, that a casual question is taken by a client as an indication of deep concern or even affection or that a slight delay in starting the session is treated as a deliberate insult. The term *transference* derives from the Freudian assumption that the client reacts to the analyst as though he or she were the client's parent. In other words, the individual's past in the form of an ingrained expectation that authority figures will be abusive (as were one's own parents) or a strong wish that the therapist will dispel one's misery (the parent one desperately yearned for) will unconsciously obscure the real person and intentions of the therapist.

Existential psychiatrists such as Medard Boss (1963) agree with Freud that the client's attitudes and feelings toward the therapist may be immature or constricted because of earlier, difficult experiences. Nonetheless, they insist that his or her feelings are actually directed at the therapist (Halling & Dearborn Nill, in press) and that the latter is not an incidental or accidental target.

The notion of countertransference speaks to the reciprocal nature of the therapeutic relationship. The therapist cannot help but be caught up in the client's conflicts and expectations, at least periodically, because of unresolved difficulties from his or her own past. Insofar as the therapist reacts in a more intense fashion than the client's behavior warrants, this experience can help him or her gain important insights into the client's situation.

In recent years, innovators within the psychoanalytic tradition have explored the effect of disturbed family relations on the child's emerging sense of self at various stages of development. They seek to portray the way their adult clients relate to others and to themselves as a consequence of unsatisfactory childhood conditions. These innovators include neo-Freudians (e.g., Harry Stack Sullivan) and object-relations theorists (e.g., Melanie Klein, Donald Winnicott, Margaret Mahler, and Heinz Kohut) as well as psychoanalytic phenomenologists (e.g., Atwood and Stolorow).

With reference to object-relations theorists, Brice (1984) explains that the term *object* is used advisedly because it is not relationships with actual, "external" people but an individual's "inner" or psychic representation of others as well as of his or her own self that are studied. We agree with the object-relations theorists that any person's self-relationship is complex in structure and revolves around a spectrum of intentions such as maintaining self-esteem and that one's relationship to oneself emerges out of interactions with others. It is also true that a variety of agendas pervade interpersonal relationships and that often disturbed persons perceive others through very narrow perspectives of psychological self-interest and protectiveness. But these observations do not justify dichotomizing human existence into two realms of inner and outer, of "psychic representations" of people on the one hand, and "actual" people on the other.

Atwood and Stolorow along with other innovators are hindered by their own embeddedness in psychoanalytic abstractions as well as their sometimes tenuous understanding of phenomenology (Wertz, 1985). Nevertheless, their clinical insights are frequently perceptive, as is shown in their interpretation of what we have called interpersonal drama:

> Perhaps the most general statement that can be made about experience and conduct from our theoretical perspective is that patterns of conduct serve to actualize the nuclear configurations of self and object which constitute a person's character. Such patterns of conduct may include inducing others to act so as to fill roles that replicate key characteristics of object representations. (Atwood & Stolorow, 1981, p. 198)

These writers are suggesting that human behavior may be motivated by the desire to maintain one's deeply felt sense of self and others. To keep experience within boundaries of the tolerable (often equivalent to the familiar), it is necessary to draw others into the web of dramatic plots already central to one's life. For instance, a client who views him- or herself as victim and others as either victimizers or advocates (object representations) may go to considerable lengths to induce a new acquaintance to play a role appropriate to this particular plot. If the client were to realize that he or she victimized others, or was not primarily a victim, the result would likely be much anxiety and confusion. Seeing oneself as a victimizer would be tantamount to being guilty rather than innocent, and seeing self as competent would be unnerving insofar as it

is an entry into a radically unfamiliar perspective on the world and oneself.

The attempt to induce another to play a specific role in the context of psychotherapy is described vividly by Yalom and Elkin (1974, pp. 44–45). The therapist Irvin Yalom worked with a young woman, Ginny Elkin, who in one session emphasized how little progress she was making, describing herself as someone who waits for her lover to make decisions about their relationship. Yalom struggled to avoid either falling into the role of rescuer or feeling overwhelmed by the helplessness Ginny expressed. He attempted to goad her into being a decisive, hopeful adult, but with little success. In a sense, Yalom was as caught up as Elkin in trying to get the other to fit into a particular plot.

Another therapist, Peter Lawner (1981), describes a client whose long and elaborate explanations left him, as therapist, confused and distracted rather than with any real understanding of his client's situation. After the session, Lawner started to wonder if the purpose of the explanations was to keep him at a distance so the client could avoid the disturbing thoughts and experiences apt to emerge in a more intimate relationship.

We have been emphasizing how clients engage others in their own dramas out of psychological necessity, taking the part of stage directors or drama coaches. This is only half the story, and by itself it is misleading. As we have mentioned, the dramas of life have their origin in a family context. Systems theory, as applied to family therapy, has focused on how the individual client and the therapist alike act within a larger pattern of behavior that resists change (e.g., Skynner, 1981). Systems theory asserts that a collective family drama depends for its existence on each member playing his or her role. The drama is not directed by one specific person, though, at a given moment, any family member may be especially instrumental in keeping it intact.

Minuchin (1974) describes a family in which each member, in turn, resisted exploring the possibility that the depressed father might really be a competent person. Insofar as the father was competent, each person in the family would lose the role of caretaker in relation to him, and one of the focal points for the family—concern about the father's condition—would be lost. Therapists who work with alcoholics and their families use the term *codependence* to refer to the whole family's investment in one member's disturbance (Schaef, 1986).

Critical Incidents and Phases

Although careful study of a person's current interaction with others, including family, helps to make his or her actions understandable, a more complete understanding emerges only as the historical dimensions of the person's life become evident. Our fourth principle suggests that knowledge of critical incidents and stages in an individual's past may provide a deeper awareness of what is happening in the present. Obviously, this is not a novel idea. Psychoanalysis has relentlessly sought to show that much of human behavior is a function of past events. However, our position is not that the past causes the present nor that one's hopes and expectations for the future have little significance for the conduct of one's life. Rather, as J. H. van den Berg (1972) points out, "The past is what was, as it is appearing now" (p. 82). The past as lesson and memory shapes the forward movement of human life.

By the same token, as a person's present attitudes and circumstances change, so does his or her recollection of the past. In psychotherapy, for example, clients may remember more of the pleasant aspects of childhood as their growing self-acceptance allows them to develop more satisfactory interpersonal relations. In speaking of a child's response to his or her life events and circumstances, Merleau-Ponty (1964) writes, "It is never simply the outside which molds him; it is he himself who takes a position in the face of external circumstances" (p. 108). This perspective is important to keep in mind as one interprets a person's life—especially his or her past—because human beings, no matter how disturbed, are not just victims of circumstances.

The case of Allen E., a 15-year-old boy whose "school phobia" is described in Goldstein and Palmer (1975), provides an example of how knowledge of a lesson from past experience illuminates baffling current behavior. Allen had been successful in academics and athletics and was well liked by his peers and teachers. Over a period of a year, he stopped attending school regularly, often leaving after morning classes. He intercepted notes sent by the school to his parents who did not realize that their son was skipping classes until the end of the school year. When Allen entered therapy, it gradually became apparent that difficulties in his parents' marriage had led him to believe his father might be having an affair, and the family might break up.

Allen's concern was greatly increased when he came home early one day to find his mother letting a strange man out of the house. He assumed his mother was having an affair and took on the responsibility for checking on her by returning home from school early, observing the house from a distance. Other factors had prompted Allen to avoid school as well. Uneasy about his own budding sexuality, he found the sexual references and joking of his classmates repugnant, and he felt safer satisfying his compulsion to masturbate at home than in the school washroom. But discovering "evidence" of his mother's affair was critical in leading him to assume guardianship

over her behavior and responsibility for holding the family together.

A similar example is provided by Jules Henry (1965) in his classic study of five families, each with a seriously disturbed child who had been institutionalized. Henry spent a week with each family, observing their daily interaction and interviewing members of the household.

During his visit with the Jones family, Henry noted a good deal of arguing and bickering between Edward Jones (a dentist) and his wife Ida. The disagreements between Edward and Ida were played out in a dramatic and surprising way one evening when Henry went with them to a Bible study group. During the meeting, Dr. Jones castigated the group for being unwilling to consider his views, criticized St. Paul for not having humility, and declared that all human beings are evil. When his wife asked if his mistrust of fellow human beings extended to her, he said yes. She replied that, under the circumstances, she might as well go out and have an affair (Henry, 1965, p. 46). At first sight, Dr. Jones's behavior appears bizarre as well as socially inappropriate. We do not have room to do justice to Henry's subtle and careful interpretation of this incident on the basis of further discussions with Edward and Ida about their relationship and their childhoods. However, we will summarize the main themes relating to Edward's mistrust.

According to his own report, Jones's mother was "hard, brilliant, well-organized, violent and vengeful. She disciplined her children vigorously, and if they deviated from her tough moral criteria, she cut them down with ridicule" (Henry, 1965, p. 39). Edward developed a reluctance to receive anything from anyone and sought safety in isolation. After all, the person on whom he depended the most attacked him fiercely. Further, he had gotten sick on his mother's milk, and his life had been in danger until alternate nourishment was found. Erik Erikson's (1968) contention that the basic developmental issue during the first year of life is attaining a sense of trust and that its absence is indicated by behavior such as refusing food fits Edward's situation all too well. When Edward met Ida, he thought he had finally found a woman who would not attack him and on whom he could depend. But the contentment of their first months of marriage, at least as he remembered them, ended when their son Tommy was born. Ida naturally gave much attention and energy to Tommy, and Edward interpreted her shift of focus as a betrayal. She eventually gave in, however resentfully, to her husband's insistence that he be first in her life and neglected their son. It was this son who was later hospitalized.

Perhaps none are so ready to attack symbols of hope (e.g., St. Paul) as those who have hoped and been deeply disappointed. The secret wish that hope might be justified remains, but it is nevertheless feared because to become open to possibility means setting oneself up to be destroyed. By attacking the other members of the Bible group, as well as his wife, Dr. Jones protected himself from his own desire for closeness and "demonstrated" how untrustworthy others are by getting them angry at him.

So far we have described critical incidents more than critical phases. But the two are mutually implicated. Allen E. was at a difficult transitional stage between childhood and manhood when he came home and discovered his mother with a strange man, and Edward Jones's reaction to the birth of his first child was rooted in a fundamental mistrust festering since the critical first year of his life. In general, a stage or a phase is a period of life that is apt to be characterized by the presence of, and a concern for, a specific challenge or problem—a "crisis" in Erikson's (1968) perspective. For instance, in midlife many people become especially mindful of their mortality and the limits of their own powers.

Familiarity with the literature on issues and stages in human development is very helpful for anyone who wants to understand disturbed behavior. We refer interested readers to Briod's Chapter 7 in this volume as well the following excellent texts that have an experiential emphasis: Erikson (1968), Kagan (1984), Kaplan (1978, 1984), Knowles (1986), and Sullivan (1953).

Embodiment

There is an embodied dimension to all our actions. For this reason, we have referred to disturbed behavior rather than using expressions such as "mental illness" throughout this chapter. At this point, we want to explain our reasons for avoiding reference to mental illness as well as clarify our fifth principle—embodiment. Although it is sometimes meaningful and helpful to make a distinction (as long as it is not absolute) between physical and psychological "illness," psychological disturbances are not primarily mental phenomena. Expressions such as "he makes me sick" and "responsibility weighs heavily upon her shoulders" speak to the unity of the mental and physical. Phenomenologists in particular have shown that the separation of human beings into two realms of body and mind, as in the philosophy of the seventeenth-century thinker Rene Descartes, is contradicted by human experience. Merleau-Ponty (1962) writes of the "body subject" as a way of conveying the intertwining of the physical and the mental, and of "corporeal schema" to refer to our intimate, preconscious attunement to the world around us. He has elaborated on the implications of this for one's understanding of others:

> We must abandon the fundamental prejudice according to which the psyche is that which is accessible only to myself and cannot be seen from the outside. My "psyche" is not a series of "states of consciousness" that are rigorously closed in on themselves and inaccessible to anyone but me. My consciousness is turned primarily toward the world, turned toward things; it is above all a relation to the world. The other's consciousness as well is chiefly a certain way of comporting himself toward the world. Thus it is in his conduct, in the manner in which the other deals with the world, that I will be able to discover his consciousness.
>
> If I am a consciousness turned toward things, I can meet in things the actions of another and find in them a meaning, because they are themes of possible activity for my own body. (Merleau-Ponty, 1964, pp. 116–117)

Merleau-Ponty's position is confirmed by everyday observations. The other's tone of voice, facial expression, and posture convey that he or she is distressed, depressed, or joyful. This is, of course, also true with respect to persons who are seriously disturbed.

Norma MacDonald (1960), in describing her experience of a schizophrenic episode, refers to an exaggerated awareness of things to which she would ordinarily pay no attention. Over time, she became attentive to how fatigue and lack of rest made her more susceptible to psychological disturbances. Renee, in *Autobiography of a Schizophrenic Girl* (Sechehaye, 1951), writes of very frightening periods when her own body and the world around her became unreal and machinelike. These changes in the person's bodily being are also, as Merleau-Ponty states, evident to the observer. The following description by Steen Halling of a therapy session illustrates the importance of paying attention to clients' embodiment:

> One of my clients had a habit of talking incessantly during each session, filling the room, as it were, with his words. I experienced his talkativeness almost as an onslaught and wondered how he could catch his breath while speaking virtually every second. As I observed him more closely, I noted that while he was speaking with rapidity, his face was surprisingly lacking in expression, except that he looked like he was partially holding his breath. In one session, I directed him to stop talking and to consciously breathe in and out slowly while attending to his feelings. At first he was startled at my suggestion, but he followed it nonetheless. Almost immediately, his expression changed, and as his breathing deepened, he looked fearful and frightened. The avoidance of feelings was made possible by his "running" while sitting, and as this defense was momentarily put aside, we were able to discuss some of the issues and feelings he had previously regarded as unthinkable.

The "defense mechanisms" of which Freud wrote are clearly bodily as well as psychological transformations. We might say that, whereas meanings refer to the world, they are carried in the body. A number of psychotherapists have emphasized the levels of meaning one carries at a bodily level and how one can gain access to them to enable a resolution of conflict (e.g., Gendlin, 1964, 1981; Lowen, 1958). For our present discussion, we want to emphasize how attentiveness to another's bodily being and to our own bodily reaction to him or her is crucial for developing understanding of the other, whether the other is normal or "abnormal."

EXTENDED CASE STUDY: THE CASE OF PHIL

The following description of a relationship that Judy Dearborn Nill developed with a client during her clinical training demonstrates how the five principles of understanding just discussed are implicit in the actual process of coming to know another person. Their first meeting starts uncertainly and sets the scene for the unfolding relationship:

"Is *she* going to yell at me too?" The lean young man with wavy black hair and intense brown eyes jabbed a finger at me. The finger shook, as did his voice, with apparent outrage. I shifted uncomfortably in my chair. My limited knowledge of diagnosed schizophrenics had prepared me to expect bizarre behavior, not hostility. Would I be able to work with Phil?

We had just been introduced by my supervisor, Phil's counselor for the 2 months he'd been living at the large psychiatric halfway house to which I'd come to do an internship. For the next 9 months—20 hours per week—I was to be Phil's counselor (i.e., case manager). He was one of seven residents assigned to me for the duration.

I took a deep breath and settled back to observe my supervisor's response to Phil. "Calm down," Ted said evenly. "Nobody is going to yell at you."

Phil shot me a suspicious look. "I know who you are. You're a spy for the VA" [Veterans Administration]. Crouching on the edge of his seat, he snapped his attention back to Ted. "You're trying to get me kicked out of here, aren't you?"

Ted shook his head. "I'm not trying to get you kicked out. I am trying to introduce you to your new counselor. Judy here . . ."

"J . . . just one more p . . . person," Phil interrupted in a loud stutter, "to boss me around and yell at me and refuse to help me!"

"Now listen, Phil." Ted leaned forward. "I'm telling you, no one wants to boss you around or yell at you or . . ."

"Yes, you do," whined Phil. By now his whole body was trembling. I wondered if he felt frightened as well as angry.

"Listen to reason, Phil . . ."

This exchange continued for another 10 minutes or so. No matter how persistently Ted tried to placate him, Phil wasn't buying. He countered everything Ted said with complaints about unreasonable rules (requiring him to enlist in a Veterans Administration day treatment program which, according to Phil, would prevent him from

attending college), staff persecution (yelling), and neglect (refusing to help).

At the mention of neglect, I got an idea and thrust myself into the conversation. "It might be an advantage to work with me, Phil," I said. "Since my case load is much smaller than Ted's, I'll have more time for you."

He stared at me for a long moment. "Will you help me get into school or will you try to talk me out of it?" His tone was somewhat less sharp.

I breathed a sigh of relief, willing to promise the moon if Phil would give me a chance. "Of course, I'll do everything I can to help," I assured him, standing up with the intention of ending the exchange on a positive note.

When Phil stood up, I extended my hand. For an embarrassing several seconds, I thought he would refuse to take it. At least he reached out. His grasp was firm. As Phil walked out the office door, I collapsed on my chair, suddenly aware of how tense I'd been. I felt both exhilarated by the challenge of Phil and afraid of unwittingly contributing to his negative view of the world.

Phil's hostile behavior has a context; it is directed at his new counselor ("Is *she* going to yell at me, too?"). We see throughout this account how the counselor is part of the field to which the client responds. Further, the interaction is colored for both parties by the meaning each brings to it. Initially for Phil, the presence of his new counselor signifies "one more person to boss me around and yell at me and refuse to help me." For the counselor, Phil is a potential threat to her future as a therapist ("My limited knowledge . . . had prepared me to expect bizarre behavior, not hostility. Would I be able to work with Phil?").

Phil's bodily being is an integral aspect of the counselor's response to him and of her attempt to interpret his intentions ("His finger shook, as did his voice, with apparent outrage. I shifted uncomfortably in my chair"). Phil, in turn, reacts to her nonaggressive bodily presence ("His tone was [now] somewhat less sharp"). She then responds to Phil's slightly relaxed demeanor ("I breathed a sigh of relief [and] extended my hand"). The perceptible release of anger on one side and anxious tension on the other leads to the foundation of a working relationship ("At last he reached out. His grasp was firm").

For the next several days, Dearborn Nill sought to develop a plan for relating to Phil based on observations of how he interacted with other staff. Although he responded negatively to attempts to "lay down the law" and was not convinced by arguments, he did seek out staff persons for attention and assistance. Unfortunately, his expectation of meeting rebuff often created its own fulfillment. His confusion and disorientation led him to continually ask the same questions, which greatly annoyed the staff:

During this time, it occurred to me that Phil was at least as frustrated as the staff persons who tried to deal with him.

What would happen, I wondered, if he got everything he wanted? I was determined to find out. I would give him the undivided, positive attention he seemed to crave. I would refuse to get caught up in defending myself or the staff against his accusations of neglect and ill will. I would avoid contradicting, arguing, and giving ultimatums. I would follow through on all promises.

I had no expectations of Phil or my plan other than a strong belief that I could eventually disarm him and win his trust. He was so quick to impugn others' motives, so disoriented and lacking in basic survival skills, I felt sure he would probably have to be institutionalized or under supervisory care for the rest of his life.

The counselor's opportunity to observe Phil in relation to others illuminates the purpose behind his irritating behavior. "He was so . . . disoriented and lacking in basic survival skills" that Phil's repetitious questioning of staff—no matter how negative the results—seemed to provide him with a sort of temporary reassurance that he was on the right track. Often another's purpose (the functional aspect of behavior) is more easily discerned when one is not immediately involved, not the recipient of annoying or uncooperative actions. The counselor begins to wonder what might occur if the apparent object of Phil's disruptive behavior (to be reassured, to get positive attention) were achieved.

One of the first challenges she faced was getting Phil to attend a day-treatment program as required by the halfway house. Knowing what would not work, she presented the requirement as binding on her—if she could not get Phil's cooperation, she would not be doing her job. In addition, she pointed out how the day-treatment program need not interfere with Phil's goal of entering college. Phil eventually agreed to go.

At the halfway house, Phil continued to complain that the staff were against him and did not listen to him. Finding argument with Phil useless, she tried another approach:

> I discovered that, more than anything else, Phil wanted to be listened to respectfully, without interruption, as he aired his side of any conflict. He felt attacked and misunderstood; he honestly couldn't see how his behavior might provoke the responses he got. In the hope of conveying to Phil my understanding, I let him talk himself out on the staff's being "all against him," and then I told him I was very sorry such unpleasant incidents occurred. Period. To my surprise, once he felt completely satisfied that I had heard and sympathized, Phil would offer spontaneously to "try harder" next time to get along. Twice he voluntarily returned to the staff person involved and apologized for blowing up at her.

Phil's perception of himself as a persecuted victim and all others as potential persecutors involved him in a characteristic interpersonal drama. He expected others to respond to him negatively, and he drew them into the persecution plot by doing those things that resulted in his being attacked or misunderstood. He felt so vulnerable to attack that he focused only on how other actors in the drama responded to him ("He honestly couldn't see how his behavior might provoke the responses he got"). Phil's counselor hoped to revise the story line of Phil's drama by refusing to read her part according to his direction. She discovered that one seemingly minor alteration in the dialogue ("I let him talk himself out . . . and then I told him I was very sorry such unpleasant incidents occurred") could lead to a more satisfactory ending.

The next step involved getting him to talk to the staff member with whom he was upset:

> About 3 months after I met Phil, he came storming into my office after an interchange with the halfway house's recreation director, Michael. Phil went on and on about how Michael had treated him like dirt, telling Phil he was paranoid and refusing to believe anything Phil said. I asked Phil if he had considered discussing his feelings with Michael instead of with me. He said that wouldn't do any good; Michael would only "get mad" at him. Next, I asked if Phil would be willing to talk it over with Michael in my presence. He said yes, if I would keep Michael from "yelling" at him.
>
> I didn't need to. Michael listened attentively as Phil told him what it felt like to be called paranoid and how he had found suspicion to be a necessary part of his life. Michael then apologized for having termed Phil's behavior paranoid. After this incident, Phil always spoke well of Michael. I frequently saw them joking and laughing together at the "med" window and on the grounds.

Phil apparently no longer sees his counselor as a persecutor. On her recommendation, he is willing to risk having his views of another perceived persecutor change as well. Again, because the other actor in the drama (Michael) did not respond according to Phil's expectation, new possibilities of relationship open up: "After this . . . I frequently saw [Phil and Michael] joking and laughing together at the med window and on the grounds."

Although there was ample opportunity to observe Phil in his current environment, there was little background information available other than hospital discharge summaries. Phil had been a "hyperactive" child. His parents divorced during his adolescence, and he lived subsequently with his mother and stepfather. He had been hospitalized several times over the past 3 years with a diagnosis of schizo-affective disorder. His first hospitalization resulted in an honorable discharge from the Army. It was difficult for Dearborn Nill to develop a sense of the significance of these events for Phil because he seldom spoke of the past. He did, however, speak of his mother, and ordinarily in glowing terms as a "55-year-old knockout." But once he bitterly recalled that it was she who "betrayed" him into the VA hospital the last time he was committed. Dearborn Nill's impression of Phil's mother was that she seemed genuinely interested in her son's welfare. She also sent him money from time to time and invited him for regular weekend visits.

In this case, then, the historical played a minor role in gaining an understanding of the client. Phil's counselor did not read his hospital discharge summaries until after she'd been working with Phil for several months. Neither did she have much contact with the significant others from Phil's past, either directly or through Phil's discussion. However, learning that Phil had been a hyperactive child and that his mother was involved in his last hospitalization did provide some imaginative insight into possible critical incidents and phases. As Phil's social worker at the VA once remarked, "The hyperactive child grows up experiencing himself as wrong." Everything he does, everything he says, everything he is, is unacceptable—too loud, too active, too demanding. If even the few persons he dared to trust (in Phil's case, his mother) seemed to betray him, it is not difficult to envision a renewed determination on his part to suspect everyone of hostile intentions.

Phil's behavior at the halfway house slowly improved. He enrolled in a nurse's aide program and volunteered to do supervised work at the VA hospital:

In the remaining months of my internship, I received only two reports of disruptive incidents involving Phil. One was a practical joke gone sour, for which he apologized as soon as he learned he had genuinely scared someone. The other was his blowing up and threatening suicide, homicide, or both with a night staff person when he couldn't get the man's attention. Again, Phil apologized almost immediately after the incident.

I noticed in Phil a growing ability to laugh, especially at himself. For instance, Phil and his VA social worker had long had a push–pull relationship. At first Phil was convinced Sherman was out to get him, "to screw up [his] head" and get him kicked out of treatment and ultimately the halfway house. Later Phil conceded on occasion that maybe Sherman "really was trying to help." As often as not, however, Phil complained of Sherman's "gestapo techniques" and unprovoked "yelling." Then one day, toward the end of my internship, Phil came in to say he didn't quite know what to make of it when Sherman *didn't* yell. He had to remind him, "Hey, Sherm, don't you want to take your frustrations out on me?"

One of Phil's last major complaints to me about halfway house "persecution" concerned his finances. The bookkeeper, he was convinced, was "ripping [him] off." "They" weren't giving him the proper amount each week out of trust (an allowance system designed to help residents budget their spending money). Further, "they" were paying too much per month on his bills. After I thoroughly investigated the allegations, I made the mistake of trying to convince Phil his perception of reality was false. He wouldn't give an inch. Nothing I said or did made the slightest impression on him. Phil was certain he was being cheated, and I heard about it night and day. Finally, out of sheer exhaustion, I suggested he withdraw his money from trust and handle it on

his own. Phil seemed startled at the idea, but as soon as he determined I was serious, he arranged to do just that. The first month he ran out of money within a week. The next month (my last as intern) he made it almost to the end. Three months after my graduation, I returned to the halfway house as clinical supervisor. Phil requested I be his counselor again. As my new duties required a great deal more of my time, however, we did not see each other nearly as often. Besides, Phil's life at the place had settled into a comfortable routine; he was considered a model resident. Ten months later, Phil left the halfway house and married a young woman from the same facility. Within another year and a half, he was employed and had a son.

Phil's way of being-in-the-world began to change as his world changed. In turn, the world in which Phil lives is transformed as he begins to feel, think, and act differently.

Phil's new counselor, Dearborn Nill, initiated a positive change through her implicit attention to the five principles of context, embodiment, purpose, interpersonal drama, and historical perspective (listed in the original order of discussion). For example, the counselor's inference that Phil's hostility, disorientation, and demanding behavior were rooted in earlier experiences of others' misunderstanding, mistrust, and impatience led her to explore offering as much time and respect for Phil as she could muster. Phil grew more certain of getting his needs met without taking a combative stance toward everyone, and his provocative behavior diminished, first with his counselor and later with others.

As Phil began to experience his world as less antagonistic, he became increasingly able to draw forth the cooperative and supportive aspects of his environment. He undertook and completed a technical training program while fulfilling the requirements of his residence at the halfway house—activities that he had previously seen as mutually exclusive. He was empowered to resolve interpersonal conflicts (e.g., with the office staff, with Michael, and with Sherman), to work through problems on his own (e.g., sharing the lamp with his roommate, learning to budget his money), and eventually to leave supervisory care altogether.

CONCLUSION

At the opening of this chapter, we quoted Savodnik (1974) to the effect that psychiatry "pays particular attention to those people with whom other persons have trouble empathizing." Moreover, psychopathology, as the study of disturbed behavior, presents an opportunity to recognize that we are all "more simply human than otherwise" (Sullivan, 1953, p. 32). To be human, whether ordinary or seriously disturbed, is to live in a world of fundamental interconnectedness; a world in which what we do is influenced by, and has influence upon, what others do; a world wherein "self" and "other" cannot adequately be conceived as discrete entities. The struggle to understand others is, fundamentally, the struggle to understand ourselves.

The process of coming to understand more of oneself or another is extraordinarily difficult to articulate. Our fivefold framework, for example, is necessarily limited by the artificial separation—for purposes of discussion—of context from purpose, interpersonal from historical, and all four of these from embodiment. And even a far more detailed, annotated case study than space allows here could not do justice to the actual gaining of insight into a previously puzzling aspect of one's own or another's behavior.

Understanding, and the empathy it enables, is experiential. Understanding entails a living awareness of self and others that is itself contexted, purposeful, situated interpersonally and historically, and embodied. We hope this chapter contributes to readers' ongoing experiences of coming to understand themselves and others with whom they have contact both informally and professionally.

REFERENCES

Alexander, F. G., & Selesnick, S. T. (1966). *The history of psychiatry*. New York: Harper & Row.

American Psychiatric Association. (1968). *Diagnostic and statistical manual of mental disorders* (2nd ed.). Washington, DC: Author.

American Psychiatric Association. (1980). *Diagnostic and statistical manual of mental disorders* (3rd ed.). Washington, DC: Author.

American Psychiatric Association. (1987). *Diagnostic and statistical manual of mental disorders* (3rd ed. revised). Washington, DC: Author.

Atwood, G. E., & Stolorow, R. D. (1981). Experience and conduct. *Contemporary Psychoanalysis, 17*(2), 197–208.

Atwood, G. E., & Stolorow, R. D. (1984). *Structures of subjectivity: Explorations in psychoanalytic phenomenology*. Hillsdale, NJ: Analytic Press.

Benedict, R. (1934). Anthropology and the abnormal. *Journal of General Psychology, X*(59), 59–80.

Bettelheim, B. (1983). *Freud and man's soul*. New York: Alfred A. Knopf.

Blackstock, E. G. (1978). Cerebral asymmetry and the development of early infantile autism. *Journal of Autism and Childhood Schizophrenia, 8*, 339–353.

Boss, M. (1963). *Psychoanalysis and Daseinsanalysis*. New York: Basic Books. (Reissued by Da Capo Books, New York, 1982.)

Brice, C. W. (1984). Pathological modes of human relating and therapeutic mutuality: Buber's existential relational theory and object-relations theory. *Psychiatry*, May, *47*(2), 109–124.

Buber, M. (1965). *Between man and man*. New York: Macmillan.

Erikson, E. (1968). *Youth, identity and crisis*. New York: Norton.

Fischer, C. T. (1985). *Individualizing psychological assessment*. Monterey, CA: Brooks/Cole.

Fischer, W. F. (1986). On the phenomenological approach to psychopathology. *Journal of Phenomenological Psychology, 17*(1), 65–76.

Freud, S. (1960). Psychopathology of everyday life. In *Standard Edition*, Vol. 6. London: Hogarth.

Gendlin, E. (1964). A theory of personality change. In P. Worchel & D. Byrne (Eds.), *Personality change* (pp. 100–148). New York: Wiley.

Gendlin, E. (1981). *Focusing*. New York: Bantam.

Goldstein, J. D., & Palmer, J. J. (1975). *The experience of anxiety* (2nd ed.). New York: Oxford University Press.

Halling, S. (1987). The imaginative constituent in interpersonal living: Empathy, illusion and will. In E. Murry (Ed.), *Psychology and imagination* (pp. 140–174). Pittsburgh: Duquesne University Press.

Halling, S., & Dearborn Nill, J. (in press). Existential-phenomenological psychiatry and psychotherapy. In E. R. Wallace & J. Gach (Eds.), *Handbook of the history of psychiatry*. New Haven, CT: Yale University Press.

Heidegger, M. (1962). *Being and time*. New York: Harper & Row.

Henry, J. (1965). *Pathways to madness*. New York: Random House.

Kagan, J. (1984). *The nature of the child*. New York: Basic.

Kaplan, L. J. (1978). *Oneness and separateness: From infant to individual*. New York: Simon and Schuster.

Kaplan, L. J. (1984). *Adolescence: The farewell to childhood*. New York: Simon and Schuster.

Kaufman, B. N. (1980). *A miracle to believe in*. New York: Doubleday.

Keen, E. (1978). Psychopathology. In R. S. Valle & M. King (Eds.), *Existential-phenomenological alternatives for psychology* (pp. 234–264). New York: Oxford University Press.

Knobloch, H., & Pasamanick, B. (1975). Some etiological and prognostic factors in early infantile autism. *Pediatrics, 55*, 182–191.

Knowles, R. T. (1986). *Human development and human possibility: Erikson in the light of Heidegger*. Lanham, MD: University Press of America.

Kraepelin, E. (1902). *Textbook of psychiatry*. New York: Macmillan.

Laing, R. D. (1965). *The divided self*. Baltimore: Pelican.

Laing, R. D., & Esterson, A. (1970). *Sanity, madness and the family*. Harmondsworth, Middlesex, England: Penguin.

Lawner, P. (1981). Reflection on the "unknown" in psychotherapy. *Psychotherapy: Theory, Research and Practice, 18*(3), Fall, 306–312.

Levinas, E. (1969). *Totality and infinity*. Pittsburgh: Duquesne University Press.

Lowen, A. (1958). *Physical dynamics of character structure*. New York: Grune and Stratton.

MacDonald, N. (1960). Living with schizophrenia. *Canadian Medical Association Journal, 82* (January), 218–221.

May, R. (1958). Contributions of existential psychotherapy. In R. May, E. Engle, & H. F. Ellenberger (Eds.), *Existence* (pp. 137–191). New York: Simon and Schuster.

Mendel, W. M. (1976). *Schizophrenia: The experience and its treatment*. San Francisco: Jossey-Bass.

Merleau-Ponty, M. (1962). *The phenomenology of perception*. New York: The Humanities Press.

Merleau-Ponty, M. (1964). The child's relations with others. In J. M. Edie (Ed.), *The primacy of perception and other essays* (pp. 96–158). Evanston, IL: Northwestern University Press. sity Press.

Minuchin, S. (1974). *Families and family therapy*. Cambridge, MA: Harvard University Press.

Price, R. E., & Lynn, S. T. (1968). *Abnormal psychology* (2nd ed.) Homewood, IL: Dorsey.

Rosenhan, D. (1973). On being sane in insane places. *Science, 179*, 365–369.

Sadler, W. A. (1969). *Existence and love: A new approach in existential phenomenology*. New York: Scribner's.

Savodnik, I. (1974). Understanding persons as persons. *Psychiatric Quarterly, 48*(1), 93–108.

Schaef, A. W. (1986). *Co-dependence: Misunderstood—mistreated*. Minneapolis: Winston.

Scheler, M. (1970). *The nature of sympathy*. Hamden, CT: Archon.

Sechehaye, M. (1951). *Autobiography of a schizophrenic girl*. New York: Grune and Stratton.

Skinner, B. F. (1970). Answer for my critics. In H. Wheeler (Ed.), *Beyond the punitive society*. San Francisco: Freeman.

Skinner, B. F. (1974). *About behaviorism*. New York: Vintage.

Skynner, A. C. R. (1981). An open-systems, group-analytic approach to family therapy. In A. S. Gurman & D. P. Kniskern (Eds.), *Handbook of family therapy* (pp. 139–184). New York: Brunner/Mazel.

Spitzer, R. L., Williams, B. W., & Skodol, A. F. (1980). DSM-III: The major achievements and an overview. *The American Journal of Psychiatry, 132*(2), 151–164.

Sullivan, H. S. (1953). *The interpersonal theory of psychiatry*. New York: Norton.

Sullivan, H. S. (1954). *The psychiatric interview*. New York: Norton.

van den Berg, J. H. (1972). *A different existence: Principles of phenomenological psychopathology*. Pittsburgh: Duquesne University Press.

van Kaam, A. (1969). *Existential foundations of psychology*. New York: Image.

Wertz, F. (1985). Book review of *Structure of subjectivity: Explorations in psychoanalytic phenomenology. Journal of Phenomenological Psychology, 16*(1), 95–106.

Wolpe, J. (1982). *The practice of behavior therapy* (3rd ed.). New York: Pergamon.

Yalom, I. D., & Elkin, G. (1974). *Every day gets a little closer*. New York: Basic.

12

Psychotherapy and Human Experience

Donald Moss

Each human being entering the psychotherapist's office reveals a unique experience of the world, of self, and of other persons. In 1958, the landmark volume *Existence* (May, Angel, & Ellenberger, 1958) introduced the existential and phenomenological perspectives to American psychotherapists. Since then, the *meaning of the patient's experience* has been at the heart of new developments in the science and practice of psychotherapy. The present chapter takes as its theme *psychotherapy and human experience,* including but also reaching beyond the specific schools of existential and phenomenological psychotherapy, to encompass the broader family of experientially oriented psychotherapies. The chapter provides an integrative synthesis, from the standpoint of the psychotherapist, of the most useful strands within this broad psychotherapeutic tradition.

We include a number of authors who are not explicitly phenomenological or experiential in orientation but who nevertheless are masters of the art of psychotherapy and have contributed richly to understanding the significance of the *patient's experience* in the psychotherapeutic process (Bruch, 1974; Fromm-Reichman, 1950; Jung, 1985; Strupp, 1984).

This chapter is organized around the following topics: (a) Historical introduction to phenomenological and existential influences on psychotherapy, (b) fundamental principles in experientially oriented psychotherapy, (c) the therapeutic attitude, (d) helping oneself versus being helped, (e) the temporal structure of the human life, (f) the temporal process of psychotherapy in phenomenolog-

ical perspective, and (g) modalities of therapeutic intervention.

HISTORICAL INTRODUCTION TO PHENOMENOLOGICAL AND EXISTENTIAL INFLUENCES ON PSYCHOTHERAPY

The terminology and names within the large family of existential and phenomenological psychology are often confusing, so we will begin with a brief identification of psychological and psychotherapeutic schools, accenting both their divergences and overlaps. For more detail on the history and conceptual frameworks of phenomenological and experientially oriented psychotherapy, the reader is referred to May, Ellenberger, and Angel (1958), Wyss (1973), May and Yalom (1984), Yalom (1980), Fischer and Fischer (1983), Bugental (1985, 1987), and Halling and Dearborn Nill (in press).

Psychoanalysis

Experientially oriented psychotherapy would be ungrateful were it not to acknowledge its immense debt to Sigmund Freud and the subsequent psychoanalytic schools, especially the analytic psychology of Carl Jung, the will psychology of Otto Rank, and the individual psychology of Alfred Adler. The early existential and phenomenological psychiatrists showed that Freud's natural scientific orientation, with its emphasis on instincts and genetic causes, was inadequate to the understanding of human experience, yet these same critics in their practice of psychotherapy followed many of the lines of their psychoanalytic training. Many of the insights that set phe-

Donald Moss • Haight Clinic Psychological Services, 109 South Jackson Street, Spring Lake, Michigan 49456.

nomenological psychotherapy apart from psychoanalysis have also been formulated in parallel fashion by creative dissenters within the psychoanalytic tradition.

Psychoanalytic therapy encourages the patient to express whatever thought or feeling enters awareness. The purpose of psychoanalytic therapy is to: (a) bring unconscious conflicts and impulses to conscious, verbal expression, (b) transform impersonal, seemingly instinctual processes into personally "owned" motives and desires, and (c) identify and "work through" earlier traumatic experiences that contribute to present-day symptoms. The therapist relies on verbal interpretation, clarification, and confrontation of the patient's conflicts and defensive structure.

Existential

Existentialism traces its nineteenth-century roots to the Danish philosopher and theologian Søren Kierkegaard and the German philosopher Friedrich Nietzsche. In our century, existentialism influenced European psychiatry and psychotherapy dramatically after the 1927 publication of Martin Heidegger's philosophical work *Being and Time* (1962) and again after World War II under the influence of Jean Paul Sartre's (1956) *Being and Nothingness*. In psychotherapy, existential influences include the emphasis on the individual's freedom and responsibility for his or her own existence, the process of becoming an individual, the challenge to authenticity in existence, and the positive role of anxiety as a medium for change and growth.

Existential psychotherapy emphasizes the real relationship between the therapist and the patient, involving an authentic encounter in the present moment between two existing individuals. Existential psychotherapy recognizes psychiatric symptoms as meaningful expressions of a disharmony in the patient's existence, which are to be understood and not merely suppressed. It advocates an openness to the tragic dimension of human life, and not merely a naive Pollyannalike optimism.

Daseinsanalysis

The existential movement in European psychotherapy took various names—existential analysis, anthropological psychiatry, "onto-analysis," and the German name *Daseinsanalysis*. The early pillars of this movement were Ludwig Binswanger, Viktor von Gebsattel, Erwin Straus, Jurg Zutt, and Eugene Minkowski. After World War II, Medard Boss (in collaboration with Martin Heidegger) forged his own viewpoint of Daseinsanalysis, and Dieter Wyss formulated the approach of "anthropological integrative" psychotherapy. Several

European refugees from the Nazis brought a knowledge of existential analysis with them to the United States in the 1940s, but the real Americanization of existential analysis began with the 1958 publication by Rollo May, Ernest Angel, and Henri Ellenberger of *Existence,* an anthology of works by European authors.

Most Daseinsanalysts or existential analysts remain psychoanalytic in their basic clinical procedure—often utilizing a couch, encouraging the patient to a free and uncensored expression of thoughts and feelings, and intervening with verbal interpretations, clarifications, and confrontations. However, the existential analyst abandons the biological, instinctually oriented concepts of Freudian analysis and adopts a more existential interpretation of the patient's experience. Prominent American existential analysts include Rollo May (1977), James Bugental (1987), and Irvin Yalom (1980).

Phenomenological

Phenomenology in philosophy was the creation of the German Edmund Husserl, who called for a "return to the things themselves" through a clearing away of assumptions and preconceptions. This methodological "fresh start" enables the phenomenologist to suspend his or her usual experience and interpretations of the world, in order to understand phenomena "as they present themselves." This philosophical new beginning immediately impressed European psychiatrists and psychologists, such as Binswanger, Karl Jaspers, and H. C. Rümke, who were seeking new theoretical foundations to understand the human being in his or her own nature, apart from the assumptions of natural science.

The concepts of phenomenology illuminate the experience of psychiatric patients and the process of psychotherapy in several ways: (a) human behavior and experience reveal a nature different from that of natural phenomena and require a distinct "human-science" approach if they are to be understood, (b) psychic phenomena, behavior, and experience can be understood through their "intentional" structure, that is, they are meaningfully directed toward a situation or object, and (c) in order to understand and to reach a patient, the psychotherapist must enter into a mutual experiencing of the patient's unique world of experience, with its own time, space, and interpersonal forms.

More recently, the Dutch psychiatrist van den Berg (1980) defined phenomenology in psychiatry as the "science of divergent thinking" about people and their world. In other words, phenomenological psychotherapy is never content with a simple change in behavior. Rather, the patient is invited to see his or her world in a different light, to discover a novel perspective on life and relationships, and to recapture a sense of wonder in a fresh and vital way of perceiving. This transformed perception and interpretation of life events becomes the avenue for practical modifications in behavior and relationships.

Gestalt

Gestalt psychologists such as Fritz Perls radicalized psychotherapeutic technique by an emphasis on the patient's lively emotional experiencing in the "here-and-now" (Perls, Hefferline, & Goodman, 1951). Gestalt therapists have criticized "aboutism"—empty and unemotional talk about past events and distant situations, and invited patients to react intensively and in a fully physical fashion to the immediate situation with the therapist (Polster & Polster, 1973, p. 234). Gestalt therapy relies heavily on the therapeutic value of novel and divergent experiences that make no explicit connection with a past trauma or conflict. If the past emerges as an immediate issue in Gestalt therapy, it is as "unfinished business," as a preoccupation with old emotional issues that blocks effective living in the present. In this case, the patient is invited to reexperience or reenact that past so as to experience it differently and is discouraged from mere recitation or analysis of past events.

Gestalt therapy places emphasis on the process of therapy, and not on its content or issues. Role play, visualization, or an imagined reliving of an experience create a greater emotional intensity in the therapeutic session. The patient is invited to a broadened *awareness* of his or her role in creating life and relationships, invited to a deeper *ownership* of that role, and challenged to *experiment* now with new modes of behaving and relating.

Client-Centered Therapy

Carl Rogers originated the first truly American school of psychotherapy: client-centered psychotherapy. Rogers abandoned the exclusive preoccupation with the patient's past. He encouraged the therapist to respond nondirectively to the patient, to understand the patient's world of experience, and to reflect back in an affirming manner the patient's own feelings, thus enhancing the patient's self-awareness. The therapeutic procedure of client-centered therapy involves a continuous "reflection" or paraphrasing of the patient's experiences, with an emphasis on the feeling dimension: "You seem to be feeling alone and abandoned." This nonjudgmental "reflection" serves to amplify the patient's awareness and acceptance of feelings. Rogers (1951, 1959) believed that growth emerges spontaneously toward actualizing the patient's "real self," once the therapist establishes an accepting atmosphere of "unconditional positive regard."

This concept of unconditional positive regard has broadened beyond an explicit approval of behaviors or statements to convey a deep respect for the person and for the "power of life" as it seeks its own way toward fullness and growth (Willis, 1985).

Experiential

Experiential psychotherapy is a specific school of therapy and should not be confused with the broader movement of experientially oriented psychotherapies (Friedman, 1976). Experiential psychotherapy draws on elements from phenomenological, Rogerian, and Gestalt psychotherapy but transforms them from a general approach into a specific method of psychotherapy with procedures, steps, and interventions. Eugene Gendlin (1968) began with research on the process of client-centered therapy and what he called the "experiential response," a patient response that is felt deeply, bodily, and immediately at an emotional level. He refined this element in the therapeutic process further into a teachable procedure called "focusing," which guides the individual to stay concentrated and attentive to the immediate flow of feelings about his or her total emotional situation (Gendlin, 1981). Gendlin (1973) and Alvin Mahrer (1983) have designed specific sequences of steps to enable the patient to enter an "experiential state," to enhance the formation of a "felt sense" of one's situation, and to allow this felt sense to move toward deeper experiencing, self-encountering, and closure.

Humanistic

Abraham Maslow founded humanistic psychology as a "third force" within American psychology in an effort to throw the doors and windows of psychology wide open (1962, pp. vi–ix). Humanistic psychology became an eclectic meeting ground for divergent influences including existentialism, the psychology of consciousness, the encounter and sensitivity group movements, and transpersonal psychology. Maslow introduced many of the key themes of humanistic psychology and psychotherapy: the pursuit of self-actualization, personal growth, and full humanness; an emphasis on both being and becoming; and a recognition of the place of values within psychological science. He also challenged the focus in psychology on the study of abnormal and dysfunctional behaviors and insisted that psychology must include in its vision the study of truly creative, outstanding, and fully functioning human beings.

We have summarized several overlapping movements contributing to the psychotherapy of experience. On the American scene, these movements have converged to a great degree, endowing many humanistic or experientially oriented psychotherapists with a core of broadly shared beliefs about the psychotherapeutic process: (a) therapy must commence with an empathic sharing of the patient's experience of a personal world, (b) the therapist must encounter the patient in his or her full historicity—as a being with roots in the past, a home in the present, and aspirations for the future, (c) therapy proceeds most effectively through a lively, emotional, and immediate reexperiencing and mastery of key personal issues, (d) novel positive experiencing in the encounter with the therapist has a corrective therapeutic value in and of itself, and (e) the individual spontaneously moves toward health, growth, and fulfillment in a therapeutic atmosphere of safety, acceptance, and awareness. The remainder of the chapter will enlarge upon these core beliefs.

FUNDAMENTAL PRINCIPLES IN EXPERIENTIALLY ORIENTED PSYCHOTHERAPY

Being with the Patient in His or Her World of Experience

The core of the phenomenological challenge to the psychotherapist is the invitation to enter into the world and story of the patient. The patient requesting help is isolated within personal suffering and troubles, and the essential curative factor of all experientially oriented psychotherapy is to stand with the patient and bridge that isolation. If the therapist is to succeed in entering into the patient's concerns, then he or she must not only comprehend but also co-experience the patient's own unique situation.

R. D. Laing, the British phenomenological psychiatrist, emphasized the importance of understanding each human being's individual world of experience:

> Each person not only is an object in the world of others but is a position in space and time from which he experiences, constitutes, and acts in *his* world. He is his own centre with his own point of view, and it is precisely each person's *perspective* on the situation that he shares with others that we wish to discover. (Laing & Esterson, 1964, p. 19)

The Dutch phenomenologist, Jan van den Berg, showed that we can only truly illuminate the abnormal behavior of the psychiatric patient through a shared perception of his or her world, with its unique unfolding of time, its individualized landscape, and its personal populace:

> To be ill, even with just a trivial illness . . . means, above all, to experience things in a different way . . . to live in another, maybe hardly different, maybe completely different world. . . . The depressed patient

speaks of a world gone gloomy and dark. The flowers have lost their color, the sun has lost its brightness, everything looks dull and dead. . . . The patient suffering from mania, on the other hand, finds things full of color and beauty, more beautiful than he ever saw before. The schizophrenic sees, hears and smells indications of a world disaster. In objects, he observes the downfall of his existence. In the voices of people, in the blowing of the wind, he hears that a revolution is about to come. In the taste of his bread, he discerns evils penetrating the things of his world. . . . The patient is ill; this means that *his world* is ill, literally that *his objects are ill,* however unusual this may sound. When the psychiatric patient tells what his world is like, he states, without detours and without mistakes, what he is like. (van den Berg, 1972, p. 46)

Even simple behavior change, when this is the patient's goal in seeking treatment, is often impeded when the psychotherapist fails to understand the patient's world. The first step toward change that seems so trivial to the therapist, may appear to the patient as a leap into a life-menacing chasm, and repeated goal setting and establishment of rewards or punishments will be ineffectual unless this experience is recognized. Aaron Beck has taken this into account in his cognitive–behavioral therapy, calling for the therapist to listen attentively to the patient's perception of the world, before any behavioral interventions are attempted (Beck, 1976; Beck, Rush, Shaw, & Emery, 1979).

The Meaningfulness of All Symptomatology

Implied in the challenge to see the patient's situation as he or she sees it is the challenge to view the patient's most abnormal behavior and painful symptoms as containing elements of self-actualization (Moss, 1984). In early discussions in the field of phenomenological psychopathology, both Ludwig Binswanger and Medard Boss introduced this concept of self-actualization (Binswanger, 1931; Boss, 1949; Moss, 1978, 1981a). Their studies showed that even the most pathological and disturbed behaviors involve a desperate and last resort effort to come to terms with a difficult situation. Sexual perversions, according to Boss (1949), can be understood as miscarried attempts, in the face of "insurmountable worldly barriers," to achieve a "loving mode of being." Faced with an unbridgeable distance and isolation, the sexual deviate turns to ever more desperate means of making contact with another human being.

Similarly, R. D. Laing showed in his studies of the schizophrenic family that the most psychotic and delusional behaviors display "intentionality," that is, they are meaningfully directed as self-expression and genuine communication toward the family (Laing, 1959; Laing & Esterson, 1964). Otto Rank (1964, p. 4) formulated this same insight differently: A neurosis represents the individual's creative but miscarried effort to impose a control and form upon his or her world and can only be understood in the context of the individual ego's ongoing effort to develop and express itself creatively.

If the therapist is to affirm and encourage the patient's efforts to discover new solutions to his or her dilemma, then it will be necessary to look more closely at seemingly negative and disturbed behavior. Further, it is both liberating and reassuring to the individual to have the meaningfulness of one's abnormal behavior illuminated in psychotherapy and to realize that, even in personal disturbance, one has been coming to terms with life. Behavior that is in some sense adaptive or purposive nevertheless often seems irrational to the individual and can trigger deep self-doubt.

Diagnosis versus Empathy

The first level of understanding in psychological science is diagnosis and judgment. The diagnostician recognizes symptoms and signs of a disorder or disease process and categorizes the patient's behavior as indicative of schizophrenia, a major affective disorder, or a character disorder. In doing so, an unequal interpersonal relationship is established. As diagnostician, one is the authority with knowledge and skills, looking down at an object for analysis and diagnosis.

This relationship is often experienced by the patient as a put-down, a further evidence of his or her inferiority and abnormality. In many instances, the patient also internalizes this same attitude as a kind of self-judging, self-diagnosis, and self-discounting attitude toward his or her own behavior. Frequently, professionals reinforce and encourage this kind of self-analysis, without recognizing its impact on the self-esteem and confidence of a patient.

The diagnostic attitude is medically invaluable. One instance of psychological distress may demand a qualitatively different response from the next. An experience of severe depression and hopelessness following the death of a child in a previously strong and healthy woman is vastly different from a similar experience of depression and hopelessness in a woman with three previous hospitalizations for major depressive episodes and a family history of affective disorders. To diagnose means to stand back at a distance, to focus symptoms, to delineate the onset and course of the problem, and to seek to understand the problem in biological, biographic, family, and psychopathological perspectives.

Rigid adherence to this diagnostic attitude is antithetical, however, to the principles of psychotherapy. The therapist must reach the patient in his or her subjectivity or "personhood." For this to happen requires that therapist and patients also encounter one another as persons. This second level of understanding in psychological science is empathy. Although never throwing away my knowledge or expertise, as therapist I encounter and accept each patient as a person, on the same level with myself. I walk with my patients in their journey and imagine myself alongside them at the center of their world of experience.

When abnormal and even unacceptable behaviors emerge, it is not sufficient to revert to the diagnostic frame of mind, label the behavior as *schizophrenic* or *manipulative*, and medicate or otherwise *subdue* the behavior. Rather, even if such intervention is necessary, the therapist is challenged to understand first: How is the patient experiencing this moment, this place, and these persons, such that he or she acts in this fashion? Any intervention will then be informed by an empathic understanding of the person, which guides the behavior into more effective therapeutic channels. Further, empathy *validates* the patient as a person to be both understood and respected, even if the therapist forcefully restricts the patient's behavior.

The Hermeneutic or Contextual Approach

Seeking to make sense of a difficult text in the Bible or in literature, one usually explores its "context," that is, the textual passages that surround it, the historical place and events that influenced it, and the personality and style of the author. It is assumed in advance that the text means something, if only one can view it from the proper angle and in the proper setting. Interpretation out of context violates the integrity of the text and distorts the original meaning of the statements because one then interprets words, phrases, and events from one's own very different and distant perspective.

This same "hermeneutic" approach applies to the behavior of the psychotherapeutic patient. Research by humanistic and phenomenological psychologists has shown that many of the abnormal behaviors so troublesome to those around the mentally ill individual consist of meaningful responses to a difficult situation. The difficulty, however, may not be apparent to others, as it is a difficulty in "the situation as he or she perceives it." The patient's own world of experience is thus the proper context within which to interpret his/her actions, and our challenge is to illuminate this experience. This approach places a dramatic emphasis on the individual experience of the patient in psychotherapy.

THE THERAPEUTIC ATTITUDE

Phenomenologically and experientially oriented psychotherapy decrees neither a specific technical attitude nor specific treatment techniques. Rather, any therapeutic modality or technique may be applied, as long as the principles of mutuality, intersubjectivity, and kinship with the patient are respected, that is, as long as the total human involvement of the therapist is not reduced to mere technique. Further, each therapeutic intervention reflects the therapist's own grounding in a philosophy and ethic of human existence, forming a *therapeutic attitude* that guides each encounter with the patient. What follows is a review of the perspectives of several European phenomenological psychotherapists.

Albert Zacher, of the Institute for Psychotherapy and Medical Psychology, in Wurzburg, West Germany, examined the issue of therapeutic attitude in an article, which also serves as a useful introduction to the Wurzburg school of "anthropological-integrative psychotherapy" (Moss, in press; Zacher, 1985). Zacher takes as his guiding hypothesis that:

> The attitude of the psychotherapist toward his patient is shaped essentially by the theoretical concepts which he represents. The decisive influence of theory thus lies not in its explicit instructions for a therapeutic posture, but rather in its image of the human being. This image can even bring about an attitude contradicting the explicit prescriptions of the theory. (Zacher, 1985, p. 149)

Zacher introduces the general concept of a therapeutic attitude, drawing especially on Jurg Zutt's existentially oriented discussion of the "inner attitude" of the therapist. Zacher reflects on critical themes in the anthropologically oriented image of the human being. At the base of an anthropologically oriented psychotherapy lie a few central concepts: (1) The unity of body and mind, implying the personal animation of the total living body—as von Weizsacker (1947) has pointed out, there is as deep a bond between the mind and the cells of the liver as between mind and the ganglion cells of the brain. (2) The mutuality of self and other—the existence of each individual refers in its very structure to the existence of others, from the earliest phases of individuation in infancy. (3) The temporality of human existence—the human being is to the same degree one who has been, one who is in the process of becoming, and an inhabitant of the future. (4) The twin domains of the ontic and the pathic—the human being lives not only in the ontic, objective world of things and factual events but also in the pathic realm of "I should," "I can," "I may, " "I must," and "I desire." (5) Illness as a fundamental mode of human existence—being sick is not just a factual change in the physical body; rather, it involves fundamental transformations in one's "being-in-the-world," that is, in one's experience of time, space, and other persons. This final concept unifies the other concepts because only when we can envision the totality of a vital human existence can we adequately comprehend its defi-

cient forms in illness. Zacher relies here especially on Viktor von Weizsacker (1956) and Dieter Wyss (1973).

The image of the human being in anthropological psychotherapy carries its corresponding therapeutic attitude articulated variously by the chief representatives of phenomenological and anthropological psychotherapy: Von Gebsattel (1954) called for a "partnership with the patient." Von Weizsacker (1956) emphasized mutuality as the "logic of interaction" between psychotherapist and patient; he also called this psychotherapeutic dialectic a "personal intercourse." Wyss (1982), in his anthropological reflections on psychotherapy, insists that the psychotherapist must bring himself as a fellow sufferer into the relationship with the patient.

Zacher (1985) summarizes another indispensable constituent in this therapeutic attitude: The therapist recognizes that he or she also lives in the field of tension of the irresolvable antinomies of human existence. The unfathomable process of life does not stop for any person, nor are its tragedies and mysteries withheld from the expert psychotherapist. Accordingly, the therapist renounces any effort to oversimplify or reduce the problems of life to one-dimensional definitions and solutions. In other words, he or she recognizes the existence of a real relationship between therapist and patient as two human beings encountering each other in the present and does not interpret every interaction as a symptom of transference from childhood.

It is not only specifically phenomenological therapists who recognize this dialogal or dialectic quality in the therapeutic interaction. For example, see Greenson & Wexler, 1969, for a discussion of the "nontransference relationship" in psychoanalytic treatment. Carl Jung (1985) also insisted that, in the interest of enhancing the individuality of the patient, the therapist must in many cases abandon all preconceptions and techniques, in which case "the therapist is no longer the agent of treatment, but a fellow participant in a process of individual development" (p. 8).

Further, in the therapist's eyes, the illness of the patient is not merely a circumscribed pathological process but rather a transformation of the entire self- and world organization of the patient. Jung (1985) has shown that the phenomenon symptom–illness–patient–world is indivisible, or as he puts it: "When the patient comes to us with a neurosis, he does not bring a part but the whole of his psyche and with it that fragment of world on which that psyche depends, and without which it can never be properly understood" (p. 95). The therapist encounters this world of the patient as something new and unfamiliar; he or she learns to perceive its horror and wonder but does not make him- or herself at home in it. Rather, by being present to the patient, the therapist communicates that this world of illness is genuine but is not the only and true world and indeed that it is capable of transformation.

Zacher closes his essay with a passage from Viktor von Weizsacker, which in itself conveys something fundamental about the attitude of the phenomenological psychotherapist: "In order to treat the living, one must partake oneself in life" (cited by Zacher, 1985, p. 159). Thus it is not only concept and theory that form the therapeutic attitude, but, rather, the concept and attitude are reflections of a deeper existential posture of the person of the therapist. Similarly, Jung (1985) held that the therapist not only "has his own method—he is that method . . . the great healing factor in psychotherapy is the doctor's personality" (p. 88). If we could broadly characterize this existential bearing of the therapist as a person, it resembles the "Yes-saying" affirmation of life of Nietzsche's Zarathustra (Nietzsche, 1966). The psychotherapist affirms the broadest range of personal experiencing and living, confronts self-imposed barriers and restrictions, and challenges any surrender or avoidance. In contrast, von Gebsattel (1954) characterized the essence of psychopathology as a "no-saying self-constriction," that is, as the fundamental antithesis of what we are here calling the therapeutic attitude.

Self-Actualization versus Self-Transcendence

Other perspectives on the therapeutic attitude should be delineated as well. Viktor Frankl (1967, pp. 49–61), for instance, has criticized the excessive emphasis on self-actualization and self-expression in humanistic psychotherapy. These concepts, widespread today, emphasize that psychotherapy will assist the patient toward the fulfillment of the greatest number of his or her own latent possibilities (cf., an article by Markus & Nurius, 1986, on "possible selves"). This understanding of psychotherapy already marks substantial progress beyond Freud's initial strictly biological emphasis on the reduction of instinctual tensions. Yet Frankl points out that true psychological health at its upper limits is characterized by a transcendence of self-preoccupation and an orientation toward an objective world of other persons, meanings, and values, which surpass the compass of the individual person. In other words, Frankl challenges the humanistic idea that the "environment is no more than a means to the person's self-actualizing ends" (Maslow, 1954, p. 117) because this idea *devalues* the ultimate meaning of the world.

Frankl's criticism has many dimensions. Erik Erikson (1968) saw the final and highest stage of human development as the challenge to transcend one's individual perspective in the face of death and to affirm the ultimate value of the earth and of being: This is my world, and I am

of it. In a similar vein, Christopher Lasch (1979) has criticized humanistic psychology for reinforcing the prevailing narcissism of our day, pointing out that patriotism and civic virtues demand the individual sometimes sacrifice his or her own existence for the higher value of nation, of humankind, or of an ideal: "Give me liberty or give me death." Traditional religious viewpoints insist that the highest levels of human existence are realized when the individual surrenders to a meaning or value beyond oneself. Both Eastern and Western spirituality emphasize this transcending of the self as a necessary step toward higher development. Transpersonal psychology also finds the ultimate fulfillment of the human being to lie in the transpersonal, supra-human level, where strictly self-oriented needs, goals, and aspirations lose prominence.

On an immediate, practical basis, the process of therapy often involves the therapist's efforts to redirect the patient's debilitating and paralyzing self-focus, because neurosis especially is marked by an inward self-absorption. The neurotic parent, for instance, who agonizes endlessly about living for his or her children, is frequently insensitive to the actual feelings and needs of each child. Life is lived too uniformly from the focus of oneself; too often, the neurotic personalizes the acts of others and the indifferent blows of life as though they were "done to me." In this context, altruism, "going out to others," or a genuine experience of self-transcending love (or genuine religious devotion) mark a step beyond neurosis!

Self-actualization in the sense discussed by Maslow (1962) and Erwin Straus (1982) was never intended to include such neurotic self-absorption. Maslow studied the lives of outstanding or "fully functioning" individuals to illustrate the meaning of self-actualization: "These same people, the strongest egos ever described and the most definitely individual, were also precisely the ones who could be most ego-less, self-transcending, and problem centered" (Maslow, 1962, p. 140). Jung, too, intended individuation and self-actualization in a much broader sense, defining the "self" as a transcendence of the personal ego.

Yet Frankl's critique at least reminds us that the therapist must occasionally challenge the patient to look beyond his or her personal horizon to the well-being of a marital partner, the needs of a child, or the good of a community, when the patient conceives "self-actualization" in too narrowly personal a scope. Otherwise the jargon of self-actualization will only reinforce the narcissism and neuroticism of the day. Too often, the pop psychological slogans of "finding oneself," "doing what feels good," or "taking risks" are enacted at the expense of marriage, vocational commitments, or deepest personal beliefs and values. Already in 1930, in a monograph resting heavily on the concept of "self-actu-alization," Erwin Straus showed the trivialization of experience and personhood when commitments and involvements become transitory and unbinding and when broader cultural values are overthrown in favor of momentary personal urges (cf., Straus, 1982, pp. 33–48; Moss, 1981a).

The Values of the Therapist—Openness, Acceptance, and Hope

Therapeutic technique and therapeutic attitude are inseparable. The Swiss existential analyst, Medard Boss, discusses the implicit wisdom in Freud's *basic rule* of psychoanalytic technique, which requires that the patient be absolutely open and truthful in revealing everything that passes through mind or heart without any exception. In Boss's (1963) opinion, this practical advice aims at "enabling the patient to unveil himself and to unfold into his utmost openness" (p. 2).

The significance of this basic rule will stand out more clearly if we consider the attitude that Boss attempts to evoke in his patients. Boss prescribes an attitude for the psychotherapeutic patient that the philosopher Heidegger (1966) called *Gelassenheit* ("letting be-ness"). This idea of *Gelassenheit* is centuries old. Two German Rhineland mystics of the late thirteenth and the fourteenth centuries, Meister Eckhart and Johannes Tauler, recognized that much of the malaise of the individual arises from the attempt to be something in particular—to force one's fate into a particular mold. The meaning of our destiny always exceeds in scope the efforts of the individual to keep it tight in hand, and such efforts to grasp and contain fate do violence to the spontaneous emergence of our future. Eckhart and Tauler guided the individual toward a deliberate, methodical cultivation of a willful passivity, toward facing the nothingness of one's own narrow intentions and projects, and toward surrendering one's whole life over to the mystery of being. They called this openness to the mystery beyond one's individuality *Gelassenheit* (Moss, 1981b, pp. 344–345).

Boss (1963) believes this same attitude to be beneficial for psychotherapy patients, who frequently suffer from a severe self-narrowing of their openness to the world. Boss conceptualizes much of psychopathology as a loss of "world openness." In attempting to refuse some potential invitation or challenge presented by the world, the patient eventually paralyzes his or her capacity to respond spontaneously. Conversely, in therapy, Boss advises the patient to surrender conventional roles and expectations, and to surrender to unknown experiences that might seem ominous and threatening and that conventional wisdom tells one are better left alone: experiences

involving anxiety, anger, shame, despondency, and despair.

Many authors in existential and psychotherapeutic traditions have emphasized the value of fostering a similar attitude in the individual. Carl Rogers advocated "openness to experience" as a fundamental value of client-centered therapy. Even behavioristically oriented researchers have advocated an attitude of "passive volition" or "letting go" as a means of releasing physical tensions and emotional constriction and allowing one's psychophysical organismic balance to return. Less surprisingly, Gabriel Marcel, the French Christian existentialist, discussed a state of availability or receptiveness (*Disponibilité*) as the pathway to a life no longer empty and meaningless. Marcel was concerned that many existentially influenced authors, especially those guided by Jean Paul Sartre's works, emphasize an openness to anxiety as an authentic aspect of our humanness, yet fail to illuminate the path beyond anxiety. Marcel believed that a true receptivity, which is creative in its fidelity to what life presents, will ultimately transcend anxiety and issue forth into hope (Bollnow, 1984a; Marcel, 1964).

The poet Rilke (1962) also advocated that whatever uncomfortable and strange experience presented itself to one's life ought to be welcomed and nurtured, for these "are the moments when something new has entered into us, something unknown; our feelings grow mute in shy perplexity, everything in us withdraws, a stillness comes, and the new, which no one knows, stands in the midst of it and is silent" (p. 64). In his letters to a young poet, he provides a vivid image to advocate this Zarathustralike embrace of the possible: "For if we think of this existence of the individual as a larger or smaller room, it appears that most people learn to know only a small corner of their room, a place by the window, a strip of floor on which they walk up and down. Thus they have a certain security" (Rilke, 1962, p. 68). Outside this familiar zone of comfort and familiarity lies growth, and the guiding ethos of psychotherapy is to ease the individual's movement beyond this comfort zone.

HELPING ONESELF VERSUS BEING HELPED

The single greatest criteria on which the schools and types of psychotherapies diverge is the dichotomy between: (a) those approaches that in a nondirective fashion assist the patient to search through personal strengths, history, and knowledge for the means to proceed in life and (b) those that teach the patient a framework of skills and principles already designed to solve a particular problem. The first approach enhances the individual's awareness of inner resources, whereas the second provides prefabricated ideas and tools already tested by others. We might choose the examples of nondirective, psychoanalytic psychotherapy and directive, cognitive behavioral therapy as examples of the two extremes. Most experientially oriented psychotherapists identify more with the nondirective, inwardly oriented approach, yet it is too simplistic to conclude that there is no place for directive skills and techniques in the course of experientially oriented psychotherapy.

The Swiss daseinsanalyst, Medard Boss, portrayed the essence of the two extremes utilizing Martin Heidegger's (1962) concepts of "intervening care" and "anticipatory care" as two modes of relating to the patient (Boss, 1963; Moss, 1978). In the first mode, *we act for the other person.* This other person waits passively, ready to accept the help that is offered, or to reject it. The action taken is accomplished by us; the patient stands by submissively. In psychiatry, a pill is dispensed, and the patient waits for its therapeutic effect. Many active and directive therapeutic interventions and many behavioral prescriptions, however powerful and effective they may be, run the risk of robbing the patient as an individual human being of initiative and responsibility.

In anticipatory care, however, we do not intervene for the other. Rather, we anticipate the patient in his or her "ability to be." We call attention to what we see as a possibility emerging for the patient. The work then remains in the patient's hands, not ours. No ready-made solution is bestowed, but, rather, a challenge is presented.

Psychotherapy, at its best, is based on the recognition of the meaning of anticipatory care. The therapist does not influence the patient by definitive maxims or dogmas, nor does the therapist eliminate the patient's sufferings by technical means. The therapist cannot determine the direction or the extent of the changes in the person. The therapist can only assist by confronting resistances or obstacles to change, thus freeing the person for a process of change that, once begun, pursues its own course.

Thus there are dangers of the directive approaches. Already, in 1919, Freud anticipated and accepted that economic and other practical needs would create pressure for directive, short-term, practical interventions on a large scale in public clinics, to treat large numbers of persons in short measure, yet he was concerned that such techniques would force psychotherapists to "alloy the pure gold of analysis with the copper of direct suggestion" (Freud, 1963a, pp. 189–190). Jung too cautioned that "giving advice" plays as small a part in psychotherapy as does surgery in general medicine. Interestingly, Jung was unconcerned about its harm because "it has so little effect" (1985, p. 173).

Yet we might better conceive of therapeutic approaches not in a dichotomy but as distributed on a *continuum:* from those that find the "whole answer" within the patient to those that provide the "whole answer" in technique. In practice, even those schools that cultivate a rich armamentarium of prefabricated solutions to be prescribed for specific problems, such as biofeedback, behavior therapy, and cognitive therapy, can be practiced in such a fashion as to enhance the patient's responsibility and freedom over illness and life.

The biofeedback concept of "self-regulation," for instance, which derives from cybernetics and general systems theory, is often utilized to encourage the patient in biofeedback to accept the responsibility not only to regulate physical tensions and states of emotional arousal but also to become self-directing in the events of life and to become an active participant in his or her own health, well-being, and quality of life (Moss, 1986). Experiencing a small resurgence of success and confidence as he or she learns to control muscle tension, the patient gradually builds a greater sense of confidence and "self-efficacy" in managing relationships, work, and life as well. The attitude of the therapist is decisive here and will determine the difference between a mere mechanical imposition of technique and the therapeutic use of behavioral techniques as tools to facilitate a deeper process of genuine personal change.

THE TEMPORAL STRUCTURE OF THE HUMAN LIFE

From a phenomenological perspective, human life is often compared to a story, with its major and minor characters and themes, its conflicts, with their resolutions and lack of resolution, and its characteristic flavor and atmosphere that set the tone for events that will follow. The reality of the human life is not like the reality of liquids and solids in physics; it is closer to the reality of metaphor and story in literature, rhetoric, and the humanities (cf. Romanyshyn, 1982; Smith, 1987). Or, as Bugental (1985) expressed it, the human universe "is made of stories, not atoms."

The story of psychotherapy intertwines with the story of the person's life. The individual is provoked to seek psychotherapy by some moment of crisis in the course of this life, by a sense of being stuck and not carrying forward the progress of his or her life. Both psychoanalytic and phenomenological authors have shown that psychopathology includes in its fundamental structure a variety of distortions in life's temporal organization and unfolding. Psychoanalytic authors speak of a fixation in development, a "frozen history" (W. Reich), or of a regression to an earlier developmental level. Phenomenologists have spoken of a vital inhibition of becoming, an arrested development (*"vitale Werdenshemmung,"* von Gebsattel, 1954, p. 130), or a flight from self-actualization (Straus, 1982). In the absence of an inviting, future horizon, existence coagulates and flows with the sluggishness and inertness so common in depression (Straus, 1966; Minkowski, 1970). The sociopath, on the other hand, lives in an unending sequence of impulse driven "nows," forgetful of past lessons and unmoved by the future consequences of present actions. Anxiety disorders represent a different distortion of the temporalizing of life; in anxiety, the individual "possibilizes"—orienting him- or herself to the worst possible catastrophic outcome for present events. Experientially oriented psychotherapy takes seriously the individual's sense of stuckness, dread, or being blocked, moves to facilitate the patient's search for a path toward the next developmental level, and seeks to open the individual awareness for the fullness of time.

The temporalizing of each moment transpires within the larger context of the individual's total life cycle. Daniel Levinson, in his research on the course of adult development, introduces many rich and useful concepts: the life course, the "era," and the life structure (Levinson, 1986; Levinson, Darrow, Klein, Levinson, & McKee, 1978). The "life structure" is the overall pattern or design of a person's life at a given time, similar to Binswanger's (1973) "basic forms" or Boss's (1963) "world designs." The central roles or areas of life into which the individual pours time and energy and the key relationships between the individual and the world make up the life structure. Levinson shows that we can evaluate the "satisfactoriness" of an individual's current life structure, assessing both its *viability* for operating in the environment and its *suitability* for the self: "What aspects of the self can be lived out within this structure? What aspects must be neglected or suppressed? What are the benefits and costs of this structure for the self" (Levinson, 1986, pp. 10–11).

The course of life shows recurrent phases of *transition,* alternating between structure building and structure changing, as the individual faces new inner or outer challenges that necessitate a transition in his or her basic approach to life (see Levinson, 1986, for a detailed schema of adult development). Many such changes resemble an organic ripening or unfolding where one pattern or era of life builds smoothly on the previous. Other phases show more the pattern of a crisis with a radical shattering of the person's life. O. F. Bollnow (1987), in his anthropologically oriented investigations of the meaning of the human life crisis, showed that it is inherent to the nature of human life that a person's life miscarries, goes

astray, or is shattered, and, in such moments, the individual is challenged to take hold of life and find the way back to a new beginning. The human life does not merely unfold and ripen in a steady organic fashion. Rather, the individual moves forward through an effortful series of upheavals, reversals, and renewal.

Cummings (1979) writes of the "lost dream" or "lost hope": When psychotherapy can discover and reawaken such a lost dream, it serves as a powerful vehicle for mobilizing personal resources and overcoming such obstacles as addiction, negativism, or apathy. The lives of many persons entering psychotherapy are permeated by a deep and pervasive nostalgia, or sense of lost expectations; life continues its seeming progress but seems empty of its former vigor. Hermann Hesse's (1961) *Journey to the East* is an allegory of this nostalgia, especially in the figure of the aging protagonist, H. H., who begins by reminiscing and attempting to retrieve the essence of a youthful crusade. The protagonist describes at one point the sale of the violin with which he once had made such beautiful music for his companions on the journey. This becomes one of many symbols for the series of compromises he made with the practicalities of life, which led him farther and farther from the vision of his youth. Eventually, he is called before a tribunal for this betrayal of the "journey to the East" and for the "dreadful stupid, narrow, suicidal life which you have led" (Hesse, 1961, p. 109). Yet he is "acquitted" for this universally human loss of vision, something also familiar to each member of the tribunal, and challenged to pick up the thread of this lost dream and carry it forward within the context of his late adult life.

Otto Bollnow (1987), in reflecting on the search for new beginnings in the human life cycle, interpreted Hesse's allegory as an "outward depiction of the return of the human being to his essential origin" (p. 30). It is not an attempt to go back in space or in time but rather to find renewal in the present: "Inward youth is . . . something given first of all as a task. It does not come to him as a gift from the gods, but rather must first be acquired" (1987, p. 42). Taking Hesse's story as an allegory of all spiritual searching, we can see in psychotherapy, too, a search for renewal and inward youth.

One male patient, for example, with a severe and recurrent depression accompanied by repetitive self-doubts, reported to me a deep disillusionment with his life and especially his career as a government accountant. As he related the story of his earlier life, the religious fervor of his youth was evident, as was the emphasis he placed on a life of "service." He had dreamed earlier of various ways of serving others, from forestry to the ministry. This ideal of service was still a dream capable of arousing his energy and enthusiasm, but the sense of being trapped in the comfortable but meaningless security of his current work robbed his life of vitality. With this bright star of service to steer toward, his therapy became a process of *searching* for the way to restore the balance between practical needs and the ideal of service in his life. Let us turn from this consideration of the time structure of the human life to a discussion of the temporal process of psychotherapy.

THE TEMPORAL PROCESS OF PSYCHOTHERAPY IN PHENOMENOLOGICAL PERSPECTIVE

The Opening Phase of Therapy (Or, the Diagnostician versus the "Good Host")

Hilde Bruch (1974) titles her chapter on the opening phase of therapy "When Strangers Meet," and reminds us that the first visit in psychotherapy requires the same amenities of kindness, courtesy, and respect as any first social encounter but with the added dimension that this encounter is *purposeful:* "Something of positive value and constructive usefulness for the patient should come of it" (p. 5). It is in this first visit, and more generally in the opening phase of psychotherapy, that an initial sense of direction, a working alliance between patient and therapist, a sense of realistic mutual expectations, and a hope for renewal through self-discovery are created.

We discussed, previously, the impact of diagnosis on the psychotherapeutic relationship; it can create an unequal relationship of expert diagnostician and pathological specimen. The phenomenological contribution to the opening phase of psychotherapy is an approach that transcends diagnosis and enters into a deep empathic encounter with the patient.

Charles Maes (1972), in his Duquesne University seminars on phenomenological psychotherapy, introduced the useful concept of the "gift." He did so in part to counteract the myth of the "unmotivated patient"— the patient who requests psychotherapy but does not "work" in therapy in the usual energetic and clearly directed fashion. Maes insists that there is no unmotivated patient, that is, each individual is motivated; existence itself is movement. This movement is a gift that the individual patient presents to the therapist. The ethos of the gift demands receptivity and a gracious appreciation for what is given. The art and discipline of being a psychotherapist involves developing the grateful receptivity to hear, accept, and bring into illumination what kind of gift each patient brings to the consultation room.

Contemporary psychiatry has developed a rich understanding of personality structure and personality disorders to describe the "stuckness" of many patients who repeat the same self-defeating patterns in relationships, jobs, and life in general over and over through adult life, and manifest these same patterns in their relationships with frustrated psychotherapists. Unfortunately, the so-called personality disordered patient is especially likely to be labeled as *unmotivated.* The most infamous patient now is probably the patient diagnosed with "borderline" personality, a pattern that brings together many features of other personality disorders along with a lack of consistent personality structure: histrionic appeals for nurturance and attention, dramatic swings in mood, impulsive and often self-destructive behaviors, a sensitivity to abandonment, personal experiences of emptiness and fragmentation, and a chameleonlike disposition to take on the psychological coloration of any new surrounding. This diagnosis may send a team of therapists into tremors of apprehension, as each clinician recalls some classic case of a "borderline" patient appealing for assistance and then rejecting the action taken, pitting one professional against another, or plunging from lucid sanity to seeming psychosis because of a rescheduled appointment. There is a great temptation for the psychotherapist to immediately label such patients in some such stigmatizing fashion and dismiss their "disordered" behavior simply as part of the diagnostic picture—as "to be expected of such a case." Yet humanistic and experiential psychology have shown that the most self-defeating patterns are nevertheless, in some sense, adaptive and purposive, if only we can decipher the proper context toward which the patient directs his/her behavior.

Abraham Maslow originated a pyramid schema displaying the hierarchy of human needs, asserting that all human behavior tends ultimately toward the higher needs of self-actualization, individuation, and becoming-fully-human. However, he also showed that at the lower levels of the pyramid, behavior is dominated by deficiencies and the drive to complete them. The biological need for food to survive is more "prepotent" than the need for safety and security; the latter is more prepotent than the need for love or nurturance; the latter more so than the need for self-esteem; and so on. This scheme shows that whether or not the individual himself perceives this in his or her striving, gratification and resolution of a lower need open consciousness to domination by another higher need. The personality disorders are instances of an individual trapped developmentally in the grips of some lower, basic, deficiency-oriented need: "So far as he is concerned, *the* absolute, ultimate value, synonomous with life itself, is whichever need in the hierarchy he is dominated by during a particular period" (Maslow, 1962, pp. 153–154).

One of my patients, a 34-year-old woman named Ellen, who reported both childhood physical abuse and sexual molestation, was frequently diagnosed as "borderline personality." She spent a total of 18 years in therapy with seven separate therapists repeating the same basic scenario: desperate appeals for her therapist to love, nurture, and tend her unconditionally, to be her sun, moon, and stars, and to withstand every provocation and test she could put that love to. When declarations of suicidal despair and shrieks of helplessness failed to win special after-hours attention, she performed rather childlike and ineffective gestures at suicide and self-mutilation in the therapeutic sessions to display the immensity of her need. (In my first session with her, she attempted to strangle herself with a belt of thin yarn.) When she could not elicit enough "good" nurturing mothering, she blamed her own "evilness"; she then attempted to provoke punitive, "bad" mothering—pushing the therapist to "give me what I deserve." Appeals for attention to reality-based goals of social adjustment or self-actualization fell on deaf ears.

Ellen was living perpetually in the immediate fear of imminent abandonment by the one person she needed most to survive in this world. Harsh confrontation only exacerbated her feelings of abandonment and endangerment; she responded best to a consistent but gentle reinstatement of limits. Unless psychotherapy could encounter her at the level where she was living, it was fruitless. Only after years of empathic affirmation and encouragement for *the person she already was,* did she begin to transcend this blocked need for basic nurturance, and display a willingness for personal rebuilding. In effect, Ellen remained suspended for years in the opening phase of psychotherapy, hungering to engage the therapist in a relationship but never solidifying that bond. (We will discuss later phases of Ellen's treatment later in the chapter.)

Another patient, Lucy, had never experienced basic trust and security; she spent day after day in a vigilant scanning of the environment for potential aggressors and dangers. Session after session, Lucy searched my every utterance and behavior for a sign that I too was a menace. By merely labeling Lucy as a paranoid personality, one would miss the meaning and purposiveness of her behavior and miss Lucy the person in her immediate lived engagement with a menacing world. The contextual meaning of her behavior is to establish a sense of basic security in an existence that has never experienced anything but endangerment.

Anthony Barton (1985), an American phenomenological psychologist, has endeavored to understand the therapeutic attitude in the first phase of therapy concretely, as a disciplined and systematic transformation of everyday modes of being with other persons. Barton points out that, unlike the ordinary citizen, the thera-

pist characteristically "stays with" the person, world, and story of the patient, attentively, interestedly, and with a willingness to bear the problems of the patient. Where others would pull away from the patient, the therapist stays with the patient. At the point where the family member or friend may chide the patient for oddness and peculiarity and convey some variant of "come be normal like me," the therapist, in contrast, finds a way to join with and stay with the patient's individual experience. One's work as therapist begins with this joining and staying, and the therapist continues to be "at work" illuminating the patient's peculiarity, suffering, and personal story.

This persistence in being "at work" is also a fundamental constituent in the therapeutic attitude. The tools of the therapist's work are the therapeutic techniques for joining with the patient; they involve the therapist's "co-participation in creating a common field of discourse, meaning, interaction, and language focused on the patient's life" (Barton, 1985, pp. 2–3). Once these initial moves have taken place and successfully created a "common field of presence with the patient," a second set of moves commence, "in which the therapist alters, transforms, or otherwise intervenes in the unfolding of the suffering life of the patient" (Barton, 1985, p. 5). Barton believes that the greatest contribution of phenomenological psychotherapy is to the "initial moves" of joining and staying with the patient; the rich variety of techniques from the most diverse therapeutic schools can all be successful in the second stage. "As long as the staying-with and joining-with is being done sufficiently and well, any or all of these modalities of intervention will work helpfully in assisting the patient to a life of decreased misery, increased self and other understanding" (Barton, 1985, p. 5).

The Central Phase of Psychotherapy

According to Martin Heidegger (1962), the German phenomenological philosopher, one of the essential characteristics of human existence is that individuals are "thrown" into the world. They always find themselves already immersed in a situation, a history, and a network of relationships not originally chosen. This is the "facticity" or destiny of life that the strongest individual cannot erase. Psychotherapy challenges the individual to take this "thrownness" and make it in some way "my own," to take the facts and particularities and create of them a new life that is uniquely an expression of oneself.

Jean Paul Sartre (1956), on the other hand, emphasizes the freedom and responsibility of each individual for his or her entire existence. Each individual is, in some sense, the creator of his or her own situation. Sartre denies any and all limitations on the freedom of human existence and confronts, as self-deceptions, all efforts to blame others or outside circumstances for one's own discontent or suffering. Neurosis is understood as a hiding away from an awareness of the original choices by which an individual relates him- or herself to the world. The therapist's role then is to enter into a dialogue with the patient, to confront neurotic self-deceptions, and to assist the patient toward a "sense of the choices on which his or her life is based" (Halling & Dearborn Nill, in press).

Many individuals, for example, those suffering with depression, come into psychotherapy keenly aware of their "thrownness"—that some events have happened to them or been done to them but unable to take these events as background for their own responsible actions and decisions toward a new future. Others, such as those involved in histrionic and manic modes of experiencing, enter therapy "living beyond their means," in a self-aggrandizing and extravagant manner, imposing their own design on life, while ignoring the limits of their own physical, mental, and spiritual being.

The psychotherapist practices his or her art in the tension between the attitudes of Heidegger and Sartre, between a form of fatalism and an absolute idealism. On the one hand, the therapist challenges the individual to "make peace" with and appropriate as one's own the particularities of this one and only life cycle. Whether the past includes incest, the war in Vietnam, or a perfectionistic family environment, this is the individual's one and only existence, beginning point, and fund of experience. Simply to appropriate this set of facts and own it as one's personal history is already liberating. There is also a coming to terms with fate and the unchangeable. To quote the final words of Sophocles's *Oedipus at Cononnus*, the patient is challenged to accept and affirm this thrownness: "Cease now and never more lift up these lamentations, for all this is determined."

On the other hand, the psychotherapist also challenges the individual to own his or her life as an eternal product of personal choices and actions, taking responsibility for the consequences of past actions, and responsibly steering a course now toward a future only dimly seen. Like Isak Dinesen's (1961, p. 77) characters in "The Deluge at Norderney," the patient is invited to imagine that one's entire life and world is a creation of one's own imagination and is compelled to ask the question, "Are we pleased with it, proud of it then?" Emotion itself is reinterpreted not merely as a passive reaction to events but as a powerful form of acting upon the world and others, as a form of personal conjuring that colors the atmosphere of one's existence and evokes a selected palette of responses from one's companions. In this Sartrean view, emotion is a form of "magical pseudo-action, a substitute for genuine action in situations which impose

limitations on our freedom" (Halling & Dearborn Nill, in press).

Once the individual has attained a belief that this life is one's own and can become an active and freely directed creation, the individual can begin to regain access to a lost capacity for action. This sets in motion a process in psychotherapy that James Bugental (1985) has called "searching." The therapeutic dialogue at this point seeks new avenues for change, beyond the patient's current awareness. The full story of the patient's life becomes material sifted through in a search for hidden resources and potential. There is no shortcut either, to avoid the sometimes circuitous searching in this phase of personal renewal. We might think of the scene in Rodgers and Hammerstein's *The Sound of Music,* where the Abbess advises the young novice Maria, who is so confused about her own life directions. She advises Maria to "climb every mountain, search high and low, follow every by-way, every path you know. Climb every mountain, ford every stream, follow every rainbow, till you find your dream" (Rodgers & Hammerstein, 1959).

The Termination or Concluding Phase of Psychotherapy

Martin Heidegger (1962) writes that human existence realizes its greatest wholeness or consummation in man's "being toward his own death." It is in this orientation toward the fact of one's own death that the limitations and finitude of one's existence becomes most clear. Sigmund Freud (1963b) expressed himself similarly, with a Latin maxim that *"Si vis vitam, para mortem"*—If you would endure life, then prepare for death (p. 133). The medieval Christian church taught each individual the lesson of *memento mori* (remember death) as a means of placing limited and mortal goals in an eternal perspective.

These philosophical and religious lessons have implications for a confrontation with twentieth-century psychopathology. Neurotic experiencing often includes among its manifestations a loss of time perspective, with a kind of vague floating awareness that one's life is out of balance, that I will act on that problem "someday," when the time seems right. Days turn into years, and one's life slips by with a kind of unreality. The individual's loss of this time sense carries with it a loss of appreciation for the gravity and urgency of one's actions and choices. For example, while in psychotherapy, a 40-year-old divorced mother arranged for her teen-age daughter to stay with a family member for "a couple of weeks" while the mother confronted her alcohol problem, her depression, and a number of self-defeating patterns in her living. Six months later, when confronted about the time that continued to pass with the daughter out of the house, she insisted she needed at least "a couple of months" to set her work, life, and relationships in better order, so she would be free to work on the right conditions for the daughter's return.

Psychotherapy can exaggerate this sense of living outside of time, with its atmosphere of unconditional empathy and acceptance. Many patients lose a sense of how long they have been in psychotherapy, why they requested treatment in the first place, and what they want to accomplish in order to complete the process. One's lack of progress or initiative is ignored with the rationale that one is "in therapy," as though that fact alone will accomplish the desired end. The psychotherapist is equally responsible in this regard, for failing to maintain a clear awareness of direction, the passage of time, and the ultimate end point of therapy.

Psychotherapy has multiple means of reminding the patient of limits and everyday reality, however, because it, too, is temporally structured. Each session has a beginning, a middle, and an end point fixed in advance. Although many have criticized the rigidity of the traditional 50-minute hour, it nevertheless remains true that the fixed time conveys a limit to the patient. The psychotherapist accepts the responsibility to assist the patient toward his/her goals for this fixed time; then the patient must continue with the direction and responsibility of his or her life beyond this time and place. A payment of money is also expected in return for the sessions, and money in our society represents reality and "business." The therapist is not the patient's selfless mother or caretaker but rather a professional exchanging services for money. A patient who seeks to stay on at the close of the session and does not make the agreed-upon payments is revealing something about his or her fundamental attitude toward life and interactions with other persons that is of immediate relevance to the purpose of psychotherapy. The psychotherapist ignores such clues only at great cost to both him or herself and the patient.

The fact that therapy is a temporary assist to life, and is not the process of life itself, must be kept in mind by both therapist and patient from the first session, for example, through a periodic regular review of progress toward goals, time in therapy, and remaining work to be done. The most decisive reminder of the finite scope of therapy involves the setting of a target date for therapy to cease. The advocates of short-term, time-limited psychotherapy argue that the end date should be set in advance of the first session, so that the sense of reality, urgency, and limit is present in the therapeutic relationship from the first moment (Strupp & Binder, 1984). James Mann (1973) expresses profoundly the existential dimensions of the patient's time experience in time-limited psychotherapy:

> Any psychotherapy which is limited in time brings fresh flame to the enduring presence in all persons of the conflict between timelessness, infinite time, immortality, and the omnipotent phantasies of childhood on the one hand, and time, finite time, reality and death on the other hand." (p. 10)

Mann articulates this conflict in psychodynamic terms, as one between child time and adult time within each individual.

The "termination phase" is the stage of therapy when even those patients who have struggled against facing the limitations of their life or the realities of the psychotherapeutic situation are confronted directly with a heavy dose of reality. Patients' dreams and fantasies at this stage often show that the patient equates losing access to the therapist with "losing everything." Dreams of death, disaster, or world collapse are common during the termination phase.

Ellen, a patient I mentioned earlier, reported a series of vivid and disquieting dreams during this termination phase of therapy: Frequently she searched in her dreams for me—the therapist—only to find that my name was changed, or I was somewhere else, and no one would tell her where. In other dreams, she destroyed and dismembered me with violent actions; acts of love and violence alternated, and my face and the faces of several past male therapists kept fading one into another. Only when she accepted and made peace with the scheduled reduction (and eventual termination) of therapeutic sessions did she *begin* to relate to the therapist as an actual person apart from her prescripted melodrama, a melodrama that seemed so monotonous to those around her. Only in this termination phase did she make more visible progress toward the personal transformations sought in therapy; we describe this progress in the following section.

MODALITIES OF THERAPEUTIC INTERVENTION

In the early days of psychoanalysis, Freud called his treatment the "talking cure." Language has held the focal point in much of the debate over psychotherapeutic technique since Freud, yet the full range of therapeutic experiencing also relies on visual imagery and the full range of our sensory modalities, behavioral enactment of situations, and the nonverbal, affective, and personal encounter of therapist and patient.

The Place of Language in the Process of Psychotherapy

Phenomenological philosophy and psychology have deepened our understanding for the place of language in human experiencing. In the phenomenological perspective, the structure of language and reality, especially human reality, are deeply intertwined: "Language is the house of being. In its abode dwells man'' (Heidegger, 1947, p. 49). Similarly, the German philosopher Humboldt showed that our language already contains a specific view of the world (Spranger, 1909). O. F. Bollnow (1980) expressed this in the following way: ''Our whole feeling, volition and thinking have always been channeled, that is guided, by an understanding of the world and of life, indicated for us in advance by the language we speak'' (p. 187). This is true not only at the general level of cultures, with their specific languages, but of *personal languages,* where the language of the patient betrays the structure of a world that discloses no hope, a world with no words for emotion, or a world in which things happen *to* a powerless, passive individual. Bringing a new realm of experience into language or assisting the individual to linguistically define self and world differently thus have a deeply transformative power.

The anthropologist Levy-Bruhl expressed this viewpoint as follows: ''We perform a magical act when words are spoken'' (cited by Bollnow, 1980, p. 188). Bollnow (1980) has shown that naming in itself is a form of appropriation:

> By giving things names we incorporate them into our world, we make things identifiable for ourselves and thereby make them for the first time accessible to ourselves. What the name is, is in the first instance irrelevant—the main thing is that the object has a name of its own. (p. 189)

In this sense, therapeutic speaking is a direct hermeneutics of experience. It is not simply a matter of copying an experience already existing—for example, in the ''unconscious''—but rather of an original and creative articulation of something previously only latent (Bollnow, 1984b). In other words, there is not one true interpretation of the client's experience or behavior, awaiting our accurate discovery. Rather, interpretation and therapy is a constructive process in which the therapist contributes a significant amount of his or her own creativity and ingenuity: in selecting elements from the client's remarks for attention, in selecting how to phrase and rephrase the client's experience, and in choosing a ''proper narrative frame'' (Messer, 1986, p. 1267; Spence, 1984, p. 86).

Barton (1974) illustrated this principle by following the same hypothetical client through dialogues with a Freudian, Jungian, and Rogerian psychotherapist and showing how each therapist, given his or her own theoretical predelictions and personal perspective, assists the client to constitute or construct a unique and different version of self-understanding. Therapists' interpretations are, in this sense, useful fictions of value in assisting the patient toward self-understanding and not objective facts in a scientific discovery process (Meichenbaum & Gilmore, 1984; see also Messer, 1986). From the phenomenological point of view, this makes psycho-

therapeutic dialogue a hermeneutic process because, like the latter-day interpreter of ancient scriptural passages, understanding for the present day can only be arrived at through a constructive recreation that gives form to meaning only latent in the original. Gergen and Davis (1985) have elaborated a comprehensive theory of the person, based on a similar, social constructivist viewpoint.

Messer (1986) has reformulated the therapeutic purpose as follows:

> The therapist from this perspective, must lead clients to a vision of themselves and events that is different from their current view. Narrative truth emerges from the dialogue between therapist and client which provides an organizing influence in the client's life. There are clearly multiple avenues for constructing and interpreting such a narrative.'' (p. 1269)

Cognitive-Behavioral Approaches

In the 1920s and 1930s phenomenological psychiatry pioneered in showing the importance of the patient's unique ''languaging,'' interpretation, and perception of the world, in producing psychiatric disturbance (see Straus, 1982). However, phenomenology is no longer alone in investigating the place of language and cognition in therapeutic experience. Cognitive-behavioral psychotherapy and the social psychological fields of attribution theory and self-efficacy theory have also demonstrated the empirical relevance of the individual's words, names, and attributions. Aaron Beck, Albert Ellis, Fritz Heider, and Albert Bandura are key among the theorists who have made contributions in this area.

Cognitive-behavioral authors have taken the general recognition of the importance of the patient's experiencing and founded upon it an empirically based technology for modifying the patient's modes of experiencing. As a group, the cognitive behaviorists are more interested in efficient techniques for change than in understanding the complexity of human experience. As a result, they frequently reduce the relationships between experience and action, cognition and emotion, or individual and environment to a simplistic cause-and-effect sequence. Nevertheless, the cognitive-behavioral school can teach us much, for example, about the experience of depression.

Ellis (1975), Beck et al. (1979), and Meichenbaum (1977) have shown how automatic negative thoughts, negative self-attributions, and pessimistic interpretations of daily events play a major role in depressive mood and low self-esteem. Aaron Beck describes a ''negative cognitive triad'' in depression, of negative thoughts about oneself, the world, and one's future. He says of his depressed patients:

> They regard *themselves* as deprived, defeated, or diseased, their *worlds* as full of roadblocks to their obtaining

even minimal satisfaction, and *their futures* as devoid of any hope of gratification and promising only pain and frustration. (Hollon & Beck, 1979, p. 154)

In spite of the myriad of ways in which a person might interpret any life event, the depressed individual will repeatedly perceive life in a stereotyped, monotonously dark fashion, assuming that a pebble in the road will block movement for life, that any setback must be his or her own fault, and that any behavior by another is evidence that "once again no one respects or loves me."

Similarly, attribution theory shows that the qualities a person attributes to him- or herself influence that person's own thoughts, feelings, and behaviors, as well as others' reactions toward that person. Attribution of unwanted, negative qualities by others plays a role in the erosion of self-esteem, stigmatization of an individual, and exclusion of him or her from social acceptance, and the onset of depressive, affective experiencing (see Forsterling, 1986, and Heider, 1958, for further details).

The therapeutic remedy, according to both cognitive-behavioral and attribution theories, is not simply to substitute a positive and equally unwarranted attribution of qualities to the individual, but, rather, to retrain the individual to engage in realistic self-attribution. That is, the therapist teaches and models a realistic appraisal of events, realistic appraisal of self, and realistic appraisal of environment. The ultimate goal has been articulated by H.H. Kelly (1971) in the context of his discussion of attribution theory, "The attributor is not simply an attributor, a seeker after knowledge. His latent goal is that of effective management of himself and his environment" (p. 22).

The cognitively oriented social psychologist, Albert Bandura (1982, 1986), has pioneered research on the sense of self-efficacy, which seems to be a critical element in overcoming habitual behaviors and problems. "Self-efficacy" is a person's belief in his or her own ability to cope with a situation. When an individual comes to believe that he or she can do nothing to change a problem, that individual will feel helpless and behave passively. The individual's fear is not merely of the feared situation but also of a personal inadequacy in dealing with it. Even when given constructive suggestions to overcome the problem, such persons will implement the instructions ineffectually, expecting and bringing about their own failure.

Those persons who believe that past failures are due to their own personal defects are most likely to give up or merely "go through the motions" for change. Thus it is absolutely critical how an individual cognitively accounts for his or her failures, especially whether they are attributed to internal or external causes. To quote Bandura: "If people are not convinced of their own efficacy, they rapidly abandon the skills they have been taught when they fail to get quick results or experience some reverses" (Bandura, cited by McLeod, 1986, p. 49).

Bandura, Beck, Ellis, and others are thus developing through psychological research something that existential philosophers and psychiatrists have been exploring since the early decades of our century. Sartre (1956, 1962), the French existential philosopher, emphasizes the human need for a sense of agency, freedom, or choice, in his writings about human existence. To paraphrase the findings of both attribution theory and self-efficacy theory in the service of psychotherapy, we can "empower" or restore hope and confidence to a powerless and helpless patient, by assisting the patient to reappraise negative self-attributions, to experience self-efficacy, and to perceive the world more realistically and openly. Mahoney has succinctly formulated the overall cognitive approach as one of teaching the patient to be a personal scientist: "We should model and teach an intimate empiricism replete with skills' training in problem analysis, hypothesis generation, evaluative experimentation and so on" (Mahoney, 1974, p. 274).

The phenomenologically or experientially oriented therapist typically places a greater emphasis than cognitive psychologists on emotional experiencing, immediate encounter with the patient, and a deeper exploration of the anchoring experiences early in the patient's life history. However, cognitive-behavioral authors have recently placed greater emphasis on the need to give therapeutic attention to emotions independent of cognition and thus made more room in their theory and practice for the irrational dimension of affective experiencing (Rachman, 1980, 1981; Zajonk, 1984). Lazarus (1977) has also emphasized the power of imagery and the realm of the imagination in personal transformation. Finally, the cognitive-behaviorists' introduction of a practical reality-oriented approach to life can be helpful to many patients in experientially oriented psychotherapy.

The Transformative Power of the Linguistic-Visual Self-Image

The deepest task for cognitive transformation is to accomplish a radical transformation of one's experience of "self"—in its full cognitive, affective, and interpersonal dimensions. In order to illustrate the powerful personal impact of the self-image each individual constructs out of words and mental pictures, consider my client, Ellen.

Although Ellen had been variously diagnosed as borderline personality and schizophrenic, she also showed some of the characteristic profile of a multiple personality. Ellen believed that at the core of her personality was "the evil one"—which she named Corrie (for the core).

Ellen saw Corrie as all-powerful and believed that all other aspects of her personality were too weak and powerless to combat Corrie. Ellen attributed most of her self-destructive acting out and fantasies of violence toward herself and others to Corrie, and many of her own constructive goals were stifled when she would announce that "Corrie doesn't like that idea," or "Corrie would punish me if I did that." In the termination phase, when frequency of therapy was reduced gradually from twice a week to every 3 weeks, Ellen reported a dream in which a disembodied set of hands began to slash at her and me with a razor. She admitted to owning an art razor and commented that "someday Corrie will come here with the razor."

This set the stage for one of the most crucial interventions in Ellen's years of therapy; I directly confronted Ellen with the suggestion that "Corrie" was merely an interpretation Ellen was making of her own personality, that, in fact, her anger and rage were not the core of her being, that her own core was not evil and dangerous at all. I suggested to her that we might apply the Biblical guideline "By their fruits ye shall know them" and look at Ellen's own behavior that showed a repeated caring, sympathetic, and gentle attitude toward her son, toward other patients she had come into contact with, and with her mother's physical suffering. I also traced the angry and hateful reactions, which Ellen had exhibited, one after the other as secondary reactions when Ellen felt hurt, betrayed, and endangered by others. In summary, I suggested to her that those feelings and impulses she called Corrie were not her core at all, but merely a secondary reaction, and her own core was one of goodness and tenderness.

Ellen's initial response was to strike out at me with her fists to prove that "Corrie is real," that Corrie is "evil inside me." Yet, as she argued that she was evil, she also burst into tears and held my hand, wanting to believe that her core was not evil and dangerous.

This seemingly simple revision in her image of herself also upset Ellen's entire view of life and reality. Ellen remarked, "It would be a whole different way of looking at everything." In succeeding weeks, this revision in her viewpoint became extremely powerful for Ellen, as she was able to be less fearful of Corrie's retaliation and came to interpret the Corrie aspects of herself not as evil but rather as the reactions of an immature and very frightened child within her, the childlike aspect of herself that needed to be guided and limited rather than exorcised or snuffed out. She also began to refuse to surrender to her other "personifications" (she began to call them by this term and give less credence to their independent reality). Here we have a complex linguistic and visual image that Ellen had constructed of her own personality and we can see its consequences in her behavior and experiencing. Further, the consequences when she began to challenge and revise that image were quite dramatic, ranging from the altered cognitive self-definition, to weight loss and a new more feminine hair style, to increased contact with what she called "normal" people.

Modalities of Experiencing

The work of Milton Erickson (Erickson & Rossi, 1979) has contributed a heightened awareness of the diverse modalities of individual experiencing. Each individual in psychotherapy responds to the therapeutic dialogue in a manner heightened by his or her own preferred sensory and perceptual modalities. It is helpful for the therapist to pick up on clues in the patient's language that show that he or she "gets a feeling" of the problem, "sees the solution," or "hears and understands." These verbal clues show us the client's dominant sensory–perceptual modality, and by couching our response in the same modality, the pathway to empathy is shortened. This same approach can enable the patient to free up latent but blocked veins of experience.

For example, a woman undergoing evaluation for chronic pain had emphasized the factual, objective, and medical nature of her complaints and minimized any accompanying emotional experiencing. Later she mentioned an episode of physical therapy where she was lying down and then unable to get up and walk again because of severe muscle spasms. She remarked matter of factly, "I felt humiliated by the pain." I simply repeated her remark with an emphasis on the word *felt,* and again she remarked, "Yes, I felt defeated by it." Again, I simply mirrored her response but now in the present tense, "You feel defeated by it." At this moment, tears came over her and she said, "Yes and I feel anger, too. I'm angry at myself that I don't know what to do. I feel inadequate, and I'll be going through it over and over the doctor says." At this point, the simple repetition of her own remarks, with an emphasis on the word *feeling* and the present tense, amplified her experience to such an extent that she volunteered an outburst of emotions, related feelings of helplessness at being unable to control her own muscles and limbs, fears of where these spasms might attack her, and how helpless she might be to prevent herself from falling to the floor, falling in the bathtub, or drowning in a swimming pool. Both a deep sense of vulnerability and a profound terror of the spasms emerged in a woman who, up until this point, showed very little emotionality. The therapeutic dialogue here follows the guidelines of a Rogerian client-centered reflection of the patient's feelings. The Ericksonian school shows, however, that feeling is only one modality of experience and that the therapist can respond to various patients with the same kind of amplification of thought, of sensing, of seeing, because this is the client's preferred modality.

It is naive to expect that each therapist's personal favored modalities of experiencing will automatically fit with those of each patient seen in psychotherapy, but a therapist can attune further through body posture, tone of voice, facial expression, and choice of cognitive and sensory vocabulary to accomodate the patient's preferred modes of perceiving. There is already a sensitive, pre-reflective dance taking place between the therapist and patient, and whenever empathy deepens, this dance automatically attunes our experiencing to one another. We can heighten and accelerate this attuning process by deliberately choosing visually oriented remarks with a visualizing client or cognitive remarks with an intellectualizing client. Further, there are moments when we may want to go against the patient's own overinvested modality, challenging a feeling-dominated patient to think, a cognitively dominated patient to feel, and so on.

Behavioral Enactment and Therapeutic Experiencing

It is not only our words and tone of voice that attune us to the client's experiencing. Actual behavioral enactment of a situation lends greater reality and immediacy to the patient's experiencing. Another case example shows how active, directive therapeutic intervention, involving behavioral rehearsal, role play, or psychodrama, can heighten the intensity of experiencing for a client. A 15-year-old girl, Candace, revealed more in a 3-minute role play than in four previous exploratory sessions. Candace, a bright, artistic girl, with a low opinion of herself, complained of being trapped in an unwilling relationship with an older, domineering, lesbian friend, June. She was unable to convey what specific fears blocked her breaking with the friend, other than a fear of being alone. However, when I asked her to become June in a role play, while I, as Candace, declared the relationship at an end, the situation was greatly illuminated. In rapid-fire succession, June threatened suicide if Candace broke off and threatened to tell her parents everything—including sexual activity, secret contact when Candace's parents had forbidden her to see June, and gifts Candace had given June to keep her attention. She also threatened to "come out of the closet" with Candace's friends so no one else would accept Candace either. This burst of dialogue disclosed the full extent of the manipulative, coercive, and exploitative aspects of the older woman's behavior, as well as Candace's own ambivalent attachment and involvement with June.

Further, Candace was empowered by the role play to

a degree neither she nor I anticipated. She reported the following week that she had stood her ground with June, refused to leave school with her, and brushed off June's threats by repeating some of the words I had used when I played Candace.

Interpersonal Encounter

The interpersonal encounter is also ever present in psychotherapy. Frequently, the interaction between therapist and patient reproduces in immediate form, the most crucial, interpersonal, and intrapersonal conflicts in the patient's life. I will illustrate this with another case example, this one from the initial evaluation interview with a 15-year-old girl. Like Ellen, Melissa also splits off (or "dissociates") most of the anger and oppositionalism that she feels onto a personality fragment that she calls "Her." She explained that "sometimes I feel that I have two people in me. I call the other person 'Her.' When I'm upset, 'Her' comes out. I blame 'Her,' and I feel better about me, but I fight with 'Her' and soon she'll be dead."

At this point, the therapist intervened and suggested that "Her" might be an important part of Melissa, and Melissa might want to listen to Her and take seriously those feelings and urges that Her expresses. Melissa's immediate retort was, "I don't like to be angry." The therapist then challenged her more firmly, saying that she was trying to kill a part of herself that might be very important in her life, especially in becoming an adult, strong, independent woman. At this point, the therapist suspected that he was opposing Melissa vehemently enough to arouse some kind of anger or oppositional reaction and inquired whether his remarks were already stirring "Her" up. At this point, Melissa admitted that yes, she could already feel "Her" getting stronger in her throat.

In this fashion, Melissa could already see, in the first session, that the therapeutic interaction would recreate Melissa's battle with "Her" and enable Melissa to deal with "Her" in an immediate, direct fashion. Later in the session, when the therapist solicited specific goals for therapy, she stated that she wanted to learn to deal better with anger and especially to learn how to channel "Her and her feelings" more positively.

We will now turn from the example of Melissa to review the overall picture of experientially oriented psychotherapy.

Conclusion

Experientially oriented psychotherapy has entered the mainstream in American psychology and psychiatry. The present chapter began with a review of the contributions of each school within the broad family of experientially oriented psychotherapies. Next we introduced the basic principles shared by these therapeutic schools, especially their emphasis on "being with" the patient in his or her world of experience, the meaningfulness of all symptomatology, the priority of empathy over diagnosis, and the contextual, hermeneutic approach. We also highlighted the therapeutic attitude of the experientially oriented psychotherapist, which includes the principle of mutuality in the therapeutic partnership with the patient; the dual emphasis on self-actualization and self-transcendence; the therapeutic values of openness, acceptance, and hope; and the priority placed on the patient's helping him- or herself through inner, personal resources.

The human life, in phenomenological perspective, is a story unfolding in time. As such, it is susceptible to arrest, reversal, and stagnation; to upheaval, shattering, and crisis; it presents a challenge to each individual for renewal in each new era of life. It is this problematic course of each personal story that propels the individual human being to become a "patient" and to seek assistance in questioning his or her own existence.

Just as the human life is articulated in time, the course of psychotherapy unfolds in time as well. The initial challenge to the therapist is to join with and stay with the patient's experience, receiving and affirming what each patient presents as a "gift." Next the therapist and patient thread their way together between the twin challenges of accepting one's life and world as they present themselves, in all factual reality, and owning this life and world as the product of one's own choices, beyond all fact or accident. Finally, in the "termination phase," the therapist and patient face the limitations of time and situation so central to both life and psychotherapy. Accepting these limitations gives time in therapy a greater seriousness and compels the creativity of the therapeutic partners.

Psychotherapy—the "talking cure"—unfolds within a world of language and cognition, but the dimensions of embodiment, nonverbal attunement, action, and encounter have equal significance in the process of psychotherapy. We closed the chapter with the examples of Ellen, Candace, and Melissa, which bring together the therapeutic modalities of language, image, and relationship. All self-cognitions and self-images take on their deepest import for us from their most significant relationship contexts. The early child's experience of self is formed in the shadow of the parent–child relationship (Merleau-Ponty, 1964). The therapeutic relationship is the milieu within which the patient can learn to experience both life and self in a more fundamentally positive light. Experientially oriented psychotherapy is thus never a mechanical process of substituting a healthy cognition or behavior for a diseased one. Rather it is, in the deepest sense, a "corrective emotional experience," unfolding within an authentic personal encounter between two fully human individuals. Therapeutic technique lends a practical effectiveness to therapeutic intervention but only when it serves the process of reawakening a human being to the broader horizons of his or her own world and life.

REFERENCES

Bandura, A. (1982). Self efficacy mechanism in human agency. *American Psychologist, 37*(2), 122–147.

Bandura, A. (1986). *Social foundations of thought and action: A social cognitive theory.* Englewood Cliffs, NJ: Prentice-Hall.

Barton, A. (1974). *Three worlds of therapy.* Palo Alto: National Press Books.

Barton, A. (1985). *Basic theory of therapy.* Unpublished manuscript, Duquesne University, Pittsburgh.

Beck, A., Rush, A. J., Shaw, B. F., & Emery, G. (1979). *Cognitive therapy of depression.* New York: Guilford.

Beck, A. T. (1976). *Cognitive therapy and the emotional disorders.* New York: International Universities Press.

Binswanger, L. (1931). Geschehnis und Erlebnis, zur gleichnamigen Schrift von Erwin Straus [Event and experience, concerning a paper of the same name by Erwin Straus]. *Monatschrift für Psychiatrie und Neurologie, 80,* 243–273.

Binswanger, L. (1973). *Grundformen und Erkenntnis menschlichen Daseins* [Basic forms and knowledge of human existence]. Munich/Basel: Ernst Reinhard Verlag.

Bollnow, O. F. (1980). The word as decision—Aspects of linguistic philosophy. *Universitas, 22*(3), 187–193.

Bollnow, O. F. (1984a). Gabriel Marcel's concept of availability. In P. A. Schilpp & L. E. Hahns (Eds.), *The philosophy of Gabriel Marcel. The Library of Living Philosophers* (pp. 177–199). Vol. XVII. Las Salle, IL: Open Court Publishing.

Bollnow, O. F. (1984b). The discovery of language in the philosophy of the present. *Universitas, 26*(1), 21–28.

Bollnow, O. F. (1987). *Crisis and new beginning.* Pittsburgh: Duquesne University Press.

Boss, M. (1949). *Meaning and content of sexual perversions.* New York: Grune & Stratton.

Boss, M. (1963). *Psychoanalysis and Daseinsanalysis.* New York: Basic Books.

Bruch, H. (1974). *Learning psychotherapy.* Cambridge, MA: Harvard University Press.

Bugental, J. (1985, December). *Humanistic psychotherapy.* Address delivered at Evolution of Psychotherapy program sponsored by the Milton Erickson Foundation, Phoenix, Arizona.

Bugental, J. (1987). *The art of the psychotherapist.* New York: Norton.

Cummings, N. A. (1979). Turning bread into stones: Our modern anti-miracle, *American Psychologist, 34,* 1119–1129.

Dinesen, I. (1961). The deluge at Norderney. In *Seven gothic tales* (pp. 1–79). New York: Vintage Books.

Ellis, A. (1975). *A new guide to rational living.* North Hollywood, CA: Wilshire Books.

Erickson, E. (1968). *Identity, youth and crisis.* New York: Norton.

Erickson, M., & Rossi, E. (1979). *Hypnotherapy: An explanatory casebook.* New York: Irvington.

Fisher, C. T., & Fisher, W. F. (1983). Phenomenological-existential psychotherapy. In M. Hersen, A. E. Kazdin, & A. S. Bellack (Eds.), *The clinical psychology handbook* (pp. 489–505). New York: Pergamon.

Forsterling, F. (1986). Attributional conceptions and clinical psychology, *American Psychologist, 41*(3), 275–285.

Frankl, V. E. (1967). *Psychotherapy and existentialism.* New York: Washington Square Press.

Freud, S. (1963a). *Therapy and technique.* New York: Collier.

Freud, S. (1963b). *Character and culture.* New York: Collier.

Friedman, N. (1976). From the experiential in therapy to experiential psychotherapy: A history. *Psychotherapy: Theory, Research and Practice, 13*(3), 236–243.

Fromm-Reichmann, F. (1950). *Principles of intensive psychotherapy.* Chicago: University of Chicago Press.

Gendlin, E. T. (1968). Client centered: The experiential response. In E. F. Hammer (Ed.), *Use of interpretation in treatment* (pp. 208–237). New York: Grune & Stratton.

Gendlin, E. T. (1973). Experiential psychotherapy. In R. Corsini (Ed.), *Current psychotherapies* (pp. 317–352). Itasca, IL: F. E. Peacock.

Gendlin, E. T. (1981). *Focusing.* New York: Bantam.

Gergen, K. J., & Davis, K. E. (1985). *The social construction of the person.* New York: Springer.

Greenson, R. R., & Wexler, M. (1969). The non-transference relationship in the psychoanalytic situation. *International Journal of Psychoanalysis, 50,* 27–39.

Halling, S., & Dearborn Nill, J. D. (in press). Existential-phenomenological psychiatry and psychotherapy. In E. R. Wallace & J. Gach (Eds.), *Handbook of the history of psychiatry.* New Haven: Yale University Press.

Heidegger, M. (1947). *Platons Lehre von der Wahrheit. Mit einem Brief uber den Humanismus.* Bern: Francke Verlag.

Heidegger, M. (1962). *Being and time.* New York: Harper & Row.

Heidegger, M. (1966). *Discourse on thinking.* New York: Harper & Row.

Heider, F. (1958). *The psychology of interpersonal relationships.* New York: Wiley.

Hesse, H. (1961). *The journey to the east.* New York: Farrar, Straus, & Giroux.

Hollon, S. D., & Beck, A. (1979). Cognitive therapy of depression. In S. D. Hollon & P. C. Kendall (Eds.), *Cognitive-behavioral interventions: Theory, research, and procedures* (pp. 153–204). New York: Academic.

Jung, C. G. (1985). *The practice of psychotherapy. Essays on the psychology of the transference and other subjects.* Bollingen Series, Vol. 20. Princeton, NJ: Princeton University Press.

Kelly, H. H. (1971). *Attribution in social interaction.* Morristown, NJ: General Learning Press.

Laing, R. D. (1959). *The divided self.* London: Tavistock.

Laing, R. D., & Esterson, A. (1964). *Sanity, madness, and the family.* London: Tavistock.

Lasch, C. (1979). *The culture of narcissism.* New York: Warner Books.

Lazarus, A. (1977). *In the mind's eye: The power of imagery therapy to give you control over your life.* New York: Rawson Associates Publishers.

Levinson, D. J. (1986). A conception of adult development. *American Psychologist, 41*(1), 3–13.

Levinson, D. J., Darrow, C. N., Klein, E. B., Levinson, M. H., & McKee, B. (1978). *The seasons of a man's life.* New York: Ballantine.

Maes, C. (1972). *Lectures: Introduction to phenomenological psychotherapy.* Duquesne University, Pittsburgh.

Mahoney, M. J. (1974). *Cognitive and behavior modification.* Cambridge, MA: Ballinger.

Mahrer, A. (1983). *Experiential psychotherapy: Basic practices.* New York: Brunner/Mazel.

Mann, J. (1973). *Time limited psychotherapy.* Cambridge, MA: Harvard University Press.

Marcel, G. (1964). *Creative fidelity.* New York: Noonday Press.

Markus, H., & Nurius, P. (1986). Possible selves. *American Psychologist, 41*(9), 954–969.

Maslow, A. H. (1954) *Motivation and personality.* New York: Harper & Row.

Maslow, A. H. (1962). *Toward a psychology of being.* Princeton, NJ: Van Nostrand Co.

May, R. (1977). *The meaning of anxiety.* New York: Norton.

May, R., & Yalom, I. (1984). Existential psychotherapy. In R. Corsini (Ed.), *Current psychotherapies* (pp. 354–391). Itasca, IL: F. E. Peacock Publishers.

May, R., Angel, E., & Ellenberger, H. F. (1958). *Existence.* New York: Basic.

McLeod, B. (1986). Rx for health: A dose of self-confidence. *Psychology Today, 20*(10), 46–50.

Meichenbaum, D. (1977). *Cognitive behavior modification.* New York: Plenum Press.

Meichenbaum, D., & Gilmore, J. B. (1984). The nature of unconscious processes: A cognitive-behavioral perspective. In K. Bowers & D. Meichenbaum (Eds.), *The unconscious reconsidered* (pp. 273–298). New York: Wiley.

Merleau-Ponty, M. (1964). The child's relations with others. In J. M. Edie (Ed.), *The primacy of perception* (pp. 96–155). Evanston, IL: Northwestern University Press.

Messer, S. B. (1986). Behavioral and psychoanalytic perspectives at therapeutic choice points. *American Psychologist, 41*(41), 1261–1272.

Minkowski, E. (1970). *Lived time.* Evanston, IL: Northwestern University Press.

Moss, D. (1978). Medard Boss and Daseinsanalysis. In R. Valle & M. King (Eds.), *Existential phenomenological alternatives for psychotherapy* (pp. 308–323). New York: Oxford University Press.

Moss, D. (1981a). Erwin Straus and the problem of individuality. *Human Studies, 4*(1), 49–65.

Moss, D. (1981b). Transformation of self and world in Johannes Tauler's mysticism. In R. Valle & R. von Eckartsberg (Eds.), *The metaphors of consciousness* (pp. 325–357). New York: Plenum Press.

Moss, D. (1984). Individuality and belonging in the suffering family. *Journal of Phenomenological Psychology, 15*(1), 71–82.

Moss, D. (1986, November). *Action oriented and holistic counseling strategies for gifted.* Paper presented to annual convention of the National Association for Gifted Children, Las Vegas, Nevada.

Moss, D. (in press). Review of K.-E. Buhler and H. Weiss, *Kommunikation and Perspektivitat. Journal of Phenomenological Psychology.*

Nietzsche, F. (1966). *Thus spoke Zarathustra.* New York: Viking Compass.

Perls, F. F., Hefferline, R. F., & Goodman, P. (1951). *Gestalt therapy: Excitement and growth in the human personality.* New York: Delta.

Polster, E., & Polster, M. (1973). *Gestalt therapy integrated.* New York: Vintage Books.

Rachman, S. (1980). Emotional processing. *Behavior Research and Therapy, 18,* 51–60.

Rachman, S. (1981). The primacy of affect. *Behavior Research and Therapy, 19,* 279–290.

Rank, O. (1964). *Truth and reality.* New York: Norton.

Rilke, R. M. (1962). *Letters to a young poet.* New York: M. D. Herter Norton.

Rodgers, R., & Hammerstein, O. (1959). *The sound of music.* A Rodgers and Hammerstein Records, Inc., Production: Columbia Masterworks Recording.

Rogers, C. (1951). *Client centered therapy: Its current practice, implications, and theory.* Boston: Houghton Mifflin.

Rogers, C. (1959). A theory of therapy, personality, and interpersonal relations as developed in a client-centered framework. In S. Koch (Ed.), *Psychology: A study of a science. Formulations of the personal and the social context, Vol. 3* (pp. 184–256). New York: McGraw-Hill.

Romanyshn, R. (1982). *Psychological life.* Austin: University of Texas Press.

Sartre, J. P. (1956). *Being and nothingness.* New York: Philosophical Library.

Sartre, J. P. (1962). *Existential psychoanalysis.* Chicago: Gateway.

Smith, D. (1987, August). *Psychotherapy and narration: Some thoughts of Paul Ricouer.* Paper presented to annual convention of the American Psychological Association, New York City.

Spence, D. P. (1984). Five readers reading. *International Forum for Psychoanalysis, 1,* 85–101.

Spranger, E. (1909). *Wilhelm Humboldt und die Humanitatsidee* [Wilhelm Humboldt and the idea of humanity]. Berlin.

Straus, E. (1966). *Phenomenological psychology.* New York: Basic.

Straus, E. (1982). *Man, time and world: Two contributions to anthropological psychology.* Pittsburgh: Duquesne University Press.

Strupp, H. (1984). Psychotherapy research: Reflections on my career and the state of the art. *Journal of Social and Clinical Psychology, 2*(1), 3–24.

Strupp, H. H., & Binder, J. L. (1984). *Psychotherapy in a new key.* New York: Basic.

van den Berg, J. H. (1972). *A different existence.* Pittsburgh: Duquesne University Press.

van den Berg, J. H. (1980). Phenomenology and psychotherapy. *Journal of Phenomenological Psychotherapy, 11*(2), 21–49.

von Gebsattel, V. E. (1954). *Prolegama einer medizinischer Anthropologie* [Prolegama to a medical anthropology]. Berlin: Springer Verlag.

von Weizsacker, V. (1947). *Falle und Probleme* [Cases and problems]. Stuttgart: Enke Verlag.

von Weizsacker, V. (1956). *Pathosophie* [A philosophy of existence from the standpoint of illness]. Gottingen: Vandenhoeck and Ruprecht Verlag.

Willis, R. J. (1985). The 'life of therapy': An exploration of therapeutic method. *Psychotherapy in Private Practice, 3*(1), 63–70.

Wyss, D. (1973). *The psychoanalytic schools.* New York: Jason Aronson.

Wyss, D. (1982). *Der Kranke als Partner* [The patient as a partner]. Gottingen: Vandenhoeck and Ruprecht Verlag (2 volumes).

Yalom, I. D. (1980). *Existential psychotherapy.* New York: Basic.

Zacher, A. (1985). The attitude of the therapist in anthropologically oriented psychotherapy, against the background of other concepts. In K. E. Buhler & H. Weiss (Eds.), *Kommunikation und Perspektivität: Beitrage zur Anthropologie aus Medizin und Geisteswissenschaften* (pp. 149–159). Wurzburg: Verlag Königshausen und Neumann.

Zajonc, R. B. (1984). On the primacy of affect. *American Psychologist, 39,* 117–123.

V

Explorations of Central Life Issues

The next three chapters are special in that they apply the existential–phenomenological approach to issues that, although central to human life, are largely ignored within mainstream psychology.

In Chapter 13, Jager's evocative reflections on the "transformation of the passions" (i.e., fury, sexuality, pain, sleep, birth, and death) demonstrate how psychoanalysis and phenomenology provide complementary perspectives on the passions as powerful psychological and bodily phenomena. The poetic quality of his writing brings to life both the concrete manifestations and general structures of his subject matter.

Chapter 14 explores the psychology of forgiving another as it portrays the process of moving from feeling deeply hurt and angry in response to the actions of a significant other toward reconciliation and resolution of inner conflict. Further, Rowe and her collaborators describe the "dialogal–phenomenological" research method that they developed in order to do justice to a phenomenon as challenging and paradoxical as forgiveness.

Moncrieff's Chapter 15 also deals with another challenging topic—aesthetic consciousness. Seeing aesthetic consciousness as the ability to enter into a harmonious communion with reality, he discusses methodological concerns, the range and nature of aesthetic awareness, and its implications for personality integration.

13

Transformation of the Passions
Psychoanalytic and Phenomenological Perspectives

Bernd Jager

The passions rarely have been explored as genuine and positive aspects of human reality. Historically, our attitudes toward the passions have been strongly determined by our attitude toward the human body. Generally, the passions were thought of as allied to the body, and, if they were studied at all, it was with the aim of triumphing over weakness or of curing illness. From the point of view of reason and of the soul, the passions quite easily made their appearance as disturbers of the peace or as reminders of a primitive or evil past. It is only in recent times, and concurrent with the philosophical rehabilitation of the body, that the realm of the passions beckons us once again as a promising field for a reflective exploration of the human realm.

It should be understood from the start that, for the purposes of the following discussion, the passions are not defined as they are in contemporary commonsense usage, as simply strong or compelling emotions. Nor do we intend to revert back entirely to the classical conception of passion as a suffering or an agony. For reasons that will become clarified in what follows, I have adopted a classification that identifies six separate manifestations of passion, namely, fury, sexuality, pain, sleep, birth, and death. To this short list we might add, on Freud's recommendation, defecation and sucking as passionate anticipations of a mature and integrated adult sexuality.

Our inquiry begins with a discussion of Descartes's (1961) influential treatise in which *passion* is thought in opposition to *action*. A return to this classical pair in juxtaposition allows us to rethink passion as a related form of passivity and suffering. Such rethinking makes it possible to reexperience the historical connection between passion, pain, and death. Next we turn to Sigmund Freud, the visionary thinker, who did more than anyone before him, or since, to open our intellectual horizons to the world of human passions.

Psychoanalysis poses a particular challenge to phenomenologically oriented psychologists. The task is here to find a manner of approach that will remain faithful to the intentions of Freud, without thereby closing off a possible emerging dialogue with phenomenology. In the main, this means that we must read Freud's description of interacting forces, his energetics, and his description of psychological regions, his topology, as technical metaphors rather than as pseudophysical literal entities. Moreover, we meet in Freud with a humanity quite differently conceived, on the whole, from the one we meet in the brilliant pages of the French philosopher, Maurice Merleau-Ponty, who is here our main guide to the phenomenological tradition.

Freud gives us a mankind *in extremis*, close to the edge of life, near sunset and sunrise, reliving dreams, in

Bernd Jager • New School for Psychoanalysis, Santa Rosa, California 95402-6544.

the grip of neurotic symptoms, ruled by passions.[1] Merleau-Ponty presents us a mankind moving between a world of abstraction and generality, of slackened tension, on the one hand, and a world of specificity and clarity, and of heightened intentionality, on the other. Freud elaborates the distance between the life of dreams and of daily life in terms of the highly complex notion of the unconscious. Merleau-Ponty elaborates that distance in terms of a bodily life that serves as a pivot, transporting us from one realm of our existence to another.[2] In both cases, however, passion constitutes a movement between discontinuous realms that initially refuse the connecting power of intelligence or of work. Passion, so conceived, constitutes the movement between sleep and wakefulness, life and death, sexual excitation and orgasm, irritation and the transports of fury, extreme pain, and collapse into unconsciousness.

The task of this chapter is to juxtapose the two worlds of the psychoanalysis of Freud and the phenomenology of Merleau-Ponty in such a manner that it will become possible to speak phenomenologically about the life of the passions in general and about sexuality in particular. To achieve such a phenomenological approach means to offer a coherent description of sexuality and of passion that is truly *psychological*, which remains faithful through and through to actual experience and does not revert back to natural scientifically conceived forces, causes, or substances. Such a psychology will refuse to base itself on the metaphors of the physical and biological sciences. On the contrary, it will be led to discover its own metaphors as it struggles to express faithfully whatever emerges in the course of its investigations. Such a psychology, freed from the incapacitating grip of alien scientific projects, will be able to get along without natural scientific "principles" or biological "instincts" for

survival. It will be able to dialogue with natural scientific, topological, or economical points of view only after it has made its own independent survey of the field of investigation.[3]

DESCARTES'S APPROACH TO THE PASSIONS

At the beginning of our modern era, Descartes (1961) defines the passions as "agitations of the soul caused by the animal spirits of the body" (p. 122). He makes mention of a general remedy against the passions, consisting in an effort "to separate within ourselves the movement of the blood and the animal spirits to which they are usually joined" (p. 208). He also distinguishes *inner emotions* that are aroused in the soul by the soul itself and the *passions* that emerge from without the soul in the bodily realm and that always depend on some movement of the animal spirits (p. 179). The first article of Descartes's book on the passions gives us a curious glimpse of how people in the seventeenth century used the word *passion*. "To begin with," Descartes (1961) writes, "I observe that whatever takes place or happens anew is generally called by philosophers a passion with regard to the subject to which it happens and an action with regard to what causes it to happen." He continues, "Action and passion are always the same thing. We use two names for the same thing because of the two subjects to which it can be referred" (p. 108). Because Descartes conceives of human reality as consisting of two clearly separate regions of body and soul, or mind, it becomes clear that what are *passions* to the soul are *actions* from the perspective of the body. Passions are the bodily actions that the soul must endure. Passions refer us to passivity, to receptivity, and to enduring.

The Greeks of classical times would speak in a similar vein of a *pathema* as a suffering or a misfortune, that is, as something that befalls one. Descartes's use of "passion" as opposite to "action" is entirely in accordance with Aristotle's (1957) manner of speaking of *pathesis* for passivity in contradistinction to *poiesis* for activity, creation, or productivity.

The Latin *patior* refers us to suffering and subjec-

---

[1]Within the context of this essay, I use the terms *mankind* and *humanity* as synonymous despite the fact that each expression maintains its own distinct accent. *Humanity* refers us to *humus* and thus to *earth;* this term emphasizes the mortal, earthbound character of our existence. *Mankind*, like the German *Mensch*, refers to the Latin *mens* for *mind*, thus emphasizing the distinguishing human traits of planning, reasoning, and understanding.

[2]Merleau-Ponty speaks of the body as a pivot of the world to indicate bodily existence as source of whatever movement or "play" we might be able to observe in the world. For him, it is "the unperceived term in the center of the world toward which all objects turn their face" (1962, p. 82). Bodily existence is not absolutely continuous with the world nor entirely discontinuous. We might say that our bodily being introduces a gap into the world together with the means to cross that gap. Merleau-Ponty's (1962) masterly reinterpretations of the Stratton experiment with inverted lenses and of the Wertheimer experiment with slanted mirrors elaborate this vision in a convincing manner (pp. 244–251).

[3]A very provocative remark in Wittgenstein's *Philosophical Investigations* comes to mind here (paragraph 621, 1967). "What is it that remains," he asks, "after I substract from the fact that I raise my arm the fact that my arm is raised?" Can we reduce the sentence "I move my arm" so that it reads "My arm moves"? Can we adequately describe psychological processes in terms of forces, origins, causes? Does not psychology, in last instance, refer us precisely to what remains after we make the Wittgensteinian subtraction?

tion. Today we still speak of the trial and crucifixion of Jesus as a passion and of its commemoration as a "passion play." The Latin *patientia* points to a lack of spirit, to resignation and dejection. And when we counsel the sick to be *patient* we ask them to suffer without complaining too much, to bear their cross as good patients must. Our words *passivity* and *patience* still carry part of the meaning that in earlier times clung to *passion*.

FREUD'S CONTRIBUTION

Freud's contribution to the understanding of human sexuality can best be appreciated from a perspective that traces his early scientific career. Freud's earliest scientific contributions were in the field of neuroanatomy. He wrote papers on the nervous system of the crayfish and the sea lamprey. For 2 years he worked on the anatomy of the medulla oblongata, and he published his findings in three excellent papers. During a subsequent phase, Freud practiced neurology, and he again published a number of clinical studies in this area. Next, Freud's interests moved away from neuroanatomy and neurology into the wider area of clinical psychiatry. Noteworthy in this phase is his interest in hypnosis. In the summer of 1884, he made a special journey from Vienna to Nancy in France to perfect his techniques of hypnosis under the guidance of Liebault. A number of years later, in 1892, Freud (1950–1952) published an account of a successful treatment of a young mother in which he used hypnosis to overcome her anxiety about, and resistance to, nursing her newborn infant. At about that time, Freud seemed to have wearied of this technique, and he began gradually to modify it to keep pace with his growing insights into the nature of mental illness. In this manner, he slowly developed the technique of free association. He also became intensely interested in the dream life of his patients early on in his career. In the first year of this century, Freud (1938) published his great study on the interpretation of dreams that, to this day, continues to dominate psychological thought on that subject matter.

If we briefly survey the objects of Freud's early scientific interest, we observe a methodic progression from sea lampreys and crayfish to human cadavers, to dying neurological patients, to hypnotized subjects, to free-associating neurotic patients in the process of becoming conscious of their symptoms. Freud's interests thus show a shift, moving from lower animal species to human subjects and from dead anatomical preparations to increasingly alive and spontaneous subjects.

A survey of his methods shows a similar development. We see the early microscopic and anatomical techniques of cutting, fixing, and staining give way to an interest in hypnosis followed in turn by an interest in the method of free association.

It would thus appear that Freud entered upon the study of the human mind and soul by way of the backdoor, as it were. He began his studies with anatomy and physiology, with the practice associated with animal life and human death, and from that starting point he gradually moved in the direction of conscious and unconscious human life. His work never lost touch, however, with this starting point and with the dividing line between life and death. Throughout all the years of subsequent investigations, he remained focused on the limits, on fate, necessity, and death within human life. He remained preoccupied with an humanity of dusk and dawn, close to the dividing line of day and night, life and death, consciousness and unconsciousness. The humanity that unfolds in his writing appears marked therefore by a strange somnambulant quality and as if in the grip of some profound lethargy that would permit no escape into the quickening stream of everyday life. The faces of this humanity appear haunted by dawn and twilight and as if caught within the time between dreaming and awakening to the world of everyday life. The faces draw the reader both inward and backward to confront a strange counterworld that appears to run parallel to and underneath our known daily world of consciousness and life. And Freud himself makes his appearance in the guise of a modern-day Tereisias, the great blind seer who guided Oedipus's self-discovery. We might imagine him seated in the dark behind the couch, out of view of the reclining patient, yet completely alert to the slightest nuance of every spoken or unspoken word. Like Tereisias, he appears attuned to the flutter of a wing of a bird overhead, bearing perhaps a fateful message. He is attuned to minor slips of tongue, small oversights, some innocent figure of speech. Whenever there occurs a slight hesitation, an unusual repetition, a strange turn of phrase, these leave a mark upon his frame of mind that points away from everyday life in the direction of another life or another consciousness.

Freud addresses humanity at the point where, like Oedipus, it already has ceased to be king. He confronts mankind when it no longer rules and surges ahead but is caught up within the grip of a powerful recollection that inexorably pulls backward, downward, and inward. The Freudian and Tereisian word is spoken when the enthusiasm for action is already on the wane, when mankind stands before the ruins of a future that it can neither assume nor comprehend.

The Freudian word, despite the many attempts to the contrary, cannot be inserted into the ongoing stream of daily life. It can speak to us only when a self-evident progress is suddenly interrupted. It does not address itself directly to the world of work, to the adventures of coming to grips with a surrounding world of daily activities. Working and loving, one may hope, will follow in the wake of the psychoanalytic word; they are not directly addressed anywhere in the extensive Freudian opus. Freud does not speak concerning a busy humanity, bent over its tasks in the full light of day and of consciousness. His concern is for a humanity near the dividing line of sleep and wakefulness and of life and death. When, rarely, he seems to be addressing the problems and mysteries of daily activities, he does so only to remind us of the dawn and the dusk, the beginning and the end.

This mankind *in extremis* that forms the subject matter of Freudian anthropology is clearly under the sway of passions. In Freud's vision, we evince the basic human condition most clearly when we are in the grip of pain or ecstasy. From a phenomenological perspective, we can see how pain and ecstasy, understood as passion, move us from the middle and the noon of life toward the edge. Deep feelings and emotions *transport* us from the comfortable middle toward the extremities. Ecstasy leads us beyond our ordinary daily self, and pain will not allow us to reach the comfortable middle. Pain is a force that breaks our stride. Pain darkens the midday brightness, as it breaks the bright shield of our daily activities. In pain, we recoil and double over while withdrawing from the ongoing dialogue with our surroundings. Pain closes our eyes, loosens the grip on our tasks; it turns us around to face a power that draws us inward, downward, backward.

Freud never forgets about pain, nor its shadow, death. The days and nights most deeply engraved upon his youthful mind are those he spent in futile attempts to lighten the immense suffering of his friend and mentor von Fleischl. His attitude toward pain at that time was still that of the physician who wants to cure and overcome pain. For a time, he imagined to have found an answer to the problem of pain and depression through a new wonder drug called cocaine. Only later did Freud gradually come to appreciate the wider dimensions of pain and death as indomitable and necessary forces in life.

A purely descriptive approach can show us the strange affinity that pain, suffering, and passion hold for each other. Passion resembles pain first of all in that it interrupts the steady rhythm of everyday life. It draws away from tasks and projects of ordinary daily activity and directs us instead to the periphery of life and death. A psychology focused on the passionate nature of human life therefore leads us away from the preoccupations of everyday life, with its emphasis on developmental progress and problem solving and shifts our attention instead to the fateful and tragic dimensions of human life. It becomes thus necessary to read Freud's developmental theory in which the oral, the anal, the phallic, and the

genital stages succeed each other, not as a series of steps taken by the child in the mastery of his daily life but as stages in a progressing awareness of the tragic nature of human life. It becomes then possible to read this developmental theory as a series of extraordinary portrayals of human passions.

The first of these portrayals shows us the sucking infant feeding at the mother's breast. Seen through the new perspective offered by Freud, we see the sucking infant hover near the dividing line of sleep and wakefulness while nearly oblivious to the immediate surroundings. The child is drawn inward and away from us by a growing pleasure that unfocuses the eyes and leaves the soft cheeks red and glowing. We see the mouth in the grip of a passionate rhythm, whereas the tiny rose hands lie idle or clutch the mother's clothing. The entire body of the child appears drawn toward the fullness and warmth of the maternal breast. Thus seen, the sucking infant is revealed to be already a swooning lover, hovering in ecstasy near the dividing line of inside and outside, of consciousness and unconsciousness, which, irrevocably summons the dividing line between life and death.

The same face of passion appears in the next phase of development when gradually the elimination of the bowels becomes the central event in the child's life. This phase shows the same movement from an absorbed, open, noontime consciousness to the periphery of life. The child must allow the midday path of progress and involvement to be interrupted by a call from the interior, from the depth and the past. The child must turn away from both toys and companions in order to attend to a growing fullness and uneasiness. This turning in the middle of daily activity is itself already a recognition of another side of life. It shows what is already prefigured in breathing, namely, the eternal rhythmic interplay of coming and going and of limits in the midst of life. The child must allow the breakthrough of a new dimension, the revelation of another side, into the midst of work and play. There must emerge a willingness to leave a task unfinished, to tear oneself loose, to turn around and address a liminal reality that has made its appearance in the midst of playful absorption. The growing sensation in the bowels announces a turnaround; it brings into view another side to daily life that exerts its own claims. The child is required to shift the attention away from the prospects of the game, from what is social and self-evident and engages hand and foot, in order to face another, lonelier horizon. To master the bowel movement means to be able to allow the interruption of one's daily activities and to suspend the clear-eyed, world-involved consciousness and to give in to the depth, the ground, and the past. All passion transports us from the midst of life to the limits of existence, which are also its sources. Within all passion, there is a dawning of the recognition and acceptance of death at the heart of life.

The oral and the anal orientations of the child anticipate in large measure the succeeding spheres of phallic and genital sexuality. And the same face of passion reappears in all of Freud's portrayals of early humanity. We slowly begin to see what binds together the physiognomy of the developmental stages, what constitutes the striking family resemblance in the portrayals of the sucking, the defecating, the masturbating child and its counterpart: the adults in their sexual embrace. All these portrayals show a different aspect of the same face of passion and of pain that dominates all of Freud's writing. This face of passion must be understood in a vivid and penetrating manner if we are to come to a fuller understanding of Freud.

We come to understand the face of passion as a fundamental project of psychoanalytic thought in the same manner that the expressive face—the face of daily life emerging within a dialectic of seeing and being seen—constitutes a fundamental project of Sartre's (1956) and Merleau-Ponty's (1962, 1964) phenomenology. Freud is as obsessed with the face drawn inward and away by suffering or passion as Merleau-Ponty is haunted by the mirror and the self-portrait of the painter, that is, by the glance by which we both find ourselves and yet are alienated from ourselves. For him, a central enigma of human existence is exemplified in the fact that my body simultaneously sees and is seen and that it sees itself seeing (Merleau-Ponty, 1964, p. 162).[4] To begin to understand the relationship between the face of passion and the expressive-reflective face of the self-portrait means, at the same time, to formulate a meeting ground where the disciplines of psychoanalysis and phenomenology can mutually engage and enrich each other.

WORKING AND TALKING: THE DAYTIME WORLD OF EXPRESSIVE EXCHANGES

The phenomenologist lives amidst a world of expressive surfaces, amidst a world of endless references and interconnections. In this world, surfaces already con-

[4]I refer the reader here to the great essay, *The Eye and the Mind* (1964), that was completed shortly before the untimely death of Merleau-Ponty and in which he writes with particular eloquence concerning the act of painting and its significance for our understanding of the human condition. He quotes Cezanne there as saying, "Nature is on the inside. Quality, light, color, depth which are there before us are there only because they awaken an echo in our body and because the body welcomes them" (Merleau-Ponty, 1964, p. 164).

tain the promise of an interior; the frontal aspect of an object refers us to its back and to its sides, and the beginning of a melody already overflows with hints of what is to be its further course and its end. A great painting of a landscape or a seascape already contains intimations of the sound of the surf or of wind blowing through trees or even of the smell of a blooming orchard or of seaweed. Here the green of the fields or the blue of the sky does not stay obediently within its own domain; it does not limit itself to proclaiming color but begins to speak of the feel and the smell of meadows and beaches. *Color* refers here to touch, and touch spins into the outline of a sound or a smell. Every aspect of an object is here intertwined at its roots with all other aspects. The enjoyable, intelligible world is here not a whole formed by additions but forms a genuine gestalt, a dynamic configuration.

In this phenomenological sphere of investigation, the expressive surfaces of objects, or even situations, not only reflect each other but also bear everywhere the imprint of the human face. Everything *seen* speaks here in a subtle manner about the one *who sees*. All substance refers to human embodiment. All movement, distance, and measurements take as their reference a mobile subject who can cover distances, who has a certain reach, and who embodies movement. The height of a mountain refers to the viewer's ability to walk and to climb, the weight of an object to a person's ability to move objects easily or with difficulty.

Implied in what the human glance discovers is also the presence of other human beings. All perception has the fundamental character of intersubjectivity. Already to name an object, or any aspect of an object, invokes the whole of language and thereby calls into presence all those who live within and through that language. To speak of an object in a certain way means to introduce it into a particular human community of a certain era and to insert it into a particular historical movement. To see something as *useful*, as *fitting*, as *absurd*, or *beautiful* means to invoke an entire cultural perspective through which we are able to see it as such.

The phenomenologist investigates a world in which every aspect is potentially awake to all others. Every aspect of an object can be seen to refer to all possible other aspects. All objects or situations can be seen to refer back to humanity as incarnate being. And all individual perceptions can be seen to contain references to a shared world.

How different is this wide-awake world of infinite interchanges and reverberations from the somber inward-turned faces of Freud's analytic patients on the couch! How removed we are here from the inward-turned world of neurotics, from the closed eyes of the suffering and the

dreaming, from the physiognomy of those in pain or ecstasy, from the automatic movements of the sleeping and
the dying, and from the unconsciousness of passionate
lovers. How strange appears from this perspective the
incoherence of fury, the pensive inwardness of defecation, the swoon of orgasm! The world of passion draws us
to the edge of life. It pulls us away from the active center
and from our open expressive interaction with others. In
passion we grope toward each other in anger or in need,
often in blindness and confusion. It is said that love and
anger are blind and that fury can make a target of anything
and that lust, when aroused, often fails to make proper
distinctions. Passion draws us away from the communal
existence of the center and pushes us toward the edge of
life. It draws us toward birth and death, toward the gods
and the demonic, toward the beginning and the end. In the
scarce light of dawn and dusk, removed from customs and
our anchorage in tasks, we wander alone while confused
by shadows or informed by visions.

How different is life near the center, in the full light
of day, shared by others, surrounded by what is intelligible, rooted in language, informed by custom, anchored in
nearly self-evident tasks. It is the upsurge of this world
that fascinates the phenomenologist. The originality of
philosophy consists in allowing the slight distance of
wonder to interrupt this marvel of self-evidence, which is
the world of everyday existence.

It is against the background of this same world of
tasks, of language, and of light that the brooding, inward-
turned world of passion can come to reveal itself fully. It
is possible thus to place the closed-off face of passion
against the background of the lively, mobile faces of people engaged in conversation or in completing tasks together. An expressive face is above all an interface. It
exists within a dynamic interplay of expressive surfaces,
and it always forms part of an active *situation,* of a radiant
circle. Within the encompassed situation, expression is
itself a radiance that rouses what it touches from its sleep
to make it part of a living structure. Expression creates a
structure of active exchange, of giving and taking, of
touching and being touched, of showing and being given
to see. Such intertwining is not merely a blurring of distinctions between one thing and another, between self and
other; it does not derive from some feeling of oceanic
oneness in which identity is lost, but, rather, it is the fruit
of an intense collaboration, of an active structuring. We
might speak here of a generosity and reciprocity in
wakefulness and distinguish it from an intermingling
within sleep or passion. Expressiveness strives in the light
of day; it is attended by an alert consciousness. It courses
freely in an atmosphere of active giving and receiving.
The expressive face offers itself. The face cannot be self-
sufficient; it does not possess itself what it makes avail-

able for others; it remains forever ignorant of exactly how
it looks. The expressive face is a half, of which the one
who observes it forms the other. Between the two halves
lies a shared world.

In Plato's (1963) *Symposium,* Aristophanes half-
jokingly tells of an early mankind in which each individual was made up of the equivalent of two persons (pp.
542–544). These original double creatures had two
heads, two pairs of legs and arms. When these giants
would break into a run, they formed a circle and moved
along with terrific speed in the manner of clowns doing
cartwheels. This self-sufficient and eventually arrogant
race of giants angered the gods, and Zeus decided to cut
them into halves. In this manner mankind, as we know it,
came into being. Aristophanes presents us with a further,
interesting detail. The old two-headed race of giants had
formed a natural unity in which each face looked out in
opposite directions. The human realm, however, comes
into being in a mutual facing that creates a shared and
social world. Apollo was thus called upon to turn the
heads of the severed halves of the giants so that each half
could face the other and see the scars left by Zeus's knife
upon their bodies. Each wounded, severed part could
henceforth face its counterpart, and each could read his
suffering and his longing from the face of the other. The
early self-evident natural unity had been cut through, and
a new social and human unity had thus come into being.

At the beginning of human history stands the knife
that separates a primordial slumbering unity, that cuts the
umbilical cord, and separates mankind from paradise.
Thus is created the wound at the heart of mankind from
which flows language and culture. Language, as the domain of metaphor, carries us (*metaphéroo*) beyond the
abyss created by that separation and rejoins us to a world,
to ourselves, to each other. Language is our re-entering
into communion following our acceptance of an exile
from the absolute. We thus retrace the primordial movement of separation and rejoining whenever we name a
thing or enter into a fruitful relation with others.

To enter the human world of fruitful exchanges always involves the sacrifice of an assent to a primordial
loss of oneness, of omnipotence or complete self-suffi-
ciency. To take our stand within the vivifying circle of
expression means to offer to others what we have forever
lost ourselves. In dialogue, we offer others an exterior of
ourselves, of our bodily being, of our words and actions.
We are forever alienated from this exterior but nevertheless gain some access to it in our relations to others.
Within an expressive exchange, I offer a face that I can
never completely see myself. I display a style and unfold
a history whose exterior remains forever beyond my
reach. And, when I look in the mirror, I find only a faint
outline of what others see. The mirror reveals the wound

made by Zeus and the fall of Adam. It reflects the silver sword of the cherubim standing at the entrance to paradise refusing me passage to a realm where there is no division between outside and inside, mother and child, man and woman, self and other. The mirror reminds me that I never can rejoin that awkward stranger, that alter ego in front of me whose glance I can neither penetrate nor evade (Lacan 1977, pp. 1–7). The mirror, like the face of the other, offers me passage to a human world on condition that I accept the sacrifice of being marked and divided and leave behind me all claims to a paradisic wholeness and completeness. Narcissus would not accept this severance at the root of his being. He would not loose himself in expressiveness, nor would he renounce that eluding other side of his words, his deeds and glances. In refusing expressiveness, in failing to make the sacrifice necessary to enter into language, Narcissus refused the human world opened to him through Echo's beckoning. Instead of entering the vocation of language and making the sacrifice necessary to enter the human world of expression, he chose to dissolve the painful difference between the inside and the outside and to disappear into the life of nature.

Human expression constitutes the dawn of light of the human world. This dawn, which is a play of light between faces in which stands revealed for the first time a surrounding world, can break only there where human faces are both *seeing* and *visible*, both glance and incarnate presence. *To be seen* means to assume the position of an incarnate vulnerable presence that places itself under the glance of the other, whereas *to see* marks us as transcendant or metaphoric beings in the process of overcoming the traumatic abyss that separates us from ourselves, from others, and from our world. The expressive face is curiously a face that both sees and offers itself to be seen. The face of a dead man is visible, but the absence of a glance places it beyond the expressive sphere, and we are confronted by nothing more than a vulnerable carnal presence. On the other hand, expression vanishes equally the moment a human glance hardens into a stare. To be caught up in someone's stare, to be overpowered by it, means also to be reduced to impotence and to be deprived of expression. And this moment of captivation in which we lose expression is also one in which we become deprived of sight. Expression falters and comes to an end whenever either the aspect of seeing or of being seen isolates itself from the other and assumes a position of absolute dominance. An expressive face is therefore always already an active dialogue between seeing and being seen. Such a face sees by virtue of its visibility and can be seen by virtue of its never surrendered capacity to see. It is visible to the extent that it sees, and it sees to the extent that it is visible. Wherever this dialogue is broken, we see the expressive face fall apart into the two abstract possibilities of *rigor mortis* and of *stare,* of flesh and spirit, outside and inside, water and fire, earth and sun. Psychopathology essentially studies the forms of breakdown of the expressive face, the darkening of the light of conversation, the hardening of the glance into the stare, the eclipse of the glance, and the transformation of a face into something merely visible, devoid of the power to see.

TRANSFORMATIONS OF PASSION

The world of expressive interchange, of conversation, of playing and working together is also a world of masks in particular and of expressive surfaces in general. Expression always refers us to a surface so that we are permitted to think of expression as literally a *surfacing* of meaning. The dominant direction of this surfacing of meaning is horizontal. Expression comes to us from afar; it reaches us from across a distance. In contrast, the world of passion darkens the expressive surfaces, closes the horizons while it withdraws from light and distance to inaugurate the depth.

The faces of passion, the withdrawing, swooning face of orgasm, the face contorted by fury or racked by pain, the face of the sleeping and dying cannot be assimilated to the expressive faces and surfaces of the social world of tasks and language. When passion breaks through upon the world of work or in the midst of play or conversation, it causes a discomfort, a feeling of embarrassment. It is as if we are confronted by a chasm that removes us from the netherworld and that refuses to be covered or to be bridged. Passion alters the pleasant flow of conversation and the seamless stream of interconnected tasks that fill our days. Passion suddenly quickens that flow, or interrupts it and thereby announces the coming into being of a radical discontinuity within the light-dominated world of seeing, doing, and understanding. It refuses to be domesticated by the light of reason; it will not passively fit itself to the measure of tasks and the orderly arrangements of daily affairs. The face of passion does not reveal itself to the quiet probing of the detached observer; it turns its back on the expressive face of the inquiring other. It refuses to be drawn into the light of day. Passion inaugurates a reversal within the world of expression; it is the breakthrough of another side to things. Passion emerges from the depth, from the realm beyond the eye and below the light. It shatters the world of reflection and opens upon a world of sound, of reverberation. Its order is not that of tasks or of grammar; it knows little of the order of logic or temporality. Its order is the order of the flesh; its rhythm is that of spasms, of trembling, of shaking, of sobbing.

Passion is the insurrection of the flesh, of the depth, of the anonymous. It reverses the relationship that obtains in the world of expressive interchange, that is, in the world of light. There the surface dominates the depth, speaks for the depth; there the face dominates the body, and the light of the eye rules the flesh. There the face *heads* the body as the surface triumphs over the depth. But in the world of passion, the depth no longer remains mere support for a brilliant surface; it wells up and destroys the charming play of light, the brilliant outer covering of things and beings. The body in the heat of passion loses the finely sculptured features, the elegant gestures of the hand or the delightful reticence of a smile. All surface drowns in the upheaval of the body, in the upwelling of matter, and of flesh. Even language loses here its brilliant outer covering, the finely shaded wording, the witty puns, and clever allusions. The witty meanings and the charming gestures are overrun by the sound of breath and the heartbeat of the body. In passion, language is overcome by the body, gives in to the urgency of the flesh. From the depth, the flesh rises to shatter the world of mirrors overhead.

This strange upheaval affects things as well as beings. At first, it might appear as if each thing had lost its connection with whatever surrounds it, as if it had recoiled from use and meaning into an atmosphere of somber material brooding. The hammer no longer points towards the nail, the chair looks withdrawn from the desk, the curtain undulates absentmindedly in the wind. Objects reveal their materiality, and we enter a world of wood and silk and iron. We feel the texture of our clothing, the grain of wood, the feline seduction of silk. From outside the window comes the dark rustling sound of masses of agitated leaves. Everything unfolds a dark substantiality with which we are secretly linked. Objects abandon their place within a complicated verbal and productive system to reveal instead their flesh, their matter. And we ourselves commune with surrounding things no longer merely by sight, through inspection or deduction, but rather by means of a deeper kinship, through our flesh.

In the world of passion, the body is a vessel, a sounding board through which reverberates the turmoil from the depth and the surrounding. We feel the turmoil of all flesh in our flesh. The sight of bouncing breasts or of swaying hips can spread like a panic through the entire body. In the world of passion, we are communing vessels in which the upheaval collects itself, by which it sounds itself out and slowly acquires definition. All the life here spreads in succeeding waves from the depth and the center. The expressive surfaces are here transformed into the tight skins of drums or the simple blank steel of railroad tracks

to which we might press the ear to hear the rumble of an approaching event.

Passion is always an *upwelling*. The world of passion is structured around the advent of an apocalypse; it awaits the reversal of depth and surface; it anticipates a creative destruction that will sweep away the concealing surfaces to reveal the ground and the flesh of all things and all beings. Those who are angry await the coming of true fury; the dying await the upwelling of the depth and of the ground; those in great pain await the oblivion of unconsciousness; those about to sleep wait for the dark of night to wash over them. And those in the grip of sexual passion await to be overpowered and flooded by the sweet oblivion of orgasm.

Like sleep or anger, orgasmic excitation slowly gains strength as it erupts from its unknown depth to wash over all surfaces. A forceful current takes hold of the limbs, it floods over the skin, it takes possession of the face and removes from it the powers of light and reflection. The eyes grow vacant and turn upward. The mouth becomes drawn, and the muscles are taut. Only after passing through a crisis can the body relax and reawaken to the light. All passions repeat the crisis of our sexual life; all move toward their own moment of culmination and reversal. Sexuality has its orgasm as dying has its death; sleeping has its point of no return as pain has its collapse, or as fury has its transfiguration. All these passionate transformations are both radical and discontinuous. The life of passion demands leaps, discontinuous progress, transformations. If we were to envision the course of passion as a journey across the plains, we would need to imagine the crossing of a broad river. If, on the other hand, we would see it as a journey across mountains, we would need to imagine an abyss, or, if we were to think of a journey down a river, we would have to think of rapids or of narrow straits.

To move from drowsiness to sleep or from sexual excitation to orgasm or from dying to death or from irritation to true fury means to move through a *crisis of passage*. This discontintity in the road, this crisis, is frequently attended by anxiety. The Latin *anqustiae* literally refers to narrow straits, to difficult passages. We can think of orgasm as the passing through narrow straits on the way to the calm of the open sea. To fail to achieve passage through these passionate channels means to be permanently caught between two discontinuous realms.

If we remind ourselves at this point of the foreshadowing of ''passion,'' in the Latin *patior*, for suffering and enduring, we can come to understand passion as a particular aspect of a journey where the determination of will or the foresight of reason no longer can make their contribution. In this manner, passion and suffering would refer us to that aspect of the journey where the channel, whose course we follow, becomes too turbulent and too swift for deliberate and premeditated passage. It is at this point that the good helmsman, after having done all he can, ties himself to the wheel and entrusts himself to the waves to carry him. At the height of passion, the water steers the ship, and we are borne by the elements. In this manner, passion carries us "besides ourselves."

THE RADICAL DISCONTINUITY WITHIN SEXUALITY

As we have seen, the world of passion is a world of radical transformations. We can envision passion as a journey through narrow straits connecting otherwise incommunicable realms. Passion is the enduring of a transformation; it means passing from wakefulness to sleep, from life to death, from intrauterine existence to birth, from irritation to the transports of fury, and from sexual arousal to orgasm.

Passion both provokes and overcomes a crisis; it first introduces and then prevails against a radical discontinuity within human life. It thereby both separates and heals; it invokes death and brings us new life. This theme of separation and discontinuity refers to the essential structure of human passion. We find some reflection on this theme in all but the most superficial of theoretical treatments. Freud's great discovery of his late maturity as a thinker was that of the death instinct, by means of which he proclaimed separation and discontinuity as an inherent aspect of our psychological life. And already in Freud's early concern with the fears of castration is there a recognition of the fact that loss and separation form a real moment and an intimate aspect of our sexuality. Freud may have been partly guided on his way by the original meaning context of the word sexuality, which refers us to what has been cut (*sectum*). Sexuality announces itself both as a loss and as a gain, as new life and as death within life. The world of human sexuality cannot be described without reference to wounding, cleaving, or cutting (*secare*). To be a sexual being means both to be wounded and to be healed; it means to have been separated and to have found a new way to bridge that separation.

Genesis makes reference both to Adam's wounds and to his healing as the first step in his emancipation from a virginal, paradisaical, somnambulant life to a fully human, mortal existence. This wounding of Adam, which is his expulsion from paradise, is repeated in all of mankind in the form of painful separations and distinctions. It is repeated in every human birth in which the somnambulant life of the womb is shattered to make

place for mortal existence. And the same order of expulsion from the womb and from paradise is repeated in the law of incest that demands of us that we leave the safe confines of our exclusive love for the parents in order to open our hearts and minds to a wider human world. To enter upon the road that leads to a deepening of our humanity and of our culture, we are required to part from those we love, and we can persist upon that road only through the acceptance of the pain of separation. To see this clearly, we must come to understand sexuality itself as a form of leave taking from a somnambulant life in the womb of nature, from animal procreation and the life of instinct.

In Genesis, we read that immediately following their expulsion from the Garden, Adam and Eve make love so that Eve becomes pregnant with their firstborn son Cain. And, in a manner that repeats this pattern, Cain comes to impregnate his wife immediately following his fateful expulsion from the land of his father. Human sexual life implies here both the acceptance of a separation—from God, from the parents, from the other sex, from the innocence of childhood, from the natural sphere of unselfconscious animal existence—and then the overcoming of that separation through the creation of new human bonds. Sexual life *severs* us; it inflicts wounds, and we enter that life on pain of death. But it also opens to us, after wounding us, the fertile riches of a fully human existence. Expulsion thus becomes the ground for a new kind of gain, and mutilation opens the door to a new integrity. There still exists in countless non-Western societies an unvarying relationship between ritual cutting and admission to the status of adult manhood or womanhood. The anthropologist van Gennep (1969) cites countless forms of such mutilations that, once healed, become the marks of sexual maturity. He mentions, among others, the cutting of the foreskin of the penis, the pulling of a tooth, the cutting of the little finger above the last joint, the perforation or removal of the ear lobe, the perforation of the hymen, the sectioning of the perineum, the excision of the clitoris, the scarifying or tattooing of the face or of any other part of the body, and the cutting of hair in a particular fashion (van Gennep, 1969, p. 71).

A first concern in the integration of mature sexuality is that of the acceptance of separation. The power of sexuality flows from a cut and a division. The great and nearly universal symbol of sexuality is therefore that of a healed wound. Sexual intimacy becomes possible upon the basis of an *accepted* separation; only those who have accepted the wound can cultivate the healing. Only those who risk disturbing the earth may sow; only those who allow a fence to be built between themselves and others can be neighbors; only those who renounce the immediacy of things in touch and glance may find access to the world through language; only those who withdraw from a comfortable and self-evident unity may think. Mankind is a creation *per via di levare*. After an initial abundance, humanity is wrought by the knife. In the myths of the Greeks, Aphrodite, the great goddess of love, emerged from the blood of the very wound cut by Cronos when he castrated Uranos, the oppressive sky god. At the beginning of human love and at its end stands "the huge sickle with its long jagged teeth" (Hesiod, 1953, p. 58). The love goddess of the Greeks was always closely associated with knives and swords and other instruments of war that could wound or kill. She married Hephaestus, the smith who made the armor of Achilles, and she betrayed him with her love for Ares, the fair god of the sword (Grant, 1962, p. 360).

A FIRST PHENOMENOLOGY OF THE SEXUAL BODY

The ritual cutting and scarring of adolescents at the time of their admission to full manhood and womanhood forms an instance of the ritualization of the discontinuity inherent in all passionate transformations. Passion always moves between points in life that at first cannot be connected by means of industry or willpower, or logic. Passion leads us outside the ordinary daily existence of activity and expression, of tasks and conversation. It moves us beyond this world of *continuity*, of industrious and artful intertwining where death is hidden and passion is kept out of sight, toward a world of *discontinuity* ruled by death and regeneration.

If we turn from our concern for passion in general to the particular passion of sexuality, we might ask how this discontinuity is embodied in the organs of sex.

Sartre (1956) has written "that no fine, prehensible organ provided with striated muscles can be a sex organ, a sex" (p. 397). A muscular organ, such as a hand, with its responsive coordinated movements, overcomes difficulties, solves problems, points, gives signs, interconnects, and unifies. Hands link to other hands and weave and build a world. Hands explore and lose themselves in what they find and do. Those aspects of the body most closely associated with sexual intercourse appear inept and unresponsive and mostly out of place in the world of work. The rise and fall of the penis is not a feat of strength or even of agility or dexterity. Sexual activity is not a making or fashioning; it will not fit into the seamless web of daily tasks. If certain expressions, such as *tool* for *penis* and *making someone* for *sexual intercourse*, persist, it is only because the anxieties inherent in the world of passion make us wish to escape into a world of work.

But neither should we think of sexual organs as sensory organs in the specialized sense of ears or eyes. The sensory organs efface themselves completely in their respective activities. The eye retreats so that there may be a visual landscape; the ear withdraws, and in the wake of this withdrawal appear the melodic configurations and tonal qualities. To see means to subordinate the process of seeing to what is seen; to hear means to make the hearing inaudible. To truly touch is to subordinate feeling to what is touched. Sexual touching institutes a reversal of this schema; it remains remarkably "ignorant" of what it touches; it does not reveal the identity of what is touched. The sexual body refuses the intelligence of discerning or pointing fingers or of industrious hands. Sexual feelings do not retreat so that there may be a sexual landscape, in the way a hand "withdraws" to reveal what it has touched. On the contrary, sexual organs draw attention to themselves and become progressively more "troubled" as intercourse proceeds; they remain a central issue in a forceful world. The eye and ear empty themselves in the visual and auditory landscape, the hand loses itself in its work, but the sexual organs become, as it were, filled with feeling. This filling and gorging sheds a light on the peculiar temporality of the world of passion, in particular when we examine it against the background of the temporality of expression.

The world of passion offers us a *crisis of passing*. In the world of expression, light dances from surface to surface; it passes and reflects; it leaves only a vague outline of an implied past and offers only a schematic understanding of what is to come. Similarly a melody *passes*, each moment appearing against the background of what was heard while anticipating what is still to come. But in the realm of passion, feelings and sensations appear to back up and crowd in on each other, thereby creating a state of excited, vulnerable overfullness. Here we do not approach step-by-step an unfolding future but experience the inexorable coming to term of a past. Orgasm is the gradual unfolding of a fate. It proceeds not by activity through the agile intervention of intelligence or by nimble dexterity, or by virtue of a feat of strength, nor yet entirely passively in the nature of an accident, but rather through the coming to term of an inexorable fateful process. Here, more than in any other region of human life, we are haunted by a past that refuses to connect rhythmically and continuously with a future. The time of passion is discontinuous, and orgasm constitutes a leap. Passionate excitement is, at first, a collecting that suddenly transforms into a spending.

In the realm of passion, bodies becomes turgid; minds fill to the point of obsession; words drown before they can be spoken; gestures are overcome by heaviness. Everywhere we find a gorging and a thickening, a proliferation of a sweet or anxious heaviness. The mobility of this world is paradoxically occasioned by its heaviness. We are not carried here by swift feet or agile hands; we rather drift heavily and drunkenly toward an inexorable crisis. The sweet heaviness of the body finds its clearest expression in the fullness and swelling of the sexual organs. And the temporality of the world of passion is also most evident here. It is only after a long and vulnerable period of filling and stiffening that the crisis is reached, that the *passing* to the other shore can take place with sudden miraculous swiftness.

We observe this same temporal structure in all the passions. We see it when babies with flushed cheeks and after having gorged themselves with milk cross over from a state of hungry wakefulness into a state of satiation and sleep. It occurs, when in anger, after a period of soaking up insults and injustices, a brooding silence suddenly explodes into a violent outburst. And Freud's observations have made us aware how the bowel movement presents us with a similar passionate pattern in which a gradual filling and stiffening leads to an intolerable fullness and heaviness that inexorably leads up to a crisis of passage. The passionate nature of pain becomes equally evident when we understand how we can be burdened by pain to the point where we are carried over into unconsciousness. Pain can fill us to the point of bursting when only fainting can bring relief. The passionate nature of sadism and masochism also becomes evident here. We thus gain awareness of the extraordinary degree to which the different modalities of passion intercommunicate. Among the modern writers, Faulkner (1953, p. 407) has explored with remarkable insight the intercommunication between sexuality and the violence of a lynch mob. And Yukio Mishima (1958, p. 40) gives, in his *Confessions of a Mask,* a remarkable personal account of the felt relationship between the passions of pain and of sex. Clinical practice presents us with numerous incidents where violent argument appears to take the place of sexual intercourse or where it may serve the function of an aphrodisiac. In these cases, the passage from irritation to fury seems to serve as a clear analog for the passage from sexual arousal to orgasm (Brill, 1955, p. 272). In other instances, we see among people with eating disorders a similar substitution from one sphere of passionate transport to another, so that the gorging with food, followed by purging or deep sleep mimicks the arousal and the liberating crisis of the sexual sphere. Freud (1966, Chapter 21) has shown the psychological links that connect the experience of bowel movement, in which a gradually increasing pressure leads via a crisis to release, to the similar temporal cycle of a mature sexual response.

Wherever we look in the world of passion, we find a cycle in which a thickening, a stiffening, a growing full-

ness and mounting pressure gives way when the term is full and the limits are touched. When that point is reached and the shore is approached, the passionate, filled body contracts and collapses in orgasm, in birth giving, in ejaculation, in outbursts of anger, in joy, in defecation, in sleep, and in death.

It is important to note that the protracted phase of absorption, which precedes the passionate response, leaves the body in an oddly exposed self-conscious position. We meet here with the helplessness of passion during its phase of incubation while it collects and absorbs. The body on the way to a passionate crisis is already out of touch with ordinary daily life. It already lacks the responsiveness and agility required in the seamless world of work, and it appears badly coordinated and out of touch with the surrounding world. The passionate body does not belong to the light of day and the world of busy tasks. It can occupy here only an oddly exposed and awkward position. The life of passion requires withdrawal, a veiling, a protective enclave. Consequently we experience passionate situations as private rather than as public affairs. We are constrained therefore from rushing in upon lovers or from intruding upon the privacy of the toilet or from violating the space of those who suffer. We should remind ourselves that public executions were once meant not only to deprive someone of his life but additionally to inflict upon him the humiliation of a public suffering and dying. Within the realm of the passions, we are never far from the sphere of shame with its similar characteristics of awkwardness, stifled speech, constrained movements, and clogged mind. It is the fate of the passionate body and the body in shame to absorb and to allow itself to become a target. It is precisely this vulnerable permeability of the passionate body that renders possible both sexuality and shame. It is only gradually, and with the maturing of sexual relations, that the first awkwardness is overcome and that the fearful undergoing and furtive doing is transformed into a positive offering, into a giving and receiving of hospitality. But the awkwardness, the feeling of shame and reserve about sexual activity, is never entirely lost.

The reticence or guardedness that keeps sexual activity outside the routines and self-evidences of the workaday world doubtless owes something to the fact that the sexual organs link us to suffering and mortality. A feeling of strangeness, even of diabolical or divine power seems to surround the sexual areas of the body. The penis, the breasts, the vagina seldom, if ever, acquire the absolute unself-consciousness or the complete self-evidence of the hand or the shoulder. These organs in some sense stand apart from the rest of the body in the way a period, comma, or exclamation mark stand out from the text. What within the biological sphere makes its appearance as "organs of sex," appears within the psychological sphere (opened by phenomenology and psychoanalysis) as marks of discontinuity that lend coherence to our reading and understanding of the human body. There are a few instances in which the sexual significance of the body is effaced and when the marks of sex no longer punctuate a bodily text but make their appearance instead as functional units in a body machine or as the useless fleshy protuberances of an ailing body or a corpse. This effacement comes to us in painful images of mass graves, or in medical illustrations of disfiguring diseases or perhaps, in observing a psychotic person in a seclusion cell. The fact of seeing people in such circumstances leaves us disoriented and confused. Within the sight of a human body deprived of the privilege of sex, we are wanderers lost in a landscape from which the familiar landmarks have been removed. A human body that no longer upholds the privilege of sex appears scarcely human to us and seems to have reverted back to a state of uncharted and inaccessible nature.

The present context would suggest that this privilege of sex refers us to the fact that the human body is always capable of a passionate passage between incommensurate realms. In this respect, human passion differs fundamentally from animal arousal and release. Within the animal kingdom, passion is a *natural* unfolding within fully commensurate natural realities. But the human body is a *metaphoric* body, and its sexual release is at the same time also a kind of death, an act of aggression, a falling asleep, a breast feeding, and a bowel movement. Moreover, this metaphoric body makes possible the transport between the incommensurate realms of consciousness and unconsciousness, self and other, night and day, word and thing, left and right.

The human body is not merely capable of speech and poetry; in its most immediate appearance, it is already more like a poem than a thing, more like a sentence than a substance. Our expulsion from the Garden, which is also our expulsion from Nature and our entrance into the divided world of human sexuality, transforms the body as a monolithic thing into a metaphoric power. The human body marked by sex and the passage of time is not merely a means to language but is itself already language through and through.

AUTOEROTISM AND THE BODY

Within psychoanalysis, human sexuality makes its first appearance in an original movement that dissociates psychological pleasure from a biological vital function. It makes its appearance there, where a functional sucking is replaced by a purely sensual sucking. The origins of human sexuality are therefore not coextensive with the biological organism. Rather it appears further along the developmental history when the child becomes capable of prolonging the satisfaction of breast feeding by using part of its own body such as the thumb or index finger or even a piece of cloth as a substitute for the maternal breast. The origin of human sexuality is thus tied to the appearance of autoerotism. What at first is simply a pleasurable sensation attending a biological function metamorphoses in the human infant into the various forms of autoerotism that under favorable circumstances become unified under the rubric of adult genital sexuality.

Autoerotism announces itself at first as a pleasurable sensation around the mouth and as a play and interplay between the upper and the lower lips and the hand. The stimulation of this region by means of the fingers transforms the body into a surface where the separate parts, the fingers, tongue, and lips begin to relate to one another and to establish a first internal logic. Merleau-Ponty (1962) has described the human body as a "strange object which uses its own parts as a general system of symbols for the world" (p. 237). It is this strange psychological property that distinguishes the human body from all other objects, and it is, owing to this property, that we can "be at home in that world, understand it, find significance in it" (p. 237).

It is fruitful to come to think of these first delineations and this raising into significance of various bodily zones under the aegis of autoerotism as the creation of a first text in which each configuration comes to stand in a coherent relationship to all others. We can speak of a sentence only when each word in a series bears a recognizable relationship to all the others so that, altogether, they form a meaningful whole. In just the same way, we recognize a painting as a kind of text insofar as every configuration and every hue within its frame maintains a relationship to all the others. If we understand a text as something woven and thus as the meeting and intertwining of many strands—I have reference here to the Latin *textere* for weaving—and as a whole achieving internal coherence through a bringing into a relationship of each part with all the others, we may perhaps think of the Freudian autoerotic body in a similar way as a text being created through the interweaving and inscribing gestures of the hands and the lips. Only such an inscribed, symbolic body opens itself to a fully human world and becomes capable of fully human relationships. But the path leading to his symbolic body must of necessity go by way of autoerotism.

Merleau-Ponty (1964, p. 162ff.) has described the human body as inserting itself into the sensible by virtue of its reflexiveness, that is, by its power to be simultaneously both absent and present, both touchable and capable of touch, both seeing and visible. When I touch my right hand with my left, a kind of current is established that I can reverse, almost at will, thereby making it possible to experience one hand alternatively as the one that touches or as the one that is being touched (Merleau-Ponty, 1962, p. 92). This reflexiveness of the human body already anticipates the difference and underlying unity existing between self and other, between person and thing, between one sex and its opposite (Merleau-Ponty, 1964, p. 168). Between the right hand and the left, between one part of the body and another, there exists a difference, a fertile abyss, a womb from which emerges a world. If the body were a severe and absolute unity, a monolithic power, it could neither reveal itself nor reveal a world.

It is the possible privilege of one aspect of the body over all others that makes possible a reference and a relationship of signification. All signification is, in last instance, based on differentiation. A completely monolithic body in which all parts would be equal to all others and in which no part would thus be able to defer or refer to another would thereby be equally incapable of longing, of preferring one thing over another. It would be capable of neither representation nor intention. Only a differentiated body, in which one part may stand for the whole or where one part may represent another, can open upon a fully human existence.

Freud's insistence on the importance of perversion as a necessary prelude to a fully human sexuality is based on this same understanding of "the human body as a general system of symbols" in which the mouth or the anus may stand in the place of the vagina, where the hands may replace the function of an organ of sex, and where a thumb can serve as a substitute for the maternal breast. The body as a system of references is already an intentional body, capable of longing and condemned to meaning. Within this understanding, the entire world of human sexuality emerges from the interplay between mouth and breast as it is repeated in the coupling of mouth and thumb. This interplay, in turn, is transposed upon bowel movement and anal opening and is repeated in the play between hand and genital, in order to become ultimately transposed upon the mature sexual interaction between penis and vagina.

We may thus think of sexuality as movement between opposing poles of various parts of the same or of different bodies. Within this series, masturbation forms a special exemplary case. Masturbation, literally a disturbance created by the hands, can be understood within this context as a new inscription on the blank page of the body, as the disturbance of a virginal terrain that brings into being a newly differentiated sexual body. We may also think about it as a fertile self-wounding that splits apart the virginal body and the natural world. It creates new polarities, novel tensions, fresh troubles, unknown vulnerabilities, incommunicable delights; it announces the willingness of the self-evident *one* to become a self-contradictory, tension-filled *two*. Masturbation is already assent to living in twofold and forms already a prelude to coupling. This aspect of sexual differentiation does not contradict the aim toward oneness and unification that pervades the entire realm of sexuality. The human sexual realm replaces the coherence and oneness of nature by the coherence and oneness of a text. Moreover, each new erotic unity, each coherent step on the way to a mature differentiated sexuality, can be achieved only on the basis of an accepted separation and an accomplished inscription. Inherent in all human sexuality is this rupture of an unselfconscious, harmonious, and natural whole, accompanied by pain and guilt, followed by the creation of a new and textual unity.

Thus the preamble to heterosexual coitus is the separation of the sexes. The preamble to homosexual coitus is the destruction of the naive and unconditional unity of one sex. The preamble to masturbation is the breaking of the preexisting natural unity of a self-evident body.

The great crisis of sexual awakening at puberty stands under the sign of the knife that cleaves the fertile difference between self and other and that deepens an already existing reflexiveness within the body.

Both masturbation and mirror gazing play with the dual aspects of the body as both a source and a terminus for a seeing and a doing. Both games begin to explore the full reverberating circle of seeing/being seen, and of doing/being done to. We might understand Narcissus of the Greek myth as lost in nostalgia for a lost unity after discovering his image in the water. He wants to overcome the affliction of duality and dreams of an absolute seeing that will not have as its other side a "being seen" and a doing that will not inevitably refer back to a "being done to."

As we have seen before, passionate activity is a doing that maintains the closest of all possible relations to its opposite of suffering and undergoing. In the sexual sphere, we cannot become the subject of an action without immediately becoming also its object. What we do to liberate ourselves ensnares us; what we do to the other immediately shows its other side as it acts back upon ourselves. We might imagine Narcissus as a dreamer of purity and undisturbed unity who seeks beyond the human realm a seeing and doing uncontaminated by carnal duality and reflexiveness. Narcissus mourns the upsurge of a body that is both object and subject and that carries within itself the division of self and other, of left and right, of man and woman. This upsurge of the flesh disturbs the vision of a natural unity in which there is no fatal division between self and other nor between self and image nor between one part of the body and another. As he drowns and merges within his own image, he becomes a being without reflection, a ghost without a shadow. The desire to escape the inherent duality and reflexiveness of the flesh ends in a fatal collapse of the human world. Narcissus dreams of a nameless, sexless, unqualified, and undivided self-belonging while he averts his eye from the Other and from a compromising human world. Narcissus of the myth searches for a lost, nameless, sexless primordial innocence while he gradually drifts away from the circle of humanity into the stillness and self-evidence of nature.

The fantasy of being a flower is perhaps an apt metaphor for becoming completely identified with one's image. The flower does not acknowledge an image, a name, or a sex; it is wholly what it is in its appearance. And Narcissus's tragic companion Echo follows the same path when she bends the sound of her melodious voice away from the expressive circle of human language and merely repeats what is said by the other. She achieves on the level of voice what Narcissus achieves on the level of the image when she becomes a speech without a speaker and an appearance devoid of subjectivity. Eventually, the voice of Echo becomes the unself-conscious sound of nature, of the rustling of leaves, and the music of cascading water. Both Narcissus and Echo lose their access to human subjectivity as they recoil from what is about to mark them. Both revert back to unself-conscious nature at the moment when they were about to discover each other. We may understand the myth of this unhappy couple as referring to the beginning of passion at the moment when human subjectivity first emerges from the folds of nature into a first *subjective* experience of pleasure in the form of autoerotism. At this moment, there appears in sight the fateful crossroad, one of which leads to full subjectivity, whereas the other leads back to a confluence with nature.

At the heart of all passion, understood as a passageway between nature and humanity, we find a core of suffering and longing. We find here always some manifestation of a mourning over the loss of unity and the violation of primordial natural integrity. Passion dreams of virginity, as expression longs for silence. The Roman observation that all creatures are sad after intercourse no doubt refers to this loss of a primordial unity. But this unity is already disturbed in the first hunger pangs that mark the end of a dream of being and having everything. And the first awareness of the growing fullness of the bowels, which in human subjectivity becomes transformed into a "having to go," brings us within the sphere of duty and custom and a nostalgia for a natural state in which we may "let go." And no matter how intense its triumphs or no matter how deep its bliss, sexuality always

remains open to suffering, to a retrogressive longing for a mythical time when there was no need to reach and to risk in order to have available, when allegiances were self-evident, and the body was a virginal whole.

The guilt and shame over sexuality and the intensity of interdictions against sexual acts and feelings reflect their origin in a paradisiacal longing for an absence of distinctions and a final overcoming of all sense of alienation. Sexual intolerance, sexual fears, speak covertly of a desire for a wholeness without seams. Passion makes manifest the seamy side; it shows us the imprint of cutting and healing. Masturbation transforms the virginal, seamless body of the child into a self-contradictory, conflicted, charged, wounded, and problematic body. The rise of sexual desires in a friendship destroys the comfortable feeling of an unself-conscious belonging to each other, of being a brother or a sister to the other. And the onset of sexual maturity in adolescence puts a sudden strain on the unself-conscious unity of the family. Sexual ardor between the sexes creates the battle of the sexes. Wherever it appears, sexual passion appears at first as a power of discord, only subsequently to become a power of reconciliation. It not only opens an abyss within the body, between the sexes, within the sexes, and within the family, but it also throws a bridge across divided parts that makes possible new alliances and unities. If sexuality is, on the one hand, an undergoing and a suffering, a loss of integrity or even a violation, it is, on the other, also a new manner of reaching all that which appeared to have broken away. Sexuality, like language and work, gives back to us in a new way that which was lost to us in our emancipation from nature.

We see thus how human sexual passion is far from being a simple *natural* inclination and that, on the contrary, it constitutes a terrain where we come to accept being marked and divided and where we enter or refuse to enter the truly human realm. To be sexed means most literally to be cut, to become *secta pars*, a piece cut from a whole, a being deprived of an original and natural belonging to a natural whole. To enter the human sexual world, the son must consent to a new distance from his mother; the daughter must take up a less intimate stance in respect to the father. New limits are imposed; new taboos come into existence. Men and women are required to observe a new code in respect to each other that acknowledges the cut and outlines the newly imposed limits. Our entrance into the human sexual world is at the same time an exodus from a natural Garden of Eden. This new code that institutes new limits between parent and child, brother and sister, boy and girl, men and women, one part of the body and another, self and image, is at the same time metaphoric for all limits and thus brings within its train the inevitable separation between the living and the dead, mortals and immortals, the sacred and the profane, paradisiacal and worldly reality.

Our sexual life inevitably bears the imprint of the sacred, understood as that which has been unalterably set apart from profane daily life. The sacred celebrates the most fundamental conception of a limit. Whatever, in our life, touches upon the limits also touches upon the sacred as the paradigmatic realm surrounded by border markers and ruled by law and set apart beyond the reach of convenience and immediate desire. It is for this reason that a progressive naturalization and biologizing of the sexual sphere can ultimately only destroy it as a genuinely human domain.

A thoroughly rationalized, efficiently managed sexuality, a sexuality without guilt, without flashes of terror and of benediction, becomes another consumer goods, another recompense for a day's work at the office. Sexuality as a "wholesome practice," as a mere process of gratification and easing of tensions, no longer can fulfill its ancient role of manifesting the depth and the other side of things and beings. Civil, cosmeticized sexuality, with blunted arrows, neutered, becomes the solid inhabitant of the middle and the noon of life. Cut off from dawn and dusk, from the beginning and the end, and from the pain over limits, it becomes emptied of its humanity. Such a sexuality, removed from guilt and divisiveness, from suffering, from death and the gods, ignorant of height and depth, becomes a harmless "feel good," the itching of a scratch, a sucker in the hand of an idiot. Fertile human sexuality, whatever its form, must live in the awareness of the beginning and the end, of the succession of the generation, of suffering the mark that brings us division while it opens for us a human world.

REFERENCES

Aristotle. (1957). *Metaphysica* (W. Jaeger, Ed.). Oxford: Oxford University Press.

Brill, A. (1955). *Psychoanalytic psychiatry.* New York: Vintage Books.

Descartes, R. (1961). The passions of the soul. In *The essential works of Descartes* (L. Bair, Trans.). New York: Bantam Books.

Faulkner, W. (1953). *Light in August.* New York: Modern Library.

Freud, S. (1938). The interpretation of dreams. In *The basic writings of Sigmund Freud* (A. Brill, Trans.; pp. 553–629). New York: Random House.

Freud, S. (1950–1952). *Collected papers, volume V,* Chapter 3 (A. Bernays, Trans.). New York: Random House.

Freud, S. (1966). *A general introduction to psychoanalysis* (J. Riviere, Trans.). New York: Washington Square Press.

Grant, M. (1962). *Myths of the Greeks and Romans.* New York: World Publishing.

Hesiod. (1953). *Theogony* (R. Lattimore, Trans.). Indianapolis: Bobbs-Merrill.

Lacan, J. (1977). *Ecrits* (A. Sheridan, Trans.). New York: Norton.

Merleau-Ponty, M. (1962). *Phenomenology of perception* (C. Smith, Trans.). New York: Humanities Press.

Merleau-Ponty, M. (1964). In *The primacy of perception* (J. Wild & J. Edie, Eds.; C. Dallery, Trans.), (pp. 159–190). Evanston: Northwestern University Press.

Mishima, Y. (1958). *Confession of a mask* (M. Weatherby, Trans.). Philadelphia: New Directions Publishing Corp.

Plato. (1963). Symposium (M. Joyce, Trans.). In *Plato: The collected dialogues.* (E. Hamilton & H. Cairns, Eds.), (pp. 526–575). Princeton: Princeton University Press.

Sartre, J. P. (1956). *Being and nothingness* (H. Barnes, Trans.). New York: Philosophical Library.

van Gennep, A. (1969). *The rites of passage* (M. Vizedom & G. Caffee, Trans.). Chicago: University of Chicago Press.

Wittgenstein, L. (1967). *Philosophical investigations.* Oxford: Basil Blackwell.

14

The Psychology of Forgiving Another
A Dialogal Research Approach

*Jan O. Rowe, Steen Halling, Emily Davies, Michael Leifer,
Dianne Powers, and Jeanne van Bronkhorst*

INTRODUCTION

This chapter presents a phenomenological analysis of the experience of forgiving another, based on a series of interviews. We start with a discussion of the importance of forgiveness as a topic for psychological study and attempt to account for psychologists' neglect of this topic.

In order to give the reader a complete picture of how an empirical phenomenological study compares to one done in traditional psychology, we have followed the basic format for any social science research: review of the literature and the formulation of the research questions, a discussion of method, and the presentation of the results.

In phenomenological research, the method of inquiry is not preconceived but is determined by the phe-

Jan O. Rowe and Steen Halling are faculty members in the Seattle University Department of Psychology; the remaining authors, Emily Davies, Michael Leifer, Dianne Powers, and Jeanne van Bronkhorst, are graduates of the Master's program in existential–phenomenological therapeutic psychology.

Jan O. Rowe and Steen Halling • Department of Psychology, Seattle University, Seattle, Washington 98122. *Emily Davies* • P.O. Box 671264, Chugiah, Alaska 99567. *Michael Leifer* • Seattle Mental Health Institute, Seattle, Washington 98122. *Dianne Powers* • Highline Evaluation and Treatment Center, Seattle, Washington 98101. *Jeanne van Bronkhorst* • Pierce County Health Department, Tacoma, Washington.

nomenon being investigated (Giorgi, 1970). In approaching the topic of forgiving another, we found that this phenomenon, which is radically interpersonal and brings about transformative openness, could be studied most appropriately using a method characterized by open and ongoing conversation. This conversation or dialogue took place on two levels: among the researchers and between researchers and the phenomenon. In addition, because our method—dialogal phenomenology—involves a significant departure from existing phenomenological methods and has considerable promise, it is discussed in some detail.

THE IMPORTANCE OF FORGIVENESS FOR PSYCHOLOGY

The political philosopher Hannah Arendt (1958) has suggested that forgiveness is one of the two most original ideas in Western civilization. Because forgiveness, as it is commonly understood, serves to change the significance of the deeds of the past, it is evident that it has personal and social as well as clinical implications. On a personal level, Fritz Perls (1969) reminds us that the prerequisite for growing up is that we forgive our parents. Further, it is likely that the failure to forgive, not just our parents but ourselves and other people in our lives, stands in the way of our development as persons who are free of unnecessary restraints from the past and illusions of human perfection (Halling, 1979, p. 193).

Forgiveness is too abstract to study

Clinicians who have raised the issue of forgiveness in therapy typically find that it has powerful connotations for clients. One psychiatrist has asserted that successful therapy entails a reduction of bitterness, resentment, and blame (Hunter, 1978). It has been suggested that forgiving oneself and those who have been hurtful is an integral part of the very movement toward responsibility that therapists seek to promote (Close, 1970). Oddly enough, forgiveness is not mentioned as an explicit issue in the family-therapy literature. We ask, as does Martyn (1977) in her discussion of family conflict, how patterns of blame and abuse from one generation to another are going to be broken except through acceptance and forgiveness? Forgiveness, similarly, is neglected in the psychological literature on interpersonal relations. For example, Heider's (1958) classic study discusses resentment and revenge at length but is silent on forgiveness.

The social implications of the notion of forgiveness have probably been most dramatically demonstrated in this country by the life of Martin Luther King, Jr., and the movement of nonviolent action that he did so much to guide and to sustain. According to King (1963, p. 30), the power of forgiving stems from its ability to awaken the conscience of the oppressor. Whether this is in fact what happens is not a question that can be answered easily, but, clearly, thousands of people who participated in the civil rights movement in the 1960s were inspired by this vision.

For these reasons, forgiveness is a topic that merits psychological study. The present study began with a computer-aided search of the psychological literature since 1970. This search identified less than 30 articles and books where the word *forgiveness* appeared in the abstract; once those studies where forgiveness was just mentioned in a peripheral way were excluded, this number was reduced to about 10. Psychology, apparently, has chosen to treat forgiveness with benign neglect in spite of its extraordinary human importance. We would like to offer some tentative explanations for this neglect.

As Arendt (1958) has indicated, the idea of forgiveness has its origin in a specifically religious context. Perhaps psychologists assume that this issue is well taken care of by theologians, not an unreasonable assumption given how central forgiveness is to the Judeo-Christian tradition. Ironically, the notion of forgiveness seems to be one with which some theologians are not entirely at ease. The eighteenth-century English Bishop Joseph Butler once wrote that "forgiveness is a controversial virtue that is contrary to natural reason" (Trzyna, 1985, p. 7), and this comment is far from atypical. There is a further irony in that some theologians and pastoral counselors (e.g., Williams, 1961) believe that an examination of the experience of forgiveness by psychologists, especially in the context of psychotherapy, would do much to bring theological thinking closer to concrete experience and to enrich its vision.

Another possible reason for the dearth of psychological studies on forgiveness is that psychology, insofar as it has been conceptualized as a natural science, has placed priority on its method, that is, the experimental method. It has then shied away from phenomena that cannot be easily studied by this method (Giorgi, 1970), and a topic as profound and yet as resistant to definition as forgiveness clearly falls into this category. However, there is evidence that psychology is moving away from a primary identification with a natural scientific model and its underlying philosophical stances of rationalism and/or empiricism. Two recent articles in *American Psychologist* that argue for an interpretive or hermeneutical approach to the study of human conduct (Faulconer & Williams, 1985; Packer, 1985) are important examples of this movement. We place ourselves within this hermeneutical tradition.

Because forgiveness is a human phenomenon warranting study by psychologists and yet one requiring an exploration into its meaning and content, we decided to embark on a phenomenological study that would begin looking at how forgiveness is experienced in everyday living. This chapter is an account of our understanding of forgiveness, more specifically, of "forgiving another" who is perceived as having injured oneself within a context of significant relationship with that person. As indicated before, it includes a presentation of the dialogal method of research.

REVIEW OF THE LITERATURE AND THE FORMULATION OF RESEARCH QUESTIONS

Given the limited scope of the literature in psychology identifying forgiveness as a subject of discussion, our review includes studies on related topics such as blame and revenge as well as a few selected theological and philosophical writings. This literature falls into four categories: (a) experimental studies where *forgiveness* is a label for a specific behavior, (b) case studies, mainly psychoanalytic in orientation, (c) theoretical psychological discussions, and (d) theological and philosophical explorations. Literature in the last category is important because forgiveness is an interdisciplinary issue and philosophers and theologians are often basing their interpretations on observations of specific human behavior.

In the experimental category, there were two studies. Both investigations (Gahagan & Tedeschi, 1968;

Tedeschi, Hiester, & Gahagan, 1969) involve a prisoner's dilemma game situation. Within this experimental context, forgiveness is operationally defined as the giving of a cooperative response by a subject after his or her opponent has made a competitive response to a prior cooperative response. Although a simple change in behavior, along this line, may be associated with forgiveness, this phenomenon cannot reasonably be defined so narrowly because the process entails a fundamental shift in attitude. Such a shift cannot be fully explicated from an observer stance because neither the inner meaning of the act of forgiveness nor the significance of the process is directly "visible."

There were three case studies, two of which were written from a psychodynamic perspective. Hunter's (1978) article considers paranoid reactions and forgiveness as two dramatically different responses to psychological injury. He discusses how developmental factors are related to the capacity for forgiveness and describes the stages patients go through insofar as they move from blame and anger toward forgiveness in therapy. Martyn (1977) attempts to integrate psychoanalytic concepts regarding personality structure with theological concepts about forgiveness by considering the situation of an abused child who is in play therapy. Lacking a more comprehensive framework, however, from which to look at these two specialized approaches with their own technical terms, this integration is not accomplished. Close (1970), on the other hand, describes in everyday language the movement toward forgiveness of a young woman who had been sexually abused. Yet it is important to note that case studies often use the situations of a particular client primarily for illustrating a certain theory about forgiveness. Also, the struggle with forgiveness in therapy may take a different form and direction than in everyday life. For example, in therapy, obstacles to forgiveness may be resolved due to the systematic intervention of an attentive and empathetic professional.

The third category, theoretical psychological studies, is a larger one. It includes two studies on revenge (Heider, 1958; Searles, 1956), an analysis of forgiveness in families (Kunz, 1981), a manuscript that integrates the insights of the Essene Code of Conduct (The Khabouris Manuscript) with psychosynthesis (Stauffer, n.d.), Smedes's (1984) book *Forgive and Forget* (an interesting mixture of psychological insights, theological assumptions, and anecdotal material), and an article by Pattison (1965) on the failure to forgive. As the category itself suggests, these studies are not based on a systematic examination of people's experience with forgiveness.

The last category includes the work of some very distinguished thinkers: Scheler's (1973) discussion of repentance, forgiveness, and punishment; Buber's (1957) article on guilt and guilt feelings; the Jewish theologian Soloveitchik's (1984) analysis of repentance; Kolnai's (1968) exploration of the relationship between temporality, freedom, and pardon; and Westphal's (1978) study of guilt and its implications for a theology of forgiveness. Although these writings contain significant insights, they also lack psychological concreteness, and although they often make clarifying distinctions, few of them indicate what forgiveness actually is, as opposed to what it is not. Given the different angles from which they address the topic of forgiveness (and many do so in passing), they do not provide a coherent sense of the phenomenon as a whole.

We would like to consider the content of this body of literature in terms of answers provided to four questions that became central for us as we reflected on our own experience of forgiveness and the discussions of this topic in the literature. First, what is the nature of injury that gives rise to the need for forgiveness? Second, what are initial responses to this event? Third, what enables and motivates one to forgive? Fourth and perhaps most crucial, what is the essential nature of forgiveness?

Although few studies address the questions of the origin of the need for forgiveness, those that do agree that it arises from the perception that one is treated unjustly. The descriptions of what this involves vary from hurt pride (Searles, 1956) and unfair assault (Smedes, 1984) to violation of the basic structure of the relationship (Kunz, 1981). The distinction between "hurt feeling" and direct harm to oneself, for example, physical injury, is not addressed in a clarifying way. There is also the suggestion that the injury includes a violation of a shared or objective notion of order and meaning (Buber, 1957; Heider, 1958). That is, the victim will say or think that the other person acted contrary to some basic principle of justice or fairness. Smedes (1984) is the only author who doubts that an assumption of intentional harm on the part of the violator is necessarily involved.

What, then, are some of the initial responses of victims to the injury? Anger, blame, recrimination, revenge or thoughts of revenge, and helplessness are typically mentioned. Heider (1958) offers a perceptive analysis of revenge as including a concern on the part of the victim that the person who brought about the injury knows why he or she is being punished, so that the wrongdoer realizes that one's welfare or rights cannot be disregarded with impunity. The search for revenge gives us the sense, however precariously, that we need not be helpless in the face of a violation of what is important to us. Searles (1956), a neo-Freudian, analyzes revenge in a way that complements Heider's (1958) approach. He sees vengefulness as a cover for grief or separation anxiety. From this we can see that to move away from seeking revenge is to move toward the recognition of loss and the admission that the action of another has brought about a basic change in one's life.

In extreme cases, disowning of one's own hatred toward the other may lead to persecutory delusions about the person (Hunter, 1978) or to a rigid belief that the violator is totally blameworthy, especially if one insists on one's own absolute innocence (Close, 1970). Anger, in contrast, "is a sign that we are alive and well" (Smedes, 1984, p. 21), as it does not involve the kind of totalizing blame that is implied in hate and revenge. But can one really distinguish so neatly between anger and blame? And how does one account for one person's "getting stuck" in revenge, whereas someone else moves through this attitude on the way toward forgiveness? Again, we are impressed by the need for a systematic investigation of forgiveness.

What are some of the factors that facilitate forgiveness? The realization that each of us has been hurtful in our reactions to other people, thereby giving up the illusion of our own innocence, can contribute to this process of forgiveness (Close, 1970). Arendt (1958) mentions that respect or love toward the other person helps us to see beyond the other merely as wrongdoer, and Kunz (1981) suggests that a history of bonding or love in a relationship provides the basis for moving beyond blame as well as the incentive for seeking to forgive. Although the injury may disrupt a history of trust, such a history in turn may give us the reason to risk trusting again. Insofar as the prior relationship was valued, the desire for reconciliation motivates us to struggle to forgive (Martyn, 1977; Pattison, 1965), although forgiving the other does not guarantee that reconciliation will occur (Kolnai, 1968).

Pattison's (1965) assertion that forgiveness is not a superego phenomenon gives us another clue about forgiveness. It occurs on a different plane than that of ordinary moral and psychological functioning, let alone a narcissistic level of self-preoccupation (Hunter, 1978). Stauffer (n.d.) suggests that, at this level, one is in touch with one's spiritual center or higher self. And Kolnai (1968) writes that:

> Forgiveness expresses that attitude of trust in the world . . . which may be looked upon as the epitome and culmination of morality . . . the demolition of our concern about Certitude and Safety in favor of a boldly, venturesomely aspiring and active pursuit of Value. (p. 223)

In contrast, the psychodynamically oriented thinkers (Hunter, 1978; Martyn, 1977; Pattison, 1965) argue that, to a significant extent, one's developmental history determines the extent to which one is capable of an attitude of trust such as Kolnai (1968) mentions. Obviously, it does not help matters if one's parents were unpredictable in their caring and given to perfectionistic demands. Stauffer (n.d.), however, suggests people can be taught how to move past obstacles that impede forgiveness even though their prior learning has focused on blaming and repudiating.

In Scheler's (1973) view, just punishment may further forgiveness. From the victim's point of view, it is easier to forgive the other when he or she has been punished for the wrongdoing. Further, fair punishment may confront the wrongdoer with his or her responsibility leading to an admission of guilt that facilitates forgiveness and reconciliation (Westphal, 1978). Similarly, if the wrongdoers suffer a serious misfortune, one may be more apt to forgive because there has been a "balancing of acounts," and, by implication, because the other thereby becomes a suffering fellow human (Heider, 1958).

Finally, we want to look at the question of the experience of forgiveness and its implications. There is unanimous agreement in the literature that one's relationship to the past event changes and there is a renewal in one's sense of the future. This does not answer the question, though, of how the past injuries are now remembered. But with this renewal, there is a restoration of the order that previously had been violated (Buber, 1957; Kunz, 1981; Martyn, 1977). For Smedes (1984), forgiveness means reconciliation with the other, but, as we have mentioned, some writers do not agree that this is intrinsic to forgiveness (e.g., Kolnai, 1968). Nonetheless, in this act of "disapproving of [one's] disapproval of the other" (Westphal, 1978), one comes to recognize the humanity of the other person (Kunz, 1981; Pattison, 1965). Whether or not this means that one extends respect or love to the other (Arendt, 1958), it does mean that one is able to wish the other well (Smedes, 1984). Forgiveness is described as a liberating experience (Martyn, 1977) in that it involves an acceptance of self (Smedes, 1984), as well as the other, and frees one from an embeddedness in the past while providing an expanded sense of one's own identity as a human person.

In this review, our intention has been to indicate how a variety of issues pertinent to forgiveness have been considered and to identify some areas that have been neglected. For example, what is the relationship between forgiving and the situation one is in at the time of forgiving? This question, because it locates forgiveness in the context of particular lives, reminds us of a larger issue: the importance of studying how forgiveness occurs in the course of ordinary living. Without such research, the questions that are unanswered remain so, and the answers to other questions are left unconfirmed or contradictory.

Reports of specific experiences provide a basis for integrating and interpreting in a more experiential and existential fashion the sometimes abstract notion of forgiveness articulated in the literature.

METHOD: THE DEVELOPMENT OF A DIALOGAL APPROACH TO FORGIVENESS

The questions that arose from the literature review called for an exploration of how people actually experience forgiveness. In discussing how to carry out such an exploration, it became clear to us that there was a need to collect peoples' stories of their own experience of forgiveness and to study these experiences in a qualitative (i.e., phenomenological) manner.

The phenomenological study involves continual interaction between the researcher and the object of study: It is a dynamic process requiring the rigor of an ongoing reflection upon the data. To this end, the method is guided by an attitude of openness to the phenomenon as it presents itself and to one's own interaction with it rather than by a series of preconceived steps and ideas (Giorgi, 1970). Consequently, as discussed in Polkinghorne's Chapter 3 in this volume, the actual direction of a phenomenological study will differ from other studies precisely because the researchers are affected by what they study, and different phenomena call for different procedures. The dialogal method is a clear example of that which is unique to phenomenological research: One cannot separate the phenomenon from the method. The phenomenon provides a ground for the research and impacts and influences the researchers as they interact with the topic.

This study began with two givens: We were going to study forgiveness and carry out this task in a genuinely collaborative manner. The second given is particularly worth noting because it is one of the distinctive features of our research method.

One of the first steps in the development of any project is arriving at a clear formulation of its direction. Our initial concept of forgiveness, as an entity in itself, created problems. Not until we looked at forgiveness in terms of the hurt to oneself in a personal relationship did a specific direction emerge. With this focus, the question, "Can you tell us about the time during an important relationship when something happened such that forgiving the other became an issue for you?", emerged as a point of departure for the interviews. The question was phrased in such a way as to not only gather descriptions of the completed process but, also, to allow interviews with those who were in the midst of the process.

As each aspect of hurt and/or movement toward healing became articulated in the interviews, it led us to explore how that particular movement was made possible. As we were exploring *how* people are healed and *how* they bring or fail to bring resolutions and reconciliation to their lives, we found ourselves moving toward a collective understanding of the nature of forgiveness. This process was done against the backdrop of sharing our own experiences with forgiveness, questioning our own biases, reading the literature, and discussing data from interviews and written descriptions. Our inquiry brought about a beginning understanding of "forgiving another" that in turn focused further inquiry. Gradually, it became apparent that the process of our work had been grounded in our continuous dialogue with each other.

Because dialogue was at the core of our process as a group of researchers, we call our method *dialogal*. As well, we are indebted to the tradition of dialogal phenomenology, especially as it is articulated in Strasser's (1969) text. This dialogue was the basis for every step of our research: making decisions about procedures, sharing tasks, and interpreting the data. The process was never linear but rather spiraling, resulting in a more and more refined and clarified interpretation. Although difficult to capture on paper, a major turning point in our work illustrates how continuous and subtle this process is. After we had read and discussed the literature, shared our own descriptions of forgiveness, and completed and discussed the interviews, we were confronted with doing the "real analysis." Suddenly we realized that we had already done much of the analysis, that is, we had been analyzing from the beginning—in dialogue. We only had to continue returning to the data to check and expand our interpretation.

In this respect, the dialogal method differs significantly from other phenomenological methods in its process, although not in its aim. Unlike studies such as those of van Kaam (1969), Giorgi (1975), and Fischer and Wertz (1979), faithfulness to the data is fostered through open dialogue among the researchers in relationship to the data rather than through adherence to a set of explicitly spelled-out procedures.

The nature of the dialogue can be described quite specifically because it has been investigated in a systematic fashion. Leifer (1986) studied the work of our group, as well as another research group at Seattle University that followed a dialogal format. On the basis of audiorecordings of the group meetings and interviews with all of the individual researchers and inspired by Gadamer's (1975, 1976) hermeneutical perspective, Leifer (1986) suggested that the context in which research happens is constituted by three levels of dialogue: (1) preliminary, (2) transitional, and (3) fundamental.

Preliminary dialogue refers to a discussion based on

individual opinions about the phenomenon. Although this discussion has a distinct and abstract "feel," it does allow for the beginning of sharing perspectives and identifying biases and prejudgments. If the researchers are responsive to the research questions in the sense of addressing and sharing their own experiences with the phenomenon, they are drawn into the transitional dialogue. This brings the phenomenon into the group, and the members enter into the experience in a more actual or direct way that often leads to a newer, more immediate understanding of the issue in question. At this point, the identifying of common themes begins. The last level of dialogue, fundamental, arises when there is a discussion of not only personal accounts of the phenomenon but others' descriptions as well. During fundamental dialogue, there is a building on previous themes and an interweaving of these themes as they are further illuminated by the data. It is out of this dialogue that a collective understanding emerges.

Although each level of dialogue may be more apparent during a particular stage of the research (e.g., preliminary dialogue is more evident as the group begins its research), all three may be in evidence in any group discussion. It is clear, however, that only when the researchers return to the data in an attitude of openness does fundamental dialogue occur, and this kind of exploration is at the core of the dialogal method (Leifer, 1986).

For us, this dialogal method had many advantages relating both to the quality of our experience doing the research and to the quality of our interpretation. In terms of the former, we were surprised by how relatively painless the process had been. The sharing of tasks took place within a group that was emotionally supportive and respectful of individual differences and talents in the context of being committed to the project. For example, those members who were more skilled at staying focused on the practicalities of the task gave specific direction when needed; at other times, those who were more process-oriented rose to provide support and encouragement. Both seemed to be needed to proceed productively.

In a similar vein, the members' outside commitments were considered. For example, when someone needed to invest less energy in the project, this was honored. As a result of this cooperative effort, we were never "stuck" for any length of time, the level of energy and excitement remained high, no one felt unduly burdened, and we were able to move through the process more quickly than if this had been an individual endeavor. In a very real sense, the project seemed to have a life of its own and was a support for us rather than a chore.

In terms of the interpretation, working as a group allowed for a continual process of articulating, questioning, and checking of individual biases. Thus, through this "collaborative inquiry" (Torbert, 1977) the effect of in-

dividual biases on the interpretation was minimized. In addition, through dialogue, the interpretation of the phenomenon of forgiving another is enlarged. In our case, it is clear that the interpretation is not simply the aggregate of the six people's ideas. The understanding and the direction that emerged out of the individual perspectives, although obviously dependent on these individual perspectives, is not merely additive—like a tapestry, the interweaving of perspectives led to a richer and fuller picture than six individual threads.

Most strikingly, the dialogue was not merely between ourselves "about" the data but more a dialogue "with" the phenomenon. This was clearly evidenced when, well into the research, we realized our experience of forgiveness had not only been articulated further but that we had been personally moved by the phenomenon itself. For example, several members found themselves forgiving a long-standing hurt. This raises the question whether phenomena, such as hate, which involve conflict and dissension, could so readily be studied using a dialogal approach.

Even though, as mentioned previously, this project never unfolded in a strictly linear way, the sequence of steps that was taken can be outlined. We began by sharing our own thoughts and reflections about forgiveness. This allowed us to begin articulating our assumptions about the phenomenon. We further deepened our understanding by writing and sharing a description of a personal experience with forgiveness. In addition, the literature on the topic was divided among the researchers, and each person wrote summaries of the books and articles read. These summaries were shared and discussed within the group. The experiential base of the project was then enlarged by informally interviewing friends and colleagues concerning their ideas about and experiences of forgiveness. Subsequent to these steps, we felt ready to develop the interview question and begin the formal interviewing process. As we also felt the need to get to know each other better because we knew we would be working very closely together, we arranged an all-day retreat.

The retreat served two functions: (a) developing group trust and cohesion and (b) outlining the next steps of our work. We developed the interview question, decided to interview people from a variety of backgrounds and contexts of forgiveness, and agreed on the specific interviewing process: Interviews would be audiotaped and transcribed, at least one follow-up interview would be conducted, and each person in the group would be involved in interviewing people. We discussed the process of interviewing as well as our own concerns and questions. This discussion continued for the duration of the interviewing.

While interviewing the research contributors, we also read other qualitative and phenomenological studies to get a "feel" for various ways of analyzing descriptive data. The next step involved playing our taped interviews for each other and discussing issues of interviewing (e.g., how does one interview a person who gives extremely verbose and/or tangential answers?). As a way of looking more closely at the data, we decided that we would each write a narrative summary of the same transcript and compare notes.

When we met together to share our narratives, we found that most of the group had had real difficulties with the assignment. As we discussed these problems, several important questions related to analysis became evident: How do I move from what is said to what is meant? What if I overlook or do not deem important some aspect of the person's experience that is central for him or her? How do I deal with my own strong emotional reactions to the transcripts? These concerns had made most members of the group reticent to begin interpreting the contributor's experience on the basis of one transcript. We discovered, however, through sharing and discussing our hesitancy and concerns, that we could use the group for feedback and to "keep us honest," and we could always return to the data to check our analysis. In fact, many of our concerns dissolved as we voiced them, and we felt a new freedom in writing our narratives.

We then decided to divide into groups of two and continue summarizing the transcripts, attempting to move toward a more interpretive presentation for each interview. The purpose of forming the dyads was to have the person who conducted the interview work with another member of the research team. Thereby, there were two distinct perspectives on the interview. Once the summary had been written, the entire research group read and discussed it, looking for themes that were specific to the particular description. The discussion also included questioning members of the dyad who had written the summary.

Having identified themes, we began to compare the narratives to find the common themes. Slowly a tentative structure of "forgiving another" became evident. As we began writing and critiquing rough drafts of our interpretation, this structure became more detailed. This process of critiquing involved continually returning to the narratives and transcripts, the literature, and our own experience to refine, revise, and expand our interpretation in the context of dialogue with each other.

THE EXPERIENCE OF FORGIVING ANOTHER

We now turn to our interpretation of the experience of forgiving another, identifying the qualities and stages of the process of responding to harm and coping with

injury.[1] From the descriptions collected, it was evident that forgiveness is a process that begins when one perceives oneself as harmed by another and ends in a psychological, if not face-to-face, reconciliation with the one who was perceived as hurtful. In this context, two dimensions of forgiving another were evident. First, it is a process that is most immediately experienced as interpersonal; it occurs within the context of a specific event and/or relationship involving another who has deeply affected one in a hurtful way. Second, the experience of forgiving another also has qualities that transcend one's relationship with that person and open one up to oneself and the world in new ways. The specific nature of these qualities, which only become apparent toward the end of the process, led us to describe the experience as being spiritual or transpersonal as well as interpersonal.

The need for forgiveness arises when someone has acted in such a way as to bring about a fundamental disruption to the wholeness or integrity of one's life. Initially, on a deep, almost organic level, there is the tearing of the fabric of one's life, one's world. The injury that involves forgiving is one that violates a person's identity. As Fischer (1970) states, "[I]dentity is grounded in the unfolding of [one's] relationships, in the projects and plans to which [one] has assigned [oneself]" (p. 125). With the feeling of injury, this unfolding is abruptly terminated, however temporarily. The future, as it was anticipated before the event, is irrevocably changed; a particular future is experienced as lost altogether, destroyed. As one person said: "We bought some mountain property together where we once planned to build and run a retreat center. But now the vision is dead."

A more general future, one "beyond the injury," is simply not there for oneself as a possibility, except insofar as particularly engaging activities or situations take one away, momentarily, from the recollection of the hurtful event. When one does remember the hurt, the pain and the loss of future are reexperienced. Thus the injurious event and/or the relationship with the injuring person are somehow central or pivotal to the network of one's identity in such a way that the disruption impinges upon one's "only world," one's "only meaningful identity," (Fischer, 1970, p. 124) as perceived at that time.

In the face of the realization of the hurt, this disruption is profoundly felt. One feels uprooted, "off center." Upon hearing from a friend that a lover had been unfaithful, one woman stated: "As [she] talked my throat became dry and constricted. It was suddenly extremely cold in my apartment and I began to shiver. I was stunned and was unaware of how to react." Relationships to the

---

[1]Like our method, the stages involved in forgiveness are not linear; certain experiences, however, seem to be more evident and dominant at certain points during the process.

world and to others at this point are characterized by distance and disease, although most dramatically so with respect to the injuring person. The distance remains in relation to that person even after connections with friends and objects in the familiar world have been reestablished—when, for example, familiar streets no longer seem foreign and forbidding. However, the broader, metaphorical meaning of the disruption for one's life is not yet articulated and will unfold later.

On a lived level, one experiences the injury as a blow inflicted by the other. In one's perception of the event, one is very self-referential: There is the belief that the other's actions were directed toward one, that one was the target of the other's demeaning or intentionally damaging and unjust behavior. At the very least, one believes the injury to have been avoidable had the other person considered one's feelings to be important. One man said, "If she hadn't known how I felt about it, then it wouldn't have made any difference."

Oftentimes an acknowledgment of responsibility, an apology from the other person, is thought to be necessary for healing: "She could acknowledge that her position is costly to me. She could apologize, not for her decision, but for how it affects me. That'd be nice. I'd like that." Underlying the wish for an apology is often a desire for the other to be different from the person as experienced. This is often thought to be necessary—for the situation to change, the other person must first do the changing. As one woman said, "Maybe that's why I can't forgive her. She hasn't realized how much pain she has caused me. Maybe that's the price she must pay for [my] forgiveness." There may or may not be conscious recognition that the criteria set up for forgiveness, that is, what the other person would have to do in order for forgiveness to occur, are unrealistic: "She'd have to come in and announce that she had lied. . . . It would be so incredible what she would have to do [laughs], that in the end it would be totally unfeasible."

The ongoing experience of hurt entails a preoccupation with the injury. This preoccupation appears to involve two dimensions: (a) the immediate, obvious, felt experience of the hurt and (b) the metaphorical, larger meaning the injury has for one's life, for example, seeing oneself in a new way.[2] Again, the person who was hurt will not typically attempt to uncover the metaphorical meaning at this point; it is the immediate experience that draws one's attention. It is assumed the other's actions were the simple and sufficient reasons for the hurt and disruption in one's life. The hurtful interaction is remembered as the transition point between a comfortable and

familiar sense of the world and an existence that is disturbing and uprooted. One person described as follows:

> The next morning I felt a slow hideous obsession creeping into [me]. I felt it taking over my life. I felt fear and then the fear turned into a cold terrifying anger. . . . I cried and screamed at the injustice of it. . . . It wasn't fair. Why? Why? Why? I asked myself. . . . What had I done to deserve this? My questions remained unanswered, and I became angrier.

The initial hurt often is accompanied by anger; in other cases, anger becomes an issue later. In anger, there is a movement toward the other person, explosively or energetically, at least in imagination. One woman said, "All I wanted to do was lick my wounds and fight back." And another reported, "I decided to . . . confront him with my newly found information. I had every intention of showing him what a failure of a human being he was."

Along with anger, there is frequently a desire for revenge or retribution. These fantasies or imaginings carry the promise of some sort of partial balancing of an injustice; they provide, however artificially, a "future" where precipitously none had existed anymore. Especially, they offer a future in which one is no longer a victim (but the victimizer). One woman described this in detail:

> I hated him. . . . I spent time wondering how a person like myself could make contact with a professional killer. It was important to me that [he] knew why he was being killed. Should I trust my employee to tell him, or should I send him a note? . . . The perfect [plan] was to get . . . him beat up. I used to imagine the blood and mashed flesh. Then he would be told that he was to treat . . . me with respect and kindness for the rest of his life [or] he would get beaten up again. . . . This fantasy allowed me to imagine how [he] would suffer in fear for the rest of his life.

The possibility of forgiving the other seems unlikely at this point, and the anger may be perceived as extending indefinitely. One middle-aged man seemed to be in this place: "My mother is a stubborn, bigoted, disappointing woman. I don't see how I can forgive her."

If the other person and the relationship are valued, thoughts of revenge are apt to become interspersed with a wish for reconciliation. Although thoughts of the other as blameworthy may still predominate, increasingly there are moments of questioning oneself: "Did I misconstrue the intentions of the other?"; "Did I do something to bring about his or her actions?" During this phase, there are the beginnings of "unpacking" the enmeshment the hurt has caused; the self-referential perspective begins to unravel. One is able to see the other in terms apart from the immediate relationship. Preoccupation with the other's wrongdoing begins to be pierced by guesses at explanations for his or her behavior that make it more

---

[2]For a fuller elaboration of these two dimensions of experience, see Fisher's (1970) discussion of anxiety.

understandable or "acceptable." And there is a dawning awareness, to some degree, that one is participating in continuing the feelings of discomfort in relation to the other person; yet exactly how, and therefore, how to end it, is not clear. One woman wondered:

> I see the obstacle in front of me but I can't seem to move it. How do I forgive her without her showing me she knows how much pain I've experienced? How do I forgive and not forget so I can go on? How do I rid myself of the selfish demand that she acknowledge my pain?

An alternative mode of being, that of being comfortable with thoughts and feelings about the other, is not yet apparent.

Aside from concerns about restoring the relationship or the growing desire to feel peaceful rather than haunted by what happened, one may also be moved by an inner obligation to forgive; additionally, there may be a sense of guilt about being angry with the other. But one is unable to simply let go of the hurt and/or recriminations, even though at times the continuation of these feelings is viewed with some perplexity. In their descriptions, those interviewed in the midst of this process spoke more haltingly and with less clarity than later when they had forgiven. This was reflected in their style of speaking as well as in what they said. At this time in the process, some critical form of healing has not taken place, and there is a moving back and forth such that one might speak of being caught between what seems like irreconcilable opposition: hurt and anger that create distance and accepting the relationship as it is at present by somehow letting go of the past.

Letting go, although consciously preferable or at least an *ought*, does not as yet really feel possible. There is a sense of clinging to the hurt and anger, which is to be distinguished from earlier phases of more spontaneous hurt and anger. This clinging appears to have the function, partly at least, of keeping oneself away from the other while staying engaged with what might have been. As distancing implies, mistrust is often a pervasive theme. This phase may be experienced as an impasse, and one feels trapped. One man said, "I did not like the anger and rage I felt, but I also did not know how to leave behind the hurt."

To achieve resolution, one may "try" to forgive, may even say one has, only to find the old pain, anger, and confusion returning. As one woman stated:

> I wrote her . . . that I [forgave] her, . . . you see I know that not forgiving her would only destroy myself. . . . By going through the motions I hoped to *feel* forgiveness. But I continue to hang on. Perhaps it is because I feel forgiving her would mean I would have to forget what she did to me. I don't want to forget because if I do, it may happen again.

There may also be some awareness that clinging to the hurt and anger may serve to move one away from specific "inner" experiences such as grief. This grief may concern both the loss of what was and/or could have been, and, on a deeper level, the loss of a particular way of viewing oneself and the world. The latter loss is the deeper metaphorical level of meaning that is not yet entirely clear. One woman, after forgiving her father for years of hurt said, "[I] am left . . . with a deep sadness for me, for my dad, for all of us who keep ourselves separate out of hurt and fear." She went on to consider, "The avoidance of this . . . sadness may be one reason why [I] resisted forgiving."

During this time there also may be moments when one feels freed from hanging onto the injury. However, these times are fleeting and cannot be captured. One man said:

> My hurt and anger vanished as I thought about [her]. . . . I felt healed. . . . This experience was deeply moving, but I would hesitate to call it dramatic. The next day . . . I was back to my previous state, and yet I knew that something was possible even though I had no idea how to get "back there."

The resolution, in the form of forgiveness, appears to come to us in an unexpected context, often at an unexpected moment. And yet, as one is surprised by the resolution, it becomes apparent that, at some level, it was sought; one was willing to forgive and open to the possibility of resolution. It seems that this willingness is crucial for forgiveness to occur. Not imagining how he might forgive his mother, one man said, "I don't see how I can forgive anything. Maybe it's because I'm stubborn or maybe I've talked myself into not being able to back down."

Experientially, however, the moment of forgiveness appears to be the moment of recognition that it *has* already occurred. Rather than being aware of changing, one realizes that one *has* changed, one has forgiven the other. Forgiveness comes as a revelation and is often viewed as a gift. One woman reported that "I proceeded to call him and apologize for the letter he was going to receive and in the same breath I said I forgave him. When I said this I was taken by surprise. It had in a sense come out of nowhere." There may be a series of revelations, that is, one may forgive a number of aspects of a relationship independently, or the injury may be forgiven once. This may depend upon whether the injury was a discrete event or a more complicated series of happenings, as well as upon the intensity and significance of the hurt.

Previous thoughts about what conditions make it possible to forgive (e.g., if the other were to apologize) turn out not to fit the reality as experienced. The focus has been on what "the other should do" and less on what *one* needs to do in order to overcome the injury. Even when apologies were forthcoming, this did not enable people to forgive and, likewise, people forgive even without acknowledgment on the part of the wrongdoers. In a parallel vein, although the immediate experience of the hurt is very conscious, it seems doubtful that there was clarity to the broader, deeper meaning of the injury. One seems long in coming to a realization of what significance the action has in terms of one's life as a whole. As previously noted, the focus was on the wounding rather than on the underlying meaning of the injury.

The critical dimension of forgiving is that one experiences a shift in one's understanding of, and relationship to, the other person, oneself, and the world. The implications of the original situation are cast in a new light: The hurt is no longer merely an injury that another has inflicted, and that, therefore, acts as a barrier, but instead becomes appropriated as pain shared with other human beings. In some sense, it is disengaged from the "injuring" person or at least no longer solely referential to that person. One man described this awareness: "[I now felt her] as another human being who was struggling and who basically did not mean me any harm." There is an experience of reclaiming oneself, which, at the same time, involves a shift into a larger perspective. No longer does one see oneself in a relationship of victim and victimizer: One is freed from the status of being the object of another's actions and so is able to return to oneself. No longer is there only one possible connection with the other person. Like a tree, the trunk of the past branches into the future. There are alternatives, where before there were none, and this new vision reinstates choice into one's life. A sense of responsibility for one's life and relationships is recovered. After forgiving her father, one woman said:

My life immediately began to change. After spending almost 6 years in a profession which I did not enjoy, but had entered to gain my father's approval, I decided to return to school to study what I loved. By opening my mind to forgiveness, I was able to open my heart, and the transformation affected my life.

After forgiving a family member for sexual abuse, one person stated, "For the first time in my life I feel free." And another person said, "I realize that forgiveness has set me free. Free to continue my life, free to exist without pain and anger, and free to love again." The vision of newness is so compelling, so like a gift of grace, one will not choose other than to move gratefully into it. The future—an immediate sense of being on the verge of new beginnings—is again available where before it was not; the past, although neither forgotten nor rationalized away, is no longer a haunting, heavy, and troubling issue.

At the level of lived experience, there is a release of tension, yet this release is one in which one's active par-

ticipation is acknowledged on some level, although perhaps most clearly in retrospect. Thus people frequently speak of being able to "let go" of anger, hurt, and recriminations. One experiences a restoration of a sense of wholeness and of inner direction and an opening up to perceiving how other people and situations are in their own right, as distinct and separate from one's own needs and desires: "I stopped trying to pigeon-hole her into a ready made mold." One has an attitude of openness to the other, and yet feels vulnerable to him or her: "I feel more relaxed and can look her in the eye, where before I couldn't." On a reflective level, one sees the other as having acted in a way human beings do, out of his or her own needs and perceptions; there may even be the recognition that what he or she did is something one has done or could well do: "Forgiving came with acknowledging that we aren't perfect." One understands the other person, and oneself, in a new and fuller way.

The experience of forgiveness is one of radically opening to the world and others, as well as to the person who hurt one. There is a sense of arriving home after a long journey and the world is welcoming, so well remembered and yet transformed. One woman wrote:

I knew at last that home was where I was. The past was no longer menacing . . . the future was no longer foreboding. . . . [I] was no longer adrift in a sea of chaos but at the helm in a world that welcomed me. I wept for joy.

Others emerge as persons separate from oneself, and yet one's connection with them is more tangible than before. There is a clarity about one's relationship to self and others. There is a sense of relatedness and freedom that did not exist before. It is because of the transforming nature of forgiveness, coupled with the experience that this involves more than one's own will, that we are suggesting there is a spiritual dimension to forgiveness.

In summary, the experience of forgiving the person who has injured oneself is a complex multidimensional process that moves from a tearing of one's lived world through feelings of hurt, anger, revenge, confusion to an opening up to a larger experience of oneself and others. As the process is being experienced, one seems to be predominantly self-referential and tends to be preoccupied with the immediate implications of the injury to one's life, for example, the dissolution of the particular hoped-for future with the injuring party. However, once forgiveness is experienced, one realizes the larger meaning the injury has for one's existence. The sense of relief from the hurt itself seems to be only one aspect, perhaps even small, of the freedom one experiences. Suddenly, the future is fraught with possibility; one feels a fuller kinship with others and self, and one is humbled by what seems to have been a gift. Although forgiveness may be desired and even sought, part of the transforming nature of the phenomenon is the encounter with something that is experienced as more expansive, more graceful, more mysterious than ordinary egocentric living. One man articulated this phenomenon well:

> [I thought of her] this time as another human being who was struggling, and who basically did not mean me any harm. It is not accurate . . . to suggest that I just thought that; it was more like an image that emerged for me, an image that was not so much seen as it was felt. . . . Blame and anger vanished, and there was a larger dimension of this whole experience that I can only describe in religious language: a sense of transcendence, of the future opening up, of a sense of presence, not of a personal being, but of being connected to something larger than oneself and yet still having an experience of myself as me.

CONCLUSION

The research we have done has begun to unfold an interpretation of "forgiving another" that addresses the questions with which we began the research: namely, what is the nature of injury calling for forgiveness, what are initial responses to this injury, what enables one to forgive, and last, what is the essence of forgiveness. We are aware, however, that this study focused solely on hurt inflicted by someone in a personal relationship. To this end, we are continuing our work as a group to focus on other dimensions of forgiveness.

Currently, we are involved in looking at the experience of being forgiven or what is popularly described as "self-forgiveness." The tentative structure that is appearing suggests that the process of self-forgiveness is similar to forgiving another. For example, it requires more than one's will and, for that reason, is not experienced as something that one does for oneself but rather seems to come when one least expects forgiveness. Again, self-forgiveness is a transforming experience bringing one an awareness of one's humanity and connection with the world while offering new freedom and possibilities. The similarities are so striking that we are beginning to wonder if they are not simultaneous processes. That is, self-forgiveness is in the background of forgiving another and vice versa. In other words, one cannot realize one's own freedom and humanity without realizing that of the other. Hopefully the research we are undertaking and the dialogal method that has emerged will call others to explore issues related to forgiveness such as when one is hurt by an unknown other, for example, a drunk driver; forgiveness in psychotherapy; and forgiveness in political and social areas, for example, racial discrimination. Clearly, this is a phenomenon with many facets and far-reaching implications for intrapersonal, interpersonal, and political relationships, and one that calls for our rigorous attention.

REFERENCES

Arendt, H. (1958). *The human condition.* Chicago: University of Chicago Press.

Buber, M. (1957). Guilt and guilt feelings. *Psychiatry, 20,* 114–129.

Close, H. (1970). Forgiveness and responsibility: A case study. *Pastoral Psychology,* 21(205), 19–26.

Faulconer, J. E., & Williams, R. N. (1985). Temporality in human action: An alternative to positivism and historicism. *American Psychologist,* 40(11), 1179–1188.

Fischer, W. F. (1970). *Theories of anxiety.* New York: Harper & Row.

Fischer, C. T., & Wertz, F. J. (1979). Empirical phenomenological analyses of being criminally victimized. In A. Giorgi, R. Knowles, & D. L. Smith (Eds.), *Duquesne studies in phenomenological psychology: Vol. 3* (pp. 135–158). Pittsburgh: Duquesne University Press.

Gadamer, H. (1975). *Truth and method* (G. Barden & J. Cumming, Trans.). New York: Seabury.

Gadamer, H. (1976). *Philosophical hermeneutics* (D. Linge, Trans.). Berkeley: University of California Press.

Gahagan, J. P., & Tedeschi, T. J. (1968). Strategy and credibility of promises in the prisoner's dilemma game. *Journal of Conflict Resolutions,* 12(2), 224–234.

Giorgi, A. (1970). *Psychology as a human science.* New York: Harper & Row.

Giorgi, A. (1975). An application of phenomenological method in psychology. In A. Giorgi, C. T. Fischer, & E. L. Murray (Eds.), *Duquesne studies in phenomenological psychology: Vol. 2* (pp. 82–103). Pittsburgh: Duquesne University Press.

Halling, S. (1979). Eugene O'Neill's understanding of forgiveness. In A. Giorgi, R. Knowles, & D. L. Smith (Eds.), *Duquesne studies in phenomenological psychology,* V. III (pp. 193–208). Pittsburgh: Duquesne University Press.

Heider, F. (1958). *The psychology of interpersonal relations.* New York: Wiley.

Hunter, R. C. A. (1978). Forgiveness, retaliation, and paranoid reactions. *Canadian Psychiatric Association Journal,* 23, 167–173.

King, M. L., Jr., (1963). *Why we can't wait.* New York: Signet.

Kolnai, A. (1968). Forgiveness. In *Ethics, value and reality: Selected papers of Auriel Kolnai* (pp. 221–224). Indianapolis: Hackett.

Kunz, G. (1981). *Forgiveness in families.* Unpublished manuscript, Seattle University, Seattle.

Leifer, M. (1986). *The dialogal method in phenomenological research.* Unpublished manuscript. Seattle University, Seattle.

Martyn, D. W. (1977). A child and Adam: A parable of two ages. *Journal of Religion and Health,* 16(4), 275–287.

Packer, M. J. (1985). Hermeneutic inquiry in the study of human conduct. *American Psychologist,* 40(10), 1081–1093.

Pattison, E. M. (1965). On the failure to forgive or to be forgiven. *American Journal of Psychotherapy,* 19, 106–115.

Perls, F. (1969). *Gestalt therapy verbatim.* Lafayette, CA: Real People Press.

Scheler, M. (1973). *Formalism in ethics and non-formal ethics of values.* Evanston, IL: Northwestern University Press.

Searles, H. (1956). The psychodynamics of vengeance. *Psychiatry, 19,* 31–39.

Smedes, L. (1984). *Forgive and forget.* New York: Harper & Row.

Soloveitchik, J. B. (1984). *Soloveitchik on repentance: The thought and oral discourses of Rabbi Joseph B. Soloveitchik* (P. H. Peli, Ed.). Ramsey, NJ: Paulist Press.

Stauffer, E. (n.d.). *Unconditional love, will and forgiveness.* Unpublished manuscript, Diamonds Springs, CA.

Strasser, S. (1969). *The idea of dialogal phenomenology.* Pittsburgh: Duquesne University Press.

Tedeschi, J. T., Hiester, J. T., & Gahagan, J. P. (1969). Trust and the prisoner's dilemma game. *Journal of Social Psychology, 79*(1), 43–50.

Torbert, W. R. (1977). *Why educational research has been so uneducational: The case for a new model of social science based on collaborative inquiry.* Paper presented at the American Psychological Association Convention, August, 1977.

Trzyna, T. (1985). *Forgiveness and truth: Literary reflections of Christian faith.* Paper presented at Seattle Pacific University, April 11, 1985.

van Kaam, A. (1969). *Existential foundation of psychology.* New York: Image Books. (Original work published 1966)

Westphal, M. (1978). The phenomenology of guilt and the theology of forgiveness. In R. Bruzina & B. Wilshire, (Eds.), *Crosscurrent in phenomenology* (pp. 231–261). The Hague: Martinus Nijhoff.

Williams, D. D. (1961). *The minister and the care of souls.* New York: Harper & Row.

15

Aesthetic Consciousness

Donald Moncrieff

This chapter is comprised of two major sections. The first lays groundwork and is titled "Preparatory Considerations." The second focuses on some of the actual findings and is titled "Discoveries." The entire chapter attempts to share in the spirit of aesthetic consciousness as well as describe ideas related to this phenomenon.

PREPARATORY CONSIDERATIONS

Consider the following wish—"That you might see like a deaf person and hear like a blind person." What people suffering the deprivation of one sense can do, by compensating with another, is often marvelous.

This phenomenon gives witness to important potentials inherent in our ability system. The all-too-obvious fact is that we have capacities to do what we have not previously done. One of our frontiers, yet to be thoroughly explored, is this wonderful system of abilities. At this point I define *consciousness* as our ability to be aware and *aesthetic sensitivity* as our ability to relate to the beautiful. I will begin to go deeper into these abilities with an example:

> Recently, I saw the sun disappear into evening. The beauty carried me beyond my ordinary world as I imagined the sunset stretching both north and south to the poles of the earth. At both ends, it touched the sunrise circling the other side of the globe. Together, sunrise and sunset seemed to form a great ring, inexorably circling the earth, twice a day challenging every seeing person to an inner awakening. I wondered about what I experi-

enced, and I wondered about my capacity to experience it.

Here I stress the capacity itself. The point is the phenomenon of seeing; the phenomenon of hearing. Note that it is not a point made from a purely psychological perspective; it is a point made from a phenomenological–psychological perspective. To clarify this, imagine for a moment that a camera ready to take a picture becomes like a person open to the world. What if such a camera were no longer merely mechanical but could be present to itself as a person can? Think, for example, of the difference it would make to the camera if it had knowledge of its ability to accept film of various speeds. Using that knowledge to adjust for fast film, it could set its shutter speed and lens opening appropriately, thus avoiding the slow-speed, wide-opening impression that the world is total light. To know fundamental attributes of our abilities, their uses and limitations, can make all the difference between our using them well or poorly. Such phenomenological knowledge can make the difference between our seeing like a deaf person and hearing like a blind one, or our missing the point of our observations altogether.

Operational Methods

There is assumed here a distinction between natural scientific psychology and phenomenological psychology. The former is understood as the rigorous application of the natural attitude to human behavior. In other words, it is an attending to the realms of perception, feeling, thought, and judgment in an objectified and scientific way. Phenomenological psychology can be understood as a study of experienced intending once the intended is

Donald Moncrieff • 84 Glendale Avenue, Toronto, Ontario, Canada M6R 2T1.

bracketed. The goal is to bring to awareness the basic characteristics of intending consciousness. Phenomenological psychology is not to be confused with the gathering of subjective data (cf. Jennings, 1986). It is rather a lifting into awareness of what is presupposed in the gathering of such data.

Phenomenology as Science

Phenomenology ultimately uses the same ability systems as does scientific psychology and uses them with at least equal rigor. In fact, if "science" is taken to mean "knowledge at its best," phenomenological psychology is indeed a science.

By comparing ability systems, Amedeo Giorgi (1974) suggests some ways in which the phenomenological effort can be understood as scientific. The relevant questions are: What ability systems do scientists use? How do they use them in order to achieve the desired results? Obviously, scientists share the same "lifeworld" as everyone else, that is, they achieve consciousness, experience life, and discover themselves in a culture laced with myriad institutions from formal, legal ones to taken-for-granted ways of thinking and speaking. In addition, scientists develop a degree of sophistication in their perceiving the world. They abstract concepts that are then represented in words used in a living way, sensitive to polysemous possibilities. Further, meanings are shared by context, as necessarily occurs when one communicates something quite new. For example, a scientist who had more experiments lined up than he could do in a lifetime was asked how he selected the next experiment to perform. He responded by saying that he selected his next one on the basis of what he judged to be the most beautiful hypothesis.

On the other hand, scientists can fix words, as happens in a dead language. Many tend toward using words in this way because, among other things, this use affords some certitude that everyone is saying the same thing. Most contemporary scientific papers exemplify this phenomenon.

It is difficult, however, for one to speak of a living, moving, changing, pattern in fixed words. Happily, the processes by which fixed words are used rigorously, revealingly, and accurately are also available to one wishing to use words with polysemous possibilities.

One set of fixed words expresses the concepts used by statisticians. To do their task, these scientists seek measures of central tendency. When the statistical processes used to clarify and simplify extractions from numerical data are adapted for application to other areas of study and research, for example, polysemous words, then measures of central tendency expand to include all index-

es of convergence. What we get in both instances are rigorous, defensible, communicable generalizations, the value of which depends upon the accuracy of the work that went into developing them. In effect, the verbalization of such a generalization is the statement of a structure to be found in a lot of examples. In other words, with work, we can really know what we are talking about (i.e., be rigorous) no matter which word system we use.

Statistical analysis can also measure dispersion or variance, in effect, indexes of divergence in the realm of numbers. The processes thus used can also be employed to seek indexes of divergence among other types of words. This leads to the discovery of types. The patterns described here will be exemplified by what I share next.

We thus end up with generalities and typicalities. These can facilitate both our understanding of the world in which we live and our ability to contribute to the intelligent use of and improvement of that world.

Consensus

Seeking generalities and typicalities through various rigorous methods is one of my research tools. One such method is the "consensus approach." This approach is comparable to the traditional scientific use of precision and the use of experimental repeatability as a means of verification. Instead of developing an experimental pattern that can be repeated, my emphasis is on patterns that *de facto* repeat. Precision is sought by means of the purifying power of many persons working together, questioning and challenging one another.

This approach can be illustrated by the "NASA game." Participants in this game are asked to imagine themselves stranded in a disabled space craft on the moon. They will have to walk some distance to a rescue point. They have a list of items available that they can take with them, and their task is to rank-order these items from most important to least important. First, individual participants in the game rank-order the items. Then groups are formed and asked to work out an ordering agreed upon by every member within the group. Finally all groups hammer out an ordering that represents a consensus of all the members of all the groups together. The orderings are then compared to that which astronauts themselves say would be best. With high frequency, the larger the group achieving a consensus, the closer that opinion is to the astronauts' actual ordering. In other words, the working out of consensus opinions can give us an approximation to the facts sufficient at least for the early stages of an exploration. In my study of aesthetic consciousness, I utilized the consensus approach with over 200 persons, ranging from competent professionals in the arts to college students.

Privileged Observer

In addition to the consensus approach, I have relied upon another method, that of the "privileged observer." This method is an adaptation of the scientific precedure of relying upon the most highly trained and knowledgeable scientists as having greater authority in their specialities than lay persons or amateurs. By applying the sensitivity of such experts to a problem (here the teasing out of phenomenological aspects of aesthetic consciousness), much can be learned that otherwide might go unnoticed.

Using this second method involved training individuals or selecting individuals who already had achieved the personal development necessary to analyze the phenomenon being investigated. Using both methods (consensus and privileged observer) simultaneously with over a hundred people, the phenomenologically meaningful aspects of aesthetic consciousness were explored.

Using Great Thinkers

Another method was also employed—"using great thinkers." This approach is comparable to the traditional review of the literature so important to the situating of a scientific study. The emphasis here, however, was slightly different from that often used. Observations of great thinkers were brought into play so that privileged observers could make use of their viewpoints as models. These models then guided these privileged observers as they probed into the phenomenon.

Abraham Maslow's work is one source of such observations. His description of B-cognition in peak experiences provides a number of models from which explorations of aesthetic consciousness can be made. Specifically, I chose a point made in *Toward a Psychology of Being* (1967) where Maslow observes that "In B-cognition the experience of the object tends to be seen as a whole, as a complete unit" (p. 78). Maslow utilizes a visualizing model (the object is "seen") with an emphasis on the *gestalt,* or wholeness of the pattern seen. This model leads to a questioning of the one seeing. What is it about your seeing that participates in the sense of wholeness? This question is in effect an expression of my concern about the phenomenal "oneness" of the aesthetic experience.

Another significant work is Mikel Dufrenne's (1973) *The Phenomenology of Aesthetic Experience.* This book provides valuable perspectives and findings for anyone wishing to explore aesthetic consciousness in depth.

Working Premises

In addition to the methods outlined here there are also a number of premises underlying my work:

1. *Consciousness as understanding.* There are some important characteristics of consciousness as understanding that can be discerned in the following simple experiment. Either imaginatively or actually place a mark like that contained within the following parentheses (.) in the center of a clean sheet of paper. Then ask yourself what it is. Various answers are possible—a small spot of ink, a point, a dot, a period, and so on. Ask someone else what it is. Similar answers may be given. Some of the answers I have received are, "That's solitude," or "A beginning," or "A plane in the sky."

This simple experiment can reveal much about consciousness, our ability to be "with" something in a "knowing" way (*con-scire*). Phenomenologists speak of this being "with" as the "intentional" nature of consciousness. For my purposes here, I would like to point out that, in no instance, can any single answer suggested tell us what the thing is "*in itself*"—a spot of ink, a point, a period, or whatever. Each answer is correct in its own way; each tells us what the thing is for someone, but what it is in itself is not so easily stated, if it can be stated at all.

Someone might say the thing in itself is a relatively flat, roundish smudge of ink. Or someone might give the chemical formula for the ink, or a description of its atomic and subatomic structures. Even this, I contend, would not tell us what the thing is. It only tells us what it is for someone, for a chemist, or a physicist. But what it is in itself must obviously be much more. What it is in itself must also (at least in part) account for the geometrician seeing a "point" there, the punctuation expert seeing a "period," the artist seeing "solitude." What the thing is in itself is a more or less defined complex of possible relations—it is an ambiguous structure—and even this is the thing in itself for understanding.

Can we conclude that all conscious behavior is then but a concentration, or focusing, upon such ambiguous aspects of what we call an object of consciousness as suit the viewpoint and purposes of the conscious person? Not from this one experiment, certainly, but the possibility is strongly suggested. As a matter of fact, it is a possibility to which I have yet to find an exception.

2. *Consciousness as a constituent of meaning.* Meanings are derived within a viewpoint (as in the situation illustrated by the experiment just suggested). Thus consciousness is a constituent in the making of meaning, that is, the structures of whatever one is "conscious of." Phenomenologists speak of this by saying that consciousness is intentional. For the purpose of exploring aesthetic consciousness, it is especially important to note that certain aspects of consciousness are not only what are being explored, but they participate in doing the exploring. Insofar as consciousness evidences aesthetic quality

and this quality is explored, it bcomes apparent that consciousness is immediately available to itself. It manifests an amazing self-presence enabling one to achieve meaning for the word *I*.

3. *Understanding as a viewpoint.* I want to achieve rigorous, in-depth, relevant understanding, and it is this premise that is the precise viewpoint taken to explore aesthetic consciousness. Rather than approaching the phenomenon as an artist, appreciator of beauty, or a seeker of causes, my approach is from that style of consciousness generally named "understanding." That is, I want to know what the relationships that make up aesthetic consciousness are. By "seeking understanding," I mean what I do to work toward answers to "what?"-type questions. "Understanding" is the grasping of the answer to the "what?" question. Consider the following example that describes an experience involving interrelated patterns.

I am sitting in a chair. What I wonder about is the nature of my behavior such that I am enabled to achieve a sense of the meaning *chair*. I am asking, "*what* is a chair?" I participate in the relationships (grounded or concretized in wood and steel or whatever) that exist between the bodily posture I call "sitting" and the material, gravitationally related structure I call "supporting." In other words, I experience or participate in a complex system that involves the dispositions or postures I can take up with my body, one of which places the weight of my body on my buttocks, and I also know or participate in another complex system that involves complementary support structures that can more or less comfortably bear my buttocks-centered disposition of weight. I thus answer my "what?"-type question.

"Understanding," then, is that personal behavior wherein I take to myself a system of relationships. It is "getting the point." In my example, an understanding is the answer to the question, "what is a chair?" In this paragraph, an understanding is the answer to the question, "what is understanding?" In these two instances, the answer is a system of overlapping or intertwining relationships that make up a new system of relationships in its own right.

Accurate understanding, then, is the achievement of a system of relationships or a *structure* within a real-life situation. Such a structure is generally found within other structures or systems and is often made up of intertwining aspects of those larger systems, as for example, the meaning *chair*. The structure itself should not be confused with an "idea" or a "thing" that are both conceptual abstractions of the structure.

The meaning of *aesthetic* is very much like the meaning *chair*, only there are many more intertwining structures involved. To understand chair, it is enough to understand something of human body posture and mate-

rial support systems. To understand aesthetic consciousness it is necessary to understand the artwork, the appreciating of it, the creating of it, the performing of it, selfhood, ego systems, personal being-in-the-world, play, imagination, symbolization, human origination, perception, and so on.

4. *Types of behaviors.* Reductionism is an ever-present danger to one trying to understand. In order to help myself avoid oversimplifications and mistaking parts for the whole, I kept in mind Merleau-Ponty (1963), who distinguishes three types of behavior: physical, vital, and human.

This typology helps to situate aesthetic consciousness within the behavioral arena.

Physical behavior is constituted by an organism involved directly with a thing, like a frog striking for food. The stimulus–response model of behavioral–experimental psychology is closely related to this type of behavior. A predetermined instinct or response potential is at work, and little adaptability or variation is possible.

Vital behavior is constituted by an organism involved with a relationship, like a chicken conditioned to take grain from a pile marked by the lighter of two shades of gray. Considerable adaptability is involved here because the shades of gray can be varied a great deal as long as one shade is lighter than the other.

Human behavior is distinguished by the vast possibilities for adaptability implicit in the following example that also illustrates aesthetic consciousness:

> During a trip to California I spent some time enjoying the Pacific. One late afternoon I was watching the sun draw ever closer to the horizon when I noticed the sparkling path made by its light on the water. It seemed as if the glistening was meant in a special way for me. As I walked along, the path of light followed me—from the sun right across the water to me—no matter where I moved! It was so simple, yet amazing. The sun was for me a great ball containing the whole of life. I had a sense of everything directing its splendor toward me, everything in the universe was saying, "Here I am!" and showing itself to me. I felt flushed with awe.

In human behavior, the sunlight's path is seen as an expression of all relations between everything (things and relations) and the observer. In other words, the observer here is in touch with relations of relations of relations—in an open system that allows for considerably more versatility, creativeness, and imaginative play than either physical or vital behavior shows.

By way of contrast, in physical behavior, we see one part of a relation directly affecting the other part—food stimulating the frog. There is a simple participation on the part of the frog.

In vital behavior, the relational system becomes more complex. Two shades of gray are perceived as related to each other, and thus the chicken is related to a relation and acts within the limitations thus afforded. Such patterns sublate within the human behavioral pattern and are thus modified by their inclusion in the more complex structure.

5. *Presentational symbol*. Notice that the complex relational system present in the preceding example was not a representation. The sunlight's path did not represent the paths of each thing's splendor. It was a repeatable manifestation of the nature of the world's involvement with a person and vice versa, which, in its making the sun's light obviously ''for'' the observer, manifested the ''for-the-observer-ness'' of everything. The observer here reached a much deeper reality than did the chicken or frog. He participated in a meaning, a system of relationships, a structure that said something about the way many other things are. In other words, the person, in a moment only possible for humans with aesthetic consciousness, perceived a *symbol*.

The term *symbol* is used here in a technical sense. It does not mean an image or representation but rather a fundamental phenomenal presentation of unknown or mysterious aspects of the world. The presentational symbol can become representational if it is changed into a metaphor, but that complexity goes beyond my present interests.

The use of ''symbols'' as distinguishing characteristics of human behavior, is closely related to Carl Jung's (1964) use of *symbol*. He sees the symbol as being the specifically human mode of access to the mysteries of life and reality beyond the edge of everyday awareness. The symbol, in this sense, is a person's stepping stone into the co-creative achievement of higher development. The symbol is the ambiguous formation of a knowing that is on the edge of the vast realm yet unknown, though somehow anticipated.

6. *The whole as structure*. Human behavior always involves physical and vital behaviors as subsets. Thus human behavior can be analyzed in terms of these simpler structures. This, however, results in reductionism if one tries to substitute the simpler aspect for the whole. The point here is that the whole exists as a whole. The focus is on that which is greater than the sum of the parts involved, namely, the structure that sums the parts in a unique way.

Keeping the methodological considerations and personal premises shared before in mind, I now turn to aesthetic consciousness as a phenomenon. I will move from an exemplary illustration to a focus on the characteristic of ''oneness'' observed in that illustration.

DISCOVERIES

The following exemplary illustration is an account given by a young man. He includes personal details, but my interest here is in the universal patterns that are revealed. This one example is, of course, merely a starting point. Additionally, I will draw on other examples and the knowledge of privileged observers as essential parts of the search for a consensual understanding. I rely upon you to integrate your experiences with what I present:

> I was 16 at the time. It was a dreary Sunday afternoon, and I was spending my time listening to the radio and relaxing. The announcer said that a Beethoven symphony was about to be played. I felt too lazy to change the station even though my previous exposure to Beethoven's music had been quite boring for me.
>
> I was almost immediately caught up in the music. I didn't know what was happening to me. I found myself crying. My body felt like it would sink into the chair. I personally was gone, into the radio, into the music, I don't know where. I was one with the music.
>
> When the symphony ended, I came back to myself sitting in the chair. I felt exhilarated, inspired, as if what was inside were too big for my cranium. I wondered what the head pressure was all about and, slowly, I realized that I would never again be able to become involved with beautiful things in the same way as I had before hearing the symphony. From then on, I thought, beautiful things would always be more beautiful for me—and that has proven to be an accurate prediction.

There are many features of this experience that are found in every other example of aesthetic consciousness. Some of these are personhood, creativeness, performance, appreciation, symbolization, and expression. Although an in-depth look at each one of these features is beyond the scope of this chapter, what follows are the results of my delving into one central feature, that of the experienced ''oneness'' with the music.

The Oneness of Aesthetic Consciousness

I began by wondering, what does ''one'' mean in this instance? It turns out to be much easier to discover what it does not mean. For example, it does not mean a numerical 1. The young man experiencing Beethoven's music is not counting or envisioning himself or his experience to be one of a series. Nor does it mean a oneness in which the listener absolutely and wholly identifies with the music. Aspects of him, such as his sitting body, in some way seem to have been left in the chair even as he personally goes into the music. When he comes out of the music, he is aware that he has changed, evidencing a sense of continuity from before to after and thus a retained personal separateness from the music. Nor does it imply aloneness, nor a conglomeration of parts unified merely by juxtaposition.

As many privileged observers tried to search out their readings of this experience and compare it with similar experiences of their own, it became evident that the oneness involved is like the oneness of the symphony itself—as it changed dwellings, to speak poetically. It first lived in Beethoven. Then it took up residence in the score Beethoven wrote. It came alive again and again as musicians read the score. It came alive in performance after performance. Then it came alive in the life of the listener being studied.

The oneness consists of a constant series of relations amid sounds, rhythms, and the emotions of involved persons. It is the same symphony whether read in the imagination of a musician, performed by a full orchestra, or reduced to a single piano arrangement. Its oneness is a constancy even though expressed in different ways. Any change of a part, theme, or even note would change the whole. It thus becomes evident that the oneness experienced is a structural oneness. It is not the oneness of an idea or a thing. It is the oneness of a structure that includes the personhood of the listener. He says, I was "caught up in the music." "I, personally, was gone . . . into the music." "I was one with the music."

Yet this description is not to be understood as a listing of parts. Oneness has various characteristics that are all interdependent. I am considering some of these characteristics as internal constituents of the phenomenon. For this to make sense, I must also consider the phenomenon in its larger context, thus focusing my perspective on both inner and contextual patterns. I limit my considerations to the immediate presentation of relevant meaning. I am thus bracketing my presuppositions regarding mediated presentations. Paying attention from the viewpoint established by Merleau-Ponty (1963), it is clear that the observed human behavior is at the symbolic level. It puts the listener in immediate contact with experience leading him beyond his previous self.

Additional Examples Expanding This Exploration

Consider these two examples, the first provided by a 25-year-old woman, the second by a 40-year-old man:

> 1. I was standing on the top of a high hill. Ordered fields swept out before me. There were farmhouses and barns in the valley, and a river that sparkled around boats moving up or down its path. Overhead a jet left its white trail across the sky. I felt peace! It was all so uplifting, expansive! I felt one with it all, the contours, the plowing, the boating, the people who made those buildings and lived in them, the people in the jet, the whole of humanity. I felt complete, alive!

> 2. I was in a large and ancient church. It was made of huge blocks of stone carved and piled in shafts crowned with Ionic volutes. For a while everything seemed cold, gray and static. Then I began to see that the stones were shaped and piled together in such a way as to express the gravitational forces holding the building up and together.

> The flow of gravity came alive for me, up the columns, spilling out and curling at the top, holding up the great beams. The stone was flowing with strength. I felt lost in the power. The entire building came alive. I was transformed into vectors reaching right out of the earth to shape a magnificent house. In a way quite new for me, I became a work of architecture.

Using the Beethoven experience, the landscape experience, and the architectural experience together to help stimulate inquiry into each of them as instances of aesthetic awareness, the following came to light.

Upon questioning, the young man who had the Beethoven experience was able to describe his feelings of oneness with the music in greater depth. All of his interest focused on the movement of the music within him. He came together in the music, that is, his concerns were not multiple but single. He felt his concerns resonate with the music. He could easily have let himself dance with the music or act as if he were conducting the orchestra. He had no sense of his body, or vitality, or humanity being involved in any distinguishable ways. He felt simply one, together with the music. The organizational harmony of the music had become his own personal togetherness. The feeling of the experience became his being. As every note, theme, and movement fitted in a fulfilling and complementary way with every other aspect of the symphony, so, too, he felt all his interests, history, and hopes coalesce into a harmonious communion that contributed to his sense of oneness. His experience felt "one," a dynamic, creative "one" that made a new person out of him while he was in the music. This involvement left him changed for life.

The symbol, which he experienced as so intermingling with who he had been as to make him anew, was composed for him of the more general rhythms of life, its ebbings and flowings, feelings of dance and sadness, experiences of the pettiness and greatness of being human. He became, in his involvement with the music, a living, embodied, concretized philosophy of life, a gesture expressing how "it all" fits. He did not think all this out at the time; rather he experienced it in communing appreciatively with Beethoven's song about "it all." His identifying with this symbol was clearly a moving of his personal center out to the edges of all he knew. It was a lifting of physical structures into vital ones and a lifting of vital structures into human ones. It was a facing of mystery. His oneness was an open oneness with a touching presentation of the world enabling him to move out into the, as yet, unknown.

The 25-year-old woman who had lived the landscape experience revealed that she had felt her personal presence expand, drawn out as it were, by the sweeping expanse of the world around her. In the flowing of the lines accentuated by plowed fields, roads, houses, barns, winding river made navigable, and finally people in high flight, she had made a work of art for herself within her imagination. She had expressed to herself the doings of people in the expanse of what she saw. For her, the marks of humanity were everywhere. If someone else had not left them, she was making them in her vision. What she was doing was a part of what everyone else was doing. As a correlative to those parts, there was a whole within which she experienced herself coming alive, excited, and fulfilled. The work of art she made with her mind was a symbol. The physical was lifted into the vital and the vital into the human. She felt her body, her whole self, being expanded, expressing in a there-and-then way the community of humankind making its way in the world. In this, she experienced a new and personal involvement with "what is," and her own being-in-the-world was transformed.

Her struggle to put into words what she could of the depths of her experience is noteworthy. What happened to her was a new way of being conscious, yet it was simultaneously a new way of behaving. She could not distinguish her consciousness within the experience from her behavior, or vice versa. Those things that usually seemed to happen in inner and outer worlds were not separate for her.

Nevertheless, the unity that she did experience had a flowing quality about it. She could discern shifts in emphasis. She was not the plowed field in the same fullness as she was herself standing on the hill. She was not humanity flying in the same intensity of concentration as she was humanity gathered together in herself living/making the inner, imagined work of art she achieved. Yet there were no clear boundaries. She did not experience her involvement as "subjective," yet clearly it is not "objective." What had happened could not be expressed adequately in the language available to her.

The 40-year-old man who had the architectural experience found himself not wanting to talk deeply about it. He felt overwhelmed by the inadequancy of words. With encouragement, this resistance showed itself as coming from his sense of the impropriety of the category systems bound up in common words. What happened and what words expressed for him were two different worlds. He could not feel honest about imposing the world of his words upon the world of his experience beyond his initial description.

Nevertheless, he was able to make it clear that his experience was one of entering personally into already-present relationships. The forces at work relating the piled stone and the earth had been there for centuries. The architectural experience of standing upright like the columns had been part of his experience since he had begun to walk. Yet this was the first time he personally felt the uniting forces involved in each.

For him, what had been disparate coalesced, and something new emerged. He, in effect, made-became a work of art himself in his participation in the architectural art of the building. Again, the physical was lifted into the vital and the vital into the human. The building came to him like the smile on a friend's face. He resonated with it (smiled with it), and he became an uplifted and fulfilled gesture expressing gravitational action and reaction. Where he experienced himself as most alive and centered, there he opened to the world of direction and motion in gravity. Having achieved this symbol he thereafter saw buildings, trees, mountains, and people differently. Everything and everyone manifested for him a kind of dance, a play of and with gravity.

An Intertwining of Systems

While exploring aesthetic consciousness for a deeper understanding of "oneness," that oneness revealed itself as a relational system amid other systems. Which system this is depends on the other characteristics one associates with the oneness. Thus, as intertwined with structure, "oneness" appears as the oneness of structure. As intertwined with the humanness of behavior, it appears as the oneness of the symbol. It is a "oneness" that occurs in the "aesthetic field" (Berleant, 1970). That is, it is a oneness that appears within the context of a work, where creativity, appreciation, and performance are all intertwining. It is what it is as intertwined with all the other characteristics that are related within the overall phenomenon of aesthetic consciousness.

The Foundational Character of Aesthetic Consciousness

This oneness is, further, down-to-earth in character. It appears within aesthetic consciousness, appreciated as a gesture more radical than, and underpinning, the realism suggested by such abstractions as *consciousness* and *behavior,* the *subjective* and the *objective,* the *spiritual* and the *material.* It appears before we can distinguish that we are "one." It is thus the ground out of which arises our individuating strivings. Like the bonding of the newly born with parents, the aesthetic experience constitutes a harmonious beginning. Further along life's way, it is the initiation of a more mature return to community involvement. This "oneness," then, permeates life and calls our attention to many meaningful aspects of our personal presence in reality. A disruption of it seems to play a part in the development of such problems as are brought to our psychiatrists and psychotherapists (Sanford, 1984).

A pattern thus begins to emerge in which aesthetic consciousness is seen as a system of intermingled systems, or a structure emerging out of relating structures. When such structures as we mean by personhood, creativeness, performance, appreciation, symbol, oneness, wholeness, play, and expression are found intertwined so as to form a structure in its own right, we have an example of aesthetic consciousness. This is a general truth, valid at least for the experiences I have explored so far.

John Dewey made a similar observation in *Art as Experience* (1934) when he noted that experience, having run its course to fulfillment, and having thus become an experience, inevitably has some aesthetic quality. The very running of its course ensures in human experience that all the characteristics I have mentioned will be more or less present. Thus, by the complete achievement of an experience, at least some aesthetic quality is present.

Further, many of the systems of aesthetics are to be found elsewhere. For example, expression, emotion, performance, and the like are fairly evident in a dog's wagging its tail at the approach of its master. Yet, symbolism and personhood are not present, and so the expression, emotion, performance, and so forth are not the same as in aesthetic consciousness. We justifiably do not speak of the dog as manifesting aesthetic consciousness. By continuing to thus distinguish systems within systems, it becomes possible to give a generalized description of aesthetic consciousness in more detail than I am providing and to designate its typical similarities and differences from other, more or less closely related styles of consciousness.

It is also possible to distinguish typical experiences within the aesthetic realm. For example, one can distinguish aesthetic consciousness as experienced in the presence of a generally recognized work of fine art from that which is experienced in a natural setting where the "artwork" is accomplished by the appreciator within his or her mind without assistance from a fellow artist.

It is also possible to distinguish aesthetic consciousness achieved in communion with a thing from such consciousness achieved in communion with a person. This distinction, for example, can be seen as underpinning the difference between cathexis and love as developed by M. Scott Peck (1978). Aesthetic consciousness of a thing, for example, a beautiful car, can lead one to feel love for the car. Peck would call this experience a cathexis and regard it as very different from love for a person. Aesthetic consciousness of a person (not some "thing" about the person) can lead to loving that person, that is, wanting and seeking what is truly best for her or him as a person.

The point is that there are verifiable distinctions within the aesthetic realm. We have the beginnings of generalities and typicalities, which are among the essentials of valid scientific inquiry.

The Developmental Character of Aesthetic Consciousness

The experiences examined so far reveal changes in the person having them. Examination of childhood experiences reveals maturing in the ways of aesthetic experience. Everyday experience makes it evident that emotions not possible at an early age become normal at a more mature stage of development.

One possible characterization of these patterns is inspired by using a great thinker Mary Ester Harding (1965), a Jungian analyst, and her book, *The "I" and the "Not-I."* With the aid of the viewpoint developed by Harding, taken in conjunction with Merleau-Ponty's, it is possible to see the ego developing slowly. At first it is very loosely related to and limited by bodily experiences. A small child seems to identify "I" as "the experienced hungry one," or "the experienced running one," and the like. Insofar as this primitive ego truly and personally gets in touch with its unifying and identity-making center, there is aesthetic consciousness. All the constituent structures are present, intermingling in a whole structure. Creativity, appreciation, performance, symbolism, and so on are all in evidence in an overall structured way. But the type of aesthetic consciousness present is very much limited by the degree of consciousness attained and by the degree of ego emergence.

Harding (1965) goes on to single out another stage of ego development beyond the one where the ego is identified with bodily experience. In this second stage, the ego is identified with the *persona*. A "persona" sometimes takes the form of what others are assumed to think of one and sometimes the form of what one wants others to think of oneself. Often it is a combination of these two. It is the "face" people try to "save," or the front they put on for the world.

As the ego develops, it usually formulates some rather strange ideas about the Self (Jung, 1968, p. 142), that is, the unifying and identity-making center subtending the ego. Its estimate of the nature and structures of the Self are immature and often erroneous. Nevertheless, this foray into the realms of partial truth enables the ego to build its strength, get beyond "persona" identification, and accept its Self with mature responsibility. This process plays a part in becoming whole, individuating, or self-actualizing.

A Constituent of Growth

Many words are used to speak of this growth process. The issue here is that such growth occurs in conjunction with the development of aesthetic consciousness, perhaps not always, but from my observations quite predominately. When asked to tell about situations where they experienced personal growth, people most frequently describe an experience with the characteristics of aesthetic consciousness.

As the ego, mediated by aesthetic experience, contacts the Self, we begin to realize that this center of our own being is a "gift" and is of the world. It is the world present in the beginnings of our personhood. The interminglings of Self and world are such that it might be difficult to designate any clear distinctions between Self and world. Thus, as one's ego enters into greater harmony with one's Self in the context of aesthetic consciousness and as self-actualization occurs, one is simultaneously more deeply involved with the world. The symbol systems revealed in aesthetic consciousness include Self-world relations such that the manifestation of one is the manifestation of both.

In many descriptions of aesthetic consciousness, the one experiencing the relevant event says things like, "I forgot myself," "I went out of myself," or "I was oblivious to myself." Upon deeper analysis, these statements reveal that the individual lost touch with the self-life commentary that often seems to go on in the back of one's head. Leaving this small *s* self means leaving the humdrum, everyday self that one often mistakes for one's true Self. But Self in the Jungian sense, the Self that is "gift," is not lost or left. In fact, people very frequently comment that aesthetic experience brings them in touch with themselves. They learn of possibilities they never thought they had and of strengths and noble characteristics that they previously had not recognized. At the same time, they do not take selfish pride in their discoveries for they see them as gifts.

A Touching of Ego and Self

When the experiences that have been referred to throughout this chapter are explored for their developmental component, it becomes obvious that the structures just described are both relevant and helpful. The young man who had the Beethoven experience said that personal growth was clearer to him from the beginning of his reflections on the experience. The self he lost in the music was the self he "had discovered up to that time, a rather boring and insensitive self." He had no trouble identifying this self as his "ego." What became available to him (a sensitivity to beauty such as he had never dreamt possible), he experienced as a great gift. In the end, he felt more himself, more true to himself, more "together."

The woman who had the landscape experience said, "Oh yes, I developed. I felt my awareness expanding out to a realization that I am one with human kind. I don't often think of that experience anymore, but I know I'm different for it. I am more in touch with who I really am. Whenever any situation arises where my humanness is called into play, I think with greater social sensitivity than I did before my experience."

The man who had the architectural experience indicated that he, too, had grown and had discovered more about who he had always been and who he was becoming. He experienced a loss of erroneous "ego" ideas, a getting beyond his persona, and an increase in Self sensitivity. For him, his experience turned out to be a revelation of his own "earthiness," a realization of how he is himself in relation to the "dances" between everything else.

It seems, then, that aesthetic consciousness is at least one very important and natural dynamic initiating and sustaining personal development. It constitutes a contact of ego and Self enabling the ego to achieve a more responsible, realistic, and harmonious relationship with the Self. Aesthetic consciousness thus appears as a human mode of making personally meaningful contact with the deeper (symbolic) meanings of the world. It varies, of course, as persons develop from tribal behavior patterns to individuaton, to the full possibilities of responsible interpersonal relations. It is a structure powerfully present all along the way.

A SUMMARY AND CHALLENGE

In the preparatory part of this chapter, I described methods by which I sought phenomenologically relevant generalities and typicalities. Consensus, privileged observers, and great thinkers were highlighted. The structures of behavior and peak experiences were used as starting points for my study of aesthetic consciousness. My perspective on understanding was mentioned as an important premise. The self-presence of human consciousness, the nature of structure, and the nature of the symbol also were key premises for my exploration.

The discovery part of the chapter utilized the structure of "oneness" to suggest the possibility of phenomenologically illuminating all the components of aesthetic consciousness. The pattern thus revealed, the structure bonding oneness, creativity, personal presence, ego–Self contact, growth, expression, and so on becomes a detailed description of the phenomenon named "aesthetic consciousness."

Understanding this pattern then leads to an ending/beginning. One can start to appreciate the depth and implications of John Dewey's (1934) wisdom when he writes that "esthetic experience is a manifestation, a record and celebration of the life of a civilization, a means of promoting its development, and is also the ultimate judgment upon the quality of a civilization'' (p. 326).

REFERENCES

Berleant, A. (1970). *The aesthetic field.* Springfield IL:Charles C Thomas.

Dewey, J. (1934). *Art as experience.* New York: Capricorn Books.

Dufrenne, M. (1973). *The phenomenology of aesthetic experience.* Evanstan: Northwestern University Press.

Giorgi, A. (1974). *Merleau-Ponty's contributions to the meaning of behavior.* Unpublished essay, Duquesne University.

Harding, M. E. (1965). *The "I" and the "Not-I."* New York: Pantheon Books.

Jennings, J. L. (1986). Husserl revisited: The forgotten distinction between psychology and phenomenology. *American Psychologist, 41,* 1231–1240.

Jung, C. G. (1964). *Man and his symbols.* New York: Doubleday.

Jung, C. G. (1968). *The collected works: The archetypes and the collective unconscious* (Vol. 9, Pt 1, 2nd ed.). Princeton, N J: Princeton University Press.

Maslow, A. (1967). *Toward a psychology of being.* New York: Van Nostrand.

Merleau-Ponty, M. (1963). *The structure of behavior.* Boston: Beacon Press.

Peck, M. S. (1978). *The road less traveled.* New York: Simon & Schuster.

Sanford, J. (1984). *Fritz Kunkel: Selected writings.* Ramsey, N J: Paulist Press.

VI

Transpersonal Psychology

Some readers may wonder why there is a section on transpersonal psychology in a book devoted to explicating the existential–phenomenological approach because these different perspectives represent two rather distinct traditions. What follows are some reflections on their respective similarities and differences as well as our reasons for including these chapters in this volume.

First, these two traditions share a number of concerns and values. Both are dissatisfied with mainstream psychology, its methods, underlying assumptions, and preconceived restrictions on the range of topics that can legitimately be studied by psychology. But the dissatisfaction that existential–phenomenological and transpersonal psychology have is aimed at more than just the discipline of psychology; they share a critical stance towards the natural scientific conception of the person and the world and the technologically oriented culture that arises from this world-view. Both of these approaches have a desire to explore all aspects of human experience, each having its own vision and evolving plan that guide its exploration of human phenomena.

Second, even with these common concerns, there has been very little dialogue between these two traditions. Their minimal mutual awareness has not, however, been the result of a careful examination and decision process. Rather, most thinkers and practitioners within one tradition are simply unfamiliar with the literature of the other. This is not to suggest that the differences between transpersonal and existential–phenomenological psychology are minimal or to predict that greater familiarity will necessarily result in a harmonious coming together. Based on our own feelings and personal discussions regarding the relationship between existential–phenomenological and transpersonal psychology (although both editors are rooted in the existential–phenomenological tradition, Ron Valle also embraces the transpersonal viewpoint, whereas Steen Halling is more of a friendly skeptic in this regard), we believe the following issues are likely to arise in any dialogue between these two approaches.

Existential-phenomenologists may well question to what extent transpersonal psychologists really examine human experience in a systematic and open-ended fashion, and to what extent certain assumptions (many based on Eastern philosophies) are already tacitly accepted as being adequate to human experience. Further, they may wonder to what extent transpersonal psychologists have articulated and developed their own philosophical basis and methods such that they are, in fact, able to integrate insights from a wide variety of psychological and spiritual perspectives. Finally, they may wonder if the difficulties of translating Eastern thought into Western terms and realities, as well as the difficulties of understanding Eastern thought in the first place, have not been underestimated within the transpersonal community.

Similarly, transpersonal psychologists are apt to have their own questions as they read the existential–phenomenological literature. For one, they may wonder why, in spite of its roots in philosophical thinkers such as Jaspers, Kierkegaard, and Marcel and its openness to all aspects of human experience, phenomenological psychology has given such little attention to spiritual experience and self-transformation. Also, phenomenologists have given rather limited attention to Eastern thought even though there are significant parallels between aspects of existential–phenomenological thought and Eastern traditions (e.g., the later writings of Merleau-Ponty and Taoism). Transpersonal psychologists may also question whether phenomenological psychology has not come to take its own foundation too much for granted and given too little energy to an ongoing clarification of basic concepts and assumptions (a positive movement in this direction is the confluence of hermeneutics and phenomenology as discussed in Chapter 1 in this volume). Readers will undoubtedly have their own thoughts and views in response to the chapters that follow.

Valle's Chapter 16 presents an initial overview of transpersonal psychology including its history and place in Western psychology, a first phenomenology of transpersonal/spiritual experience, and basic tenets of the transpersonal approach. The chapter also presents a response to Rollo May's critique of transpersonal psychology as well as discussions of meditation, Sankhya philosophy, spiritual awareness, and the nature of love and relationship.

Wittine's Chapter 17 offers his basic postulates for a transpersonal psychotherapy. This chapter continues much of the discussion contained in the preceding chapter, especially as it applies to the clinical application of transpersonal and spiritual perspectives, as well as to the ongoing dialogue between existential and transpersonal approaches in psychology.

In Chapter 18, Frager provides an overview of transpersonal theories and systems in psychology from both Western and Eastern sources. This chapter is designed to familiarize the reader with the wide range of topics and approaches that are currently regarded as "transpersonal" and to introduce spiritual psychology as an emerging new field within transpersonal psychology.

Schneier's Chapter 19 describes her Imagery-In-Movement Method, providing the reader with an example of a promising transpersonal methodology in psychology. Schneier discusses both the therapeutic and spiritual aspects of her approach as well as its implications for both existential–phenomenological and transpersonal psychology.

The transpersonal section concludes with Metzner's Chapter 20 on states of consciousness. As the nature of consciousness is central to both existential–phenomenological and transpersonal perspectives, this chapter presents a number of approaches to consciousness that Metzner believes must be considered in any psychological approach or inquiry.

16

The Emergence of Transpersonal Psychology

Ronald S. Valle

There are more things in heaven and earth, Horatio, than are dreamt of in your philosophy.
William Shakespeare, *Hamlet*

Transpersonal psychology, as the fourth force in psychology, has emerged from humanistic psychology (the third force) in much the same way that humanistic approaches emerged from their behavioral and analytic foundations. To address the role of transpersonal perspectives within the realm of humanistic psychology seems, therefore, a natural place to begin this discussion, for humanistic psychology represents an openness to all aspects of human nature and human beings: behavior, cognition, and affect as well as transcendent experience. And it is this very openness to experience that makes third force psychology the natural home for existential–phenomenological perspectives. Yet, in spite of this openness, there remains a not-so-subtle resistance to incorporating certain approaches to the understanding of human life and human existence into the humanistic framework, that is, approaches that integrate aspects of ourselves that do not seem part of our more day-to-day conceptual, emotional, and languaged realities—the so-called transpersonal and/or spiritual dimensions.

_____

Ronald S. Valle • Graduate School for the Study of Human Consciousness, John F. Kennedy University, Orinda, California 94563.

THE FIRST THREE FORCES IN PSYCHOLOGY

From a historical–philosophical perspective, the humanistic movement was, and continues to be, both a reaction to and an attempted completion of the world-views or approaches within more mainstream, traditional psychology. Both behavioral–experimental psychology and the psychoanalytic school (interchangeably referred to as the first and second forces in psychology) represent this tradition, and, as such, have provided a solid and well-defined groundwork. It is within this context that the philosophical bases that underly the third and fourth forces have taken form in psychology.

In strict behaviorism, the human individual is treated as a passive thing with no experiential depth, a separate entity divorced from its surrounding environment, an entity that simply responds to stimuli impinging upon it from the external physical and social world. Only that which is observable and whose dimensions can be agreed to by more than one observer is allowed. Human behavior (including our verbal behavior) is, therefore, the objective focus of the behaviorist; human experience is dismissed as subjective, unmeasurable, and not the stuff of science.

In partial response, the radical behaviorism of Skinner (e.g., 1974) claims to have collapsed this rather classic behavior–experience dualism by regarding thoughts and feelings, in their manifest, observable forms, as subject to the same laws that govern operant conditioning and the roles that stimuli, responses, and reinforcement schedules play within this particular paradigm. More specifically, Skinner (1974) regards that which is felt or introspectively observed as not some nonphysical world of consciousness, mind, or mental life, but the observer's own body. He states:

> "Emotion . . . is a matter of the probability of engaging in certain kinds of behavior defined by certain kinds of consequences. Anger is the heightened probability of attack, and love is the heightened probability of positively reinforcing a loved person. (in Evans, 1968, p. 11)

In the psychoanalytic scheme, the person is given more depth. Not only is the role of conscious experience discussed, but the realms of Freud's personal unconscious and Jung's collective unconscious are acknowledged as well. The human being is thereby more whole, but is still treated as a passive entity, one that responds to stimuli from the "inside" (current emotions, past experience, unconscious motives, etc.) rather than the pushes and pulls from without. Whether the analyst speaks of the punitive nature of one's toilet training or the subtle empowerment of the mother archetype, the implicit and radical separation of person and world goes on.

Yet, the seeds for an expanded discussion of human nature have been planted here. As discussed in more detail later, transpersonal psychologists acknowledge egoic experience and self-identity as foundational necessities whereas Jung's description of archetypal realities are regarded by many as central to understanding the essence of transpersonal awareness.

It is only when we reach the third force, humanistic psychology, that the fullest range of human potential is entertained and open to investigation. Yet, within these ranks, there are various perspectives, each with its own approach to human experience and human possibilities. Let me be more specific.

Of the numerous approaches labeled *humanistic* (e.g., those of Frankl, Rogers, Perls, Bugental, and May), existential–phenomenological psychology remains, for me, the central (and essential) third force perspective. It was here, in this blend of existential philosophy and phenomenological method, that I first felt a Call (to use the Heideggerian term) to experiencing a different way of being-in-the-world, not simply a different way of thinking. The human individual and his or her surrounding environment are regarded as implicitly and inseparably intertwined; one has no meaning when treated independently of the other. The person and world co-constitute one another. Although the world is still regarded as essentially different than the person in kind, the human

being, retaining its experiential depth, is seen as an active agent who makes choices within preexisting external constraints (i.e., human freedom is a situated freedom). From this tradition come a number of concepts that call us to a new definition of human capacity: not only co-constitutionality and situated freedom, but lived structure, prereflection, the life-world, and intentionality.

For me, the notion of intentionality has been of special importance in several ways. It has helped me to understand the nature of my everyday experience, it has provided a context in which to better understand the essence of my transpersonal experiences, and, in these ways, it has provided me with a conceptual form with which to bridge existential–phenomenological and transpersonal psychology.

Intentionality directly addresses and reflects the felt quality of what we normally describe as our consciousness, awareness, or experience, and its contents. To speak of the intentional nature of consciousness is to say that consciousness always has an object (whether that be a physical object, another person, or an idea or feeling), that consciousness is always a "consciousness of." This particular way of defining/describing intentionality directly implies the deep, implicit interrelatedness between the perceiver and the perceived that characterizes consciousness for the existential–phenomenological psychologist. It is this prereflective inseparability that enables each of us, through reflection, to become aware of the meaning that was implicit for us in the situation as it was lived (i.e., to have a textured and meaningful [meaning-full] experience).

A BEGINNING PHENOMENOLOGY OF TRANSPERSONAL EXPERIENCE

Even with this acknowledgment of and sensitivity to the nature and levels of human experience, there are certain types of awareness that do not seem to be fully captured or illuminated by phenomenological reflections on descriptions of our own experience and/or our prereflective felt sense of things. Often referred to as transcendent or transpersonal experience, these types of awareness are not really "experience" in the way we use the word in daily conversation (i.e., as made up of our thoughts and emotions) nor are they identical with our prereflective sensibilities. Rather, they are in some way "prior to" both of these levels and are more of a context or "space" from which our more common experience or felt sense emerges. This space or context does, however, present itself (i.e., manifests) as an "experience," and is, thereby, known to the one who is experiencing. But implicit in this "experience" is also the direct and undeniable realization that this foundational space is not of the realm of "experiencer–perceiver" and "experienced–perceived." Rather, it is a noumenal, unitive space within which the phenomenal world and intentional consciousness manifest. In fact, it is only because of this noumenal space or ground that the constituents of which existential–phenomenological philosophy speaks are possible (including felt sense and intentionality).

I am attempting here to word that which in its very essence is unwordable, for as soon as it is "thought of" or "felt" by the one who thinks and feels, that which is unwordable becomes a mere reflection of its true essence or Self, a shadow on the wall of Plato's cave—it transforms into something else, into some "thing" that is other-than-itself. These reflections are what I believe the existential-phenomenologists normally refer to as the objects of consciousness that is thereby, indeed, characterized by intentionality.

If wording the unwordable is the issue here, then to speak of a phenomenology of transpersonal experience becomes essentially enigmatic. What does it mean to investigate descriptions of that which is prior to any thematized experience or prereflective felt sense? Yet we are who we are in this moment or, perhaps more to the point, we are who we think we are in this moment. From my particular place of self-identity, then, let me share with you my own beginning phenomenology of transpersonal/transcendent experience as I have attempted to describe and understand it based on my own observations and self-reflections. This is not to imply that there is only one way to interpret transpersonal experience, but, rather, to reflect in words the nature of my own experience of this realm.

There are six general qualities that I have come to recognize in transpersonal awareness (most often as part of my meditative practice; more on meditation later):

1. There is a deep stillness and peace that I sense as both existing as itself and, at the same time, as "behind" all thoughts, emotions, or felt senses (bodily or otherwise) that might arise or crystallize in or from this stillness. I experience this as a state of *isness* or *amness* rather than a state of *whatness* or "I am this or that." This stillness is, by its very nature, neither active nor bodily and is, in this way, prior to both the prereflective and reflective levels of awareness.

2. There is an all-pervading aura or feeling of love and contentment for all that exists, a feeling that exists simultaneously in my mind and heart. This is not a feeling laced with desire and/or expectations but, rather, an open embracing of everyone and everything just as they are. It melts into the peace when I allow myself to simply "let it all be."

3. Existing as or with the stillness and love is a greatly diminished, and on occasion absent, sense of "I." The more common sense of "I am thinking or feeling this or that" becomes a fully present "I am" or simply, when in its more intense form, as "Amness" (or pure Being; e.g., Heidegger, 1962). The sense of a "perceiver" and "that which is perceived" has dissolved, for there is no longer any "one" to perceive as we normally experience this relationship.

4. My normal sense of space seems transformed. There is no sense of "being there," of being extended in and occupying space, but, similar to the previously mentioned, simply being. Also, there is a loss of awareness of my body sense as a thing or spatial container ranging from an experience of distance from sensory input to a radical forgetfulness of the body's very existence. It is here that my everyday, limited sense of body-space touches a sense of the infinite.

5. Time is also quite different than our everyday sense of linear passing time. Seemingly implicit in the sense of stillness described here is also a sense of time "hovering" or standing still, of being forgotten (i.e., no longer a quality of mind) much as the body is forgotten. Hours of linear time are experienced as a moment, as the eternal Now.

6. Bursts or flashes of insight are often part of this awareness, insights that have no perceived or known antecedents but that emerge as complete and "full blown." These insights or intuitive "seeings" have some of the qualities of more normal experience (e.g., although "lighter," there is a felt weightiness or subtle "content" to them), but they initially have an "other-than-me" quality about them, as if the thoughts and words that emerge from the insights are being done to or, better yet, through me—a sense that my mind and its contents are vehicles for the manifestation as experience of something greater and/or more powerful than myself. In its most intense or purest form, the "other-than-me" quality dissolves as the "me" expands to a broader, more inclusive sense of self that holds within it all that was previously felt as "other-than-me."

Mystics throughout the ages have used parables, poems, and pictures to induce the kind of awareness that I have attempted to describe in terms of these six qualities. But, they also point out that as soon as there is a thought of it (i.e., a vibration in the mind), this transcendent space with its deep stillness is disturbed as the sense of One becomes the two (i.e., it becomes the knower and the known). This is the realm of intentional awareness (i.e., consciousness as a "consciousness of ").

Given this perspective, there does not appear to be any room, in a phenomenology that insists that all experience or consciousness is characterized by intentionality, for a transcendent or transpersonal experience that is, in some way, prior to intentional awareness. To speak of a transcendent or pure consciousness (i.e., consciousness without an object) that is prior to or beyond that which is given directly in human experience is to evidence the idealistic fallacy according to the existential–phenomenological psychologist and to, thereby, betray the reality that is *Lebenswelt* (the life-world). If, however, transcendent experience (or "experiencing," to use Krishnamurti's, 1956, term) is one of oneness with what one typically experiences as outside or other-than one's self (i.e., an experience of duality dissolving), then one can just as accurately speak of this awareness as "consciousness without a subject." In this case, talk of the idealistic fallacy becomes irrelevant.

It is here that I see the borderline or bridge between the humanistic and transpersonal forces in psychology, for it is here that one is called to recognize the radical distinctions among the reflective mind, the prereflective body-sense, and pure consciousness, between rational-emotive processes and transcendent-spiritual awareness. Mind, not consciousness, is characterized by intentionality and, what's more, there is, to use Franklin Merrel-Wolff's (1973) words, an authentic philosophy of consciousness without an object. It is this implicit distinction that was underlying the original stirrings of the transpersonal movement within humanistic psychology—a sense of the transintentional nature of Being, the underlying fabric, space, or ground from which all that is human emerges and on which all that is human plays. Let us trace the history of this movement (from Valle & Harari, 1985).

TRANSPERSONAL PSYCHOLOGY: HISTORY AND DEFINITIONS

The initial committee for a proposed transpersonal journal and other related projects consisted of a number of founders of the Association for Humanistic Psychology, including Joseph Adams, James Fadiman, Harriet Francisco, Sidney Jourard, Abraham Maslow, Michael Murphy, Miles Vich, and Anthony Sutich. Of these, Sutich

and Maslow may be regarded as the midwives for the articulation of the transpersonal view within the early development of humanistic psychology.

We may regard Maslow's pronouncement in support of the concept of untapped human potential, as reflected in his view that a human being must become all that he or she is capable of becoming, as the signal phrase of the human potential movement. It also provided the opening to the transpersonal perspective as suggested in Maslow's 1967 lecture, "The Farther Reaches of Human Potential," a talk cited as the first public presentation of the emergence of transpersonal psychology (Maslow, 1969). This presentation raised the perspective of optimal states and optimal values extending far beyond ordinary limits of ego boundaries, time, and space. In fact, Maslow regarded humanistic psychology as a forum for the coming back to the prime reality of human experience and human existence itself. The major emphasis rests on the assumptions regarding biologically-based higher needs that include love, beauty, and dignity. When both basic and these higher needs are fulfilled, a different picture emerges. Maslow holds that for these individuals, there is a realm "beyond."

The first term describing this newer development was Julian Huxley's *transhumanistic* as that which motivates, gratifies, and activates the fortunate, developed, self-actualizing person. Maslow referred to Hartman who spoke of the intrinsic values of truth, goodness, beauty, perfection, excellence, simplicity, and elegance, and who then commented: "What this amounts to is that this third psychology is giving rise to a fourth, 'transhumanistic' psychology dealing with transcendent experience and transcendent values" (from Harari, 1985, personal communication). This new approach not only embraced the values of humanistic psychology, but went beyond our ordinary boundaries to transcend the limits of the ego–self. This position reemphasizes the need to live by and for "intrinsic values" and to reject the view that true science needs to be value-free or neutral. In fact, peak experiences and transcendent values relate directly to the important bridge between modern science and ancient mystic/spiritual traditions.

Maslow (1968) used a hierarchical model and conceptualized such qualities as love, sexuality, and friendship as ranging upward to a rarefied atmosphere that many of us rarely if ever reach. He conceptualized a healthy society as one that possesses substantial "growth-fostering potential" and, by acknowledging and describing the essential role of transcendent awareness in understanding the nature of human being, provided a broader conception of objectivity. And, characteristic of his transpersonal vision, he speaks for the sacralizing of everyday life as a way of enhancing and fostering maximum growth and higher values. He speaks, in a sense, for his view of the "growing tip" of the population that is the healthiest and most creative—those who form the exemplar of what we all could be.

Sutich documented the history of the transpersonal perspective and its emergence. He noted that humanistic psychology was beginning to overlap and become mistakenly identified with another emerging force in psychology. By early 1968, Abraham Maslow, Viktor Frankl, Stanislav Grof, and James Fadiman had together agreed to the name *transpersonal*. Sutich (1969) formally acknowledged the birth of a transpersonal discipline from humanistic psychology via his definition of transpersonal psychology:

> Transpersonal (or "fourth force") psychology is the title of an emerging force in the psychology field by a group of psychologists and professional men and women from other fields who are interested in those ultimate human capacities and potentialities that have no systematic place in positivistic or behaviorist theory ("first force"), classical psychoanalytic theory ("second force"), or humanistic psychology ("third force"). The emerging transpersonal psychology ("fourth force") is concerned specifically with the empirical, scientific study of, and responsible implementation of, the findings relevant to becoming, individual and species-wide meta-needs, ultimate values, unitive consciousness, peak experiences, B-values, ecstasy, mystical experiences, awe, being, self-actualization, essence, bliss, wonder, ultimate meaning, transcendence of the self, spirit, oneness, cosmic awareness, individual and species-wide synergy, maximal sensory awareness, responsiveness and expression, maximum interpersonal encounter, sacralization of everyday life, transcendental phenomena, cosmic self-humor and playfulness, and related concepts, experiences, and activities. As a definition, this formulation is to be understood as subject to optimal individual or group interpretations, either wholly or in part with regard to the acceptance of its content as essentially naturalistic, theistic, supernaturalistic, or any other designated classification. (pp. 15–16)

Since this original definition first appeared, there have been a number of scholarly attempts to outline, define, and describe the nature of transpersonal theory and practice (e.g., Boorstein, 1980; Tart, 1975; Walsh & Vaughan, 1980; Wilber, 1980). Regardless of the particular way it is discussed or defined, however, it is important to realize that, when one begins to talk of the expansion of self-identity beyond the boundaries of ego, name, and form, one is implicitly or explicitly dealing with radical self-transformation as well, that is, with a qualitatively different way of seeing "human being." Questions regarding the nature of "normal" functioning and the possibility of an "optimal" physical, emotional, intellectual, and spiritual health come to the fore. One is now addressing the full range of human nature and our ultimate capabilities and potential.

Given this historical–philosophical review as a contextual backdrop, let us turn more directly to the emerging form of transpersonal psychology. There have been, and continue to be, many psychological and philosophical traditions around the globe that are, in essence, transpersonal in their orientation. These approaches are often grounded in the context of elegant and greatly detailed systems of thought, some with a rich history that literally spans thousands of years, that, as a whole, touch almost every culture on earth. These approaches include, but are not exclusive to, Vedanta, Yoga, Zen and Tibetan Buddhism, Sufism, Christian mysticism, Taoism, mystic Judaism, the spiritual traditions of Native American cultures, and the teachings of Gurdjieff and his followers (see, for example, the discussion of Sankhya philosophy presented later).

All of these disciplines (and those like them) reflect themes and variations on what Aldous Huxley (1970) called the "perennial philosophy." As such, they typically include the following premises, premises that can be thought of as comprising an identifiable structure or essence that characterizes any particular psychology or philosophy as transpersonal:

1. That a transcendent, transconceptual reality or Unity binds together (i.e., is immanent in) all apparently separate phenomena, whether these phenomena be physical, cognitive, emotional, intuitive, or spiritual.
2. That the ego- or individualized self is not the ground of human awareness but, rather, only one relative reflection-manifestation of a greater trans-personal (as "beyond the personal") Self or One (i.e., pure consciousness without subject or object).
3. That each individual can directly experience this transpersonal reality that is related to the spiritual dimensions of human life.
4. That this experience represents a qualitative shift in one's mode of experiencing and involves the expansion of one's self-identity beyond ordinary conceptual thinking and ego–self awareness (i.e., mind is not consciousness).
5. This experience is self-validating.

The roots of transpersonal thinking are quite ancient. What is new, however, is the existence of a modern transpersonal psychology whose major task is to bring these ideas from the many different cultures, times, and traditions into our own psychological language and scientific framework. This is, of course, a difficult and demanding project that, as it has progressed, has not surprisingly been challenged by a number of noteworthy thinkers. Let us turn our attention to one of these challenges.

FURTHER CLARIFICATION OF TRANSPERSONAL PSYCHOLOGY: A RESPONSE TO ROLLO MAY

Rollo May's (1986) recent critique of transpersonal psychology provides a good example of the kind of response that transpersonal theory and practice has received from contemporary psychologists. Because May is one of the more thoughtful of these critics, his commentary also provides an appropriate forum for illustrating the very dialogue in which transpersonal psychologists wish to engage their colleagues. I would like to participate in this dialogue by examining and responding to May's critique (from Valle, 1986).

The prefix *trans* literally means both *beyond* and *through* as well as *across*. With this in mind, I feel that May (1986) misses the central point when, in reference to transpersonal psychology, he concludes that "it is a contradiction in terms to think one can make a psychology by throwing out or 'leaping across' . . . the person" (p. 87). Rather than discarding or "throwing out" our humanness, transpersonal psychology calls each of us to acknowledge that there is more to being human than just the behaviors, thoughts, and emotions that one expresses through his or her personal awareness and individual ego-identity. Self-identity and the process of individuation are truly essential aspects in understanding the human individual, personal aspects that are central to the transpersonal psychologist's practice, inquiry, and investigation. In addition, however, there is an extensive literature, both ancient and modern, that affirms the existence of human experience that is beyond the level of personal self-awareness, experience in which identity is not confined to the individual mind or more limited sense of self. These aspects or potentials, which express themselves through the medium of our personal emotions and thinking mind, are also a key part of the transpersonal psychologist's interests.

Transpersonal psychology, therefore, calls us *through* and *beyond* our more familiar level of ego awareness to a critical examination of the very ground from which our behaviors, thoughts, and emotions emerge as forms or manifestations. This foundational, shared reality has been metaphorized and/or conceptualized in a number of ways. Psychologists and philosophers alike have spoken of unity, intuition, oneness, noumenal reality, the collective unconscious, spiritual presence, mystic union, archetypal awareness, and others.

It is in this sense that I understand Abraham Maslow's appeal for "a Fourth Psychology, transpersonal, transhuman, centered in the cosmos rather than in human needs and interests, going beyond humanness [and self-]

identity" (May, 1986, P. 87). Maslow asks us to understand all of our humanness in this broader context, not to limit our vision (and, therefore, our understanding) to only a part of what and who we can be. Transpersonal psychology can be seen, therefore, as having two tasks: (a) to reinvestigate human behavior and human experience in this broader context to see which principles remain unchanged and which must be reformulated, and (b) to investigate the principles that govern the transpersonal realm itself and reveal its essence and nature.

May (1986) claims that the term *transpersonal* implies "that we can 'leap across' the negative aspects of human behavior, the expressions of the 'ego' . . ." (p. 88) and, thereby, that transpersonal psychology seeks to avoid or discard the negative aspects of human nature (e.g., cruelty, sadness, evil, anxiety, and suffering). My understanding is quite different. To truly understand the nature of the human individual, one must first acknowledge the full range of our humanness, which includes our negative aspects, our positive aspects, and the phenomena that are beyond the personal. Only from within this broader, transpersonal context can one begin to understand the true nature of any particular human behavior or experience. It is from this perspective that the transpersonal psychologist questions and examines all aspects of human nature, not only what we hide in the darkness of our shadow, but that which makes us noble and good as well (e.g., altruism, humility, forgiveness, joy, and love).

In fact, transpersonal psychology sees our "light" and "dark" sides as two sides of the same coin. One cannot understand one without embracing the other, for the very meaning of darkness depends on recognition of the light, and light has no meaning without shadow. In practical terms, the transpersonal psychotherapist is just as likely to help a client own and recognize his or her unresolved grief or unexpressed anger as to help a client embrace his or her capacity for compassion or desire for selfless giving.

Underlying this approach is an implicit assumption that seems a necessary characteristic of any truly transpersonal perspective: that a basic component of being human is the process of or movement toward self-transcendence as a radical change in one's most basic sense of self, as a process that (as discussed before) involves the transformation of intentional awarenesss itself. The forum for this transformation can take many forms, including art, being close to death, natural beauty, sex, religion, a birth, or any other potentially self-transforming human experience. And it is this characteristic or belief that separates transpersonal psychology from any other school or specialty area in the field. Human behavior and experience will never be fully understood without a conscious awareness and account of this process in any and all of our investigations.

In this context, the mind and its contents can be viewed as another part or subsystem of a greater whole. May (1986) claims that transpersonal psychology "confuses both psychology and religion" by taking "a point of view which goes beyond humanness" (pp. 88–89). For me, it is just the opposite. Transpersonal psychology helps clarify both psychological phenomena and transcendent experience (which may or may not involve some religious interest) by providing a broader framework that incorporates them both. To view human behavior, thought, emotion, and intuition in harmony, both theoretically and experientially, with our transcendent awareness is to envision a more complete and qualitatively different view of the human condition. It is only from this more complete perspective that the full range of human phenomena and our place in the universe can be understood.

In his closing section entitled "The New Humanism," May (1986) acknowledges Thomas Mann who proclaims that the "inner value and beauty of the human being lies precisely in the fact that he belongs to the two kingdoms of nature and the spirit." May goes on to express his ideal of "a world in which our loneliness will tie us together with our fellows" and "perfection and imperfection will cancel each other out." (p. 90). Grounded in the awareness of our spiritual essence and longing for a world where, in compassion and without judgment, we all stand together, May expresses a transpersonal vision. Seen in this light, May's comments call me as a transpersonal psychologist to ask: "What is it that calls us through our loneliness to a vision beyond our personal needs?"

What follows is an exposition of one classical transpersonal/spiritual schema—Sankhya philosophy. This presentation is offered both to ground the present discussion of transpersonal psychology in an exemplary philosophical treatise and to illustrate how transpersonal/spiritual ideas can be systematically described and applied, especially with regard to the understanding of mind and consciousness.

SANKHYA PHILOSOPHY

Let us look at the nature of Sankhya thought that, as one of the primary Indian philosophical systems, underlies the core of Yoga practice and philosophy (see, for example, Arya, 1986, Rama, 1982, Tigunait, 1983). Sankhya philosophy, which may be regarded as a cosmology/theology as well, sees all levels of reality and

phenomena as governed by two principles: the conscious and the unconscious. In existential–phenomenological terms, these principles are the implicit structural constituents of existence itself. The conscious principle (*purusha*) represents the formless, transcendent–spiritual aspects of reality—pure consciousness comprised of the essences of awareness, life, and will. On the other hand, the unconscious principle (*prakriti*) reflects the substantial, material aspects, the forms or shells of the world as it appears to our senses. In this system, then, both conscious, living spirit and inert, lifeless matter are necessary for understanding the existence and appearance of the phenomenal world.

Spiritual ignorance becomes, therefore, the failure to recognize this core distinction in all that exists. How, one may ask, do purusha and prakriti, which are separate and utterly different in their essential nature, interact?; that is, how can purusha that is eternally free and self-sufficient be made to assume the limitations that are necessarily involved in the association with matter? It is through the deprivation of knowledge or, rather, the loss of awareness of its eternal and essential nature. The manifestation of the phenomenal world is, therefore, the inevitable result as purusha forgets its true Self and begins to identify and become increasingly involved with matter.

The nature of mind. The implications of this approach for understanding the nature of mind is potentially profound. In traditional Western thought, there is very little if any distinction made between the mind or mental activity (thoughts and emotions) and consciousness or awareness. In fact, they are often used interchangeably in a very misleading manner.

Sankhya philosophy, however, makes this distinction very clearly and does so in a way that is quite foreign to those of us raised in a Western culture. Mind is treated as part of prakriti (the material realm) and not as a part or derivative of purusha (pure consciousness). The manifestation of prakriti is seen to range over a wide spectrum from its dense physical appearance as objects and things of the world (e.g., the physical body) to its most subtle, least tangible form as "stuff of the mind" (i.e., thoughts, emotions, and intuition).

Our bodies seem to have life, therefore, and our minds appear to be conscious because of spirit's identification (or, better, misidentification) with these forms, not because of properties inherent in the forms themselves—our bodies reflect the energy and life of purusha, and our minds manifest purusha's awareness and will. That is, our mental processes are active and alert only because of the purusha–prakriti interaction, prakriti's natural state being unconscious and inert. We mistakenly believe, because of our various desires (i.e., attractions and repulsions to worldly objects and ideas), that we are the forms, body and mind, and become, therefore, forgetful of our true Self. This forgetfulness, this identity with the ego–self alone, is the essence of spiritual ignorance (*avidya*) in the yogic scheme.

Consider a brown paper bag that contains an electric light bulb. When the light is switched on, the whole bag glows. If we liken the paper bag to the mind and the light bulb to purusha or the spiritual Self within, the confusion begins to dissolve. If one attributes the luminous quality or glow of the bag to the bag itself, one mistakenly equates mind with consciousness. If, however, one realizes that the bag glows brightly only because of the light within, then the problem is solved. Consciousness is purusha, mind is prakriti, and, therefore, mind is not consciousness.

As is probably quite obvious by now, there is very little agreement or overlap between Sankhya philosophy and the psychological theorizing that characterizes much of Western thought, including both the behavioral–experimental and existential–phenomenological schools. Why is this so?

The major point of difference surrounds the nature of mind. Within the behavioral–experimental realm, the mind and mental processes are, at best, viewed as "internal" intervening variables (by the cognitive psychologists) that stand between the impinging stimulus and the observable response. Thoughts and emotions are reduced to the role of mediator, standing between the stimulating environment and the behaving organism. It is human behavior that becomes the central focus because the experimental psychologist insists on understanding only that which complies with an objective, physical universe. It is, therefore, only human behavior that is observable, measurable, and of a kind that is possible for more than one observer to agree on its existence and characteristics.

To many behaviorists, mind is regarded as an epiphenomenon of the neurochemical brain where mental processes often serve as "noise" in the system that makes the experimental task of accurately describing the causal bases of behavior all the more difficult. In either case, consciousness and mind are used interchangeably and treated either as intervening variables (in an objective, behavioral way) or as a nuisance that must be summarily dismissed if science is ever to make progress in this area. This whole way of thinking represents a rather remarkable reductionism, especially when viewed in the light of the Sankhya system.

The existential–phenomenological approach takes a much-needed step forward by addressing human consciousness as a psychological phenomenon that is not only quite worthy of scholarly investigation, but one that

must be examined in order to truly understand the nature of human being. As stated before, consciousness is regarded as intentional in nature and, although more sensitive than the behavioral–experimental rendition, this treatment of consciousness still falls short of the Sankhya vision.

In short, existential–phenomenological psychologists seem to confuse mind and consciousness. What they refer to as consciousness is what Sankhya philosophy treats as parts and processes of mind. In comparison with the pure "Amness" of purusha, the intentional "I am this" quality of the self-identified mind is more than simply analogous to the insistence that consciousness is always a "consciousness of" as the existential–phenomenologists claim. It is, to put it simply, a property of mind, not consciousness. That is, intentionality characterizes mind as an inherent quality of this subtlest material form (i.e., prakriti), but it offers little with regard to understanding spiritual experience and/or pure awareness *per se*. However one metaphorizes this qualitative difference, Sankhya calls us to recognize the important distinction between mind and pure consciousness if we ever hope to understand the full range of human potential. This distinction is one which existential-phenomenology fails to make.

Implications. Because Sankhya philosophy regards the mind as the subtlest manifestation of the material realm, the mind becomes a borderline area or bridge between the world of form and formless spirit. It is the mind that lies closest to one's spiritual awareness, and it is through the mind, therefore, that one can most easily discover the true Self that waits within.

What are the implications of adopting a perspective of mind and spiritual awareness such as this? If mind is not consciousness and spiritual ignorance is the misidentification of spirit with the form in which it reflects (i.e., the mind), then true knowledge or self-realization can only come via the awareness of this mistaken identity through the dissolution of this misidentification. Given this perspective, meditation has been suggested, over thousands of years in many different forms in many different cultures, as a practical method for working with the mind in order to bring about this change in awareness (i.e., true self-transformation). Let us look at one form of meditation, sitting with eyes closed, as an example of these practices.

The actual meditative practice begins with concentration. As a process, concentration involves giving the mind one thing to focus on such as a word, syllable, or mantra that one repeats silently in one's mind or a visual image such as a candle flame, picture, or yantra. Although a subtle and difficult art to master, concentration is not, as many believe, a dull and tedious task. In fact, the experience of successful concentration is quite pleasurable and satisfying in both the physical and emotional sense.

As one practices concentration in a systematic fashion, two things begin to occur with increasing frequency and intensity: the general content and distracting noise of the mind is reduced as the mind becomes quieter during the practice, and, from the context of this relative stillness, one begins the natural process of watching (witnessing) all thought and emotion from a perspective or place of peaceful nonattachment, slowly breaking one's identification with the contents of the mind. With continued practice and awareness, one eventually acquires the ability to bring one's mind to one-pointedness or pure focus at will. This ability to focus the mind at will is a prerequisite for true meditation, that is, meditation as the effortless flow of timeless awareness. It is in this flow that the nature of reality and existence is revealed.

Consider the following example as an illustration of this process. A solid block of uncut marble has an infinite number of potential statues that could be chiseled and cut from it through the efforts of a skilled sculptor. The block is likened to purusha—infinite potential, formless, unmanifest spirit. The moment one statue is created, however, this one existing form negates the possibility of the appearance or manifestation of any one of the infinite number of other forms that could have been created from this same block of marble instead. To the extent that one form is revealed, all of the rest are veiled; to the extent that purusha identifies with prakriti, the phenomenal world appears/exists as it does.

It is in this sense that our identification with any one physical form (person or object) or mental form (thought or emotion) denies infinity (i.e., the act of creation is also a negation). It is in this way that identification with the products of our minds keeps the realization of our spiritual Self at a distance; by solely identifying with our thoughts, we forget the Divine. And so, in this way, the practice of meditation invites spirit into your life.

The experiences attained via this meditative discipline are developmental in nature, they are well-known and described in great detail by those who have walked this path, and they are self-validating. Through these meditative experiences, one comes to realize the nature of thought and emotion including their origin, manifestations, progress, and, perhaps most importantly, what is necessary to bring about their cessation. Meditation can be seen, therefore, as the means to gain control of the modifications of the mind. As such, meditation also becomes a practical means for ending human suffering by helping us to disidentify with our attractions and re-pulsions to things in the ever-changing phenomenal world.

REFLECTIONS ON LOVE AND RELATIONSHIP

With this perspective literally "in mind," much of the work of humanistic psychology can be seen in a new light. In our openness to and encouragement of emotional states, for example, we risk attachment to these forms and begin to see them as ends in themselves. By ignoring the presence of living spirit as pure consciousness, we reduce ourselves, once more, to "things" in what amounts to a radical emotional materialism done in the name of humanistic approaches to psychology. At best, we understand these states more completely via descriptive–phenomenological analysis, but, within the closed system of mind as our sole identity of "who we really are," we come no closer to the truth of it all. By identifying only with the ego–mind, the transcendent aspects of affective phenomena remain obscure.

When approached from a transpersonal perspective, however, love and the essence of interpersonal relationship take on new meaning. When we say "I love you," for example, we really mean "I need you to be a certain way. If you are not, then I won't love you anymore." This "being in love with" is, of course, not love but need, a conditional state of mind that is filled with fear of both broken expectations and of true love itself.

The intentionality of mind is evident in conditional love, for "being in love" is always a "being in love with" someone or something else (i.e., some other-than-self); conditional love always has an object. The perception of "other" (i.e., perceived duality) is a constituent of intentionality and, thereby, of conditional love as well.

As the process of disidentification proceeds, however, perceived "otherness" begins to dissolve and, with it, expectations for the other as well. "Being in love with" transforms slowly into a "being in love" (together with the other). Rather than needing another as a focus for the attribution of one's loving feelings (i.e., the other as cause of or reason for these feelings), one begins to experience love simply by being in the presence of an other. Not only is the perception of "other" less evident here, but the feeling of love is no longer as dependent on whether or not the other fulfills one's expectations.

When the perceived separateness of "self and other" has dissolved and one's identity is secure in the spiritual Self, "being in love" becomes simply "being love."* This is the realm of unconditional love, for it is only here that there is no perceived "other" to have any conditions for. With no "other-than-self," it is then meaningless (from this perspective) to speak of any "object" of awareness—whatever there is, there's only one of it (i.e., the "perceiver" and the "perceived" have dissolved). Whereas intentionality, indeed, characterizes the "ego-self-identified" mind, the realm of spirit, of pure consciousness, is a truly transintentional reality.

Equating this level of "being love" with spiritual awareness is not, of course, a new idea. It has often been said that "God is love" and that spiritual realization is identical with pure bliss and peace. The mere physical presence of certain individuals who have gained mastery of their minds, and, thereby, their self-identity, can have a profoundly calming effect on the hearts and minds of those around them. This loving presence is a felt presence; it is tangible and the natural result of meditative practice.

Although we all touch this place of unconditional love on occasions, love of this kind seems very rare. All of our lives we follow the implicit cultural prescription that true love is something that we must work hard to find. We are led to believe that if we put forth constant effort, that if we seek and search while remaining keenly attuned to the actions and words of others, that with a little bit of luck, we will eventually meet that "right" someone with whom we will fall in love. It is not pride, lust, and emotional need that we miss—there are more than enough situations in which we can choose to be with these—but love. How many of us worry that we will never experience this connection with another human heart, that, no matter how hard we try, we will never find this uniquely human place of shared intimacy and inspired affection? We despair that we shall live a cold life alone, a life untouched by the warmth and light of love.

Seeing this predicament in the context of unconditional love, however, I suggest that things are not like this at all! In fact, the real situation is just the opposite of how we think it is! Rather than looking for love, we expend most of our energy keeping ourselves from loving one another, numbing ourselves to the opportunity to experience true intimacy at every moment with everyone we meet. Our ego defenses—denial, projection, rationalization, repression, and the rest, our self-conscious feelings, our awkwardness, penchants, and fears, and just our random flitting thoughts—"Will she touch me?", "Does he care?"—all serve to keep away that which we proclaim we crave the most. The ego–self keeps itself going in this way, keeps itself real. For if it were to embrace the fierce reality that all is love, it would lose its sense of false control and dissolve back into the Oneness that is God and Love. Right here on the level of one-on-one relationship, our separate selves throw up fear to fuel the masquarade that we are all separate beings in search of elusive love.

If two individuals come together with a sensitivity to the relationship between their respective ego–selves and the nature of love (as described before), then a new understanding of human relationship can emerge as both begin to see that, ultimately, the only reason to be with another human being is to awaken to one's spiritual Self or, closer to the level of felt experience, to remember the love that is one's essential nature. With conscious intent, two individuals can agree to use their being together as a vehicle or means to help one another step out of his or her unconscious reactivity into the strength and warmth of clear choice and self-awareness. What exists here is the possibility for a true spiritual relationship or spiritual marriage (e.g., Vissell & Vissell, 1984) that is manifest in, but essentially independent of, the particular form of the social relationship or roles of the individuals so committed.

With mutual intent, my wife Valerie and I have consciously chosen to live our marriage in this way and find ourselves, thereby, on an exquisitely difficult, fascinating, confusing, fulfilling, exhausting, joyful, and often painful journey (Valle & Valle, 1984). Of the many insights I (we) have gained and continue to gain in this process, the following stands out as most worthy of note in the present context.

The nature of expectations both for the other person and for the relationship itself repeatedly presents itself as a central issue in most of our interactions. Whether it involves working out our daily schedules (dinner, employment concerns, car repairs, or feeding the dog), agreeing on how we will be with our three children, or how we will express our love and affection for close others in our lives, it has become quite clear to me how often I experience pain when the reality of the way things are comes up against the way in which my mind insists on clinging to a certain view of the way things should be (see Levine, 1982). It seems that expectations always lead to suffering because, at some time in some way, things always turn out differently than we wanted them to be, especially with regard to the words, feelings, and actions of our partner.

It is here, in the day-to-day concerns that relationship brings to my attention, that I see a central truth in my life most clearly—that our essential nature is love. When I do not experience love in the moment for whoever or whatever I am with, to the extent that my mind has set up the separation of "self" and "other" in any situation, I am partially dead in that moment, not fully alive. When my mind clings out of fear of the change to come, fear of the next unknown moment, my heart contracts and closes to the other. It seems difficult for the heart to remain open in an atmosphere of self-created apprehension. It seems that when the love that we are is denied and sacrificed on the altar of perceived "self" and "other," a separation or vacuum appears in the heart, and fear rushes in to fill this space. My self-reflections tell me that, no matter how many forms my feelings take, in the end there are only two things in my experience: fear and love. It is always one of these two that I must choose.

The ways in which I cover or dilute my love with fear are also entwined in this matrix of experience. When Valerie, for example, says or does something that I respond to with a painful feeling of some kind, it is so simple, even automatic, at times to say to her: "You made me angry!" (or "depressed" or "confused" or "jealous" or whatever). I have come to regard this kind of reaction as an insanity plea. It is true spiritual craziness to see oneself as emotionally dependent on the whim of an other. No one can make me feel anything I do not choose to feel (however conscious or unconscious that choice might seem to be in the moment). Here is one clear way in which we choose to be a "victim," give our personal choice and, therefore, our power to the "other," and, out of fear, close our hearts, not only to the other, but to ourselves as well.

A recourse to this situation is to regain mastery of our own reactions, emotional and otherwise. It is an art to give our feelings room to be what they are, room to rise up in our awareness and fully manifest in our experience, and, then, to fall away when they are ready to go. In this way, one begins to see that feelings come and go of their own accord, in tune with their own rhythms, and that if one does nothing to them, does not react to or contract around them, they naturally dissipate and dissolve in time. There is really nothing to do when a feeling arises except to let it be and, with this realization, to remember that one has choice regarding when or if to express the feeling in word or deed.

Being this way with one's emotional life is, admittedly, most difficult to live at times, especially with feelings we experience as very painful. Yet, what other choice do we have? Repressing feelings or compressing them with judgment (e.g., "Anger is bad. I shouldn't feel angry.") only pushes them down and guarantees they will return another time with even greater force. Freely expressing them, on the other hand, only reinforces their power and, therefore, also increases the likelihood of their later return, as well as contracting the heart and increasing the suffering of the individual who is seen as their object. Once again, one has chosen fear instead of love.

Being with a relationship in this way, one quickly sees that the journey is far more intrapersonal than interpersonal, that the key dialogue is between one's self and the Voice within, and what a blessing it is to be with another person who loves God more than he or she loves you. To live one's life from the heart and to take responsibility for one's own feelings and reactions is to remember and access a deeper part of one's self, a transpersonal Self that somehow lies behind, in the very foundation of, who we think we are.

CONCLUDING THOUGHTS

How many of us can love as the sun loves? Unconditionally, the sun shines on everyone, giving its light, heat, and life to saints and murderers alike. As psychologists who study human emotion and human life, as personal beings who continually relate to others as if they were somehow separate from ourselves, I call each and every one of us to this task of self-transformation. Being ever aware of body, mind, and spirit and sensitive to their subtle interplay, I call you to access your will consciously to choose love in all situations, to say "no" to anger, jealousy, and depression and "yes" to love, to manifest this empowered heart that is nothing other than your true spiritual Self. In this way, we will someday surely meet one another without fear, truly open, in Love.

REFERENCES

Arya, U. (1986). *Yoga-sutras of Patanjali,* (Vol. 1). Honesdale, PA: Himalayan Press.

Boorstein, S. (Ed.). (1980). *Transpersonal psychotherapy.* Palo Alto, CA: Science and Behavior Books.

Evans, R. I. (1968). *B. F. Skinner: The man and his ideas.* New York: Dutton.

Heidegger, M. (1962). *Being and time.* New York: Harper & Row.

Huxley, A. (1970). *The perennial philosophy.* New York: Harper & Row.

Krishnamurti, J. (1956). *Commentaries on living; First series.* Wheaton, IL: Theosophical Publishing House.

Levine, S. (1982). *Who dies?; An investigation of conscious living and conscious dying.* Garden City, N Y: Anchor.

Maslow, A. H. (1968). *Toward a psychology of being.* New York: Van Nostrand Reinhold.

Maslow, A. H. (1969). The farther reaches of human nature. *Journal of Transpersonal Psychology, 1,* 2–10.

May, R. (1986). Transpersonal or transcendental? *The Humanistic Psychologist, 14*(2), 87–90.

Merrell-Wolff, F. (1973). *The philosophy of consciousness without an object.* New York: Julian.

Rama, S. (1982). *Choosing a path.* Honesdale, PA: Himalayan Press.

Skinner, B. F. (1974). *About behaviorism.* New York: Vintage.

Sutich, A. J. (1969). Some considerations regarding transpersonal psychology. *Journal of Transpersonal Psychology, 1,* 11–20.

Tart, C. T. (Ed.). (1975). *Transpersonal psychologies.* New York: Harper & Row.

Tigunait, R. (1983). *Seven systems of Indian philosophy.* Honesdale, PA: Himalayan Press.

Valle, R. S. (1986). Transpersonal psychology: A reply to Rollo May. *The Humanistic Psychologist, 14*(3), 210–213.

Valle, R. S.,& Harari, C. (1985). Current developments in transpersonal psychology. *The Humanistic Psychologist, 13*(1), 11–15.

Valle, R. S., & Valle, V. A. (1984). Spiritual marriage. *Yoga Journal,* November-December, 12–14.

Vissell, B., & Vissell, J. (1984). *The shared heart; Relationship initiations and celebrations.* Aptos, CA: Ramira.

Walsh, R. N., & Vaughan, F. (Eds.). (1980). *Beyond ego: Transpersonal dimensions in psychology.* Los Angeles: J. P. Tarcher.

Wilber, K. (1980). *The atman project: A transpersonal view of human development.* Wheaton, IL: Theosophical Publishing House.

17

Basic Postulates for a Transpersonal Psychotherapy

Bryan Wittine

The Greeks had a word, *pou sto,* meaning a place to stand, a ground, base, or set of principles from which to operate. The purpose of this paper is to suggest a *pou sto* for the practice of transpersonal psychotherapy (Grof, 1985; Vaughan, 1986; Wilber, 1977, 1980).

It is common knowledge that the beliefs and state of mind of the therapist—both conscious and unconscious—determine to a great extent the nature of the therapy and, in particular, its outcome. Therefore, I believe it will be useful to make explicit some of the fundamental assumptions held by many transpersonal therapists.

As I see it, transpersonal therapy is an approach to healing/growth that aims to bridge the Western psychological tradition, including psychoanalytic and existential psychological perspectives, and the world's perennial philosophy. Huxley (1944) defined the perennial philosophy as:

> . . . the metaphysic that recognizes a divine Reality substantial to the world of things and lives and minds; the psychology that finds in the soul something similar to, or even identical with, divine Reality; the ethic that places man's final end in the knowledge of the immanent and transcendent Ground of all Being.'' (p. vii)

More specifically, I am referring to the perspective of an esoteric or mystical tradition that Huxley and others (Schuon, 1975; Smith, 1976; Wilber, 1977) believe un-

derlies the world's religious doctrines with their cultural and historical idiosyncracies. This esoteric perspective permeates the whole approach of the transpersonal therapist. What differentiates transpersonal therapy from other orientations is neither technique nor the presenting problems of clients but the spiritual perspective of the therapist.

The word *transpersonal* (from the Latin *trans* meaning beyond and through and *persona* meaning mask or personality) has been defined as referring to states of consciousness extending beyond the customary ego boundaries and the ordinary limitations of time and space (Grof, 1985; Walsh & Vaughan, 1980). Fadiman (1980) suggests the word *transpersonal* can also be used to characterize the entire process of growth *through* the personality to spiritual states of being. I believe it can also be recognized quite simply as an amalgam of transcendental and personal. Seen in this light, a transpersonal approach seeks to help clients integrate the transcendental or spiritual and personal dimensions of existence, to help them fulfill their unique, creative individuality while pointing toward their rootedness in the nontemporal, formless, depth dimension of being.

The following five postulates are an attempt to weave Western psychology and the perennial wisdom. They form a *pou sto* for transpersonally oriented clinical work. I suggest transpersonal psychotherapy affirms: (a) the need for healing/growth on all levels of the spectrum of identity—egoic, existential, and transpersonal; (b) the therapist's unfolding awareness of the Self, or deep center of Being, and his or her spiritual perspective on life as

Bryan Wittine • Graduate Program in Transpersonal Counseling Psychology, John F. Kennedy University, Orinda, California 94563.

central to the therapeutic process; (c) the process of awakening from a lesser to a greater identity; (d) the healing, restorative nature of inner awareness and intuition; and (e) the transformative potential in the therapeutic relationship not only for the client but for the therapist as well. In this chapter, I will discuss these postulates and some of the themes suggested by each.

In considering them, however, I wish my readers to be aware of two important points. First, these postulates are my *pou sto*, the frame of reference through which I work with my clients. They do not comprise the belief system of every transpersonal therapist. They are where I stand at this point in my life. Although I believe most transpersonal therapists would substantially agree with me, each is also likely to differ in many ways according to his or her individual perspective.

Secondly, when reading mystical literature, words such as *Self* and *Being* must not be taken literally and confused as things or objects. According to the world view of the perennial philosophy, what these words point to eludes objectification. Our true nature cannot be known completely by the mind, for the experience of the Self is beyond the range and reach of conceptual, dualistic thought. Even giving it a label and calling it the *Self* can be misleading, for this implies our true nature is an *it*, a thing or object separate from an observing subject.

In order to be truly known, transpersonal dimensions of consciousness must be directly experienced. Transpersonal experiences occur as we transcend the "eye of the flesh" and the "eye of the mind" and awaken our "eye of contemplation" (Wilber, 1983). The elusiveness of perennial philosophers tends to frustrate those of us who have yet to discover realities outside our ordinary sense perceptions, and strictly rational conceptualizations; nevertheless, the perennial philosophy explicitly states that only individuals whose vision penetrates behind the veil of worldly appearances can experientially verify mystical realities.

POSTULATE 1

Transpersonal Psychotherapy is an approach to healing/growth that addresses all levels of the spectrum of identity—egoic, existential, and transpersonal.

"Who am I?" and "What am I?" are the central questions addressed in the field of psychology. The quest to find answers to these eternal questions is as ancient as the questions themselves. Inscribed above the door to the Temple of Apollo were the words, "Man, Know Thyself!" Self-knowledge was the aim of the mystery schools in ancient Greece and Egypt. In the Europe of the Renais-

sance, alchemists turned inward to practice their "Great Work," the goal of which was to discover the philosopher's stone, a symbol for a true Self lying behind and beyond our surface personality. The Hindu Vedas and *Upanishads,* some esoteric Christian teachings, the sayings of the Buddha, and in modern times psychoanalysis and existential–humanistic psychology—at the heart of each of these are the simple questions, Who am I? and What am I?

And the answer? Wilber (1977, 1979), one of transpersonal psychology's most influential and prolific exponents, suggests it depends entirely upon where we are identified in a spectrum of identity. Our identification is determined by where we draw the boundary line between what we identify as "I" and what we exclude as "not-I." In other words, when I describe myself, I am identified with everything on the inside of that boundary line. Everything not me is outside.

The Self, or depth dimension of Being, is the true nature and condition of all sentient beings. As a result of our conditioning, however, we limit ourselves and our world and turn from our original nature to embrace a boundaried existence. "Our originally pure consciousness," Wilber (1979) wrote, "then functions on various levels, with different identities and different boundaries. These different levels are basically the many ways we can and do answer the question, 'Who am I?'" (p. 5). In other words, the world of individual forms is an appearance of the Self.

Borrowing from Wilber (1977, 1979) and Walsh and Vaughan (1980), I emphasize three levels, dimensions, or bands in this spectrum—the egoic, existential, and transpersonal—extending from the strictly isolated and individual to the wholly inclusive and universal. I view them as interpenetrating levels in a "hierarchy of wholes." The higher dimensions go beyond, yet include the lower. Just as a cell is a tiny life existing within the larger life of, say, the brain, and the brain is a smaller life existing within the greater life of the physical body, so too our egoic identity is one component of our greater existential self, and our existential self functions within a still greater, all-encompassing transpersonal reality. The transpersonal may not be truly known while we are exclusively identified at the existential level, just as the existential self is only partially experienced when we are exclusively identified with the ego.

Egoic Identity

I define egoic identity as a stable, relatively constant, and enduring system of mental self- and world constructs that gives us the sense of being particular beings separate from other particular beings.

If we take the view of the perennial philosophy, as

developed by Wilber (1977, 1979), that an individual is first a Buddha and becomes an ego, then we are born as pure Being, completely open, innocent, and undifferentiated from nature and mother. But we cannot live our lives in this state of unconscious, undifferentiated oneness. We must survive in the world. So, under the influence of primary caretakers, we "fall" from our "sinless" state in unconditioned Eden into the "sin" of egoic separateness.

Our mental-egoic identity is a whole constellation of concepts, images, self- and object representations, identifications, subpersonalities, and coping and defense mechanisms associated with the feeling of being separate persons, different from all other persons. This system of mental constructs is fashioned from the early interactions between our inborn and unfolding givens—our capacities for bodily pleasure and pain, thought, perception, memory, movement, affect, and the like—and the environmental inputs of primary caretakers and life experiences. The various parts of our self- and world construct system are the building blocks of our house of personality. How we consciously and habitually organize, perceive, and give meaning to ourselves and our world are conditioned by the structure of our mental-egoic self.

Theories of character structure are basically psychoanalytic (Horney, 1950). Recent innovations are the psychiatric classifications of DSM-III (Millon, 1981) and the neoanalytic approaches of ego psychology (Blanck & Blanck, 1974, 1979), object relations theory (Horner, 1984; Kernberg, 1975; Masterson, 1976, 1985; Miller, 1981), and psychoanalytic self-psychology (Kohut, 1971, 1977; White & Weiner, 1986). My conception of the mental-egoic identity is fundamentally the same as Masterson's (1985) "real self," a term he used to designate "the sum of self and object representations with their related affects" (p. 21).

As I see it, one primary task of transpersonal psychotherapy is identical to that of many other Western psychotherapies: to facilitate the emergence and development of a stable, cohesive egoic identity when this is needed by the client. Many individuals come to therapy needing a clearer sense of who they are as separate, distinct individuals. Their self-identity can be described as preegoic. They are identified almost entirely with certain acceptable aspects of their total selves (what Jung called the *persona*) and deny, repress, or project their unacceptable aspects (Jung's *shadow*). Their self-definition is vague, distorted, and significantly limited; their boundaries, shifting and unstable. Consequently, these understructured individuals either form addictive, symbiotic relationships that are highly intense and chaotic, or withdraw into an ivory tower, becoming estranged from others. Both types feel extremely vulnerable in a world of overwhelming proportions.

As Masterson (1976) puts it, "Their capacity to love is crippled by the need to defend themselves against intimacy by clinging and/or distancing; their satisfaction at work is crippled by the need to avoid individuation" (p. 3). They are usually struggling to break free from archaic ties and conflicts with introjected parental and early authority imagos and consolidate a realistic sense of themselves, others, and the world.

Developing a stable egoic identity, or concepts of self and concepts of others that are realistic, integrated, and whole, gives them a firmer inner foundation from which to form more satisfying relationships and adjust to ever-present psychosocial pressures. When they learn to stand as separate, independent persons, they can enter into more fulfilling relationships rather than becoming enmeshed in the identities of others or distancing themselves out of the dread of self-fragmentation and loss of their already impoverished feeling of individual selfhood.

These clients usually come to therapy with polarized views of themselves and the world. Their identities are caught in extremes of good and bad, right and wrong, either this or that, and they neglect to see the full spectrum of possibilities between the extremes. Two case examples illustrate my point. One, an emotionally distant, detached man with a schizoid trend in his personality could not experience his personal needs and feelings because he was terrified he would lose control. As a child, he learned his needs and emotions were dangerous; they upset his perfectionistic mother who threatened him with her illnesses and her possible death if he needed nurturance or expressed anger. Another male client, tender but passive, rejected being assertive and going after what he wanted because to do so made him like his aggressive, dominating father who humiliated both him and his mother. In this pre-egoic state he was unconsciously enmeshed with the mother. He also engaged in grandiose success fantasies, all of which would be realized in some distant tomorrow. However, continuing to see his father as all bad and having rejected him completely, he also rejected the power and practicality he needed to realize some of his dreams.

These men were seeing things in black and white and missing the color in between. The first had disowned his entire emotional nature. The other had split off his aggressive impulses and became, in his own words, "a sweet man with no balls." Their respective journeys in psychotherapy helped them realize that living at the extremes of emotional distance or passivity out of a fear of becoming hysterical or aggressive and dominating is self-defeating. Each in his own way went beyond preegoic splits to the cohesion and integration of ego. Thus work at the egoic level builds boundaries, integrates polarizations, replaces nonfunctional concepts of self and other, and modifies character structure so clients can interact with others and the world in a more fulfilling way..

Existential Identity

Once individuals with preegoic identities have developed a more realistic conception of themselves and others, a more cohesive egoic identity, they can embark on a process that takes them further on the journey of self-discovery, that of unfolding their existential self, or their true inner individuality.

Other clients enter therapy with a more stable, cohesive self-definition. They have a relatively solid feeling of being particular persons separate from others. For them, problems and concerns develop not so much because they have too little structure but because *they have too much*. Their difficulties come from being overboundaried, not underboundaried. They have become overly rigid and defended in their self-definition and patterns of living. I am here referring to the differentiation made by psychoanalytic metapsychology between preneurotic and neurotic characters. The work of transpersonal therapy for the so-called neurotic character is focused on emancipating a deeper "existential self" from the prison of the mental ego's constricting armor.

What I am calling the existential self[1] has been termed the "real self" by Horney (1950) and the "I-process" or the "essential being" by Bugental (1981). Horney (1950) says:

Whatever the conditions under which a child grows up, he will, if not mentally defective, learn to cope with others in one way or another and he will probably acquire some skills. But there are also forces in him which he cannot acquire or even develop by learning. You need not, and in fact cannot, teach an acorn to grow into an oak tree, but when given a chance, its intrinsic potentialities will develop. Similarly, the human individual, given a chance, tends to develop his particular human potentialities. He will develop then the unique alive forces of his real self: the clarity and depth of his own feelings, thoughts, wishes, interests; the ability to tap his own resources, the strength of his will power; the special capacities or gifts he may have; the faculty to express himself, and to relate himself to others with his spontaneous feelings. All this will in time enable him to find his set of values and his aims in life. In short, he will grow, substantially undiverted, toward self-realization. And that is why I speak . . . of the real self as that central inner force, common to all human beings and yet unique in each, which is the deep source of growth. (p. 17)

[1] I am using the term *existential* in this chapter in a restricted sense. May (1983) wrote, "Logically as well as psychologically we must go beyond the ego-id-superego system [the mental-egoic identity] and endeavor to understand the 'being' of whom these are expressions." He also wrote, "Being is to be defined as the individual's 'pattern of potentialities.' These potentialities will be partly shared with other persons but will in every case form a unique pattern in each individual" (p. 17). May is clearly referring to a pattern of intrinsic individual potentialities and not to spiritual realms that transcend the individual.

Horney claims the real self is the "original force toward individual growth and fulfillment," the "spring of emotional forces, of constructive energies, of directive and judiciary powers." This "alive center," she says, "feels more real, more certain, more definite" with every experience we have of it.

For Bugental, the primary characteristic of the "I-process" is "feelingful awareness." He differentiates this "I" from the mental-egoic self with its images and concepts of what we and the world are. To Bugental (1981), the mental-egoic self is a construct of awareness, a perceptual object, whereas the "I" is the "livingness," the being who is aware:

Most basically, the *I* is . . . feelingful awareness. . . . But, . . . our awareness discloses other aspects of our being: we are finite; we have the potential to take action; we can choose from among actions and non-actions that which we will make actual; and we are separate but related with other men. These, clearly, are aspects of the *I-process*. The being of the individual person is what we point to by the term *I* or *I-process*. It is possible, for discussion purposes, to think of the *I-process* chiefly as combined awareness and choicemaking, with the other attributes subsumed under this composite function. (p. 204)

In general, it seems to me clients unfold the inherent potentialities of their existential self as they confront what Bugental (1981) terms the existential givens or the conditions of being human. As human beings, we are embodied, finite, capable of making choices and taking action, and separate from, but related to, others. Each human being is subject to these conditions of existence whether or not he or she pays attention to them. "When a person is aware of himself and world and lives in accord with these conditions of being alive, he is a harmonious part of all being. When, however, he distorts some of the conditions of his being, he loses that very being in the process" (Bugental, 1981, p. 15). In *Existential Psychotherapy,* Yalom (1980) argues convincingly that the root of many neuroses is the inability to face these realities.

The fact of our embodiment means we are subject to youth, maturity, and age, to continual change, to illness and health, to all the joys and anxieties of being physical and dwelling on planet earth. Because we are embodied, we are also finite. Nothing embodied is permanent. The one certainty of our earthly life is that it will end; the greatest uncertainty is when. We are subject to fate, to life's contingencies, to limits and endings. Despite all our efforts to control our lives, what will happen and when are ultimately beyond our knowing.

During this limited time in which we are alive, we act and choose. We are free to make choices, take action, be creative, and discover meaning and purpose. Our lives are precious, or as some Tibetan Buddhists have put it, they are "auspicious occasions." We are responsible for the living of our lives. Although there are obviously limits to our freedom, each of us has far more potential for life than we let ourselves know.

Finally, we are separate, distinct individuals, yet in some way related to all other persons and all living things. We make our choices and take action in relationship to other people in close connection and to the world at large. We are capable of having both our individual identities and intimate relationships.

In my own clinical practice, I often find that as clients encounter these givens, they become more aware of themselves, other people, and the world. They begin to prize authenticity and gradually make their outer behavior and communication congruent with their inner thoughts and feelings. They come to treasure a way of life ruled by the dictates of their "alive center," the existential self, and less by the need for approval or direction from outside authority—a kind of healthy narcissism, if you will.

More specifically, we can speak of clients unfolding potentialities in three areas: *personal power, love,* and *creativity.* Clients who encounter the existential givens begin to awaken to a greater feeling of personal power. They realize they are neither victims of the world nor the aggressors. Rather, transcending the victim/aggressor syndrome, they discover the courage to affect life in meaningful ways; they become more proactive than reactive, more choiceful and purposeful, more spontaneous and passionate in their living. They are willing to live "on the edge," to take greater risks to shape life according to their desires, and to accept full responsibility for their wants, desires, and actions.

Similarly, when identified with their existential center, these people begin to give and receive love without losing themselves to others or maintaining overly rigid boundaries. Having come to a greater acceptance of their separateness, they are less dependent and absorbed in others and more centered in themselves, as well as more realistically aware of others. They are "self-ful," and not selfish. Consequently, they are able to enter into interpersonal relationships with an ability to care wholeheartedly for both themselves and for the other.

Finally, existentially identified individuals seek to express themselves creatively in ways which contribute to the life of their times. They experience a surge of creative energy and long to be expressive in activities that are usually meaningful not only to themselves but to their families and to society. Often they are keenly motivated to offer something of themselves that will affect significantly the lives of others and society as a whole. A change of profession is not unusual because they begin to recognize a need to express what is intrinsic to them as unique individuals. In this regard, Krishna's counsel to Arjuna in

The Bhagavad Gita (Saraydarian, n.d.) is especially appropriate: "It is better for a man to perform his own dharma [the law and truth of his being] imperfectly than to perform another's perfectly. It is better to die in one's own dharma. To do the dharma of another is dangerous" (p. 31). Shakespeare put it even more succinctly: "To thine own self be true."

The task of transpersonal psychotherapy at this level is to help loosen the hold of the rigidified mental ego so that the dharma of the individual may come forth. Clients gradually liberate their energies from the superstructure of their conditioned mental-egoic identity and put them in the direction of actualizing the skills, talents, and functions that are uniquely their own. Rather than remaining the persons their primary caretakers wanted, or the culture deemed they should be, they begin to make choices based on what they feel and want, and express who and what they more essentially are. If it is their dharma, the truth of their being, to be musicians or creative artists or athletes, they begin to actualize and express these intrinsic capacities—just as it is the dharma of dogs to bark, of fires to burn, and of the earth to turn on its axis.

Transpersonal Identity

In transpersonal psychology, it is assumed our mental-egoic and existential selves are incomplete. When our identity is primarily egoic, we are identified with a mental conception of who we and the world are, a conception determined substantially by the self- and object representations formed through interactions with primary caregivers during childhood. In the vernacular, we are "living in our heads" and split off from our intrinsic individuality and our physical bodies. When our identity is existential, we have begun to confront and accept the givens of human life—that we are embodied, finite, free, and related—but we are still individuals and therefore at the same time separate from others, the environment, and the universe. According to the perennial philosophy (Vaughan, 1986; Wilber, 1977, 1979), we cannot be truly whole until we awaken to the wholeness of a deeper level of identity, the Self.

The perennial philosophy tells us that we come from (or are grounded in) the One Self, that we are estranged from or unaware of our origin, and can return, not by learning something new, but by remembering our true identity. Each historically conditioned religion has its own way of saying this. For example, in Christian mysticism we are to marry Christ as our Beloved and enter the Kingdom of Heaven. Buddhists, who espouse the doctrine of *annatta,* or the nonexistence of any sort of separated self, speak of awakening to our original condition, Buddha nature, which is ultimately empty and void. In the yogas of India, the goal of the journey is to realize Atman, the ground of personal being (God immanent), which is one with Brahman, the ground of universal Being (God transcendent). In this chapter, I speak of the realization of the Self, or the nontemporal, formless, depth dimension of Being, which is both immanent and transcendent.[2]

Although definitions are misleading because of the reasons I mentioned earlier, concepts can be useful to point toward our true Self. Here are four useful ways for thinking about the Self:

1. The Self is pure transcendent consciousness, beyond all boundaries and all subject–object distinctions. It is nontemporal, changeless, formless, indivisible, and whole. As pure, transcendent Being, the Self is the essence of the entire world, of all worlds, inner and outer, and all levels of identity, high and low, above and below. As Mind (Big Mind or No-Mind to Zen Buddhists and Universal Mind in some systems of Western metaphysics), the Self is the source of all individual minds. According to Brunton (1943), a modern philosopher of the perennial wisdom, it is the origin of the separate self-sense, the personal feeling of "I" and everything associated with the individual personality. The Self gives birth to the ego, contains and sustains it for some time, then calls it back to Itself again at death.

2. The transcendent Self is shared, not individual. There is but one Self residing in the hearts of all persons, not a different Self for each individual. There are not billions of Selves, but one Self in billions of forms. Persons who realize the Self often say they become aware of their essential unity with all living things, that their seeming individuality is really an inseparably interrelated part of one wholeness, and that love, unchanging and eternal, links all parts together.

3. Immanent within the individual, the Self can be experienced as a true "I," or a deep center of being and consciousness distinct from everything associated with the separate, personal ego (Assagioli, 1965; Deikman,

[2]It is beyond the scope of this chapter to detail the many levels of transpersonal consciousness mapped in both Eastern and Western sacred traditions. The reader is referred to Green and Green (1971), Smith (1976), and Wilber (1977) for contemporary overviews, and to Aurobindo (1955), Bailey (1925), Fortune (1935), and Govinda (1960) for cartographies of specific spiritual traditions. My own thinking has been influenced significantly by integral philosophy (Aurobindo, 1949; Chaudhuri, 1965, 1974; Satprem, 1968); occult metaphysics (Bailey, 1934; Case, 1947; Fortune, 1935; Scott, 1935); Buddhist meditation practice (Goldstein, 1976; Trungpa, 1976b); and *A Course in Miracles* (Anonymous, 1975), a Gnostic-Christian rendition of the perennial wisdom.

1982). If the ego is defined as "a constellation of self-concepts along with the images, fantasies, identifications, subpersonalities, motivations, ideas, and information related or bound to the separate self-concept" (Wilber, 1980), the Self is what is left insofar as one is completely disidentified from these. The experience of disidentification from the ego is that of being consciousness itself, the context or field in which egoic processes occur, transcendent to, and therefore capable of, observing all thought, feeling, sensation, and experience. As I will later discuss, this deep center of Being is often experienced paradoxically as both individual and universal.

4. The Self is a source of love, wisdom, and creative inspiration within the individual, like a fountain or a natural spring arising from within the earth (Assagioli, 1965). Intuition comes from and leads to this higher presence in the human being. So do our inner promptings toward integration, synthesis, and wholeness of being (Jung, 1959). In some contemplative traditions, such as Tibetan Buddhism (Evans-Wentz, 1958), esoteric psychology (Bailey, 1934), and Christian mysticism (de Mello, 1978), this source is visualized as an inner Buddha or Christ, an angel, sage, divine child, or warrior of the light. The 22 major trumps of the Tarot cards and various Tibetan tanka paintings are also symbolic representations of various aspects of the Self. The meditator visualizes these images, dialogues with them, and eventually becomes absorbed in the states of consciousness they symbolize. Answers to deeply and sincerely asked questions may come from the Self or from superconscious regions of the psyche *through* these transpersonal wisdom figures (Assagioli, 1965; Progoff, 1975).

When our egoic and existential needs are generally met, many of us, therapists and clients alike, thirst for a greater life. We may have everything we want—a loving spouse, children, a house in the suburbs, two cars, plenty of money, the American dream. We may have actualized and expressed much of the creative potential. Yet, after fulfilling our material goals and achieving a feeling of personal significance, still we recognize the unsettling feeling of a "divine discontent." This experience of inner poverty is not limited to those who have become successful in the terms of our society. The sense that something intangible and enigmatic is missing in our lives, something we cannot put our finger on, can come to anyone at anytime.

In the course of psychotherapy, some clients begin to recognize a profound truth: No matter how great they will ever become, how much they will ever possess, and whatever they will ultimately accomplish, still they will never be fulfilled. The first of the four noble truths of

Buddhism—the impermanence, pain, and insubstantiality of embodied existence—becomes starkly, even shockingly felt. As a result, prompted by an inner imperative, their attention begins to turn to spiritual questions.

Transpersonal experiences sometimes occur in my practice of psychotherapy when the client incorporates one or more of the existential givens into his or her being, or in a very profound way penetrates beneath a well-entrenched defensive pattern. These individuals quite naturally begin to consider their relationship to God, ultimate Mystery, their place in the evolutionary scheme of things, life after death, parapsychological phenomena, and spiritual disciplines. Archetypal experiences, encounters with deities and spiritual guides, and complex mythological sequences sometimes emerge in their dreams and imagery, as Grof (1985) has so thoroughly documented. Very commonly, clients encounter childhood God concepts deeply embedded in their psyches and discover greater freedom to question and search in the transpersonal dimensions of their being upon letting go of these concepts.

One motif involves the experience of an inner, transpersonal center. Clients say this center of Being is still, radiant, and calm, yet dynamic and mysterious, and is sometimes likened to a sanctuary in the midst of the ever-changing whirlwinds of thought, feeling, sensation, fantasy, imagery, and everyday occurrences normally associated with egoic and existential life. With practice, clients can withdraw into this refuge for sustenance and nourishment, then return to the world and participate in their daily activities in a clearer, less reactive way. As one client put it, "Coming here is like taking a vacation on a tropical island. It is quiet and peaceful, yet teeming with life—life as potential, life coming into being, life decaying and returning to the ground. I come here not only for sustenance but because I know I will be inspired."

Clients who discover the deep center say here they are most truly themselves. The experience is one of being "I" as pure subject, a center of consciousness and being, and not of self as object. Although clients say this center is most uniquely them, that is, the essential person, and that their bodies and personalities are witnessed as objects, paradoxically, the center is simultaneously transcendent. Something more universal than the individual, yet not wholly other than the individual, is felt. One man said, "I am me and not me, both at once. I feel most myself, yet something infuses me, something bigger than I. I am it, it is me, and we are other to each." He also said, "I am all of a piece. I am whole. And I am one with you [the therapist] and everything." And finally, "Coming here is coming home to where *God lives me.*"

For one woman, encountering existential realities transformed her fear of the unknown into a reverence for universal Mystery. This woman expected the worst and armed herself against impending threats by watching her own and others' every move. Her childhood was typical for those with a paranoid self- and world construct system. Abused as a child, she learned to see herself as a vulnerable little force in a world where strong people attacked and got the better of the weak. As a child, the client learned to protect herself and ward off all surprises. She did so by becoming vigilant and prepared. In childhood, this was self-preserving. Now in her adult life, she was using the same defense to ward off the reality that she could never know with complete certainty what would actually happen in her life, no matter how hard she tried to be prepared. She could try predicting the future (indeed, she was a student of a noted psychic) and take precautions as fully as possible to ward off possible dangers; still, she could never know with complete certainty what would happen and when.

Slowly she realized if she did not let go of some of the very vigilance that had protected her as a child, she would never find fulfillment. This realization terrified her. By choosing life, she would be vulnerable to so many unknowns. Yet, upon confronting this human reality as fully as she could, she began to feel a profound, quiet strength, like "a mountain." She became convinced life would turn out for the good, that she probably would survive physical death; but something of the unknown would always be unknown. She called this unknown dimension the "Sacred Mystery." For her, this Mystery could be sensed, appreciated, loved, even worshipped. But it could never be conquered or completely known. This, to her, was the Divine.

It is not uncommon for awareness of the Self to begin unfolding through techniques of active imagination and symbolic visualization (Assagioli, 1965; Gerard, 1964; Hannah, 1981). Clients can be asked to visualize a symbol or scene and let their imagination unfold a story. This is what happened for Conrad, a 34-year-old executive at a major publishing firm who daily interacts with famous writers and executives. When he began his therapy, everything about him, from his clothes to his walk, gave the appearance of a slick, stylish, impeccable, well-controlled businessman. But beneath the "veneer," as he put it, Conrad was lonely. No one really knew him. Those closest to him could not penetrate his suit of armor. And neither could Conrad.

In therapy, Conrad worked hard to get beneath his veneer. But as he did, time and again he came to an anguished feeling of emptiness, of not being enough, of being nothing. Only after many sessions could he stay there and experience these feelings without turning away from them. Finally, during a particularly painful self-confrontation in which he let go to the emptiness, I asked him to imagine a swamp with a figure emerging out of its murky depths. The figure was small, like a gnome, covered with leaves and mud and "a slimy green crud that reminds me of nose snot." He trembled when he saw it. The gnome washed itself off, and there, under the mud, was a Divine child surrounded by a halo and radiating warm feelings of love and understanding. Conrad burst into sobs so strong the tears spurted from his eyes. He wept with joy as he and the child began an "energetic exchange." Gradually, Conrad felt his consciousness absorbed into the boy and becoming one with a field of light. He said again and again, "This is me, the being I was before I was born."

Following this session, Conrad went to a church close to my office. He wanted to be alone and savor the sacred feeling. The church was locked, but he sat outside on the lawn, weeping gently and sketching the entire vision: the swamp, the murky figure, and the golden child. From that time on, his interpersonal relationships began to change for the better.

Some Differences between Existential and Transpersonal Identities

Attributes of the transpersonal Self appear to broadly cluster around themes of love, will, and creativeness, in a manner similar to those of the existential self. However, the transpersonal qualities are more universal than their existential counterparts. They extend beyond the frame of reference of the separate, individualizing person to include humanity, the planet, and the cosmos.

For example, when our self-sense is merely egoic or existential, loneliness and isolation can dominate our experience. Love between individuals is personal, subject to jealousies and heartaches. At times, we acutely feel our separateness from each other and the rest of creation. Not so with the discovery of the Self. When we open ourselves to transpersonal identity, we begin to discover we are perpetually united in the core of our being with the whole of creation and ultimately can never be separated from those we love. Brotherhood, in the mystical sense, acceptance, and loving kindness begin to infuse our consciousness and become more dominant in the living of our lives. This does not mean we will never again be subject to grief and despair. On the contrary, the world's greatest mystics suffered a great deal, as any casual reading of some of their biographies will reveal. We inevitably return to our egoic and existential awareness but can never forget what we have experienced. This experience of transcendent love and unity leaves us with wonder and often radically transforms our mental-egoic identity. For

example, we are likely to become more loving and respond more compassionately to our own suffering and the suffering of others.

Similarly, at the egoic or existential levels, meaninglessness can be pervasive; yet, as we open to transpersonal identity, we sense human and planetary evolution are under the direction of some greater authority—in Christian terms, the will of God. Greater peace of mind unfolds when we align our personal will with the heartbeat of a universal Will. Feelings of meaninglessness gradually diminish as we sense our place and function in the cosmic scheme of things.

Finally, at the egoic and existential levels, we often experience ourselves as mentally limited, in the dark, not smart or creative enough in comparison to other people we know. Yet, as we open to transpersonal identity, we are sometimes astonished to discover an abundant storehouse of creative ideas available to us and find that, by tapping this reservoir, there is the possibility of greater wisdom and understanding. In addition, our perceptions heighten, and we become more vividly alive. We begin to see beyond mundane appearances into deeper levels of meaning, whereas at the same time remaining well aware of everyday realities and demands. By comparison, regular egoic mental processes appear slow and even dull.

The Intermingling of Themes from the Levels of Identity

One final point before leaving Postulate 1. It is essential to keep in mind that the egoic, existential, and transpersonal levels of identity are interpenetrating levels in a "hierarchy of wholes." Because these levels are interpenetrating, *the life concerns of clients can involve all levels simultaneously.* This point is often underemphasized in hierarchical and developmental models of human functioning but becomes apparent when one applies these models to clinical work. The issues discussed by clients in the course of psychotherapy do not necessarily revolve consecutively around preegoic, then egoic, then existential, then transpersonal themes. More often, themes from the various dimensions are intermingled.

For example, the life concerns presented by clients with borderline personality organizations are likely to center on preegoic and egoic themes. As therapists, we support the integration of their all good and all bad self- and object representations and nurture the emergence of a solid, cohesive identity. Although the content of therapy for these clients will be primarily egoic, discussion of existential and transpersonal themes when they are presented by the client can enhance their healing process. Similarly, other clients who have already developed cohesive intrapsychic structures may be struggling with issues concerning authenticity, personal freedom, separateness, and life meaning. Hence, the major areas for exploration in their therapy will be existential. However, in most individuals, ego-level work is rarely, if ever, completed; consequently, these clients may not only work on egoic blocks but also explore transpersonal questions as a result of or as a way to confront the existential issues that concern all human beings.

A specific example will clarify my meaning. A 35-year-old male client complained of difficult relationships with male friends. He chose as friends distant, controlling men who were unable to respond to him in a consistently sensitive, caring manner. The client yearned to relate deeply and personally to these men and to receive warmth and tender care from them. But this type of deep friendship seemed unobtainable from the men he sought out, leaving him feeling frustrated and hurt. He already sensed he was asking men for a degree of intimacy and closeness that bordered on a love affair and, in some respects, was looking for something that was not of this world. He also knew, at least intellectually, that he was seeking to develop attributes of his masculinity mirrored by qualities he saw in friends. However, the exploration of the pattern of his relationships with men required that he open up to far deeper dimensions of his inner world than he expected.

He explored his childhood nuclear dynamics (egoic level). His father was distant and austere and dangled love and nurturance in front of the boy like a carrot. No matter how the client would try, he could never get the prize. Then, when he became an adolescent, the father abandoned the family, leaving the son feeling alone and unprotected.

Existential themes also informed the client's explorations: For example, the fact that someone could abandon him so abruptly and with such completeness prompted the boy to close down his hopes for ever developing a relationship with a male. He yearned for deep contact, but the risk was too great. If an attachment really developed, it could be destroyed, leaving him feeling alone all over again. This led him to explore his separateness, isolation, and estrangement from others and the "zone of psychic emptiness," experienced as an inner vacuum or hole in his being, which lay beneath his yearning for deep male contact.

Then began a series of associations involving Christian mystical themes, including the archetypal image of Christ as the perfect lover who wounds the client with love and then goes away, thus involving the client in a spiritual game of hide and go seek. When these associations began to unfold, the client's searching in his inner world became more restless, more insistent and forceful

than before. The client began to perceive himself as the beloved bride of Christ, pining away for his lost lover and yearning to be dissolved in the bliss of Divine union. In one session, he actually prayed for Christ to come from deep inside him and pull him firmly back down into the very center of his being. This yearning is exemplified in *The Spiritual Canticle* of St. John of the Cross (Kavanaugh & Rodriguez, 1979, p. 410), which holds special meaning for the client:

> Where have You hidden,
> Beloved, and left me moaning?
> You fled like the stag
> After wounding me;
> I went out calling You, and You were gone.
> Shepherds, you that go
> Up through the sheepfolds to the hill,
> If by chance you see
> Him I love most,
> Tell Him that I sicken, suffer, and die.

As the therapy progressed, these themes became intermingled in the client's communications. In a single therapy hour, he would start anywhere along the spectrum—with egoic, existential, or transpersonal aspects—and weave together the other elements until they became a composition with many variations on a single theme. He would start, say, with the subjective feeling of loneliness and isolation, then would speak of a close friend with whom he felt frustrated and angry. He would draw psychodynamic references to his relationship with his father or speak of qualities of his own inner male projected onto the friend. He would bring in the archetypal references, then tap again the feeling of emptiness and lack. Gradually these variations came together into a single constellation. The various levels—egoic (references to childhood), existential (references to isolation and emptiness), and transpersonal (the Christian motif) came together as a unit, until he realized he was yearning, not for a person, but for attributes of his own transpersonal essence, the Christ in this instance being symbolic for the courage, strength, potency, and loving passion (the "blood of Christ") of his own Higher Self. This Self, he realized, was not something outside of himself. It was neither a separate object he could reach for nor an external entity that would grab hold of him and pull him down deep into itself. The client began to witness a collapse of the subject–object differentiation between transcendent self and individual personhood.

As these themes were described again and again, not in a mere "talking-about" mode but in a deeply experiential way (see Postulate 4), the client became more and more aware of these transpersonal attributes within himself and began to bring them forth. His relationships with all people, men and women, improved, and he became more fully committed to a spiritual path of daily meditation.

POSTULATE 2

Transpersonal psychotherapy recognizes the therapist's unfolding awareness of the Self and his or her spiritual world-view as central in shaping the nature, process, and outcome of therapy.

As I see it, therapy can be considered transpersonal insofar as the therapist seeks to realize the Self, the deep center of Being. As I mentioned before, what differentiates transpersonal therapy from other orientations is neither technique nor what clients talk about. The difference lies in the centrality of the therapist's consciousness and his or her spiritual orientation to life. The therapist's state of mind and orientation inform his or her therapeutic stance.

Early in the movement's history, Sutich (1976), one of the founders of transpersonal psychology, proposed that transpersonal therapists are characterized by their dedication to a spiritual path. Many leading figures in transpersonal psychology believe the meditative practices in Buddhism, Hinduism, Taoism, Christian mysticism, Sufism, and other traditions are unsurpassed for expanding awareness and awakening to our true nature. However, the concept of path need not be limited to a formal spiritual tradition. As I see it, a path is a course of action or conduct entered into specifically for the purpose of cutting through the ego-mind and opening to the Self. Given that definition, activities such as gardening, writing, painting, indeed the whole of daily life, are spiritual practices *if*—and this is a big *if*—they are approached with mindfulness (in the Buddhist sense) and entered into specifically to expand one's awareness of the depth dimension of Being.

Research into the effects of meditation (Shapiro & Walsh, 1984) suggests disciplined, consistently practiced meditation helps individuals to become less defended, more impartial and even-tempered, compassionate and loving. Disciplined meditators tend to become more open and alert, with enhanced perceptual accuracy and ability to make choices and take action. Intuition, mindfulness, forgiveness, compassion, the ability to register psychic impressions, and to discern the value and source of intuitive guidance—all of these are attributes that unfold to

one degree or another as meditators become more open to the depth dimension of Being.[3]

If an individual seeking to become a transpersonal therapist practices meditation or other psychospiritual exercises, the likelihood is that a spiritual perspective will gradually characterize his or her outlook on life, and transpersonal attributes will begin to permeate his or her being. Eventually a transpersonal context will inform his or her therapeutic approach.

For example, one constellation of transpersonal attributes that gradually suffuses the consciousness of an individual opening to the Self includes unity, love, and brotherhood. If, as I postulated earlier, the Self is shared and not individual—that is, if there is only one Self with countless individual manifestations—then, at the transpersonal level, all living things are our one Self. Clients and therapists alike are manifestations of the Self we share. Although a client in psychotherapy is a unique and distinct individual at the egoic and existential levels, at the transpersonal level he or she is us, we are he or she. At least two manifestations of the shared Self are in the consulting room—the therapist and the client—and possibly more, for the client can be a couple, a family, or a group. In short, there is one Self in the consulting room in two or more bodies.

Some clinicians may misinterpret what I advocate as an enmeshed or narcissistic state of mind. The misunderstanding is likely to result from a confusion of levels in the spectrum of identity. At the egoic and existential levels, therapist and client are indeed separate and distinct and will always remain so. Therapists must maintain their own integrity and help clients unfold theirs. Although this separateness is kept in the foreground of awareness, transpersonal therapists can also seek to recognize what many have discovered through the practice of spiritual disciplines: From the perspective of the transpersonal level, this separateness is an appearance, not a fact. I suggest this recognition of essential unity, when it is directly experienced by the therapist, can radically affect the therapeutic relationship, for it undercuts the separated self-sense and utterly transforms the therapist's view of him- or herself, the client, and the world.

[3] A metaphor may clarify my meaning. The Self is sometimes symbolized by the sun radiating out rays of light in all directions. The rays of light are the Self's various attributes. In addition to those listed here, transpersonal attributes include beauty, compassion, courage, universality, freedom, brotherhood, goodness, goodwill, inclusiveness, openness, harmony, joy, bliss, light, love, truth, serenity, peace, service, spaciousness, stillness, strength, synthesis, wholeness, and wisdom. As one draws inward toward the deep center of Being, one's personhood is said to become imbued by qualities such as these, just as one grows warmer the closer one gets to the sun.

Insofar as we view our clients egoically, we tend to see them as separate individuals different from ourselves. We see complex patterns of characteristics, subpersonalities, self-images, impulses, drives, motivations, and the like that, in many ways, are quite different than our own. But, from a transpersonal perspective, these make up their mental-egoic identity, formed through the interaction of their inborn givens and the press of primary caregivers. If we are viewing our clients only in this way, we are witnessing a limited part of their total selfhood. We are seeing the clothes they wear, their personalities, not their spiritual essence. We are missing the Christ, Buddha, or godliness within them and our essential unity with them. Insofar as we awaken to transpersonal identity, however, we also experience our essential unity with all human beings and living things. In the eyes of a therapist on a path of self-realization, therefore, the person seated opposite the therapist is not just a constellation of personal characteristics; he or she also becomes an individualized expression of the Self we share.

What are the implications of this viewpoint? I believe there is something very important in this principle, but it is frustratingly out of grasp unless the therapist has begun to awaken to his or her deep center of Being. Essentially, it is this: More than anything else, our clients need to be seen and felt as the Self they truly are, which is no different than the true Self we are. As I see it, through this recognition of the client's and our own true identity we hold an expanded vision of who the client is and what he or she is capable of. If our frame for holding the client is broad, the client is aided to relinquish some of the crippling egoic self- and world constructs and beliefs that underlie his or her presenting and ongoing concerns and to enlarge his or her sense of identity. Recognition of the client's true nature, inner light and beauty, creativeness, power, and dignity, through eyes that are accepting, appreciative, and unconditionally loving—all of which Assagioli (1965) contends are attributes of the Self—is the heart of healing in transpersonal psychotherapy.

Goldsmith (1959), a spiritual healer of some renown, believed healing occurs when the Christ of the healer touches the Christ of the client, when the Buddha is seen through the eyes of the Buddha. Thus spiritual healing results when the healer enters an expanded state of consciousness in which there is only the Self. A client requesting healing receives it because he or she has reached out to the consciousness of a practitioner who understands that there are not a client consciousness, a practitioner consciousness, and a Self-consciousness. There is only one consciousness—the consciousness of the Self. Vaughan (1986) speaks of something akin to this as "healing awareness." The therapist who is on a path of

Self-realization can practice penetrating beneath the appearance of egoic and existential separateness, individual symptoms and behavior to the reality of the client's Being. The therapist can practice looking through the eyes of the Self into the heart of the individual and see there the Self.

It is a truism that the state of mind of one individual can affect that of another for good or for ill. The kindly doctor with a soothing bedside manner can help to ease the pain and suffering of a frightened patient through the magnetism of his friendliness and radiance of strength and goodwill. The teacher who is open and loving can inspire others to learn far more than one who is controlling and defensive. Many meditators report their practice tends to be more evocative when they sit in the presence of an inspired, Self-realized individual, or an advanced practitioner than when they meditate by themselves or with each other. I suggest a therapist who is unfolding awareness of the Self and recognizing his or her unity with the whole of creation tends to develop a healing presence along these lines. A therapist whose mind is becoming attuned to deeper realms of Being and who realizes, if only for brief moments, the essential unity of all living things, is gradually more open, spacious, and accepting than one who is not and is likely to have a corresponding effect upon the state of consciousness of the client.

The therapist's healing presence is also characterized by a marked degree of intuitiveness. According to contemplative traditions, intuition unfolds as one's consciousness expands. Intuitive awareness can be likened to a lightening bolt that cuts through one's linear, analytical, problem-solving mode and opens one's perceptual windows to a vision of one's true nature. Intuition is often described in the spiritual traditions as a quiet voice that whispers its guidance when the mind is still. The therapist who meditates can make use of his or her intuition in psychotherapy if he or she will pose such questions as "How do you want me to proceed?" to the Self as a source of wisdom and guidance and wait patiently for inspiration. In this way, the Self can guide the therapist in his or her work. It seems to be the case that if the therapist can become aware of the guidance of the Self, the therapy will progress as far along in the process of Self-realization as the client desires, guided by the Self for which the ally has been the therapist.

The therapist's spiritual awareness and reliance upon the wisdom and guidance of the Self may or may not be made explicit to the client. When a client is spiritually inclined, therapists may find it useful to openly discuss the possibility that a higher healing power than either client or therapist may be operative, even to the extent of using such religious terms as God, Christ Consciousness, Buddha Nature, and Spirit. With clients who are uninterested in things of the spirit, therapists should keep their intention to be guided by the Self to themselves. I do not believe that any attempt should be made to force one's own belief system or meditational practice on a client.

POSTULATE 3

Transpersonal psychotherapy is a process of awakening from a lesser to a greater identity.

According to *A Course in Miracles* (Anonymous, 1975), "What you think you are is a belief to be undone." In *The Dhammapada* (Byrom, 1976), the Buddha taught:

> We are what we think.
> All that we are arises with our thoughts.
> With our thoughts we make the world. (p. 3)

In the perennial philosophy, self-identity and sense of the world at the egoic and existential levels in the spectrum of identity are viewed as arising from our thoughts and beliefs. As it is stated in *The Avatamsaka Sutra* (Namgyal, 1986):

> The mind is like an artist;
> It creates
> All existential realms.
> All these are created by the multifarious mind. (p. 8)

In transpersonal therapy, healing involves the realization of a greater identity that comes to light when we relinquish our unquestioned conceptions of self and world. As I expressed earlier, these conceptions of identity are the constructs of our consciousness. According to the perennial philosophy, these constructs are not our true identity.

To help his disciples realize the deep center of Being, Ramana Maharshi (1972), one of India's greatest saints, taught a method of spiritual practice entitled self-inquiry. In this practice, we meditate upon the question, "Who am I?" and reject every answer provided by the discursive mind. By doing so, we probe ever deeper into the self. For example, if, upon asking the question, we hear within ourselves our own name, we reject this ("No, that is a name I have been given") and inquire again ("Who is the 'I' who has been given this name?"). Perhaps the next response that comes is an image of ourselves as a warrior of the light or some other archetypal figure. This too we reject and plumb deeper, saying, "No, this is an image of myself. Who is the 'I' who has this image?"

Those who practice this method within a broader context of spiritual development claim to descend into the

self beyond the egoic and socially adapted levels to the more authentic layers of their being, from egoic to existential to transpersonal identity. The principle behind this practice is identical to the third postulate of transpersonal psychotherapy: By gradually relinquishing our exclusive identification with our preegoic identity, we can awaken to our egoic identity; by relinquishing our exclusive identification with our limited egoic self- and world structure, we can deepen to our existential identity; by relinquishing our exclusive identification with our embodied individual self-sense, we can eventually transcend to our true identity as the Self, the origin and source of all our experience.

In *Opening to Inner Light,* Metzner (1986) published his amplifications of several metaphors that are applicable to this process. Building upon metaphors from the *Brihadaranyaka Upanishad,* Metzner discusses the process of transformation "from dream state to awakening," "from illusion to realization," "from darkness to light," "from the unreal to the real," "from imprisonment to liberation," "from fragmentation to wholeness," "from separation to oneness," "from being in exile to coming home." In my practice, I have found that, as clients relinquish an old identity and awaken to a new, more expanded state of being, these motifs frequently emerge in their dreams, imagery, and free associations. I also find it useful to introduce clients to these metaphors, for example, by telling transformational myths and fairy tales, thus providing different ways clients can give meaning to the process of transformation they are undergoing.

According to Bailey (1950), a British exponent of the ageless wisdom in the theosophical tradition, any such development, from the lesser to the greater, "is indicative of the livingness of the inner divine entity [the Self]" (p. 1). Seen in this light, the levels in the spectrum of identity are not only interpenetrating dimensions that together constitute a person's wholeness of being but stages in a "transpersonal-izing" developmental process. When our self-concept evolves from preegoic to egoic to existential to transpersonal identity, we are undergoing the progressive stages of a transpersonal growth process. Each movement is transpersonal, for, in each, we are becoming more awake, self-realized, enlightened, liberated, and whole. With each transcendence of who we thought we were, we come closer to who we are, until ultimately, paradoxically, we come home to the Self we never left.

This postulate has important implications for the conduct of transpersonal therapy. As therapists, we do not necessarily use specific practices to help clients have transpersonal experiences. Rather, following the metaphor of the proverbial onion that is gradually unwound, we compassionately yet persistently help our clients identify and let go of those self-definitions and patterns of living that are impeding enhanced self-awareness and the emergence of a greater identity.

That greater state may be egoic, existential, or transpersonal, depending upon the locus of the client's identity when he or she began the therapy. It is greater only in that it is in advance of the client's present state. A deeper identity already exists. As Wilber (1980) sees it, this deeper structure of identity is not created but lies *enfolded* in the client's unconscious *as potential waiting to be unfolded*. Clinical experience suggests it is evoked when the client confronts the defenses and unwinds the constructions of his or her bodymind that hinder its emergence. In this sense, transpersonal therapy is grounded in the teachings of the perennial philosophy. As *A Course in Miracles* (Anonymous, 1975) puts it, "The search for truth is but the honest searching out of everything that interferes with truth" (p. 267). For example, the *Course* also states the meaning of love is beyond what can be taught. What is possible, however, is to remove the blocks to love's presence, which is our natural inheritance. The task, therefore, is not specifically to create a greater identity. Ever greater dimensions of identity simply are. Rather, our task is to seek out and eliminate the barriers, defenses, and blockages within ourselves that we have built against them.

The Dark Night

If, in the course of therapy, the resistances and defenses of the lesser identity are gradually relinquished, clients are likely to enter a "dark night" or crisis of awakening. They become acutely aware that their old way of life has little to offer, that its cost in terms of aliveness and creativity is enormous. Old structures are recognized as worthless and self-defeating and cherished illusions as imprisoning. The old identity gradually unravels and falls apart. Feelings of anxiety, emptiness, darkness, and chaos are the result, for *nothing appears right away to take the old identity's place*. In short, clients begin to undergo a crisis of death and rebirth (Grof, 1985; Metzner, 1986).

One such crisis involving annihilation and abandonment occurs when a preegoic client awakens to his or her egoic identity (Johnson, 1987). Bugental (1981) recognizes another involving a confrontation with the void occurring as a client transforms from egoic to existential identity. St. John of the Cross (Kavanaugh & Rodriguez, 1979) called a similar transition the dark night of the senses and characterized it as a normal stage in spiritual growth when a spiritual seeker, having tired of the "things of the senses," cannot yet depend upon consolation from the "things of God." This is one of many types of transpersonal crisis (Wittine, 1982). In my experience, no matter where a client's locus of identity is found at the start of therapy, a dark night unfolds as he or she awakens to any greater identity. Wherever clients begin, the crisis of awakening is a time of transition between the dissolution of the old and the emergence of the new. In other words, a dark night is a natural rite of passage inherent in psychotherapeutic change.

This is not the place to detail the dark night as it is found in psychotherapy. I can do no more than briefly describe the feelings many clients experience and follow that by suggesting how a transpersonal therapist might support the client through this stage. If the therapeutic journey undertaken is thoroughgoing in its exploration of their psychic depths, clients inevitably realize that some aspects of their old self- and world-construct system function like a suit of armor crippling them and squeezing the life force out of them. Because the emergence of a new self inevitably involves the destruction of present securities, they feel their whole existence is held in the balance. Consequently, the existential anxiety that Rollo May (1983) described as "the experience of the threat of imminent nonbeing" intrudes into conscious awareness. Clients become aware that their present existence, which at least offers safety and security, is becoming uprooted, and they are terrified they may lose themselves and their world and become nothing. Even a fragmented self, or a life in captivity, is better than no self, no life at all. As May (1983) put it:

> Anxiety occurs at the point where some emerging potentiality or possibility faces the individual, some possibility of fulfilling his existence; but this very possibility involves the destroying of present security, which thereupon gives rise to the tendency to deny the new potentiality. (p. 111)

In addition to the eruption of anxiety, a pervasive feeling of emptiness or voidness can also dominate our clients' inner life during the dark night. Often this voidness has pervaded the background of their lives all along. It existed half consciously behind the self they were trying to be. As one client described it, "There is nothing inside me except cold, desolate open space. All I can feel is a great vacuum—a yawning, hungry abyss. That's my only ground. It's all I am."

As the old self- and world-construct system is shed, a deep feeling of loss often emerges. Life no longer makes sense. Clients may feel arid. Richness is missing in their lives. Much of the world and everything in it appear to be unreal. There is no point to anything; there is nothing to live for, to long for, to aspire to and become.

As they loosen their hold on their old self-identifications, images of birth and death sometimes emerge in their dreams, fantasies, and free associations. Depression is likely; so also are moments in which suicide is considered as a way out. Some are surprised by a murderous rage directed toward parents and other authority figures to whom they surrendered their personal authority, power, and capacity to make choices, and unconsciously became willing prisoners. Many clients become angry with the therapist for being the herald of awakening. "Why," they feel, "can't you let me sleep?"

None of these emotions need to be dramatic. As most clinicians are well aware, emotional expressiveness does not necessarily determine the depth at which a client is working. Many clients work very quietly at this point. However, this phase of therapy is usually characterized by a heightened intensity and a sense that something important is happening that is beyond either the therapist's or the client's conscious control.

It takes both an open heart and great skill to guide a client through this crisis of awakening. The attitude of the therapist toward the experience of transformation affects how the client will, in the words of the *I Ching,* "cross the great water." It is imperative that therapists realize *this is a healing crisis, not a pathological one.* The client *is* falling apart; however, this crisis also heralds the birth of a new person. I believe one of our greatest functions as therapists is to act as midwives to this birth.

As therapists, we must be prepared to remain psychologically present and supportive with our clients during this experience of giving birth. The most basic preparation we can have is to have undergone our own dark nights and, through them, to have learned that birth follows death. Without our own experiences and an attitude of hopefulness, our clients' feelings of death and voidness can bring forth our own anxiety, and we can unknowingly abort their transformation process. We may become defensive in any number of ways. I think our defenses typically grow out of our own feelings of helplessness and an inordinate need to force order onto chaos. What is required of us as therapists is that we be present and accepting of raw emotion and trustful of the psyche's natural healing processes. Trungpa's (1976a) guidance is particularly relevant:

> Any state of mind . . . is a workable situation. . . . Chaotic situations must not be rejected. Nor must we regard them as regressive, as a return to confusion. We must respect whatever happens to our state of mind. Chaos should be regarded as extremely good news. (p. 69)

Keeping an open heart is also crucial. As therapists, we need to have faith and confidence in the client's ability to give birth to the new identity. Although it is painful and disturbing for the client to undergo these experiences, the anxiety and emptiness can be befriended. If they are confronted with an attitude of loving kindness and accepted into oneself as fully and as unflinchingly as one can, a greater self-identity and a renewed feeling of personal power will emerge out of the darkness.

Clients often say that what they value most during these times of darkness is our belief and trust in them and our encouraging them to keep faith with themselves, to hang in there and encounter the anxiety and voidness as directly as possible. As they wander namelessly, apparently without identity, through the valley of the unknown, what they appreciate most is our willingness to be their support and friend rather than our clinical interpretative skill, important as that often is. As therapists, we can be empathic and express deep care and respect for their suffering, while also making explicit our conviction, born out of our own journeys through the unknown, that they can emerge on the other side of the dark night with a greater sense of self and capacity for life, while, at the same time, keeping the most cherished aspects of what they are leaving behind. The inward experience of darkness, emptiness, and death, this very void, is in actuality the womb out of which their greater identity—whether egoic, existential, or transpersonal—eventually can be born. Maintaining our faith and confidence in our clients' process and making these explicit can be our clients' beacon as they walk through the darkness and awaken to this greater identity.

POSTULATE 4

Transpersonal psychotherapy facilitates the process of awakening by enhancing inner awareness and intuition.

According to the perennial philosophy (Huxley, 1944), the truth lies within, and salvation comes by expanding our inward awareness. To turn attention inward and "self-ward" and become more fully aware of our inner realms is a natural human capacity transpersonal psychotherapy makes full use of. Learning to live directly from an inner center and from one's internal sense of things is in itself restorative and healing. However, in most of us, this capacity is blunted. As Bugental (1981) notes, we have lost our inner sense of being. Our attention is dominated by external happenings or by the mental events of our analyzing, reasoning mind. Many people in our Western culture minimize the importance of inward awareness and are frightened by the thought of what they might find lurking in the depths of themselves. Consequently, they rarely pay attention to their internal sense of things.

Many spiritual traditions teach us we can realize a greater reality through intuition, which is defined by H. Wildon Carr (quoted in Bailey, 1932) as "the apprehension by the mind of reality *directly as it is* and not under the form of a perception or conception, nor as an idea or object of the reason, all of which by contrast are intellectual apprehension'' (p. 26; italics added). However, to develop intuition and know the intrinsic wisdom of our deeper wellsprings, we must relinquish the dominance of our judging, analyzing mind and shift our attention away from its exclusive focus on the objective world. We must become more aware of our interiors. Many, if not most, human beings can access deeper levels of inner wisdom and intuit within themselves whatever they need to make their lives more the way they really want them to be, if they will only turn inward.

As Perls (1969) noted, ''Awareness per se—by and of itself—can be curative.'' A number of psychotherapists with humanistic and/or phenomenological orientations (Bugental, 1978, 1981; Gendlin, 1978; Mahrer, 1983, 1986; Perls, 1969; Progoff, 1975, 1980; Van Dusen, 1972; Welwood, 1982) have developed techniques of evocation based on this principle. Each of these practitioners, in his own way, encourages clients to (a) center their attention on a genuine life concern, often as it is experienced in bodily felt sensations, (b) open their awareness as fully as possible to whatever they are inwardly experiencing in the here-and-now, and (c) describe what they discover as if experiencing it for the first time—from the vantage point that Suzuki (1970) called ''beginner's mind.'' When clients allow themselves to be as fully as possible in their stream of awareness and give simple, unbiased, naive, primitive, nonexplanatory descriptions of whatever they find within their awareness, they make new discoveries in *energetically charged* flashes of direct knowing. I emphasize ''energetically charged'' because these flashes are far more than mental insights. They are keenly felt with one's whole being, including the physical body and the emotions.

Any and all channels to the interior can be used— physical sensations, feelings, emotions, memories, thoughts, imagery, dreams, fantasies, visions. To the extent that these channels are blocked, constructive healing forces are also blocked. When awareness is trusted and our clients' natural capacity for inner searching is freed, they discover intuitively—that is, by way of a direct, bodily felt knowing from deep within themselves—greater possibilities and meanings. Clinical experience (Bugental, 1978; Gendlin, 1978; Mahrer, 1986) suggests that these intuitions, *when experienced with one's whole organism,* are themselves restorative and healing.

A teaching story told by Bugental (personal communication) is often useful in explaining to clients how we want them to inwardly search during the therapy hour. Think of a man living on an oasis in the middle of a desert. For years, the water from an underground spring has sustained him and his family and flocks, keeping thirsts quenched and the soil for planting rich. But one day the spring runs dry. His only choice is to find another spring. He begins to search close to the spot where members of his family have satisfied their thirsts for years. But he is disappointed. He expands his search to other parts of the oasis but discovers there is very little water left anywhere. Very soon, this oasis will turn to sand. Fearing for his own and his family's survival, he is forced to abandon his close surroundings and strike out into uncharted territories. So he gathers a few belongings and some cheese and dried meat and begins to wander. He searches far away from his desert oasis. He even searches in places where he least expects to find it. One day, as he searches in the most unlikely and surprising of spots, ''Eureka!'', he discovers the water of life.

Water is here used in its archetypal significance, as a symbol for wisdom and knowledge intuitively derived. The same motif can be found at the heart of some fairy tales. For example, at the start of the Brothers' Grimm (1944) tale, *The Water of Life,* the king is ill and his lands are barren. His son must find a special water to restore the old king's health. The hero searches far and wide and encounters numerous trials and obstacles before discovering the water and returning home to his sickly father. When clients, like the desert man and the old king, feel inwardly impoverished and genuinely concerned about the emptiness and aridity of their lives, they spontaneously search for and find the water of life.

When this teaching principle is followed, both therapist and client are searchers on a shared expedition into the well of the inner world. However, it is the client who is the central figure in the inward search; the therapist is primarily a guide. What is held in highest regard is the expansion of awareness and a thorough description of the inward experiences occurring right here and now in the client; analysis and interpretation of these experiences, according to some theoretical system of the therapist, are useful but of secondary importance. In order to guide the inner search, the therapist suspends conceptual frameworks as much as possible, tries to be open and adventurous, and follows the flow of the inward experiencing—in his or her client, of course, but also in him- or herself—wherever it goes.

POSTULATE 5

In transpersonal psychotherapy, the therapeutic relationship is a vehicle for the process of awakening in both client and therapist.

As I see it, transpersonal psychotherapy differs from other therapeutic approaches in the kind of attention it gives to the relationship between therapist and client.

This relationship can be seen not only as a vehicle for the client's awakening but for the therapist's as well.

Whoever our clients are, whatever their character structure and the concerns they bring to therapy—they are really quite the same as us (i.e., we share the same human condition). We are not only doctors curing the illness of some sick client separate from us nor simply guides leading other people to some greater degree of authenticity and identity. Every person who comes to transpersonal therapy also offers us an opportunity to heal our own wounds and to realize more fully our own authenticity. In their healing, we are also healed; in our healing, they too are healed.

To expand on this, it is sometimes useful to assume that everything is projection. What lives inside us determines what we see outside ourselves in our world. As *A Course in Miracles* (Anonymous, 1975) puts it:

> Projection makes perception. The world you see is what you gave it, nothing more than that. But though it is not more than that, it is not less. Therefore, to you it is important. It is the witness to your state of mind, the outside picture of an inward condition. As a man thinketh, so does he perceive. (p. 415)

Similarly, in a Tibetan Buddhist text (quoted in Namgyal, 1986, p. 60), it is written:

> An external phenomenon is perceived
> Differently by differing levels of consciousness.
> A body of enchanting beauty
> Is looked upon differently:
> A wandering yogin perceives it as a corpse;
> A sensual man perceives it as an object of lust;
> A dog looks upon it as food.
> These are three different perceptions.

From the viewpoint of the therapeutic relationship, this is the basis of transference and countertransference phenomena, especially when defined as the total emotional reaction of the client to the therapist, and vice versa, in the treatment situation (Kernberg, 1975). I suggest that transpersonal psychotherapy expands upon the psychoanalytic interpretation of this phenomenon. In psychoanalysis, it is assumed it is possible for the analyst to perceive the client from an objective vantage point, that being a completely objective witness is not only desirable, but possible. To the contrary, I believe it is *impossible* to perceive another person except through one's perceptual system, which, except possibly in the higher states of spiritual enlightenment, is always colored to one extent or another by one's state of mind and the profound context of largely unconscious beliefs that predetermine our way of living. Everything that is perceived is always perceived from the point of view of someone, and the observer inevitably colors what he or she is observing according to his or her own unconscious material and deeply embedded context

of beliefs. In order to make this explicit, some practitioners of transpersonal psychotherapy have renamed the transference–countertransference phenomenon *mirroring*, meaning we see ourselves reflected in the other.

Whatever a client's character structure or concern, it is useful to assume that he or she reflects back to the therapist some aspect of the therapist. One important key for discovering what in the therapist is being mirrored is by examining the therapist's emotional reactions to the client. The therapist is always reacting to the client in one way or another, including the possibility that having no emotional response at all is simply another kind of reaction. By analyzing his or her own emotional reactions, the therapist discovers how the client acts as a mirror so that the therapist can see his or her own interior processes and, thereby, learn about his or her own unconscious material. In this way, the client is a gift to the therapist, offering the therapist an opportunity to reclaim a portion of him- or herself.

Let us take an example. A client with a preegoic character structure, with narcissistic, hysterical, and paranoid tendencies, talks about how his employees are victimizing him. They do not trust him to make sound business decisions and are making the choices he himself should be making. In the therapy situation, he is emotionally chaotic and in continual crisis, and when his female therapist attempts to intervene in any way, the client dauntlessly defends himself. The therapist is aware that the same chaos and defensiveness the client manifests in the consulting room are probably what his employees mistrust in him. The therapist may or may not feel inside herself some of the same mistrust they experience toward the client. It is, of course, essential for the therapist to access her emotional reactions, but there is more.

My point is that this client offers his therapist the opportunity to work with some of her own preegoic residual material, in whatever form it takes. Her material is likely to be quite different than the client's. She may not act out her hysteria as much as the client, but she nonetheless has her own hysterical pattern. Perhaps she is frightened of emotional chaos and therefore feels compelled to keep a tight leash on the expression of her feelings. Perhaps the client reminds her of her mother who was given to mood swings of depression and elation. Perhaps, as a child, she took on the task of keeping her mother's emotions harmonized, of cheering her up when she was low, and calming her down when she was nervous or agitated. Otherwise, the therapist would not have received the nurturance and attention she needed. Now, with this client, she feels compelled to soothe and calm, even suppress his chaotic emotional processes.

Whatever the pattern may be, the client is offering the therapist the possibility of healing her own unresolved hysteria. Through the therapist's own inward searching, done in her own therapy or in some other growth process, she can discover the subpersonality her client is mirroring back to her and work with that.

The Native Americans have a saying, "Don't judge another person until you've walked a mile in his moccasins." In my experience as a therapist, teacher, and supervisor, when therapists try to experience things through their clients' eyes, they also become aware of how their clients mirror them. Then, when they work on what their clients mirror, they become more capable of empathizing and guiding clients in their inward search. For this reason, transpersonal supervision may utilize techniques involving the same inward searching process that the client uses in therapy. In one such technique, developed at Naropa Institute in Boulder, Colorado, therapists can be taught to appreciate the client's phenomenological world by entering a meditative state and describing as fully as possible the client's body (face, build, clothes, characteristic movements, gestures, and actions), speech (rhythm, intonation, range, often used words and expressions), and mind (how the client sees him- or herself and the world, feeling states, degree of self- and other awareness). Van Dusen (1972, pp. 18–43) offers a similar practice that is applicable to therapeutic supervision.

The purpose of these techniques is for therapists to gain an intense awareness of the client and discover that the whole nature and quality of a person's life can be found in the details of his or her face, movements, gestures, voice quality, and actions, and in speculations about his or her self- and world concept. By guessing freely what it might be like to be the client, by shifting impressions as new ones come, and by doing so spontaneously and openly while in this meditative state, two things very often happen. First, therapists enhance their awareness of the client. But, in doing so, they tend to discover those ways in which they are similar to the client. By focusing upon these similarities in themselves, by discovering new and more compassionate ways of approaching them, and by looking for deeper meanings for these mirrored qualities in themselves, therapists discover a whole new way of being with these similar qualities in the client. The result is a deepening of empathy and appreciation of the client's inner being.

As therapists discover new ways of approaching the qualities in themselves that are mirrored by their clients, they also discover a greater range of possibilities for interacting with those aspects of the client in the therapeutic context. The interventions they make with their clients can duplicate the interventions they make with themselves. When therapists repeat to clients what they say to heal their own unhealed selves, clients are often uner-

ringly aided in breaking through their own characterological patterns. I have often found that when my interventions emerge from my own inwardness, my clients feel truly seen, felt, and heard.

The therapist also mirrors the client. As part of their therapy, clients will have the opportunity to reclaim disowned portions of themselves through the mirroring process. They see themselves in a mirror the therapist holds up. That mirror, when expertly handled by the therapist, becomes for the client a means of awakening to a greater identity.

To illustrate, let us begin by remembering that, at no point, are therapists doing therapy with someone who is entirely different than themselves. I believe this fact is in the background of a client's awareness and often comes to the foreground toward the end of the therapeutic journey. In the background of their conscious awareness, clients know their therapists are quite similar to them; therapists are part of the same human condition and are, therefore, handling life as best they can, always less than perfectly, and dealing with the same life concerns. Clients know therapists struggle with egoic issues like self-esteem and have yet to integrate many disowned portions of their shadow. They know therapists are human beings subject to illness and death, that they make the best choices they can and act in as informed a way as they know how but are often off the beam in handling their own existential concerns. And they know that therapists are tremulous in the face of transcendental mystery, for despite their glimpses of a greater Reality, very few therapists are spiritually enlightened. Whether or not they are consciously aware of it, clients also know therapists are qualified to be therapists not because they are different or better, not because they are experts on how to live life, but by virtue of their training and the many years they've struggled to free themselves from some of the very same self-concepts and life patterns that deaden all human beings and keep them separate from that supreme synthesis—the Self.

These are basic facts about therapists, and clients know them. When they see their therapists in ways other than these, they are projecting something from their own inner world onto the therapist. Mirroring, then, can be viewed as any deviation from these basic facts. Clients may idealize their therapists, see them as ultimate authorities or rescuers, as all-powerful or all-knowing. They may cast therapists as mother, dad, teacher, or some archetypal figure, perhaps even as the higher Self. It may be useful, even essential, for them to cast their therapists in these roles for a while during the course of the therapy, and therapists may need to accept the transferences, allow them to happen, and work within them, as Kohut (1971) advised. However, they are not perceiving the therapist's inner Being. They are clients' transferences and eventually they must reclaim their projections in order to be whole. As in other forms of therapy, a milestone in transpersonal therapy occurs when the client begins to recognize the therapist first as a mirror reflecting back his or her object representations (mother, dad, authority) and then as a living, breathing human being with his or her own very human strengths and frailties—egoic, existential, and transpersonal.

Closing Remarks

I believe transpersonal therapists have yet to clarify the *pou sto* of their orientation. It is essential for transpersonal therapists to be explicit about the principles and assumptions to which they subscribe and out of which they interact with their clients, for it is well known that the beliefs of the therapist affect the process and outcome of psychotherapy. Just as our unconscious, unquestioned conceptions of ourselves and our world restrict us from living the lives we want and knowing our true identity, so our beliefs and assumptions about clients and the process of psychotherapy stamp irrevocably how we interact with them, what we expect them to do in therapy, and the outcome of the therapeutic journey.

It seems crucial to me that readers do not see these postulates in isolation but as a contextualization for other therapeutic approaches. For example, in my mind, psychoanalysts are practicing transpersonally oriented analysis if they are dedicated to a spiritual path that informs their therapeutic work. They may subscribe to these five postulates or others, while, at the same time, remaining true to those aspects of psychoanalytic theory and technique that they recognize as essential to their practice. Similarly, I see the postulates for existential–humanistic psychotherapy formulated by Bugental (1981) as fitting well into the context I describe in these pages.

As transpersonal therapists, we must be explicit in our assumptions if we are to contribute to a comprehensive approach that addresses the whole human being— ego, existential, and spiritual. Consequently, the five postulates offered are definitions of a preliminary model, starting points for the development of an integrative theory for transpersonal psychotherapy.

REFERENCES

Anonymous. (1975). *A course in miracles*. Vol. I. *Text*. Tiburon. CA: Foundation for Inner Peace.
Assagioli, R. (1965). *Psychosynthesis*. New York: Hobbs-Dorman.
Aurobindo, R. (1949). *The life divine*. New York: Dutton.
Aurobindo, R. (1955). *The synthesis of yoga*. Pondicherry, India: Sri Aurobindo Ashram Press.
Bailey, A. A. (1925). *A treatise on cosmic fire*. New York: Lucis.
Bailey, A. A. (1932). *From intellect to intuition*. New York: Lucis.
Bailey, A. A. (1934). *A treatise on white magic*. New York: Lucis.
Bailey, A. A. (1950). *Education in the new age*. New York: Lucis.
Blanck, G., & Blanck, R. (1974). *Ego psychology: Theory and practice*. New York: Columbia University Press.
Blanck, G., & Blanck, R. (1979). *Ego psychology II: Psychoanalytic developmental psychology*. New York: Columbia University Press.
Brunton, P. (1943). *The wisdom of the overself*. New York: Samuel Weiser.
Bugental, J. F. T. (1978). *Psychotherapy and process*. New York: Random House.
Bugental, J. F. T. (1981). *The search for authenticity* (Enlarged edition). New York: Irvington.
Byrom, T. (1976). *The Dhammapada: The sayings of the Buddha*. New York: Random House.
Case, P. (1947). *The Tarot: A key to the wisdom of the ages*. Richmond, VA: Macoy.
Chaudhuri, H. (1965). *Integral yoga: The concept of harmonious and creative living*. Wheaton, IL: Theosophical Publishing House.
Chaudhuri, H. (1974). *Being, evolution, and immortality: An outline of integral philosophy*. Wheaton, IL: Theosophical Publishing House.
Deikman, A. J. (1982). *The observing self: Mysticism and psychotherapy*. Boston: Beacon.
de Mello, A. (1978). *Sadhana: A way to God*. St. Louis: Institute for Jesuit Resources.
Evans-Wentz, W. Y. (Ed.). (1958). *Tibetan yoga and secret doctrines*. London: Oxford University Press.
Fadiman, J. (1980). The transpersonal stance. In R. N. Walsh & F. Vaughan (Eds.), *Beyond ego: Transpersonal dimensions in psychology* (pp. 175–181). Los Angeles: Tarcher.
Fortune, D. (1935). *The mystical Qabalah*. London: Ernest Benn.
Gendlin, E. (1978). *Focusing*. New York: Bantam.
Gerard, R. (1964). *Psychosynthesis: A psychotherapy for the whole man*. New York: Psychosynthesis Research Foundation.
Goldsmith, J. (1959). *The art of spiritual healing*. New York: Harper & Row.
Goldstein, J. (1976). *The experience of insight: A simple and direct guide to Buddhist meditation*. Boston: Shambhala.
Govinda, A. (1960). *Foundations of Tibetan mysticism*. New York: Weiser.
Green, E., & Green, A. (1971). On the meaning of transpersonal: Some metaphysical perspectives. *The Journal of Transpersonal Psychology, 1*, 27–46.
Grimm, J., & Grimm, W. (1944). *The complete Grimm's fairy tales*. New York: Pantheon.
Grof, S. (1985). *Beyond the brain*. New York: State University of New York Press.
Hannah, B. (1981). *Encounters with the soul: Active imagination as developed by C. G. Jung*. Boston: Sigo Press.
Horner, A. (1984). *Object relations theory and the developing ego in therapy*. New York: Jason Aronson.
Horney, K. (1950). *Neurosis and human growth*. New York: Norton.
Huxley, A. (1944). *The perennial philosophy*. New York: Harper & Row.

Johnson, S. (1987). *Humanizing the narcissistic style*. New York: Norton.

Jung, C. G. (1959). *Man and his symbols*. New York: Doubleday.

Kavanaugh, K., & Rodriguez, O., (Trans.). (1979). *The collected works of St. John of the Cross*. Washington, DC: Institute of Carmelite Studies.

Kernberg, O. (1975). *Borderline conditions and pathological narcissism*. New York: Jason Aronson.

Kohut, H. (1971). *The analysis of the self*. New York: International Universities Press, Inc.

Kohut, H. (1977). *The restoration of the self*. New York: International Universities Press, Inc.

Maharshi, R. (1972). *The spiritual teaching of Ramana Maharshi*. Boulder: Shambhala.

Mahrer, A. (1983). *Experiential psychotherapy*. New York: Brunner-Mazel.

Mahrer, A. (1986). *Therapeutic experiencing*. New York: Norton.

Masterson, J. (1976). *Psychotherapy of the borderline adult: A developmental approach*. New York: Brunner-Mazel.

Masterson, J. (1985). *The real self: A developmental, self, and object relations approach*. New York: Brunner-Mazel.

May, R. (1983). *The discovery of being*. New York: Norton.

Metzner, R. (1986). *Opening to inner light*. Los Angeles: J. P. Tarcher.

Miller, A. (1981). *Prisoners of childhood* (subsequently published as *The drama of the gifted child*). New York: Basic.

Millon, T. (1981). *Disorders of personality*. New York: Wiley.

Namgyal, T. (1986). *Mahamudra: The quintessence of mind and meditation*. Boston: Shambhala.

Perls, F. (1969). *Gestalt therapy verbatim*. Lafayette, CA: Real People Press.

Progoff, I. (1975). *At a journal workshop*. New York: Dialogue House.

Progoff, I. (1980). *The practice of process meditation*. New York: Dialogue House.

Saraydarian, T. (Trans.). (n.d.). *The Bhagavad Gita*. Agoura, CA: Aquarian Educational Group.

Satprem. (1968). *Sri Aurobindo or the adventure of consciousness*. New York: Harper & Row.

Schuon, F. (1975). *The transcendent unity of religions*. New York: Harper & Row.

Scott, C. (1935). *An outline of modern occultism*. London: Routledge & Kegan Paul.

Shapiro, D., & Walsh, R. (Eds.). (1984). *Meditation: Classic and contemporary perspectives*. New York: Aldine.

Smith, H. (1976). *Forgotten truth: The primordial tradition*. New York: Harper & Row.

Sutich, A. (1976). The emergence of the transpersonal orientation: A personal account. *The Journal of Transpersonal Psychology, 1,* 5–19.

Suzuki, S. (1970). *Zen mind, beginner's mind*. New York: Weatherhill.

Trungpa, C. (1976a). *The myth of freedom*. Boston: Shambhala.

Trungpa, C. (1976b). Foundations of mindfulness. *Garuda IV* (pp. 17–46). Boulder: Vajradhatu.

Van Dusen, W. (1972). *The natural depth in man*. New York: Harper & Row.

Vaughan, F. (1986). *The inward arc: Healing and wholeness in psychotherapy and spirituality*. Boston: Shambhala.

Walsh, R., & Vaughan, F. (1980). *Beyond ego*. Los Angeles: J. P. Tarcher.

Welwood, J. (1982). The unfolding of experience: Psychotherapy and beyond. *Journal of Humanistic Psychology, 22,* 91–104.

White, M. T., & Weiner, M. B. (1986). *The theory and practice of self psychology*. New York: Brunner/Mazel.

Wilber, K. (1977). *The spectrum of consciousness*. Wheaton, IL: Theosophical Publishing House.

Wilber, K. (1979). *No boundary: Eastern and Western approaches to personal growth*. Boston: Shambhala.

Wilber, K. (1980). *The Atman project*. Wheaton, IL: Theosophical Publishing House.

Wilber, K. (1983). *Eye to eye: The quest for the new paradigm*. New York: Doubleday.

Wittine, B. (1982). *The crises and conflicts of spiritual awakening*. Unpublished doctoral dissertation, California Institute of Integral Studies, San Francisco.

Yalom, I. (1980). *Existential psychotherapy*. New York: Basic.

18

Transpersonal Psychology
Promise and Prospects

Robert Frager

INTRODUCTION

This survey of transpersonal psychology focuses on three major domains—the psychology of personal development, the psychology of consciousness, and spiritual psychology. These three main areas overlap to form the field of transpersonal psychology.

The psychology of personal development includes those models of human nature found in: (a) psychoanalysis and neo-Freudian personality systems, (b) the body-oriented models of therapy and growth developed by Wilhelm Reich and others, and (c) the positive, growth-oriented models of Maslow and humanistic psychology. We examine not only the theoretical formulations but also the practical applications to individual growth found in each system.[1]

The psychology of consciousness is devoted to mapping and exploring different states of human functioning, such as dreaming, meditation, drug states, and parapsychology. Spiritual psychology consists of the study of the models of human nature found in the world's religious

traditions and the development of psychological theory that is consistent with religious and spiritual experiences. One area of major interest is the integration of the concept of the deep Self within both psychological and spiritual models of human nature.

The transpersonal approach to each of these areas is based on an interest in studying human capacities and potentials and a fundamental premise that these capacities are far greater than our current understanding and theorizing. Transpersonal psychology does not consist simply of the content of the three areas listed previously. It is also a point of view, a perspective that can be applied to a wide variety of areas, not only in psychology but also in anthropology, sociology, and other disciplines involving human behavior.

As one example of this interrelated approach, Vaughan (in Walsh & Vaughan, 1980) has described transpersonal psychotherapy in terms of context, content, and process. The transpersonal context in therapy is determined by the therapist's beliefs, values, and intentions. It includes interest in expanding self-awareness and the sense of the self, and a belief in the possibility and desirability of inner transformation. Transpersonal content refers to experiences of different states of consciousness, especially those experiences in which the individual experiences a transcendence of the ego or personality. Transpersonal process refers to the process of moving from one stage of identification to another. The first stage is identification with the ego and includes developing self-esteem, ego strength, and the like. The second stage is that of disidentification with roles, posses-

---

[1] I am indebted to Arthur Hastings for his seminal suggestion to organize the field of transpersonal psychology into the three domains of the psychology of personal development, psychology of consciousness, and spiritual psychology.

Robert Frager • Institute for Culture and Creation Spirituality, Holy Names College, Oakland, California 94619, and Institute for Transpersonal Psychology, Menlo Park, California, 94025.

sions, activities, and relationships. The third stage is one of transcendence or identification with the Self.

Ron Valle (see Chapter 16 in this volume) has listed five basic premises that summarize the perspective of transpersonal psychology. If we look closely at each premise, we can see how the fundamental assumptions of transpersonal psychology are significantly different from the assumptions of traditional Western psychology. We can also see how these premises tie together the various areas of transpersonal psychology.

The first premise, that there is a transcendent reality, brings transpersonal psychology more into the domain of philosophy and comparative religion than psychology. One of the fundamental (but rarely conscious) assumptions of psychology and Western science in general is that the universe is essentially fragmented, accidentally created, and meaningless (see, for example, Tart, 1975a).

In his discussion of the perennial philosophy, Aldous Huxley (1945) argued that the world's religious traditions agree that human beings are part of the fundamental wholeness or unity of the universe. As many Indian philosophers have put it, each individual is like a wave in the ocean. The waves rise out of the ocean and then fall back into it. At one level, each wave is an individual and separate form. At another level, there is only the ocean, and the waves are not really separate at all. As with the first premise, traditional psychology holds very different assumptions. These include the assumption that human beings are only their bodies and nothing more and that we are each locked within our separate nervous systems; therefore, each individual is isolated from all others and from the surrounding environment (see Tart, 1975a).

The notion that it is possible to experience directly this higher order reality is also diametrically opposed to traditional psychological assumptions. First of all, in maintstream psychology there *is* no higher order reality. Second, being locked within our separate nervous systems, we are incapable of *directly* experiencing anything; all our experiences are filtered through our nervous system and also affected by our past experience.

According value to other states of consciousness also runs counter to the traditional psychological and scientific assumption that our ordinary waking consciousness is the best and most rational state and that therefore all other states are inferior, irrational, or pathological (see Tart, 1975a). The idea that the experience of other states of consciousness may be self-validating, is, according to traditional psychological assumptions, but an example of the irrationality (or even pathology) to be und in altered states of consciousness. Again, being ked within our own separate nervous systems, we cannot possibly have genuine noetic, numinous, or self-validating experiences.

Teilhard de Chardin (1970), the well-known twentieth-century philosopher and theologian, has outlined the fundamental task of transpersonal psychology:

> It is essential that we wake up a certain number of aspirations still half-conscious in ourselves, if we wish to experience at its full the passion for the ultra-humanization towards which we are impelled by the very drift of the Universe. . . . So far (and for good reasons) the psychologists have been concerned primarily with the medical task of freeing the individual patients from their hidden or buried complexes. But now the time has come, for . . . exploring and tapping the mysterious cores where still lie, untouched, the most powerful energies of the human soul. (pp. 110–111)

It is the intention of this survey to present a transpersonal perspective within three interrelated domains and to understand transpersonal psychology as a discipline that combines and blends the concerns and approaches of these domains.

PSYCHOLOGY OF PERSONAL DEVELOPMENT

Today, a wide variety of processes of personal development is available through self-help groups, self-help books, and churches, synagogues, social service organizations, and community centers. Many of these processes are derived from the psychotherapeutic treatment of neurosis, now taken into nontherapy contexts and used to help healthy people improve their levels of functioning and self-understanding. Other processes stem from therapies and disciplines that focus on improving physical functioning. Still others have developed within this new growth-oriented context, which has often been described as the human potential movement.

Psychotherapeutic Approaches

The techniques and insights of psychotherapy were, at first, restricted to small numbers of the affluent and curious. Today, the benefits of psychotherapy are accessible to almost everyone. This includes the analysis of unconscious motivations and of other processes not normally accessible to conscious understanding. This section examines the contributions of psychotherapy from a transpersonal perspective. We first examine the analytic ground on which so many later systems are based. This includes the seminal contributions of Sigmund Freud, Erik Erikson, and Carl Jung. We also examine the work of Alice Miller, who brings an analytic approach to some of the great obstacles and distortions of personal development.

The Analytic Ground

Psychoanalysis. Psychoanalysis, the beginning of modern psychotherapy, is not generally considered transpersonal. In fact, most transpersonal psychologists recall Maslow's division of psychology into four "forces," with the mechanistic determinism of psychoanalysis and behaviorism on the one hand, and the rich, growth-oriented complexities of humanistic and transpersonal psychologies on the other. However, Maslow did insist that, for him, transpersonal psychology was not a rejection of either behaviorism or psychoanalysis but rather added to and was built on to the other two. Although psychoanalysis has often been criticized for its emphasis on the irrational and unconscious determinants of human behavior, Erich Fromm has pointed out that Freud was optimistic in his belief that the ego could be strengthened and that the unconscious could be made conscious. "Reason, so Freud felt, is the only tool—or weapon—we have to make sense of life, to dispense with illusions and establish our own authority" (Fromm, 1959, p. 2). As suggested by Freud's (1933, p. 80) famous dictum, "Where id is, there let ego be," he was dedicated to bringing unconscious processes into the light of consciousness, a goal very much in harmony with the transpersonal theme of understanding and expanding consciousness.

Erikson's Developmental Model. Erikson (1963) extended Freud's developmental model throughout the entire life cycle, from childhood to adult and old age. His model is essentially one of healthy development, outlining the kinds of issues and challenges faced by every individual.

Erikson's developmental model is based on the model of embryonic development where each stage is a turning point in which certain strengths and skills are tested. The basic principle in this model is that each stage can develop only when the previous stage has laid the foundation for it.

Earlier stages do not have to be "perfectly" handled for development to continue. However, serious difficulty at one stage is likely to distort development later, the successful resolution of the crisis at each stage impelling the individual on to the next. In each stage, earlier strengths and skills are confirmed and integrated, as new attributes are developed and tested.

Erikson has also added a brilliant formulation of the "virtues" developed at each stage. Erikson uses virtue in its old sense, as in the virtue of a medicine, referring more to potency than morality. The individual emerges from each crisis with an increased sense of inner unity, clearer judgment, and increased capacity to function effectively. The virtues discussed by Erikson are, in chronological

order, hope, will, purpose, competence, fidelity, love, care, and wisdom. Erikson examines, in an integrated way, both the positive and negative possibilities inherent in each stage of development. He includes both pathology and normality and also the real possibilities of development beyond average functioning.

Another important contribution of Erikson's has been his psychobiographies—Martin Luther (1958), Mahatma Gandhi (1969), Maxim Gorky (1963), Adolf Hitler (1963), George Bernard Shaw (1963), and Sigmund Freud (1964). His studies of major historical personalities have included not only their personal development but also the psychological impact they had on their generation and on society. Here, too, Erikson can serve as a model for transpersonal psychologists. If we want to understand the full range of human experience and potential, we need to study in depth those extraordinary individuals who exhibit this range.

Jung's Analytic Psychology. Carl Jung can be considered the first transpersonal psychologist. It was Jung who first used the term *transpersonal* in 1917, when he wrote of the "transpersonal unconscious" as a synonym for "collective unconscious." For Jung, the collective unconscious "contains the whole spiritual heritage of mankind's evolution, born anew in the brain structure of every individual" (Jung, in Campbell, 1971, p. 45).

According to Jung, the unconscious contains rich and valuable psychic material as well as the repressed traumata and irrational untamed passions that were Freud's primary focus. Jung emphasized the importance of developing a deeper interchange between conscious and unconscious processes.

The collective unconscious contains psychic structures or archetypes. These are universal forms or patterns that tend to organize psychic material. Jung also called the archetypes "primordial images" because they often correspond to mythological themes found in the legends and folklore of many cultures. Symbols generated by common archetypes include the perfect circle, the flawless gem, the "he-man," and the wise woman.

The archetypes are somewhat like the streambed whose shape determines the characteristics of the river and its flow. "They form a bridge between the ways in which we consciously express our thoughts and a more primitive, more colorful and pictorial form of expression. . . . These 'historical' associations are the link between the rational world of consciousness and the world of instinct" (Jung, 1964, pp. 47–48). A given archetype may be associated with a wide variety of symbols. For example, the mother archetype embraces each individual's real mother and also all other mothers and nurturing figures. This includes women in general, mythic images such as the Virgin Mary and Mother Nature, and also symbols of nurturing such as the ''Motherland'' and ''Mother Church.'' An understanding of Jung's approach to archetypes can yield great insight into the power and meaning of dreams and other potent symbols and images.

The central archetype in the psyche is the Self. It is the center of the entire psyche, linking our conscious and unconscious processes. The Self is a deep, inner guiding factor. At early stages of self-exploration, the Self can seem small and inconsequential or even alien to the conscious mind. Individuation, or self-development, is a major concept for Jung.

One important part of this process involves development of a dynamic relationship between the ego, the center of consciousness, and the Self. ''The ego receives the light from the Self. Though we know of this Self, yet it is not known. . . . In reality its experience is unlimited and endless. . . . If I were one with the Self I would have knowledge of everything'' (Jung, 1975, pp. 194–195).

So, in a sense, Jung agrees with Freud that psychological growth is a matter of becoming more conscious. ''No matter whether people think they are individuated or not, they are just what they are: in the one case a man . . . unconscious of himself; or in the other case, conscious. The criterion is consciousness'' (Jung, 1975, p. 377).

Jung saw analysis as an inner journey, as an inner growth process. ''The main interest of my work is not concerned with the treatment of neuroses but rather with the approach to the numinous. But the fact is that the approach to the numinous is the real therapy and inasmuch as you attain to the numinous experiences, you are released from the curse of pathology'' (Jung, 1973, p. 377).

Rethinking Childhood: The Work of Alice Miller.

Alice Miller is a Swiss psychoanalyst who has written brilliantly about childrearing and childhood. Miller (1984) maintains that Freudian theory is correct in asserting that everyone is shaped (although not necessarily determined) by childhood, that all neuroses are rooted in childhood, and that classic analytic techniques are effective in making possible the reenactment of the drama of childhood that allows a blocked maturation process to begin. She argues that Jung and most neo-Freudians do not place sufficient emphasis on the significance of these early childhood experiences.

Miller differs from classic psychoanalytic thought in several important areas. She rejects Freud's drive conflict theory of neurosis in favor of his earlier theory that neurosis stems from the repression of real, early traumatic experiences. Parents are not only objects within a patient's psyche; they are also real persons who may have caused their child real suffering.

Miller (1981) points out that all children have a primary need to be accepted as they really are, to have their feelings and sensations acknowledged and accepted. If they are deprived of this, as adults they will search for what their own parents could not give them—someone who is deeply aware of them and who respects and admires them. This search can never fully succeed because it is tied to a situation locked in the past, to the time when the self was forming. As parents, such adults unconsciously seek gratification for their own childhood deprivation from their children. They fail to provide an atmosphere of tolerance and acceptance for their own children as unique individuals, and they pass their emotional problems along to the next generation. At its worst, this process leads to emotional, physical, or sexual abuse.

Accommodation to the needs of a psychologically deprived parent leads to the development of the ''false self'' (Miller, 1981). In order to gain and hold the parent's love, the child reveals only what is expected and eventually fuses with what is revealed and loses touch with all other aspects of self.

Miller's (1984) ground-breaking study of the abuse suffered by Adolf Hitler as a child is a masterpiece and should be read by anyone interested in the roots of violence and evil. Miller illustrates the extent of the emotional and physical abuse that Hitler suffered as a child, and that, amazingly enough, has been denied or downplayed by virtually all of his biographers (for example, Hitler was beaten by his father every single day of his childhood, and he was almost beaten to death at the age of 11).

Miller sees the imprisonment of the true self within the prison of the false self less as an illness than as a tragedy. She has convincingly shown the damaging role that society has played in this process in her analysis of what she has called ''poisonous pedagogy,'' a system of moral, intellectual, and religious beliefs centering around the notion that children are naturally amoral, violent, or even wicked. These beliefs tend to justify various forms of mental and physical cruelties under the guise of *child rearing*. Two common examples of poisonous pedagogy are ''Spare the rod and spoil the child'' and ''Children should be seen but not heard.''

The result of such pervasive attitudes is the suppression of the natural vitality, creativity, and feeling in the child. As adults, we then do our best to rid ourselves of the child within us, to deny our weakness, dependency, and helplessness, while also suppressing our real selves and our vitality and creativity.

Miller's (1983) fundamentally optimistic, transpersonal orientation is reflected in the last line of *For Your*

Own Good, "For the human spirit is virtually indestructible, and its ability to rise from the ashes remains as long as the body draws breath" (p. 279).

Body-Oriented Approaches to Therapy and Growth

Freud discovered that tremendous insight and life change can result from having clients lie on a couch and talk about themselves. Similarly, Wilhelm Reich and others discovered that systematically focusing on the body in therapy is also extremely effective in gaining therapeutic insight (we are, after all, bodily beings). Other ways of working with the body focus more on personal growth *per se*. These include the system developed by Feldenkrais and the Eastern disciplines of hatha yoga, t'ai chi, and aikido, all of which are reviewed later.

All of these approaches are devoted to enhancing human functioning and improving human capacities far beyond the limits of the average person by increasing our awareness of our bodies. All work with the breath as well, relating the breath to the concept of life force. They also advocate "nondoing," learning to let the body operate naturally and smoothly, favor relaxed and "natural" movements and posture, and teach the individual to reduce habitual, unnecessary tensions in the body. Mind and body are treated as a single whole, an ongoing psychophysiological process in which change at any level will affect all other parts. Similarly, the spiritual traditions of Yoga, Buddhism, and Sufism (discussed in the section on spiritual psychology) treat the body as a vehicle for purification, prayer, and meditation.

Reichian Therapy. Wilhelm Reich was a great psychotherapeutic pioneer in his insistence on the unity of mind and body. Reich's work has inspired many traditional and transpersonal therapists to include the body in therapy (see, for example, Grof, 1985). Reich's lasting contributions seem to be in his discovery of the physical armoring process and its interaction with psychological processes and also his discovery of biological energy and the importance of releasing energetic blocks.

Reich began as a Freudian psychoanalyst. He was initially interested in elaborating on Freud's original conception of character, which he concluded was formed as a defense against anxiety created by the child's strong sexual feelings and consequent fear of punishment. He focused his early efforts as a psychotherapist on working with character defenses (Reich, 1976), the habitual pattern of psychological distortions and defenses found in each individual. He discovered that each pattern of character defense was associated with a specific pattern of muscular tension and rigidity, or muscular armoring.

As a consequence, Reich began to devote his attention to loosening the muscular armoring in order to speed the therapeutic process. As chronically tense muscles were loosened, patients often spontaneously relived old traumatic situations or experienced a variety of strong physical sensations. Reich concluded that these sensations were due to movements of newly freed biological energy, or orgone energy.

In time, Reich devoted himself to research on orgone energy, both in individuals and in nature (Reich, 1973). Reichian therapy developed as a biophysical approach, including the use of deep breathing and manipulation of tense muscles to mobilize blocked energy and to release associated blocked emotions.

Bioenergetics. Alexander Lowen, the co-founder of bioenergetic therapy, combined Reich's fundamental concepts of bioenergy and energy release with more traditional psychoanalytic terminology. Bioenergetics is designed to help people become more aware of their bodies and to help them enjoy fully the life of the body. It includes work with the basic bodily functions of breathing, moving, feeling, and self-expression. Lowen (1975) writes:

> A person who doesn't breathe deeply reduces the life of his body. If he doesn't move freely, he restricts the life of his body. If he doesn't feel fully, he narrows the life of his body. And if his self-expression is constricted, he limits the life of his body. (p. 43)

Feldenkrais's Work. The evolutionary development of the human body and human behavior provides the foundation for Feldenkrais's work. In his first book, *Body and Mature Behavior* (1950), Feldenkrais begins with a detailed physiological and evolutionary examination of human erect posture and discusses the development of the cerebral cortex in relation to the older portions of the human brain. His system was developed to enhance physical functioning rather than as a form of therapy.

The essential role of learning in virtually all of human behavior is a major theme for Feldenkrais. Also, human functioning always involves movement and activity. An old Chinese proverb says, "I hear and I forget, I see and I remember, I do and I understand." Feldenkrais's work focuses on learning and understanding through doing. His learning exercises are called "awareness through movement" and generally consist of a series of small movements that combine to form new and efficient ways of carrying out complex actions like sitting, standing, and walking.

Hatha Yoga. Hatha yoga exercises were originally developed as a preparation for meditation. Today, especially in the West, hatha yoga mainly consists of the practice of yoga postures that promote greater health, flexibility, and vitality (see, for example, Majumdar, 1964). Posture practice enables the individual to sit relaxed and motionless for long periods of meditation. The postures also help develop a firm and flexible spine, stimulate various glands and internal organs, and are excellent means of reducing tension.

One of the goals of classical hatha yoga is to purify and strengthen the body as a vehicle for vital energies. The more energy that is available, the healthier and stronger the individual, and the more effective one's spiritual practices. Traditional hatha yoga practices include washing and cleansing the nasal passages and the digestive system, breathing exercises, fasting, a pure and vegetarian diet, concentration, and meditation exercises.

T'ai Chi Ch'uan. T'ai chi ch'uan is a Chinese exercise system that, like hatha yoga, was devised as an adjunct to spiritual practice. T'ai chi also promotes health, vitality, and self-defense. It has been said that t'ai chi practice leads to the flexibility of a child, the health of a lumberjack, and the peace of mind of a sage. One major aim of the practice is to develop ch'i, or vital energy. The student must learn to relax completely while practicing the t'ci chi movements so ch'i can flow unobstructed. Eventually, every movement becomes coordinated with the flow of ch'i. The student also learns to center energy and balance in the area of the navel and to move with a straight, supple spine and relaxed neck.

Also, the mind must be calm and concentrated on the movements (t'ai chi has been called a moving meditation). It is important, therefore, in t'ai chi practice to have slow, fluid movement in harmony with an inner flow of ch'i. In the t'ai chi classics (Chen & Smith, (1967, pp. 106–111), it is written:

> In resting, be as still as a mountain; in moving, go like the current of a great river.
> When you act, everything moves, and when you stand still, everything is tranquil.

Aikido. Another spiritual and martial art, aikido was founded in the 1920s by Master Morihei Ueshiba. Master Ueshiba had studied many of the traditional Japanese martial arts and was also deeply involved in the practice of spiritual disciplines from the Buddhist and Shinto traditions. He developed aikido as a way of self-development and inner growth as opposed to the traditional martial arts emphasis on becoming strong and defeating others (Ueshiba, 1963).

There is no competition in aikido, the aim being to learn to harmonize with the movements of a partner rather than to see who is stronger. A basic aikido principle is that the mind leads the body. The student learns to blend and redirect a partner's energy rather than fight force with force. Aikido might be translated as "a way of harmony of vital energy." *Ai* means to unite or harmonize; *ki* is vital energy; and *do* means path or way.

In aikido and t'ai chi, it is important to use mind and body in harmony. This harmony is reflected in relaxed and fluid, yet powerful, movement, in mental focus and concentration, and in centering, or awareness of the navel and lower abdomen. In China and Japan, the naval area is thought of as one's physical, energy, and emotional center. The better the concentration and movement from this center, the more fluid and powerful one's actions.

Humanistic Psychologies

The field of humanistic psychology was the first major field of psychology to focus explicitly on human potentialities. It was established to provide an alternative to the two dominant positions in psychology in the 1950s—psychoanalysis and behaviorism.

Maslow's Self-Actualization Psychology

Abraham Maslow was a major theoretical organizer in this new field. He argued that it is more accurate to generalize about human nature by studying the finest examples of humanity, the "growing tip," the healthiest and most creative people. He engaged in various preliminary explorations of "self-actualizing" people, loosely defining self-actualization as "the full use and exploitation of talents, capacities, potentialities, etc." (Maslow, 1970, p. 150).

Another of Maslow's basic concepts is that of the peak experience. Peak experiences are intense, joyous, and exciting moments in each of our lives, and may include our reactions to a beautiful sunset or listening to a moving piece of music, as well as feelings of deep satisfaction after creatively completing a challenging job.

As part of the process of Maslow's (1971) evolution from humanistic psychology to transpersonal psychology, he added the study of transcendence to his work on self-actualization. He found that some self-actualizing individuals had many transcendent peak experiences, whereas others had them rarely if ever. He discovered the transcending self-actualizers are more aware of the sacredness of all things and of the transcendent dimensions of life in the midst of daily activities. Also, they tend to think more "holistically" and are better able to transcend dichotomies than "merely healthy" self-actualizers.

Maslow (1968) was the first to write about the need for transpersonal psychology:

> I should say also that I consider Humanistic, Third Force Psychology to be transitional, a preparation for a still "higher" Fourth Psychology, transpersonal, trans-human, centered in the cosmos rather than in human needs and interest, going beyond humanness, identity, self-actualization and the like. . . . We need something "bigger than we are" to be awed by and to commit ourselves to in a new, naturalistic, empirical, non-churchly sense, perhaps as Thoreau and Whitman, William James and John Dewey did. (pp. iii–iv)

Colin Wilson (1972) has clearly illustrated Maslow's importance: "Maslow was the first person to create a truly comprehensive psychology stretching, so to speak, from the basement to the attic. . . . Maslow's achievement is enormous. Like all original thinkers, he has opened up a new way of *seeing* the universe" (p. 184).

The Human Potential Movement

In the 1960s, the academic field of humanistic psychology was swept up into what has been called the human potential movement. Influenced by psychedlic drugs and Eastern mystical traditions, many of those involved in this movement experimented with every possible method or technique that promised to enhance human growth and development—the movement had a strong emphasis on experience. Out of a desire to avoid arid intellectualism, rationality and intellectual understanding were often ignored in favor of emotional or physical expression that has severed, unfortunately, to isolate humanistic psychology from the academic mainstream.

The first and most important institution devoted to the human potential field was the Esalen Institute, founded in 1962. Within a few years, Esalen developed a national reputation as the avant-garde center for encounter groups and other intense, emotionally charged workshops. Workshop leaders experimented with new therapeutic and growth-oriented techniques, often claiming that they were able to facilitate more personal change in an intense week or weekend than was possible in years of conventional therapy.

The human potential disciplines, such as encounter groups and other intensive workshops, aim explicitly at "personal growth," increased awareness, and the like and regularly evoke ecstatic and transpersonal experiences as well (Murphy, 1969). They share certain fundamental features with traditional contemplative and transpersonal disciplines in that they focus attention upon unfamiliar aspects or possibilities of one's experience, attempt to break perceptual constancies, require surrender to formerly resisted perceptions or feelings, and

facilitate increased vitality, power, joy, and a greater sense of meaning and freedom. All techniques and disciplines aimed at personal development may become integral parts of one's inner journey, leading toward transcendence of limitations and exploration of the limits of human capacities (i.e., they may be used within a transpersonal perspective).

THE PSYCHOLOGY OF CONSCIOUSNESS

William James on Consciousness

William James, the founder of American psychology, was profoundly interested in consciousness. James (1890) was critical of his colleagues who tried to reduce human experience to discrete bits and pieces:

> The traditional psychology talks like one who should say a river consists of nothing but pailsful, spoonsful, quartsful, barrelsful, and other moulded forms of water. Even were the pails and the pots all actually standing in the stream, still between them the free water would continue to flow. It is just this free water of consciousness that psychologists resolutely overlook. (p. 255)

James (1890) observed that our inner life is constantly changing. We never have the exact same thought twice. Yet consciousness is also continuous; each thought is influenced by our preceding thoughts, and consciousness itself is affected by attention and by will.

Will, which James defined as a combination of attention and effort, is the critical ingredient in all meaningful action. He felt that an idea automatically produces action unless another idea conflicts with it. Will allows one to hold one choice among conflicting alternatives long enough to allow action to occur.

In James's (1890) view, the mind is far richer and more complex than our emphasis on ordinary waking consciousness would lead us to believe. Normal waking consciousness is but one special type of consciousness. All around it "there lie potential forms of consciousness entirely different" (p. 288).

Grof's Developmental Model of Consciousness

Stanislav Grof is a European psychiatrist who has written extensively on LSD research and altered states of consciousness. Grof (1985) has described the major characteristics of psychedelic experiences. These include transcendence of space and time, transcendence of distinctions between matter, energy, and consciousness, and transcendence of the separation between the individual and the external world.

In analyzing the content of LSD experiences, Grof (1975) distinguished four major types of experience, which are of universal significance—abstract, psychodynamic, perinatal, and transpersonal:

1. Abstract, or aesthetic, experiences are primarily sensory, for example, experiencing sounds and colors more vividly than usual.
2. Psychodynamic experiences involve the reliving of emotionally charged memories from various periods of the individual's life. They also include symbolic experiences that are similar to dream images that are understandable in psychoanalytic terms.
3. Perinatal types of experience deal with birth and death. In some cases, LSD subjects relived elements of their birth, sometimes in astonishingly correct detail. Grof (1975) found that perinatal memories tended to form constellations, or collections of memories, that share the same strong emotional charge or other important similarities. Memories of physical traumata, generally associated with birth, appear to be more important than the psychological traumata that are traditionally the major focus of psychotherapy.

The role of physical trauma provides one explanation for the power and effectiveness of Reichian and other therapies that work directly with the body. Grof (1985) himself has recently developed a system of therapy that involves neo-Reichian breathing, evocative music, and body work and often results in the reliving of previously unconscious perinatal experiences.

Grof discusses four major stages of the birth process. The first stage, derived from the fetal development in the womb, is associated with lack of boundaries and symbols such as the ocean and Mother Nature. Negative experiences connected with this stage are symbolized by pollution and contamination.

In the second stage, the beginning of labor, the cervix is not yet dilated. It is associated with feelings of anxiety and threat from an unidentifiable source and also a sense of being caged or trapped, with no exit.

The third stage involves the movement of the fetus through the birth canal; it is symbolized by struggle for survival, crushing pressure, and suffocation.

In the fourth stage, the experience of birth, the agonizing struggle finally ends in feelings of relief and relaxation. It involves the ''death–rebirth experience'' and may be symbolically experienced in visions of light and beauty or by a sense of liberation and salvation.

4. Transpersonal types of experience involve the sense that one's consciousness has expanded beyond the usual ego boundaries and transcended the limitations of space and time. These include ancestral memories, mem-ories of life in a prior incarnation, and the experience of merging completely with another person or group. Other phenomena include experiences of extrasensory perception (ESP) and visions of archetypal forms such as demigods and demons.

Grof (1985) argues that there is a close relationship between spirituality and the exploration of different levels of consciousness. He has found that working through early traumatic memories tends to open the way to perinatal and transpersonal experiences and that these levels of experience are followed by a deepening inner sense of spirituality. Conversely, those who have profound spiritual experiences find work with personal truama and other issues much easier.

As with Alice Miller's work, focus on early experience provides an essential foundation for both psychological growth and spiritual awakening. From this perspective, we can see that transpersonal psychology must include an integrated view of the full range of human experience, from childhood trauma to adult spirituality.

Paradigm Shifts and the Study of Consciousness

Grof (1985) found that many transpersonal experiences seem to contradict the principles of Western science. Individuals have reported transcending all physical boundaries, communicating directly with other people and other life forms, and so forth. Grof (1985) has argued that the older, materialistic paradigm of Western science must be replaced by a modern paradigm, one that is compatible with both modern theoretical physics and also with consciousness research.

Thomas Kuhn (1962) originally defined a paradigm as a set of values and beliefs shared by members of a scientific community, where theory and research developed within the community will all be consistent with these fundamental values and beliefs. A paradigm is a context within which one works. Kuhn points out that once a paradigm is developed and accepted, it generally inspires a period of scientific progress.

However, there eventually comes a time when recognition of the limitations of a given paradigm gives rise to a search for a new paradigm. Theories and applications derived from the current paradigm no longer work as well as they did. Anomalies are discovered, new data that cannot be readily explained by the old theories, and the paradigm no longer meets its own criteria for success. The adoption of a new paradigm involves a new way of seeing. Like the perceptual shift that occurs while viewing a reversible gestalt figure, once it happens, it happens completely.

In Kuhn's view, there is almost inevitably resistance to the new paradigm on the part of those attached to the old one. Because the two paradigms operate on different assumptions and postulates, there is often fundamental disagreement concerning the nature and definition of important problems and the criteria for correct solutions. Advocates of the new paradigm are then accused of using "unscientific" methods or studying "unscientific" problems.

Grof (1985) has pointed out that relativity theory and related developments in physics form a new paradigm that is not compatible with the old Newtonian model of the universe. In relativity theory, space and time are not separate; they are interwoven. The flow of time is not uniform and absolute but depends on the position of the observers and their velocities relative to the observed event. Atomic physics has conclusively demonstrated that matter is not solid at the subatomic level. Still other theories, such as quantum mechanics, work with logical discrepancies and notions of probabilities rather than absolute existence of subatomic particles. Grof points out that the transpersonal experiences he has studied are inconsistent with the Newtonian model—that is, they constitute anomalies in Kuhn's sense—but are fundamentally compatible with the new paradigm in physics.

Not everyone shares Grof's views. In *Einstein's Space and Van Gogh's Sky* (1982), Larry LeShan, a psychologist, and Henry Margenau, a theoretical physicist, posit that modern psychology needs to develop its own new paradigm. The authors begin by examining the roots of nineteenth-century science. The point out that when modern science began to develop in the seventeenth and eighteenth centuries, the dominant world view was that God, who is fundamentally rational, created a rational cosmos. The job of science was to understand that God-given rational structure.

Early approaches to science contained three fundamental assumptions. First, because scientists began by investigating those things that could be seen, touched, and counted, the whole universe was assumed to be quantitative. Quantification was not seen as a human activity that imposed a somewhat arbitrary order on the universe. It was considered to be part of reality itself.

A second assumption was that everything in the universe functions through cause and effect. More specifically, it was believed that the past is the complete cause of the present, that all action is the result of an interplay of forces from the past. It was absurd and inconceivable even to entertain the idea that the future influences the present or that there is such a thing as an uncaused event.

One implication of this second assumption is that the cosmos is predictable. Theoretically, if we know enough about the past and present, we can predict what will happen next. The writing of a great symphony, the fall of a specific leaf, and the painting of the Mona Lisa all could be predicted if only we had enough knowledge.

A third assumption is that everything could be explained mechanically. The cosmos is like a giant clockwork and can be explained by a mechanical model. In fact, because the universe is mechanical in nature, this is the only valid kind of explanation.

These three assumptions can be summarized as a belief in quantification, cause and effect, and the need for mechanical models. LeShan and Morgenau (1982) point out that these assumptions have *never* worked for psychology.

First of all, the attempts that psychologists have made over the last 100 years to quantify inner experience have failed. The behavioristic attempt to distinguish between inner and outer "behaviors" has essentially ignored the basic data of psychology, which is our inner experience. It is fundamentally impossible to quantify feelings so that we could state precisely "I am twice as happy as you," or "she has half the pain that he does," or "Rembrandt was three and a half times better than van Gogh."

Predictability is also a fundamental problem. Predictability rests on the idea that the past is the complete determinant of the present, even though, for human beings, purpose and future goals are of major importance. Some psychologists have insisted that teleology, the notion that behavior is purposeful and therefore influenced by future goals, is "unscientific." This level of explanation clearly does not apply to the movement of billiard balls and other inanimate objects, but that is no reason to discard it in studying human behavior. The same human act may have a totally different significance depending on its purpose (for example, picking up a telephone to call a hospital and ask after a sick child, to phone in a business order, or to whisper to a lover).

LeShan and Margenau's Theory of Consciousness

Physicists routinely work in three different domains, each requiring a different description of reality. First is the "see–touch" realm, or the realm of objects that can be perceived by the senses. Second is the microcosm, things too small to be seen or touched, even theoretically. Third is the macrocosm, things that are too big or too fast to be seen or touched, even theoretically.

LeShan and Margenau (1982) write:

> In this realm [the macrocosm] we must use a different description of reality in order to deal scientifically with

the data. In the microcosm the new "metaphysical system" is the "correct" one—it is the "true" description of reality. . . . Which system is *really* the correct one? It depends on the realm dealt with. The assumption that there is one "true" definition of *all* reality is outworn. (pp. 17–18)

The authors add two additional realms for psychology. The fourth realm is that of the meaningful or goal-related behavior of living things. This includes the behavior of organisms seeking food, avoiding danger, mating, and so forth. The fifth domain is that of human inner experience.

Within the last two decades, social scientists have gradually come to realize that the paradigms of both "common sense" and also nineteenth-century physics were not adequate to deal with complex data involving human beings. We also began to understand that physics was using different models of reality to deal with new and different kinds of data. LeShan and Margenau (1982) argue that the models of reality constructed by physicists to fit their data are not adequate for dealing with meaningful behavior or inner experience. We need to develop our own models and not borrow those designed for a completely different realm of data.

The authors developed some general principles for the development of theoretical models in the domain of human consciousness. The following are issues that any full psychology of consciousness must consider:

1. The observables in the realm of consciousness (the authors' term for the fundamental "data" of personal experience) will not be as sharply defined and distinguishable as in the sensory realm. The realm of consciousness contains "processes" rather than "things."
2. The observables cannot be quantified so as to compare mathematically one person's experience with another's.
3. Observables have no "public access"; they can only be observed directly by one person.
4. The observables cannot be seen or touched; therefore, they cannot be described in terms of size, shape, or location. We cannot ask, for example, "How large is a fear?" or "Where do I feel love?"
5. Because the observables of the consciousness realm cannot be quantified or located in space, the ways they interact will differ from the interaction of objects in the sensory realm.
6. The principles of space and time are different from the sensory realm. Space is personal space, and time is personal time. So far, no mathematical systems have been found to be applicable to either.

7. Principles of conservation do not apply (for example, "matter and energy are neither created nor destroyed"). New ideas can truly be created.
8. Mechanical models do not apply. Observables in this realm cannot be visualized as "push–pull" parts of a machine.
9. Purposes and causes exist as observables in the realm of consciousness. Free will is also an observable experience in this realm, although it has no counterpart within the sensory realm. Therefore, individual behavior is not fully predictable.

Tart's Model of States of Consciousness

Another major contributor to the psychology of consciousness is Charles Tart. Tart (1975b) has developed a systems theory approach to the study of consciousness, believing that each identifiable state of consciousness contains stabilizing processes that serve to maintain it. These include specific focuses of attention, positive and negative feedback, and limitations of the range of psychological and physiological functioning to those activities that maintain the state.

Tart suggests that awareness is a major component in activating many of the structures found within certain states of consciousness. Many psychological structures require much awareness, or attention, while they are developed, and then become habitual and require very little attention (for example, tying one's shoes, driving a car, or other habits). Tart hypothesizes that, in any given state of consciousness, attention is repeatedly and automatically drawn to those structures that are crucial in maintaining that state. This is one of the major sources of stability of states of consciousness such as the waking and meditative states.

Alteration in stages of consciousness follows a three-step process. The first step is to disrupt the current state. Some states are more stable than others. For example, a loud handclap may wake you from a deep sleep, but it probably will not alter a waking state of consciousness.

The second step is to apply what Tart calls "patterning forces," that is, stimuli that tend to move the disrupted system toward the pattern of the desired state of consciousness. Once a given state is disrupted, it is possible to move into a variety of other states. For example, a person sitting quietly and becoming more and more relaxed may move from the waking state into sleep or into a hypnotic or meditative state. This depends on physiological state (e.g., tired or not), mental activity (repeating a hypnotic formula, focusing on a mantra, daydreaming, etc.), and a variety of other patterning factors.

The third step is restructuring into a new, stabilized state of consciousness. Some people new to meditation, for example, may become so excited that their mantra is "working," that they slip right back into waking consciousness; that is, their meditative state did not become stabilized.

Tart's model indicates that we need to consider both inner change within a single state of consciousness and also change involving a shift from one state to another. For example, many psychological patterns may be extremely difficult to alter because they are connected to a stabilizing matrix of interrelated systems within a given state of consciousness. In order to change these patterns, we may have to disrupt that state, perhaps to work within another state of consciousness in which the pattern is not so well stabilized.

It can be said that *all* significant change involves some disruption of our state of consciousness and that all permanent change involves a stabilizing restructuring of consciousness. Carl Jung (in Jacoby, 1959) has described this process from a psychotherapeutic perspective:

> All the greatest and most important problems of life are fundamentally insoluble. . . . They can never be solved, but only outgrown. This "outgrowing" proved on further investigation to require a new level of consciousness. Some higher or wider interest appeared on the patient's horizon. (p. 302)

Wilber's Developmental Model

Ken Wilber is another major consciousness theorist. He has attempted to portray the entire spectrum of consciousness in a single, integrated model. Wilber (1977) lists four major stages in the evolution of consciousness—shadow, ego, existential, and mind.

At the first stage, we identify with a limited mental *self-image*. We each accept as "mine" those thoughts and feelings that are consistent with our self-image. Other inner processes are rejected as "not-me" and repressed, denied, or projected onto others.

At the second stage, the boundary is drawn between mind and body. We identify only with the mind, not with the total organism. At this level, we are likely to say "I *have* a body" because the body lies somewhere outside our sense of self.

At the third stage, the boundary line is drawn between organism and environment. Everything inside the skin is "me," and everything else is not. In other words, we identify with a sense of self that is separate from the rest of the universe. There is a fundamental dichotomy between self and other, organism and environment.

Between the third and fourth stages lies what Wilber calls the "transpersonal bands." Here occur processes that go *beyond* the individual. These include the phenomena of ESP, out-of-body experiences, and also many peak experiences. In all these cases, there appears to be an expansion of the self/not-self boundary beyond the skin boundary of the organism.

At the fourth stage, we finally realize what Wilber (1979) calls "the ultimate metaphysical secret . . . that there are no boundaries in the universe" (p. 31). This state has been called the territory of no boundary by Wilber and unity consciousness or cosmic consciousness by others (Underhill, 1961). Wilber (1979) writes that "once the primary boundary [between self and not-self] is understood to be illusory, one's sense of self envelops the All—there is then no longer anything outside of oneself, and so nowhere to draw any sort of boundary" (p. 47).

Wilber suggests that different forms of therapy address the splits found at each level of the spectrum. Ego-level therapies focus on healing the split found at the shadow level by establishing communication between conscious and unconscious processes; these include most traditional approaches to psychotherapy. Existential-level therapies seek to extend identity to the total organism; most of the approaches of humanistic and existential psychology fit in here. Transpersonal band therapies deal with archetypal and mystical experiences; Jungian and transpersonal therapies are among the few that include work at this level. At the level of mind, the "therapies" that seek to heal the split between the individual and the cosmos are the world's great spiritual traditions, which are discussed in the next section on spiritual psychology.

Wilber (1980) suggests that consciousness develops in two related processes. First, there is the outward arc, the process of personal, ego development from subconsciousness to self-consciousness. This process begins with the undifferentiated consciousness of the newborn. Differentiation between the infant and the environment proceeds gradually, eventually resulting in the development of the sense of a separate body-ego self. As the child matures, a mature self-concept develops. The highest level of development in this process is the attainment of integration of ego, body, shadow, and personality.

The second major process is the inner arc, the process of transpersonal spiritual development from self-consciousness to "superconsciousness." In this process, consciousness extends beyond the body–mind into various realms or levels. These include the realm of psychic experiences, the realm of religious and archetypal experiences and the realm of direct experience of the Divine. The final realm is that of absolute unity, in which consciousness itself is transcended.

In his book, *The Atman Project*, Wilber (1980) suggests that all of evolution and personal development represents a movement toward the state of cosmic unity. He writes,

> Development is evolution; evolution is transcendence . . . and transcendence has as its final goal Atman, or ultimate Unity Consciousness in only God. All drives are a subset of that Drive, all wants a subset of that Want. . . . And this entire movement of evolution simply continues from unity to unity until there is only Unity. (p. ix)

In his writings, Wilber has done an extraordinary job of synthesizing material from a wide variety of areas and disciplines. Some transpersonal psychologists have come to consider his work as *the* major theory in transpersonal psychology. However, his work is open to critical commentary in several areas.

First, Wilber provides an extremely linear model of evolution and growth, one that does not match the frequently described process of inner growth in which change is far from a linear, unidimensional process. Jung (1939), Grof (1985), and others have pointed out that, most commonly, issues continue to resurface as the individual changes and then are dealt with at finer or more subtle levels.

Secondly, Wilber tends to interpret freely concepts from Hindu, Buddhist, and other religious traditions, at times out of context or without reference to original texts. For instance, he frequently juxtaposes the term *Atman* (the Hindu concept of an undying, imperishable Self) with the term *sunyata* (a Buddhist term for the nature of reality, a major characteristic of which is the impermanence of all things, including the self). This ignores the real differences between these two terms and the traditions from which they are taken (see, for example, Wilber, 1980, p. 101).

Third, Wilber coins much of his own idiosyncratic terminology. Although he often refers to ideas and concepts from many other fields, he rarely discusses any other theories or relates his own ideas to relevant theories in mainstream psychology of social science. Consequently, his influence outside of transpersonal psychology has been extremely limited.

A Critique of Hierarchical Models of Consciousness

One assumption made by Wilber and by other transpersonal theorists is that there is a "perennial" psychology or philosophy. In such general models, the world and the psyche are generally categorized in hierarchical terms (e.g., Wilber, 1980). There are different "levels" of world and self. The "higher" levels are described as better—as more real, more effective, or more "spiritual."

One important drawback to such broad hierarchical models of human development is the lack of any empirical evidence or even cogent and convincing evidence. Also, the hermeneutic tradition in modern philosophy insists that ideas and concepts only have meaning *within* a given tradition and language. To set up an arbitrary system of universal categories is to risk violating the unique meanings and realities of individual traditions and texts.

Another criticism of these models is that their hierarchical structure leads to the potential devaluing and even oppression of societies or groups ranked as "lower." This also includes "lower levels" of the psyche, such as the body, the emotions, and sexuality. These models typically value the urban, the intellectual, and the masculine. They devalue the tribal and rural, the physical, and the feminine.

Rothberg (1986) outlines pitfalls or dangers one should be aware of in developing any perennial model in transpersonal psychology: (a) ignoring empirical facts in favor of "higher truths"; (b) reifying abstract concepts of "higher levels"; (c) devaluing the "lower levels" of the earth, the body, the emotions, and the like; and (d) using a hierarchical model to justify oppression of individuals and groups ranked as "lower."

An alternative to the linear hierarchical model is to conceive of each level as a different "domain" or "mode of knowing." In this approach, spiritual growth could also consist of increasing one's understanding and functioning within a given domain. Also, different levels can be seen as connected or included within each other. In this way, there is no reification of the spatial *metaphors* of "ascent," "hierarchy," or "higher/lower."

Matthew Fox (1979) suggests that the hierarchial, "Jacob's-ladder" model has become dominant in Christian spirituality. It has led to separation of clergy from worshippers and a looking *up* to heroes, saints, success, and status. Another consequence has been the separation of compassion from justice, as "justice" became "judgment" (and control) in the hands of the ladder-top authorities. Fox suggests that instead of the climbing of Jacob's ladder, we consider dancing Sarah's circle, her celebration at the birth of Isaac. The circle is non-hierarchical and is also a celebration of birthing, creating, fruitfulness, and laughter.

SPIRITUAL PSYCHOLOGY

For many professionals, interest in transpersonal psychology developed as a consequence of personal spiritual experiences in the Jewish or Christian traditions or as a result of exposure to one of the Eastern spiritual traditions, such as Yoga or Buddhism. These latter traditions offer sophisticated theoretical descriptions of human experience and states of consciousness. In addition, they facilitate powerful spiritual experiences through prayer, meditation, and other practices (i.e., they offer a practical, experiential spirituality). Many transpersonal psychologists have reported having their view of human nature and human potentials significantly expanded through their exposure to spiritual concepts and practices. Because they have been unable to integrate such views within the traditional fields and approaches of psychology, many have turned to transpersonal psychology.

Spiritual psychology is an emerging new field within transpersonal psychology. It is an attempt to develop a psychology that does full justice to mysticism and spirituality, one that studies the deeper or transcendental Self, the ground for the most profound subtle and mystical experiences (see, e.g., Ajaya, 1983; Arasteh, 1980).

The term *mysticism* has many different meanings. In its original sense, mysticism is the art of the spiritual life whose aim is union with the Divine. Mysticism refers to experience that cannot be put into words; the terms *mystic* and *mystery* share the same root, the Greek *myein,* ''to close the eyes.'' In her classic book, *Mysticism,* Underhill (1961) refers to mysticism as ''the expression of the innate tendency of the human spirit towards complete harmony with the transcendental order; whatever be the theological formula under which that order is understood'' (p. xiv).

In their survey of the literature of spontaneous mystical experiences, Pahnke and Richards (1973) found nine interrelated categories:

1. Unity. Experience of an undifferentiated unity, internal or external.
2. Objectivity and reality. An authoritative sense of insight about reality, gained through direct experience.
3. Transcendence of space and time. Includes loss of orientation in space or time, and/or a sense of transcendental perspective that is beyond time.
4. Sense of sacredness. A sense of the infinite, of inspiring realities.
5. Deeply felt positive mood. Feelings of joy, love, blessedness, peace, which may be quiet or exhuberant, mild or intense.
6. Paradoxicality. Experiences that violate common sense or logic, such as the experience of an ''empty unity'' that somehow contains all reality.
7. Alleged ineffability. A frequent claim that language is inadequate to contain or even accurately reflect the experience.
8. Transiency. The mystical state of consciousness is clearly temporary, in contrast to daily experience and also psychosis.
9. Positive changes in attitude and/or behavior. Includes changes in attitudes toward oneself, toward others, toward life, or toward mystical consciousness itself. May result in a change in life-style and long-term goals.

A frequent theme in the literature of mysticism is the radical self-transformation that occurs in the mystical process.

> It [mysticism] implies, indeed, the abolition of individuality; of that hard separateness, that 'I, Me, Mine' which makes of man a finite isolated thing. It is essentially a movement of the heart [or the deeper Self], seeking to transcend the limitations of the individual standpoint and to surrender itself to ultimate Reality. (Underhill, 1961, p. 71)

The following are some preliminary assumptions for this new field of spiritual psychology:

1. Ordinary waking consciousness is only one, special type of consciousness. Other states of consciousness, such as those found in meditation and in mystical experiences, are no less valid. In fact, some spiritual traditions (Tart, 1975a, p. 78) maintain that the waking state of the average person is neither truly awake nor conscious; the average ''awake'' individual selectively perceives only a part of the internal and external environments and generally responds mechanically and partially as well.

The states described in the world's spiritual traditions seem in many ways to be superior levels of functioning, including greater self-awareness, a more accurate perception of the world, more energy, increased intuitive sensitivity and inspiration, and a greater capacity for creativity. As mentioned earlier, most psychologists believe strongly that ''rational,'' waking consciousness is the highest state of consciousness. As a result, there has been a systematic devaluation of, or disinterest in, virtually all forms of mysticism and spirituality in psychology.

2. The Newtonian–Cartesian model of a purely materialistic and mechanical universe may be useful for certain limited kinds of scientific research, but it is not the appropriate model for spiritual psychology. Different cosmologies have been developed within each of the world's religions. Aldous Huxley (1945), in *The Perennial Philosophy,* suggests that all of these traditions agree that:

> The divine Ground of all existence is a spiritual Absolute, ineffable in terms of discursive thought, but (in certain circumstances) susceptible of being directly experienced and realized by the human being. . . . The last end of

man, the ultimate reason for human existence, is unitive knowledge of the divine Ground. (p. 21)

Any model of the universe that is suitable for spiritual psychology must include both meaning and the Divine.

3. Human experience frequently shifts between the sacred and the profane, that is, between a view of the world as filled with meaning, mystery, and the Divine and a mechanical, dispirited view of the world.

4. The deep Self is the very essence of what it is to be human. At the core of our humanity is our relatedness to God. Thus religious faith and the mystical quest are not irrational or neurotic (although they *can* be misused in the service of a neurosis). On the contrary, they are manifestations of our deepest and truest selves.

Many mystics have described the deep Self as the Divine element in each individual. St. Catherine of Genoa (in Huxley, 1945, p. 11) wrote, "My Me is God, nor do I recognize any other Me except my God Himself." Similarly, St. Bernard (*ibid.*), "In those respects in which the soul is unlike God, it is also unlike itself." One of the central tasks of spiritual psychology is the study of the deep Self and its relation to the rest of the psyche.

5. The world's religions have been built on the genuine mystical experiences and inspirations of their founders. Although these religions may have changed greatly over time and the original message distorted by ignorant or self-seeking followers and organizations, this does not change the fundamental experiential truth of the original religious messages.

Although religions may share certain basic truths, this does not necessarily mean that the mystical experiences of all religions are identical. Two cups dipped in an infinite ocean might not bring up the same contents.

6. The radical self-transformation described in the mystical literature is an essentially healthy process and a central area of study for spiritual psychology. The notion of transformation as a major, qualitative change in the adult psyche is not a part of the traditional psychological view of human nature (with the possible negative exception of psychosis). However, in many ways, it can be argued that such transformation is the culmination of healthy adult development.

Metzner (1986) outlines the various symbols and metaphors used in many traditions to describe this transformational process. These are changing from caterpillar to butterfly, awakening from the dream of "reality," uncovering the veils of illusion, emerging from captivity to liberation, purification by inner fire, moving from darkness to light, progressing from fragmentation to wholeness, journeying to a place of vision and power,

returning to the source, dying and being reborn, and unfolding the tree of one's life.

Aspects of Selected Spiritual Traditions

As must be evident from the preceding discussion, what we know about the current state of spiritual psychology has come more from the great mystics and the world's spiritual traditions than from psychology itself. Each mystical tradition has developed a practical psychology, a sophisticated picture of human nature that provides a context for understanding the Self, mystical experience, and self-transformation.

In the following section, we will look at four spiritual traditions—the creation spirituality of the Judeo–Christian tradition, Yoga, Buddhism, and Sufism. The theory of human nature found in each of these traditions is sometimes explicitly formulated, and sometimes it is implicit in descriptions of spiritual growth and transformation. As with the variety of personality theories in psychology (e.g., Frager & Fadiman, 1984), all of these theories have something to offer. After all, each is based on hundreds of years of observation of human nature. The concepts and insights of one tradition may be particularly relevant to some people at a given stage of their lives. At other times, the insights and ideas of different traditions may prove more helpful.

One of the important functions of each spiritual tradition is to make the process of the spiritual journey explicit. This is valuable for several reasons. First, it shows those embarked on the mystical quest that they are not alone. Our culture, with its valuing of the profane over the sacred, leads those who have mystical experiences to feel isolated. Second, knowing about the process keeps you moving when, inevitably, you get "stuck" or feel in need of inspiration. Third, the essence of all spiritual guidance is to "name" the journey. Fourth, a solid, clearly articulated mystical grounding supports the prophetic struggle, the struggle for justice and for the actualization of spiritual ideals in the world.

Creation Spirituality

The creation spirituality developed by Matthew Fox (1979, 1980, 1982, 1983) represents a return to an ancient religious paradigm, one that goes back to the earliest text of the Bible, the psalms, the Hebrew wisdom literature, and to Jesus and much of the New Testament. It also draws extensively on the great Christian mystics, such as Meister Eckhart.

Drawing primarily on the work of Meister Eckhart, Fox (1983) has outlined the four stages of the spiritual journey. These are the via positiva, the via negativa, the via creativa, and the via transformativa. He points out that this model conceives the spiritual journey as a cyclical spiral rather than as a linear progression. One meets each of these four paths over and over again on the way.

The via positiva is the beginning of all genuine mysticism. This path involves loves for creation and awe at its splendor and immensity. God can be experienced in and through creation, which is not antithetical to the world of spirit. Eckhart has written that " 'isness' is God" (in Fox, 1983, p. 39). That is, there is a Divinity in all that is; all that exists comes from a Divine source. The universe can be seen as a training ground for love. We fall in love with the beauty and the wonderful gifts found in creation. And, if love is part of the essence of the Divine, we must experience love deeply to come close to God.

The via negativa is a balance and a complement to the via positiva. The via negativa is multidimensional and nonlinear. It includes such seemingly disparate experiences as darkness, nothingness, silence, pain and suffering, letting go, receptivity, and letting be. The mystical refusal to reduce paradox to dichotomy embraces both the light of the via positiva and the dark of the via negativa. Thus, Meister Eckhart (in Fox, 1980) wrote, "The ground of the soul is dark" and also "Where understanding and longing end, it is dark but God *shines* there" (p. 126).

Everyone on the mystical journey must deal with darkness and unknowing. One of the great struggles of the mystics is to let go, to be open, empty, and receptive in order to plumb the depths of self. Fully experiencing our suffering and pain is an important way of letting go. Yet, in our culture, we do all we can to avoid them. Valium is our most popular prescription drug. Studies of grief have shown clearly that we can only drop suffering after embracing it, softening into our pain and truly experiencing it (see, for example, Levine, 1982). Unfortunately, an almost universal reaction in our culture is to immediately deaden such pain with drink, drugs, or distractions.

Humor is also part of this stage. It is a letting go of our seriousness and of the image our ego wants to present to the world. Those who do not take themselves too seriously have a better chance to become free, and the separateness of self and other seems to dissolve in the joy of shared laughter.

The via negativa must be built on the positiva, or else it can become antilife and antispirit. Pruning can strengthen a tree and make it grow and produce more. But if the tree is not strong and healthy to begin with, pruning can kill it.

Meister Eckhart (in Fox, 1983) wrote, "Outside of God, there is nothing but nothing" (p. 149). We are nothing, except for our innermost being, except for what is from God in us. If we do not name and accept our nothingness, we become controlled by it, and then we rush to fill it—with worthless activities and busyness. The more we become empty, the more possibilities there are. The more we become empty, the more we can be filled with God.

The via creativa results from a combination of positiva and negativa that leads to a breakthrough to our own creativity. In one sense, this creativity is the image of God within us, God as infinite potential manifesting differently through each person.

Many of the mystics have been extraordinarily creative. They have been great poets and also imaginative writers who have given birth to rich new ideas and modes of expression (Fox, 1983). This is especially fitting because God is the essence of creativity and of birthing. To get in touch with God within us is to give birth—to create, to express ourselves in poetry, prose, art, and music. "We are all meant to be mothers of God. For God is always needing to be born" (Eckhart, in Fox, 1983, p. 222).

The via transformativa includes the other three paths. It requires a combination of compassion and justice to create a better world for everyone. Actions that stem from this sense of compassion include (a) realization of the interconnectedness of all creation and a reverence for all existence; (b) a sense of celebration, joy, and play—which gives depth and sacredness to all of life, and life to all ritual; and (c) a love of healing and opposition to injustice.

This path includes commitment to evolving a spirituality that supports the principles of justice, equality, and care for the earth. It includes an understanding of how the hierarchical fall/redemption tradition has lent itself to rationalizing slavery and oppression of "lower" peoples and cultures and of a devaluing and misuse of the earth.

This path includes the forms of spirituality of those who have been oppressed and devalued—women, native peoples, minorities, workers, and peasants. These spiritual traditions have much to teach us, including humility, eros, earthiness, and interdependence.

Creation spirituality is, of course, not the only tradition of Christian or Jewish spirituality. There are Ignatian, Charismatic, and Pentacostal spiritualities to name but a few other Christian approaches. Jewish spiritual traditions include Hassidism and the Kabbala. I have outlined the work of Fox here as one example of the rich resources Western spirituality has to offer transpersonal psychology. Fox has attempted to provide a spiritual paradigm that supports our quest for wisdom and survival. His work bears serious consideration by anyone interested in spiritual psychology.

Yoga

Yoga is the foundation of Indian mysticism. It includes a wide variety of religious and spiritual practices, such as meditation, asceticism, service, and devotional chanting. The classic principles of Yoga were systematized by Patanjali about 2,000 years ago in the *Yoga Sutras* (see, e.g., Arya, 1986; Taimni, 1961). Over the centuries, many different approaches to Yoga have been developed.

The goal of Yoga is to calm body and mind in order to realize the Self within. Yoga means "to join" or "to unite"—the union of the ego-self with the one Self, of the individual with the Divine. The Self in each individual is a part of transcendent Spirit, which is pure consciousness and knows no limitations or qualifications. Spirit includes consciousness within and beyond the universe. The Self is to Spirit as the wave is to the ocean, a form that the ocean takes on for a time. Although Spirit is conceived of as formless, it is not limited to formlessness. The great yogi Ramakrishna (in Nikhilananda, 1948) once said to a student, "You believe in God without form; that is quite all right. But never for a moment think that this alone is true and all else false. Remember that God with form is just as true as God without form" (pp. 61–62).

The yogic concept of mind includes all thought processes. In most people, these processes are unceasingly active and seemingly uncontrollable. When the mind is finally quieted through the discipline of Yoga, it clearly reflects the Self, as the waters of a still lake reflect the moon.

Control of the mind is only possible when the subconscious tendencies (*samskaras*) are controlled because these tendencies shape mental activity. They are created by past experiences, from this life and past lives. Mental habit patterns gradually form subconscious tendencies, for example, one who is frequently angry develops subconscious tendencies toward anger and becomes more and more prone to respond angrily.

Therefore, in order to control and still the mind, Yoga practitioners must completely reform their consciousness. Otherwise, subconscious tendencies will continue to affect the mind, sprouting suddenly like long-dormant seeds. Through intensive spiritual discipline, it is possible to "roast" such seeds and destroy their potential influence.

There are many different schools of Yoga in India today. Each approach is designed for seekers of different temperaments. Bhakti-Yoga stresses devotion and love of God as the way to self-transformation. Yogananda (1968), a great devotional yogi, has written:

He is the nearest of the near, the dearest of the dear. Love Him as a miser loves money, as an ardent man loves his sweetheart, as a drowning person loves breath. When you yearn for God with intensity, He will come to you. (p. 1)

Techniques used in Bhakti-Yoga include devotional meditation and contemplation, chanting, and ritual worship.

Jnana-Yoga is the yoga of the intellect. It is a discipline of rigorous self-analysis, a path suitable for those with a clear, focused intellect. The jnana-yogi finds the Self by learning to discriminate between what is perishable and imperishable, limited and infinite.

Self-scrutiny, relentless observance of one's thoughts, is a stark and shattering experience. It pulverizes the stoutest ego. But true self-analysis mathematically operates to produce seers. (Yogananda, 1972, p. 51)

The jnana-yogi strives for constant inner awareness. By seeking out the underlying source of all thoughts and experiences, the yogi eventually discovers the Self. "By steady and continuous investigation into the nature of the mind, the mind is transformed into that to which 'I' refers; and this is in fact the Self" (Ramana Maharshi, in Osbourne, 1962, p. 113).

Hatha-Yoga (discussed previously) is, in a sense, the yoga of the body. It includes practices designed to purify and prepare the body for spiritual states of consciousness. The body is seen as a vehicle for subtle life energies, or *pranas*. These energies underlie all our activities and experiences, from digestion to the most profound meditation. The disciplines of Hatha-Yoga are designed to strengthen, coordinate, and control these energies, enhancing physical, mental, and spiritual functioning.

Hatha-Yoga is often closely associated with Kundalini-Yoga (see, e.g., Krishna, 1967; Radha, 1981). Kundalini is considered to be the finest form of subtle energy. It is activated, or "awakened," in advanced spiritual states. Highly accomplished yogis learn to control their kundalini energy and to move this energy up the spine through six consciousness centers (*chakras*) and then to the seventh, the crown center of the head. As each chakra becomes energized, or awakened, the yogi experiences different spiritual states of consciousness.

Yogis who have mastered kundalini can often awaken this energy in others. However, the student must be ready to handle this experience. Through meditation, purification, and other practices, the student's mind becomes strengthened so that higher states are not overwhelming, and, also, the student's body becomes subtly strengthened so that it can handle the influx of energy that accompanies such states.

Karma-Yoga is the yoga of action and service. It involves learning to act selflessly without attachment to gain or loss, success or failure. It requires will and discipline to overcome our selfishness, pride, laziness, and the like.

Karma means action and also the effects our actions bring. Everything we do is karma, and all our acts—physical and mental—leave their marks on us. The great Hindu scripture, the *Bhagavad-Gita,* teaches that only worship and action without attachment are free from the ties of karma.

> The world is imprisoned in its own activity, except when actions are performed as worship of God. Therefore you must perform every action sacramentally, and be free from all attachments to results. (Prabhavananda & Isherwood, 1951, p. 45)

Karma-Yoga brings about the purification and letting go of the self that is an important ingredient of the mystic's journey.

Raja-Yoga, literally "royal yoga," emphasizes the development of mental control and meditation. The classic discipline, outlined in Patanjali's *Yoga Sutras,* consists of eight "limbs" or stages—abstentions, observances, postures, subtle energy control, sensory interiorization, concentration, meditation, and illumination. As with many mystical systems, these are not hierarchical, linear stages. The student is generally working on several limbs at any given time.

The abstentions and observances form a code or set of guidelines, the foundation for yoga practice. They include nonviolence, truthfulness, nonstealing, continence, noncovetousness, purity, contentment, self-discipline, self-study, and devotion to God.

The goal of Raja-Yoga is mastery of deep meditation in which the mind has become completely concentrated and only the object of meditation remains in the consciousness of the meditator. The result of this practice is illumination when the mind has become totally calm, inward, and focused, reflecting only the qualities of the Self.

Yoga is essentially a system of complex and sophisticated practices designed to transform body, mind, and consciousness. The aim of all these practices is to direct the flow of consciousness back to its source, the Self. The different schools of Yoga use different human capacities to accomplish this—physical descipline, will power, devotion, self-analysis, mental discipline, and control of subtle energy. Compared to most other mystical traditions, Yoga seems to offer a wider variety and greater number of *practical* techniques and exercises.

One well-known Western psychologist who has studied Yoga in great depth is Ram Dass. Two of his books, *Be Here Now* (1970) and *Grist for the Mill* (1977), provide a Western interpretation of Yoga philosophy and principles and an integration of Yoga thought with modern psychology.

Zen Buddhism

Zen is a school of Buddhism, a branch that emphasizes meditation and spiritual practice in addition to the ritual practices found in all Buddhism. Zen is based on the fundamental concepts of Buddhism—impermanence, selflessness, dissatisfaction, the four noble truths, and the noble eightfold path. The following discussion is an interpretation of these basic concepts taken primarily from the Zen perspective (see, e.g., Kennett, 1976).

One of the major characteristics of existence, according to Buddhist thought, is impermanence. This doctrine holds that *nothing,* including all material things, ideas, and theories, is permanent or lasting; everything is in flux. Thus there can be no unalterable truth because what is true in one situation will not hold when that situation inevitably changes. It is our resistance to this inherent change that is the source of our grief and suffering.

Applying this principle to the notion of Self yields the doctrine of selflessness, which holds that there is no immortal soul or imperishable Self within each individual. We are each a collection of attributes—intellect, emotions, body. All of these are impermanent and constantly changing. There is, however, the Buddha nature in each individual. The Buddha nature is in everything and is as large as the entire universe, embracing all beings and all creation.

In the initial experience of enlightenment, Zen students first truly realize their Buddha nature. In later stages, everything is seen to possess the Buddha nature; any distinction between the religious and the worldly then disappears. At a still later stage, the notion that everything is holy is transcended; everything *is.* Dogen, the founder of one of the great Japanese schools of Zen, described this process as follows:

> When one studies Buddhism one studies oneself; when one studies oneself one forgets oneself; when one forgets oneself one is enlightened by everything, and this very enlightenment breaks the bonds of clinging to both body and mind, not only for oneself but for all beings as well (Dogen, in Kennett, 1972, pp. 142–143).

The third basic characteristic of existence is dissatisfaction or suffering. This comes from our limited ego, which seeks permanence and pleasure in a world of impermanence and change. Buddhism teaches that the problem is not with the world but with our wish to have the world be other than it really is.

This principle of dissatisfaction is also the first of the four noble truths. The second truth is that dissatisfaction is a result of our desires, or cravings. We are caught up in craving for the attainment of pleasure and craving for the avoidance of pain. The stronger the craving, the more intense the dissatisfaction.

The third truth is that elimination of craving brings the extinction of suffering and dissatisfaction. Eliminating craving does not mean extinguishing all desires. Our basic healthy needs, wants, and desires are normal and necessary. Craving is unhealthy; it involves becoming controlled by our desires and feeling miserable if they are not satisfied.

The fourth truth is that there is a way to eliminate craving and dissatisfaction. This way is the noble eightfold path, also known as the middle way. The middle way avoids the extremes of seeking the greatest possible sense gratification on the one hand, or self-mortification and life-denying asceticism on the other. The Buddhist ideal is moderation.

The noble eightfold path consists of right speech, action, livelihood, effort, mindfulness, concentration, thought, and understanding. Right speech includes truthfulness and avoidance of harmful speech. Right action includes abstaining from killing, stealing, and dishonesty; it also means acting to help others. Right livelihood refers to earning one's living from activities that benefit others and do not harm them (for example, not engaging in the killing of animals or selling arms). Right effort means using one's will to produce wholesome states of mind and to avoid unwholesome states. Right mindfulness is to be aware of the activities of mind and body. Right concentration is to keep the mind "one pointed" in meditation. Right thought includes detachment, love, and nonviolence. Right understanding is the understanding of the four noble truths. The highest level of such understanding is only reached through personal experience of these truths as a result of the most profound study and meditation.

Buddhism is nontheistic. It talks about the activities of the mind, not about the Divine. This might seem to conflict with those forms of mysticism based on devotion to God. A devout Buddhist might argue that the Divine is truly transcendent, that no approach or description is even barely adequate, and that Buddhist thought approaches the Divine and all of creation as ever-changing process.

Sufism

Sufism is Islamic mysticism. It has assumed different forms over many centuries as Islam spread to different cultures and civilizations. The aim in Sufism is to transcend the self and to "lose" oneself in God.

There are different stages of growth outlined by various Sufi teachers. These stages are not linear, and the student may be working at any given time on issues from more than one stage:

1. Initial awakening. This stage begins when one concludes that the external world is not fulfilling. It is the beginning of a basic, spiritual reorientation of values, and the realization that prior goals have little meaning or value. This has also been called the stage of repentance. Junaid of Baghdad, the great ninth-century Sufi master said, "There are three meanings of repentance. The first is guilt and remorsefulness, the second freedom from habits, and the third cleansing oneself from injustice and animosities" (in Attar, 1907, Vol. II, p. 32).

2. Patience and gratitude. Patience is one of the greatest virtues. It is essential for living in the present, without which no spiritual work is possible. Without patience, real prayer or meditation are impossible because attention is never in the present moment.

Patience is half of faith. If you remember that all things come from God, then your trust in God's love and mercy should lead you to wait patiently for whatever gifts are meant for you.

Gratitude is also related to remembrance that all things come from God. One Sufi master has commented:

> If you make a distinction between the things which come from God you are not a man on the path of the spirit. If you consider yourself honoured by the diamond and humiliated by the stone, God is not with you. (Attar, 1961, p. 99)

3. Fear and hope. Fear is fear of God. It is not fear of being punished or sent to hell. Rather, it is the fear lovers feel when they are concerned that something they might say or do might cause the beloved to love them less. If you remember that the Beloved witnesses all your thoughts and actions, this fear will transform your life. The Sufi master Shibli (in Shafii, 1985) stated, "Each day that I was overcome with fear, the door of knowledge and insight opened to my heart" (pp. 183–184).

In *Freedom from the Self,* a seminal comparison of Western psychology and Sufism, Shafii (1985) writes, "The essence of Sufism is hope" (p. 184). Focus on your faults, and shortcomings can be paralyzing. Hope allows you to see yourself clearly and honestly, without becoming paralyzed.

Ghazzali, the prominant Sufi philosopher, wrote with great psychological insight about hope:

> Know that everyone who expects something good in the future is experiencing hope. The ignorant do not differentiate between hope, wish, and false hope or self-deception. If one acquires good seed, plants it in plowed grounds, weeds and waters it regularly, relies on God's will to keep away pests and blights, and expects a harvest, this expectation is hope. If one does not search for good seed nor plant in good earth nor weed nor water, and still expects a harvest, this is called false hope or self-deception. If one puts a good seed in the earth and weeds,

but does not water, and waits for rain, particularly in an area of little rainfall, this is called wish (in Shafii, 1985, p. 184).

4. Self-denial and poverty. Self-denial means to serve others instead of always putting yourself first. It is to serve in order to please God, not to please others or to be rewarded or praised. Service to others comes naturally if you remember that everything in the universe comes from the Creator.

Poverty means lack of attachment to possessions rather than ownership of goods. It is freedom from wants and desires. It is far easier to drop your possessions than to drop the attachment to them. Inner poverty is one of the highest spiritual states. It is to have nothing in your heart but God.

5. Trust in God. At this stage the person seeks everything from God, not from the world. Ghazzali (in Shafii, 1985) has listed three different degrees of trust. The first is the kind of trust a person places in a doctor or lawyer, knowing they are well-trained and highly skilled. The second is the trust of a child in its mother. It is a total trust and reliance on the mother—spontaneous, automatic, and unconscious. The third degree is to be like a corpse in the hands of a mortician. There is absolutely no resistance to whatever happens to you, no wish or expectation.

> This is not like a child who calls upon the mother, but like a child who knows deeply that even if he does not call for the mother, the mother will be totally aware of his condition and will look after him. This is the ultimate degree of trust in God. (in Shafii, 1985, p. 227)

In addition to the preceding stages of growth, we are also working constantly with different levels of the soul. According to various Sufi teachers, there are seven different souls in each person—the mineral, vegetable, animal, human, angelic, secret soul, and the Soul of the secret of secrets.

The mineral soul is basically static and inert. The activities at the level of the vegetable soul include the simplest forms of response to the environment and ingestion of nourishment. The activities at the level of the animal soul include desires, passions, and mobility. The functions of the domain of the human soul include cognition, self-awareness, and future planning. The activities at the level of the angelic soul include prayer, devotion, and love of God. The secret soul includes prayer and devotion at a deeper and more sincere level. Finally, there is the Soul of the secret of secrets, which is the Divine in each individual. As God is infinite, beyond time and space, so is this level of soul. It actually transcends all of this material creation, yet is paradoxically a part of each of us.

These various souls are not actually distinct from each other. They are somewhat like facets of a single gem. They are within each other, and each is evolving. In each individual, the souls are integrated in either the human soul or one of the higher level souls.

Our experience is strongly affected by which soul is dominant at a given time. For example, in dreaming, each soul functions differently. Dreams produced by the vegetable and animal souls concern fulfillment of desires. If you go to bed hungry, you may dream of eating. Dreams produced by the human soul include complex symbols and require some skill to analyze. Dreams from the angelic soul also involve symbols. They are archetypal or numinous dreams, or what Jung (1961) called "high dreams." Dreams from the secret soul are literal and easy to understand. They are actually spiritual experiences, such as meeting with great saints or visiting holy places. Dreams from the Soul of the secret of secrets include the visions of the prophets; they are direct messages from Divine realms.

Another set of categories frequently used in Sufism is that of the different levels of one's inner nature, or *nafs*. These can be related both to the stages of growth and levels of soul mentioned previously.

The term *nafs* refers to a process, not an inner state ormental structure. In Arabic, its meanings include "breath," "essence," "self," and "nature." It is the result of the interaction of body and soul. The soul becomes an exile from the realm of spirit when it enters the body and becomes imprisoned in the material world. The body by itself is inert. It contains various organs and instruments of action but not the power to fulfil its own physical urges. That power comes from the soul.

First is the commanding *nafs*. This is the realm of the physical and egotistic desires, including rage, greed, sensual desires, and envy. At this level, the individual is completely dominated by these desires. There may be lip service to religious or social ideals, but, in reality, the individual is motivated solely by ego and physical desires.

Second is the accusatory *nafs*. At this level, the individual is still dominated by wants and desires, but now the person repents from time to time and *tries* to follow higher ideals. Personal needs still dominate.

Third is the inspired *nafs*. Now, the individual is truly motivated by ideals such as compassion, service, and moral values. Though not free of the power of the desires and ego, this new level of motivation significantly reduces their power for the first time.

Fourth is the tranquil *nafs*. The old desires and attachments are no longer binding. This is akin to the stage of trust and gratitude. The ego–self begins to let go at this stage, allowing the individual to move toward merging with the Divine.

Fifth come the fulfilled and fulfilling *nafs*. Here the individual has become truly religious. Prayer, service, and spiritual pursuits are highly motivating and are now preferred to the desires of the body and the ego.

Finally, there is the perfected *nafs*. Here, all sense of individuality and separateness is dropped. At this stage, the individual has fully realized that only God exists, that there is nothing other than God, and that any sense of individuality or separateness is an illusion.

Themes in Spiritual Psychology

The spiritual traditions just covered above contain a number of similar themes. In all of them, there is an apparent tension between the worldly and the Divine, the sacred and the profane. All agree that it is not the world that is the problem but our attachment to it. Although this attachment to the worldly is seen as a spiritual obstacle, the world is also honored as a Divine creation or as a manifestation of God. A spiritualized relationship to the world facilitates the mystic's journey.

These spiritual traditions share the belief that one needs to transcend the individual ego-self to find the Self or to find God. The means differ in form but not in function. All of the traditions we have covered provide means of turning one's attention inward. By developing self-understanding, the grip of the ego and attachment to the world is loosened. Through the development of deeper self-knowledge—from prayer, meditation, service, and the like—the seeker gradually becomes more and more aware of the Self within, or of God within and without. In dealing with pain and suffering, the seeker becomes free of fear and restriction to the self-protective and limited ego-self's ways of relating to the world. In developing love and devotion, the individual is inspired to new levels of service and understanding and to the experience of God as the Beloved behind all love.

One of the tasks of spiritual psychology is to continue to examine the world's spiritual traditions. Each tradition sheds light on different facets of the spiritual journey. More detailed study of the spiritual and psychological experiences described in different traditions can lead us to a clearer picture of the process of spiritual growth and development and to an understanding of how this process is affected by different spiritual practices and cultural and religious traditions.

CONCLUSIONS

We have reviewed the three major domains of transpersonal psychology—the psychology of personal devel-

opment, the psychology of consciousness, and spiritual psychology. Each of these domains, taken separately, has been studied within other fields of psychology. The psychology of personal development includes both fairly traditional approaches to psychotherapy and also the field of humanistic psychology. Much of the psychology of consciousness has been studied in the separate fields of parapsychology, hypnosis, and biofeedback. The content of spiritual psychology has been the domain of the psychology of religion.

Taken together, these domains reinforce each other and provide a context and scope for transpersonal psychology. The basic premise of transpersonal psychology is that we do not yet know the extent of human potential. This sense of the vastness and potential power within each individual brings to psychotherapy and to human growth a transpersonal context. This approach brings to the study of human consciousness a sense of exploring the depth and breadth of human experience, rather than isolated or special experiences. And the transpersonal perspective brings to spiritual psychology an understanding that the great mystics and spiritual traditions have tremendous relevance in our exploration of the depths and potentials within each of us.

REFERENCES

Ajaya, S. (1983). *Psychotherapy east and west.* Honesdale, PA: Himalayan International Institute.

Arasteh, A. (1980). *Growth to selfhood: The Sufi contribution.* London: Routledge & Kegan Paul.

Arya, U. (1986). *Yoga-sutras of Patanjali.* Honesdale, PA: Himalayan International Institute.

Attar, F. (1907). *The Tadhkiratul-Auliya.* London: Luzac.

Attar, F. (1961). *The conference of the birds.* London: Routledge & Kegan Paul.

Campbell, J. (Ed.). (1971). *The portable Jung.* New York: Viking.

Chen, M., & Smith, R. (1967). *T'ai chi.* Rutland, VT: Tuttle.

Erikson, E. (1958). *Young man Luther.* New York: Norton.

Erikson, E. (1963). *Childhood and society.* New York: Norton.

Erikson, E. (1964). *Insight and responsibility.* New York: Norton.

Erikson, E. (1969). *Gandhi's truth.* New York: Norton.

Feldenkrais, M. (1950). *Body and mature behavior.* New York: International Universities Press.

Fox, M. (1979). *A spirituality named compassion.* Minneapolis: Winston Press.

Fox, M. (1980). *Western spirituality.* Santa Fe, NM: Bear.

Fox, M. (1982). *Breakthrough; Meister Eckhard's creation spirituality in new translation.* Santa Fe, NM: Bear.

Fox, M. (1983). *Original blessing.* Santa Fe, NM: Bear.

Frager, R., & Fadiman, J. (1984). *Personality and personal growth.* New York: Harper & Row.

Freud, S. (1933). *New introductory lectures on psychoanalysis.* New York: Norton.

Fromm, E. (1959). *Sigmund Freud's mission.* New York: Harper & Row.

Grof, S. (1975). *Realms of the human unconscious: Observations from LSD research*. New York: Viking.

Grof, S. (1985). *Beyond the brain: Birth, death and transcendence in psychotherapy*. Albany: State University of New York Press.

Huxley, A. (1945). *The perennial philosophy*. New York: World.

Jacoby, J. (1959). *Complex, archetype, symbol in the psychology of C. G. Jung*. New York: Pantheon.

James, W. (1890). *The principles of psychology* (2 vols.). New York: Holt, Rinehart & Winston.

Jung, C. (1939). Conscious, unconscious, and individuation. In *Collected works* (Vol. 9, Part 1). Princeton, NJ: Princeton University Press.

Jung, C. (1961). *Memories, dreams, reflections*. New York: Random House.

Jung, C. (Ed.). (1964). *Man and his symbols*. New York: Doubleday.

Jung, C. (1973). *Letters*. Princeton, NJ: Princeton University Press.

Jung, C. (1975). *Letters, Vol II: 1951–1961*. Princeton, NJ: Princeton University Press.

Kennett, J. (1972). The five aspects of self. *Journal of the Zen Mission Society, 3*, 2–5.

Kennett, J. (1976). *Zen is eternal life*. Berkeley, CA: Dharma Publishing.

Krishna, G. (1967). *Kundalini: The evolutionary energy in man*. New Delhi: Ramadhar & Hopman.

Kuhn, T. (1962). *The structure of scientific revolutions*. Chicago: University of Chicago Press.

LeShan, L., & Margenau, H. (1982). *Einstein's space and Van Gogh's sky*. New York: Macmillan.

Levine, S. (1982). *Who dies? An investigation of conscious living and conscious dying*. Garden City, NY: Anchor.

Lowen, A. (1975). *Bioenergetics*. New York: Penguin.

Majumdar, S. (1964). *Introduction to yoga principles and practices*. New Hyde Park, NY: University Press.

Maslow, A. (1968). *Toward a psychology of being*. New York: Van Nostrand.

Maslow, A. (1970). *Motivation and personality* (Rev. ed.). New York: Harper & Row.

Maslow, A. (1971). *The farther reaches of human nature*. New York: Viking.

Metzner, R. (1986). *Opening to inner light: The transformation of human nature and consciousness*. Los Angeles: Tarcher.

Miller, A. (1981). *The drama of the gifted child*. New York: Basic.

Miller, A. (1983). *For your own good: Hidden cruelty in childrearing and the roots of violence*. New York: Farrar, Straus & Giroux.

Miller, A. (1984). *Thou shalt not be aware: Society's betrayal of the child*. New York: New American Library.

Murphy, M. (1969). Education for transcendence. *The Journal of Transpersonal Psychology, 1*, 21–32.

Nikhilananda, S. (Trans.). (1948). *Ramakrishna: Prophet of new India*. New York: Harper & Brothers.

Osbourne, A. (1962). *The teachings of Ramana Maharshi*. London: Rider.

Pahnke, W., & Richards, W. (1973). Religion and mind-expanding drugs. In J. Heaney (Ed.), *Psyche and spirit* (pp. 109–118). New York: Paulist Press.

Prabhavananda, S., & Isherwood, C. (1951). *The song of God: Bhagavad-Gita*. New York: Mentor.

Radha, S. (1981). *Kundalini, Yoga for the west*. Boulder, CO: Shambhala.

Ram Dass (1970). *Be here now*. San Cristobal, NM: Lama Foundation.

Ram Dass (1977). *Grist for the mill*. New York: Bantam.

Reich, W. (1973). *The function of the orgasm*. New York: Touchstone.

Reich, W. (1976). *Character analysis*. New York: Pocket Books.

Rothberg, D. (1986). Philosophical foundations of transpersonal psychology: An introduction to some basic issues. *The Journal of Transpersonal Psychology, 18*, 1–34.

Shafii, M. (1985). *Freedom from the self: Sufism, meditation and psychotherapy*. New York: Human Sciences.

Taimni, I. (1961). *The science of yoga*. Wheaton, IL: Quest.

Tart, C. (1975a). *Transpersonal psychologies*. New York: Harper & Row.

Tart, C. (1975b). *States of consciousness*. New York: Dutton.

Teilhard de Chardin, P. (1970). *Building the earth*. New York: Avon.

Ueshiba, K. (1963). *Aikido*. Tokyo: Hozansha Publishing.

Underhill, E. (1961). *Mysticism*. New York: Dutton.

Walsh, R., & Vaughan, F. (1980). *Beyond ego: Transpersonal dimensions in psychology*. Los Angeles: Tarcher.

Wilber, K. (1977). *The spectrum of consciousness*. Wheaton IL: Quest.

Wilber, K. (1979). *No boundary*. Los Angeles: Center Publications.

Wilber, K. (1980). *The Atman project*. Wheaton, IL: Quest.

Wilson, C. (1972). *New pathways in psychology: Maslow and the post-Freudian revolution*. New York: Mentor.

Yogananda, P. (1968). *Sayings of Yogananda*. Los Angeles: Self-Realization Fellowship.

Yogananda, P. (1972). *Autobiography of a yogi*. Los Angeles: Self-Realization Fellowship.

19

The Imagery in Movement Method
A Process Tool Bridging Psychotherapeutic and Transpersonal Inquiry

INTRODUCTION

It has been said within the Zen tradition: "If you meet the Buddha, kill him." The reference is an admonition to accept no concepts, no ideas, no dogma but only one's own direct experience of the spiritual, for the true Buddha lives within. If transpersonal psychologists are to benefit from the esoteric psychologies that are at the root of many spiritual traditions, they must surely value this admonition, for if spiritual experiences are more than myth and legend, they should emerge in any thoroughgoing and open-ended investigation of consciousness.

However, research into spiritual experiences is no easy task, for the spiritual development of an individual is an inner journey through many different levels of awareness characterized by subtle shifts in experience that may or may not have any obvious behavioral referents (for example, see Metzner's Chapter 20 in this volume). It is a delicate process that is not amenable to the typical laboratory and control methods of experimental psychology. In contrast, the research approach of phenomenological psychology defined by Valle and King (1978, p. 15) as seeking "to reveal the structure of experience through descriptive techniques . . . asking the question '*what?*'" and seeking to "*understand* phenomena" offers much promise.

In addition to being phenomenological in approach, the particular method chosen will have to be one capable of evoking transpersonal experience. As Tart (1975) has pointed out, there are certain experiences not accessible to ordinary waking consciousness, and, in order to investigate them, one must develop a "state-specific science" that enables both subject and researcher to enter an altered state and explore the dimensions of that domain from within that experience.

Furthermore, to allow an exploration of the process of spiritual unfoldment, the method will have to be capable not only of accessing particular spiritual experiences but of catalyzing a transformative journey through many levels of awareness, much as the many meditative and/or contemplative practices employed by esoteric traditions do. By providing a "vehicle" of transformation, the method chosen will assist the seeker in the journey toward realization of the highest spiritual experiences.

The imagery in movement method (IMM), which I developed in 1977, meets these criteria for a research tool. It is a synthesis of several awareness or consciousness-exploring techniques into one four-step process. The methods incorporated into IMM are psychotherapy techniques originally designed to help clients uncover the unconscious or only partially conscious sources of their psychological difficulties and to resolve

Susan Schneier • Graduate School for the Study of Human Consciousness, John F. Kennedy University, Orinda, California 94563.

these difficulties. The specific techniques incorporated will be discussed in a later section of this chapter.

This chapter presents IMM, its origin in my own experiences, sources that contributed to it, and case material that demonstrates the process of the psychospiritual evolution it catalyzes. This will be followed by a brief discussion of the method's usefulness as a tool for transpersonal inquiry and its possible value as a method for phenomenological research.

ORIGIN OF THE METHOD

In 1974 I experienced a sudden and amazing shift in my own consciousness (without the use of any drugs). After attending a month-long intensive seminar on the exploration of consciousness conducted by the Esalen Institute, I suddenly experienced a shift in my awareness from a predominately verbal, linear, rational, and everyday mode, experienced primarily in my head, to a high-imagery, holistic, pattern-oriented, and intuitive mode of experiencing located more in my whole body. As my consciousness shifted, so did my experience of the world. Previously, I had inhabited a world of separate things moving about in time and space in ordinary ways—a profane world. Suddenly, I found myself in a world that looked the same but felt quite different. It was a world of interpenetrating energy fields, suffused with meaning and significance, with artistic and poetic nuances—a sacred world.

During the approximately 6 months that followed, I found myself often in this "other mind" and thinking/experiencing in a wholly different way. Instead of thinking in sentences, much as if I were writing, images—inner sights, sounds, smells, feelings of movement, body sensations—were the substrate of my thought process. My body seemed to be playing a much larger role in my thought process than ever before, using not only kinesthetic and proprioceptive imagery but also actual movements and postures to mimic and somehow "grok" the movements and postures of others and of things in my environment. Using this new "language" of imagery and movement, I found myself especially able to think in patterns and to appreciate the interconnectedness of ideas, people, and other experiences in my life—whatever I was directing my attention toward.

I also had the feeling that, in contrast with my usual way of understanding things, which was somehow a view from the outside, with this new language I was able to understand by *standing under*. By using my imagery process and my body, I could take on the form of something and use my very being to create an analogy to its struc-

ture. Through analogy and metaphor, I could then appreciate things from the perspective of the *inside*. This new way of thinking/being led me to a series of profound insights about my life, my work, and finally about the process of thinking itself.

I soon found a number of writings that seemed to refer to exactly the shift I had experienced, each proposing that consciousness was experienced in two modes characterized by different and complementary ways of orienting toward the world, each serving different functions (see Deikman, 1974, for a review of these writings and Samples, 1976, for a description of this "other mind").

In 1980, after 6 years of exploring related topics in the research and clinical literature and experimenting with developing a method for inducing shifts between these two modes, I proposed a theory of "metaphoric mind" or what I chose to call "analog mode" based on the analogical and pattern-making experiences described above (Schneier, 1980). This theory provides the cognitive framework for IMM. Although space precludes a detailed discussion of this work here, it is important to say that the proposed "analog mode" was postulated to be specialized for "world breaking and world making," and to be the mode of body/mind necessary for accessing dreams, fantasies, intuitions, creative visions, and spiritual experiences. This mode was held to be necessary for personal transformation, connecting empathically with others, and for accessing transformative insights. Many different states of consciousness were understood to comprise this mode, including daydreaming, dreaming, hypnosis, meditative states, psychotic states, and so forth. By contrast, "digital mode" was viewed as specialized for "world sustaining" and as the linear, rational state of body/mind necessary for accomplishing the tasks of everyday life and communicating within an established cultural consensus. I assumed that it, too, consisted of a number of discrete states of consciousness. Clearly, both ways of knowing/experiencing were vitally important with the important questions being when to use each and how to bring both to bear on any issue of concern.

IMM was created with the intention of developing a tool that could be used to shift back and forth between these two "modes" at will. To access the analog mode, three therapeutic techniques were combined. Therapy methods that turned attention inward and accessed imagery (of all modalities) were combined with methods that promote awareness of the bodily sensations accompanying these images and with methods such as role play and psychodrama that can be used to enhance the reality of these inner experiences by bringing them into outward expression. To allow for a shift back to the "digital" mode, I developed writing and thinking exercises that assist in translating the language of metaphor to that of rational insight.

Since 1977, four fellow psychotherapists and I have met on an almost weekly basis in 2- to 3-year segments, to use the method to explore our own consciousness. Charmian Anderson, Don Mariacher, Donna Scott, Aron Spilken, and I have used ourselves as "guinea pigs" in developing and refining the method. Although IMM was originally designed to be a tool for shifting modes of consciousness, we found that using it in an open-ended way on a regular basis evokes a process of transformation that leads through one's deepest psychological conflicts and out the other side to profound transpersonal experiences. Recognizing this, we began to use the method with selected clients. This chapter draws upon my experience with my own students and clients as well as my colleagues' experiences in using the method with their clients. To date, I have personally used IMM to explore the unfolding of the psyche in some 80 individuals.

THE IMAGERY IN MOVEMENT METHOD: A PROCESS TOOL

IMM is a four-step process that can be used to explore any topic or question of concern or to simply open investigation into the structure and fabric of one's current consciousness. The four steps of IMM are as follows: (1) *expression*—doing an abstract color drawing either spontaneously or in response to a particular question one wants to explore; (2) *mapping*—exploring the body sensations, thoughts, images, and feelings associated with the different colors and shapes of the drawing and getting a preliminary understanding of the meanings of these elements and what the drawing as a whole reveals about the inner psychological situation; (3) *fantasy-enactment*—taking an imaginary journey into the most compelling element in the drawing and physically enacting the flow of images that present themselves (i.e., engaging in a psychodrama); and (4) *verbal translation*—using a series of questions designed to uncover the symbolic meaning of the elements in the drawing and the events in the fantasy and further questions to determine how these symbols relate to one's current life situation.

IMM is generally a facilitated process, although an individual trained in using the method can work alone. Typically, it is done one-on-one with a trained facilitator or in a small group of four or five people who have been trained to co-facilitate each other. When I have facilitated individuals, I have done it in 2-hour sessions on a weekly basis. Small groups have usually met for approximately

3-hour sessions and occasional weekend marathons. Even a few sessions can be useful to gain insight into and resolve a particular issue, whereas years of work may be required to evoke and sustain a process of personal or spiritual transformation.

Step One: Expression

In *expression,* any self-created art form can be used, such as sculpture, dance, poetry, or music. However, the easy availability of paper and colors (crayons, pastels, magic markers), the fact that a tangible product is produced and endures past the moment of expression, and the ease of this form of expression that requires no more talent than the ability to "doodle," makes drawing the usual method of choice.

The opening instructions are:

Look at the colors. You'll find one that your eyes are attracted to. Let your hand pick up this color and draw whatever it likes until you feel finished. Then look again, find the next color, and do the same. Keep doing this until the drawing feels done.

Initially, when the client is apt to draw stereotyped images of concrete objects as they were taught in grade school, I recommend that the drawing be an abstract one. Later, this restriction is unnecessary and may, in fact, be detrimental to the free expression of the client who is taken with a particular image he or she wants to express.

Typically, there is initial resistance in clients who fear they cannot draw or cannot think of anything to draw. Usually this fades quickly when the facilitator reassures the client that "this is not art" and "absolutely anything will do" and further that "just let your hand do whatever it wants." In fact, to the amazement of people who have had no previous artistic experience, an abstract color drawing often emerges easily. A person inexperienced in using art as a personal process may have no idea initially of what the drawing means and may relate to it almost as if someone else had done it.

The purpose of expression is to make the implicit explicit. It is my experience that a kind of "aura" of nonverbal experience accompanies our waking consciousness. This aura is comprised of what is "in the back of my mind," "on the tip of my tongue," what "haunts me," my "sense of things," "an intuition," or that "feeling in my guts." Like a microscope or telescope that can bring something fuzzy into sharp focus, the drawing helps to bring the entire gestalt of our momentary ground of being into view.

It is important to the success of the drawing process, as it is throughout the use of this method, for the facilitator to focus on helping the unfolding of the drawing process but not to, in any way, prejudice the content of the exploration or the direction in which it flows. Therefore, the facilitator is careful not to suggest anything to draw or to influence the process by expressing his or her own emotional reactions to the client's unfolding drawing.

Step Two: Mapping

In *mapping*, the suitability of the language of color and form to represent inner experience becomes obvious. Here the client begins an exploration of (a) each element of the drawing as well as (b) the overall organization of the drawing itself.

The facilitator assists with the first part by suggesting that the client "look at a particular color or shape, turn your attention inward, and report to me what images, body sensations, feelings, and thoughts present themselves to you." The client may need some help in learning to focus inward and to "catch" the experiences that flit by. When asked to look at a particular color of the drawing, he or she may at first report that he or she experiences "nothing." Asked to introspect again and to report anything at all that happens, a typical response might be: "I saw a pattern of light and dark" or "Well, I feel a tingling in my throat; is that what you mean?" With encouragement and some practice, clients soon begin to access and report their inner experience.

The facilitator helps the client to explore the full sensory experience associated with each element of the drawing—not just visual images but also auditory, olfactory, kinesthetic, and proprioceptive images. Sometimes the client is encouraged to briefly "step into that part of the drawing and tell me what is happening" as that instruction is often powerful in assisting him or her to switch into the imagery stream. In addition to noticing imagery of all modalities, the client is encouraged to notice and report thoughts and emotional feelings that accompany these images.

When these analog-mode experiences have been accessed, the client is then encouraged to be receptive to the symbolic meaning of each element of the drawing. He or she is instructed to "ask yourself what the meaning of this part of the drawing is and listen to the answer." Typically, in the same way that the drawing simply flows out without effort, the "meaning" of a particular part of the drawing simply "pops into" the client's head; either he or she actually imagines "hearing" a voice that says it (for example, "it's your hostility") or sees a visual image of the meaning written in words ("seeing" a typewriter printing out "your hostility").

Sometimes, when asked for a meaning, the client

may reply, "I don't know." It is often very effective here to give a simple instruction to access the appropriate mode by saying "that's your verbal (digital) mind, and it doesn't know, ask your imagery (analog) mind what it means."

It soon becomes apparent, as different graphic elements of the drawing are explored, that every color and shape in the drawing encodes a body of sensate phenomena that share in a common theme or meaning. Although these meanings are obtained readily and apparently without any deep reflection on the part of the client, subsequent work on the drawing reveals that they are not mere "labels" or superficial explanations of parts of the drawing. Nor are they merely "projections" or "made-up" explanations. Rather, they prove on further exploration to be powerful concepts that shed light on the apparently disparate images and fantasies associated with that element of the drawing, providing a very incisive statement about that aspect of the client's inner experience.

When the exploration of each element of the drawing has been completed and the client has accessed images, feelings, and the symbolic meaning for each part, he or she is then facilitated in discovering the overall statement being made by the drawing. This is done by asking a variety of questions that assist the client in accessing overview material, such as "What is the story of this drawing?, What issues are expressed in it?, What is the relationship between the parts of the drawing?, and What is the title of the drawing?" In this last part of mapping, the client often has a series of "aha" experiences as he or she realizes that the drawing is indeed a "map" of his or her inner landscape.

Let us consider an example of the entire process of mapping. A client of mine, who I shall call Crissa, on one occasion rendered the drawing reproduced in black and white in Figure 1. The original drawing consisted of a dark blue dot, partially surrounded by a black hazy semicircle, with some yellow–gold flecks in the upper right-hand corner of the drawing. She reported that, when looking at the blue dot, she experienced a feeling of tension in her stomach, a kinesthetic sensation of being "scrunched down," a coldness throughout her body, a constricted feeling in her heart, a feeling of loneliness, and an image of sitting on a cold, blue-and-white linoleum floor. These sensations and images triggered a memory of being 3 years old in the family kitchen and being yelled at by her mother. When I asked her what all this symbolized, she heard the word *withdrawal* in her mind's ear and then, more precisely, *self-protective withdrawal*.

Going further, Crissa then explored the black and found that it triggered sensations of being in a wet fog-filled night air, an image of a dark street and a shadow that

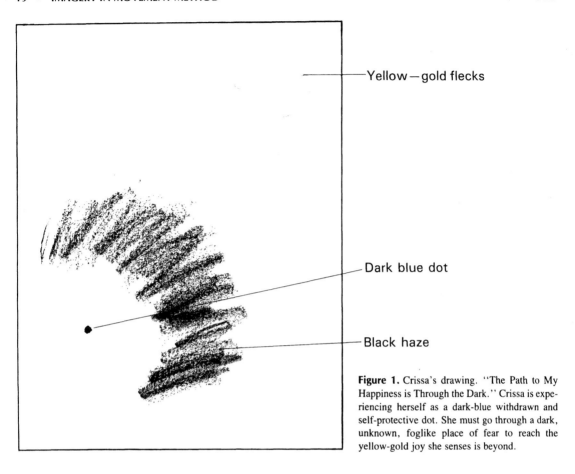

Yellow—gold flecks

Dark blue dot

Black haze

Figure 1. Crissa's drawing. "The Path to My Happiness is Through the Dark." Crissa is experiencing herself as a dark-blue withdrawn and self-protective dot. She must go through a dark, unknown, foglike place of fear to reach the yellow-gold joy she senses is beyond.

flits by, and feelings of fear. The symbolic meaning that came to her for all this was "an unknown fear—something that haunts me."

Moving to the yellow–gold flecks, Crissa then noticed in her mind's eye "sunlight glinting off the water, a warm happy sunshine feeling, the smell of hot dogs and suntan c'l, the sound of children laughing and splashing in the water, a memory of being away at summer camp." To all this she ascribed the meaning *spontaneity*.

Not only did every color and shape soon acquire depth and meaning, but it also became obvious that, by virtue of their placement on the page in a particular geometrical relationship to one another, Crissa's entire inner psychic situation was being represented. When asked, "What's happening in this drawing?", she said:

> I'm feeling lonely and withdrawn, but the only way I'll get back to that happy and spontaneous place I used to know is if I go through this unknown fear of something that I've avoided for years. I don't know what it is, but I know I must go through it.

On being asked, "What is the title of this drawing?", her whole experience came into sharp focus. She replied, without hesitation, "The path to my happiness is through the dark."

As in expression, the facilitator makes every effort to not influence the content of the material that emerges but only to facilitate the process. Thus the facilitator will *never* comment on or interpret the associations that are reported by the client. This effort to avoid interpretation is even reflected in the way in which the questions are phrased.

The purpose of mapping is orientation. In contrast with other imagery-oriented psychotherapeutic methods that simply ask the client to access an image without the intermediate step of doing a drawing, this method provides the context in which the various images emerge. It provides a psychological snapshot of the state of the client's inner reality at a given moment in time—a "map" of the inner landscape. Furthermore, it also reveals the dynamics of the psyche by implying the direction of growth—Crissa knew, for example, that she must go through the black to reach her yellow gold.

Step Three: Fantasy Enactment

In *fantasy enactment,* the client is asked to identify the "most charged" part of the drawing and to "step into" that part of the drawing and report "what's happening." At first, the facilitator assists the client in accessing an ongoing stream of images. Later, he or she helps the client to enact the fantasy that then unfolds. For example, Crissa chose to "step into" the blue dot of her drawing in her imagination, and, at first, noticed only a feeling of sitting on a cold, hard floor. A major part of the facilitator's role is to focus the client's attention on the sensory details that first present themselves. I did this by taking off from whatever information Crissa gave and then asking questions such as "What does the floor look like? What's happening around you? How does your body feel? How are you dressed? What do you smell? What do you hear?" In so doing, I was careful to pace and time my questions so they did not disrupt her process but helped to ease her more deeply into her experience.

Gradually, the scene became more and more vivid. Crissa saw herself as a 3-year-old child, wearing a soiled little white dress, sitting on a blue and white tile floor, smelling rancid bacon fat, seeing and hearing her angry mother at the stove, yelling at her. As the scene got sharper and clearer by virtue of promoting sensory focusing, it began to unfold before her like an inner movie. She watched as the images presented themselves without any apparent direction from her conscious mind.

When she felt comfortable enough to move yet deeper into this experience, I initiated the "enactment" phase of the process by asking her to get up and act out the scene as it unfolded—to do a spontaneous psychodrama guided by the sensory imagery, feelings, and thoughts that were emerging for her. At this point in the process, the facilitator helps to intensify this experience by acting out any roles that the client requests. Crissa wanted me to yell at her in a particular way characteristic of her mother and to make a sound like pots and pans being rattled with irritation to amplify the sensory images she was having. As the psychodrama unfolded, Crissa recalled that her mother had slapped her and could see the visual image of it but was not connecting emotionally with the memory. She asked me to help enact it, and even though we used a pillow to protect her from any actual hurt, we managed to reenact the scene with sufficient realism to trigger her feelings. She reexperienced the coldness of the interaction with her mother and cried bitterly while visualizing her mother storming out of the kitchen and leaving her to cry alone.

Characteristically, the moment there is bodily engagement in the process of exploration, a dramatic shift occurs in the client's experience. Suddenly the scene becomes all too real. There is an experience of being at a frightening edge and not knowing what will happen next. The client often experiences his or her body moving spontaneously and without any conscious forethought. It is almost as if his or her body develops a life of its own and the client finds him- or herself fighting, jumping up, collapsing, crying. The client *becomes* the process, becomes the fantasy unfolding itself. Usually, the experience reaches its own resolution, and, in the process, the client who has surrendered to it experiences tremendous catharsis and insight that is at once intellectual, emotional, and embodied. Again, the facilitator is careful when assuming a role in the fantasy enactment to not rely on his or her own impulses or spontaneous ideas for guiding the drama but to confine the dramatization to the specific words, gestures, and intonations requested by the client.

Typically, one of two types of fantasy sequences unfold: either a memory experience or a waking dream. Like Crissa, clients may suddenly find themselves reliving a memory in very vivid detail, remembering details (the trim on a dress) that have long since been forgotten. Often memories are retrieved from the first few years, not infrequently including birth experiences. Once one scene or "frame" from a memory is retrieved in full sensory detail, the entire movie or memory sequence usually unfolds.

Alternatively, the fantasy sequence may be a waking dream—a story that unfolds itself much as a night dream might. Sometimes it is a symbolic dream. For example, in a subsequent session, Crissa felt drawn to enter her blue dot again, and this time found herself in the midst of a polar landscape, freezing to death on the snow. Encouraged to stay with the sensory experiences, she lay down on the floor curled up into a little ball, complained of feeling cold, and then reported that she was experiencing inner sensations in her face and body of lying in the crunchy, icy hardness of snow. She could feel the biting cold air, the deep chill in her bones, and a desperate longing in her heart. As the scene came alive, she got up and enacted wandering hopelessly, moaning and crying for help, searching for warmth and shelter but finding nothing but endless white. Finally, she reported to me that she was going to "lie down in the snow to die," and lying down on her back with arms and legs spread out, she experienced a profound sense of surrender. Suddenly, with the amazement typical of someone experiencing the spontaneous unfolding of an inner fantasy, she reported to me that she saw a small golden ball of light within her that gradually was growing brighter and brighter, warming not only her body but the surrounding scene, melting snows and bringing green shoots forth from the ground.

Instead of this highly symbolic experience, Crissa might have had what I call a "literal waking dream" in which realistic, plausible events (past or future) that have not actually happened are experienced. These waking dreams remake reality in ways that resolve the issue expressed in that part of the drawing. For example, Crissa might have had a fantasy in which she found herself back in the kitchen but this time rewriting the actual memory by enacting the telling of her mother, in a quiet and loving way, that she will not be treated so poorly, although she is truly sorry that life has been so hard on her.

Regardless of whether the fantasy is a waking dream (symbolic or literal) or a memory experience, it remains true to the *theme* or *meaning* given to that part of the drawing that was the entry point to the fantasy. Thus the blue dot that symbolized "withdrawal" in Crissa's drawing led to the memory experience in the kitchen, a symbolic waking dream of the polar fantasy, and could have led to the "redo" literal waking dream just proposed. In each case, the material elicited would provide yet more information on the theme of withdrawal.

Typically, memory experiences trace the roots of this theme in early life experiences. In this case, Crissa's "withdrawal" was traced to an early experience with an angry mother. From my experience with hundreds of hours of fantasy enactments, I have concluded that each color or shape in a drawing provides access to both the formative experiences that developed the theme represented by that graphic element as well as all later experiences that have become associated in the individual's memory with that theme. These findings dovetail nicely with those of Grof (1976) who reports that LSD-catalyzed research into consciousness reveals the presence of such constellations of memories and fantasies around a common theme that he calls "COEXs" or "systems of condensed experiences."

For example, when I asked Crissa later in the session to "slide backwards in time along this 'blue' feeling and see a scene from the earliest time you felt this way," she accessed a still earlier image of being a newborn infant refusing to suck bitter milk, whereas further explorations of the blue dot led to a rapid succession of later memory scenes in which she felt that way—an image of being in school and being reprimanded by a teacher, a painful time with a boyfriend who left her, and a recent memory of being told she was not doing well at work. All these experiences were readily available, simply by exploring the theme of "self-protective withdrawal." As Grof (1976) reports, it was the work with Crissa's infant experience that finally proved to be the most powerfully transformative, for it was the template or prototype experience

around which all the others constellated. These memories reveal the origin of the conflict represented in that part of the drawing and, when relived, allow the body to release the patterns of holding that have kept the associated feelings from being expressed.

Waking dreams that emerge when the client "enters" a particular color or shape in the drawing express the issue represented by that part of the drawing and attempt to resolve it. Symbolic waking dreams place the issue in a larger context and provide wisdom about its resolution, whereas literal waking dreams provide one with an opportunity to rehearse different behavior. Thus Crissa's polar fantasy suggested to her that warmth cannot be found in the environment but exists within and is, in fact, sufficient to enliven not only her own body but the environment in which she finds herself. This same insight could have been expressed in a literal waking dream such as the one I proposed above that she might have interpreted as finding within herself the ability to love herself by refusing to accept abuse while also loving and "warming" her haggard mother.

One can see, in Crissa's experience, intimations of the power of this process in both furthering self-development and ultimately moving toward transpersonal experience. In the midst of her worst pain, at a time when there was nothing left to do but die, a powerful image of guiding warmth appeared to Crissa. This is typical of many experiences I have had with clients and has led me to have a deep faith in the self-healing and self-transcending qualities of the psyche.

The purpose, then, of fantasy enactment is none other than self-transformation. When both memory and waking dream experiences have been accessed, the client understands the source of the issue, has become aware of how the body has participated in holding that issue, and has seen the solution to the issue within the larger context of his or her life. Thus Crissa experienced the roots of her current feelings of coldness and withdrawal from others in her early experiences with her mother and was reassured by her own psyche that she had sufficient warmth within herself to support her through the worst lonely times. She was encouraged by this realization to face the next step in her work—exploring the black and hazy part of her drawing that represented an unknown fear blocking her way to spontaneity. With the conclusion of the fantasy-enactment work, the client turns from accessing material to using the methods of verbal translation to understand the relevance of that material for their daily lives.

Step Four: Verbal Translation

In *verbal translation*, the client is assisted in understanding or "reflecting upon" the experiences that have

IMAGERY-MOVEMENT WORK ANALYSIS SHEET   Name_____ Date _____Session_____

Title of Session: *My path of happiness is through the dark*   Sketch of drawing(s):

Summary: *My dark blue dot of withdrawal is freezing to death and is incapable of accepting warmth of nurturance. I must journey through an unknown black haze, to reach my yellow-gold flecks of summer happiness. However, I have a golden ball of light within — my all pervading, sweet-smelling spirit that like a bell's tone can always be heard to guide me. I will not freeze in this inner landscape, for spirit's warmth will melt my snows and bring green shoots forth from my earth.*

Major themes of session:

- *Withdrawal in the face of unkindness*

- *desperate searching for love from the outside*
- *inability to accept nurturance despite need.*
- *finding nurturance through Spirit within*

Current life details and relevance to session themes:

- *I've withdrawn from Joe since he wouldn't lend me the money*
- *I don't feel he cares about me*
- *I haven't been willing to accept anything else from him.*
- *Been going camping alone and feeling really strong and peaceful inside... Maybe I don't need his support - financial that is --- as much as I thought.*

Figure 2. Verbal translation exercise: Summary sheet (completed at end of write-up).

unfolded during the preceding explorations. Typically, the client involved in fantasy enactment is very absorbed in the experience. Often he or she seems to forget both the facilitator and the surroundings and to be completely swept up in the enactment, appearing almost hypnotized. Powerful emotions are expressed as vivid scenes are enacted. At the conclusion of the fantasy enactment, the client is often visibly shaken and moved. He or she seems to be in an altered state and, according to my thinking, has indeed been in the "analog mode."

To help the client "come back to reality," the facilitator will, at this point, ask some very general questions about the process that has unfolded. In Crissa's case, I sat with her quietly and then gradually asked questions such as "How was that for you? What do you think is the meaning of that polar scene fantasy? How does it relate to the memory in the kitchen? How does this blue-dot theme

apply to your current life? What in your life reminds you of this memory and fantasy?"

When asked gently and after the client has quieted emotionally, the questions serve to move him or her back into everyday reality. You can see the faraway look in the client's eyes fade as he or she focuses more clearly on the facilitator and objects in the room. Typically, clients will wipe their faces, adjust their clothing, and straighten their body posture. They seem to put away their feelings. All this signals to me that they have returned to everyday consciousness or the "digital mode" and are sufficiently oriented to "reality" to be able to leave the session. To facilitate further reflection on and integration of the fantasy and imagery material that has emerged, the client is given "homework"—a writing exercise using forms (see Figures 2 and 3) that have been specially prepared to help stimulate and structure this writing.

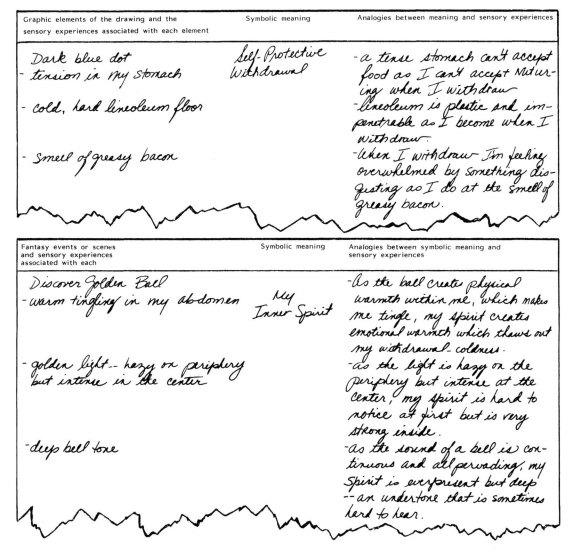

Graphic elements of the drawing and the sensory experiences associated with each element	Symbolic meaning	Analogies between meaning and sensory experiences
Dark blue dot - tension in my stomach - cold, hard linoleum floor - smell of greasy bacon	Self-Protective Withdrawal	- a tense stomach can't accept food as I can't accept Nurturing when I withdraw - linoleum is plastic and impenetrable as I become when I withdraw. - when I withdraw I'm feeling overwhelmed by something disgusting as I do at the smell of greasy bacon.

Fantasy events or scenes and sensory experiences associated with each	Symbolic meaning	Analogies between symbolic meaning and sensory experiences
Discover Golden Ball - warm tingling in my abdomen - golden light -- hazy on periphery but intense in the center - deep bell tone	My Inner Spirit	- As the ball creates physical warmth within me, which makes me tingle, my spirit creates emotional warmth which thaws out my withdrawal-coldness. - as the light is hazy on the periphery but intense at the center, my spirit is hard to notice at first but is very strong inside. - as the sound of a bell is continuous and all pervading, my spirit is everpresent but deep -- an undertone that is sometimes hard to hear.

Figure 3. Verbal translation exercise: Crissa's session write-up forms for analyzing the sketch and for analyzing fantasy enactments.

The form is in three major parts: a section for reflecting on the graphic elements of the drawing and the experiences that emerge during mapping, a section for reflecting on the major events in the fantasy enactment, and various summary sections in which the client reflects on the overall process and its significance for his or her current life. The sections for the drawing analysis and the fantasy analysis are the same in form. Both ask the client to break the experience into meaningful chunks. For the drawing, the client must identify the main graphic elements that have significance, whereas, for the fantasy, the equivalent would be major events and/or scenes.

For example, in Crissa's case she identified the blue dot, the black haze, and the yellow–gold flecks as the major graphic elements of her drawing. When analyzing the memory, she chunked it into "sitting on the cold floor," "mother yelling at me," "being slapped," and "alone and despairing." Analyzing the polar fantasy into events, she identified "alone and freezing," "searching for warmth," "giving up to die," "discovering the golden ball," and "the shoots sprouting up around me" as the major chunks of the fantasy.

Next, the client notes all the sensory experiences and feelings associated with each of these elements or events, simply recording them below the element or event/scene that triggered them. For example, Crissa wrote underneath the blue dot (see Figure 2): "tension in my stomach, a cold, hard linoleum floor underneath me, smell of greasy bacon, feeling of apprehension." Underneath "discovering the golden ball," she wrote "warm, tingling in my abdomen, beautiful golden light—hazy on periphery but intense in the center, sound of deep bell tone which is continuous, unchanging, and all pervading, smell of incense, feeling of awe."

Then the client asks him- or herself what the symbolic meaning of that element or event is, "listens" for an answer, and records that answer under the column labeled *symbolic meaning*. Some of these meanings will have already emerged spontaneously during mapping or other phases of the process. However, here they are written down and viewed with a clear reflective mind. As we know, Crissa's symbolic meaning for the blue dot was "self-protective withdrawal." Reflecting on the symbolic meaning of discovering the golden sphere, she realized it represented "finding my inner spirit."

The chunking of the drawing and fantasy into meaningful elements and events, the identification of the sensory experiences and feelings as well as the identification of the symbolic meaning associated with each element or event are preparatory to the next, and most important, part of the write-up: tracing the analogies. As with the rest of verbal translation, tracing analogies is accomplished through open-ended questioning. After some initial education into the nature of analogical thinking, the client is asked to answer the question: "Why did your imagery mind choose this particular sensory experience to represent that symbolic meaning?" and to write the answer to that question for each sensory image that emerged for that element in the "analogies" section of the form.

For example, for the blue dot, Crissa asked herself why her imagery mind chose "tension in my stomach," "cold, hard linoleum floor," and "smell of greasy bacon" to represent the symbolic meaning of "self-protective withdrawal." Her answers are shown in Figure 2:

My withdrawal is like tension in the stomach because when the stomach is tense it can't take anything in or digest anything and when I withdraw I close off all source of nurturing from everyone, even those who are not threatening me. My withdrawal is like a cold, hard, linoleum floor because I harden myself not allowing anyone to touch me emotionally. I become cold and show a smooth, plastic surface which is impenetrable to others. This withdrawal occurs when I feel overwhelmed by something I don't want to take in, something that makes me feel disgusted and nauseated as does the smell of greasy bacon, the remnant of a dead animal.

Regardless of whether one is analyzing a graphic element in the drawing, a scene or event from a memory, or one from a waking dream, the same process of tracing analogies is followed. When the fantasy is a symbolic one, such as Crissa's polar fantasy, this process of un-

covering the symbolic significance of the events is not so surprising. What is most interesting, however, is the discovery that even with memories, every event and every scene can be ascribed a symbolic or general meaning. Thus even "literal" events have indeed "become symbolic." For example, Crissa's experience of being slapped by her mother had come to represent "rejection" to her. The sensory details associated with that memory become the defining characteristics for representing rejection for her. Thus the abrupt, distracted, and back of the hand way she was slapped represents her brand of rejection—a feeling of being unimportant:

She gives me only the hard side of herself and hides her palm, the softer side, from me. It is a distracted action which shows me she doesn't even care enough to pay attention to being angry at me and take the time to hit me directly. The smell of bacon in the air further symbolizes this aspect of rejection—it is an old rancid smell of fat that has been left to spoil, as I was left to spoil.

Another individual might have used a bright-red shape to symbolize rejection and found it to be associated with images of being yelled at for being "too dumb." For this client, "rejection" would be permanently associated with feelings of not being good enough and with a very face-to-face, engaged, and relentless verbal abuse. The one word *rejection* would label two very different experiences for these two clients.

After fully exploring the drawing and the fantasy in this way, the client then moves on to fill out the summary parts of the form: first identifying the major themes that have emerged during the work and then clarifying how these themes relate to his or her current life situation. In Crissa's case, the themes were "rejection by an uncaring potential nurturer," "discovering source of strength within," and so forth. Considering how these themes related to her current life, she realized she had cast her boyfriend in the role of this uncaring nurturer because he refused to help her with a financial crisis and that she needed to stop trying to get him to take care of her and, instead, connect with her own inner strength.

This tracing of themes and how they are being played out in the current life situation is very important to the therapeutic use of this method because it is here that the client sees how the inner life and structure are reflected in his or her daily world. It reveals why the client does this particular drawing at this particular time.

Finally, in the summary part of the form, the client brings together both the imagery and fantasy material that has emerged in working with the drawing and fantasy enactment and the symbolic meanings and their relevances to his or her current life situation, using this material to write an integrated summary of the insights that have emerged in the session. As is true of tracing the analogies, writing the summary is powerful in evoking an experience of greater wholeness or expansion. The client witnesses and simultaneously experiences him- or herself on many levels, seeing his or her current life and past life through the symbolic and imagery representations that organize all of these experiences.

Verbal translation ultimately returns the client to his or her ordinary life situations, renewed with insight from the excursion into imagery and fantasy. Crissa, for example, understood how her past experience was like a filter through which she viewed her current relationship with her boyfriend and also that she had what she needed within herself. She then chose to develop her awareness of this strong side and stop desperately trying to manipulate her partner into giving something to her that she alone could give to herself. Viewing him with fresh eyes, she was then in a position to decide whether she wanted to stay in or leave the relationship. With the "filter" removed from her perception of him, she decided to stay.

It is in verbal translation that the client can have a new expanded sense of him- or herself. In our culture, we are usually in one or the other mode of consciousness: Either we are talking, thinking, or writing in everyday consciousness (digital mode) and relatively unaware of our inner sensations, images, and feelings, or we are drifting into that inner world (analog mode)—whether through daydreaming, dreaming, reverie—and letting go of the world of everyday thought. However, the client in this stage of the process is both thinking about his or her life in rational ways (i.e., what the images mean and how they apply to daily life concerns) *and* remaining fully in touch with the images, sensations, and feelings associated with those meanings. The experience reported is one of profound insight and inner expansion—of "being at a shimmering edge"—the edge of contact and communication between what the client experiences as two very different "minds."

A PROCESS OF UNFOLDING

Used over time, IMM catalyzes the development of a vocabulary of color and form for each person. Repeatedly, an individual will select a particular palette of colors that has come to represent different aspects of his or her psyche. The drawings then reveal the evolving relationship between these aspects. Typically, these aspects will change in color and shape and move in position with respect to one another on the page as the inner psychological situation changes.

For example, over the space of a year, Crissa did a series of drawings in which the dark-blue dot of her first drawing grew larger and bulbous as she reported that the blue was "thawing out" and felt like the kind of "pins and needles" one experiences as a limb that has been

extremely cold warms up. The black haze took over as the most "charged" part of the drawing, and, as she became more familiar with the issues it represented and could "see" them more clearly, it grew smaller and more sharply defined. Still later, the black turned to gray and faded out, and the blue assumed a flower shape as it changed in meaning from "self-protective withdrawal" to "my integrity which can never be damaged." The gold flecks came to light on top of the flower symbolizing an integration of her spontaneity and joy with her previously withdrawn integrity. In the last phase of our work together, a new salmon-colored shape emerged. She identified this color with a spiritual aspect of herself that had a feminine/motherly quality to it.

These changes in Crissa's drawings are typical of the process of transformation in other clients. Often, there is a shift in the color or shape that the client will identify at the beginning of the fantasy enactment as the "most charged" part of their drawing. The client may still include that aspect of his or her psyche in the drawing, but it is no longer the place of interest, conflict, or attention in the drawing or in his or her life. Crissa's focus moved from the dark blue to the black, and toward the end of her work, although these colors were still part of her drawings, it was the new salmon-colored spiritual aspect that attracted her attention.

As in the example of Crissa's work, new colors may emerge, or the significance of old colors may change. Sometimes one sees the phenomenon of the colors becoming "washed clean" of meaning. As the old images, memories, fantasies, and feelings associated with a color become fully conscious and integrated, the color may become engaging in and of itself because of the quality of light and energy it possesses.

What is most remarkable is that "something" in the psyche appears to be self-healing. Without direction or interpretation from the facilitator with regard to the content of the session, "something" presents the key issues, works on those issues, and resolves them, and then "something" moves on to present the next issue. Like layers of an onion being peeled, the psyche appears to peel off its issues spontaneously, going deep into old pains and suffering and reliving them, and then resurfacing into joy, love, creativity, and freedom. As the drawings change, so does the behavior, although sometimes a change in drawings presages—by 6 months to a few years—a change in behavior. There are many idiosyncrasies in the way in which each person's process unfolds. Regardless of these differences, the process appears to move steadily in the direction of increasing joy, freedom, and capacity.

In keeping with transpersonal models of the development of consciousness (e.g., Wittine's model of ego, existential, and transpersonal levels of consciousness; see

Chapter 17 in this volume), informal research with IMM demonstrates a process that works through personality issues and then widens into ever-expanding and more inclusive levels of consciousness.

THE EMERGENCE OF THE TRANSPERSONAL

Transpersonal means "over, beyond, or through" the personal and refers to all experiences in which we transcend the ordinary boundaries and limitations of our personalities (See Valle's Chapter 16, Wittine's Chapter 17, and Frager's Chapter 18 for expanded discussions of transpersonal psychology). In working with clients, I accept as "transpersonal" any material the client identifies as such, whether by that name or by words such as "holy," "spiritual," "sacred," or more idiosyncratic terms. I do not measure the client's experience against any definition of levels of spiritual awareness and may, therefore, be studying the growing edge of a particular client's spiritual awareness rather than any "ultimate" state of spiritual realization.

Symbols of the Spiritual

It is interesting to note the many different ways in which spiritual experience is represented in drawings and fantasies. For each person and at different points in any given individual's evolution, spiritual experience takes many forms. For one man, the spiritual was represented as a blue kidney shape that he called the "blue soul pool." It was a place where one could "constantly change form. . . . One minute you could be a man, the next, water in a stream, the next, the sky." Upon entering it, one first "felt a boundary with water and then not, and then became one with it—no matter how you move there's no resistance."

For another, it was "a field of yellow flowers." Walking through it during her fantasy enactment, she reported, "The light is so intense I cannot look for more than an instant . . . I feel a warmth inside . . . a glow . . . I sense my power, knowledge, truth . . . I am enfolded with love . . . I feel energy emanating from my head which is light, airy, and joyfully empty. . . . I throw my arms up and my head back as I run through the field."

Yet another drew a white circle—a "shining sphere." As she stepped into it, "rays of light fanned out from the center, breaking through the darkness. . . . I felt an inner opening and expansion inside. . . . It was as if tight bands had dropped off and I was filled with light. . . . I had gotten in touch with an inner, soft,

powerful, loving part of me that I was unaware of before."

Although, for many, the symbols led to highly idiosyncratic visions, for some they led to more traditional religious images. For example, one client reported: "As I stepped into the yellow color, I saw a gold palace with huge heavy golden doors with sculptured figures. . . . Entering the great hallway, I stood and looked into a mirror wondering what I was doing here. Two angels came and asked me to follow. They opened another door and I was flooded with a white light, very bright and intense. I walked inside and saw Christ sitting on a throne. He had long hair, flowing robes, and very loving eyes. I was very surprised to find myself there and to encounter Christ; it was an incredible experience."

Upon completing a drawing, most clients have no idea what they will encounter when they "enter" a particular color or shape. This is as true for spiritual aspects of the psyche as for repressed early experiences. As the individual enacts the unfolding imagery, his or her entire being participates in the experience. One woman saw an intense light in a fantasy enactment and found herself shaking, crying, and experiencing energy streaming through her body as she envisioned the light entering her. A man, upon hearing the Buddha's laugh, allowed himself to laugh and be filled with irrepressible joy. A second woman saw herself standing in an unusual posture and, when she assumed this posture, suddenly felt flooded with a new experience of centeredness, presence, and power. A third woman saw herself going through a process of melting, evaporating, becoming fog, and then becoming nothing. As she allowed this process to become vivid and real for her, she experienced a transformation in her sense of self from being an individual point of consciousness to being a field of consciousness.

Assagioli (1972) has reported that there is as much fear of the sublime as of the repressed. My work with clients has confirmed this observation. Just as cathartic work on past issues results in personal transformation, fantasy work on spiritual issues also results in self-transformation. Although working on one's personality issues usually leads to better integration with the world of others, clients who begin to work on spiritual aspects of themselves can experience transformations in attitudes and beliefs that may be difficult to integrate into their daily lives.

For example, one client repeatedly "entered" a "golden aspect" of her being that led to experiences of "being one with all humanity." During these experiences, she would "see and know" that every event was chosen by all participating parties. She was, however, a criminal lawyer whose job depended on proving one person innocent and another guilty. Were she to take her new insights seriously, her entire life-style that she had spent years developing would be threatened. Were she to ignore these insights, she would have to put aside the most powerful and important experience of her life. She was understandably frightened and ambivalent about further work on this golden aspect of herself, yet unable to abandon it entirely.

Although there is much individuality in the nature of symbols that emerge in exploring spiritual experience, some generalizations can be made about the phenomena that present themselves. The most common colors chosen to represent the spiritual realm have been white, yellow, gold, silver, and various shades of blue and purple. Sometimes, however, it has been a combination of all colors that has been used to represent this aspect of being. Spheres, lines radiating out from a center or forming a "V" shape, organic flowing forms (like plants or water in streams), spirals, diamonds, and triangular forms have been the most common shapes. For some clients, it is specific colors and shapes like these that carry spiritual meaning. For others, it is a personal mandala, which brings together in a balanced and symmetrical design many different colors and forms, which is used to represent spiritual experience. The mandala, by representing different aspects of the psyche in balance, symbolizes a state of inner wholeness, centeredness, and balance associated with spiritual levels of awareness.

"Stepping into" the spiritual elements of a drawing, clients experience an immediate shift in body experience and emotional attitude. They feel as if they are expanding physically—when relaxed into, this expansion can be extremely pleasant. It can, however, be frightening when the individual contracts in an attempt to control it, and this can result in a series of jolts or shocks. Often there is mention of feeling a loss of body boundary or as if one's body is changing form. Frequently, there is an experience of "energy"—both "more energy" and "energy of a higher vibration." This energy can be seen as coming from an outside spiritual source or from the center of one's being and is often associated with a very brilliant light—sometimes too brilliant to bear.

Sounds can play an important role in these experiences. Some are all-embracing "total" sounds—like a deep roaring, the sound of the ocean, or the sound of the entire universe. Alternatively, the sounds are of light, clear music and very beautiful melodies.

The emotions and feelings associated with these experiences usually include love, joy, awe, amazement, and sometimes either a fear of the unknown or its opposite—a sense of recognition and familiarity as if one had experienced or known this before and had forgotten it. There is often a feeling that everything is as it should be, that, after all, everything is all right. Sometimes there is sadness, usually at the unnecessary suffering, confusion, and loneliness that has been part of one's life in the face of the newly revealed perfection of things.

The Process of Spiritual Unfoldment

Some of the people I have worked with have spent months to years using IMM and never encountered any experience that they labeled as spiritual or even extraordinary. Everyone did, however, have some experiences that they felt were extremely positive. Typically, they were images or fantasy sequences of natural things—sun, sky, ocean, growing plants—that made them feel more relaxed, happy, or expanded. One wonders if, with sufficient time, these experiences would have developed into spiritual feelings.

Others, frequently after many months or even years of difficult explorations of unhappy childhood experiences and feelings, suddenly came upon graphic images and fantasies that they explicitly identified as spiritual. These people often went through a battle with themselves with regard to accepting these experiences. Some became cynical and doubting; others were afraid.

Still another group of people began using IMM during what appears to have been a "spiritual opening"—a sudden breakthrough of transpersonal material into their conscious experience. These individuals have then gone through alternate periods of "dark" and "light." Beginning with drawings that led to intense spiritual feelings and realizations over a period of weeks or months, they then appeared to forget these experiences as their drawings led them into periods of intense work on childhood wounds. Eventually, spiritual aspects returned in their drawings, and they expanded their sense of themselves, shifted toward the positive in mood and attitude, and reevaluated their excursion into the "dark" as a "necessary lesson."

Then there are those individuals who have begun their work drawing only spiritual aspects. These individuals often appear to use spiritual images as a defense against early childhood pain, before initiating a descent into childhood wounds. However, after a long and difficult descent, they have gradually returned to their spiritual beginnings, validating these experiences from a much deeper perspective.

Finally, there has been a group of individuals who have included spiritual aspects in all their drawings from the beginning to the end of their work. Their self-drawings have been mandalas showing dark and light aspects of their being, and they have viewed their work as a process of increasing integration of these opposites. These people may represent the most developed stage in the evolution toward spiritual realization in that they have never lost sight of this aspect of their beings.

In all cases, it is very clear that spiritual unfoldment is a long and delicate process in very much the same way that psychotherapeutic work is. Assagioli (1972) has identified two stages in psychotherapeutic work: a period of "personal synthesis" in which psychological issues are addressed and worked through and a period of "spiritual psychosynthesis" in which there is a process of re-centering around a "higher self" as one disidentifies with the personality and reidentifies with the spiritual center of one's being. This is a fitting description of the process one observes in clients working with IMM.

It is important to note that this process of "spiritual psychosynthesis" has many stages, and one can observe for a given individual that numerous symbols of spirit emerge over time, each representing different spiritual aspects and states. It is clearly a journey, as reported in the esoteric psychologies. Each emerging color or form represents a clearer, more encompassing, and more profound experience of "Spirit."

Case Example: The Relationship between Psychotherapeutic Work and Spiritual Unfolding

By external standards, Linda appeared to be doing quite well when she began working with IMM. She was an apparently successful lawyer with a very responsible position in a law firm that paid well. However, she felt stifled, bored by her work, and unable to assert herself in the workplace. She had been married and divorced and, although she was currently in a relationship, she felt very ambivalent about her boyfriend. She felt she could neither love nor truly express herself in her work and had a chronic illness that had taken a turn for the worse.

Her drawings for several years were dominated by black, blue, red, and a cold whiteness. Images of being an innocent baby animal trapped by a hunter haunted her. She was self-critical, self-judgmental, and was indeed trapped by an inner hunter.

Over time, the source of this self-hatred came to revolve around fantasies of being split between an abusing man and a degraded, sexualized woman. Many waking dreams revolved around this theme. She also had a series of drawings and waking dreams that revolved about an image of a demon child—a child with vital green eyes that were somehow terrifying.

Gradually, memories that were at the root of these waking dreams were uncovered—memories that were previously totally unconscious—of being sexually abused as a 3-year-old child and of both enjoying and being rageful about the abuse and of wishing that her abusive father

would die. When, by awful coincidence, he did die shortly after her "wish," she became terrified of her own vitality and power. The demon child was born—an ever-alert, ever-watchful, and ever-constricted and self-hating self. Its sexual vitality as well as its power, hidden within, could nevertheless be seen. It was represented by the color green, shining out from its demonic eyes.

A pink, alive, squiggly baby part of herself, a vulnerable part—the part that had allowed the abuse—was portrayed as encased in black rage and locked away behind tank-green barriers. She had no sympathy for this "baby."

Upon realizing, as a result of her work with IMM, that she had been living the life of the demon child since that event, fearing her vital green because of a child's magical thinking, Linda did a series of drawings in which green began to explode out, along with the pink. She reported an increasing feeling of power at work and an increasing willineness to be open at the same time.

Periodically, purely positive images would emerge. There was an image of a primeval forest, triggered by stepping into a darker green in one of her drawings. The forest was a symbol for "passion, love of life, abundance, fertility, bursting forth, expanding." She reported that "the only thing that stands between me and living in the forest is fear; part of the fear is that it is not the right thing to do; it is straying too far into the unknown." Quickly, the positive images would once again be buried in the work on painful issues.

Meanwhile the relationship with her boyfriend began to blossom and eventually led toward marriage plans. Working on opening her heart to her partner-to-be, she drew her feelings about him. What emerged was the pink, squiggly vulnerability, the vital, sexual green, and the serenity of light blue. However, there were also disruptive colors—an orange and the tank green that symbolized anxiety and self-protectiveness, respectively. She reported, "I don't have the ability to fantasize transcending. I can't sustain the experience. I can touch it . . . get a quick glimpse of it—like jumping up as high as I can looking to see . . . but I can't sustain it."

After many more drawings and much work on her childhood wounds, Linda had a dream in which a Great Spirit Doll came to her and she had a fantasy of merging with it. As she worked on the dream using the fantasy-enactment process, she reported, "It's so powerful—so much spirit—so much light. It floods me with light. Light pushes everywhere right into my head, but it stops where my eyes are. I say 'No.' Something has to remain watchful, alert, and rational and can't get overwhelmed by that."

More imagery/movement sessions revealed that the Great Spirit was associated with her abusive father who, despite his behavior, had a very loving presence. As a result, Linda did not trust the spiritual. She no longer trusted this ''white light'' and was afraid it would take over, that she would become as corrupt and powerful as her father had been and would seek revenge for the pain she had suffered—perhaps on her mother who was still alive.

Understanding how her spiritual experience had become coupled with the memories of abuse, Linda began to move still further into her freedom. She drew a beautiful image with pink vulnerability, clear sky blue, as well as the previously frightening vital green. She reported that the blue represented the fear of being alive and that it was the color of the sky, very clear and pure, and she felt she could ''grow tall in that color.''

Shortly after saying this, she called this idea *grandiose* but nevertheless followed an impulse to complete the drawing by adding a silver mountain to it. Of this she said:

> The idea of transforming shame, fear, pain, and invalidity into a majestic mountain is very powerful; it feels like a reach. What it symbolizes is not there yet; there is a sense of longing and frustration, hard for me to have faith that I can *be* something without *doing* something. But I know, really know, it's the only way it can happen. I don't know when that will be, but I'll know when it is . . . when I have the mountain inside of me and it's an alive thing and not a piece of rock.

This client went on to marry, have a child, and change her workplace to one where she could be more creative and expressive. She left after just having placed a foot into the transpersonal realm, just having established a relationship with it.

Other clients have had much more dramatic processes of spiritual unfolding than Linda, but she is a particularly good example of the way in which IMM can lead one from more usual psychological issues into transpersonal experiences. Her case thereby suggests that this method may serve as a potential bridge between psychotherapeutic work and transpersonal inquiry.

A PROCESS TOOL WITH MULTIPLE PURPOSES

As mentioned previously, IMM was designed to assist individuals in bringing both digital and analog modes of consciousness to bear on an issue of concern. The value of drawing as a quick entry point to the world of images and feelings is well-known among art therapists, Jungian analysts, and many clinical psychologists. Recent research and theory on the ability of line (Rhyne, 1979), color (Sharpe, 1975), and geometrical relationship (Arnheim, 1966) to encode feeling and thought supports these clinical observations.

The fantasy-enactment stage of IMM uses a combination of Jungian and body-oriented methods to access inner experiences, and role-playing and drama methods for vivifying them. More specifically, I use Jung's method of ''active imagination'' (Jung, 1968) to assist clients in accessing waking dreams but have clients physically enact the images they are observing because I am personally convinced by body-oriented therapists, such as Reich (1968), that it is through movement that we express feeling and through the lack of movement that we block it. Asking clients to enact a fantasy either facilitates emotional expression or increases awareness of the blocks to that expression. To intensify further the fantasy enactment, I incorporated Gestalt role-playing models that help the client to ''become'' different aspects of him- or herself (see Perls, Hefferline, and Goodman, 1951) and Moreno's (1946) technique of psychodrama that uses the therapist and group members to play ''roles'' in scenes from a client's life, employing whatever props, sounds, or effects are necessary to enhance the reality of the experience.

Doing the drawing, exploring the sensory associations and body sensations during mapping, and the fantasy enactment all assist the client in gaining access to inner experience and deepening into this experience. To assist in contextualizing those experiences, accessing symbolic meanings for each part of the drawing and elucidating the overall organization of the drawing were incorporated into the mapping phase of IMM. Through these aspects of mapping, the client is led directly to his or her own interpretation of drawing, in contrast to many art-therapy methods that give much of the responsibility for interpretation to the therapist. In this way, the expression and mapping stages of IMM provide the client with the context in which the fantasy enactment unfolds. When he or she then explores a particular region of the drawing, and, therefore, a particular aspect of his or her psyche, the other aspects are not forgotten. In addition to strengthening the cognitive aspect of the process through expression and mapping, IMM also includes the verbal translation work at the conclusion of the process. This work elucidates the analogies to one's current life situation, grounding the fantasy work in the practicalities of one's daily experience.

Although I know of no other therapeutic or process tool that uses the methods developed in mapping and verbal translation, these methods were inspired in part by the perspective of the cognitive therapists. This therapeutic orientation (see Beck, 1979) posits that it is the meaning we ascribe to a situation that determines our reaction to that situation. IMM is especially powerful in assisting the client to become aware of his or her meanings, for it provides a graphic representation of the inner world, of the meanings and experiences that have structured that world, and a clear understanding of how that private reality is a filter through which we encounter our current reality.

IMM as a Research Tool

Although IMM was not originally designed to function as a research method, it holds some promise for both transpersonal inquiry and for the more general field of phenomenologically oriented research. From my work with clients, it is apparent that IMM enables individuals to access and explore spiritual experiences in the presence of another. This seems essential if one is to have a reasonable expectation of studying spiritual experience. Otherwise, we are dependent on either retrospective reports of what the experience was like, inducing experiences with drugs, or attempts to make complex physiological measurements of advanced meditators or other individuals who are purported to have attained "advanced" levels of spiritual awareness.

Furthermore, by catalyzing a client's process of spiritual unfoldment, one can observe both different levels of awareness and different symbols of the spiritual as they emerge over time. For any given individual, therefore, IMM provides an opportunity to observe the way in which his or her personal issues and conflicts interweave with transpersonal experiences and concerns, the progression and development of spiritual symbols and experiences, the influence of early childhood events and relationships on his or her spiritual symbols and spiritual issues, and the effects of emerging spiritual concerns on his or her everyday life and behavior.

The phenomenological approach is one that accepts human experience as given in our everyday lives, prior to any interpretive reflection, and aims to explicate the meaning of particular experiences within that lived world both for individuals and groups of individuals, searching for essential meanings that are common to human experience (e.g., Van Kaam, 1959). Although IMM has usually been used in an open-ended way, one could easily adapt it to a phenomenologically oriented research study by simply asking the subject to do an abstract drawing of the topic being researched. For example, rather than asking the subject to answer a series of questions on the topic of "really feeling understood" as in Van Kaam's (1959) study, one could ask him or her to draw that experience. By then using the process questions appropriate to mapping that assist the subject in accessing his or her previously nonverbal experience, a very complete expression of that experience could be obtained. A subject

would be able to provide visual, auditory, olfactory, proprioceptive, and kinesthetic images as well as thoughts and feelings associated with the drawing and, thereby, with the topic of "really feeling understood."

IMM may also hold special promise as a method for exploring body–world relationships. Moss (1978), in discussing the theories of Merleau-Ponty and other phenomenologists interested in body experience, has stated that the "lived body" is a "body disposed to possible actions" (p. 85) and that "there is a world for each embodied organism, a world formed by the organism's bodily attitude and activity toward its world (p. 86)." During the fantasy-enactment phase of IMM, it becomes evident that each part of a drawing both represents a particular aspect of the drawer's "psyche" and provides access to particular bodily states including postures, movements, and energetic experiences associated with that aspect. For example, a client's experience of stepping into a light-blue part of a drawing that represents the "higher self" might lead to feelings of expanding, relaxing, and drifting in space. This would reflect a very different bodily sense of the world than, perhaps, entering a red part of the drawing that represents the "angry self" and that involves a bodily sense of being thwarted and confined and wanting to "break out." Indeed, every part of the drawing has bodily states associated with it. Thus the drawing itself would provide an opportunity to explore the phenomenology of the body–world relationship.

IN CONCLUSION

Much time has elapsed since I discovered the "other mind" in me. The method that I developed as a result of that experience has been used successfully as a psychotherapy and growth tool, a means of enhancing communication in couples, families, and work groups, and as a method for accessing intuitions as well as creative and spiritual resources. It is my hope that it can also serve as a research tool for the exploration of human consciousness.

REFERENCES

Arnheim, R. (1966). *Toward a psychology of art*. Berkeley and Los Angeles: University of California Press.
Assagioli, R. (1972). *Psychosynthesis*. New York: Hobbs, Dorman & Co.
Beck, Aaron T. (1979). *Cognitive therapy and the emotional disorders*. New York: Guildford.
Deikman, A. (1974). Bimodal consciousness. In R. E. Ornstein (Ed.), *The nature of human consciousness* (pp. 67–86). San Francisco: W. H. Freeman.
Grof, S. (1976). *Realms of the human unconscious: Observations from LSD research*. New York: Dutton.

Jung, C. G. (1968). *Analytical psychology: Its theory and practice*. New York: Random, Vintage.

Moreno, J. L. (1946). *Psycho-drama*. New York: Beacon.

Moss, D. (1978). Brain, body and world: Perspectives on body-image. In R. S. Valle & M. King (Eds.), *Existential-phenomenological alternatives in psychology* (pp. 73–93). New York: Oxford University Press.

Perls, F. S., Hefferline, R. F., & Goodman, P. (1951). *Gestalt therapy: Excitement and growth in the human personality*. New York: Julian.

Reich, W. (1968). *Character analysis*. New York: Farrar, Straus & Giroux.

Rhyne, J. (1979). *Drawings as personal constructs: A study in visual dynamics*. Unpublished doctoral dissertation, Santa Cruz, University of California.

Samples, R. (1976). *Metaphoric mind: A celebration of creative consciousness*. Reading, MA: Addison-Wesley.

Schneier, S. (1980). *Metaphoric mind*. Unpublished manuscript. San Francisco.

Sharpe, D. T. (1975). *The psychology of color and design*. Totowa, NJ: Littlefield-Adams.

Tart, C. (1975). *States of consciousness*. New York: Dutton.

Valle, R. S. & King, M. (1978). An introduction to existential-phenomenological thought in psychology. In R. S. Valle & M. King (Eds.), *Existential-phenomenological alternatives for psychology* (pp. 3–17). New York: Oxford University Press.

Van Kaam, A. L. (1959). Phenomenal analysis: Exemplified by a study of the experience of "really feeling understood." *Journal of Individual Psychology 15*(1), 66–72.

20

States of Consciousness and Transpersonal Psychology

Ralph Metzner

The purposes of this chapter are (a) to situate current thinking on consciousness in the field of transpersonal psychology, (b) to formulate a distinction between states, levels, and stages of consciousness, and (c) to propose a heuristic model for the study of altered states of consciousness. Transpersonal psychology is concerned primarily with those aspects of human experience and behavior that lie beyond the personal, interpersonal, and social aspects studied in other psychological schools. Following Walsh and Vaughan (1980) in their distinction between transpersonal context, content, and process, I see the study of consciousness and its transformations as the central content area for transpersonal psychology.

The question as to the most appropriate and fruitful methodology for consciousness research or transpersonal psychology in general is still very much an open question, and my personal belief is that the approaches derived from phenomenology and the conventional quantitative psychological research methods have complementary contributions to make to this endeavor. As Hilgard (1980) notes:

> Among philosophers of science, a position better described as critical realism has gradually replaced the various forms of positivism, including operationalism. Critical realism allows a place for phenomenological thinking without assigning a privileged place to the knowledge available through introspection.

It should be noted that phenomenologists in the philosophical tradition of Husserl argue that phenomenological psychology should be based on the description of lived experience and not on introspection.

Having stated something of my own methodological predilections, I would like to further address the question, What is research? To *research* an area, whether in the sciences or the humanities, is to "search again": Initially, we explore some territory or field, as we *search* out landmarks and key features using our own observations and perceptions; then we *re-search*, we go over the same territory as a cartographer or surveyor might in order to be able to communicate and explain our findings to the larger community of scholars or scientists. Some have spoken of this same distinction as between exploration and explanation or between hypothesis generating and hypothesis testing. Phenomenological research is similary and implicitly concerned with two phases: first, the lived experience as described in the individual's own words and second, the explication of the inherent structures or themes of that descriptive text, for the purpose of communicating with others.

In transpersonal psychology, the *search* is the quest for personal growth, or spiritual understanding, or self-realization, as it has been described in the world's spiritual traditions, and as it is pursued today, whether assisted by a psychotherapist, guided by a guru, or carried out individually. Two recent books might be cited as examples of consciousness research from a transpersonal psychology perspective. In *Opening to Inner Light* (Metzner, 1986), I present 10 classical metaphors of the

Ralph Metzner • California Institute of Integral Studies, 765 Ashbury Street, San Francisco, California 94117.

process of self-transformation as described in Asian and Western philosophical–religious traditions. In the book *Transformations of Consciousness* (Wilber, Engler, & Brown, 1986), the authors describe transformations of consciousness, both psychopathological, in the direction of psychic disturbance, and psychotherapeutic, in the direction of psychic health, from the perspective of Wilber's integrated developmental model (of which more will be said later).

In his review of the history and current status of consciousness in psychology, Hilgard (1980) pointed out how serious psychological interest in the topic, outlawed since the beginning of the century by the alliance between behaviorism, positivist philosophy, and operationalist methodology that dominated academic psychology for half a century, came back into mainstream psychology by several roads. One was the gradual rise of cognitive psychology through studies in perception (Miller, Bruner, Neisser), imagery (Holt, Singer), psycholinguistics (Chomsky), and information-processing models derived from cybernetics. Another was the growing interest in Piaget's model of stages of cognitive development, as distinct from Freud's pyschosexual and Erikson's psychosocial stages. The numerical increase in researchers working in this general area, from the disciplines not only of cognitive psychology but the neurosciences, computer sciences, and linguistics has been so dramatic that a new field, *cognitive science,* has been born and now claims the allegiance of many experimental psychologists interested in problems of perception, learning, and cognition (see also Gardner, 1985).

The concept, *states of consciousness,* became a focus of research interest in the 1960s with the advent of psychedelic or "consciousness-expanding" drugs and with discoveries linking brain electrical activity and the sleep–dream cycle. The rapid eye movement (REM) phenomenon was the operationalist's dream: an objective method for the study of subjective experience. The notion arose of a normal, ordinary, baseline, or consensus state of consciousness (Tart, 1972) and the various altered states, or alternate states (Zinberg, 1977), as modulations of that baseline state. The altered states (ASCs for short) studied within this new framework range from the familiar everyday states of dreaming and sleeping, through various moderately usual states involved in creativity, daydreaming, biofeedback, or hypnosis, to the unusual and rare states triggered by psychedelic drugs, meditation, mystical experiences, and sensory isolation. This afforded a new framework or classification system for these different states of consciousness. However, as Hilgard rightly pointed out, classification does not imply causation: By saying that someone is in an altered state we have not given any explanation but merely a description or

categorization. Many hundreds of studies have been done during the past 20 years on ASCs within this kind of general framework, and several multiple-author books have been published (Davidson & Davidson, 1980; Goleman & Davidson, 1979; Pope & Singer, 1978; Sugarman & Tarter, 1978; Valle & von Eckartsberg, 1981; Wolman & Ullman, 1986).

Several important theoretical contributions to this literature should be mentioned here. Andrew Weil (1972) suggested that there exists an innate human drive to experience periodic episodes of non-ordinary states of awareness and that this could be seen in certain childrens' behavior, such as spinning, and in adults' experimentation with consciousness-altering agents. Roland Fischer (1971) put forward his so-called arousal model in which he arranged ecstatic and meditative states on a "perception–hallucination continuum." This continuum varies in degrees of ergotropic and trophotropic arousal, and Fischer used both neurophysiological and experiential data to define the points along this continuum.

Another contribution was Charles Tart's "systems approach" to states of consciousness, expounded in his book *States of Consciousness* (Tart, 1975). According to this view, consciousness is defined as consisting of "*structures* or *systems* of the mind/brain that act on information to transform it in various ways." A discrete state of consciousness is a "dynamic pattern or configuration of psychological structures" (p.5); and, in altered states, this pattern differs experientially from the *baseline state.* Tart also proposed that "state-specific sciences" are necessary in order to organize and evaluate knowledge that one might obtain in an altered state.

Another major theoretical contribution to this field is the work of Stanislav Grof (1976, 1985) who, starting from his findings with LSD psychotherapy (both psycholytic and psychedelic), developed a classification model of the kinds of experiences subjects have in such therapy: These range from aesthetic experiences, psychodynamic childhood-related insight experiences, and "perinatal" experiences associated with four different substages of the birth process, to transpersonal experiences. These latter, in turn, were divided into extensions within the framework of "objective reality," both temporal (e.g., ancestral memories) and spatial (e.g., animal identification), and extensions beyond objective reality (e.g., spiritistic, extraterrestrial, archetypal experiences). This model represents a comprehensive classification of states of consciousness *according to content* that is not necessarily limited to psychedelic-induced states.

In many ways, it appears that the new interest in the study of states of consciousness, to date still limited to a small minority of psychologists, is a kind of reconnection with the interests of William James who is increasingly being acknowledged as the father of American psychology. In his *Varieties of Religious Experience*, first published in 1902, James (1936) gave a masterful account of religious transformative ("conversion") experiences, weaving together the literature of mysticism with published phenomenological accounts of such experiences. "Exceptional mental states" was a long-standing area of interest for James, and his previously unpublished and fascinating 1896 Harvard lectures on this topic, including sections on dreams, hypnotism, automatisms, hysteria, multiple personality, demoniacal possession, and witchcraft, have been published in an annotated edition (Taylor, 1983).

The burgeoning interest in states of consciousness during the 1960s and 1970s was accompanied by a turning to the philosophical literature of the Asian traditions that, in their systems of meditation and yoga, contain remarkably sophisticated and complex models of human experience. The following are important examples of this kind of conceptual and cross-cultural bridge building. Leary, Metzner, and Alpert (1964) adapted the *Tibetan Book of the Dead* as a metaphoric account of psychedelic experience. Goleman's (1977) book, *Varieties of Meditative Experiences*, suggested a twofold classification of meditation paths derived from the Theravada Buddhist school to develop a comparative analysis of several different Eastern and Western teachings. Ken Wilber's (1977, 1983) series of books have developed what he calls a "spectrum model" of consciousness that attempts to integrate Western psychology's developmental stages with several different Eastern teachings on levels of development. Metzner's (1971) *Maps of Consciousness* described several systems of consciousness development from both the Asian and the Western esoteric tradition and compared them to Western psychology.

All these works could equally well be described as examples of transpersonal psychology, or East–West psychology. The latter is a field explicitly devoted to this kind of cross-cultural comparison and integration.

STATES, LEVELS, AND STAGES OF CONSCIOUSNESS

Historically and philosophically, there have been two main metaphors or analogies for consciousness. One is a *spatial or geographical metaphor:* Consciousness is like space (as the Buddhists emphasize); It is like a terrain that can be mapped out, one can have a "cartography" of consciousness. The notion of going or being on an inner journey, of exploring inner worlds, of being in a "different state" or "in another world" all implicitly assume this metaphor. The other is a *temporal or biographical metaphor:* Consciousness is like the river of time. Expressions such as "stream of thought" (William James) or "flow of experience" imply this temporal metaphor. It is interesting that time and space, which Kant said were the *a priori* categories of all experience, should provide the primary (implicit) analogies for the understanding and description of consciousness and its modifications.

I offer the following definition: "A person's *state of consciousness is the system, context, or field* within which the different aspects of the mind, the contents of consciousness, including thoughts, feelings, sensations, perceptions, images, memories, and so forth, function in patterned interrelationships." A state of consciousness then is *altered* if the functioning of these interrelated elements is significantly different, for a definite period of real time, from the mode of functioning in the *baseline* state. The baseline state is also referred to as "ordinary," "waking," or "normal" consciousness. As Tart (1975) has pointed out, this normal state is culturally relative; we learn, through conditioning and modeling, what are the normally expected and consensually validated experiences in our culture. Hence I follow the suggestion to call this baseline *consensus consciousness*, which implies that different cultures may have a quite different range of states and levels of consciousness to which they have access.

I suggest that the major *content categories* of consciousness—what we experience when we are "in" a certain state of consciousness—are the following: thoughts/ideas/beliefs/attitudes; feelings/emotions/ moods; sensations/perceptions/images; sense of time and space; sense (or image) of body, and sense (or image) of self. Tart (1975) has a list of "ten major subsystems [collections of related structures] that show important variations over known d-ASC's" (p. 5). His list mostly overlaps with mine, except that he distinguishes exteroception (perception of external stimuli) and interoception (perception of internal body stimuli) as two different perceptual structures. He also lists memory and subconscious as separate systems. I regard memory as being part of the major categories I named before; thus we can have remembered (past) thoughts, remembered feelings, and so on. Similarly, I do not see subconscious contents as a separate category; instead I assume we have both conscious and unconscious cognitive, affective, and perceptual contents (processes, structures).

State of consciousness refers to an experience that has a definite beginning, a certain duration in "real" or clock time, and an ending, at which consciousness returns to the baseline. During that period of time, the various content components are functioning in a different than usual mode: Thoughts, emotions, and perceptions are all changed. We do not say we are in an altered state if only our thinking has changed, if we changed our mind, or adopted a different set of beliefs; nor would we recognize an altered state if merely our feeling or mood is changed. But if both thought and feeling are different, and if, in addition, perception is changed, particularly perceptions of the world of time and space (e.g., greater perceptual depth, colors enhanced, sounds different, time flowing more slowly), then we are clearly in a different state. If, in addition, the body image and the self-image are different, as they are in mystical, psychotic, and psychedelic states, then we have profound and radical alteration of the total state of consciousness—a state in which the normal, consensual framework of our view of reality has been suspended, eliminated, or transcended. It is characteristic of such profound ASCs that the person experiencing them is at a loss for words to describe them. The mystical experience is invariably described as ineffable, which supports the notion that linguistic categories are "state-specific"; that is, they cannot be applied to the experience of an altered state.

States must be distinguished from traits. Psychologists speak of "state anxiety" (how anxious you are now) and "trait anxiety" (how anxious you generally tend to be). William James was careful to make a distinction between having a religious experience and developing traits of saintliness—the two are not necessarily correlated. Traits are relatively enduring dispositions to think, feel, perceive, and act in certain ways, whereas states have a definite duration in time with a discernible beginning and ending during which psychic functioning is noticeably different.

Traits may be regarded as antecedents of altered states; they are part of the predisposing *set* or *attitude* that can be a major determinant of the content of an altered state. For example, introverts experience an alcohol intoxication very differently than extroverts. Trait changes may also occur as a consequence of an altered state; there may be changes in behavior, habits, or attitudes, following an altered state. On the other hand, some altered states may occur, even profound ones, and leave the individual's outer behavior relatively unchanged; perhaps only the attitude or predominant feeling tone is different.

Within the context of psychotherapy, or spiritual growth disciplines, the more enduring personality (trait) changes are of course more interesting, as well as more difficult to bring about, than temporary altered states. The spiritual traditions of East and West almost unanimously suggest that one should avoid being seduced and distracted by the glamor of "visions," "illusions" (*makyo*), "powers" (*siddhis*), and special experiences, and keep up one's spiritual practices until lasting changes in consciousness (perspective, understanding, attitude) are brought about.

States must be distinguished from levels. States, as already noted, are divisions of psychic time; we are in a sleep state, a waking state, a dreaming state, a trance state, and so on for certain definite periods. Levels of consciousness, on the other hand, which are also referred to sometimes as "planes" or "dimensions" of consciousness, are structural features of the human psyche. Whereas Western academic psychology has tended to blur or ignore this distinction, the Indian and other Asian traditions have been quite clear on the distinction.

Thus in the *Upanishads* and Vedanta texts, we read of the five *koshas* ("sheaths," "envelopes") that surround the central, formless, imperceptible, unknowable, illumined spiritual Self, or *Atman* (Deutsch, 1969). These sheaths are arranged in increasing degrees of subtlety: The densest is the sheath made of food—the physical body; next is the sheath made of *prana,* or subtle energy; next is the sheath made of *manas,* which is sensori-motor mentality and imagination, what some call "desire-mind"; the fourth level "up" (speaking metaphorically) is the sheath of *vijnana,* or understanding, intelligence, knowing mind. The fifth *kosha* is composed of pure *ananda,* bliss, or joy. Sometimes two additional levels above these five are mentioned—a sheath composed of pure awareness (*chit*) and a sheath composed of pure being (*sat*).

I am not concerned here with determining the truth or validity of this particular metaphoric conception of psychic structure. I only wish to point out that the same Upanishad texts that describe and refer to these *koshas* also refer to four different states of consciousness and describe the relationship between them. The first state is the waking state (*jagrat*) in which we are identified with the "food sheath," the physical body. Next is the dream state (*svapna*) in which we are aware of and identified with the sheaths or bodies made of *prana, manas,* and *vijnana,* life energy, sense mind, and understanding. These three together are sometimes referred to as the "inner action organ" (*antahkarana*). In the deep, dreamless sleep state (*sushupti*), we are aware of the bliss sheath, in other words, a state free of particular thoughts or images, a state we experience as pleasurable. The fourth state in Vedanta, know as *turiya* or the "fourth," is entered during deep meditation and is equated with *samadhi,* a unitive state of absorption, where subject–object distinctions are transcended (Deutsch, 1969).

Other Asian and Western esoteric teachings (sometimes referred to as the "perennial tradition") have similar structural models, although the descriptive terms used may differ and the number of levels may vary. According to theosophy and related teachings in the West, there are seven planes of consciousness that correspond with seven "outer" planes of reality. These are usually depicted in graphic form as arranged in horizontal layers, like the image of a cake, with the physical or material body or "vehicle" as the lowest and densest, the "gross body" in the quaint language of nineteenth-century occult philosophy. Other planes are referred to as etheric, astral, mental, causal, subtle, intuitive, buddhic, atmic, and so on. They are regarded as relatively permanent features of the psychic landscape that one traverses during meditation. During a given state of consciousness, such as a dream, a meditation, or a drug state, we may be in, or tune in to, or be identified with one or more of these inner levels or dimensions of our psychic totality. These inner sheaths or bodies are assumed to always be there even when our awareness is not tuned to that particular frequency (to use the favored radio metaphor of contemporary esoteric literature).

The very ancient shamanic cultures in all parts of the world speak of three "worlds"—the upper world, middle world, and lower world—that can be visited by the shaman in a "journey" or trance (Halifax, 1982). Here, "journey" is a metaphor for the "shamanic state of consciousness" (Harner, 1980) just as "trip" became the 1960s' metaphor for the psychedelic state. "Lower world" and "upper world" are metaphors for the realms, or domains, or planes, or levels of consciousness one visits, or dwells in, *during* such altered states.

The evidence supports the need for distinguishing states and levels, as can be inferred from the following observations: (a) the same state, for example, an LSD-induced "trip" or a shamanic journey induced by drumming, can lead the individual to very different realms or levels of consciousness (e.g., hell, paradise, the astral plane); and (b) the identical level or dimension of consciousness (e.g., *nirvana*, or the "body of bliss") can be approached or entered in different states, or from different states—for example, in meditation, on a psychedelic trip, or during a spontaneous mystical rapture.

The Western philosophic and religious traditions also have multidimensional models of the human psyche. The medieval European Christian notion was of the human being as a four-tiered being consisting of spirit, soul, mind, and body (Smith, 1976). The four worlds of the Jewish Kabbalistic tradition are called emanation (*aziluth*), creation (*beriah*), formation (*yezirah*), and action (*asiah*). Later developments in European philosophy favored a three-level model consisting of body, mind, and soul; or the gross, the subtle, and the causal realms (Wilber, 1983). With the philosophical revolution formulated by Descartes, Western thought opted for a two-tiered, dualistic framework: the human soul was a "rational soul," hence equated to intellect or "thinking thing" (*res cogitans*), to be distinguished from material objects and bodies that consist of "extended substance"

(*res extensa*). In twentieth-century thought, positivist philosophy and behaviorist psychology conspired to reduce the two levels to one: Only physical behavior was judged to be susceptible to scientific observation, and hence only the physical realm and body were "real." This leap from epistemological preference to ontological prejudice could perhaps be expressed, in recognition of Descartes, in the motto *"I behave therefore I am."*

Contemporary depth psychology also has a conception of levels of consciousness—what psychoanalytic theorists refer to as Freud's "topographical model": the conscious, the preconscious, and the unconscious. To these, a Jungian would want to add the distinction between personal unconscious and collective unconscious. Psychoanalytic theorists observe the same distinction between states and levels when they say that, in dreams or in schizophrenia (both altered states), the contents from the unconscious may overflow into the conscious, or dominate conscious thinking.

States of consciousness, and levels, must be distinguished from stages of consciousness development. Whereas levels of consciousness refer to the permanent structures of the psyche, stages refer to a progressive development of some kind, a path of growth or spiritual development that has many steps or stages. Western psychology has concerned itself with the stages of psychological development from infancy to childhood and through the various stages of the adult life cycle ending with old age and dying. Eastern traditions, on the other hand, have concerned themselves with possible levels of consciousness development beyond the socially well-adjusted norm, culminating in a stage variously referred to as a sage, a master, an adept, or a saint. Those who imagine that a Yoga or Zen master is always in a state of enlightenment or bliss or *nirvana* are confusing stages and states. There is every reason to suppose that advanced adepts still cycle through sleep and dream phases of consciousness and also enter, at different times, into deeper states of meditation. The nineteenth-century Indian saint Ramakrishna, for example, would often spontaneously enter a state of *samadhi* while talking to his disciples and would then return from that state (Mukerji, 1973).

On the other hand, those who describe spiritual development as consisting of a step-by-step ascent through fixed levels of consciousness are confusing levels and stages. Ken Wilber, who made a heroic attempt to bridge Western and Asian theories of development by formulating a continuous succession of stages, with the transpersonal "bands" following the existential and personal bands (of the spectrum), drew a forceful distinction between levels as permanent, enduring components and stages as transition phases of consciousness (Wilber, 1983). But, nevertheless, his whole model postulates a succession of stages that one goes through that correspond to the levels or bands on the spectrum.

There are two grounds for questioning the validity of this conception. One is Wilber's application of child development as an analogy to spiritual development: according to his model, one adds the spiritual stages to the completed cycle of child development, thereby continuing the progression. As an alternative, some view spiritual development not as the acquisition of new kinds of cognitive skills, or even transcendence of prior levels, but rather a kind of interior development analogous, perhaps, to the process of ripening. Another ground for questioning his model is the possibility that persons in more advanced stages of development might not simply be on a high plane of consciousness all the time but rather have the ability to access many more levels than the ordinary person and function effectively at those levels. This kind of notion is implicit in the concept of the magician or magus who travels between heaven and earth and uses the powers of many realms. I believe that it will be one of the tasks of transpersonal psychology in the next decades to arrive at some consensus as to the nature, number, and characteristics of different levels of human consciousness, the stages of development one passes through, and the varieties of altered states one might experience.

A HEURISTIC MODEL OF ALTERED STATES OF CONSCIOUSNESS

Heuristics are open-ended procedures and strategies in both everyday reasoning and scientific investigation (Wimsatt, 1986) that function as guidelines and supports to discovery; they are distinguished from algorithms that are closed systems of logical inferences from axiomatic premises. In proposing a heuristic model for the study of states of consciousness, I want to emphasize that the model (Figure 1) is not explanatory and not reductionistic; it does not explain or explicate the underlying principles or mechanisms by which the system operates. However, it is useful for ordering and comparing observations made, and it may also facilitate new insights and understanding.

The model is an extension or generalization of what was referred to earlier as the "set and setting hypothesis" in psychedelic research. This hypothesis, which was originally formulated by Leary, Litwin, and Metzner (1963), and has since been widely accepted by researchers in that field, states that the particular contents of psychedelic experiences are a function of the individual's *set* (expectation, intention, personality, mood, values, attitudes, beliefs) and the *setting* (context, physical and social environment, expectations and behavior of others present,

especially any guide, therapist, healer, or teacher). The drug was said to be a trigger, or catalyst, of the change in state of awareness but not to have any content *per se*. Psychedelics were also referred to as "nonspecific awareness amplifiers."

The generalized set-and-setting model states (as a heuristic assumption) that for all altered states and the ordinary, consensus reality state, the *contents* of consciousness (i.e., the particular thoughts, feelings, images, perceptions, sensations, etc.) that we experience are determined primarily by the set (the internal factors mentioned before) and the setting (external environmental factors). The agent, stimulus, or procedure that induces the transition to an altered mode of functioning may be called "trigger" or "catalyst"; there is no direct or obvious relationship between known characteristics of the catalyst and the subsequent changes. Psychedelic drugs are obvious catalysts, as are hypnotic induction procedures, meditative techniques, sensory isolation, rhythmic drumming, powerful emotions, music, and so forth. Even in situations of altered states where no obvious trigger can be observed, it is heuristically useful to assume there is one and to search for what it was that induced the crossing of the threshold into an altered state.

Having stated the basic assumption, we must immediately qualify it: In the case of the ordinary, normal states (waking, sleeping, dreaming) with which we are all familiar, there may not be an identifiable trigger. One could postulate, in reductionist fashion, that there is a certain concentration of neurotransmitters (e.g., serotonin) in certain brain systems that triggers falling asleep or waking up. My preference is to say that these alterations of consciousness are *cyclic*; that is, at certain phases and points of the circadian (24-hour) cycle, we transition from sleep to waking and vice versa; and we cycle through dream states following the ultradian (90-minute) cycle, which also modulates the waking state (Rossi, 1986). This still leaves open the possibility that there may be unusual sleep, dream, or waking phases that are triggered by identifiable catalysts (e.g., the alarm clock that wakes us up or the sedative that puts us to sleep).

In Figure 1, an arrow, which roughly signifies "influences," goes from "set" to "setting," pointing to the obvious fact that the intentions, beliefs, and expectations of the individual will influence the choice of setting or context. Thus it could be said that intention (set) is primary over environment (setting) as a determinant of human experience and action. This assumption is supported by a study that showed that instructions ("set") given to subjects merely to pay attention to their subjective experience, without any other alteration of external stimuli, can induce a mild ASC with sensory changes similar to those in psychedelic states (Hunt & Chefurka,

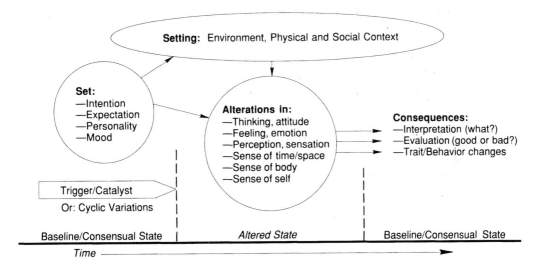

Figure 1. General model of altered states, showing the transition into an ASC being triggered or catalyzed by an external stimulus (or by cyclic variations), and the contents of the ASC determined by factors of set and setting.

1976). "Spontaneous altered-state effects can be elicited in short time periods via subjective set alone" (Hunt & Chefurka, 1976, p. 876). Perhaps there is a parallel here to phenomenology's insistence on the primacy of intentionality.

Although no general consensus exists as to the number and classification of altered states, the heuristic model here presented does offer a framework within which comparative investigations can be conducted. To conclude this chapter, I will briefly review how this model applies to the major presently recognized kinds of altered states.

As already indicated, I regard *waking, sleeping,* and *dreaming* as states that vary normally and regularly on the psychobiological circadian and ultradian cycles, rather than being "triggered." *Daydreaming* is probably not enough of a change in overall psychic functioning to be regarded as an altered state but may consist, rather, in a switch to a more fantastic, imaginal, "primary process" mode of thought following the same ultradian cycle as night dreaming. This idea is supported by the studies that show that our thinking becomes more fantastic and dreamlike every 90-minutes or so (Rossi, 1986). These cycles only account for the timing of the altered mode of consciousness, as the trigger functions in other, more anomalous states. As far as the *content* of dreams (night or day) is concerned, it is incontestable that intention and setting are the major determinants of content. Our dream contents are shaped by prior thoughts, feelings, and other experiences and they are also influenced by environmental factors such as sounds, temperature, and ambiance.

In the case of *hypnosis*, although the long-standing debate still continues as to whether it involves a special state or not, the present model merely holds that *if* there is a change of state, the trigger is apparently the induction procedure (verbal or nonverbal); the contents are a function of the subject's internal set; and the hypnotist's instructions are the primary setting factor. The neodissociationist view of hypnotic phenomena put forward by Hilgard (1986) implies the existence of a kind of parallel stream of awareness and that the individual in the hypnotic trance can be induced to switch back and forth between these modes, each one affording access to different information but unaware of the other. Multiple personality disorder (MPD) is generally assumed to involve dissociative processes similar to hypnosis, with the difference that here we have stable personality structures that coexist in the same individual, each with incomplete or no knowledge of the others, in other words, dissociation within the ordinary waking consciousness state (Beahrs, 1982). The process of one or another of a multiple set of personalities taking control over the ego and the body is known as *switching* and is analogous to the crossing of a threshold into a different state of consciousness.

In the Asian systems of *meditation*, we encounter a whole range of methods for bringing about changes in consciousness and a whole series of descriptions of different states attained by these methods. Here the trigger or catalyst for the ASC is the meditative technique, whether this be the *concentrative*, where one focuses attention on some internal or external stimulus and gradually becomes more and more absorbed in that object of concentration, or the *insight* or *mindfulness* kind, in which the meditator merely observes the ongoing processes of awareness (such as the flow of breath or the stream of thought) and gradually becomes less and less identified with these processes (Goleman, 1977). Clearly, the intention and predisposition of the meditator is the prime factor in these states, and this is influenced by training and tradition; the setting, the characteristics of the environment, and the meditation teacher or guru are equally important. Although early Western research on meditation tended to equate it with relaxation and/or self-hypnosis and to look for applications in the areas of stress management, health maintenance, and cognitive efficiency, recent work has been more sophisticated, distinguishing between different forms of meditation on both electrophysiological and psychological variables. Concepts such as "deautomatization" (suspension of automatic, habitual modes of perception) and "attention redeployment" (shift from external to internal orientation) are being used to account for the state changes that may occur in meditation (Shapiro & Walsh, 1984).

The nature of the *psychedelic drug* experience has already been discussed in the framework of the present model. Here, the differing roles of trigger, set, and setting are clear and easily distinguishable. The broader class of *psychoactive drugs*, which includes stimulants, depressants, and narcotics, can also be regarded as catalysts of ASCs; here it appears that the content of the experience is much more limited and invariant, and thus the pharmacological trigger plays a relatively greater role (and set a lesser, though not insignificant, role).

Environments of *sensory isolation*, or sensory deprivation as it was called in the early studies, are clearly capable of triggering quite profound altered states. As with dreams and hypnotic trances, the content and value of the experience is a function of the individual's preparation and intention. Environments with restricted sensory input have a long history in the religious and contemplative traditions as adjuncts and supports to spiritual insight and mystical experience (e.g., the hermitage, monastic cell, solitary desert vision quest). And the reports of lost explorers or sea voyagers have supported the notion that unexpected and profound transformative experiences are possible in such environments, their nature and content very much a function of attitude and predisposition.

Under the general heading of *sound* as a trigger of altered states, there is a vast variety of phenomena that have yet to be studied extensively. Drumming appears to be among the most prevalent triggers in shamanism, next to hallucinogenic plants and solitude vision quests (Halifax, 1982; Harner, 1980). The drumming facilitates a "shamanic state of consciousness" in which the shaman goes on a "journey" to obtain healing or diagnostic information or spiritual counsel. It has been proposed that the steady beat drumming produces auditory entrainment of cerebral and perhaps also cardiac rhythms. Likewise, in many spiritual traditions, incantations and invocations of spiritual energy or presence are accomplished through singing, *mantra,* or prayer. Chanting and singing have been important in religious ceremonies (e.g., Gregorian chant, hymns, gospel spirituals) since ancient times.

Psychotic states, though not included in most discussions of ASCs, clearly belong there, especially if one considers the initial stage or "break," or acute onset of schizophrenia. In the framework of the heuristic model, we can here consider schizophrenia (and other forms of psychosis such as paranoia, mania, depression) neither as disease, as in the medical model, nor as a communication disorder, as in the psychosocial model, but as a certain kind of extreme ASC that may or may not result in long-lasting personality changes. Although the "psychotomimetic" theory of psychedelic states equated psychosis and the effects of psychedelics, it is now accepted that there is only a partial overlap between these two experiences; *some* hallucinogenic experiences (the so-called bad trips) have psychotic-like features.

The trigger for a psychotic ASC might be a stressful interpersonal or environmental event occuring within the biological context of genetic predisposition as well as the social–familial context of chronically ambivalent "double-bind" sorts of communication patterns; in some instances, a specific trigger might be hard to find or be apparently absent. The presence of psychic, religious, or transpersonal elements in some schizophrenics has led several investigators to develop alternate models for the understanding and "treatment" of this condition. The Jungian analyst John Perry (1974) has pointed to the mythic overtones of self-renewal in psychotic process. The Grofs (1986) have developed the concept of *spiritual emergence* in which a kundalini syndrome, a shamanic journey, mythic renewal, psychic opening, emergence of karmic patterns, and possession states can be seen as powerful, inherently transformative altered state experiences that may not lead to psychotic disintegration if they are supported and respected, rather than treated and aborted with antipsychotic medication.

A number of twentieth-century accounts of *mystical experiences* have described such states in language relatively free from the theological and dogmatic assumptions of any one particular religion; William James, with his survey of religious conversion experiences, Bucke's concept of "cosmic consciousness," and Maslow's "peak experience" might be cited as examples. Psychoanalysts have tended to give pathological interpretations of religious experience, categorizing them as examples of "regression," "primitive thinking," or "delusions of grandeur." Such attitudes are likely to result in misunderstanding and inappropriate treatment of individuals who are having such experiences. Transpersonal psychologists who have studied this area have concluded that unusual transcendent and mystical experiences may be much more common than one would think (Thomas & Cooper, 1981).

Several authors have proposed criteria for identifying mystical experiences, that is, common themes that occur in the personal accounts of such experiences. Lukoff (1985) has identified criteria for differentiating mystical and psychotic experiences, with the possibility of overlapping features (i.e., mystical experiences with psychotic features and psychotic states with religious features). It seems clear that either state can be triggered by psychedelics or other catalysts, or can occur without the presence of any identifiable trigger. Also indisputable is the notion that the content of such experiences is a function of set and setting. The word *psychedelic* does not refer to a particular kind of experience but rather to a trigger of different kinds of experience.

The concept of altered states has also played a significant role in parapsychology; numerous studies have been done to test the idea of *psi-conducive states*, that is, states of consciousness in which psi capacities such as telepathy or clairvoyance manifest more easily or strongly. Dreams, hypnosis, meditation, psychedelics, and biofeedback have all been shown to facilitate psi under certain conditions (Krippner & George, 1986; Tart, 1977). *Psi* refers to perceptual phenomena that appear to violate the constraints and conditions of ordinary perception; thus, it does not appear that there is a special psi state but rather that in various types of ASCs, psi perceptions can be facilitated. The one exception to this conclusion are *out-of-body experiences* (OBEs) that are comparable to what the occult literature refers to as "astral projection" and that clearly involve major alterations of perception of body, self, time, and space. Gabbard and Twemlow (1986) have published an important paper describing and differentiating the reported phenomenology of OBEs from other similar states of "altered mind/body perception," including depersonalization, autoscopy, schizophrenia, and near-death experiences (NDEs).

Through the work of Raymond Moody, Kenneth Ring, and others, the prevalence and phenomenological features of *near-death experiences* have been extensively studied and described (Ring, 1984). Here, the trigger of the altered state is the sudden and unexpected awareness that one is dying or dead, and the characteristic features are constant across many different personality characteristics and prior religious beliefs of the individual. In this situation, set and setting seem to play a relatively minor role in determining content. Indeed, this is one situation in which the deliberate preparation

for or induction of the altered state is physically impossible and humanly undesirable.

There are other kinds of altered states that have been identified. In particular, some believe that ASCs may occur in creative activity as well as some forms of psychotherapy and biofeedback. Analogously to the role of ASCs in psi, I would postulate that certain states facilitate the creative *inspiration* phase, with the *expression* phase requiring focused waking consciousness. I suggest that one regard creativity, psychotherapy, and learning as areas of *application* of altered states, rather than being another class of ASCs. They are areas in which ASCs may spontaneously occur and also be purposefully utilized or applied. Thus techniques derived from hypnosis, meditation, yogic *pranayama*, shamanism, and psychedelics have all been employed in psychotherapy to bring about changed states of consciousness with therapeutic import. Most of these same techniques have also been employed in learning situations, as for example in the *suggestopedia* of Lozanov (Ostrander & Schroeder, 1979) in which a relaxed, receptive state is shown to facilitate learning. Biofeedback, as commonly applied, does not seem to induce an ASC, although the use of EEG hemispheric synchronization feedback may induce a kind of deep trance analogous to some meditative and hypnotic states.

The cross-cultural study of *trance states* may yield further valuable information. It appears that, besides hallucinogens and drumming, techniques of breath and ritual dance movement are also widely used to induce trancelike states (Wavell, Butt, & Epton, 1967). "Speaking in tongues," or glossolalia, is another set of phenomena that has been analyzed from the perspective of altered states of consciousness (Goodman, 1972). The ability of certain body postures to induce special states, as found in shamanic practice, has also been demonstrated experimentally (Goodman, 1986).

There is, in addition, a universal human experience that has not, as far as I know, been extensively studied from an ASC perspective, although it clearly would be both appropriate and interesting to do so. I am speaking of the experience of "falling in love," in which thoughts, feelings, and perceptions (of time, space, body, and self) are all altered in significant ways in response to the "trigger" of the beloved person and in which the contents of consciousness are clearly determined by set and setting. Some work has been published on sexual orgasm as an altered state (Davidson, 1980).

I have attempted, through this brief survey of a variety of altered states of consciousness, to indicate the heuristic utility of the generalized set-setting-trigger model in researching and understanding these important phenomena of human experience. The heuristic research model here presented does not specify or limit the methodological assumptions or procedures one wishes to adopt. The various altered states can be, I believe, usefully and productively studied within this framework, whether one uses survey and questionnaire methods, group comparisons and correlations with personality variables, or whether one uses the phenomenological method of close and detailed empathic inquiry into the nuances of a particular individual's phenomenal experience.

REFERENCES

Beahrs, J. (1982) *Unity and multiplicity*. New York: Brunner-Mazel.

Davidson, J. M. (1980). The psychobiology of sexual experience. In J. M. Davidson, & R. J. Davidson, (Eds.), *The psychobiology of consciousness* (pp. 271–332). New York: Plenum Press.

Davidson, J. M., & R. J. Davidson (Eds.). (1980). *The psychobiology of consciousness*. New York: Plenum Press.

Deutsch, E. (1969). *Advaita Vedanta*. Honolulu: University of Hawaii Press.

Fischer, R. (1971). A cartography of the ecstatic and meditative states. *Science, 174* (4012), 897–904.

Gabbard, G. O., & Twemlow, S. W. (1986). An overview of altered mind/body perception. *Bulletin of the Menninger Clinic, 50*(4), 351–366.

Gardner, H. (1985). *The mind's new science: A history of the cognitive revolution*. New York: Basic.

Goleman, D. (1977). *Varieties of meditative experience*. New York: E. P. Dutton.

Goleman, D., & Davidson, R. J. (1979). *Consciousness: Brain, states of awareness and mysticism*. New York: Harper & Row.

Goodman, F. D. (1972). *Speaking in tongues*. Chicago: University of Chicago Press.

Goodman, F. D. (1986). Body posture and the religious altered state of consciousness. *Journal of Humanistic Psychology, 26*(3), 81–118.

Grof, S. (1976). *Realms of the human unconscious*. New York: E. P. Dutton.

Grof, S. (1985). *Beyond the brain*. Albany, N Y: SUNY Press.

Grof, S., & Grof, C. (1986). Forms of spiritual emergency. *Spiritual Emergency Newsletter*. Menlo Park, CA. C.I.T.P.

Halifax, J. (1982). *Shaman—The wounded healer*. New York: Crossroads.

Harner, M. (1980). *The way of the shaman*. San Francisco: Harper & Row.

Hilgard, E. R. (1980). Consciousness in psychology. *Annual Review of Psychology, 31*, 1–26.

Hilgard, E. R. (1986). *Divided consciousness* (2nd edition). New York: Wiley.

Hunt, H. T., & Chefurka, C. M. (1976). A test of the psychedelic model of altered states of consciousness. *Archives of General Psychiatry, 33*, 867–876.

James, W. (1936). *Varieties of religious experience*. New York: Modern Library.

Krippner, S., & George, L. (1986). Psi phenomena as related to altered states of consciousness. In B. B. Wolman & M. Ullman, (Eds.), *Handbook of states of consciousness* (pp. 332–364) New York: Van Nostrand Reinhold.

Leary, T., Litwin, G. H., & Metzner, R. (1963). Reactions to psilocybin in a supportive environment. *Journal of Nervous & Mental Disease, 137*(6), 561–573.

Leary T., Metzner, R., & Alpert, R. (1964). *The psychedelic experience*. New Hyde Park, NY: University Books.

Lukoff, D. (1985). The diagnosis of mystical experiences with psychotic features. *Journal of Transpersonal Psychology, 17*(2), 156–181.

Metzner, R. (1971). *Maps of consciousness*. New York: Collier Macmillan.

Metzner, R. (1986). *Opening to inner light*. Los Angeles: J. P. Tarcher.

Mukerji, D. G. (1973). *The face of silence*. London: Servire Publications.

Ostrander, S., & Schroeder, L. (1979). *Superlearning*. New York: Delta.

Perry, J. W. (1974). *The far side of madness*. Englewood Cliffs, NJ: Prentice-Hall.

Pope, K., & Singer, J. (Eds.). (1978). *The stream of consciousness*. New York: Plenum Press.

Ring, K. (1984). *Heading toward Omega*. New York: William Morrow.

Rossi, E. L. (1986). Altered states of consciousness in everyday life: Ultradian rhythms. In B. B. Wolman & M. Ullman, (Eds.). *Handbook of states of consciousness* (pp. 97–132) New York: Van Nostrand Reinhold.

Shapiro, D. H., & Walsh, R. (Eds.). (1984). *Meditation: Classic and contemporary perspectives*. New York: Aldine.

Smith, H. (1976). *Forgotten truth—The primordial tradition*. New York: Harper & Row.

Sugarman, A. A., & Tarter, R. E. (1978). *Expanding dimensions of consciousness*. New York: Springer.

Tart, C. (Ed.). (1972). *Altered states of consciousness*. New York: Doubleday.

Tart, C. (1975). *States of consciousness*. New York: E. P. Dutton.

Tart, C. (1977). *PSI—Scientific studies of the psychic realm*. New York: E. P. Dutton.

Taylor, E. (Ed.). (1983). *William James on exceptional mental states*. Amherst, MA: University of Massachusetts Press.

Thomas, L. E., & Cooper, T. (1981). Incidence and psychological correlates of intense spiritual experiences. *Journal of Transpersonal Psychology, 12*(1), 75–85.

Valle, R. S., & von Eckartsberg, R. (Eds.). (1981). *The metaphors of consciousness*. New York: Plenum Press.

Walsh, R., & Vaughan, F. (Eds.). (1980). *Beyond ego, transpersonal dimensions in psychology*. Los Angeles: J. P. Tarcher.

Wavell, S., Butt, A., & Epton, N. (1967). *Trances*. New York: E. P. Dutton.

Weil, A. (1972). *The natural mind*. Boston: Houghton Mifflin.

Wilber, K. (1977). *The spectrum of consciousness*. Wheaton, IL: Theosophical Publishing House.

Wilber, K. (1983). *Eye to eye*. New York: Doubleday Anchor.

Wilber, K., Engler, J., & Brown, D. (1986). *Transformations of consciousness*. Boston/London: Shambhala.

Wimsatt, W. C. (1986). Heuristics and the study of human behavior. In D. W. Fiske & R. A. Shweder (Eds.), *Metatheory and social science* (pp. 293–314). Chicago: University of Chicago Press.

Wolman, B. B., & Ullman, M. (Eds.). (1986). *Handbook of states of consciousness* New York: Van Nostrand Reinhold.

Zinberg, N. (Ed.). (1977). *Alternate states of consciousness*. New York: Collier Macmillan.

Name Index

Subject Index

Abandonment, 122, 204
Ability system, 245, 246
Abnormality, 179, 181. *See also* Psychopathology
Abyss (Merleau-Ponty), 229
Active imagination, 275, 325
Adult development, 202
Aesthetic consciousness, xiii, 215, 245–253
  development of, 252
  and psychological growth, 252
Aesthetic experience and civilization, 254
Aesthetic field, 251
Aesthetic sensitivity, 245
Affirmation, 93
Akido, 294
Alcoholics, 185
Altered states of consciousness (ASCs). *See* Consciousness
American Psychological Association, xiii, 160
American Psychologist, xiii
Amnes, 259
Analytic psychology (Jung), 291–292
Anatomy of a text, 18-22
Anger, 48, 51, 128, 135, 136, 210, 227, 240
Annatta, 273
Anxiety, 13, 29, 30, 113, 127–136, 164, 171, 282
  anxious experiencing, 134–135
  being anxious, 29–30, 48
  and Freud, 131
  the other being anxious, 135
  and self-understanding, 134
Anxiety disorders, 202
Approach, 90
  in testing, 165
Appropriation (through language), 207
Apraxia, 72
Archetypal dreams, 307
Archetypal experiences, 275
Archetypes, 258, 291–292
Architecture and culture, 30, 31
Aristotelian categories, 158, 165
Art, 119–120
  and phenomenology, 221

Assessment, 157–178
  sample report, 173–176
  traditional process, 167–170
  See also Human science assessment
Association for Humanistic Psychology, 260
Atman, 274, 299–300, 323
Atoms, as constructions, 20
Attachment, 265
Attitude
  of the actor, 28–29, 30
  of the observer, 28–29, 30
  of science, 17–22, 37–38
  of text, 17, 20
Attribution theory, 142, 207–208
Attunement, nonverbal, 211
Authenticity, 166–167
Autism, 184
Autobiography, 116
Autoerotism, 228
Avatamsaka Sutra, 280
Awakening, metaphors of, 280
Awareness, 42, 195
  reflective, x–xi
  See also Consciousness
Awe, 323

B-cognition, 247
Beginner's mind (Suzuki), 283
Behavior, 4
  change, 196
  covert, 4, 64
  expressive, 84
  human and animal, 31–33
  sampling of, 138
  scientific view of, 25–26
  types of (physical, vital, and human), 248–249, 250, 251
  See also Behaviorism
Behavioral analysis, 182
Behavioral enactment, 210
Behaviorism, ix–x, 3, 5, 25–26, 33, 43, 74, 94, 139, 160, 180, 182, 257, 261, 291, 297, 330, 333
  and mind, 264